GUSTAVE DORÉ
a Biography

by **Dan Malan**

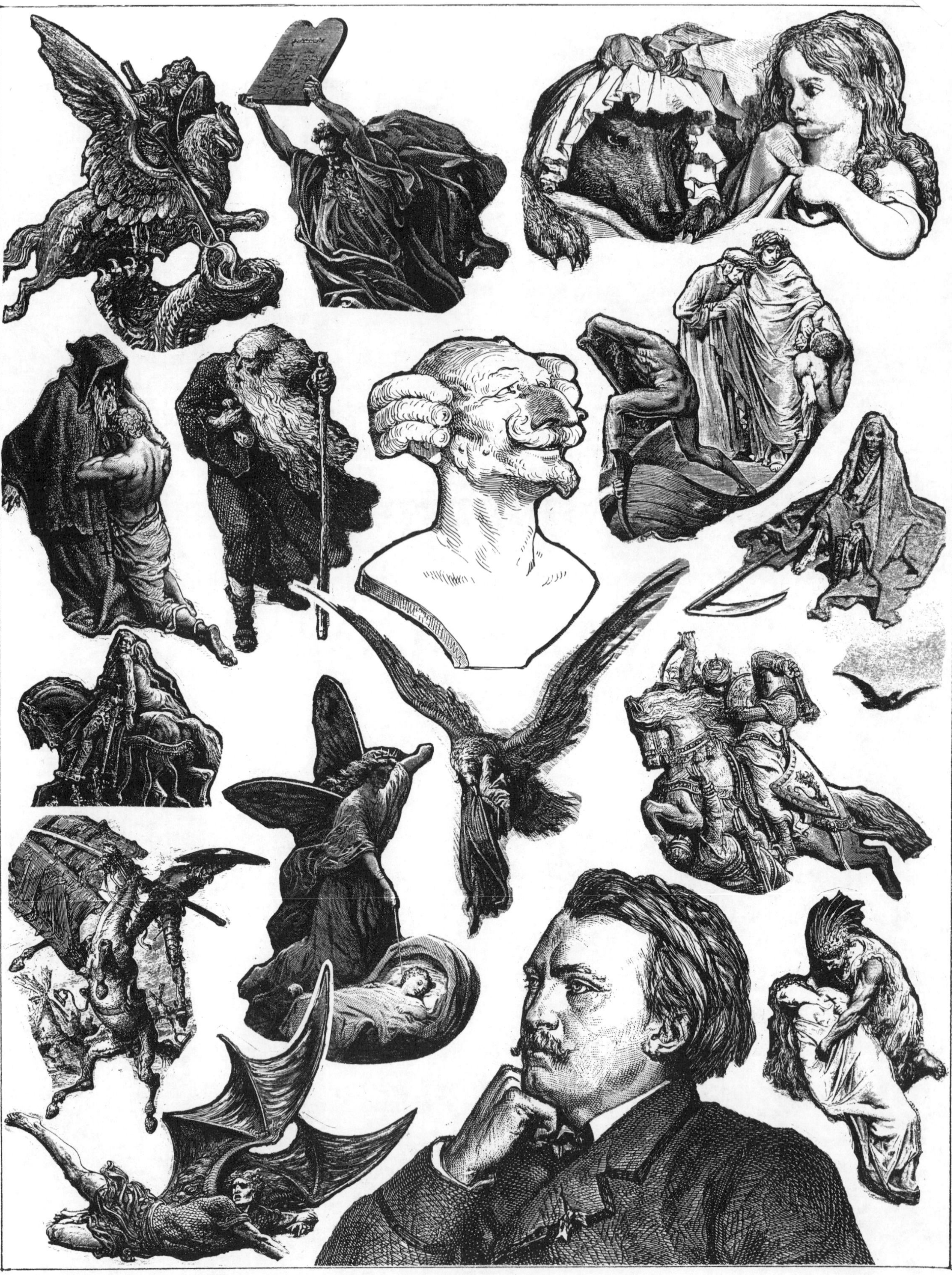

GUSTAVE DORÉ

a Biography

by **Dan Malan**

MCE Publishing Co.
St. Louis
1996

ISBN 1-888957-02-6

Printed in the U.S.A.

First Edition

Published by:

MCE Publishing Co.
7519 Lindbergh Drive
St. Louis, MO 63117
voice (314) 781-2319
fax (314) 781-0699

Library of Congress Cataloging-in-Publication Data

Malan, Dan.
Gustave Doré : a biography / by Dan Malan. -- 1st ed.
p. cm.
Includes bibliographical references and index.
ISBN 1-888957-02-6 (pbk.)
1. Doré, Gustave, 1832-1883. 2. Engravers--France--Biography.
3. Illustrators--France--Biography. I. Title.
NE650.D646M35 1996
769'.92--dc20
[B]
96-9340
CIP

TABLE OF CONTENTS

 cover of 1st Jewish edition of the ***Doré Bible*** (1874) 11x17, 25 lbs., heavy gilt full morocco

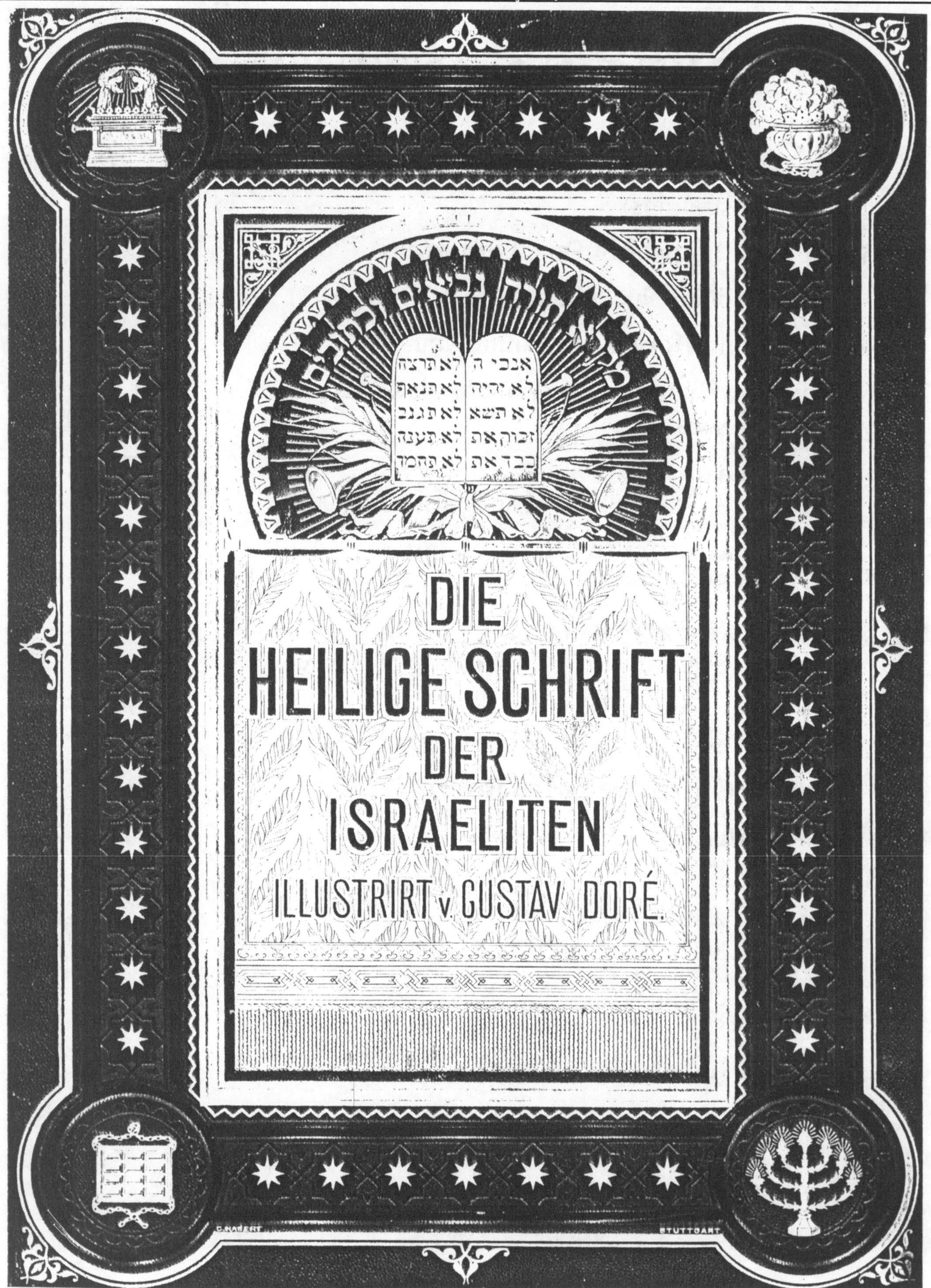

ILLUSTRATIONS (by page # & quantity)

 cover of 1st English edition of Doré's ***Don Quixote*** (1866) heavy gilt brown cloth

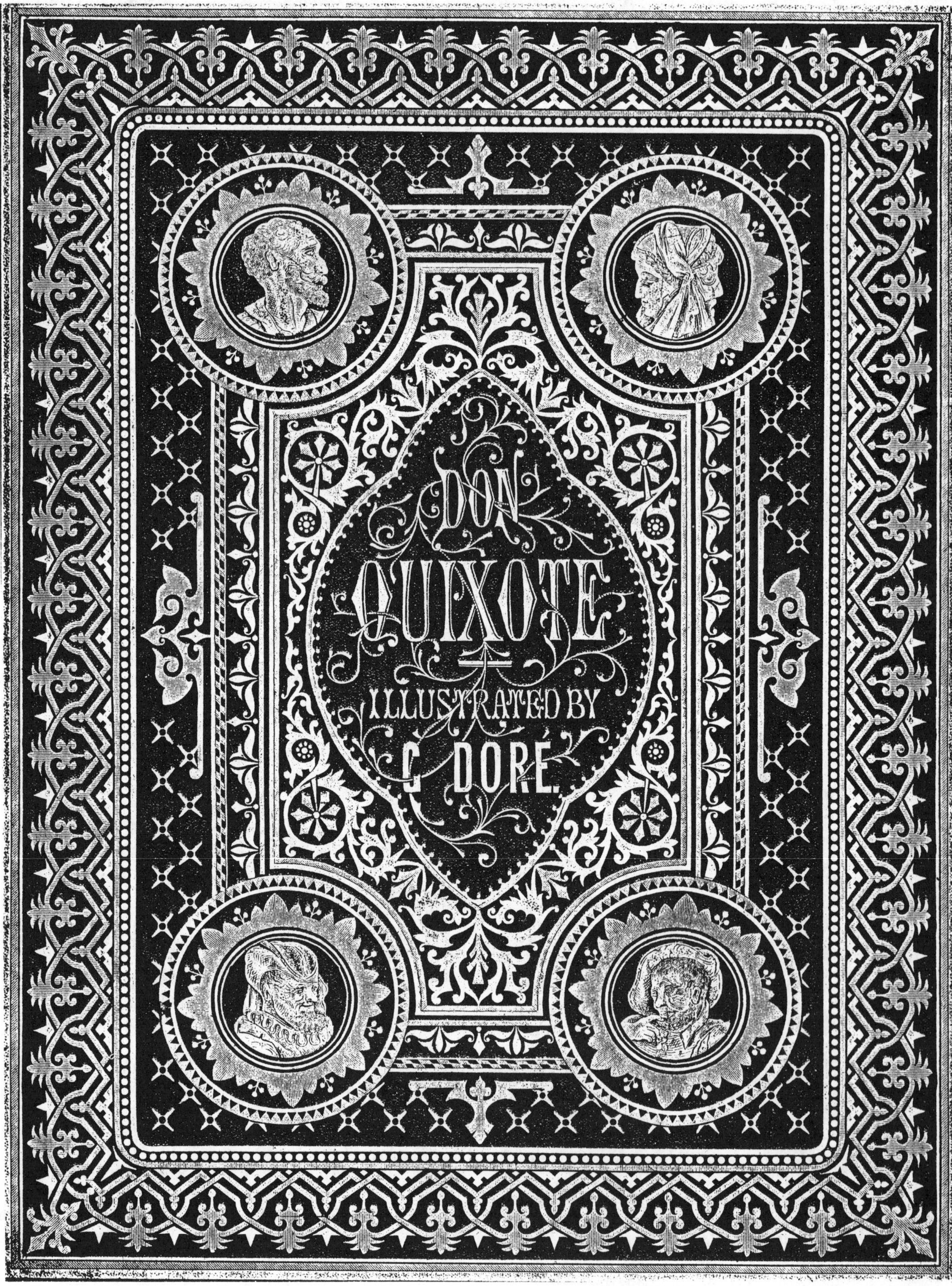

FIRST BOOK EDITION of DORÉ ILLUSTRATIONS

* = English 1st book edition; major folios & 4tos are underlined; new illos in reprint editions: ***Rabelais-Taine-Segur-Bible-LaFontaine***

Year	No.	Title
1847	105	**Doré:** *The Toils of Hercules*
'51	155	**Doré:** *Three Malcontent Artists*
	175	**Doré:** *An Unpleasant Pleasure Trip*
'52	134	**Lacroix:** *Bibliophile Jacob*
	19	**Brot:** *Alone in the World*
'53	24	**Byron:** *Complete Works*
'54	6	**Brot:** *The King's Executioner*
	10	**Brot:** *Doctor of the Heart*
	500	**Doré:** *The History of Holy Russia*
	105	**Rabelais:** *Gargantua & Pantagruel*
	20	**Doré:** *The People of Paris*
	24	**Doré:** *Parisian Menagerie*
'55	11	**Gerard:** *The Lion Hunter*
	30	**Sherer:** *Gold Prospectors*
	425	**Balzac:** *Droll Stories*
	64	**Taine:** *Mineral Waters of the Pyrenees*
	11	*The War in the Orient (Crimea)*
'56	13	*The Legend of the Wandering Jew*
	12	**Dumas:** *The Duke of Savoy's Page*
	30	**Gastineau:** *The French in Africa*
	14	**Girardin:** *Tales of an Old Maid*
	8	**Haussmann:** *Insurrection in China*
	20	**Lafon:** *Jaufre the Knight*
	9	**Noir:** *The Bronze Man*
	24	**Reid:** *Wilderness Home*
	48	**Perceval:** *Memories of a Young Cadet*
	12	**Plouvier:** *Sabbath Choruses*
'57	12	**Lafon:** *National Legends*
	20	**Segur:** *New Fairy Tales*
'58	8	**Dumas:** *Jehu's Companions*
'59	20	**Doré:** *Gallic Follies*
	31	*The War in Italy*
	20	*Battle for Italian Independence*
	324	**Malte-Brun:** *Worldwide Geography*
	12	**Montaigne:** *Essays*
'60	137	**LaBedolliere:** *Modern Paris*
	271	**Taine:** *The Pyrenees* (see 1855)
*	5	**Shakespeare:** *The Tempest*
'61	29	**Aimard:** *A Ball of Francs*
	158	**About:** *King of the Mountains*
	76	**Dante:** *The Inferno*
	52	**Dumas:** *Complete Works*
	6	*Garibaldi & the Italian Volunteers*
	34	**deKock:** *Monsieur Dupont*
	12	**Malo:** *Songs of Yesteryear*
	203	**Saintine:** *The Pathway of Children*
'62	12	*The Album of Gustave Doré*
*	36	**Ainsworth:** *All Round the World*
	42	**L'Epine:** *Captain Castagnette*
	31	**Laujon:** *Tales & Legends*
	42	**Perrault:** *Fairy Tales*
	158	**Raspe:** *Baron Munchausen*
	165	**Saintine:** *Mythology of the Rhine*
'63	24	*History of France*
	44	**Chateaubriand:** *Atala*
	377	**Cervantes**: *Don Quixote*
	177	**L'Epine:** *Croque-Mitaine*
	9	**Segur:** *New Fairy Tales* (see 1857)
'64	11	**Marx:** *One Minute Story*
'65	20	*Sinbad (Arabian Nights)*
	4	**Moore:** *The Epicurean*
'66	60	**Gautier:** *Captain Fracasse*
*	50	**Milton:** *Paradise Lost*
	228	*The Holy Bible*
	37	*The Holy Bible* (2nd ed)
'67	334	**LaFontaine:** *Fables*
*	303	**Doré:** *200 Sketches*
*	2	**Hugo:** *Toilers of the Sea*
	11	**Terrail:** *The Mayflower Page*
'68	60	**Dante:** *Purgatory & Paradise*
	21	**LaFontaine:** *Fables* (see 1867)
*	37	**Tennyson:** *Idylls of the King*
'69	6	**Feval:** *Gold Prospectors*
	7	**Lamothe:** *Martyrs of Siberia*
'70	10	**L'Epine:** *Knight Good-Times*
*	9	**Hood:** *Poems*
*	34	**Manning:** *Spanish Pictures*
*'71	5	**Jerrold:** *Cockaynes in Paris*
*'72	180	**Jerrold:** *London, a Pilgrimage*
'73	13	**Lachatre:** *History of the Popes*
*	7	*Man among the Monkees*
	614	**Rabelais:** *Works* (see 1854)
'74	306	**Davillier:** *Spain*
*'76	42	**Coleridge:** *Rime of the Ancient Mariner*
'77	100	**Michaud:** *History of the Crusades*
'79	46	**Ferry:** *The Forest Ranger*
	28	**Delorme:** *Gustave Doré* (first bio)
	618	**Ariosto:** *Orlando Furioso*
*'83	26	**Poe:** *The Raven*
	19	*Society of French Watercolorists*
*'85	66	**Roosevelt:** *Life of Gustave Doré*
*'91	73	**Jerrold:** *Life of Gustave Doré*
*'93	25	*The Doré Gallery: Illustrated Catalogue*
1907	95	**Doré:** *Versailles & Paris in 1871*
1930	39	**Valmy-Baysse:** *Gustave Doré*
*1996	45	**Dickens:** *A Christmas Carol*

 Doré (1832-1883) at approximately ten-year intervals (circa 1850, 1860, 1870 & 1880)

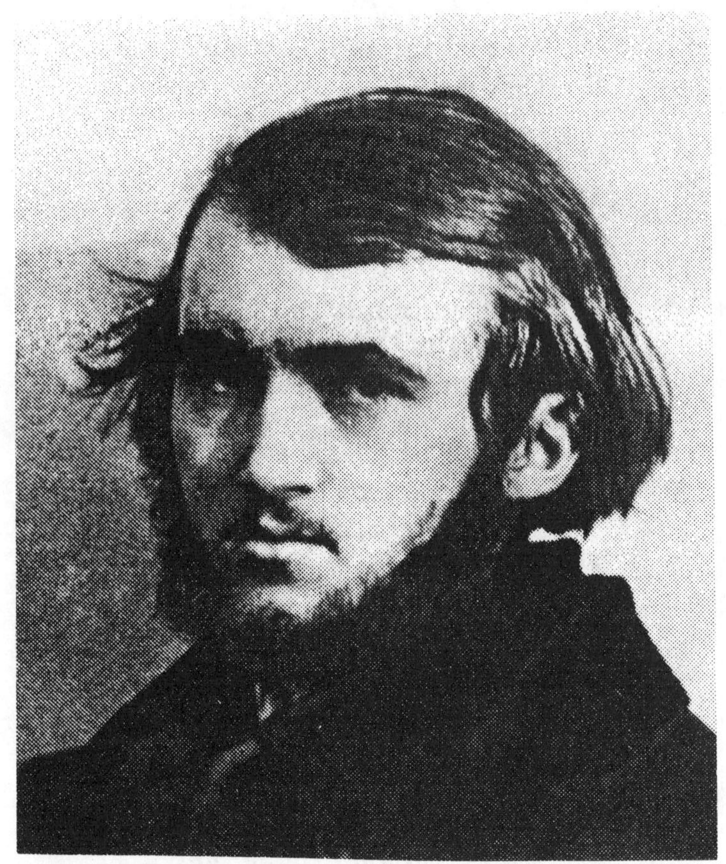

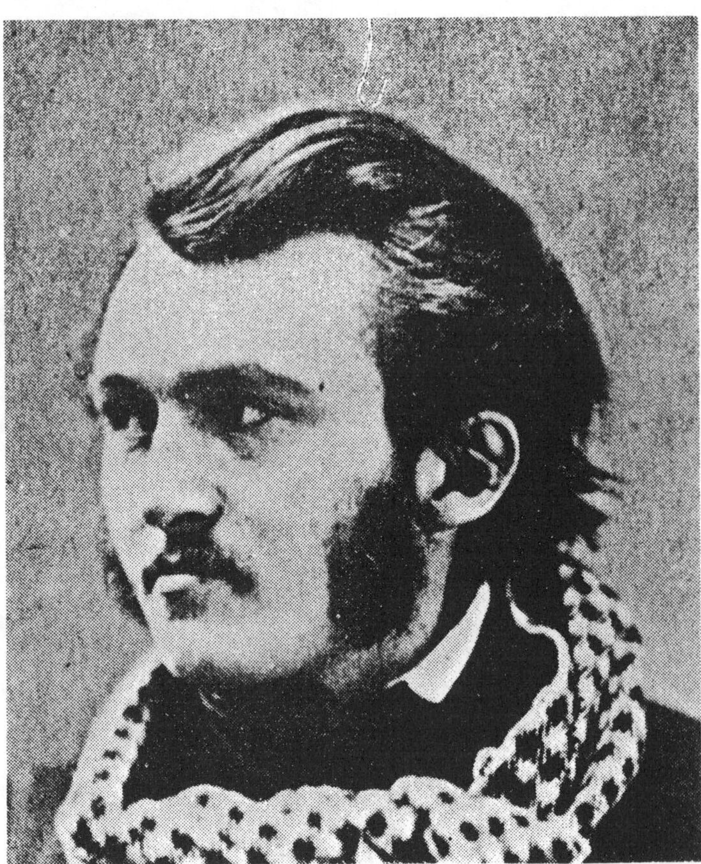

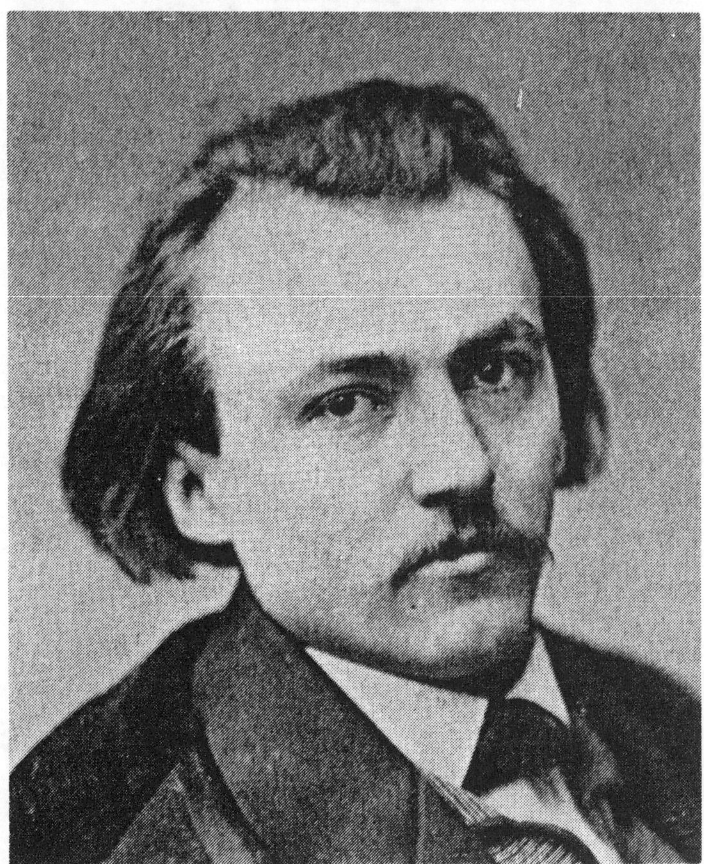

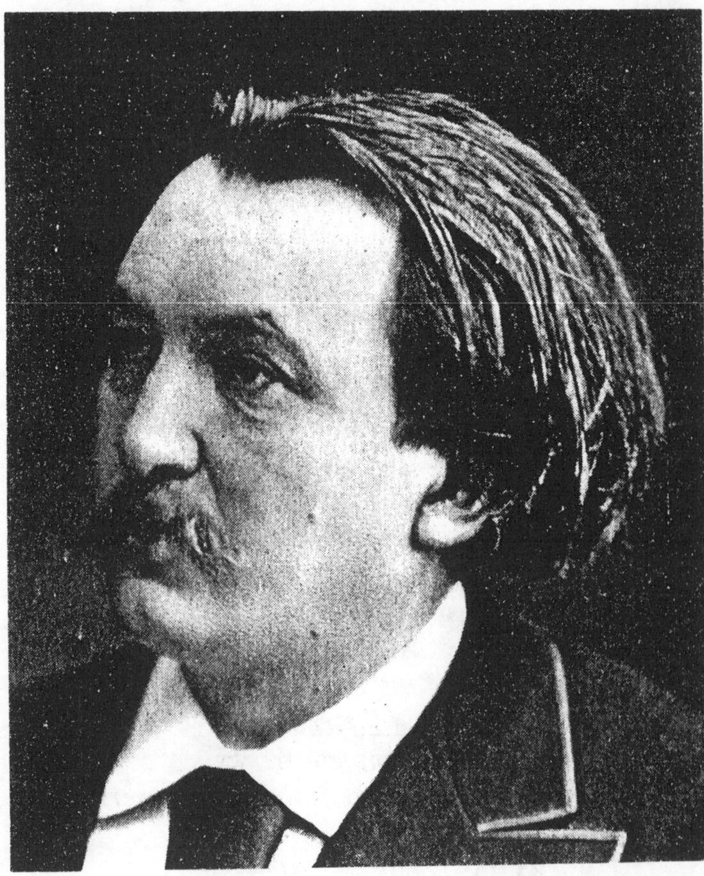

Major Biographical & Bibliographical Sources used herein (see also page 91)

(for complete bibliographic information, see Dan Malan: *Gustave Doré - Adrift on Dreams of Splendor*)

Amer.Cat.	*The American Catalogue* (Frederick Leypoldt, New York, 1870 on)
Art Inst.-Chic.	The Art Institute of Chicago (extensive file reference information on 1896 Doré Gallery)
Brit.-Mus.	British Museum Catalogue (267 folio volumes + supplements) (see also NUC)
Cassell	Simon Nowell-Smith: *The House of Cassell*, 1958, Cassell-London, p.80-106.
Clapp	Samuel Clapp: *Gustave Doré*, 1983, Hazlitt, Gooden & Fox-London, 126 pages.
Clement	Clement & Hutton: *Artists of the 19th Century*, 1884, Houghton-Boston, p.212-215.
D.Gal.	*The Doré Gallery: Descriptive Catalogue of Pictures*, 1868-1900, London/NY/Chicago+
Delorme	Rene Delorme: *Gustave Doré*, 1879, L.Baschet-Paris, 104 pages.
Deze	Louis Deze: *Gustave Doré-Bibliographie*, 1930, Marcel Seheur-Paris, 166 pages.
Duplessis	George Duplessis: *Catalogue des Dessins...G.Doré*, 1885, Cercle de Libraire-Paris, 218 pages.
Edwards	Amelia Edwards:*Gustave Doré-Personal Recollections*, in 1883 *Art Journal*-London, p.361-365, 389-394.
Eng.Cat.	*The English Catalogue* (London, 1856 on)
Farner	Konrad Farner: *Gustave Doré, der Industrialiste Romantiker*, 1963, Kunst-Dresden, 667 pages.
Fonds	Adhemar/Letheve: *Inventaire du Fonds Francais apres 1800* (V7), 1954, Bibliotheque Ntnl.-Paris, p.1-56.
Forberg	Forberg & Metken: *Gustave Doré*, 1975, Rognier/Bernhard-Munchen, 1,536 pages.
Gosling	Nigel Gosling: *Gustave Doré*, 1973, David & Charles-Newton Abbot, 112 pages.
Guratzsch	Guratzsch & Unverfehrt: *Gustave Doré*, 1982, Harenberg-Dortmund, 389 pages.
Hachette	Jean Mistler: *La Librairie Hachette*, 1964, Hachette-Paris, p.116-155.
Herendeen	W.H.Herendeen: *The Doré Controversy,* in 1982 *Victorian Studies*, p.305-327.
Jerrold	Blanchard Jerrold: *The Life of Gustave Doré*, 1891, W.H.Allen-London, 415 pages.
Kaenel	Philippe Kaenel: *Gustave Doré-Realiste/Visionnaire*, 1985, Tricorne-Geneva, 104 pages.
Kunzle	David Kunzle: *History of the Comic Strip-19th Century*, 1990, Univ.CA Press, p.105-141.
LeBlanc	Henri LeBlanc: *Catalogue-Gustave Doré*, 1931, Ch.Bosse-Paris, 558 pages.
Lehmann	Helmut Lehmann-Haupt: *The Terrible Gustave Doré*, 1943, Marchbanks-NY, 48 pages.
Lehni/Clapp	Nadine Lehni & Samuel Clapp: *Une Introduction a la Sculpture de Gustave Doré* in *1991 Bulletin de la Societe de l'Histoire de l'Art Francais*, Paris 1992, p.219-253.
Manhattan	Manhattan Storage: *Collection of Paintings ... Gustave Doré*, 1947 auction, 7 pages.
Marie L.	"Marie L.": *Reminiscences of Gustave Doré*, 1893, Doré Gallery-NY, 40 pages.
Muir	Percy Muir: *Victorian Illustrated Books*, 1971, Praeger-NY, p.220-227, 241-244.
North-Peat	Anthony North-Peat: *Gossip from Paris: 1864-69*, 1903, Kegan Paul-London, 7 Doré references.
NUC	National Union Catalogue (754 folio volumes in 1955 + supplements) (from U.S. library card catalogues)
OCLC & RLIN	(Computer searches of U.S. Libraries/Universities/Art Museums (combined listings of 1200 Doré editions)
Ollier	Edmund Ollier (35p. *Gustave Doré Memoir* in) *The Doré Gallery*, 1870, Cassell-London.
Paris-1878	*The 1878 Paris International Exhibition*, 1878, Gebbie/Barrie-Philadelphia, p.64-68.
Paris-1974	(Jean Adhemar): *Gustave Doré*, 1974, Bibliotheque Nationale-Paris, 4 page folding sheet.
Ray	Gordon Ray: *Art of the French Illustrated Book*, 1982, Pierpont Morgan Library-NY, p.326-48.
Renonciat	Annie Renonciat: *La Vie et l'Oeuvre de Gustave Doré*, 1983, ACR-Paris, 299 pages.
Richardson	Joanna Richardson: *Gustave Doré, a Biography*, 1980, Cassell-London, 176 pages.
Roosevelt	Blanche Roosevelt: *Life & Reminiscences of Gustave Doré*, 1885, Cassell-NY, 502 pages.
Rose	Millicent Rose: *Gustave Doré*, 1946, Pleiades-London, 68 pages.
Strahan	Edward Strahan: *Etudes in Modern French Art*, 1882, R.Worthington-NY, p.73-74.
Stranahan	C.H.Stranahan: *A History of French Painting*, 1888, Scribner-NY, p.414-426.
Strasbourg-83	(Nadine Lehni): *Gustave Doré*, 1983, Musee d'Art Moderne-Strasbourg, 343 pages.
Strasbourg-93	(Nadine Lehni): *Gustave Doré, une Nouvelle Collection*, 1993, Ed.Musee-Strasbourg, 101 pages.
Tebbel	John Tebbel: *A History of Book Publishing in the United States* (V1-V2), 1972+, R.R.Bowker, various.
Valmy	J.Valmy-Baysse: *L'Art et Vie de Gustave Doré*, 1930, Marcel Seheur-Paris, 347 pages.
Van Gogh	*The Complete Letters of Vincent van Gogh,* 1958, N.Y.Graphic Society-CT (15 Doré references).

Major Abbreviations used herein:

bio = biography	eng = engraving	litho = lithograph	#-B, #-b = number of full-page plates, vignettes
chrono = chronology	illo = illustration	mag = magazine	pts. = parts edition (m=monthly; w=weekly)
ed = edition or editor	intro = introduction	sc = sculpture	repro = reprint or reproduction

Footnotes: This book contains zero footnotes! Whether they are at the bottom of a page, the end of a chapter, or the end of a book, it is very distracting to readers to have to jump all over a book, often just for one detail. This book eliminates lengthy footnotes, and important shorter footnote material is included briefly in parentheses in the text of the book itself.

12 (top left) Red Rose Collection 46" x 67" throw rug taken from *The Ancient Mariner* plate #26 (no Doré credit)
(top right) Marks of Distinction rubber stamp taken from *The Apocrypha* plate #15: Heliodorus (no Doré credit)
(bottom left) Time Magazine (Feb.14, 1994, pg.57) taken (& altered) from *Red Riding Hood* (no Doré credit)
(bottom right) M.H.deYoung Memorial Museum (San Francisco) *Doré Vase* placed at front entrance July 1994.

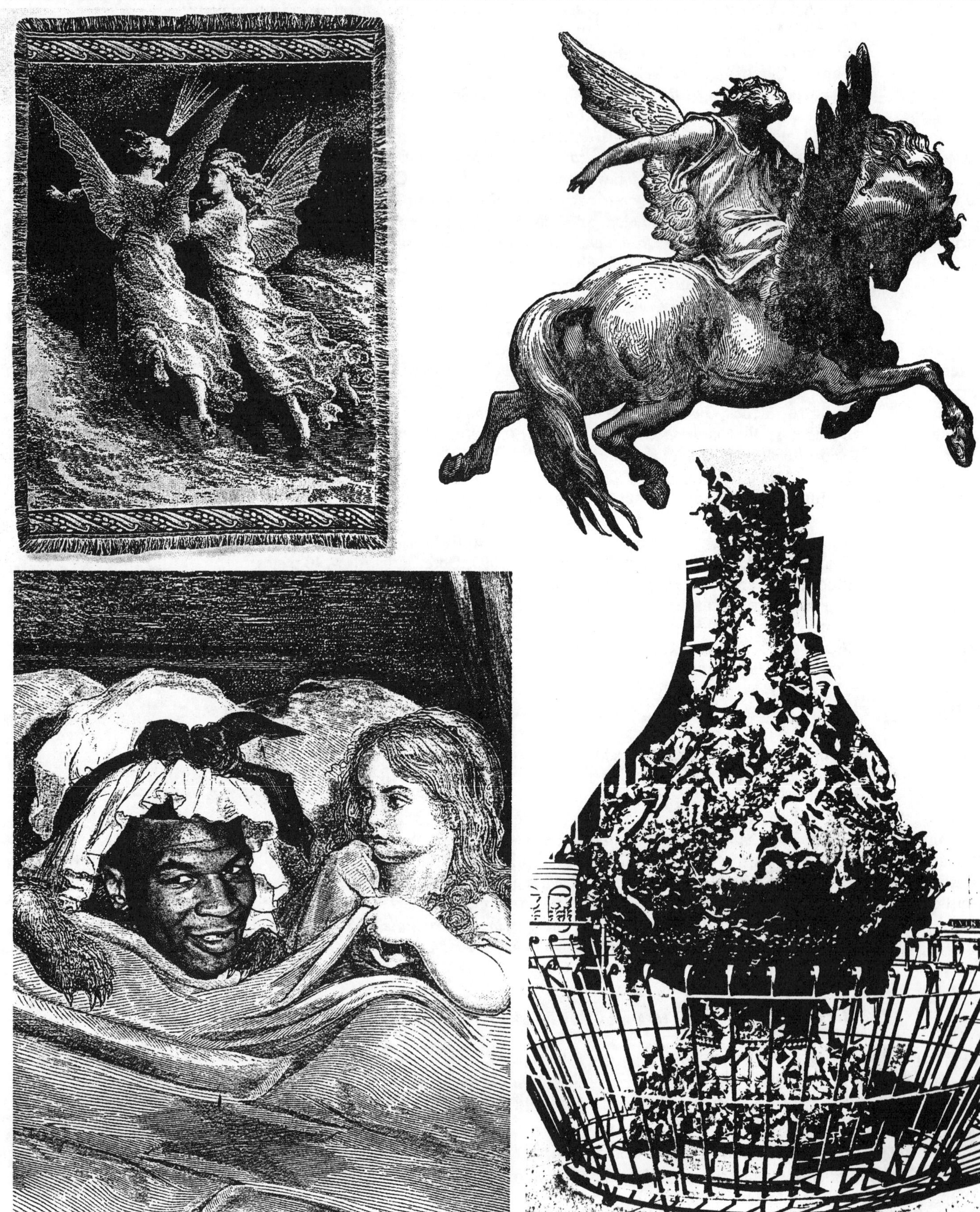

1. INTRODUCTION - DORÉ IS ALL AROUND YOU

Gustave Doré (1832-1883, pronounced Doe-Ray) is one of the great hidden treasures of the art world. His 10,000 engravings and 3,000 book editions make him by far the most prolific and popular illustrator of all time. At the time of his death, he was literally the most famous artist in the world. It was asserted that even though he was French, his folios could be found in any English-speaking household where they could spell the word "art." Yet a half-century later he was virtually unknown. Controversy surrounded him - individuals, groups, and countries have fought over him. The goal of this book is a more balanced assessment of Doré's artistic achievements.

Doré did over 8000 wood engravings, 1000 lithographs, 700 zinc engravings 70 steel engravings, and 50 etchings. Yet he still found time for 400 oil paintings, 600 watercolors, 900 mixed-media sketches, and 30 major works of sculpture. No one has ever questioned his status as the most prolific of illustrators. Yet fame and wealth never satisfied him. He was obsessed with the one thing he could not attain - he wanted the French fine art establishment to acknowledge him as a great painter. It it hard to deny that much of their criticism was biased and personal. They all knew Doré as that renegade boy-genius cartoonist who would not take lessons, who had no school, who would not use a model, who would not paint from nature, but who somehow without their "blessing" became more wealthy and famous than any of them.

The level of Doré's fame can be easily documented by the number of editions of his illustrated works. At the age of 15, he burst upon the Parisian artistic scene as a boy-genius cartoonist, at a higher rate of pay than than Honore Daumier made at the height of his career. By 1860, Doré was France's greatest illustrator, but still unknown outside its borders. Then came the Doré folios, and between 1861-1900, over 1700 Doré book editions were published, an average of a new Doré edition every nine days! He was so popular that the rate of editions actually increased in the decade after he died.

In 1861, Doré revolutionized the art world by taking the "art of the people" (illustration) and elevating to the level of fine art, through a series of literary folios, beginning with his 20 lb., 13" x 17" folio of ***Dante's Inferno***, containing 76 full-page engravings. Before that, high-quality art folios involved enormous expense, with steel engravings from commissioned paintings. Doré drew directly onto wood blocks and trained a school of wood engravers to produce artistic effects rivalling steel engravings. Doré essentially produced black-and-white paintings. Such a volume was still very expensive, and Louis Hachette, the most prominent French publisher, refused to finance it. Doré had to pay for the edition himself. Even then, Hachette warned him that he are throwing his money away and that he would be lucky to sell 100 copies. A few days after the book went on sale, Doré received a short message from the eminent Mr. Hachette: "Success! Come quickly! I am an Ass!" Far from selling 100 copies, there have now been 200 editions of Doré's illustrations for ***Dante's Inferno***.

The 200 editions of "Doré's" *Inferno* make it one of the most popular sets of illustrations of all time. But it is only third on the Doré list, behind 300 editions of his ***Don Quixote*** illustrations, and 700 editions of his ***Bible*** illustrations. The only non-Doré set of illustrations that compares with these are Sir John Tenniel's illustrations for ***Alice in Wonderland***, of which there are over 400 editions. But there is a big difference. Tenniel was the original *Alice* illustrator, whereas Doré was illustrating works which other artists had been illustrating for centuries. Yet the Spanish regard the Frenchman Doré as the definitive ***Don Quixote*** illustrator, as do the Italians for his *Dante*, while his ***Bible*** illustrations are by far the most popular religious illustrations of all time.

Doré's genius was seen in six artistic qualities which he possessed to an extraordinary degree: imagination, creativity, photographic memory, rate of production, dramatic intensity, and topical versatility. Some of the topics Doré covered were social commentary, social satire, political satire, fables, fairy tales, travel, knighthood, the Crusades, horror, mythology, fantasy, religion, literature, and poetry. Here is a partial list of the great authors and literary classics Doré illustrated:

Arabian Nights
Ariosto's ***Orlando Furioso***
Balzac's ***Droll Stories***
The Bible
Lord Byron's ***Works***
Cervantes' ***Don Quixote***
Chateaubriand's ***Atala***
Coleridge's ***Ancient Mariner***
Dante's ***Divine Comedy***
Dickens' ***A Christmas Carol***
Alexandre Dumas' ***Works***
Gautier's ***Captain Fracasse***
Thomas Hood's ***Poems***
Hugo's ***Toilers of the Sea & Hunchback of Notre Dame***
LaFontaine's ***Fables***
Michaud's ***The Crusades***
Milton's ***Paradise Lost***
Montaigne's ***Essays***
Moore's ***The Epicurean***
Perrault's ***Fairy Tales***
Poe's ***The Raven***
Rabelais' ***Gargantua & Pantagruel***
Raspe's ***Baron Munchausen***
Reid's ***Desert Home***
Segur's ***New Fairy Tales***
Shakespeare's ***Macbeth & The Tempest***
Tennyson's ***Idylls of the King***

But that is just the tip of the iceberg. Doré's illustrations have been extensively "borrowed" and inserted into works by others:

Aesop
Johann Sebastian Bach
Jean Cocteau
Dinah Mulock Craik
Cecil B. DeMille
Brothers Grimm
Thomas Hardy
Ernest Hemingway
Washington Irving
Carl Jung
Jack London
Sir Thomas Malory
Karl Marx
Herman Melville
Plato
William Prescott
Sir Walter Scott
Mary Shelley
Harriet Beecher Stowe
Eugene Sue

Now that all of Doré's illustrations are in the public domain, dozens of new books use his engravings each year, by authors ranging from Billy Graham to Anne Rice to Howard Stern.

Another indication of the extent of Doré's popularity can be seen in the languages in which his editions appear. It is almost impossible to find a European language in which there were no Doré editions. Some Doré editions were major events. The 1887 Greek edition of Doré's ***Paradise Lost*** folio was the first Greek edition of that title. Here are the Doré edition languages, with the number of editions for the most popular languages. Notice that even though Doré was French, there are over twice as many English as French editions:

Doré sketches from ages 5-8: - *The Ant & the Moth* (2); - local people around Strasbourg (2); - animals: *Monsieur Fox* (1); - Mdm.Braun's dog: *Fouilloux* (2).

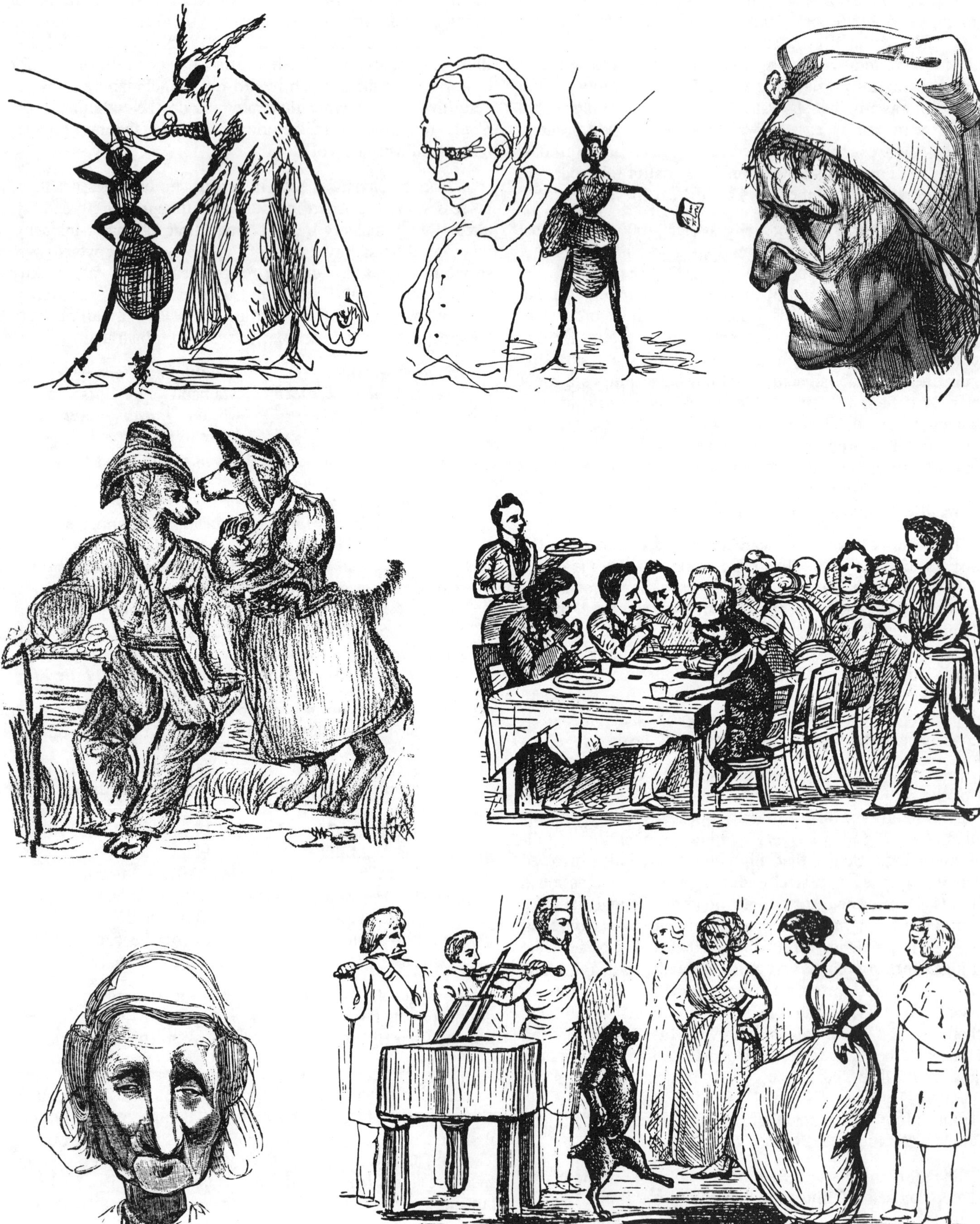

English	(1500)	Portuguese	Japanese	Chinese
French	(700)	Norwegian	Catalan	Icelandic
German	(200)	Finnish	Latvian	Slovakian
Spanish	(200)	Danish	Ukranian	Esperanto
Italian	(130)	Polish	Yiddish	Armenian
Dutch	(50)	Greek	Serbian	Estonian
Russian	(50)	Czech	Croatian	Lithuanian
Swedish	(40)	Hungarian	Bosnian	Rumanian
Hebrew	(30)	Bulgarian	Flemish	

The popularity of Doré's illustrations can be shown by the number of known editions of each title. These editions are detailed in my bibliography, ***Gustave Doré - Adrift on Dreams of Splendor***. Here are his most popular titles (f = folio):

Author/Title	Engravings	Editions
The Bible	(265)f	(700)
Cervantes' ***Don Quixote***	(377)f	(300)
Dante's ***Inferno***	(76)f	(200)
Dante's ***Purgatory & Paradise***	(60)f	(180)
Milton's ***Paradise Lost***	(50)f	(100)
Tennyson's ***Idylls of the King***	(37)f	(100)
Perrault's ***Fairy Tales***	(42)f	(100)
Raspe's ***Baron Munchausen***	(158)f	(100)
Davillier's ***Spain***	(306)f	(80)
Coleridge's ***Rime-Ancient Mariner***	(42)f	(70)
LaFontaine's ***Fables***	(355)f	(70)
Rabelais' ***Gargantua & Pantagruel***	(719)f	(70)
Balzac's ***Droll Stories***	(425)	(60)
Poe's ***The Raven***	(26)f	(30)
Michaud's ***The Crusades***	(100)f	(30)
Saintine's ***Mythology of the Rhine***	(165)	(30)
Jerrold's ***London, a Pilgrimage***	(180)f	(25)
Hood's ***Poems***	(9)f	(25)
Chateaubriand's ***Atala***	(44)f	(25)
Segur's ***New Fairy Tales***	(29)	(25)
Taine's ***Tour through the Pyrenees***	(335)	(25)
Ariosto's ***Orlando Furioso***	(618)f	(20)
Beranger's ***Legend-Wandering Jew***	(13)f	(20)
Arabian Nights	(20)	(20)
About's ***King of the Mountains***	(158)	(20)
Doré's ***History of Holy Russia***	(500)	(20)
Gautier's ***Captain Fracasse***	(60)	(20)
Malte-Brun's ***Geography***	(324)	(20)
Reid's ***Desert Home***	(24)	(20)

In the period of the 1860s-80s, publishers could increase sales of a book by adding one Doré illustration to 100 by other artists, and then stating on the title page, "Illustrated by Doré and others." But by the turn of the century his engravings had been re-reprinted so many times that the quality of many prints looked like mud. So publishers stopped promoting him. Then particular countries would "rediscover" him generations later. Now publishers do not promote his name, they just use his engravings because they are free and still widely appreciated. Doré is now the opposite of the commercial art world, where the name of the artist is more important than the appearance of the art. Would a Monet painting be any less beautiful if it turned out to have been painted by an unknown artist? Today, many people love Doré's art without knowing his name.

So if we do not see his name, how can we find the Doré art that is still all around us? You just have to know where to look. Besides new editions featuring Doré, here are some of the ways his engravings and other artwork are used in various forms of pop culture, or in more traditional formats:

Magazines	(***Time Magazine*** cover - 12/18/95)
Movies	(***Seven*** - Brad Pitt & Morgan Freeman)
Book Covers	(Anne Rice: ***Lasher*** - paperback)
Art Displays	(**Poe Museum** - Richmond, VA)
Paintings	(Sotheby's - sold as high as $600,000)
Sculpture	(***Doré Vase***: San Francisco Art Museum)
Comic Books	(Doré series by **Tome Press**)
Angel Books	(almost all contain Doré engravings)
T-shirts	(***The Bible, The Raven***)
Videos	(***The Raven, The Ancient Mariner***)
Slide Sets	(***London-a Pilgrimage, Divine Comedy***)
Internet	(***Rime of the Ancient Mariner***)
Audio CD	(J.S.Bach with ***Bible*** graphics package)
CD-ROM	(***Bible*** engravings)
LP Albums	(***Don Quixote, Fairy Tales***)
Bookmarks	(***Don Quixote***, etc.)
Throw Rugs	(***Rime of the Ancient Mariner*** - 46x67)
Rock Posters	(***Dante's Inferno, Ancient Mariner***)
Postcards	(Angels, Biblical, Paintings, Sculpture)
(Politics)	(Doré ***Russia*** satire used as propaganda)
Jigsaw Puzzles	(***Don Quixote***, by Intl. Polygonics)
Postage Stamps	(France:***Fairy Tales***, San Marino:***Dante***)
Theatre Promos	(***Man of La Mancha, Moby Dick***)
Rubber Art Stamps	(***Dante***, ***Bible***, Angels)
Silver Relief Plates	(***Don Quixote***)
Educational Filmstrips	(***The Crusades***)
Religious Publications	(almost every religious group)
Stained Glass Windows	(in churches, cathedrals, etc.)

In recent years, Doré has finally gained respect in Europe as a painter. For the 1983 Doré centennial, there were major exhibitions in Paris, Strasbourg, Le Havre, Bourg-en-Bresse, Geneva, Hanover, and London, exhibiting several hundred Doré works of art. There have also been major Doré reference books in French by Renonciat and in German by Forberg & Metken. This was finally balanced out with my 1995 major reference work on Doré, the first ever in English. This present volume is more of an introduction to Doré. But if you need in-depth bibliographic Doré information, see my book: ***Gustave Doré - Adrift on Dreams of Splendor*** (ISBN 0-9631135-8-5).

Doré sketches from age 10: - animal stories in style of J.J.Grandville (3); - *Miroflor & Mistenflute* (2); - mythology story: *The Life of Jupiter* (1); - *Dante's Inferno* (1).

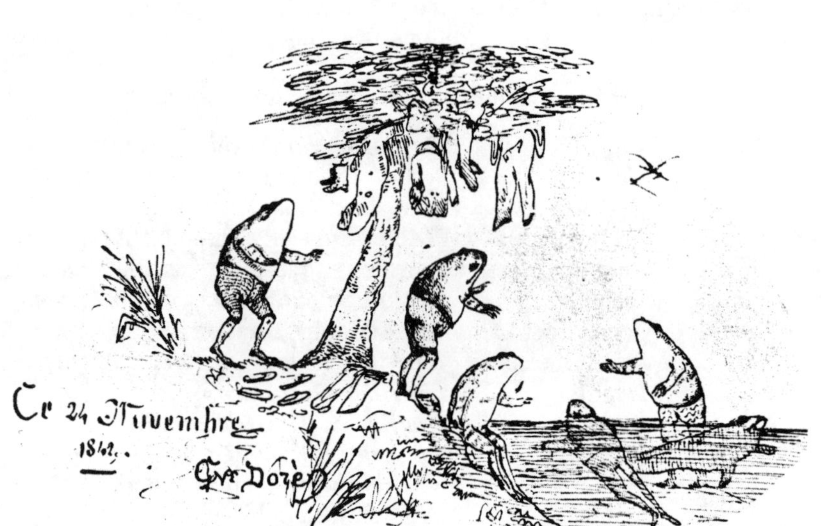

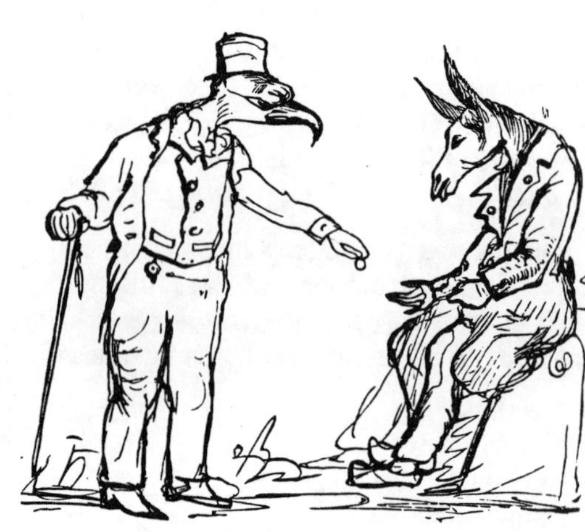

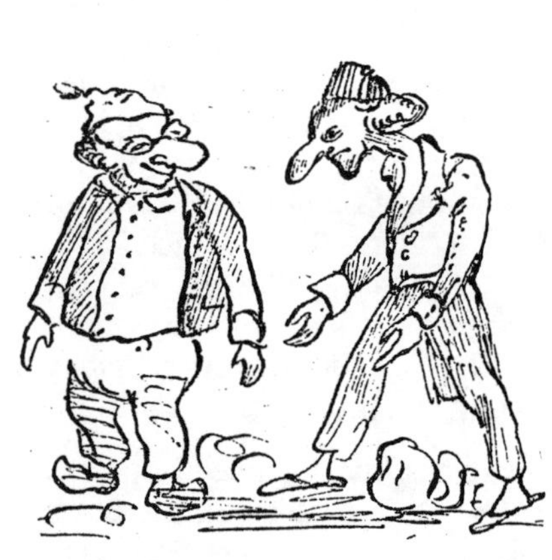

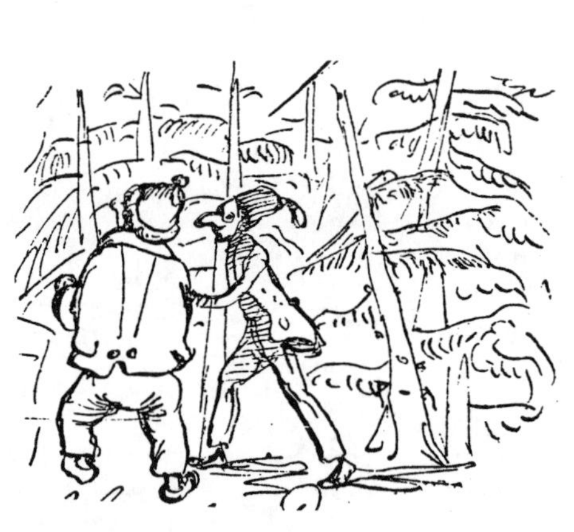

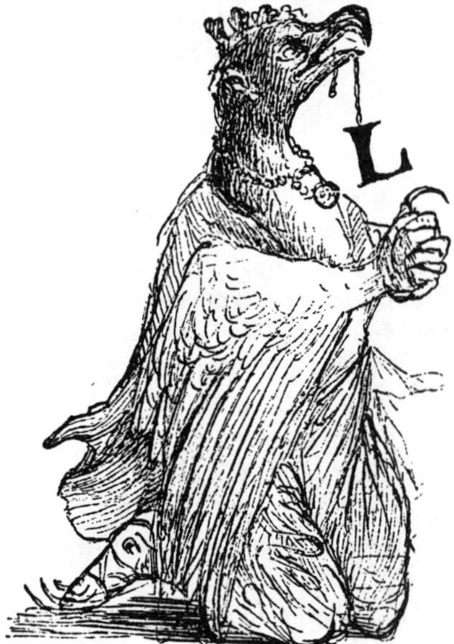

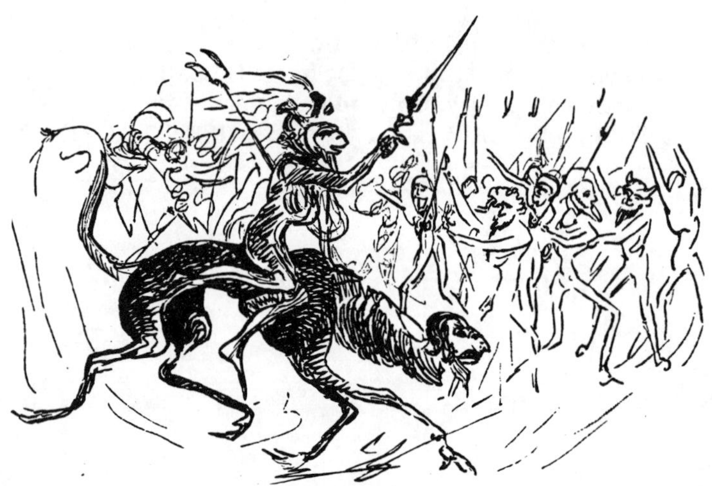

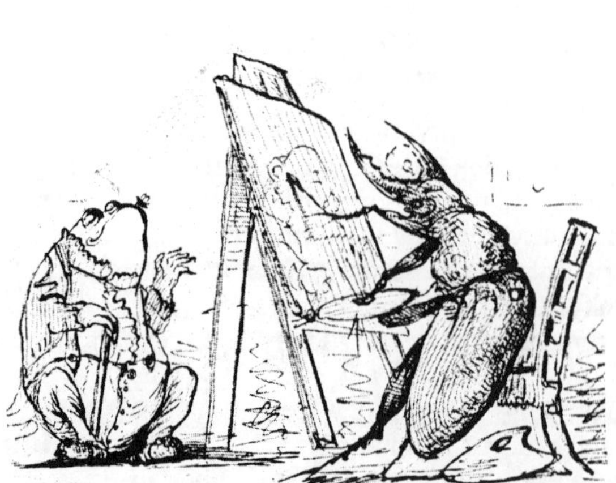

2. A BOY WHO EXPECTS TO BE FIRST IN HIS CLASS

Louis-Auguste Gustave Doré was born January 6, 1832, and died January 23, 1883. To this day many reference books incorrectly list the dates and names. But his birth certificate is reproduced in Roosevelt and LeBlanc. The birthdate error was partly his own fault. He once wrote that he was born January 1, 1833. Doré had a photographic memory, yet he apparently forgot his birthdate. He is often referred to as Paul Gustave Doré. Paul may have been a nickname, but it was not one of his legal names. Many reference books list his first name as Gustav. That error came from English researchers referring to German Doré editions rather than the original French.

Gustave was born in the French town of Strasbourg, right on the German border. His art was often said to have German characteristics, but he was a Frenchman through and through. After his home town was lost to Germany in 1871 (at the end of the Franco-Prussian War), he vowed never to return to a German Strasbourg, and he never did. It has also been asserted that his family name was originally Dorér, and that he was descended from the great 15th century illustrator Albrecht Durer. That is a nice anecdote, but I have yet to see anyone list any type of documentation for it. If you repeat a possibility long enough, it sounds like a fact. The name Doré means "gilded," which led to endless remarks about "the golden boy" or "the golden year" but especially to the enormous profits so many legal and illegal publishers made off of Doré.

Gustave's father, Pierre Louis Christophe Doré, a civil engineer, married Alexandrine Braun. They had three sons in quick succession - Ernest (who became a composer), Gustave, and Emile (who became a military officer). They were upper-middle-class, and the glue that held the family together was the beloved nurse Francoise, who, as she would later relate, saw Gustave enter the world and saw him leave it. Her age is never given, but she must have been at least 80 when Gustave died. Doré did a watercolor painting of her in 1881. If ever a movie is made of Doré's life, Francoise would make the perfect narrator. Early Doré biographers Roosevelt and Jerrold were fortunate to have such an eyewitness to almost everything Doré ever did, at least in France. Many researchers since have added bibliographic details, but few have ever been able to add to the biographical information Roosevelt and Jerrold obtained from Francoise and a host of other Doré intimates, including his brothers and two boyhood friends, Arthur and Ernest Kratz. The Doré brothers and the Kratz brothers were all about the same age, and they were all inseparable friends.

The stories of Gustave Doré's childhood are legendary. It was said that from the age of four, Gustave was never seen without a pencil in his hand. He always wanted his pencils sharpened at both ends. Jerrold (p.6) actually claimed that as an infant, instead of crying, "I want a bottle," Gustave cried, "I want a pencil." His earliest dated drawing was from 1837, when he was five. Everyone around him was astounded at his early artistic prowess. Gustave's first teacher, Mr. Vergnette, awarded him first prize in a contest when Gustave was five. Gustave made a series of drawings of insects behaving as humans, entitled "A Boy who expects to be First in his Class." Gustave often drew his assignments rather than writing them. There are stories of teachers having trouble communicating to the class and asking young Gustave to come up and draw it on the board so the other students could understand it. The only real division of opinion was among his parents, his mother being his greatest fan (she would remain so until her death), and his father being his greatest critic, wanting him to be an engineer. The great irony is that at the father's untimely death a few years later, Gustave at 16 was already making enough money as an artist to support the entire family! Doré has to rank among the greatest of artistic child prodigies. The great French illustrator J.J.Grandville saw Doré's work at age 12 and predicted greatness for him. But Grandville could never have guessed that just a few years later, that little child would be more famous (and more highly paid) than he.

The three Doré boys were all talented, but Gustave far exceeded his brothers in intelligence, talent, and charm. It would be an understatement to say that his mother spoiled Gustave, she worshipped him! Their emotional bond was so great that Gustave barely outlived her. Freud would have had a field day analyzing their relationship. Yet Gustave was a very giving person. There are many documented stories of his great compassion for the poor at a very young age, such as the time he came home from school without his shoes, and told his mother how after school he met a poor boy who had no shoes, and all Gustave could think of was - "What luck! We wore the same size!" That compassion would come to fruition in his adult charity work at local children's hospitals, and in his 1872 ***London, a Pilgrimage***, hailed by many as the greatest visual expression ever of the social class struggle. That book (of which there are many recent reprints) should be required reading for all sociology students.

Gustave was so talented and so impressionable that each new experience catapulted him to new creative dimensions. At the age of seven, he saw his first opera - ***Robert le Diable***. He loved the music and the drama, and went around singing and performing the scenes. Not only did he become a life-long fan of opera, but it also stimulated his interest in the supernatural. He drew angels as easily as if they had been standing in front of him, and perhaps they were. His early sketches were in two major categories - local people, and imaginary scenes: animals in human situations, monsters, angels, flights of fancy, etc. Besides his artistic genius, he also showed great musical and athletic talents. Doré became an accomplished tenor, violinist, acrobat, and mountain-climber. His abilities seemed limitless.

If Doré had not gone into art, he would almost certainly have gone into theatre. As a child he often organized the other students into theatrical productions. He would make costumes, props, scenery, and backdrops. Perhaps his greatest theatrical accomplishment came at the ripe old age of eight. Strasbourg dedicated a monument to Johann Gutenberg on November 13, 1840. There was a parade and each guild designed a float, with the printers' guild in the lead. Gustave was enthralled with the festivities. Shortly thereafter, Mr. Vergnette assigned a major class project, and Gustave suggested that the class recreate the Gutenberg Parade. The other students thought it impossible, but Gustave replied, "Nothing is impossible. I will take charge of the whole affair, and will be responsible for everything. You will see what I can do. We will make it a grand success." (Roosevelt, p.29) Arthur Kratz then related the amazing scope of eight-year-old Gustave's accomplishment:

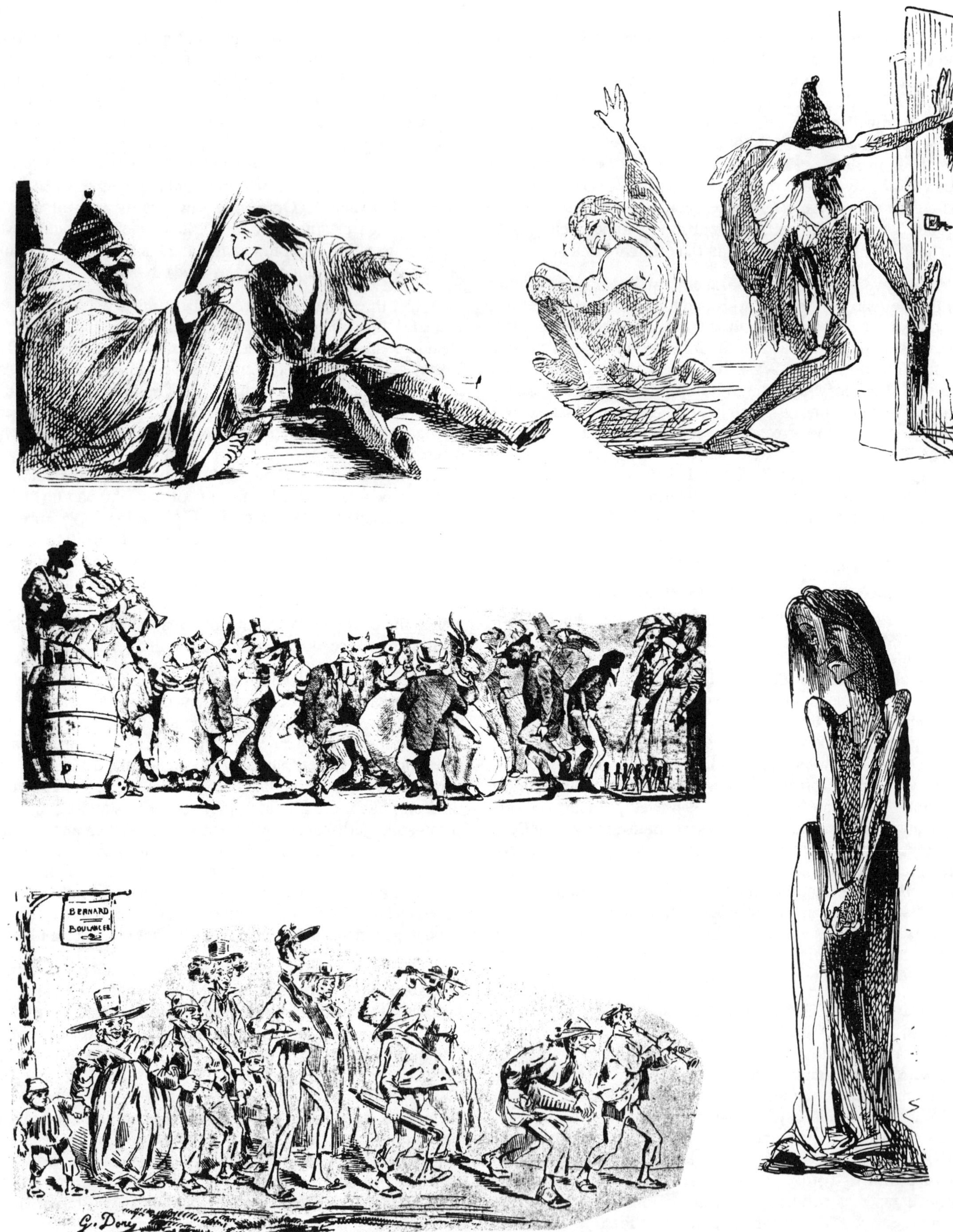
BERNARD
BOULANGER
G. Doré

Let me tell you about the fete which we got up under his direction. About one p.m. on the appointed day everything was ready, and we marched round the cathedral square after having shown ourselves to the professor. There were the four chariots drawn by some of the school boys, the rest of whom filled the cars, representing different corporations. Gustave was at the head of his chosen guild, and dressed himself in a characteristic costume, himself in a characteristic costume, including a Rubens hat, with paper ornaments. His whole get-up was that of a medieval artist. The respective masters of the guilds were chosen from amongst ourselves by him, and he prepared them for the parts they had to play. For instance, I personified the chief cooper, and he taught me the trick that was always performed at the fetes of the coopers' guild. Some of the Alsatian mountaineers were extremely adroit in the performance of this particular trick, which consisted in turning round a glass full of beer inside the rim of a cask-hoop without spilling a drop of liquor. Gustave, who was wonderfully dexterous, had learned how to do this to perfection from an old barrel-maker. Well, he got me up in my part, and I headed my guild in the car, twirling the glass in the hoop to the best of my ability. The printers' association was in the hands of Ernest Doré, Gustave's oldest brother, who played a very important part in the fete.

Not only had Gustave organized and completed the preparations for the celebrations, but he had decorated the chariots inside and out. He painted four banners, each of nearly two yards in length and one in breadth; one for each corporation. He drew the insignia from memory. The printers' banner displayed presses, newspapers, and so on, and that of the coopers' their old craft symbols; but the most marvellous of all was that which waved above his own triumphal car. He had accurately painted the ancient lantern of the Peintres-verriers, in the form of a star, with coloured glass points, and at its base he reproduced a well-known stained glass window of the cathedral. It was decorated with a design in arabesques environing the gorgeous banner's margin; and in a corner, underneath all, was inscribed his own name, "G. Doré fecit."

We marched round the square, stopping every now and then to work at our various trades. The gardeners made up bouquets, and threw them to the crowd; bulletins were issued from the printing-press, and flung about; I did my hoop trick, and made believe to drink deep draughts of the foaming beer of Strasbourg; but Gustave outdid us all. He made sketches of people in the crowd, which he launched to the right and left with great dignity. Only when someone exclaimed that he or she recognized a striking likeness did I realize that Gustave was making real drawings. He was the quaintest sight I ever set eyes on, and I think I can see him now, perched on his car, with his extraordinary hat, his fantastic garments, his head bent on one side; striking his attitude and quickly making his sketches, which he distributed to the applauding throng. We finally drew up before the Pension Vergnette, and went into the house, where we presented the four banners to our school-master, and Gustave made an elaborate speech in honour of the accasion. The Professor and his family were delighted; but when they saw the paintings on the banners, and some of the sketches which Gustave had strewn about him in the Place, their enthusiasm knew no bounds. From that day forth I felt sure that my gifted schoolfellow would never become an actor. It was obvious that Gustave Doré was cut out by nature for an artist, and all who knew him foretold that he would one day adopt painting as a career. I have heard of many precocious youths, but never have I known such a prodigy as Gustave Doré proved himself to be, when quite a little child, planning and successfully carrying out a marvellous imitation of the Fete of Gutenberg as he executed from memory.

Even Gustave's father was astounded at his total recall of the tiniest details, when they went on trips together. Many days later he could draw amazingly accurate depictions of scenes and people they had met. When Gustave was told stories he could immediately visualize and draw them, even if they were pure fantasy. He loved Bible stories, fairy tales, mythology, old legends and literary classics. He began combining memory and imagination; he could precisely draw an actual event, but when the real story ended, he would keep it going without hesitation from his imagination. His visual stories existed in a dimension outside of reality or unreality - they existed in the dimension of creativity. As his stories progressed, real people might become animals or insects. He began to have a fascination for winged creatures - angels and demons, fairies and cupids, that would become one of the dominant themes of his great literary folios.

When Gustave was nine, his father's occupation caused them to move to Bourg, in the Alps. This added a new natural setting to the Black Forest region he had loved so well. He loved nature so much that he once fell asleep in the forest by himself, and awoke to frantic adults searching for him. In Bourg he had a new teacher, Grandmottet, who was just as impressed as Vergnette had been. At the age of nine, Gustave's reputation had preceded him to his new school. His teachers often commented that they had never seen a child more talented, cheerful, and full of life. But he did get into trouble because he was so impulsive and dreamy. When he first got oil paints, he could not wait to find a canvas. He grabbed the first item he could find to paint - a chicken! He somehow managed to paint the entire chicken bright green. A short time later he was dismayed to come across a mob of hysterical superstitious peasants who were certain that the chicken had come from the devil. His father had to go to great lengths to convince them

 Les Travaux d'Hercule, by Gustave Doré, 1847 lithographic album (first published work - age 15!)

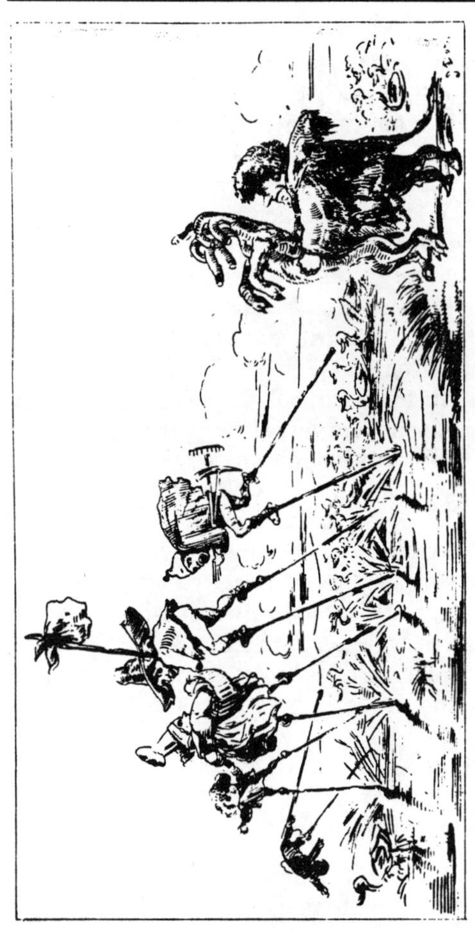

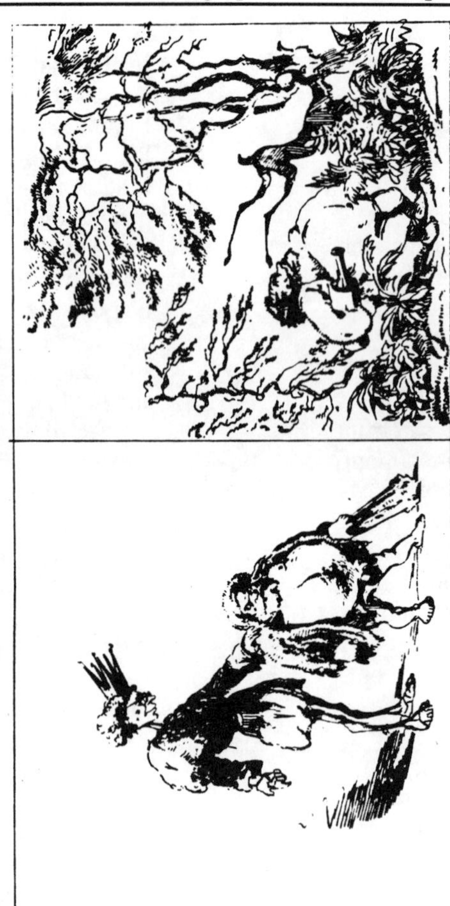

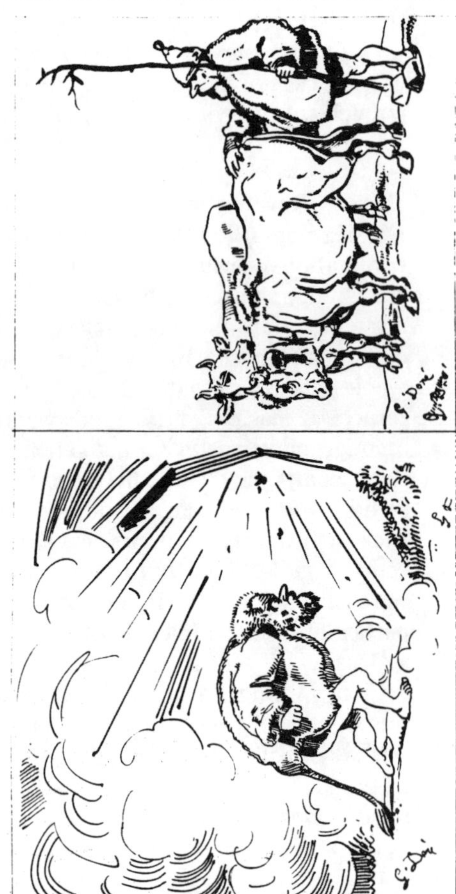

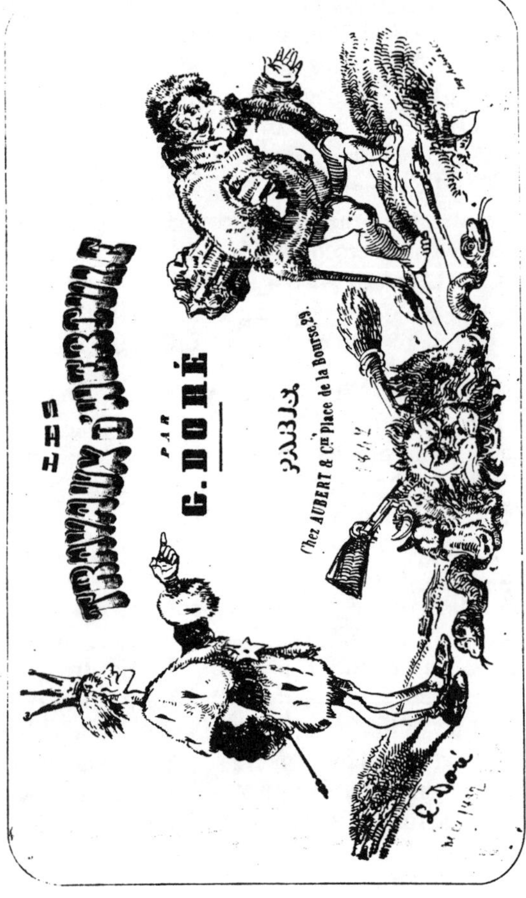

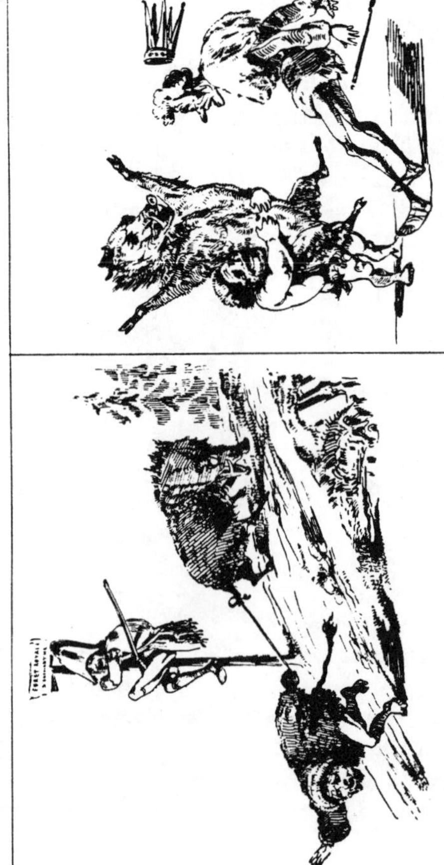

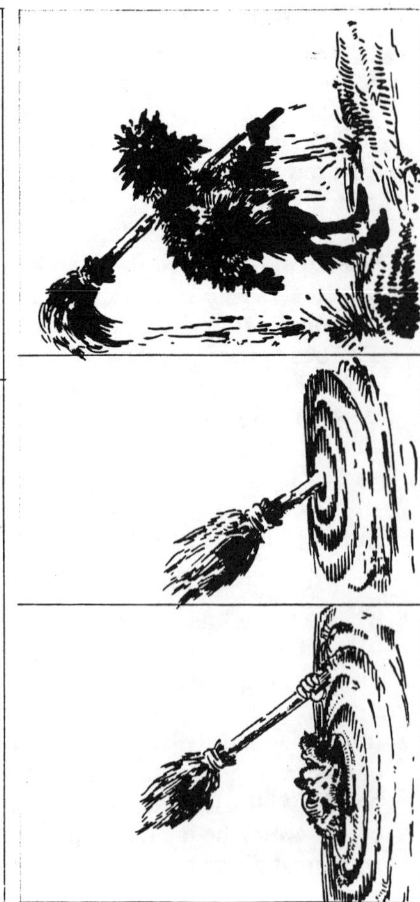

that his son was not demon-possessed, just goofy. An elderly woman then put a curse on Gustave, stating that just as his painting had made other people suffer, so painting would make him suffer. To the day he died, he believed in that curse.

Gustave's father hardly had to push Gustave to do well in school, since Gustave was always overachieving. His reward for school success was going on trips with his father, which Gustave relished. They would explore the Vosges forests and mountains. While his father take care of civil engineering work, Gustave immersed himself in nature, exploring or laying in the grass for hours drinking in the scenery. Per Roosevelt (p.47) "There was not a tree of the forest that he had not studied, not a flower that grew by the wayside, but its name and perfume were known to him, not a herb nor healing plant so cunningly hidden in the mountain clefts but his eye could detect it and his hand pluck it from its lurking-place. He knew where the wood-birds nested and nightingales sang; he knew the track of the deer and the haunt of the squirrel."

It was in Bourg that his father seemed to ease up on his opposition to Gustave's artistic pursuits. In the little town of Ceyzeriat, near Bourg, Gustave was able to borrow actual lithographic stones, to make his first "official" engravings. It is often said that his first published work was at the age of 15, but that was his first commissioned work. He began personally engraving and printing lithographic stones at the age of 12. He did hundreds of childhood drawings. Although there are many sketches of local individuals, his forte quickly evolved into picture-stories. Here is a summary of his amateur picture-stories between the ages of 5-13:

- 1837	(age 5)	***The Ant & the Moth*** (school story)
- 1839	(age 7)	***Rencontre de Monsieur Fox***
- 1840	(age 8)	***Fouilloux*** (Madame Braun's dog)
- 1842	(age 10)	J.J.Grandville-style animal stories
		Miriflor & Mistenflute (tourists)
		Jupiter (mythology)
		Dante's Inferno
- 1844	(age 12)	***Calypso & Telemachus***
- 1845	(age 13)	Bourg society lithographs

We have already discussed the 1837 story of the ant and the moth, Gustave's earliest dated drawings. The 1840 work was bound into a brown leather sketch-book and presented to Madame Braun, a close friend of the Doré family. She showed that very book to Blanche Roosevelt after Doré's death in 1883. It shows the all-too-human adventures of Madame Braun's dog, including sitting at the table eating with the rest of the family, and waltzing with Mrs. Doré. In 1842, after the move to Bourg, there was a major increase in Doré's picture-stories. He was inspired by Grandville's 323 anthropomorphic animal drawings in ***Scenes de la Vie Privee et Publique des Animaux*** (serialized from 1840-42; 2V book edition in 1842, by Hetzel/Paulin of Paris. see Ray, p.273-275) That motivated Gustave to begin work on his own animal stories. He created three similar books with a total of 57 animal drawings. These are the drawings which Grandville himself happened to see, and with which he was so impressed. Forberg reprinted 36 of Doré's 57 early animal drawings (p.1321-1335).

Next, Gustave's fascination with mythology led him to a series of drawings of the life of ***Jupiter***, the Roman equivalent of Zeus. Next came Doré's first attempt at ***Dante's Inferno***. It contained ten pages of combined text and illustrations. It is interesting to compare those crude 1842 drawings with the 1861 engravings which made him world-famous. His travel adventure comedy, ***Miriflor & Mistenflute***, was the beginning of many Doré satires on tourism in magazines and in his lithographic albums over the next decade. In 1844, Gustave did his second literary classic in 10 pages of text and illustrations. This time it was ***Calypso & Telemachus***, but this one was in much more of a humorous vein than his 1842 Dante. In 1845, he did those Bourg lithographs of various social scenes, which are now shown at Doré exhibitions.

Most of Doré's childhood drawings have been reprinted in some major Doré reference work - Roosevelt, Jerrold, Valmy, Deze, Farner, Forberg, Renonciat & Strasbourg-1983. It is fascinating to follow the development of his raw artistic genius without art lessons. Some critics have said that during Doré's professional life, he made too much money, and that it motivated him to overproduction. But the artistic ouput from his childhood shows that his rate of artistic production was an inner obsession unrelated to money, which he could not have restrained even if he had wanted to. Doré was never motivated by money. Money only represented the means by which he could continue to express his artistic creativity.

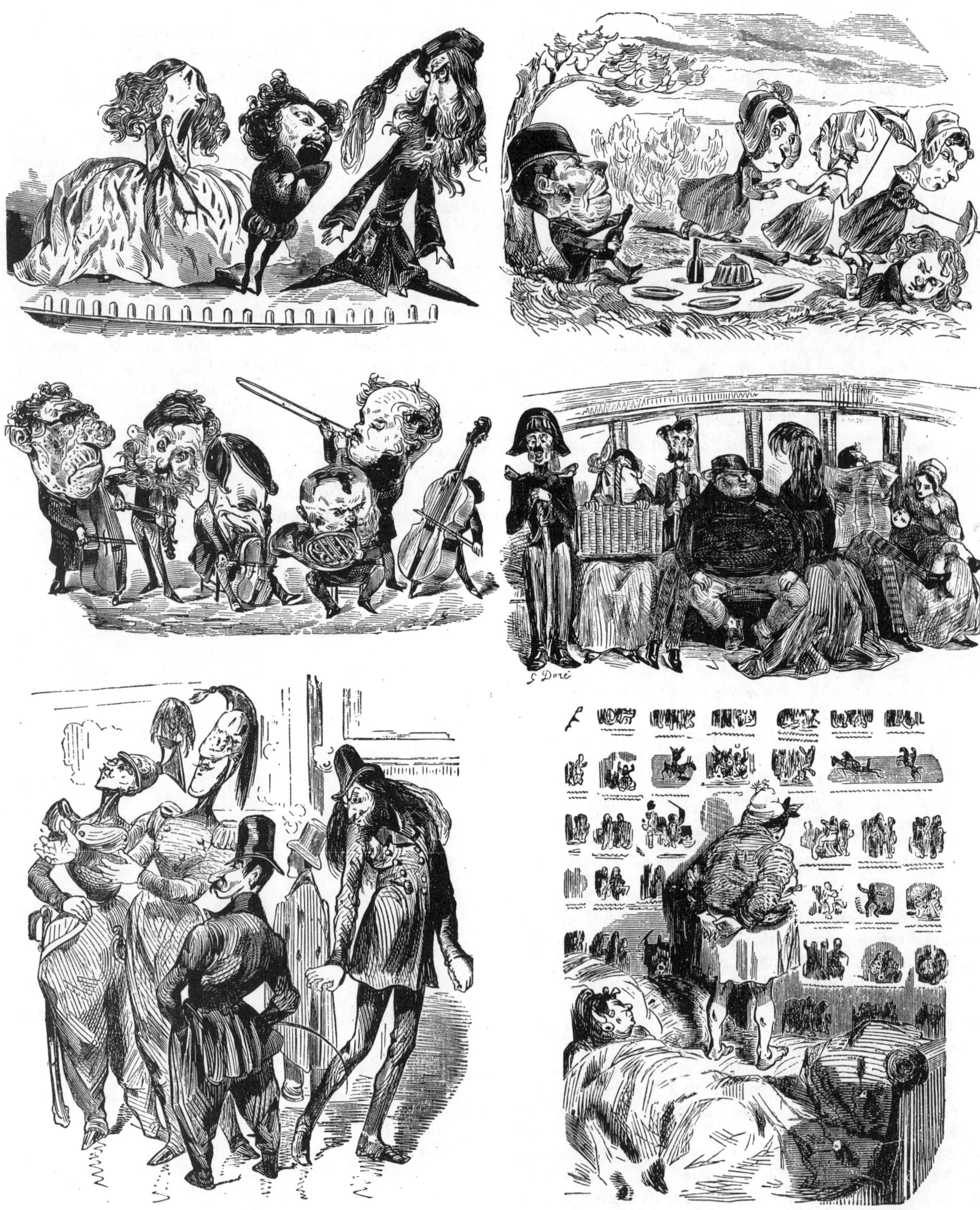

This artist wonders how the idiots can admire Horace Vernet as they do.

Aubert's coloured caricatures will continue to delight children of all ages.

3. THE BOY-GENIUS CARTOONIST (1847-53:AUBERT)

The story of how Doré became famous at the age of 15 is almost mythical. In September of 1847, Gustave visited Paris for the first time, with his family. Being so impressionable, he immediately fell in love with Paris, and determined to remain there. His creative mind shifted into overdrive, trying to figure out how to get his family to go along with such a arrangement. One of the many places in Paris that fascinated Gustave was a publishing company named Aubert. In their windows they displayed illustrations for forthcoming books. Gustave was convinced that he could do better illustrations than the ones on display. So he hatched a plan. The next day he pretended to be ill, and convinced the family to go out sight-seeing without him. He then set to work and made several drawings at his usual lightning speed. He was about to take Aubert by storm.

You must remember that Gustave looked very young. Theophile Gautier stated that at fifteen, the thin little Gustave looked no more than ten or twelve. In many ways he acted like a little child, so impulsive and playful. Picture that little child, with a set of drawings almost as big as himself, marching right into the House of Aubert, past the stupified employees, into the office of the white-haired publisher Charles Philipon. Gustave dropped his drawings on Philipon's desk and asserted, "This is how those illustrations should look!" Philipon was shocked at Gustave's boldness, and amazed at the quality of the drawings. He did not believe that the little boy in front of him actually did the drawings, especially when he learned that Gustave had never taken an art lesson. He insisted that Doré make some drawings right then and there, and called in other employees to watch. Can you picture that group of adults staring at a mere child making sketch after sketch in seconds? They saw a boy who was supremely confident, talented, and uninhibited. Paris had never seen such a veritable Mozart with a pencil. Philipon's attitude changed from disbelief to abduction. He would not let Gustave leave. He sent employees to track down the gruff Monsieur Doré. Imagine Gustave's childish delight as Philipon pleaded with his father to let Gustave stay in Paris, where he would be well paid to draw cartoons. Because of Gustave's age, his father had to sign the contract that made Gustave a professional artist. The contract called for Gustave to work exclusively for Aubert for a minimum of three years. Gustave would be paid 40 *francs* per page for the first year, increasing to 50 *fr* and 60 *fr* in the second and third years. To put that in perspective, the most the great cartoonist Honore Daumier ever earned at the height of his fame was 40 *fr* per page. By the age of 17, Doré was the highest paid cartoonist in France! Because of his age, Gustave was only required to do a page a week, but he always did much more. Philipon was to find Gustave a home and see that he finish his schooling, at the famous Lycee Charlemagne in Paris. But Gustave's father died in 1848, and his mother and brothers came to live with him in Paris. Gustave at 16 was supporting his entire family.

Philipon was convinced he had found a gold mine. He was about to launch a new illustrated humor weekly - ***Journal pour Rire***. The first official issue was February 5th, 1848, but on December 27, 1847 they published a 4-page promotional "specimen" number, the back page of which contained 13 Doré vignettes. But even before that, on December 14, 1847, they announced the publishication of Doré's first book edition -

Les Travaux d'Hercule

The Labours of Hercules was a Doré parody of Greek mythology. It was published by Aubert, Philipon's brother-in-law and business partner, who in the introduction had this to say about the new Parisian artistic sensation:

> ***The Labours of Hercules*** have been designed, drawn, and lithographed by an artist 15 years of age, who has taught himself drawing without a master, and without classical studies. It has appeared to us that this is not the least curious fact about this original album, and we have desired to cite it here, not only in order to specially interest the public in the works of this young draughtsman, but also to mark the point of departure of M. Doré, whom we believe to be destined to take distinguished rank in art.

Hercules was an oblong lithographic album, essentially a comic book. The 46 pages contained 104 illustrations, plus the full-page cover illustration. It was *Album Jabot* #12, the first comic-book series, begun a century before ***Superman***. The case could be made that Doré's ***Hercules*** was actually the first comic-book superhero. Doré's ***Hercules*** is listed in the French and German Comic Book Price Guides. Comic books really began in the 1830s. The Swiss teacher, Rodolphe Topffer, began making cartoon picture-stories to entertain his students. He did not invent cartooning, but he developed the ideas of telling an extended story using sequential art panels. His art was rather crude, but it caught on, and so began the *Album Jabot* series. Other artists in the series were Cham and E.Forest. Doré had seen some of those comics. From 1847-54, Doré was France's most popular comic-strip artist, for books and magazines. In the mid-1850s he evolved to more serious literary illustration, and thereafter seemed embarrassed by his comic-strip origins. The mantle of comic-strip art then passed to Wilhelm Busch of Germany, and eventually to the Sunday comic strip "funnies" we still see today.

Before we move on from ***Hercules***, we must comment on its rarity. The undated Aubert edition from 1847 was the only French edition. Ray (p.329) describes that edition as being "of legendary rarity." Ray himself was fortunate enough to acquire Michael Sadleir's copy. Ray died a decade ago, but I have not been able to track down his copy. Kunzle (p.109) states, "No copy could be found in the United States; neither the British nor the French national library catalog lists it." Kunzle himself reprinted part of it, the first time (1990) any of it had been translated into English. After 75 years of obscurity, the original book was finally reprinted in German in 1922 by Rentzch of Zurich. There was another German reprint in the 1980s. But the real credit for exposing the book goes to the 1975 German Doré pictorial guide by Forberg. Among the 2,000+ Doré illustrations reproduced therein is the entire French & German text of ***Hercules***. That led yours truly to translate the entire work into English and finally publish thc first English edition of ***Hercules*** in 1992. Unfortunately, it is now out of print. Samuel Clapp of London owned a copy of the French edition, until he sold his entire Doré collection to the Musee d'Art Moderne in Strasbourg, which then put his collection on display (see Strasbourg-1993).

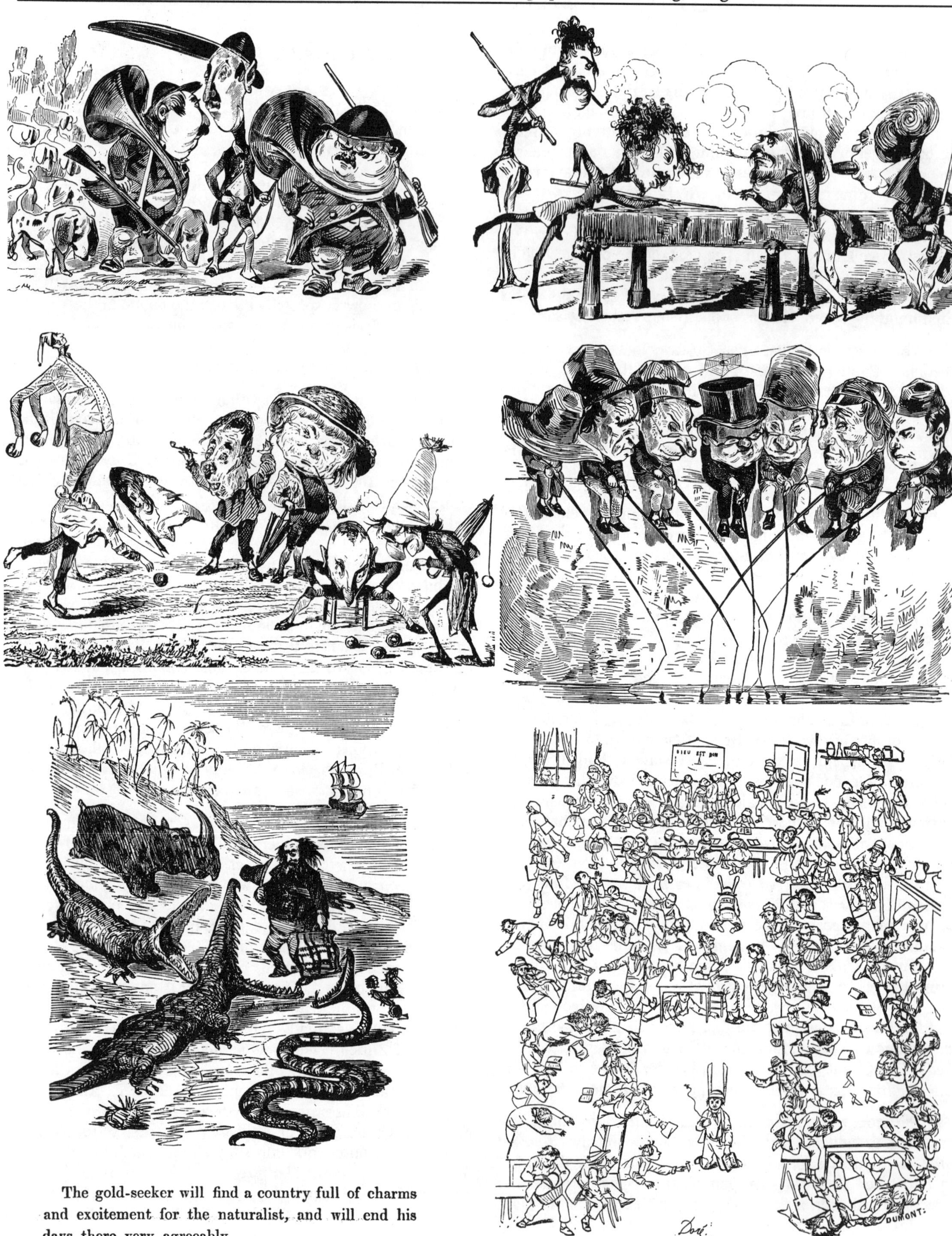

The gold-seeker will find a country full of charms and excitement for the naturalist, and will end his days there very agreeably.

Journal pour Rire

Doré did not just do drawings, he was creating everything about the art - the topics, the content, the captions, the stories; and at a rate that amazed all around him. Here is his rate of production of original illustrations for the years 1847 to 1853, when he was between the ages of 15-21. He had 1,880 published illustrations by the time he was 21. Over the seven years that is an average of 270 illustrations per year, and this was his slow period. In the decade after that, he averaged about 500 illustrations per year, even though he was by then producing hundreds of full-page folio engravings. During his entire life he produced art at a frantic rate, and it eventually took its toll.

1847: 118
1848: 253
1849: 148
1850: 289
1851: 544
1852: 332
1853: 176

Journal pour Rire was a non-political humor magazine. Previous publications like ***Charivari*** had emphasized political satire. In that era, such pursuits could land artists, writers, and publishers in jail. But Philipon tried very hard to be non-political, hardly an easy task in yet another year of French revolution. Doré was also as non-political as possible. Kunzle has done some impressive research into Doré's early comic-strip period. He comments on Doré's magazine art (p.106):

> Philipon recognized in this facile child-artist the very embodiment of the spirit of his new journal - carefree, light-hearted, unreflective, excited but not disturbed by the political ferment. The gamin of journal caricature, still a schoolboy, Doré reveled in the revolution, as might any child who did not suffer from it. His style was one of variably systemized graffiti, and he showed already the fertility that would become his hallmark, reputation, and notoriety.

But just how successful could a publication be that featured a child-artist? ***Charivari*** at its peak had a circulation of 3,000. In March of 1848, the brand-new ***Journal pour Rire*** already had a circulation of 9,000. By May of 1849 it reached 14,000. Doré was not the only artist, but he was certainly the prime attraction. He did lithographs and then increasingly wood-engravings. He used two major styles: a page full of small comic-strip vignettes, or one large outline illustration cartoon. The second style was borrowed from Dicky Doyle in London, working for ***Punch***, but once again Doré improved on the quality, just as he had done with Topffer's style. From 1848-1850, Doré did nothing but magazine illustrations. It was a pattern that would repeat itself throughout his life. He would exhaust the creative potential of a particular medium and then move on to a new artistic direction or medium.

In LeBlanc's massive (and rare) 1931 Doré bibliography, he actually counted and labelled every Doré illustration in every French magazine, identifying the first printing of each illustration and all reprints. Over a 10-year period, Doré did 1,408 illustrations for Philipon, about half of his magazine output. In 1856 the name was changed to ***Journal Amusant***. For a decade Doré parodied every aspect of French society, and in the next decade he did more literary and travel engravings. Philipon was not slow in profitting from Doré's popularity. Since he owned the rights, he kept repackaging Doré and other ***Journal pour Rire*** artists. In 1848 and 1849 he issued book editions - ***Album du Journal pour Rire***, reproducing ***Journal pour Rire*** art. Each volume had hundreds of Doré engravings. Then in 1851 he published a series of booklets called ***Ces Chinois de Parisiens*** ("Chinese in Paris" - the series title had no connection to booklet contents), again reprinting ***Journal pour Rire*** illustrations. Doré illustrations appear in ten of those editions. But the real shocker was his 1851 publication of ***Papier peints comiques***, which was wallpaper! Wallpaper full of illustrations from ***Journal pour Rire***. There were three different versions of it. Then in 1853 he came up with another series of booklets - ***Petits Albums pour Rire***, with different titles but many of the same illustrations. Doré illustrations appear in seven of those editions. That was the end of Philipon editions, but by 1867 Doré had become world-famous, and English publishers were desperate for any Doré illustrations. So Frederick Warne of London issued a quarto album entitled ***200 Sketches, Humorous & Grotesque*** (it actually contained 303 illustrations), reprinting Doré 1849-52 ***Journal pour Rire*** art. They even updated Doré's captions to make them fit 1860s London. In their preface, they tried to assert that Doré's comic-strip art was actually superior to his literary folios:

> Among the many drawings by Gustave Doré which have been published in England and elsewhere, comparatively few represent the artist in the direction in which his real strength is generally confessed to lie. "As a grotesque designer," says one of the principle London literary journals, "he has no living rival, and few equals in former times;" but the works "with illustrations by Doré" put forth to show his excellence, not unfrequently present him in that phase in which his peculiar talent is not exhibited to advantage.

200 Sketches was reprinted several times. Some of the English captions are quite witty. Some of those illustrations have been reprinted in recent years in the U.S. magazine ***Coronet*** (1938), in Forberg (1975), in a Dover Press edition called ***Doré Spot Illustrations*** (1987), and in Kunzle (1990).

Des-Agrements d'un Voyage d'Agrement

By 1851, Doré had more time on his hands, with the completion of formal schooling. That year he did two more satirical lithographic albums, or comic books. Both are quite rare, but were reprinted in their entirety in Forberg, and partially by Kunzle with English text. The first of these was a spoof of tourism. ***Des-Agrements d'un Voyage d'Agrement*** basically means "The Unpleasantries of a Pleasure Trip." It was also oblong, but whereas ***Hercules*** was about 6½x10 with 105 large illustrations on 46 pages, ***Des-Agrements*** was about 10½x14 with 175 small illustrations on 24 pages. It was the culmination of years of poking fun at tourists in ***Journal pour Rire***. Gustave had spent his childhood in serious interaction with nature, and he divided travellers into two groups - serious nature lovers (like himself) and bumbling novices completely dependent on resorts and guides. Kunzle reprinted about a fourth of ***Des Agrements*** in English, and he points out (p.122) how cinematic Doré was, in a scene where tourists interact with poets who are lost in contemplation:

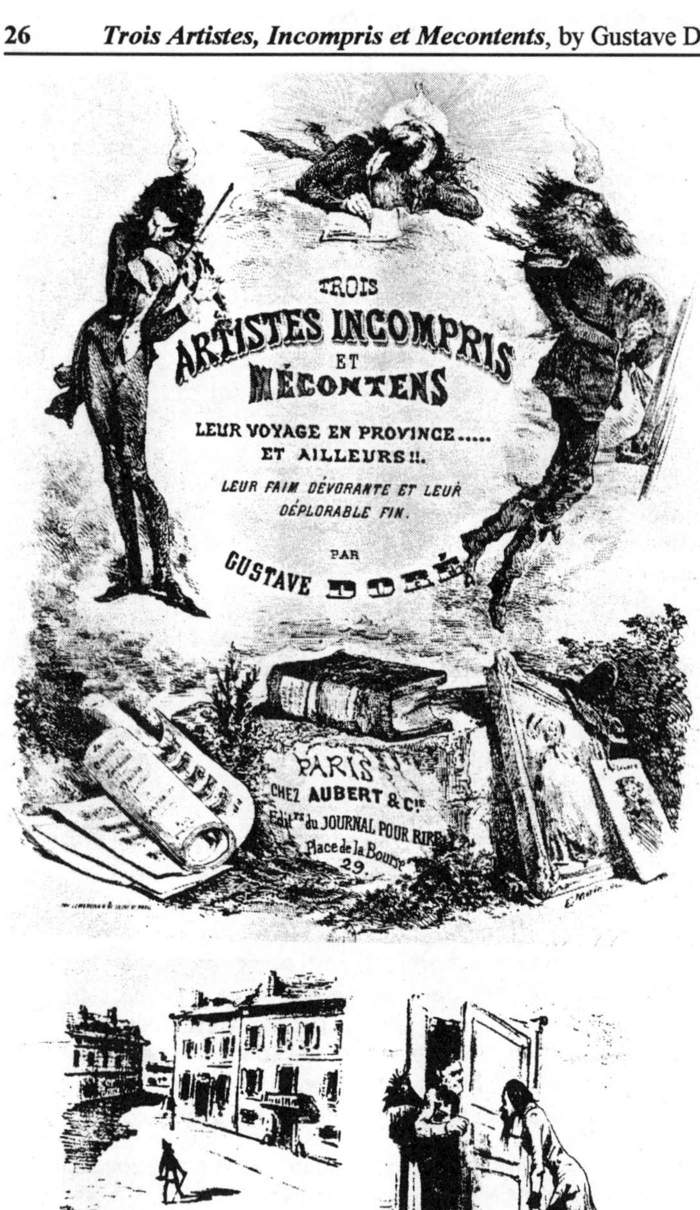

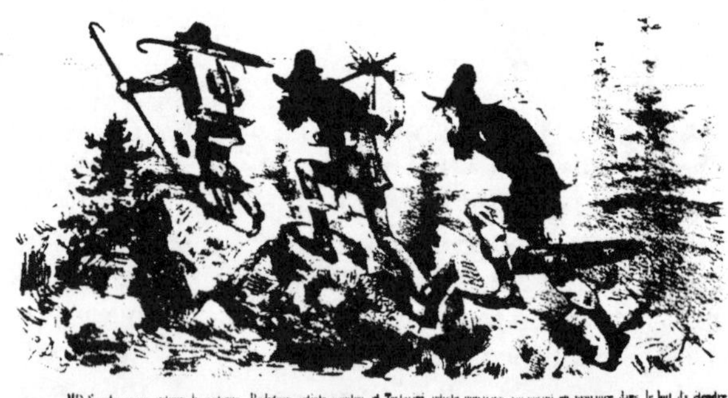

Mrs Sombrecoeur, auteur dramatique, Badigeon artiste peintre, et Tartarini artiste musicien, voyageant en province dans le but d'étendre leur réputation, [illegible] par un chemin pareil à celui de la gloire.

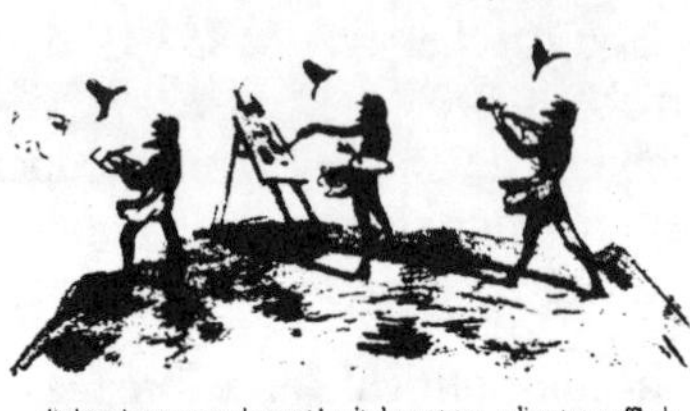

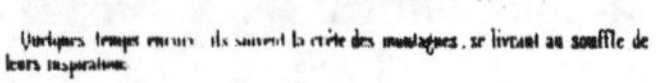

Quelques temps encore, ils suivent la crête des montagnes, se livrant au souffle de leurs inspirations.

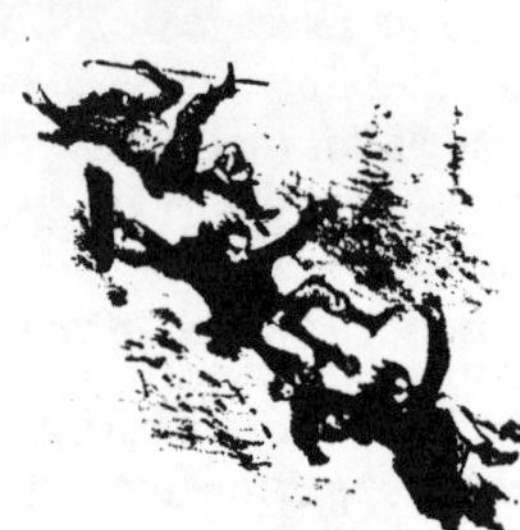

Et au terrain glissant de la rêverie.

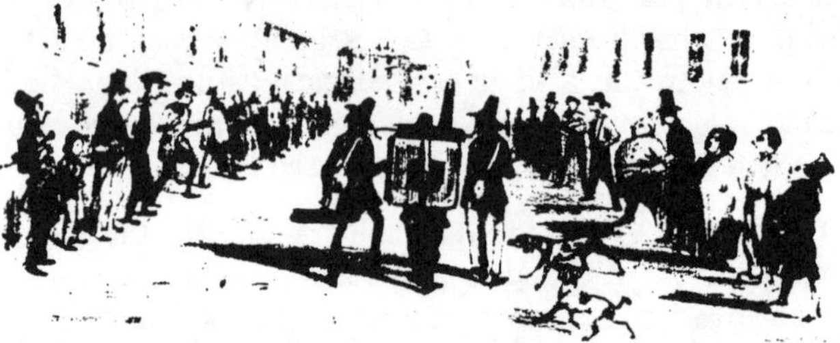

Forts de leurs inspirations, ils font une solennelle entrée dans la ville de B....... au grand étonnement des [illegible] qui n'ont jamais vu 3 barbes entrer comme ça sans rien dire.......

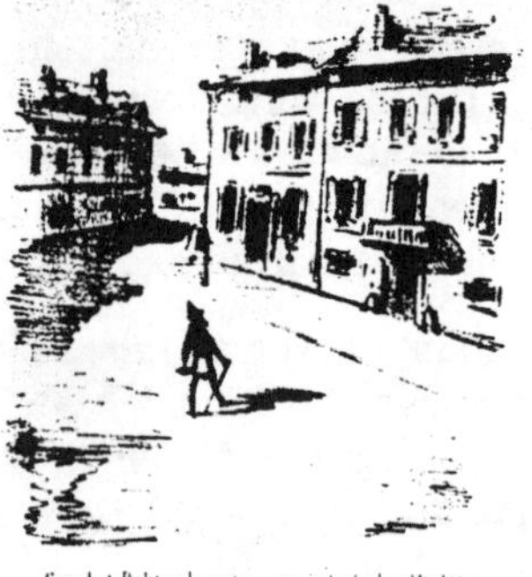

Cependant Badigeon le peintre, songe à aborder le public libéral de cette ville [illegible] à juger du public par les murs qui le recouvrent, l'accueil sera froid.

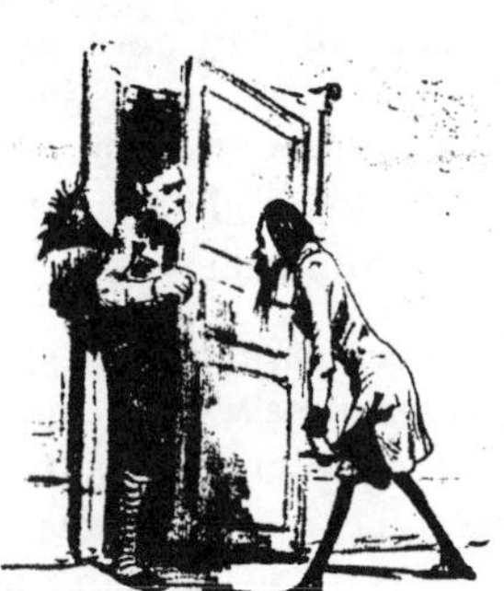

Partout les domestiques lui répondent [illegible] aux portes que tout le monde est daguerreotypé, et que l'on ne reçoit ni artistes ni commis voyageur.

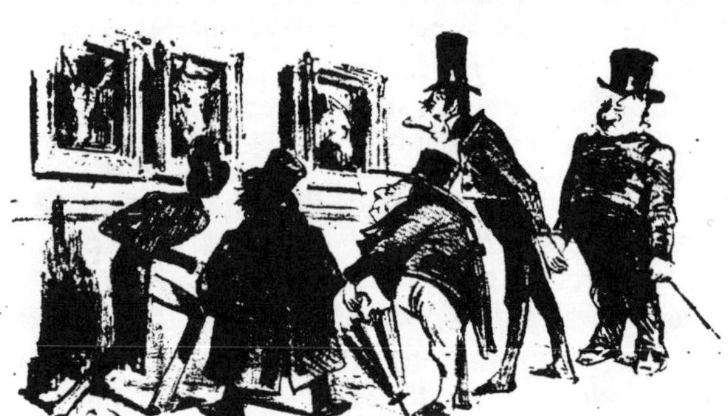

A la vue des études d'animaux que Badigeon a faites dans les campagnes d'alentour, les bourgeois de la ville, admettent ce talent et se décident [illegible] tirer leur portrait.

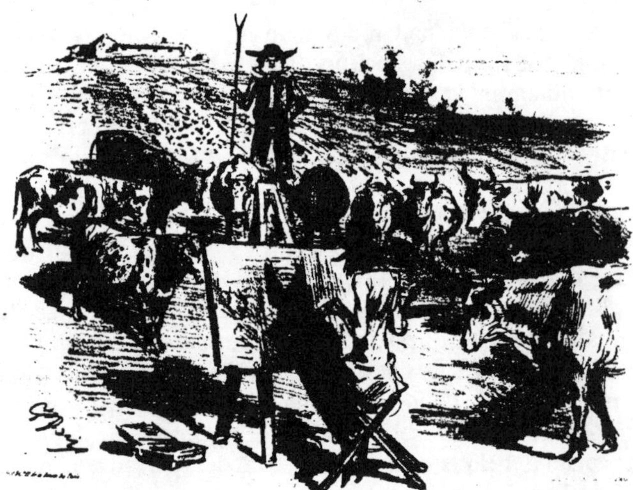

Rebuté par la ville, Badigeon obtient à la campagne des commandes assez considérables _ il fit le portrait d'un riche fermier entouré de ses biens.

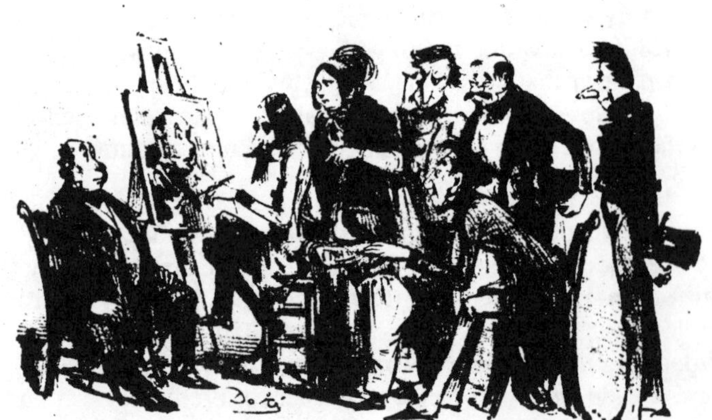

Alors commence pour Badigeon sa carrière de portraitiste _ heureusement pour lui que dans ses débuts, il ne manque ni de sages conseils, ni de bons avertissements. Il en est accablé.

This particular episode is one of the most cinematic Doré ever devised, showing in quick succession six similar scenes, three in medium and three in close-up view, of the progressively crumbling ruin. The terror of the tourist is contrasted with the composure of two German poets, who become literally rooted to a free-hanging segment of the topmost arch - an emblem of romantic aloofness and a loftily precarious existence.

Doré never lost his love of nature, in his travels in Alsace, in the Alps, in the Pyrenees, in the Scottish Highlands, etc. Later on we will look at one of the most beautiful travel books ever made, the massive 1874 ***Spain***, by Doré & Baron Charles Davillier, the illustrations of which have found their way into editions of Ernest Hemingway, Alexandre Dumas, William Prescott, Theophile Gautier, and dozens of other authors. There were only three known editions (all undated) of ***Des-Agrements***, all from the 1850s, and each by a different publishers - Aubert, deVresse, and Fechoz & Letouzey.

One interesting scene in ***Des-Agrements*** is where tourists happen upon a great young artist who is creating an enormous landscape painting out in the woods. The artist is, of course, Gustave Doré. He saw no problem in shameless self-promotion in a humorous work. It is ironic that he often argued that he did not need to paint from nature because he had everything he needed in his memory. His treatment of an aspiring artist in ***Des-Agrements*** was in sharp contrast to his other book that came out at the same time -

Trois Artistes - Incompris et Mecontents

This other 1851 lithographic album was not oblong, but was otherwise similar in size and content - 10x13½ with 155 small illustrations on 25 pages, plus a classic cover. The title reads "Three Artists - Misunderstood Malcontents," the story of a painter, a poet, and a musician, setting out to attain fame and fortune, and finding the common people to be less than cooperative or appreciative. It is also quite a witty story. ***Trois Artistes*** is also rare, but it was also reprinted in its entirety in Forberg, and Kunzle translated about a fifth of it into English. The only problem with those Forberg reproductions is that they reduce the originals by over 50%. It is also unfortunate that Kunzle's English versions do not include the entire books.

Trois Artistes really came back to haunt Doré. It was easy for his as a teenager to poke fun at unappreciated artists. Two decades later, Doré would be the misunderstood malcontent painter. In ***Trois Artistes***, Doré saw artistic rejection coming from uneducated country folk. But that would hardly compare with his own artistic rejection by the French art establishment. They did not forget how Doré mocked them for years when he was just a cute kid making fun of everybody. A decade later that young anti-establishment cartoonist thought that the art establishment should praise his paintings. To add salt to their wounds, by the 1860s Doré was already more famous and wealthy than most of them. In one early Doré cartoon, he pictured a rejected artist with the caption: "This artist wonders how the idiots can admire Horace Vernet the way they do." Not many years later that was exactly what Doré was saying about Ernest Meissonier. It has often been said that everything came too easy to Doré, that he did not "pay his dues." Doré paid his dues after he became famous. The day came when he finally realized that there was absolutely nothing he could do to make the French art establishment accept him. It is so unfortunate that he could not be satisfied with everything else he attained. He became obsessed with the one thing he could not have. But we are getting ahead of our story here.

When last we left Doré's personal life, he was enrolled in the prestigious Lycee Charlemagne. He did very well there, and had as fellow students the likes of Edmond About and Hippolyte Taine, both of whose works he later illustrated. But living in Paris was like a perpetual dreamland. In his younger years he had to create a dream world; now it existed right in front of him. He became famous almost overnight. He liked the attention, but not nearly as much as he loved the art of Paris. He practically lived in the Louvre and other museums. In what free time he had (besides being a full-time student and full-time artist), he would gaze for hours at art treasures. He did not make sketches, but he did write notes about dates and other details. He still would not take art lessons. He was firmly convinced that he could draw anything, either from memory or imagination. In 1848, at the age of 16, he had two drawings displayed at the Salon, the government financed art exhibition. His father died unexpectedly toward the end of 1848, and his mother and brothers and Francoise moved to Paris to join him. They settled in St. Germain, on the Rue St. Dominique, in the home built by his maternal grandfather. Gustave did early oil paintings of his father and of Charles Philipon. Some of his earliest friends, in addition to his schoolmates, were Paul Dalloz, Paul Lacroix, and Nadar, the photographer. Dalloz wrote that in his early Parisian years, Doré "...went into the fashionable world, to the first nights at the theatres, to musical parties, and to official receptions and balls; but diversions - even the wild gaieties of the Caveau - were never permitted to interfere with his art." (Jerrold, p.55) These were the days when Doré was not sure if he was a boy or a man. He had a little bedroom off of his mother's bedroom (which remained so until her death), and they discussed everything, in the early morning and late at night. He was gradually settling into the routine that would rule his entire adult life - his emotional dependence on his mother. It affected all his romances and near-romances, but we will cover all of that in a later chapter.

Bibliophile Jacob

The year 1851 saw the end of Doré's exclusive contract with Aubert. They stayed on very good terms, but Doré never liked being tied down. The transition away from Aubert and comic-strip art began with Doré's friend, Paul Lacroix. Lacroix was a popular French author, under the pseudonym Bibliophile Jacob. In fact, he was popular before Doré was born. Lacroix was born in 1807, and his father was a celebrated poet before him. His brother Jules was also a famous writer, and his brother-in-law was a chubby little fellow named Honore de Balzac. Lacroix was a father-figure for Gustave after he lost his father. Lacroix knew the Doré family before Gustave was born, and had seen some of Gustave's amazing drawings at the age of six. So he was delighted when Gustave came to Paris in 1847. Lacroix said that by 1848 "...all Paris was alternately

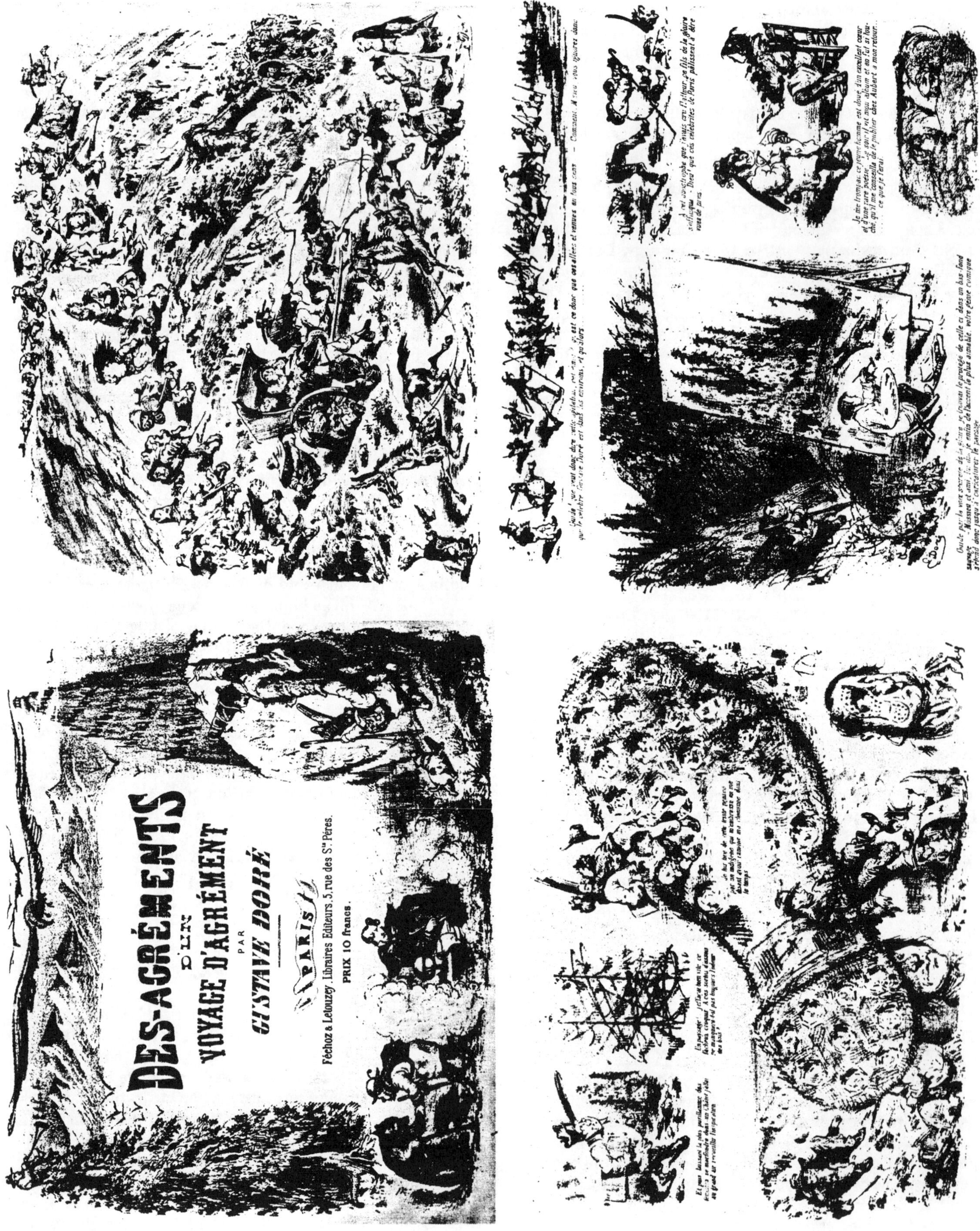
DES-AGRÉMENTS
D'UN
VOYAGE D'AGRÉMENT
PAR
GUSTAVE DORÉ
PARIS
Féchoz & Letouzey, Libraires Éditeurs, 5, rue des Sts Pères.
PRIX 10 francs.

laughing and crying over his marvelous works." (Roosevelt, p.91) Lacroix often visited Doré, and after seeing hundreds of unpublished illustrations Doré had done in his "spare" time, suggested that Doré do some illustrations for an upcoming illustrated set of Lacroix's works. He then gave Doré a set of his works to read for illustration ideas. Lacroix picks up the narrative from there (Roosevelt, p.92):

> He came to see me a week or two later. "Now," I said, "let us talk of my story. Have you read it, or even begun it?" "Oh," he replied cheerfully, "I mastered that in no time, and the blocks are all ready!" "What blocks?" I shouted, rising hastily from my chair in astonishment. "Ready with what?" "Your woodcuts," he answered calmly; "they make just three hundred. Here are some of them." and he commenced extracting numberless pieces of wood from pocket after pocket, "and the rest are in a basket at the door."
>
> All the while he was carelessly piling up pieces of wood on my table. I was so amazed that I could not, and, in fact, dared not show my feelings, for he was in such tremendous earnest. I think I can see him now as he stood before me, fire flashing from his beautiful eyes; his colour coming and going, while his face shone with the light of genius and enthusiasm; his slim hands diving swiftly into his pockets, each time bringing forth a block of wood enriched by a perfect marvel of design and skilful draughtmanship. I picked up one or two without commenting on their value. "Take them to Du Tacq, the editor," I said brusquely, "and let us see what he decides."
>
> "Very well," he replied; ... When he was gone I took up the blocks, and - I could not help it - the tears started to my eyes on looking at them. He was so gay and light-hearted, and did everything with so little effort, though so young, taking his talent - genius, I might say - as such a matter of course that there was little hope of inducing him to study seriously. I went to Du Tacq earlier that I should have otherwise done, because I was anxious to know what he thought of the drawings. He said -
>
> "I have not words to express myself adequately in speaking of such marvels. They are all admirable, and some are such beautiful specimens of work that I have appropriated them and taken them home to Mdm. Du Tacq. I did not tell young Doré this. I merely looked at them and made some commonplace remarks, asking if he could and would reproduce those particular drawings. He readily complied, thinking, no doubt, I was not quite satisfied with them; but judge for yourself. Those I have selected are so fine and exquisite that they resemble the figures in a Velasquez. I was not satisfied because I was enchanted. I would never have allowed any engraver to touch them. They are to-day with my wife, framed, covered with glass, and hang in the place of honour in my salon, as if they were the rarest works of Raphael or Michel Angelo. I have had some experience with wood-designers, but never have I seen anything in any way to compare with the amazing talent and precocity of this lad. He has a great future before him."

The ***Oeuvres Illustrees du Bibliophile Jacob*** was issued in 30 parts from 1851-1852, and then in a 5-volume set. It contained 134 Doré illustrations, plus many others by Celestin Nanteuil, Edouard Frere, Bocourt, Mettais, Hadamar, Schann, and Vessiot. It was published by J.Bry of Paris. Doré did several books for J.Bry in the next few years, including ***Lord Byron, Rabelais,*** and ***Montaigne***. Despite the high praise by Lacroix and Du Tacq, ***Bibliophile Jacob*** is not considered amongst Doré great works. There are three ways to explain this. First, that they were still very good, but do not compare with the art form Doré was to develop during the 1860s. Second, that there was a flood of wood engraving in French (and English) publishing at this time, making the average wood engraving at the time a low quality item, and thus Doré's illustrations looked very good by comparison. Third, that there were serious problems with what engravers did to the drawings artists delivered to them. This is borne out by many other 19th century illustrators, including the leading "Pre-Raphaelite," Dante Gabriel Rossetti. Lacroix goes on to point out this very fact in his ongoing narrative in Roosevelt (p.94): "It was a curious sight to see the boy scolding and haranguing men three or four times his age because they worked badly. He even attempted to show them the right way to engrave, and gave them elaborate instructions in an art he had never learned himself." By the 1860s Doré had developed his own "school" of engravers. Lacroix points out how delighted Doré was to find young engravers who were both talented and cooperative. (Roosevelt, p.96) Some Doré critics have stated that Doré was "completely dependent" upon those engravers to "improve" his drawings. Excuse me? The reason Doré's school of engravers was so good was because he trained them! It is true that sometimes he did not fill in all the details of simpler objects, such as trees, because he had already worked with his engravers about how to do those items. LeBlanc (p.201) also points out the low quality of the ***Bibliophile Jacob*** engravings. That early Doré work is now very rare and obscure. Forberg reproduced 17 of those illustrations (p.163-179).

Lord Byron

Shortly after completing the illustrations for ***Bibliophile Jacob***, the same publisher (J.Bry) asked Doré for illustrations to Byron. Doré only did 24 of those, and ***Oeuvres Completes de Lord Byron*** was issued in monthly parts in 1852-1853. It probably represents the all-time low for engraving quality on Doré's works. Perhaps Doré was still fighting with those same engravers. Most of them would not even put Doré's name on the engravings. There were three 1850s editions of the book, but there are no copies in any American library. Roosevelt (p.145) relates how difficult it was in 1884 to even find the copy in the Bibliotheque Nationale in Paris. Roosevelt points out that since Doré drew directly onto the wood blocks, which eventually wore out from the printing, that there is no way to ever really tell what his original art looked like. Forberg did reproduce eight of those illustrations (p.243-250). J.Bry was the transitional publisher between comic-strip art for Aubert and the leading French publisher Hachette, who took Doré on in 1855, and who later published his major folios. You might say that Doré "outgrew" Aubert and then J.Bry.

(top row) ***Bibliophile Jacob,*** by Paul Lacroix (1851-52) (bottom row) ***Works of Lord Byron*** (1853)

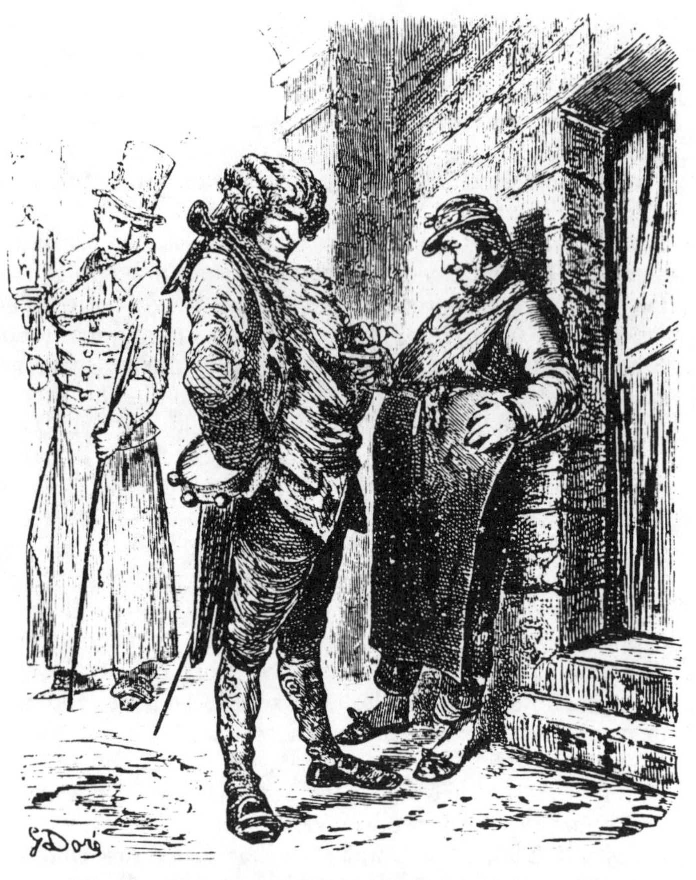

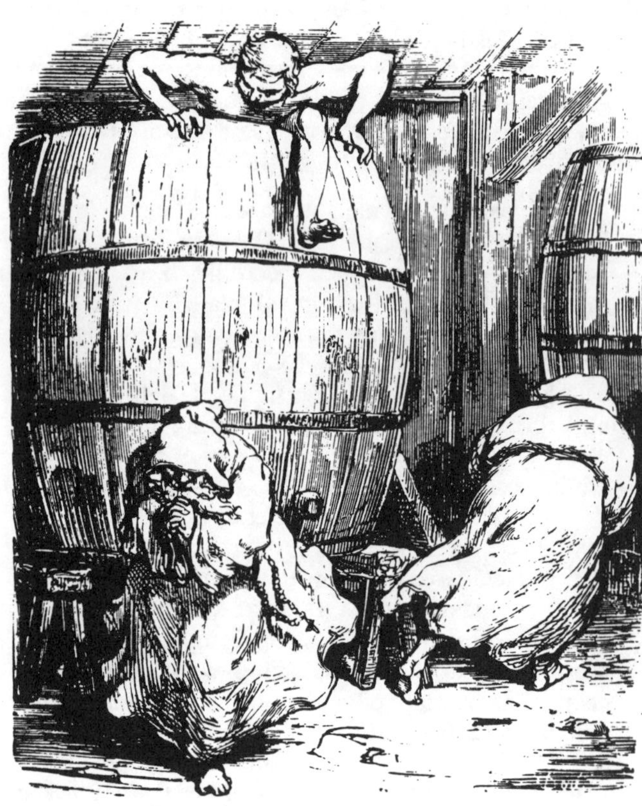

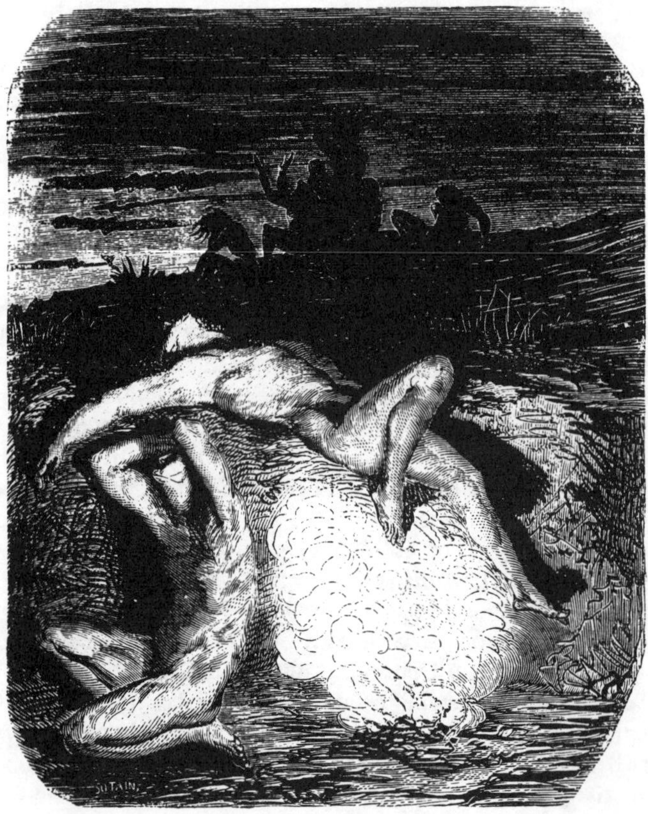

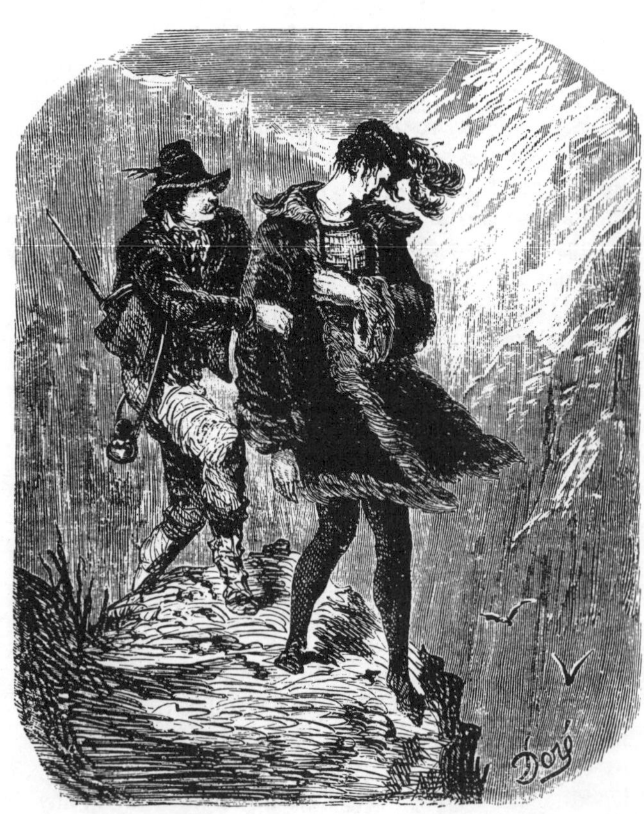

In the transition period 1851-54 Doré went from being a comic-strip cartoonist to being a serious literary illustrator. So ***Bibliophile Jacob*** and ***Byron*** are really significant only as part of that transition. But by 1854 some bad habits had developed in Doré's life, caused primarily by his ego. Dispite constant encouragement from Paul Lacroix and Theophile Gautier to take art lessons, to use models, and to paint from nature, Doré refused to see or accept any difference between illustrating and painting. He thought that his photographic memory and imagination could solve everything. He also got in the habit of fighting with anyone who disagreed with him about his talent in general or any particular work of art. In the process he began alienating his friends. He retained many famous friends, but most of them were much older than him. They eventually began to die off, and in the artistic/literary world, "another generation arose that knew not" Doré. He seemed to have unlimited talent, but his worst enemy was his own ego. He would lash out at friends if they inadvertently referred to him as a "draughtsman." Lacroix recalled from 1848 the first Doré oil painting he ever saw. Doré had painted a pretty little scene of a fisherman, but unbelievably enough, he painted it entirely in gray! Doré seemed to think that gray oil paint was like lead in a pencil. Doré had painted a b&w drawing! Lacroix thought it must be a joke, and laughed, which Doré did not take very well. Here is how Lacroix put it (Roosevelt, p.102):

> He was furious at me. I told him that the drawing was quite correct, and the subject a very agreeable one; but that no human being calling himself an artist had ever painted a picture all of one colour, and that colour an unnatural one.

How could such an artistic genius have such a major flaw? Was it possible that he had unlimited talent in black & white, but was color-blind? What an incredible irony! But how then did Doré end up doing several hundred paintings - in colors? Or did he simply think in b&w, and then had to retrain himself to think in color? I believe that Doré did have a sort of color-blindness, that he could not see soft and subtle color shades. Doré was exactly the opposite of impressionism, which is almost entirely dependent on soft color shades. It is possible that Doré could only see the major color shades. Doré was constantly using his other extraordinary talents to make up for this major weakness. Shortly before Doré died, he did gain some respect as a sculptor, where color was not an issue. Many people (like van Gogh) have asserted that Doré was one of the greatest b&w artists who ever lived. It could also be asserted that Doré's two greatest enemies were color and his own ego.

Shortly after Lacroix laughed at Doré's gray fisherman, Doré's mother came to live in Paris, and it appears that Doré sought emotional consolation from her. It was not very long before Lacroix was invited for dinner, and then taken to Doré's studio where he was shown 25 enormous canvasses, with greatly improved coloring, per Roosevelt (p.103):

> "Look," he said triumphantly, striking his boyish forehead - "Look at these. Twenty-five pictures, mostly all landscapes and all - all, M. Lacroix, painted by me alone in this studio." Raising his voice he added, "Models, forsooth! Your old hobby! Bah! my mind is my model for everything. Mother understands me, and she tells me that I am a great artist."

That last sentence by Doré should keep psychoanalysts occupied for decades. Doré then proceeded to tell Lacroix not to tell anyone that he had done them all in just a few days, because people would think that anything done that quickly could not be good. Is it possible that Doré's mother helped him in identifying the color shades? If it was true, it was a secret they took to their graves. But whatever his problems with color, he never did take art lessons, he never did use a model, and he never did paint from nature. His photographic memory and imagination did indeed appear to him to be limitless.

In many ways it was actually a disadvantage for Doré to become the boy-genius artistic sensation at such a young age. No one denies that he had formidable talent for one so young. But there are two things he did not have, and which his initial success prevented him from attaining - maturity and serious art training. Of course, relating his youthful accomplishments makes an exciting story, but most of the suffering he would encountered later on in life came from his having been too successful too quickly. Could he not have achieved all that he did and more, but a few years later, after he learned a little patience? But others argue that Doré's accomplishments came from his artistic genius being unencumbered and unrestrained. No one can ever prove what might have been, but it is true that his being so successful so young allowed him almost unlimited artistic freedom.

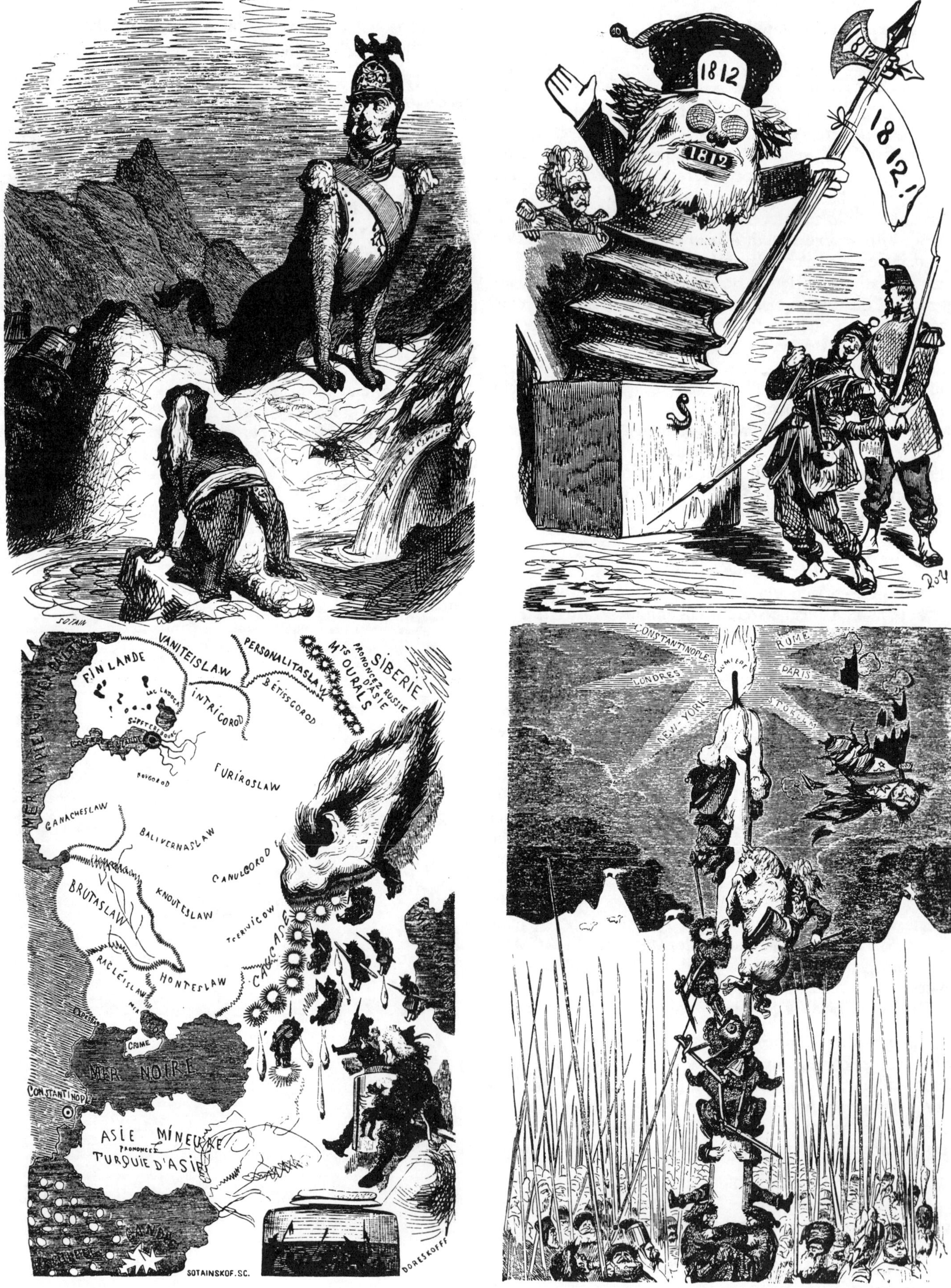
1812
1812
1812
1812!
SOTAIN
ROY
FINLANDE
VANITEISLAW
PERSONALITASLAW
SIBERIE
PRONONCEZ RUSSIE D'ASIE
MTS OURALS
LAC LADOGA
INTRICOROD
BÉTISSGOROD
S.T PETERSBOURG
NOVGOROD
FURIROSLAW
GANACHESLAW
BALIVERNASLAW
CANULGOROD
BRUTASLAW
KNOUTESLAW
CAUCASE
RACLÉISLAW
HONTESLAW
ODESSA
CRIME
MER NOIRE
CONSTANTINOP
ASIE MINEURE
PRONONCEZ
TURQUIE D'ASIE
SOTAINSKOF.SC.
DORESKOFF
CONSTANTINOPLE
ROME
LUMIERE
LONDRES
PARIS
NEW-YORK

4. FROM COMIC-STRIPS TO LITERARY CLASSICS (1854-60)

The years 1854-1860 were transitional for Doré in many ways - from boyhood to manhood (or a reasonable facsimile thereof), from comic strips and lithographic albums to literary vignettes, and from Aubert to J. Bry to Hachette. Additional transitions would follow - from literary vignettes to literary folios to oil painting to watercolor to sculpture, from French to English, and from secular to religious art. Doré was always in transition because he was never satisfied with success. His restless genius always needed a new challenge.

Histoire... de la Sainte Russie

This title was Doré's final comic-strip art. The full title was ***Histoire Pittoresque, Dramatique et Caricaturale de la Sainte Russie*** (J.Bry, 1854, 8½x12, 500 illustrations). It was also his only political satire book. The ruthless satire in ***The History of Holy Russia*** was prompted by the then-ongoing Crimean War. The definitive research on this title was done by Kunzle, who points out that it was by far the longest story in a comic-strip format in the 19th century. Kunzle asserts (p.129): "It is also, by any standards, one of the funniest and most imaginative, deploying a dazzling array of graphic devices. Finally, it is the most thoroughly political, polemical, and topically relevant graphic work of Doré's vast oeuvre." It actually came out shortly after *Rabelais*, but we are covering it first to finish this genre, before we move on to his literary triumphs. It also marks the end of his career as a writer. He "wrote" four books: ***Hercules, Des-Agrements, Trois Artistes,*** and ***Russia***, all comic-strip satire. I do not count three other titles which are just lithographic plates with captions.

After the Crimean War ***Russia*** faded into obscurity, with no French reprint editions and no translations for over 60 years. But World War I brought it back to life. The Germans discovered it and used it to mock the French alliance with Russia. The 1917 German edition of ***Das Heilige Russland*** deleted 23 illustrations which made the czar look too much like the kaiser. The March 1917 introduction was written the same month the czar abdicated. Germany assisted Lenin in returning to Russia. Then when peace negotiations between Germany and Russia began in early 1918, the German goverment ordered copies of ***Russia*** bought up and destroyed. (Kunzle, p.132) But this stimulated German interest in Doré between the world wars, when some 40 German Doré editions were published, including several biographies, plus the first German editions of Doré's ***Rabelais, Balzac,*** and ***Hercules***.

The circumstances surrounding 20th century editions of Doré's ***Russia*** have all the trappings of a prolonged spy novel, with a recurring pattern of editions published for political ends, and then suppressed when political winds changed directions. There were German editions in 1933 and 1937, and Hitler, Goering, and Goebbels were actually involved in the debate about whether to promote the book because it was anti-Russian and therefore anti-communist, or to suppress the book because it was anti-czar and therefore technically pro-communist. But when Hitler made his secret pact with Stalin in 1939, the logic was reversed and the book suppressed. Then the logic was reversed again with Hitler's invasion of Russia. But most warehouse copies were destroyed by allied bombing raids, and the balance frantically destroyed in 1945, as Russian troops were approaching Berlin.

Chapter three of this prolonged spy novel involves the cold war. In the March 5, 1951 issue of ***Life Magazine*** there was a lengthy article, *Like Czar, like Commissar*, which was the first English translation of 60 of the ***Russia*** illustrations. In the introduction, U.S. General Walter Bedell-Smith (who signed the Nazi surrender in 1945, and was U.S. Ambassador to Russia from 1946-49), made the claim that Doré's ***Russia*** illustrations were inserted into a 1930s Soviet edition of another French book about Russia, the Marquis de Custine's ***Russie en 1839***. According to Bedell-Smith, the Soviets were following Hitler's plan "B" logic that since Doré's illustrations were anti-czar, that made them pro-communist; but they found out all too quickly that the Russian people identified Stalin with the czar. Kunzle (p.133) asserts: "I know of no evidence to support Bedell-Smith's allegation about a suppressed Soviet edition." But it could just show that the communists were very good at suppressing books. But no reference book or library has ever reported an actual copy.

Recent decades have seen a flurry of editions of Doré's *Russia* - French editions in 1967, 1970, 1974, 1980 & 1991; a 1970 German edition with an important postface by Francois Bondy, British editions in 1971 & 1972, a 1971 American edition with an important introduction by Harvard Professor Richard Pipes, and partial reproductions of Doré illustrations from *Russia* in Forberg (67), Dover's ***Doré Spot Illustrations*** (67), and in Kunzle (37). Anyone seeking more information on this fascinating story should read the entire chapter in Kunzle (p.123-134). As Pipes, Kunzle, and many others have pointed out, Doré's ***Russia*** is actually a satire on despotism, which is now and will always be an important topic. Almost all Doré titles had many editions in the first 50 years and then tailed off. But ***Russia*** has been just the reverse pattern.

Rabelais: Gargantua & Pantagruel

This was Doré's first great literary success. In ***Byron*** and ***Lacroix***, Doré's artistic imagination had not been sufficiently challenged, and keep in mind that they represented the first time his artistic expression had been limited to someone else's text. In 1853, Doré requested full control of illustrations for an edition of the classic French satire ***Rabelais***, of which his friend Paul Lacroix was to be editor. J.Bry balked at turning over such a classic to one so young, and it took major support from Lacroix to carry the day. Still, J.Bry issued it in a cheap format on thin show-through paper Jerrold called "tea-paper," similar to onion-skin paper but lower quality. Doré was again furious with the engravers. J.Bry employed many low quality engravers, and they resented Doré's efforts at improving their product. The next year (1855), Doré moved on to publishers with better engravers, particularly Hachette. Various French publishers had sharply different attitudes about engraving quality. Remember how Du Tacq raved about Doré's ***Lacroix*** blocks? That was before they were engraved. Probably the only reason Doré went with J.Bry at all was because they were the first publisher who gave him a chance to do any serious literary illustration work.

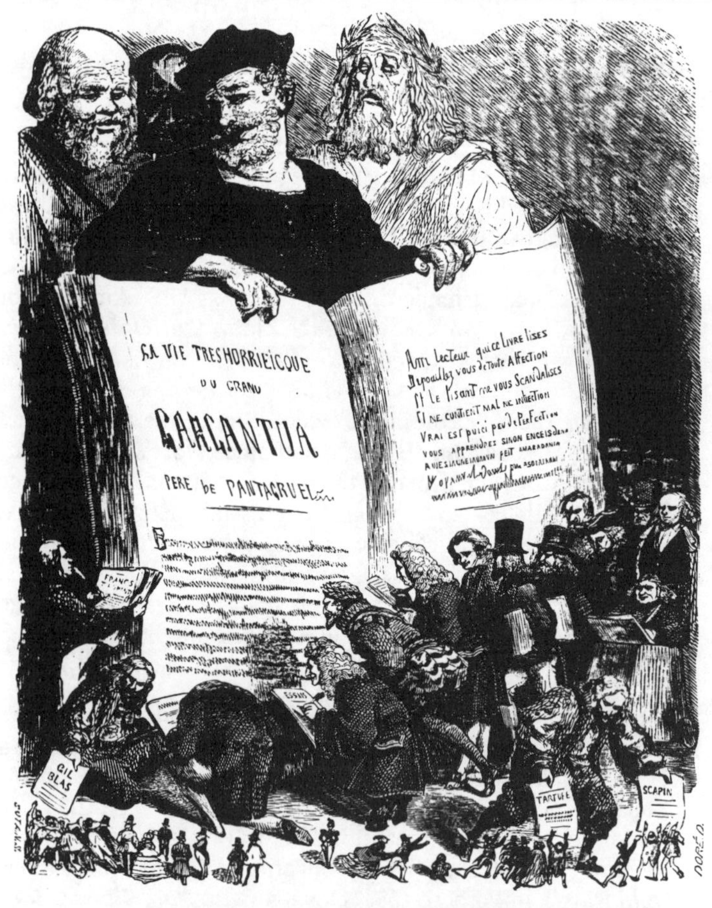
LA VIE TRESHORRIFICQUE
DU GRAND
GARGANTUA
PERE DE PANTAGRUEL
Ami lecteur qui ce livre lises
Depouillez vous de toute affection
Et le lisant ne vous scandalises
Il ne contient mal ne infection
Vrai est qu'ici peu de perfection
GIL BLAS
TARTUFE
SCAPIN

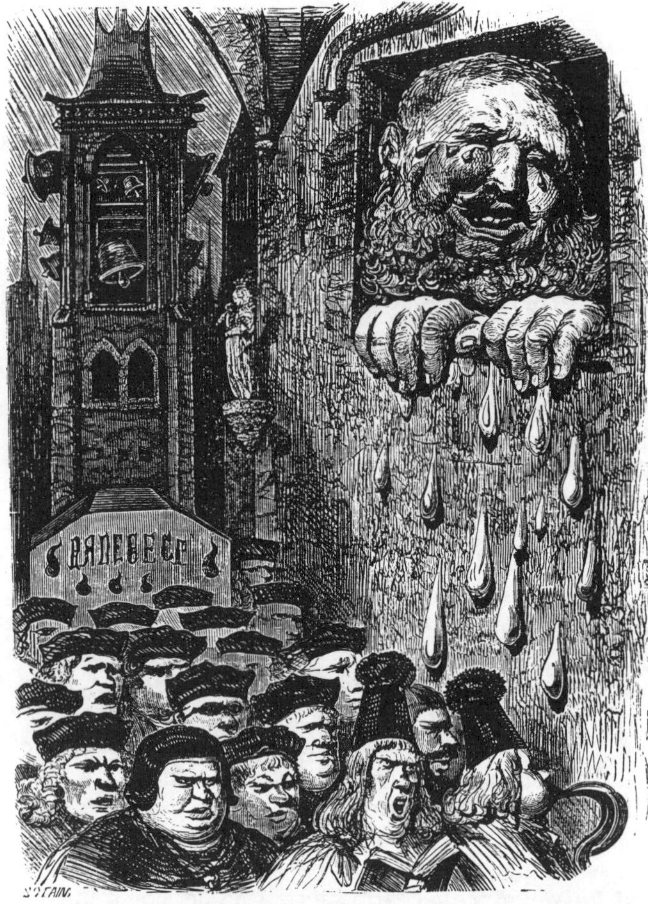

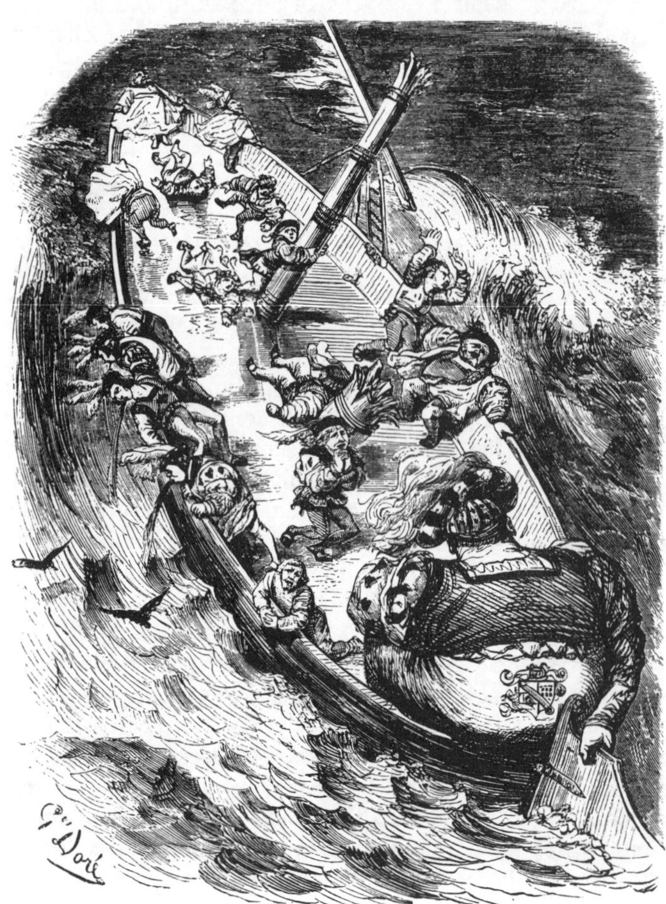
G. Doré

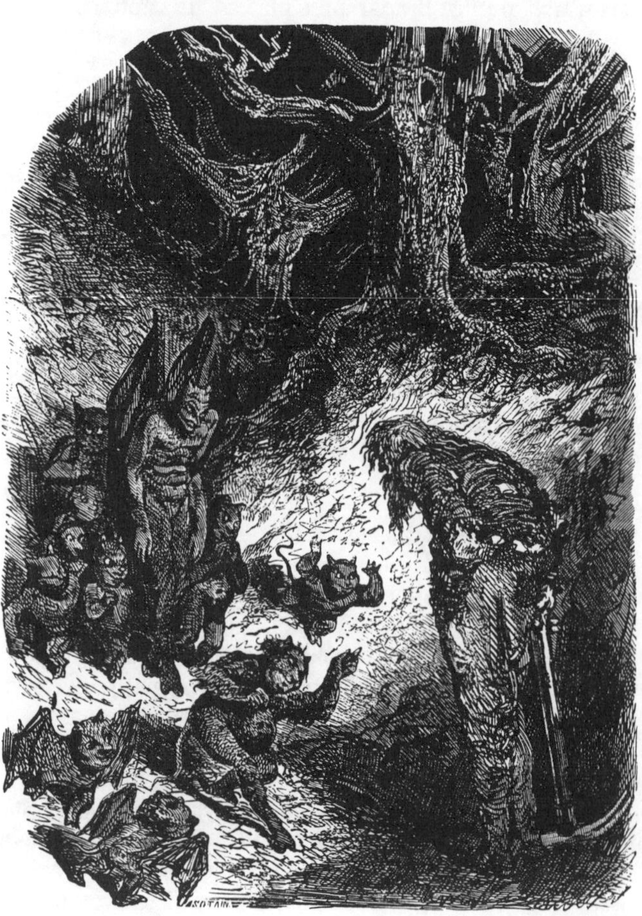

Despite the edition quality, Doré's ***Rabelais*** was a great success. It was issued in weekly parts, and in 7 booklets, and in one 7½x11 volume for 10 *fr*. It was the talk of Paris, the first real glimpse they had of what Doré's imaginative genius could do with literary classics. Many Parisians did not believe that a young comic-strip artist could do so well in a much more serious field. Doré would continue to amaze them for decades, with his ability to make the world of imagination become a visual reality. While his magazine comic-strips were very popular, his pre-***Rabelais*** books did not sell that well (and all are extremely rare). But there have been over 60 editions of Doré's ***Rabelais***. He once again drew them directly onto wood blocks, which were printed so many times that the blocks wore out. There were 14 full-page engravings and 91 vignettes in the text. There were new editions almost every year. In 1858, J.Bry issued a cheap 2 *fr* edition, in a 2-volume 6x8½ format with only 44 of the 105 illustrations. When the English edition finally came out in the 1870s, it was in a smaller 5½x7½ format with only 50 illustrations, and with many original vignettes made into full-page plates. For the English edition, Doré re-draw many blocks that had worn out.

By the 1870s, the rights to Doré's ***Rabelais*** had moved on through several French publishers, eventually landing with the Garnier Freres firm. They then conceived one of the most ambitious Doré editions ever undertaken. They had Doré do 604 new ***Rabelais*** illustrations, including 61 full-page folio engravings. In 1873 Garnier issued a 2V 13x17½ ***Rabelais*** folio with 719 illustrations, priced at a staggering 200 *fr*, and a limited Deluxe Edition at 300 *fr*. It was so expensive that there were no foreign editions. In fact, Garner immediately began issuing a much cheaper quarto version (10½x13) in 140 weekly parts from 1873-75 at ½ *fr* per part, resulting in an 1875 2V edition, with "only" 674 illustrations. Those folio editions are a major art treasure, and very difficult to find. It was not until 1978 that Dover Press issued an illustration-only edition with 252 of those engravings, and the next year the Franklin Library included 158 of those in their ***Rabelais***.

But back in 1854, Doré was revelling in his new success as a literary illustrator. This was truly a best-seller, and other publishers began beating his door down to offer him contracts to illustrate other works of literature, particularly stories set in the middle ages and involving satire. He only did one more set of illustrations for J.Bry, 12 vignettes for the ***Essays of Montaigne*** in 1859. His horizons were expanding, as least in the field of illustration. His social horizons also expanded. One of the first and most enthusiastic reviews of his ***Rabelais*** illustrations was by none other than Alexandre Dumas, in the July 8, 1854 issue of his new magazine ***Le Mousquetaire***. It led to a warm friendship, which endured until Dumas' death in 1870. Another influential new 1854 friendship was with Theophile Gautier, who remained Doré's closest friend until his death in 1872. Doré was now rubbing shoulders with some of the world's literary giants. Doré would also later develop a close friendship with Victor Hugo, then in exile.

La Menagerie Parisienne
Les Differents Publics de Paris

Les Folies Gauloises

These three oblong lithographic albums all contain full-page satirical cartoons with Doré captions. They are Doré's book editions by Philipon/Aubert (Doré did contribute heavily to one more of their magazines, *Musee Francais-Anglais*). They are all about the same size, in the 10½x13½ range. All are undated, but ***Menagerie*** and ***Publics*** are almost certainly 1854, while the date of ***Folies*** continues to be debated, but it was probably 1859. The evidence in favor of an earlier ***Folies*** date was that Doré's style had changed considerably by 1859, but perhaps he drew them earlier. These lithographic albums are very rare. Most copies were long ago taken apart to sell individual lithographs. There are also full-color versions of ***Menagerie*** and **Publics**, and those are particularly desirable. Only ***Folies*** exists in English, entitled ***Historical Cartoons***, an undated 1868 edition by J.C.Hotten. In 1947, ***Menagerie*** was republished in French, German, Dutch, and Spanish.

Menagerie and ***Publics*** contain 24 and 20 lithographs, respectively. They are a more gentle satire on French society, more witty than biting, much in the spirit of Honore Daumier. Doré seemed to be mellowing (or perhaps wearying from the strident tone of ***Russia***) and these lithographs are now often reprinted in books about French history and culture. But ***Les Folies Gauloises*** (literally "Gallic Follies") is a biting attack on the excesses in French history. It also has 20 lithographs. Amusingly, the English edition of ***Folies*** actually asserts that the illustrations are of British history, adding a new full page of text by Thomas Wright to accompany each illustration. The English edition is fairly low quality, but it is the only edition anyone has a realistic chance of acquiring. Forberg (p.1163-2000) reprinted 14 *Menagerie*, 10 *Publics*, and 13 *Folies*. Ray was once again (p.329-333) forunate enough to get Michael Sadleir's copies, and Ray speaks very highly of these Doré lithographic albums. Ray's book is from the 1982 display of his massive collection of French illustrated books at the Pierport Morgan Library in New York. Most intact copies of these albums are now in libraries and museums in France.

Honore de Balzac: Droll Stories

Rabelais and ***Balzac*** provided an amazing 1-2 punch for Doré's assent from boy-genius comic-strip artist to serious adult literary illustrator, at the ripe old age of 23. Each new success spurred him on to greater accomplishments. Up until 1854, all Doré's illustrations had been for two publishers. The year 1855 saw five new Doré publishers: Societe Generale, Librairie Nouvelle, Gustave Barba, Bulla, and the premier French publisher - Hachette.

With Societe Generale, Doré had better cooperation on ***Balzac*** - better engravers, better paper, and the freedom to do as many illustrations as he saw fit (425 for ***Balzac***, compared to 105 for ***Rabelais***). It even had a numbered list of every engraving, with caption, engraver, and page number. One of the most often (over) quoted anecdotes about Doré pertains to the ***Balzac*** illustration on page xv entitled *Les Bons Proupos des Religieuses de Poissy*, engraved by Best. In drawing a tiny vignette of a long building, Doré got tired of drawing in

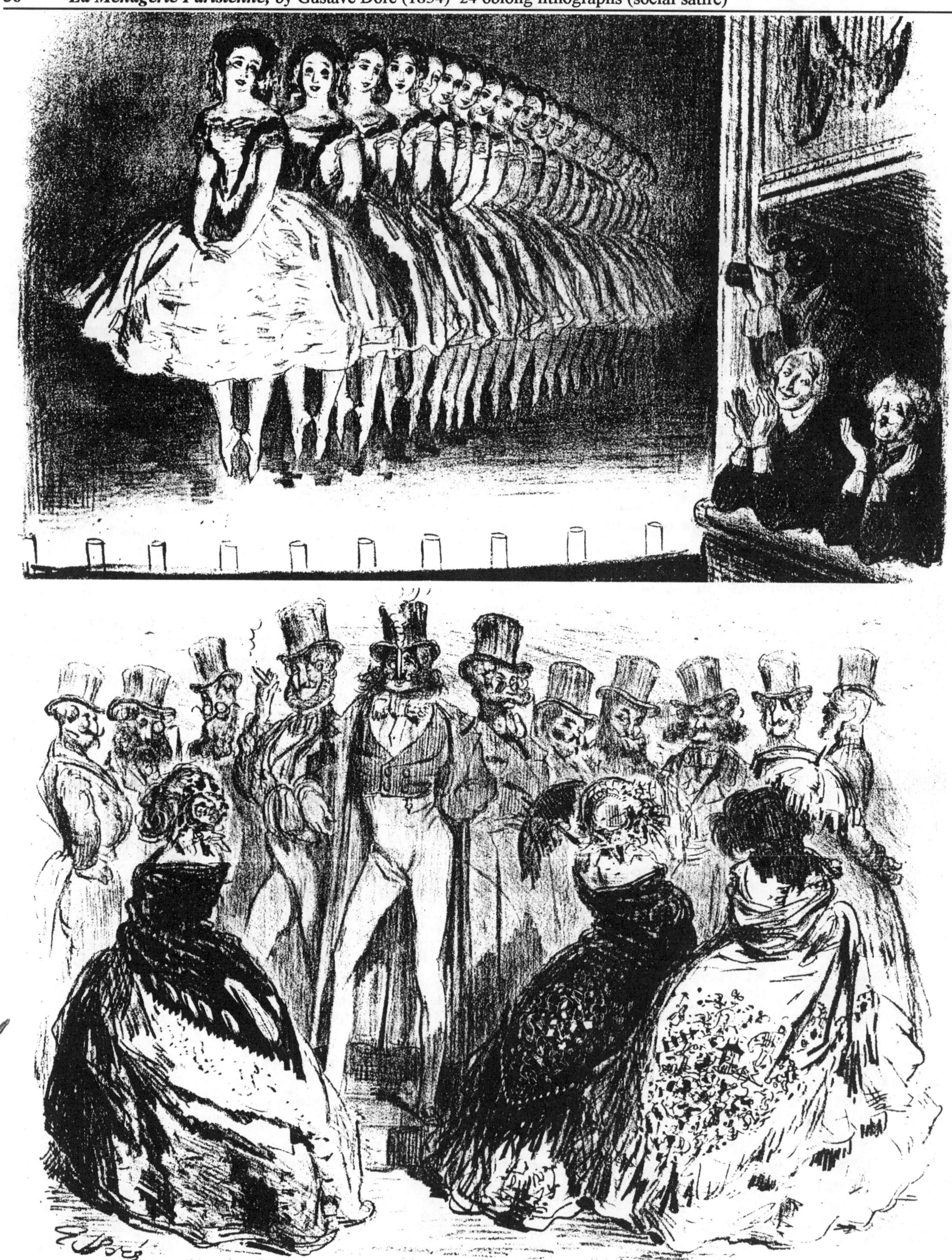

all the tiny windows, so he just stopped and put a little note to the engraver at that point: "etc." indicating that the engraver should finish putting in all the little windows. Poor Mr. Best has really given engravers a bad name by (you guessed it) engraving in the actual word "etc." on the side of that little building. It went undetected initially because it was a small engraving, and the "etc." actually prints backwards.

Balzac proved to be Doré's most popular small book by far. It was only 5½x8½, and there have been about 60 editions in French, English, German, Dutch, Spanish, and even one in Serbo-Croatian. Many people are surprised when they see it, expecting all Doré's famous books to be folios. The French version is ***Les Contes Drolatiques***, and the Societe Generale de Libraire first edition, dated MDCCCLV (1855), lists itself as "5th edition," meaning that it is the 5th edition of ***Contes Drolatiques***. There were several printings of that "first" Doré edition. LeBlanc (p.42) shows seven variations of the 1855 edition. The first printing is very simple - the title page lists "424" instead of "425" Doré illustrations, have forgotten to count the frontispiece. There were 103 full-page engravings, and 322 vignettes. ***Balzac*** is full of engravings of grotesque faces, often similar to 1960s horror movies. Doré's ***Rabelais*** and ***Balzac*** illustrations are full of grotesque horror and black comedy, delighting the French. Decades later, when Doré was famous in England, he encountered great hostility to these early drawings from John Ruskin and others. Today there are still many art critics who like Doré's early art style better than his folios. But why compare apples and oranges?

There is great deal of confusion about both French and English editions of Doré's ***Balzac***. There was an 1860 ***Balzac*** edition, published by J.C.Hotten of London, but in French, which also calls itself "5th edition." ***Contes Drolatiques*** was not even translated into English until 1874. Then two French publishers (Garnier & E.Caen) each list an 1861 "6th edition." Garnier acquired the rights to Doré's ***Balzac*** in 1857 from Balzac's widow. Per Anthony North-Peat, British Attache, in his ***Gossip from Paris 1864-69*** (p.324): "Madame de Balzac authorized him to do so by letter, on condition that no artist but Doré should be allowed to illustrate her husband's work." But Garnier tried to stretch her words by also publishing in the 1860s a cheap unillustrated edition (since no other artist had illustrated it), which brought a lawsuit from the copyright owner M.Levy. In 1869, the judge ruled that Garnier had only acquired rights to the Doré version. You will recall that Garnier was the one who in 1873 published the beautiful but very expensive Doré ***Rabelais*** folio. Since they also had the rights to the Doré ***Balzac***, they issued an 1873 *Balzac* edition and gave one away with each ***Rabelais***. In 1926, Garnier issued a 7x9 numbered Limited Edition ***Balzac*** on vellum paper, bound in 3/4 vellum over painted boards.

English language ***Balzac*** editions are more confusing than the French, due to undated editions by many publishers, and illustrations ranging from the full 425 down to 15. The title page of the first English-language edition is not dated, but the introduction is dated January, 1974, stating that it is the first English translation of ***Contes Drolatiques***. But most reprint editions also have undated title pages, but retain that same dated introduction. For collectors, the important thing to look for is the phrase "with the whole 425 illustrations." The first reprint editions that have all 425 illustrations are the 7x10 Bibliophilist editions from the 1930s. While ***Rabelais*** and ***Balzac*** were highly praised and represented new direction for Doré, they led to several years of doing literary vignettes of which he was not particularly proud. On top of that, many publishers would commission him for one title, and then later on usurp the illustrations and insert them into other titles.

Jules Gerard: Lion Hunting

This minor Doré book marks the beginning of his many travel engravings. The French version is called ***La Chasse au Lion***, and the full English title is ***Lion Hunting and Sporting Life in Algeria***. Doré did 11 vignettes for the 1855 Librairie Nouvelle edition. They did two 1855 editions, a 246 page, 10½" high January edition, and a 254 page, 6½" high March edition. There were several French reprint editions. There is an 1856 English edition by Lambert, but those illustrations are not by Doré. The first Doré illustrated English edition is the undated 1860s edition by Bell & Daldy. There is also an undated 1870s edition by Ward/Lock.

Musee Francais-Anglais Illustrated London News

Doré contributed heavily to one last Philipon magazine, but the illustration style is very different. By 1855, Doré could not be coaxed into doing any more comic-strip art. It appears that ***Russia*** drained the last of it out of him. But the Crimean War was still a big issue, and Philipon came up with the idea of a magazine to be published simultaneously in Paris and London, featuring their joint foray into Crimea, and other areas of mutual interest. So began ***Musee Francais-Anglais***, which ran 64 monthly issues from 1855-1860, with 174 Doré engravings through 1858. It was Doré's first British exposure, and he made sure they saw that he was a serious illustrator. He did 47 lithographs and 127 wood engravings. Most of the lithographs were large battle-scenes of Sebastopol, Balaklava, Alma, Inkermann, etc. Many were double-page, and one for Sebastopol was actually a 4-page fold-out; with the magazine being a folio to begin with, the lithograph was perhaps 20x28. Some lithographs were engraved from Doré oil paintings. Of course, Philipon made the most of Doré's ***Musee*** engravings, publishing two reproduction books: ***20 Grandes Lithographs*** and ***100 Gravures***. As with so many other early Doré editions, those two bound volumes are quite scarce. Forberg did reprint 48 Doré ***Musee*** engravings (p.1015-1037 & 1288-1300).

Another major event that was covered in ***Musee*** was Queen Victoria's visit to France in 1855. This led to Doré's first meeting with Blanchard Jerrold, who would become a very significant lifelong friend. Jerrold, in turn, introduced Doré to Herbert Ingram, editor of the ***Illustrated London News***, and Jerrold convinced Ingram to contract with Doré to do illustrations for his publication. Doré did at least 15 drawings for Ingram from 1855-56. He may have done more, but many engravings were not signed. But it would be a dozen years before Doré actually set foot on British soil.

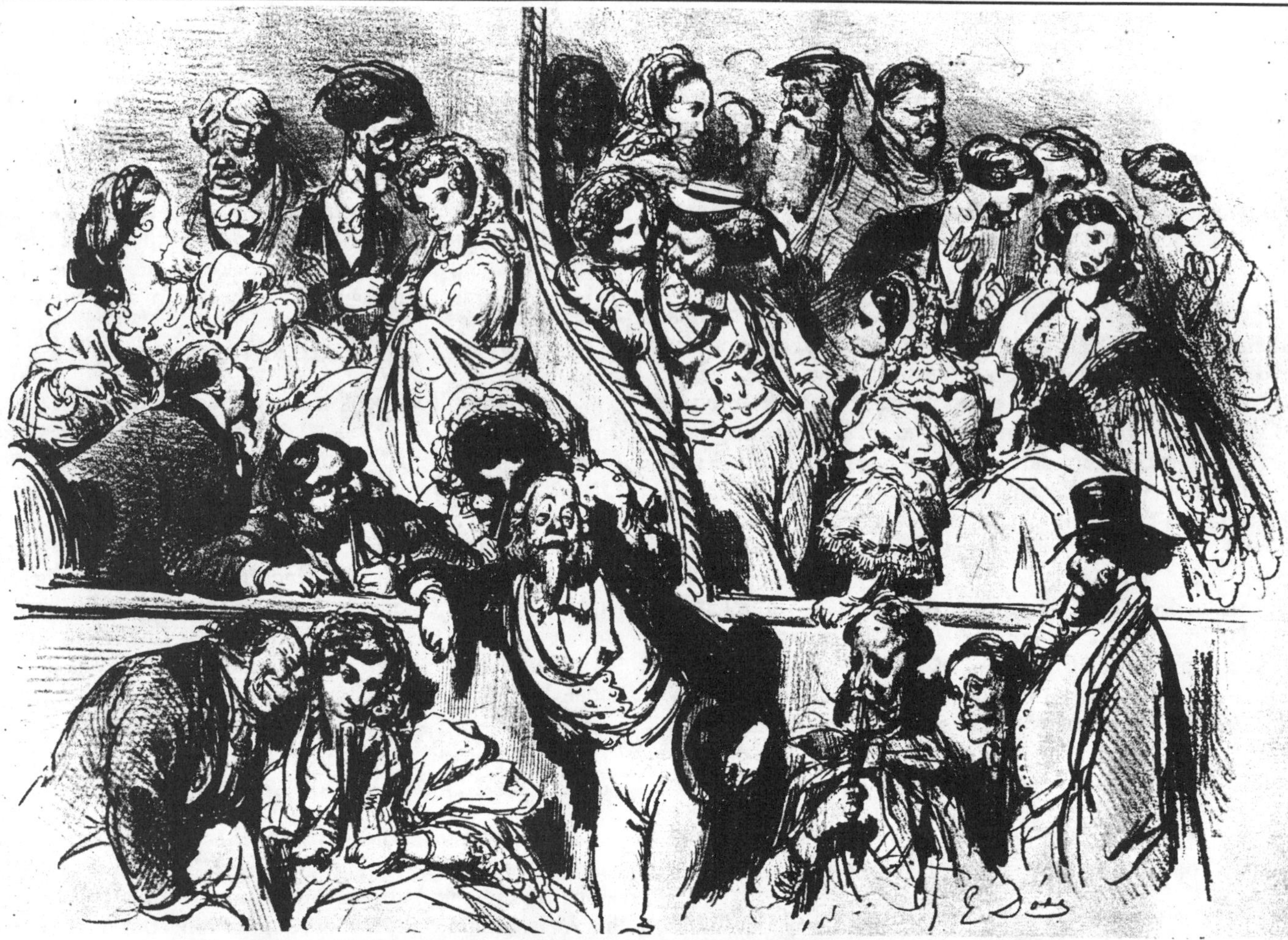

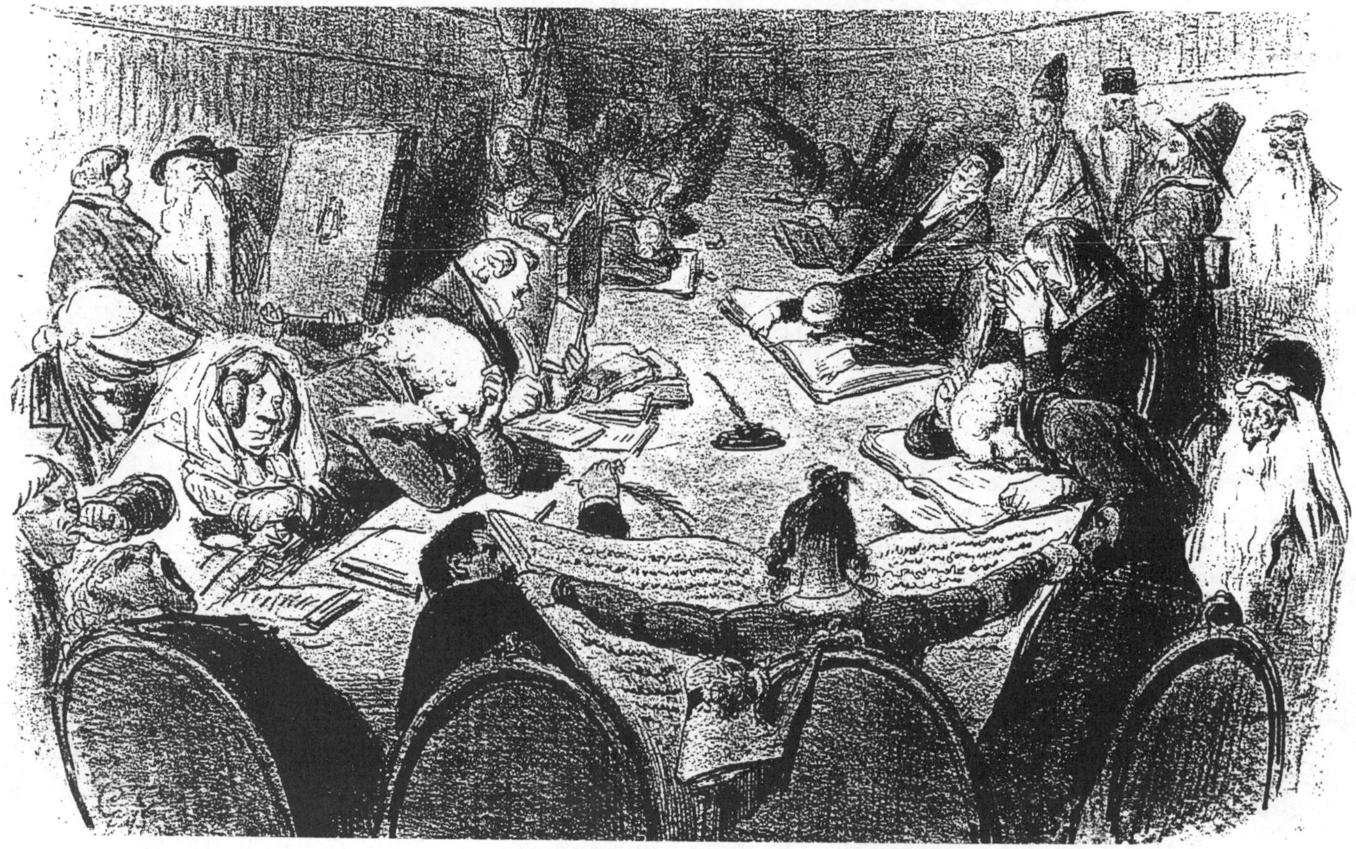

Journal pour Tous
Semaine des Enfants

While not much came of Doré's initial British contact, events were swirling around him in Paris. Just as Charles Philipon in 1848 had seen Doré as a major player in the success of his new humor publication, so Louis Hachette in 1855 was eyeing Doré as a significant part of his new literary publication. Hachette was starting a high-quality publication that would serialize works of literature, and he knew just how important the illustrations would be in its success. On April 7, 1855 he launched ***Journal pour Tous***, containing the best recent French, English & European literature. From 1855-63, Doré did 362 original ***Journal pour Tous*** engravings. Many works Doré illustrated in those serials were later published in book editions - ***Feval, Terrail, Aimard, About, Ferry***, plus ***Sinbad the Sailor***. He also did 16 ***Macbeth*** engravings which for some strange reason have never found their way into any book edition, othere than a few of them shown in reference works like Forberg. But perhaps most amazing was the set of 45 engravings Doré did in 1861 for ***Dicken's A Christmas Carol***. That set of engravings includes the very first drawing ever made of Tiny Tim. Not one of those engravings has ever been printed in any book, not even a Doré reference book. At least that is until now. By the time you read these lines, MCE Publishing Co. will have published the very first book edition of Doré's ***Christmas Carol*** engravings.

One other trend that began in ***Journal pour Tous*** was the re-using and re-engraving of Doré's illustrations for use in other works. Some people call this pirating, some call it doctoring, some call it butchering. But ***Journal pour Tous*** reprinted 100 of their Doré illustrations, and LeBlanc (p.392-393) shows exactly how one of those was doctored twice. LeBlanc actually attempts to trace the use, re-use, and re-captioning of every one of Doré's magazine illustrations. Job should have had such patience. Doré quickly tired of all that high volume hack work, and had already secretly started his folio engravings, but could not get anyone to publish them, because these publishers were specializing in cheap editions.

But Hachette was so pleased with the success of his new literary magazine that at the beginning of 1857 he saw fit to launch another one, ***Semaine des Enfants***, this one geared toward even younger readers. The premier story featured Doré illustrations for the Comtesse de Segur's ***Nouveaus Contes de Fees*** ("New Fairy Tales"). It was her first published work (she was already in her fifties), and it was so popular it was published in book form that same year, and 20 more volumes of her writings quickly followed. But ***Semaine des Enfants*** also quickly deteriorated into the "get as much mileage as possible out of each illustration" syndrome, with Doré's illustrations not only being re-used, but also jumping back and forth between the two magazines, and between book editions and magazine serials. It is no wonder that so many people thought that Doré had done 100,000 illustrations. They seemed to be seeing his illustrations everywhere. But Hachette was doing nothing more than Philipon and dozens of other publishers before him had done. The public wanted illustrations. It was the 19th century equivalent of television. The public wanted visual entertainment, and the more publishers strove to meet demand, the more quality deteriorated. The amazing thing was that Doré was able to emerge from all of that and produce an art form (literary folios) in which the quality was far above the demand. Is it really any wonder that Hachette and everyone else was so stunned by both the quality and the success of Doré's ***Dante's Inferno*** in 1861?

Hippolyte Taine: A Tour of the Pyrenees

It was Theophile Gautier who coined Doré's nickname, "gamin de genie" (boy-genius). It was in Gautier that Doré met his match in intellect, talent, personality, and expression. In 1855, Doré, Gautier, and Paul Dalloz (then editor of ***Moniteur Universel***) took a trip to the Pyrenees, combining business with pleasure, since Doré was to illustrate the book by his old schoolmate Taine. That trip was one of the most enjoyable Doré ever had - adventures, conversations, pranks, sights, etc. Gautier even matched Doré's childish playfulness, then switching to intellectual discourse. Gautier and Doré were forever debating whether the true basis of aesthetics was the beauty of nature or the beauty of women. They often related various tales about adventures on that trip.

But the incident they all remembered best was in a little town called Urrugne. They went to the livery stable and talked them into the loan of a royal coach and the best horses. Then they disguised themselves as servants. Doré and Dalloz stood on the back dressed as grooms. Gautier, who was very stout and could appear pompous and imposing at will, drove the coach. They shut up the coach so that no one could see inside. It was very hot, but they kept up their stiff appearance. They drove into town proclaiming, "Make way for the distinguished visitors to Urrugne!" Soon a huge crowd gathered, trying to find out who was in the coach. They drove all around town to attract as many people as possible, and then pulled up in front of the principal hotel in the town. By then the crowd was so great they could barely avoid running over them. The three of them got down, saluted the crowd, opened the door of the coach, and then marched into the hotel, bowing to the right and left. The crowds gathered closer and closer to the coach, waiting for the distinguished guests to alight. Finally, one courageous soul peeked into the coach, and emitted a howl of rage upon finding it empty. But most of the crowd took it very well, laughing and carrying on. Inside the hotel, the three "servants" thought they would die of laughter. All this is in Roosevelt, chapter 20. Doré was always the acrobat, walking on his hands and doing handsprings. That was simply his way of celebrating everything, even a successful practial joke.

After reading that chapter in Roosevelt about Doré's trip to the Pyrenees, you would be astonished to read in another reference book (Muir, p.244), concerning Doré's illustrations for ***Taine***: "Doré had in fact never been to the Pyrenees and his drawings for Taine were made from photographs." Muir has a major section on Doré (which we will discuss later), but it is quite negative - Muir uses over 100 negative adjectives in his dozen pages on Doré. Even today, many people still resent just how popular Doré was. But where could such an overt

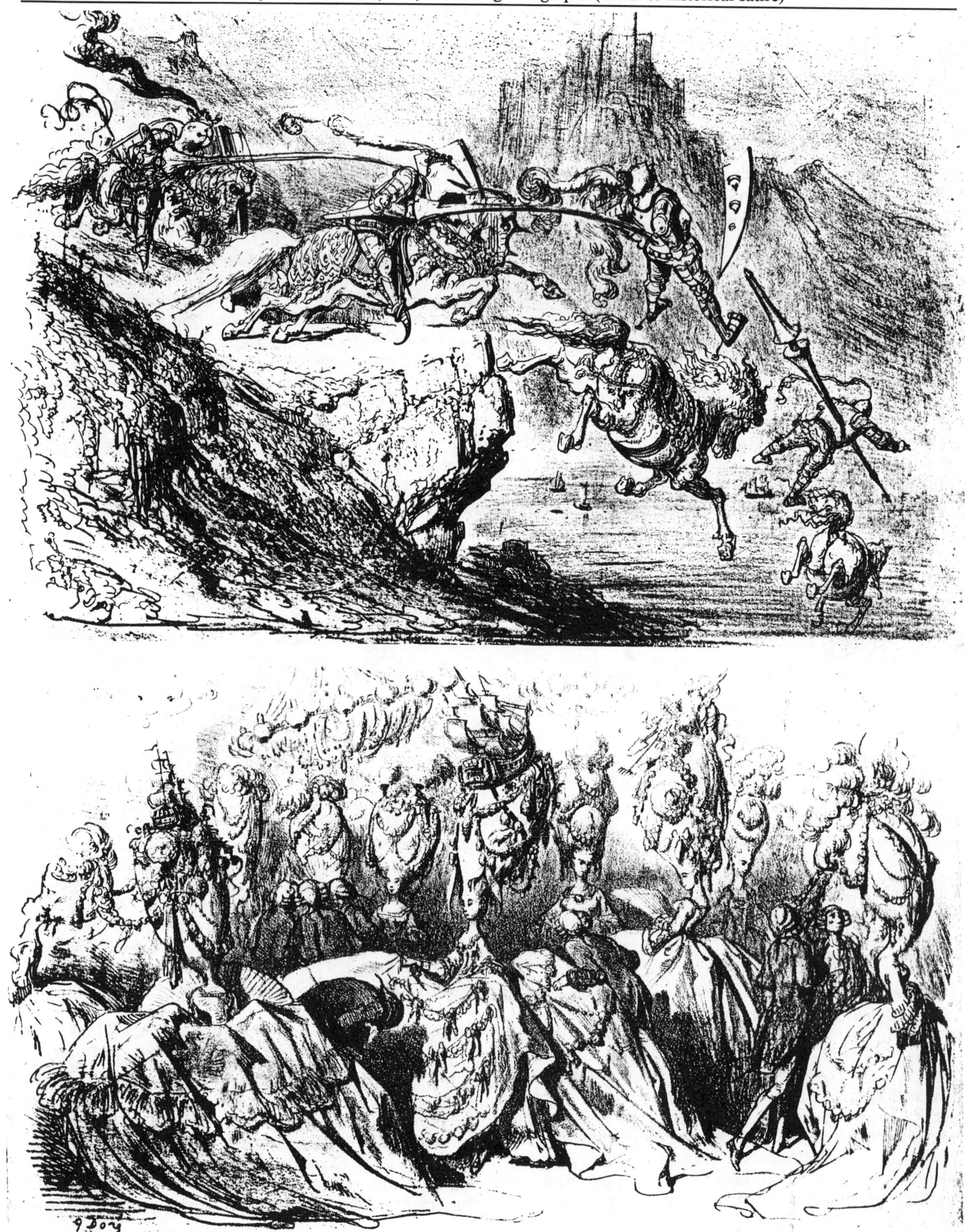
G. Doré

error come from. It comes from reading Jerrold without reading Roosevelt. Jerrold (p.99) relates the letter he received from Taine in 1883 shortly after Doré's death, in which Taine states: "We never made a journey to the Pyrenees together. When he illustrated my little book he had nothing more, I believe, than photographs of the country. It was M. Hachette who brought us together..." Of course Taine was not lying. He had not been on that trip to the Pyrenees, and was guessing about the photographs. Even though Muir lists Roosevelt as a major source, he missed that entire chapter. Research on Doré is especially difficult because Doré does not evoke neutrality.

This was Doré's first book edition for Hachette. The 1855 version was entitled ***Voyage aux Eaux des Pyrenees***, referring specifically to the mineral waters of the Pyrenees. Doré did 64 illustrations for that edition. In 1860, Hachette expanded the book to cover the whole Pyrenees region, changing the title to ***Voyage aux Pyrenees***. For that edition Doré did an extra 279 illustrations. It is quite possible that the photographs Taine surmised were for this expanded edition. They used 56 of the 1855 illustrations, making a total of 335 in the 1860 edition. Later editions have only 164 illustrations.

Technically, there are no British editions of ***Taine***. In 1865, 24 of the ***Taine*** illustrations were used in J.G.Edgar's novel ***Cressy & Poictiers***, published by Beeton of London. Then in 1867, 115 of the ***Taine*** illustrations were used in Henry Blackburn's travel book, ***The Pyrenees***, published by Sampson/Low of London. Then in 1874, New York publisher Henry Holt finally issued the ***Taine*** text in English, but with only 258 illustrations. Then in the 1892, the ***Blackburn*** text was republished as part of ***Artistic Travels***, but using only 48 ***Taine*** illustrations. Doré also did many landscape paintings of the Pyrenees. Some of those are in the Musee Pyrenees in Lourdes. There was a 1975 book by Marguerite Gaston called ***Images Romantique des Pyrenees***, published by the museum, featuring a Doré watercolor on the front cover, in which they praise Doré's illustrations and paintings of the Pyrenees.

Captain Mayne Reid: Desert Home
Comtesse de Segur: New Fairy Tales

Although Hachette's two literary magazines were full of Doré illustrations, they actually published very few Doré book editions before his ***Dante's Inferno*** folio in 1861. Besides the 1855 and 1860 ***Taine*** editions, ***Reid*** and ***Segur*** were the only Hachette Doré books before 1861, and both of them were also serialized in their magazines. The 1856 ***Reid*** edition, entitled ***L'Habitation du Desert***, contained 24 Doré illustrations in a little 5x7 format. They then serialized it in 1860 in ***Semaine des Enfants***. But the serialized version contained 50 Doré illustrations. The 26 extra engravings were "borrowed" from ***Aimard*** and ***Ferry***. But ***Reid*** was very popular, and Hachette's 1925 edition was the 23rd edition. Apparently, there was only one English edition (by T.Nelson of Edinburg, 1869). There were two early Polish editions in 1864 and 1872, published in Varsovie (Warsaw). The story is actually set in America. By the mid-19th century, Europe viewed the U.S. west as an exotic, romantic locale, and many European authors wrote adventure stories set in the U.S. west, including Mayne Reid of England, Gustave Aimard of France, and Karl May of Germany. Doré illustrated several books set in America (the best being ***Atala***), but he never visited the U.S.

As we saw earlier, ***Segur*** was the first work serialized in ***Semaine des Enfants*** in 1857. But the 20 book illustrations in the 4½x7 book edition in 1857 entitled ***Nouveaux Contes de Fees*** were all different from the 14 magazine illustrations. The 1863 reprint edition had 29 Doré illustrations, adding nine of the 14 magazine illustrations. They also added seven illustrations by Jules Didier plus ten tiny unsigned vignettes, making a total of 46, which was the standard for future editions. Hachette's 1924 printing was the 25th edition. There were a couple English editions, but there was little foreign interest in the title. The ***Reid*** and ***Segur*** vignettes were hardly amongst Doré's finest, but 25 French editions of each shows that they were certainly popular there.

It should also be pointed out just how popular the Comtesse de Segur was in France. Sophie Rostopchine was the daughter of a Russian Count who married a French Count (Segur). The Czar of Russia was her godfather. At 55, she began writing stories to entertain her grandchildren. Hachette "took a chance" on her, and she proceeded to enthrall a whole generation of French children. There are many stories about children stopping her on the street to kiss her, and of children weeping at her death in 1874. She wrote 20 children's books in 18 years, all of which were profusely illustrated by Hachette and reprinted many times. In 1974 there was an English edition of ***Segur*** (with nine Doré illustrations), retold by Beatrice Schenk de Regniers, entitled ***The Enchanted Forest***.

The Legend of the Wandering Jew

Today, few people have ever heard of this story, but it was quite popular in the 19th century and earlier. It is the story of a Jewish cobbler who mocks Jesus on his way to the cross. Jesus places a curse on him - he will "wander forever." That man later becomes very devout, and finds himself in the predicament of having supernatural powers of invulnerability, but with no power to affect anything around him. Today it sounds like something out of ***The Twilight Zone***. He sees the suffering of the world, with no ability to help. For centuries people claimed to see him passing through, and he became sort of a good-luck charm. The tale was especially popular in France after Eugene Sue's 1845 4-volume novel of the same name (***Le Juif Errant***), which contained 83 full-page plates and 600 vignettes by Gavarni, in a 8vo volume.

So what could Doré do to outdo Sue and Gavarni? Doré came up with perhaps the highest ratio ever of size of edition to amount of text, producing a 16x24 book containing only 24 lines of verse. He did 12 of the largest wood engravings ever made - 12x16. Reference books state that the boxwood trunks on which wood engravings were usually made were rarely larger than 7x9, and these do not show lines that should be visible if four sections were pasted together. It is a mystery. There was also a 19x25 lithographic poster made from the cover, which was deleted from reprint and foreign editions. The text was a 24-line poem by Beranger, so they added a few fillers. Here is the line-up, from the 1856 title page:

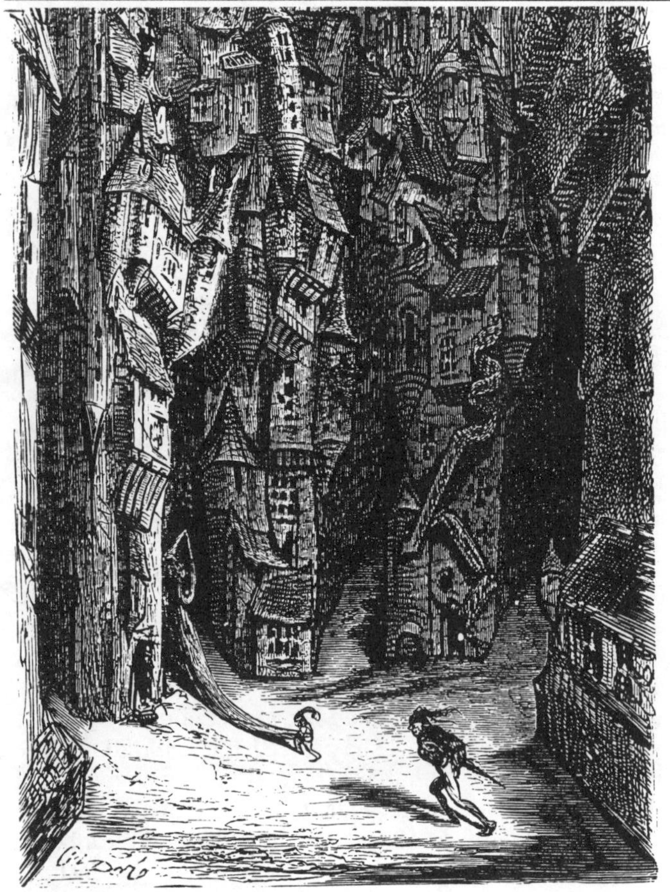

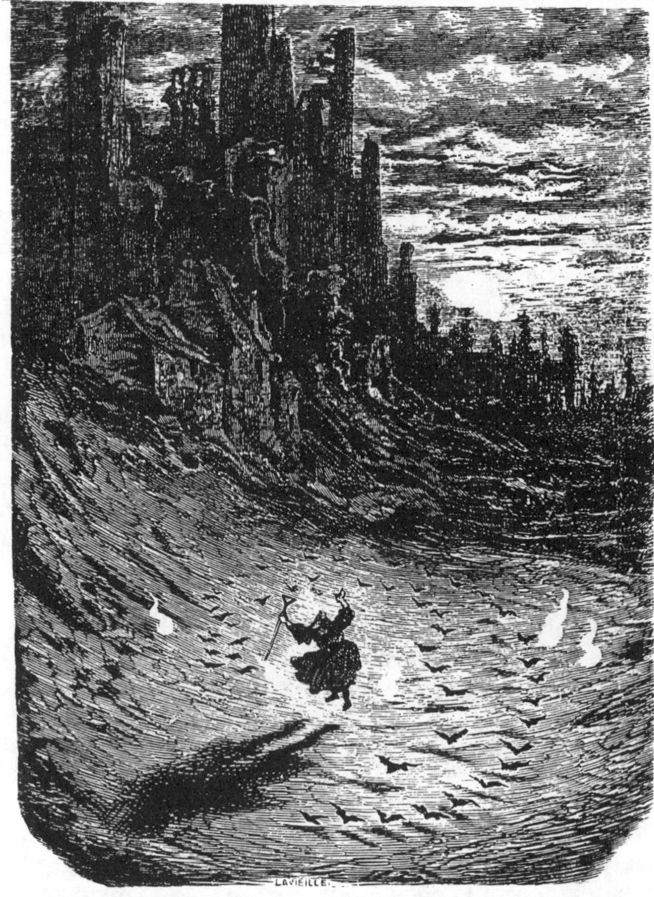

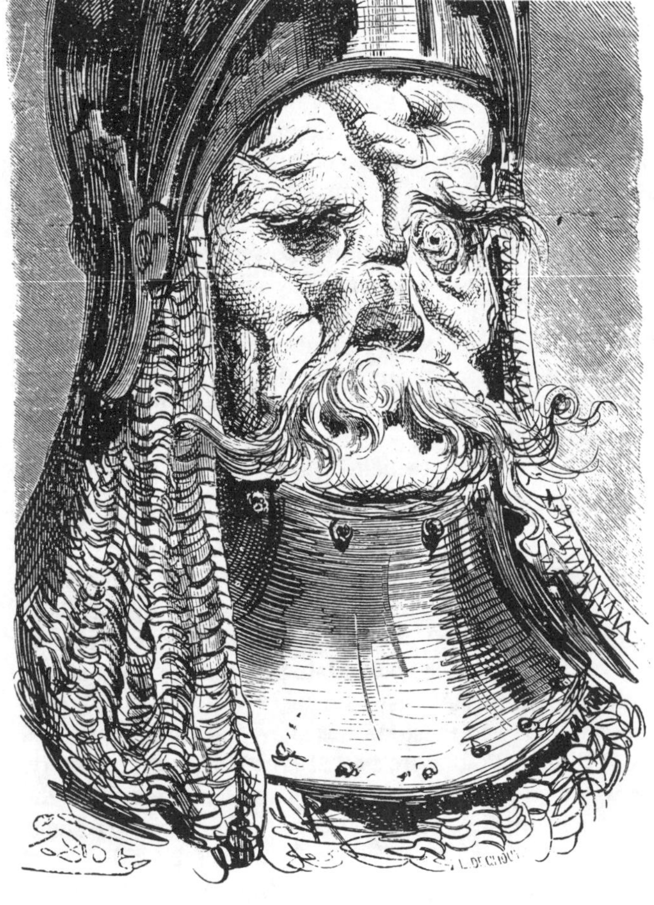

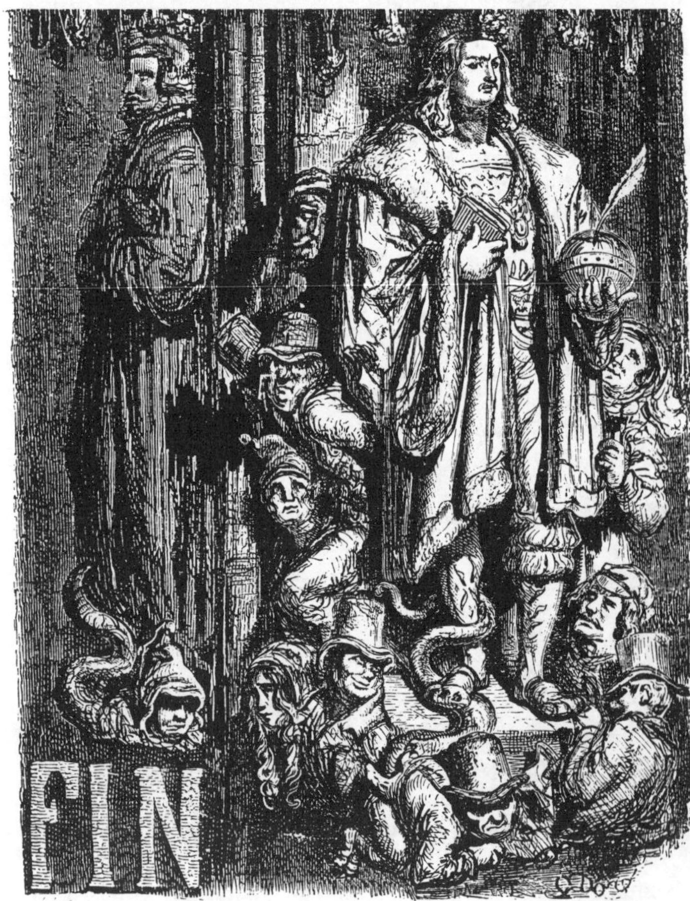
FIN

drawings:	Gustave Doré
engravers:	F.Rouget, O.Jahyer & J.Gauchard
printer:	J.Best (he of the *Balzac* "etc." fame)
prologue:	Pierre Dupont
epilogue:	Pierre Dupont
preface:	Paul Lacroix (Bibliophile Jacob)
bibliographic notice:	Paul Lacroix
ballad:	Pierre-Jean de Beranger (24-line text)
music:	Ernest Doré
publisher:	Michel Levy freres

For years, bibliographers had trouble deciding who to list as the author. Although Beranger wrote the poem, Dupont was often listed as author because he wrote the prologue. It was also listed an anonymous. Now Doré is usually listed as the author, since the text is really just captions. The book "is" the Doré engravings. Most bibliographies list 15-20 titles as being "by" Doré. The enormous engravings combine religion, horror, mysticism, fantasy, adventure, and morbid humor. It was the first edition to show wood engraving's true potential. This is where Doré began to take popular art and elevate it to the level of fine art. Even today, rare-book libraries often mislabel Doré folio wood-engravings as etchings, lithographs, or steel engravings for inclusion in fine art departments. They are often shocked to learn they are "only" wood engravings.

There was one major drawback to the ***Wandering Jew*** engravings - they were just too big; not aesthetically, but for practical reasons. There were only three French editions. The first English edition was in 1857 (Addey). Frederick Leypoldt of Philadelphia (who would later start *Publisher's Weekly*) published a portfolio of all 13 illustrations in 1863, but that is extremely rare. The major English-language edition was the 15½x22 Cassell in 1866. English editions eliminated almost all the introductory sections. Then each decade saw a different size set of engravings. In 1873, George Gebbie (Philadelphia) photographically reduced the engravings to 4½x7, and issued them in a 6x10 edition. In the 1880s, U.S. publishers issued an intermediate-size 12x15 edition, with 9x12 engravings. Then in the 1890s, P.F.Collier of New York actually inserted Doré's illustrations into an edition of Eugene Sue's novel, even though Sue's novel is a completely different story. They reduced Doré's illustrations to an almost microscopic 2¾x3¾, nearly an 80% reduction. There were about 20 editions of Doré's ***Wandering Jew*** in the 19th century, but none in the 20th. The story may have died out, but Doré's illustrations do still turn up in art reference books or Doré anthologies.

Mary Lafon: Le Chevalier Jaufre
Mary Lafon: Fierabras-Legende Nationale

We often hear of 19th century women authors using a male pseudonym. Here we have the opposite. Mary Lafon's real name was Jean-Bernard Lafon. It is hard to understand why a 19th century man writing stories about knighthood would use a female pen name. These two titles were published in 1856 and 1857 by Librairie Nouvelle. Both are 7x10½. ***Fierabras*** contained 12 Doré engravings. It was not reprinted (except for a magazine serialization). ***Jaufre*** is a significant title with several reprint editions. It is Doré's first knighthood title, a precursor of his ***Cervantes, Tennyson,*** and ***Ariosto.*** The 1856 first edition contains 20 Doré engravings, which are 5x7½ and signed. Those are very important details, because in 1926 a French publisher found a large quantity of that edition, but unbound and unillustrated. They inserted reproduction illustrations which were reduced and unsigned (and less desirable to collectors), and had the books bound and offered them for sale. There was also an 1876 French reprint edition disguised as a new book by means of a different title - ***Le Chevalier Noir*** ("The Black Knight").

The 1856 ***Jaufry the Knight*** edition (Addey of London) was the first English-language edition of any Doré book. In 1857, an obscure New York publisher, Wiley & Halsted, published the first American Doré edition. They took eight of Doré's 20 ***Jaufry*** engravings, cropped off the edges (including Doré's signature), and then added in the name of their own engraver, J.W.Orr. There was not one word mentioning Doré. Anyone looking at it would certainly have thought that J.W.Orr did the illustrations. Orr did not even re-engrave them. That version has seen several editions, but still with nary a mention of Doré. Meanwhile, in London in 1858-59, another publisher, James Blackwood, borrowed the 20 Doré ***Jaufry*** illustrations and used them for two new books written by fictitious authors to fit the engravings - ***The Adventures of St. George***, by William Peacock, and ***Boldheart the Warrior***, by George Pardon. At least they did give Doré credit. Then there was an 1869 edition by Thomas Nelson of London, Edinburg & New York, who titled it ***Geoffrey the Knight.***

Doré did one other title for Librairie Nouvelle, an 1856 8vo of Mme.Emile de Girardin's ***Contes d'un Vieille Fille***. It contained 16 total engravings, seven by Doré and nine by G.Fath. Those Doré engravings are probably superior to his ***Segur*** illustrations, but the book was much less popular. That title also saw an 1856 English edition by Addey, entitled ***Stories of an Old Maid***. There were also 1866 and 1880 French reprints, but that was it. Forberg reprinted six of Doré's seven illustrations (p.180-186).

Alexandre Dumas: Page du Duc de Savoie
Alexandre Dumas: Compagnons de Jehu
Alexandre Dumas: Oeuvres Completes

It is a shame Doré never did an edition of one of Dumas' major works. But it has often been stated that publishers could not afford both an expensive author and an expensive illustrator, not did they need both for a book to sell. That is also why Doré never illustrated Jules Verne, and why he did very little for Victor Hugo. It is why Doré's books tend to be a strange mixture of the greatest classics to be found (in the public domain), plus lesser-known current authors. Doré did do a nice set for Gautier, but the only major folio Doré ever did for a "major" current author was for ***Tennyson***. And people wonder by that publisher (Moxon) squeezed every nickel out of every possible marketing strategy (no, they did not print wallpaper). Doré's last great folio (***The Raven***) was scheduled to be released practically to the day that the Poe copyright expired.

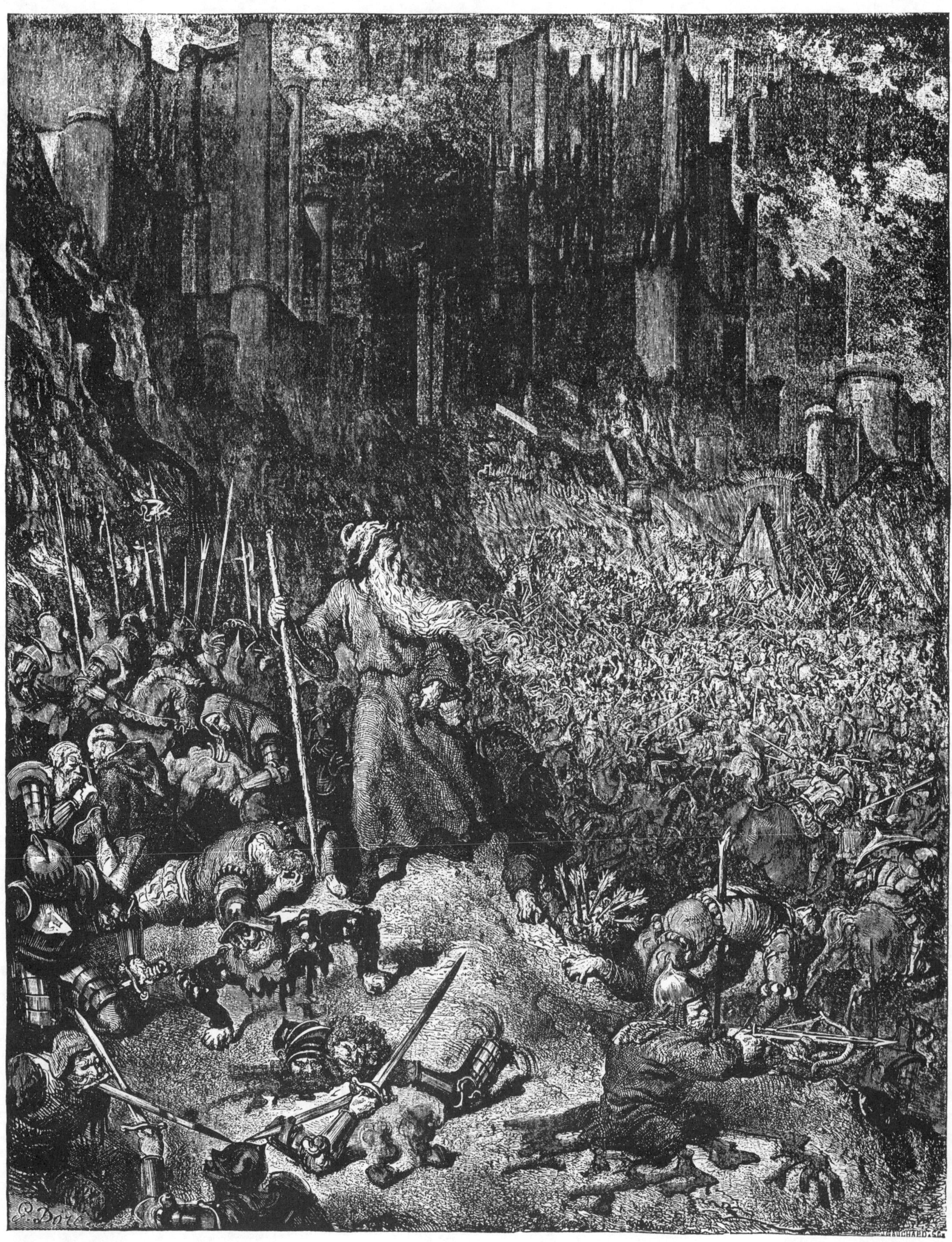

Doré did 12 vignettes for ***The Duke of Savoy's Page*** and eight for ***Jehu's Companions***. They are nothing to write home about. Of course they were also serialized in magazines. Then they were incorporated into the lengthy sets of Dumas' ***Complete Works*** in the 1860s. For that set they went through Doré's other magazine serials and figure out how to borrow 52 Doré magazine engravings for other titles to be inserted into some of Dumas' minor short stories. So most any French Dumas set could have some Doré illustrations. LeBlanc lists the original source for all the borrowed Dumas engravings. It took him 12 pages to list all of them (p.93-104). There were also many other illustrators in those sets. Finally in the 1890s, a 50-volume Dumas set by Little/Brown of Boston which used some of the Doré illustrations. So some later English Dumas sets may contain some Doré illustrations.

There is another Dumas title which claims to have Doré illustrations, from the 1950s. The 1958 British edition is entitled ***From Paris to Cadiz***; while the 1959 U.S. edition is entitled ***Adventures in Spain***. This is one of those attempts to "create" another book by a great author. They put together letters Dumas wrote while vacationing in Spain in 1846 to create a title. It does contain six Doré illustrations, reprinted from ***Davillier's Spain***. But all of the illustrations state that they are courtesy of the Metropolitan Museum of Art, from a 1919 gift by Mrs. A. S. Sullivan. Apparently, she donated either a copy of the ***Spain*** folio, or some original sketches.

Victor Malte-Brun: Geographie Universelle

From 1854-1860, Doré produced over 3500 published illustrations, a blinding rate. Between 1857-59, he did 324 vignettes for the Malte-Brun ***Geography***. All the engravings are in an oblong 4½x5½ uniform style. For Doré, they were fairly simple, but they have a charm to them. They feature people more than scenery. The set was first published in 108 weekly parts, then in six 8x11½ volumes, and then in two volumes, by Gustave Barba. It was also full of colored maps. There were reprint sets, plus booklets for most any particular country, region, or continent, in almost any combination you can imagine. But no foreign editions have ever been found.

La Guerre de l'Independence d'Italie

By 1859, French military focus had shifted from Russia to Italy. The effort to help the Turks against the Russians ended in 1856, and the effort to help the Italians against the Austrians began a couple years later. But Doré was not about to do another comic-strip version of this story. Both his book and magazine illustrations were now in the serious vein. For the Italian war, Doré produced large battle scene lithographs and even oil paintings. The Italian War prompted ***Journal pour Tous*** in 1859 to issue weekly supplements to numbers 218-232, for which Doré contributed 31 large illustrations, many of them double-page. Those 26 supplements were then bound into one 4to volume, entitled ***La Guerre d'Italie***. Doré was also contributing to another magazine by this time, ***Le Monde Illustre***, published by the Librairie Nouvelle. Most of the 87 original illustrations he did for them were from 1859-1861, a great many of which also involved the war in Italy. Quite a few books about the war were published within a short time, and many of the Doré illustrations contained therein were reprinted from magazine illustrations or from other books. But one that contained all original Doré engravings was ***Batailles et Combats de la Guerre de l'Independence d'Italie***, published by Bulla Freres in 1859. It was an oblong folio, and contained 20 oblong 11x16 (or double-page 16x22) Doré lithographs of Italian battle scenes. Another significant book was the 1861 Goupil folio, ***Garibaldi et les Volontaires Italiens***, for which Doré made six large illustrations. There are other titles for which Doré's involvement was limited or uncertain. They were not reprinted or translated, but many of his battle scenes have been reprinted in reference books.

William Shakespeare: The Tempest

This contains only five Doré engravings, but the undated 1860 edition is very significant. It is Doré's first book art commissioned from London, and about the last time that he played second fiddle in title billing, behind Birket Foster. Doré's 1856-1857 British editions had not made much of an impression, and few Londoners remembered him in 1860. And to think that just six years later British magazines would proclaim 1866 the Doré year. ***The Tempest*** is a very rare book; LeBlanc, Muir and many others were unable to find it. There are actually two versions of the 7½x10 Bell & Daldy edition; one with very ornate cover lettering, and another with standard block lettering, both publisher's cloth. There is also an undated New York edition, probably 1861, by D.Appleton.

LaBedolliere: Nouveau Paris
LaBedolliere: Environs du Nouveau Paris

These two books are practically one two-volume title - a light-hearted look at life in Paris, done for Doré's friend, Emile de La Bedolliere (not to be confused with French poet Charles Pierre Baudelaire, living at the same time). Doré did 67 engravings for ***Nouveau***, which came out in 26 weekly parts, beginning in January of 1860. Doré did 70 engravings for ***Environs***, which came out in 24 weekly parts, beginning in November of 1860. Both are undated, as are reprint editions, which can be differentiated by the change in address of the publisher Gustave Barba. There are no foreign editions, and few Doré reference works ever contain any of these illustrations. It was just more Doré filler work, as he was quietly working on his ***Dante's Inferno*** folio.

This is a good place for an overview of Doré's work up to 1860. The years 1847-60 were marked by high quantity and occasional high quality. If Doré had stopped at this point, he would have been known as one of the best 19th century French illustrators. But he was still virtually unknown outside of France. Here is a list of the major magazines to which Doré had contributed up through 1860 (by the ripe old age of 28). Doré's magazine contributions basically ended by 1861, with the one exception of the ***Davillier:Spain*** series for ***Tour du Monde***, which became a major book folio in 1873. We will cover that title in a future chapter.

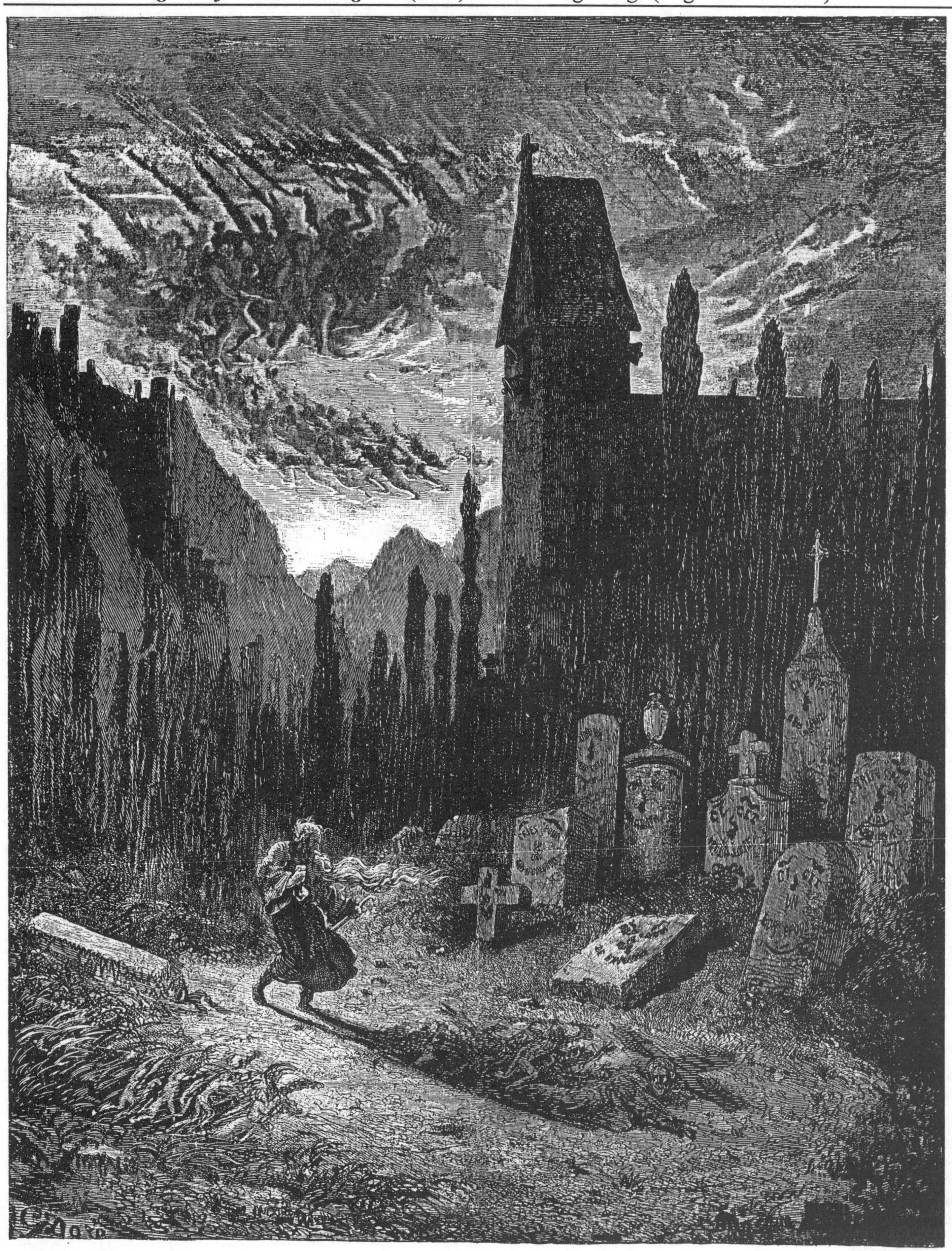

years	magazine	illos: new / repro
1848-1855	*Journal pour Rire*	1379 / 3
1851-1853	*Almanach pour Rire*	34 / 3
1851-1862	*l'Illustration*	36 / 11
1852-1853	*Almanach-Journal pour Rire*	32 / 0
1855-1862	*Journal pour Tous*	362 / 100
1855-1856	*Illustrated London News*	15 / 0
1855-1860	*Musee Francais-Anglais*	171 / 18
1856-1868	*Petits Journal pour Rire*	0 / 743
1856-1858	*Journal Amusant*	29 / 23
1856-1883	*Le Voleur Illustre*	7 / 114
1857-1866	*Semaine des Enfants*	82 / 185
1857-1861	*Le Monde Illustre*	87 / 67
1860-1873	*Tour du Monde*	368 / 0

By 1860, Doré had produced 2300 magazine engravings and 2900 book engravings. In this book list we are not listing books which are just sets of bound magazine illustrations, or repackaged as comic-strip booklets. For multi-volume sets, the year listed is when the set was finished. Some minor titles listed here have not been mentioned in the text.

year	author / *title*	illos
1847	*Les Travaux d'Hercule*	105
1851	*Des-Agrements d'un Voyage Agrement*	175
	Trois Artistes Incompris et Mecontents	155
1852	Paul Lacroix: *Bibliophile Jacob*	134
	Alphonse Brot: *Seul au Monde*	19
1853	Lord Byron: *Oeuvres Completes*	24
1854	Alphonse Brot: *Le Bourreau du Roi*	6
	Alphonse Brot: *Le Medecin du Coeur*	10
	Rabelais: *Gargantua & Pantagruel*	105
	Histoire...de la Sainte Russie	500
	La Menagerie Parisienne	24
	Les Differents Publics de Paris	20
1855	Balzac: *Contes Drolatiques*	425
	Jules Gerard: *La Chasse au Lion*	11
	John Sherer: *Les Chercheurs d'Or*	30
	L'Affaire d'Orient	5
	Episodes de la Guerre d'Orient	6
	Taine: *Voyage aux Eaux des Pyrenees*	64
1856	Mayne Reid: *L'Habitation du Desert*	24
	Mary Lafon: *Le Chevalier Jaufre*	20
	Girardin: *Contes d'un Vieille Fille*	7
	La Legende de la Juif Errant	13
	Dumas: *La Page du Duc de Savoie*	12
	Benjamin Gastineau: *France en Afrique*	30
	A.Haussmann: *L'Insurrectin en Chine*	8
	Louis Noir: *L'Homme de Bronze*	9
	Victor Perceval: *Memoires-Jeune Cadet*	48
	Plouvier/Vincent:*Refrains du Dimanche*	12
1857	Mary Lafon: *Fierabras*	12
	Segur: *Nouveaux Contes de Fees*	29
1858	Dumas: *Les Compagnons de Jehu*	8
1859	Malte-Brun: *Geographie Universelle*	324
	Les Folies Gauloises	20
	Michel de Montaigne: *Essais*	12
	Batailles-Guerre-Independence-Italie	20
	La Guerre d'Italie	31
1860	LaBedolliere: *Nouveau Paris*	67
	LaBedolliere: *Environs-Nouveau Paris*	70
	Taine: *Voyages aux Pyrenees*	335
	William Shakespeare: *The Tempest*	5

During the 1850s, Doré's obsession with being a "great artist" rose and fell in reaction to particular events. He began to develop hostility toward certain French artists who received undue levels of praise, according to him. Doré had always been the best at everything, and it galled him to see his works ignored, rejected, or criticized, while others (whom he judged to be inferior to himself) were praised to the high heavens. His problem was not with older artists like Eugene Delacroix. Doré and Delacroix were both in the inner circle of the composer Rossini, and there is no record of any friction between them. But the mantle of France's greatest artist was passing from Delacroix to Ernest Meissonier, and with every mention of Meissonier's name, Doré ground his teeth a little harder. Today, Meissonier is hardly considered the greatest 19th century French artist, but back then he was particularly famous for his Napoleon paintings. The narrative is picked up by Paul Lacroix, in Roosevelt (p.166-167), in the year 1854:

> He (Doré) also began at this time to develop a characteristic which I regretted to observe in one so young, especially a lad of his remarkable natural gifts. He conceived an early dislike for all artists, sculptors, draughtsmen, and people of that class. As to painters, Meissonier and Gerome positively stuck in his throat. When he heard of the fabulous prices paid to those artists he wanted to tear his hair with rage. He never seemed to realize the fact that age and experience could make any difference to the achievements of great successes, and measured public appreciation by what he felt he had within him, never missing an opportunity to say that he alone was unappreciated. He nearly had a convulsion one day on hearing that Meissonier had received 200,000 francs for a single picture.
>
> "What!" he exclaimed, - "a thing like that! Now look at me. I can paint; I know I could paint better than Meissonier, at any rate. Have I ever been paid 200,000 francs for anything? No, and I never shall be. (note: Doré highest payment for a painting was 150,000 francs for *Christ Leaving the Praetorium*, in 1872) The fact is that no one understands me. I shall live and die misunderstood, or never comprehended at all, which is worse."
>
> I cannot tell you how it vexed me to hear him go on in this way. When he had one of those fits, it was useless to try to argue with or console him, and I used to say to myself, "Why can't he be content? Why will he fill his head with ideas about painters which can only render him unhappy?" But he would persist in tormenting himself, and I trembled when I reflected what must be in store for him should he encourage this chronic discontent in preying upon him.
>
> I could not but marvel at the change that had taken place in him. His real nature was gay, sunshiny, and tender. He entertained sympathy for every one outside of his own profession, but never heard of

(top) Lafon: ***Jaufrey the Knight*** (1856) 20 wood engravings (original illo size 5x7½)

(bottom) Lafon: ***Fierabras - Legends*** (1857) 12 wood engravings (original illo size 5x7½)

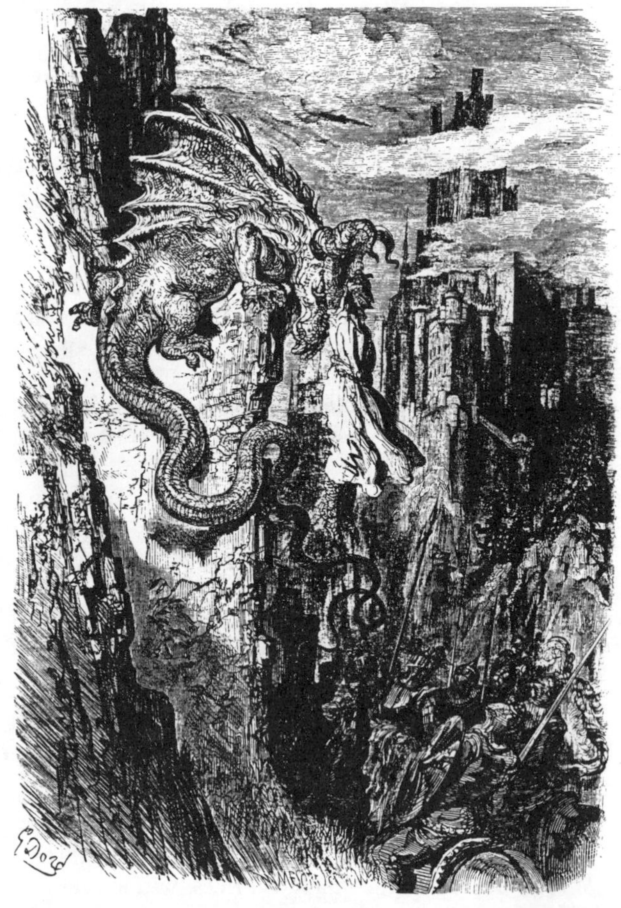

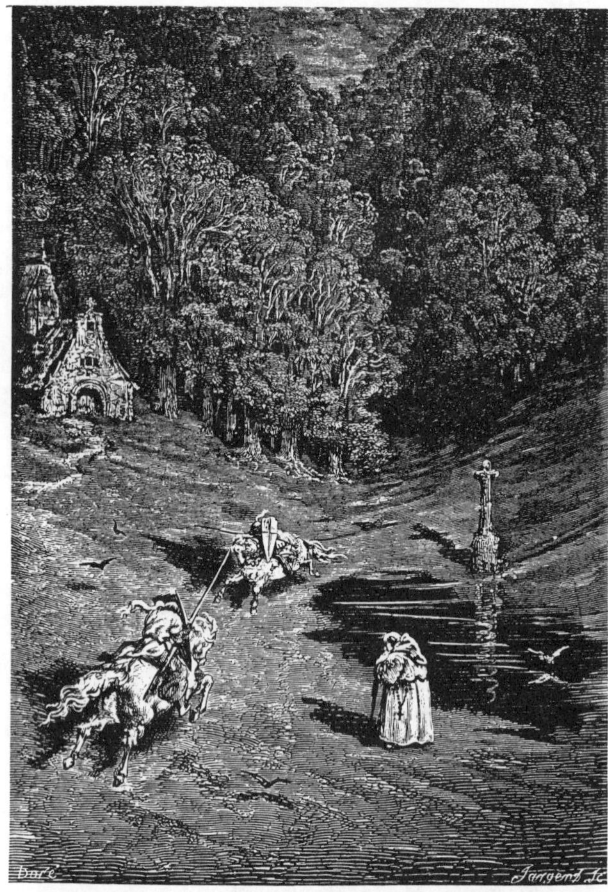

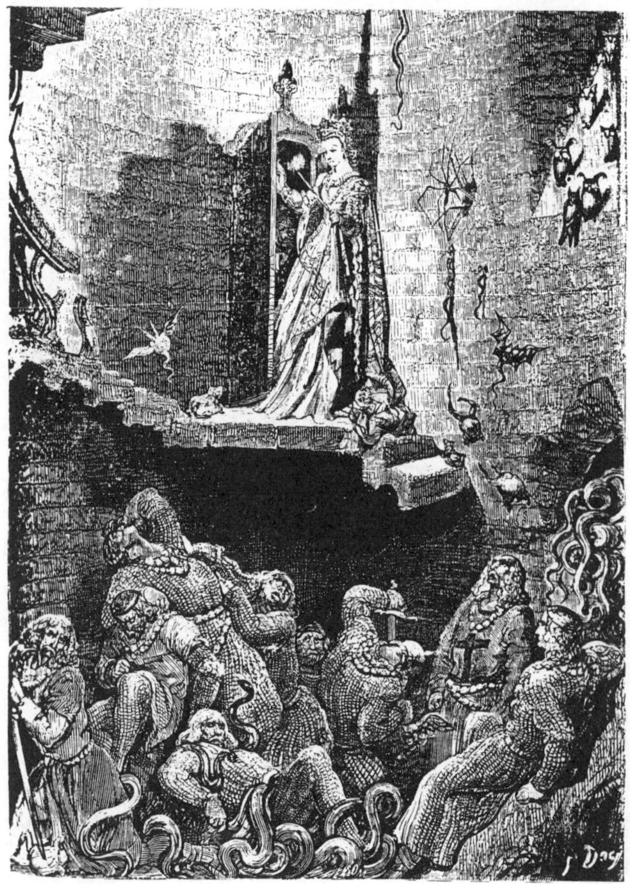

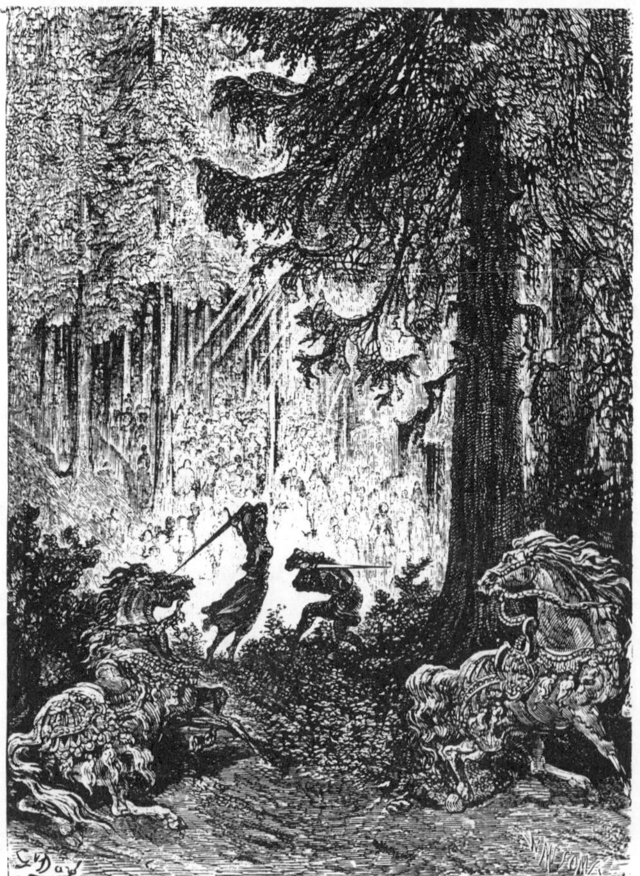

> any other artist's success without brooding over it jealously and unhappily. In those days his mother had a hard time with him, and I think only the profound love they bore each other filled up every other void in their lives. No matter how abrupt Gustave might be with others, his adoration for her had reached a point which made him indifferent to everything and everybody else. She thought with and for him, and he took her counsel anent all that concerned him. It was the most extraordinary reciprocity of affection that I have ever known. Determined as he was in his relations with others, he yielded in all respects towards her. I hoped and imagined that he would get over his unpleasant tendency to rail at artists and painters in general; but the next time I saw him after the hue and cry over the 200,000 francs paid to Meissonier, he began again at once to abuse that artist. Not only had he not forgotten the incident above alluded to, but I speedily realized that he had been brooding ever since over Meissonier's success; and I was prepared to tell him plainly that I felt ashamed to see a lad of his talent developing such a disposition.

Notice how Doré referred to himself as a misunderstood artist, just three years after his own satire on that very topic. Soon his ego and emotional dependence on his mother began to produce major negative consequences. Doré told Lacroix, per Roosevelt (p.168): "I am going to paint a series of pictures representing the abominations of Paris, you know, with all the old streets, all the wretches and outcasts." Soon Doré invited Lacroix to see those completed paintings:

> On looking at his new work, *Paris as it is*, I grew more and more astounded, for there were 12 colossal canvases, some of them more than half the height of the room. They were extraordinarily well executed, and as before, he had painted them in less time that it takes most artists to prepare their brushes and canvas. Here his effects were not derived from colour, but from the grouping of the personages and the drawings, which were beyond all praise. Of the twelve pictures each one was more horrible than the other - all were positively sickening in their realism. I could not bring myself to believe that he had imagined and painted such vivid scenes is so short a time.

Notice that Doré still did not have a sense of color, but his skill in other areas made up for it. Theophile Gautier also praised the paintings. In a short time two Americans had been located who wished to buy all 12 paintings, to take them on a travelling American show. They offered Doré 110,000 francs for the 12 of them. Doré was very proud of the offer and bragged about it to Lacroix and Gautier. Remember that in 1854, Doré had absolutely no reputation as a painter. This was to be a major step for the future of his anticipated career in painting. But he had not reckoned on his mother's reaction to the offer. Roosevelt (p.170) gives her chilling reply:

> "They have offered you 110,000 francs? Then you should not accept the offer, for it means that they will pay more. Ask them for 140,000. It is quite clear that people who can pay 110,000 francs can always pay 140,000."

At that point both Lacroix and Gautier protested vigorously, realizing what a major step it was for a painter with no reputation to make such a sale of a group of paintings. But her reply to their protests was beyond chilling:

> "I have given you my opinion. Gustave is always being done by everybody he has to do with; only his mother appreciates him at his great value. He is easy-going, and would, like a fool, accept the first offer these men make to him. And you - you counsel him to prove that he thinks nothing of his own work by selling it to the first bidder, and at the price the latter proposes to give! It is simply ridiculous, and I will not hear of such a thing. Besides, as I said before, people who can pay 110,000 francs can just as well pay 140,000. If they refuse to give more they are only trying to get the better of Gustave. I have spoken, and that settles it - 140,000 francs or nothing."

The Americans pleaded with Doré to understand the enormous expenses they would entail in getting the paintings to America, and in setting up and advertising the travelling show. But his mother's word was law, and they left sadly and empty-handed. His mother still had her game-face on:

> "The will come back. They were only trying on the old game. My poor Gustave, how little you really know the world! It was only a trick. I tell you they will come back; for I well know that anyone who can pay 110,000 francs for pictures can always pay 140,000. They will come back."

She was as wrong as she could possibly have been. Not only did they never come back, but Doré lost an invaluable chance at major artistic exposure. Over a dozen years would pass before Doré would get another serious offer for his paintings. The fact is that 110,000 francs was a very good offer, all things considered. Doré's emotional dependence on his mother was so great that he could not even suggest to her what a terrible mistake she had made. It is believed that Doré actually destroyed all those paintings, not so much because he felt bad when he saw them, but because his mother might feel bad if she saw them. You would think that such an event would make him question his emotional dependence on her. But as the years went by, he actually became even more emotionally dependent on his mother. It could almost be described as emotional incest. Doré was opting for her version of emotional reality rather than an adult view of physical reality. Anytime the topic of the Americans came up, Doré's mother would immediately lash out at them as though they were some sort of despicable slime.

The events of the 1850s were almost enough to make Doré give up on painting. It is not that he was a bad painter, but he thought that since he had been so successful as a comic-strip cartoonist, and then as a literary illustrator, that he should have the same tremendous success as a painter. But

(top & middle rows) Malte-Brun's ***Geography*** (1857-59) - 324 wood engravings (original size 4½x5½ oblong)
(bottom) ***Garibaldi & the Italian Volunteers*** (1861) - 6 lithographs (original size 16x22 oblong)

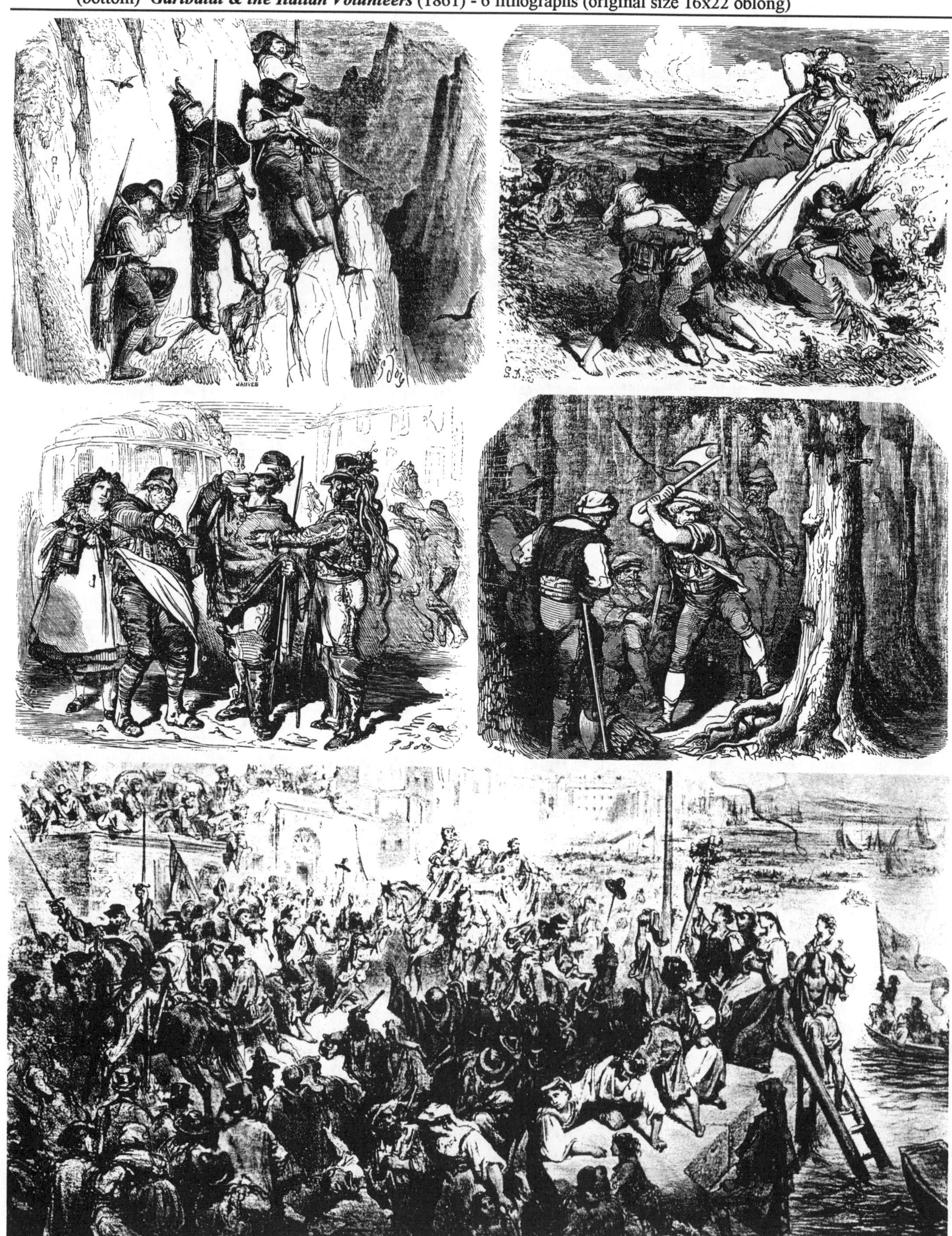

the rules of that game were different. The dramatic wit and outlandishness that made him stand out as an illustrator did absolutely nothing for him as a painter. Doré's paintings even had the benefit of influential friends who wrote supportive articles for him. But there were no other reviews, and there were no buyers, and there were no medals. Doré may have been an average painter, but there were thousands of painters, and to Doré average meant failure. We mentioned that he had submitted two drawings to the 1848 Salon. He submitted individual landscape paintings in 1850 and 1852, and another oil painting in 1853. But his first major effort was in 1855. For the 1855 Salon, he did three oil paintings - ***The Battle of Alma, The Prairie,*** and ***Soir*** (Evening). But Doré expected fireworks to go off when people saw his paintings. He had submitted a fourth painting (***The Death of Rizzio***), but it was rejected by the jury panel. Doré should have been happy just to have his paintings exhibited. How many other 23-year-olds could boast three paintings there? But he had started at the top, and anything else was the bottom. In 1857, he submitted ten oil paintings to the Salon, mainly landscapes. That year he actually won an Honorable Mention, for his massive ***Battle of Inkermann,*** over 15 feet high. It is now in the Musee Nationale de Versailles. But the reviews criticized the color, and said that Doré "lacked school." Doré made no more submissions to the Salon until 1861.

It may be difficult to reconcile the spoiled-child tantrum-throwing painter Doré with the playful, carefree, kind-hearted illustrator Doré. Throughout his life, he remained essentially child-like. But there are many stories of Doré's kindness and charity, as in Roosevelt (p.240):

> One day a workman fell from a scaffolding into the street, and sustained severe injuries. Next door was Doré's studio, who was just entering the latter when he witnessed the accident. The man uttered a loud cry, and then gasped out, "My poor wife! who will give her bread whilst I am in the hospital?" Doré had just been paid for a piece of work, and without a word emptied his pocket. "Here are 500 francs, my friend," he said, "if no other help comes to you, send to the address on this card. Courage, and better luck."

Let us draw the curtain on this chapter in his life with another story from his travels, from Roosevelt (p.162-163):

> A characteristic incident marks the trip to the Netherlands. At one of the frontiers, near midnight, Doré could not find his passport. In vain he gave his name, Doré, to the stiff officer, but he would not let him pass. At last an isolated gleam of intelligence penetrated his dutiful and official obtuseness. At the full name, Gustave Doré, he smiled triumphantly, as much as to say, "I have you now." His words were: -
>
> "If you are Gustave Doré, it will be easy enough to prove it. Make me a sketch of - of anything you see at hand."
>
> Continental travellers who grumble at having even to show their keys, will be lost in sympathy for the poor artist, obliged at such an unhallowed moment to evoke the muse; but he did it. Drawing a note-book from his pocket, he did not sketch the people about him, but, going to a window, looked out upon the street; and some persons standing at that moment in conversation unconsciously served for models. In a few seconds he handed a perfect sketch of them to the officer, whose hat was in his hand whilst he allowed the artist and his party to proceed. A proper passport was made out for the Doré family, but the official kept the little sketch as a personal recollection of the famous artist.

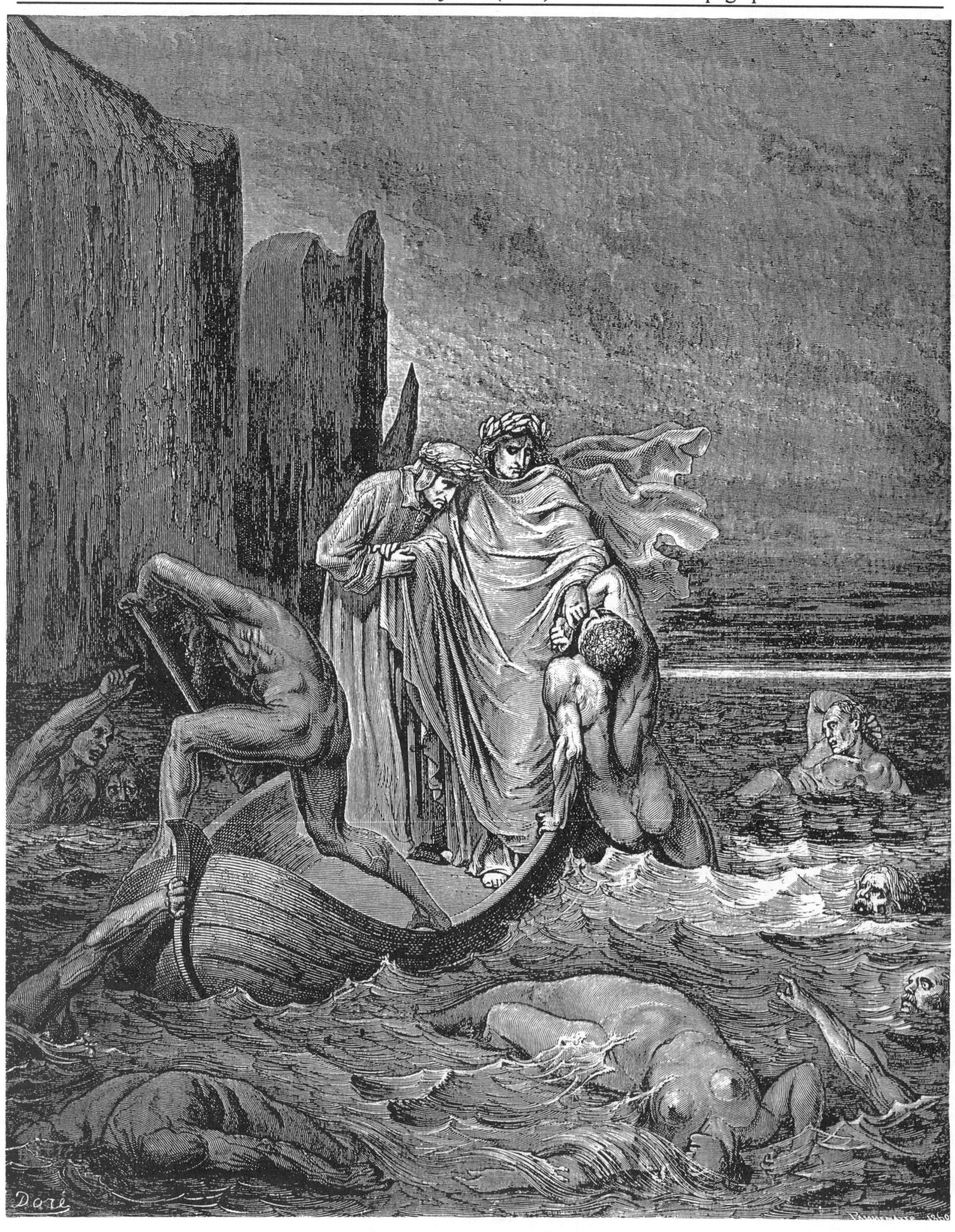

5. THE DORÉ LITERARY FOLIOS (1861-64:HACHETTE)

The story of the Doré folios does not actually begin in 1861 with ***Dante's Inferno***, but in 1856 with ***The Wandering Jew***. We mentioned how the events of 1854-55 made Doré feel rejected as an arist. ***The Wandering Jew*** folio became an outlet for the frustrated painter inside him. To Doré, those 12x16 wood engravings were not illustrations, they were b&w paintings. If he could not make the illustrator into a painter, he would make painting come to illustration. That is the true significance of the Doré folios - they were not engravings of paintings, they are painting illustrations. Doré's b&w artistic skills, coupled with inadequacies as a painter, and an ego that could not tolerate being a rejected painter, drove him to a new type of illustration. It should not come as a surprise that in the 1870s, Doré made many paintings from the scenes in his folio engravings. For the last two decades of his life, Doré existed in a strange limbo between illustration and fine art, and it was difficult to tell where one ended and the other began.

Dante's Inferno

Roosevelt and Jerrold claim that Doré began working on ***Dante's Inferno*** in 1855, and finished it in 1857. But all the dated engravings list 1860. Perhaps he began his research in 1855 and worked on the blocks from 1857-1860. Doré did engrave a few of the blocks himself. But this was the period when he was beginning to develop his "school" of engravers, personally selected and trained by himself to maximize the advanced effects he was trying to achieve upon the blocks. A survey of ***Inferno*** plates shows that his two favorites, Pisan and Pannemaker, were already doing the lion's share of the engravings. But over 20 engravers worked on those 76 plates, a number of which show his famous white-on-black effect.

But the real pre-publication story was the search for a publisher. Publishers were beating Doré's door down, begging him to do work for them, but when he suggested something unconventional, they all took a hike. His dream of a lavishly illustrated literary folio was just too expensive. The eventual retail price of ***Dante's Inferno*** was 100 *fr*. During the 1850s, Doré's most expensive book was ***The Wandering Jew***, which sold for 12 *fr*. The rejection of Doré's literary folio idea had one major difference with his rejection as a painter - he could offer his engravings directly to the public. He could pay for a book edition himself, and let the public decide its fate. After searching in vain for a publisher, he came back to Hachette and said he would pay for the edition himself. The grand old man, Louis Hachette, was still pessimistic. He tried to give Doré fatherly advice - "I have been a publisher for 30 years, and I am telling you that you are throwing your money away. You will be lucky to sell 100 copies." But this time Doré was confident of his artistic abilities, per Roosevelt (p.111):

> Doré selected a famous poem, immortal by reason of its intensely genuine imaginative character as a true vision, a narrative of things actually seen by the mortal eye of the narrator, but a poem which is at the same time the most cruel, the most ferocious, the most diabolical in the whole range of the world's literature. He selected it, not to revel in its horrors and its cruelities, but because he felt and saw with Dante, and his imagination could master and interpret the mystical vision without flinching. Besides, the *Inferno* was essentially a pictorial poem. It presented a series of grand and awful scenes, capable of the highest artistic treatment. Doré had no idea of freezing the blood of "the gentle dames of Paris," but a very distinct determination to offer to the world a signal proof of his power as a poetic artist.

There is some disagreement about the initial print run of the 1861 Hachette folio edition of ***L'Enfer***. LeBlanc (p.78) says it was 3,000, but in the reference book on ***La Librairie Hachette*** by Jean Mistler in 1964, he states (p.153) that they printed just 1,000 copies in French (and Italian) and 800 in Italian (only). The simplest way to differentiate listings for the two versions is by the Italian word for "Paris" = "Parigi." The ***Hachette*** book details Doré's heavy expenses in production and printing, and how the contract specified that Doré would receive 60% of the gross sales, Hachette 15% for distribution, and the bookseller 25%. Mistler had access to the Hachette archives, and found there a letter from July 17, 1863, from a Mr. Robin to Hachette, seeking to buy the rights to some sort of theatrical production by means of projection out of Doré's illustrations to ***Dante's Inferno***. Was that not a precursor to the film industry? Doré's ***Dante's Inferno*** has influenced the theatre, from the British actor Sir Henry Irving in the 1890s, to films by Henry Otto & Harry Lachman in the 1920s-30s, to Jack Nicholson in ***The Witches of Eastwick*** in the 1980s, to Brad Pitt & Morgan Freeman in ***Seven*** in 1995.

The 13x17 ***Inferno*** folio finally appeared in 1861. It was over 2" thick, of the highest quality paper, weighing about 20 lbs. At first they only bound 100 copies, to minimize Doré's losses. Doré held his breath. Just a few days later, he received that message from Louis Hachette, "Success! Come quickly! I am an ass!" But let us have a little sympathy for Mr. Hachette. For so many years the trend had been toward cheaper and cheaper books. Remember, this book came out at almost exactly the same time as the launching of ***Dime Novels***. The first U.S. edition of Doré's ***Dante's Inferno*** sold for $25-$60, depending on the binding. What most of the publishing field had missed was the growing middle-class, and their twin desires for cheap editions but also for high-quality art-books.

Louis Hachette had underestimated the success of Doré's ***Dante's Inferno*** just slightly. He thought it would sell 100 copies. It has now sold about 200 <u>editions</u>! Besides French, it has been published in English, Italian, German, Portuguese, Spanish, Dutch, Russian, Finnish, Swedish, Yugoslavian, Latvian, Bulgarian, Rumanian, and Chinese. Doré supplanted the great Botticelli as the definitive illustrator of Dante. To this day there is a steady stream of new Doré editions in Italian. On the 700th anniversary of the birth of Dante (1965), San Marino issued four postage stamps with Doré engravings.

The first edition sold out in a couple months. It was an unqualified success, both commercially and critically. Paris was filled with reviews, tripping over each other in heaping praise upon Doré's achievement. This was now the third level of praise Doré had experienced: in 1847-48 as a clever boy-

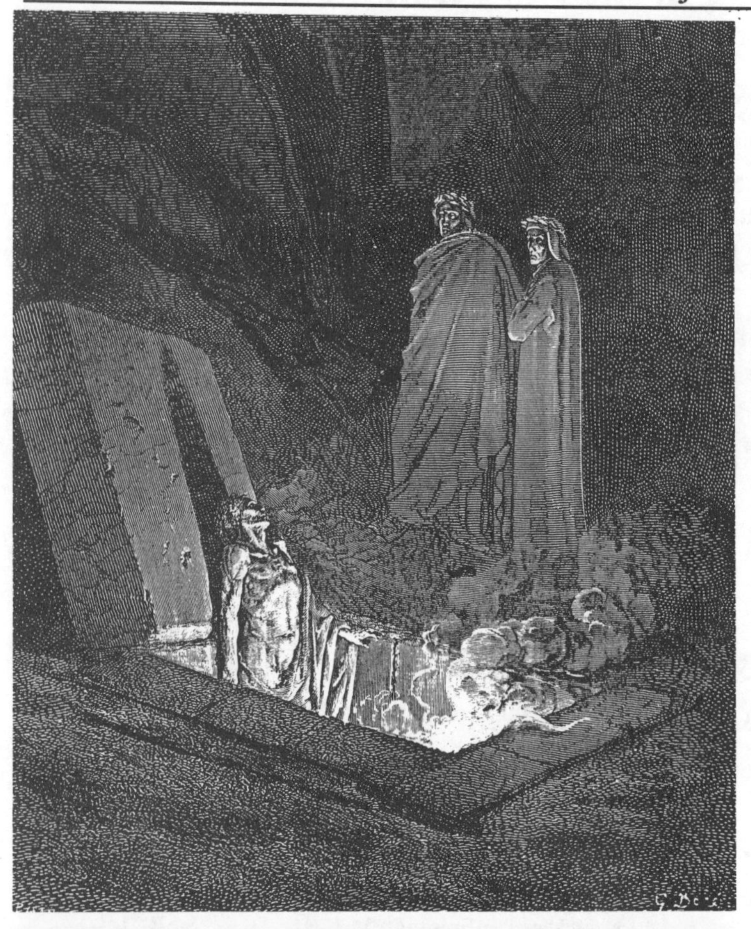

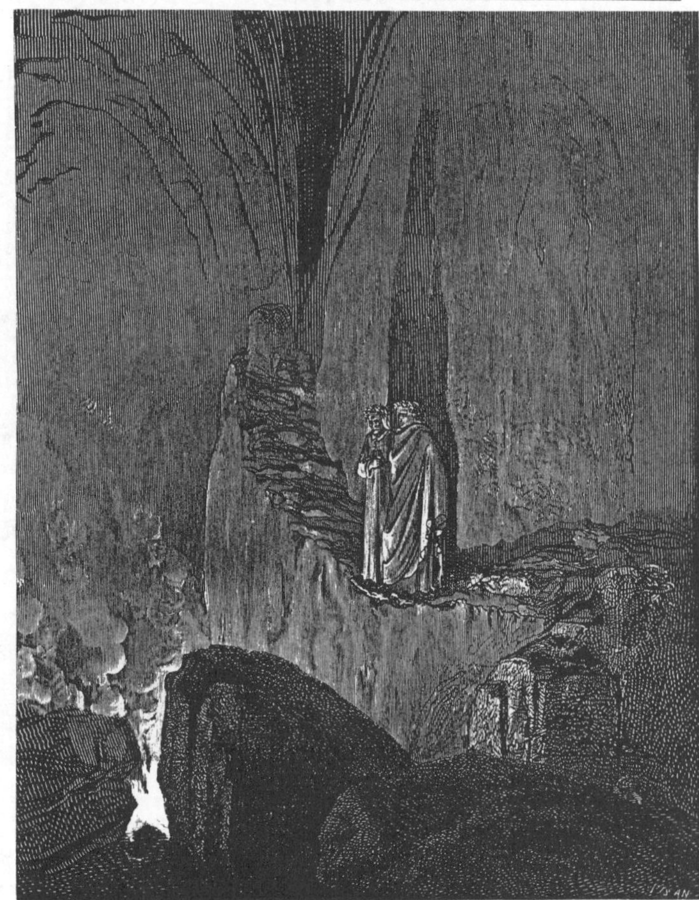

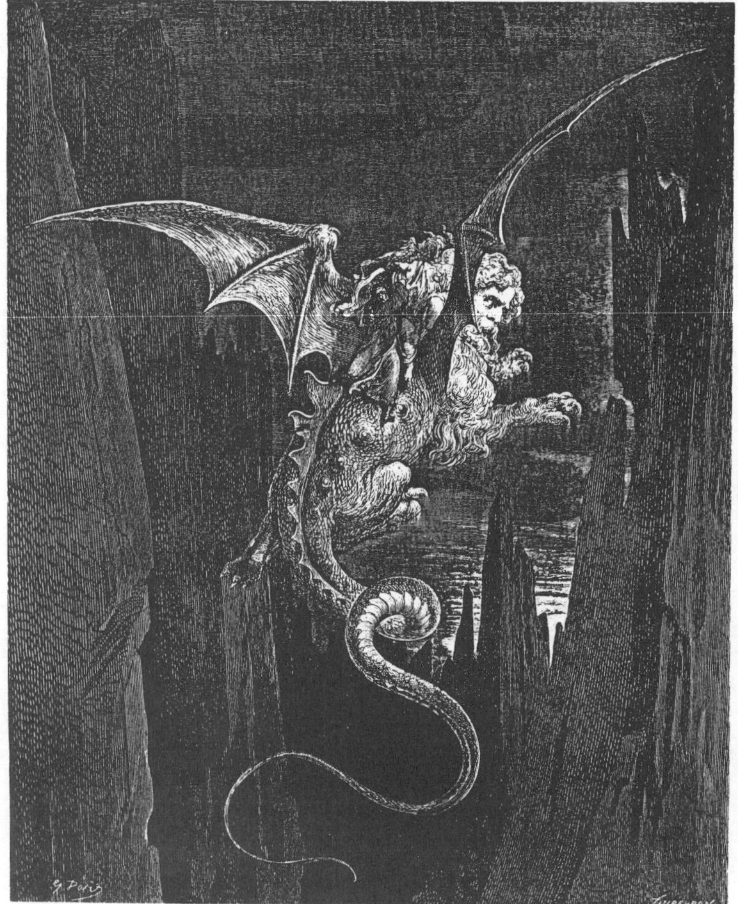

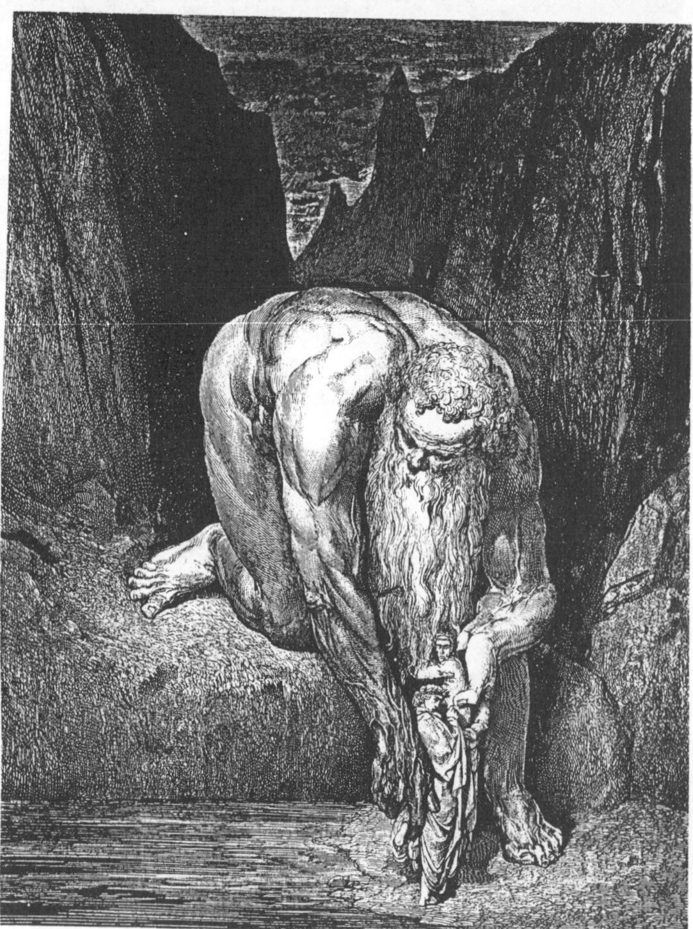

genius comic-strip artist of ***Hercules*** and ***Journal pour Rire***, in 1854-55 as the serious literary illustrator of ***Rabelais*** and ***Balzac***, and now this. France was now proclaiming Doré to be the greatest illustrator in the world, and within a few years the rest of the world would catch up with that proclamation. Doré had defied all the critics and had achieved a level of artistic expression that was undreamed of. Up to that point, Doré had been competing against other illustrators. From that point on, other illustrators could only dream of being compared to him. Now publishers were again knocking on his door, but now it was not to say, "we would like for you to illustrate this" but "we would like to publish anything you want to illustrate." The lion's share of his folios went to Hachette.

The second edition followed the next year. Hachette published several editions in folio format before reducing the size. In 1868, Doré completed Dante's ***Divine Comedy*** with ***Purgatory & Paradise***. We will get to that later. Eventually the two parts were combined. In 1866, the first English folio edition appeared in a slightly smaller 12x15. Cassell, Petter & Galpin became the "authorized" English publisher of most of Doré's folio editions. Doré was even more of a gold mine for Cassell than he was for Hachette. Cassell published over 20 editions of his ***Dante's Inferno***. Cassell published over 200 Doré editions. Their first ***Inferno*** edition was published in December of 1865, and the British reviews outdid the French. British publications like ***The Art Journal*** proclaimed 1866 as "the Doré year." By 1868, Doré was much more famous in England than any British illustrator.

In America, Doré started off a bit more slowly. In 1863, Frederick Leypoldt of Philadelphia, the eventual founder of ***Publishers Weekly***, got an edition of the French ***Inferno*** and published a portfolio of ten of Doré's engravings. Two years later he published another edition with all 76 engravings. These were entitled ***The Dante Album***. Those portfolios are extremely rare. Prior to the 1891 international copyright law, U.S. publishers helped themselves to anything commercially viable coming from Europe. In 1867, the Boston firm DeVries & Ibarra published English and Italian ***Inferno*** editions. In 1868, another Boston firm, J.E.Tilton, published J.W.Black's ***Photogravures from Doré's Dante***. All those early editions are very rare. In late 1867, Cassell came on the scene with a newly opened U.S. office, and began publishing the Doré ***Inferno*** by subscription only in 25 monthly parts at $1 each. They included a notice telling how to get the parts bound. That was the first "official" U.S. edition. By the 1880s, Cassell editions were down to 10½x13½ and the market for the more expensive edition dried up. The 1882 edition was $6 and the 1888 edition was $4. Cheaper 1880s editions sold like proverbial hotcakes, and over a dozen "cheap" U.S. publishers began issuing Doré editions. Editions kept getting cheaper and cheaper, both in price and quality, and after the turn of the century, they died off. In more recent years there have been several editions by Crown, Pantheon, and Dover, and even in comic-book format by Tome Press.

After ***Inferno*** was so successful, close friends expected to see Doré on top of the world, but he seemed to be almost pouting. The papers were full of declarations of his supremacy as an illustrator, but Doré quickly became obsessed with the lack of official recognition by his country. For some years it had been discussed that Doré's accomplishments made him worthy of inclusion into the Legion of Honour. It was childish of him to pout over being able to walk around with that "little scrap of red ribbon in his button-hole," but he had certainly achieved more than many others who had been so honored. One close friend who saw Doré's dejection was Paul Dalloz, and after getting an earful from Doré and his mother, he set out and cornered the Minister of Public Instruction. This is how Dalloz related the scene to Roosevelt (p.226):

> I asked him if Gustave Doré's name was included in the list of persons selected for decoration. He hemmed and hawed, finally replying that they had thought about it, but that Doré was so young, and there were so many candidates for distinction, etc. Of course he had a dozen reasons ready; but eventually he asked me for some particulars about Doré, and promised that he would think the matter over. He seemed so well disposed that I left him, craving his permission to return in a quarter of an hour, and tore off to Gustave's house. Entering his studio, I vociferated, "Give me a copy of all your works!" and without further explanation carried off enough to fill my carriage. Again I invaded the Minister's room, a lackey following me, staggering under the weight of two armfuls of books.
>
> "What are these?" exclaimed Mr. B_____, aghast, pointing to the pile of volumes.
>
> "Some of the works of a young man of 28," I replied, "and this is not a quarter of all that Gustave Doré has done."
>
> The Minister took up one and scanned it closely, then another, and another, turning over page after page. Time passed; presently he picked up the *Inferno* of Dante, and went through it to the end, without speaking a word. Then he opened it again, laid his hand impressively on one of the illustrations, and said -
>
> "Not a word more! Let this speak for him. His own talent says more than could a multitude of friends. For Gustave Doré not to belong to the Legion of Honour would be an insult to himself and an injustice to the country that gave him birth."
>
> Ah! that was well said. I returned to Doré with the copies of his works.
>
> "Here, you great baby," I said, embracing him, "take your books; laugh, sing, eat, drink, sleep, and lament no longer. You will have the Cross of the Legion of Honour, not through any influence of mine, but through your own real talent and labour."

Edmond About: King of the Mountains

Edmond About was one of Doré's schoolmate friends from the Lycee Charlemagne in 1848. How quickly a dozen years had passed. About had become a prominent writer and journalist. His best known novel was ***Le Roi des Montagnes***, in 1857. In 1860 it was serialized in ***Journal pour Tous***, with 56 Doré vignettes. The 5th book edition in 1861, published by

(top) full-size detail (bottom) reduced illustrations from Perrault's ***Fairy Tales*** (1862) - 42 full-page plates

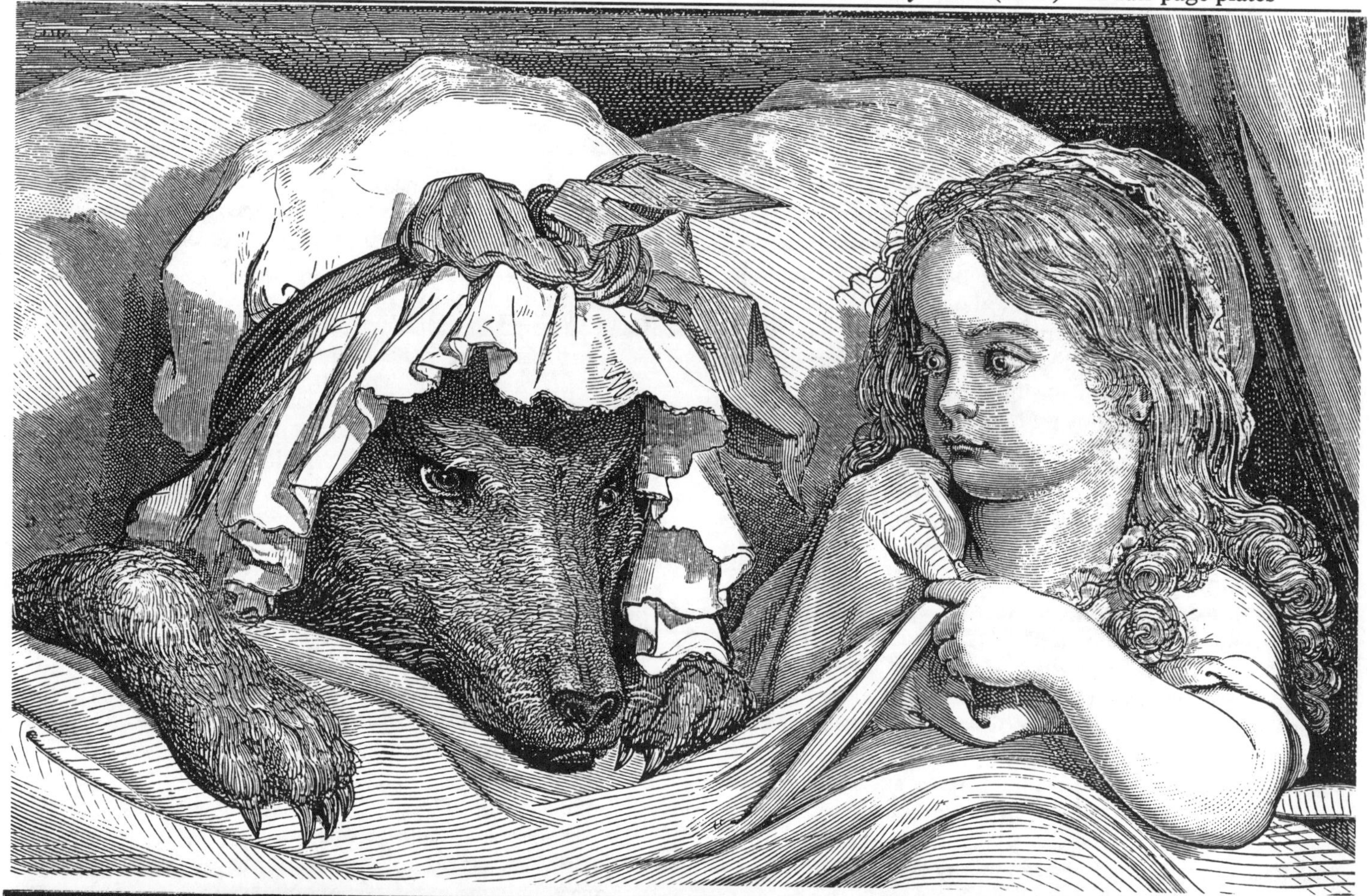

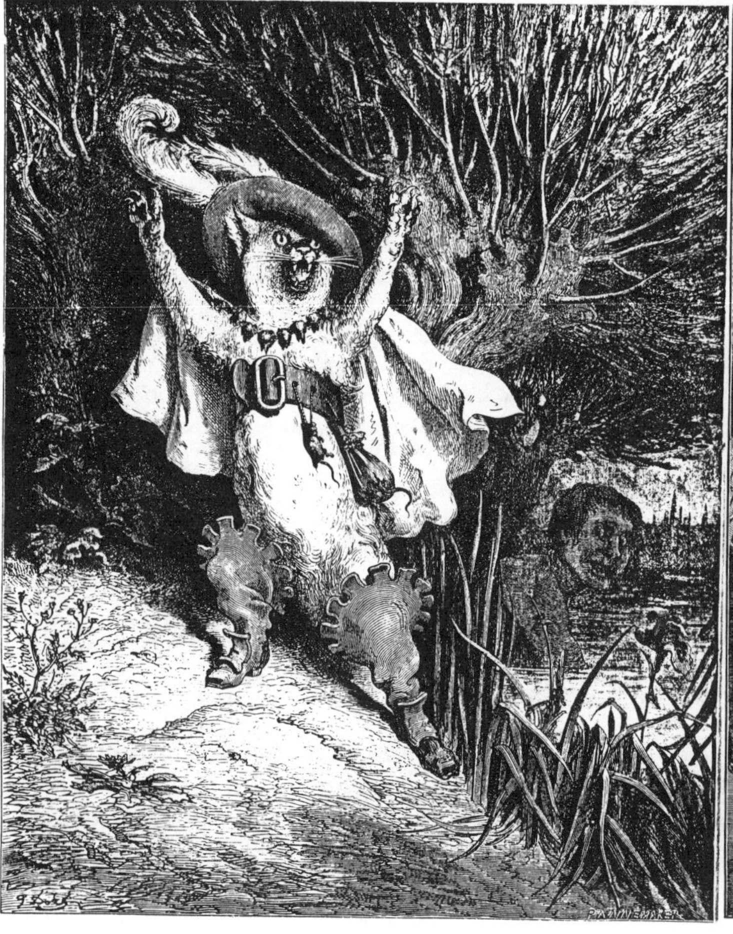

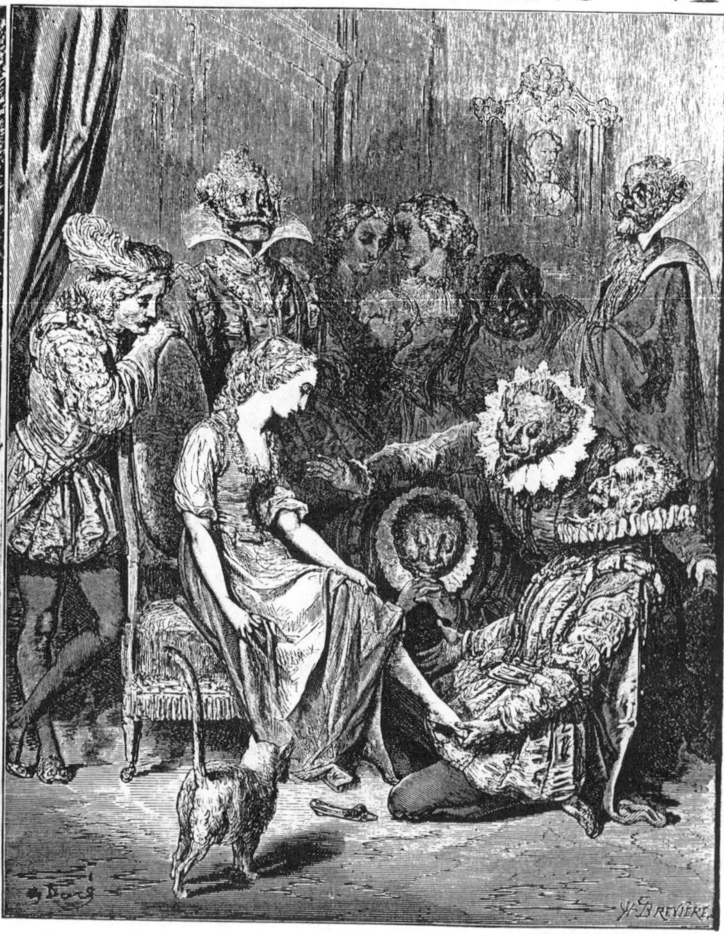

Hachette, was the first illustrated edition, containing 158 Doré illustrations, including the ones from the serial. These illustrations were just the opposite of the ***Inferno***; they were light, funny simple sketches. It is about the famous bandits in the Greek hills (who are also highly respected businessmen) and of three people they kidnap - a wealthy British woman and her lovely young daughter, plus a poor German botanist in love with the daughter. There have been about 20 French editions with the Doré illustrations. English publishers could not decide whether to call the story *King of the Mountains* or *The Greek Brigand*. There was even an edition in Esperanto, the synthetic language of a century ago that has now lost its significance due to the prominence of English.

X.-B. Saintine: Le Chemin des Ecoliers
X.-B. Saintine: La Mythologie du Rhin

Saintine's full name was Xavier-Boniface Saintine. It is a confusing name, and he is sometimes listed under Xavier. Doré illustrated two of his books in 1861-62 for Hachette. They have the same basic content - German mythology and folktales. The 203 illustrations for ***Chemin*** and the 165 for ***Mythologie*** are all different. Some foreign editions combine the illustrations. They are mainly small vignettes. The title ***Chemin des Ecoliers*** means something like "the Pathway of School Children" which has no connection to the content. It was not reprinted. There were French ***Mythologie*** reprints. English reprints are confusing. The only official editions are by Scribner of New York, of Saintine's ***Myths of the Rhine***, in 1875. But the British, being so independent, did not like Saintine's text, so Daldy & Isbister published ***River Legends***, with text by E. H. Knatchbull-Hugesson, at the same time, but with only 42 Doré illustrations. Knatchbull-Hugesson's name is also confusing. Sometimes he is listed under Knatchbull, sometimes under Hugesson, sometimes under some nobility title, and other times under "Brabourne." Not to be outdone by British name confusion, Lippincott of Philadelphia published about 280 Doré vignettes from the two original books with a new text, ***The New Hyperion***, by Edward Strahan, also in 1875. Strahan was actually Everett Shinn. Scribner then took to borrowing (without credit) ***Saintine*** illustrations for Frank Stockton books. This was a common pattern. There is no end to the titles which have borrowed Doré engravings.

Wm.F.Ainsworth: All Round the World

Back in 1860, Hachette began their travel periodical, ***Tour du Monde***. At first they had Doré do illustrations for China (13), Norway (10), the U.S. (9), Africa (6), and others (6). Some of the U.S. illustrations pertain to George Catlin's work on Indians. In 1861-1862, the British publisher W.Kent came out with a 4V set called ***All Round the World***, with text by William F. Ainsworth (not the author of ***Dick Turpin*** and ***Tower of London***; his name was Wm. Harrison Ainsworth). The set had hundred of engravings, including 36 by Doré from ***Tour du Monde*** before the ***Spain*** serial started. But in 1862, Doré had no name recognition value in London, so they did not list his name on the title page, and even scratched his name off his own engravings. But by the time that set was reprinted in 1866 by Wm.Collins, Doré was a very big name in London, and from then on he was featured on the title page and his name magically reappeared on his engravings. The set was reprinted into the 1890s. An 1872 edition by C.Griffin disguised the book with two new titles: ***The Earth Delineated with Pen & Pencil***, and ***Wanderings in Every Clime***. Though all the Doré illustrations are from a French magazine, there is no French book edition of that title or any similar title.

Charles Perrault: Fairy Tales

This 1862 title marks the first of many publishers who wanted to be able to feature a Doré folio. The publisher J.Hetzel (who edited his own editions under the pseudonym P.J.Stahl) would very shortly become famous as the exclusive publisher of the works of Jules Verne; but in 1862 he made quite a name for himself with this Doré folio of Perrault's ***Contes de Fees***. What was amazing about this work was not so much that it was another critical and commercial success, but that these engravings could possibly have been done by the same illustrator who had just done ***Dante's Inferno***. After the hefty 100 *fr* price tag on the ***Inferno***, ***Perrault*** looked like a bargain at 60 *fr*. But ***Inferno*** had 76 engraving, compared to only 42 for ***Perrault***, and much less text. But they were about the same binding size. Once again, papers were full of praise for the new work. Saint Beuve, in ***Nouveaux Lundis***, described it as "a gift-book fit for a king." He noted that the illustrations had a German air about them, influenced by the scenery of Doré's childhood, and from Grimm's ***Fairy Tales***, themselves derived from Perrault. One minor criticism was of Doré's illustrations of the faces of women. Doré seemed to have trouble drawing beautiful women; his women tended to have thin, plain faces, lacking in personality. Later on we will look at some theories about what might have caused that.

Once again, this proved to be an extremely popular set of illustrations, with about 100 reprint editions worldwide. Hetzel published folio editions almost every year. In recent years there has been another flurry of French editions, but much smaller, about 5x7. There were also editions in English, Spanish, German, Italian, Russian, Danish, Swedish, Dutch, and Hebrew. In this work, Doré illustrated nine of Perrault's tales. Most French and other European editions printed all 42 engravings. But English editions chopped it up shamelessly. No English edition has ever printed all 42 illustrations. Some editions delete the more obscure tales; others delete some of the illustrations for some of the tales. Here is the full list:

frontispiece & title-page vignette	(2)
Hop-o'-my-Thumb (or *Tom Thumb*)	(11)
Sleeping Beauty (*...in the Wood*)	(6)
The Donkey-Skin	(6)
Puss-in-Boots	(4)
Blue-Beard	(4)
Little Red Riding Hood	(3)
Cinderella (or *The Glass Slipper*)	(3)
The Fairy	(2)
Ricky of the Tuft	(1)

 reduced illustrations from ***Baron Munchausen*** (1862) - contains 158 Doré illos.

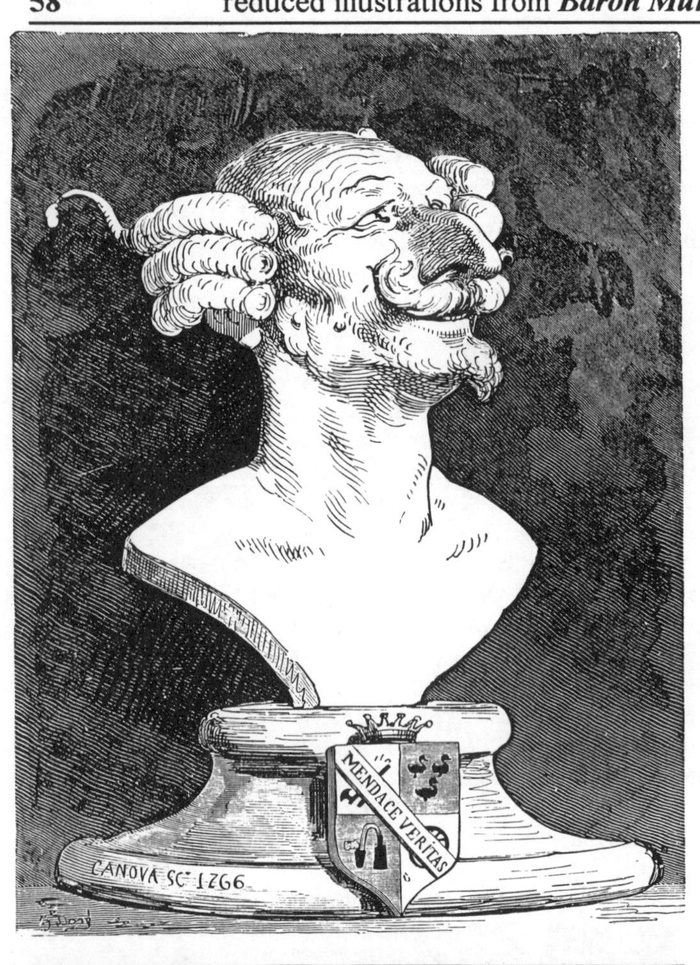

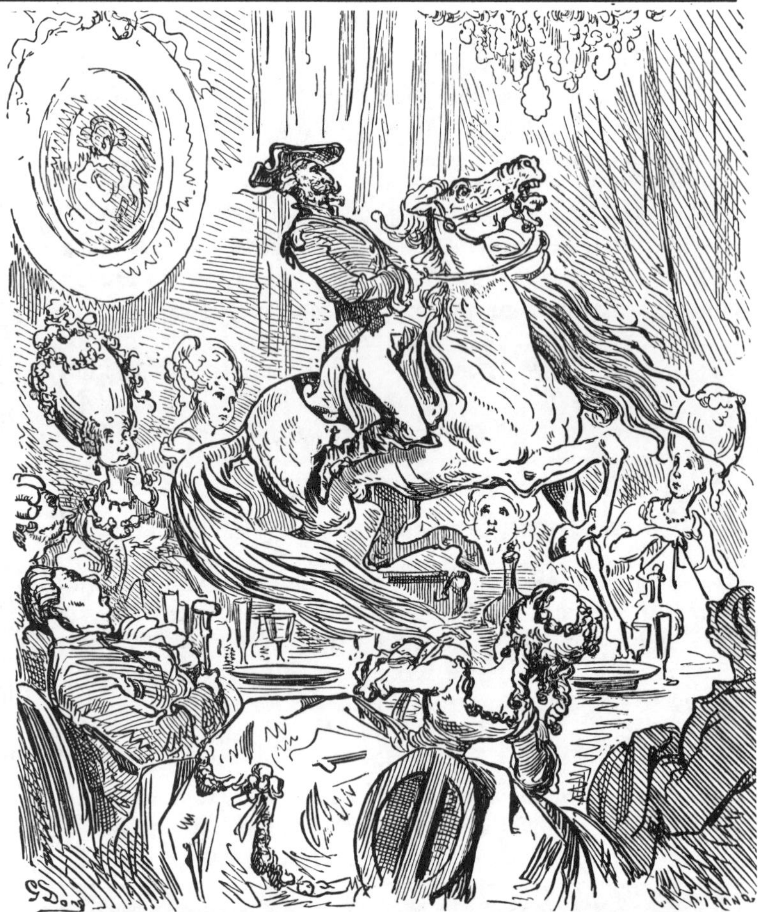

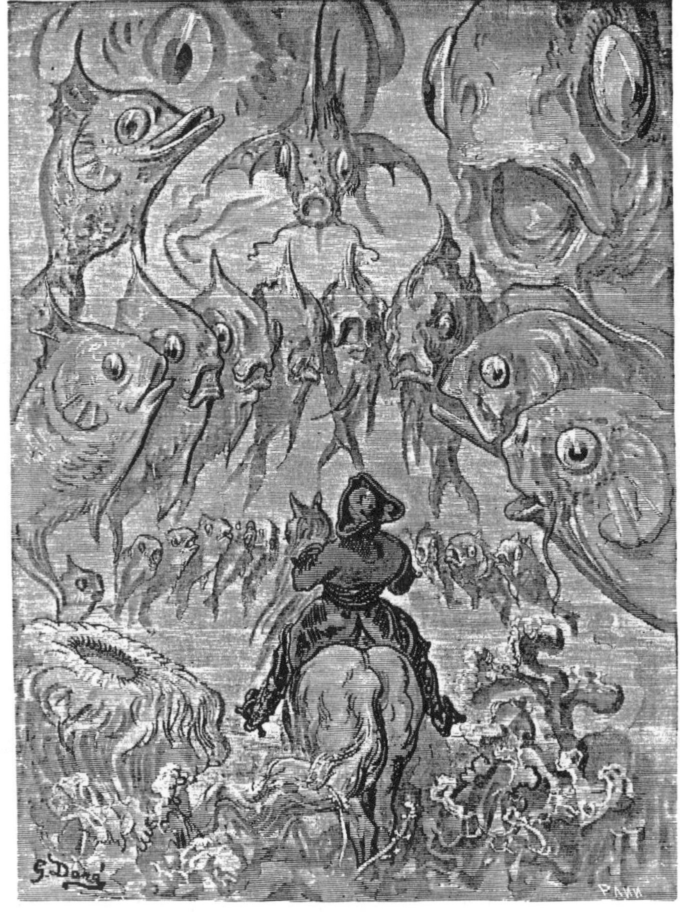

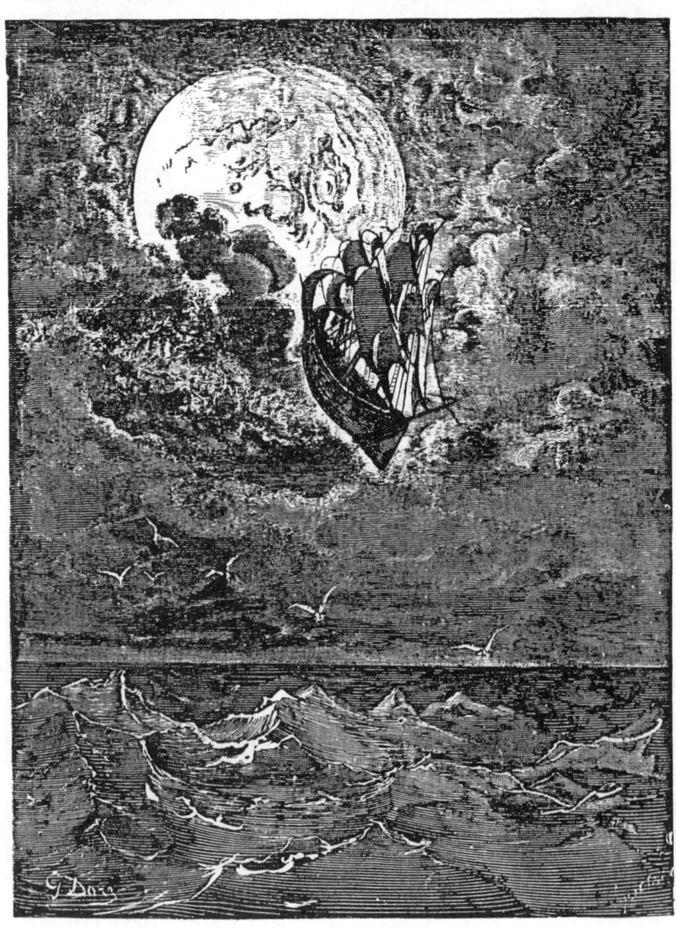

The first English edition of Doré's ***Perrault*** is confusing. Tom Hood (the younger) translated it in verse, and there is no mention of Perrault. It is entitled ***The Fairy Realm***, by Tom Hood. It only included 24 of the 42 illustrations, and only five of the nine tales. There is also confusion about the date and publisher. The first edition included a November 1865 Hood introduction, but there is no title-page or copyright date. It was published in December of 1865, and reference sources are divided as to whether that is officially an 1865 edition or an 1866 edition, because if there had been a date on the title-page, it would have been 1866. This is so frustrating. It was common practice to publish books at Christmas-time, but date them the following year. Bibliographers are often confronted with double-listings. The publisher of the first edition was Ward, Lock of London. They published one edition and then sold the rights to Cassell, who published an 1867 edition, also undated, still containing that dated introduction. Many people swear that the Cassell edition was 1865, which only goes to prove that you should not swear. Both editions are 10½x13. Many French Doré folios became English quartos. Then when Cassell went to reprint the title in 1872, they repackaged it (again). They changed the book title from ***The Fairy Realm*** to ***Fairy Tales Told Again***, and instead of listing Tom Hood they stated, "by the author of ***Little Red Shoes***."

Each English-language publisher felt the need to have a different-sounding book of fairy tales, and so you can find the Doré illustrations in ***Popular Fairy Tales, Standard Fairy Tales, Old-Fashioned Fairy Tales, Grimm's Fairy Tales, Mother Goose Fairy Tales, The Big Book of Fairy Tales, French Fairy Tales,*** and even ***Perrault's Fairy Tales***. Then in 1945, Louis Untermeyer did a new translation of Perrault, and that Didier edition included Doré illustrations. But there are three different edition titles; the first two were combined into the third. ***French Fairy Tales*** (1945) contains 15 Doré illustrations, ***More French Fairy Tales*** (1946) contains 13 different Doré illustrations, and ***All the French Fairy Tales*** (1946) combined the two.

Also in 1946, there was an exhibition of 12 Doré oil paintings, based on his ***Perrault*** illustrations, at the James Vigeveno Galleries in Los Angeles. In their 8-page catalogue, they list all 12 painting titles, and they show four of them. What was so strange about those paintings is that they had never ever been mentioned in any Doré reference work. Leblanc (1931) claimed to be a comprehensive bibliography of Doré's illustrations and original art, but he only listed 133 oil paintings. Now we know the total to be closer to 400, with most of the others listed in Doré Gallery catalogues or in recent exhibition books or in auction records. But additional Doré paintings do seem to appear out of thin air. These 12 oil paintings, all on the same theme, turned up half-way around the world 80 years later, with no previous mention of their existence. They have now been selling at major auctions for nearly 50 years, at prices in the $5,000-$20,000 range.

That Vigeveno catalogue led to an error in my reference book ***Gustave Doré - Adrift on Dreams of Splendor***. Their catalogue listed one painting as being based on the nursery rhyme ***Peter, Peter, Pumpkin Eater***, and on page 61 of my book I repeated that error. It appears that they were looking at an untitled painting with a large pumpkin, which was actually the Fairy Godmother scene from ***Cinderella***. Remind me to never again go by anything but original source documents.

In 1983, France finally issued a postage stamp to Doré, and they chose the famous double entendre engraving from ***Blue-Beard***. It is amazing that folks in Victorian England did not catch that fairly obvious risque meaning. In the February 14, 1994 issue of ***Time Magazine*** (p.55 & 57), they used two Doré ***Perrault*** illustrations, without giving him credit. Doré's ***Perrault*** illustrations keep turning up in new fairy tale books. The most popular illustration is the one of Little Red Riding Hood in bed with the wolf, which somehow came to represent the relationship between men and women. It was even used in a book by Carl Jung, to express hidden meanings.

L'Album de Gustave Doré

This was Doré's final lithographic album, very different from the earlier ones. These were not humorous cartoons. These were art lithographs, some based on Doré paintings. The 12 lithographs are about 8x10. Doré engraved all of them himself, and all are very high quality. The folio was published by Goupil of Paris. The lithographs were also available in a color version. It is now almost impossible to find them in book format, the lithographs having long ago been separated and sold individually. You would be lucky to find even one individual print. There were no reprint editions.

Doré's great popularity in 1862 by made it possible for his artistic ego to be stroked by such a *livre d'artiste*. The publisher Hetzel complained that plate #6 (*L'Ogre*) was very similar to one of his *Perrault* engravings. The (*Andromede*) plate was a different view of, his famous 1868 painting, which sold in 1989 for over half a million dollars. Doré returned many times to the theme of a beautiful naked woman chained to the rocks, about to be devoured by a monster, with a knight swooping in to same her. This album is unique among Doré's books. Of the 12 lithographs, Forberg reprinted two of them and Renonciat reprinted two others.

The Adventures of Baron Munchausen

Doré again displayed his versatility, going from horror to fairy tales to fine-art lithographs to comic adventure. This marked his third new 1862 publisher - J.Hetzel, Goupil, and now Charles Furne. The ***Munchausen*** quarto was a bargain 20 *fr*, with 32 full-page plates and 126 vignettes. There have been about 100 editions of these lighthearted illustrations in French, English, Dutch, German, Italian, Danish, Spanish, Portuguese, Swedish, Norwegian, Russian, Hebrew, Yiddish, Ukrainian, Latvian, Polish, and Bulgarian. English editions usually list Rudolph Eric Raspe as the author, but German editions list Gottfried Auguste Burger as the author, while most French editions list only Theophile Gautier as translator, and many other countries list no author at all.

The early French editions are about 9x12 and undated, but the first edition can be determined by the publisher name Charles Furne by itself, while the reprint editions list the

(top row) reduced illustrations from L'Epine's ***Captain Castagnette*** (1862) - contains 42 Doré illos.
(bottom row) reduced illustrations from L'Epine's ***Legend of Croquemitaine*** (1863) - contains 177 Doré illos.

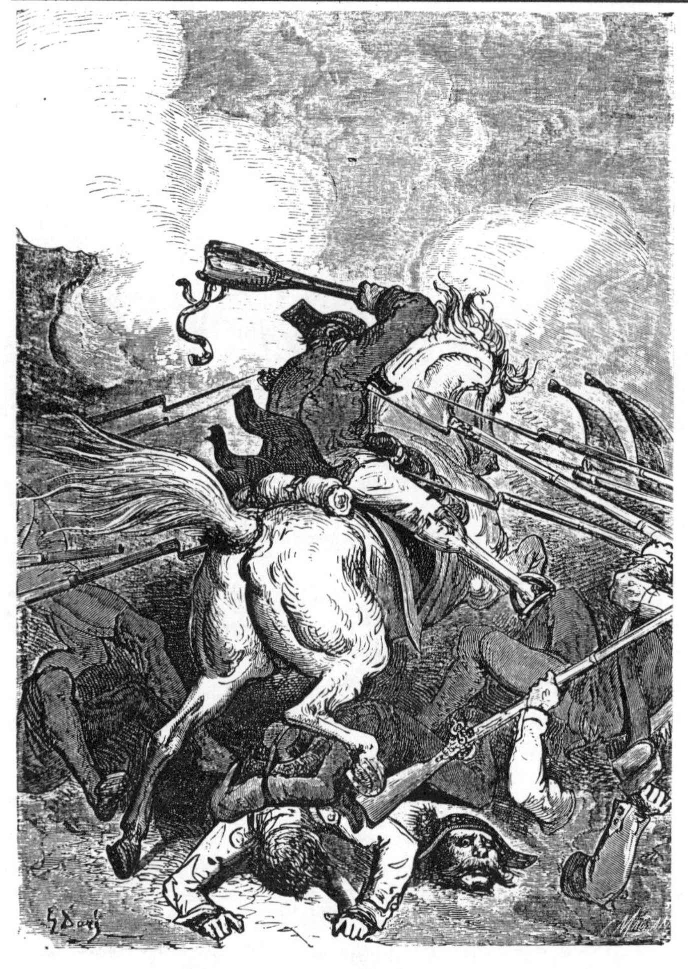

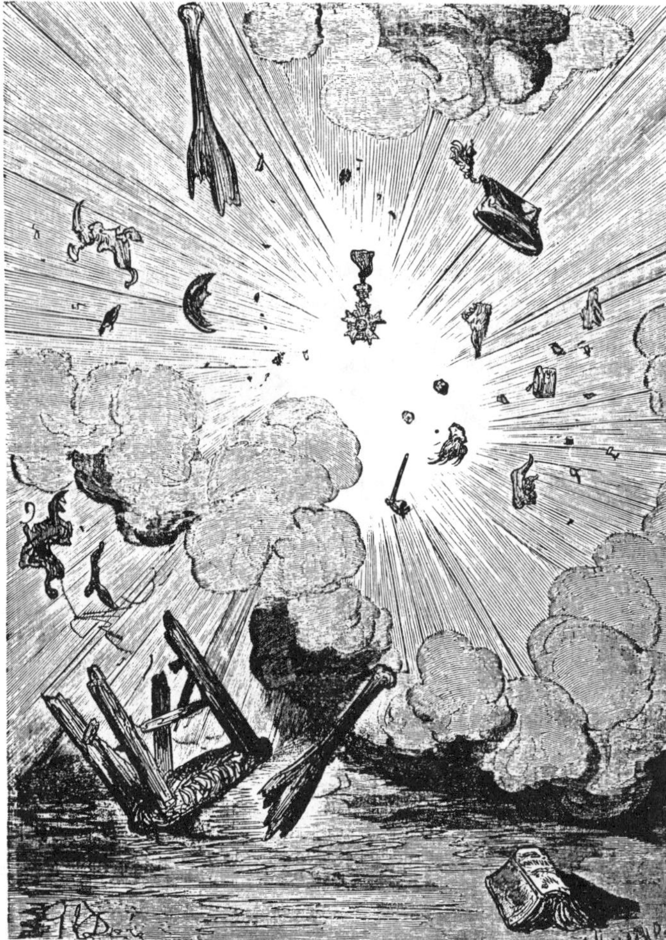

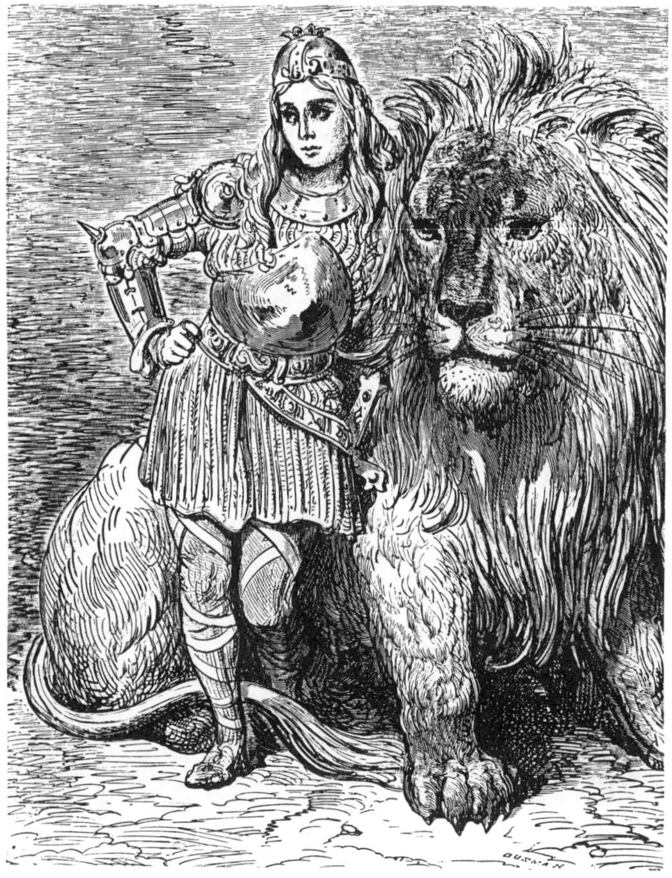

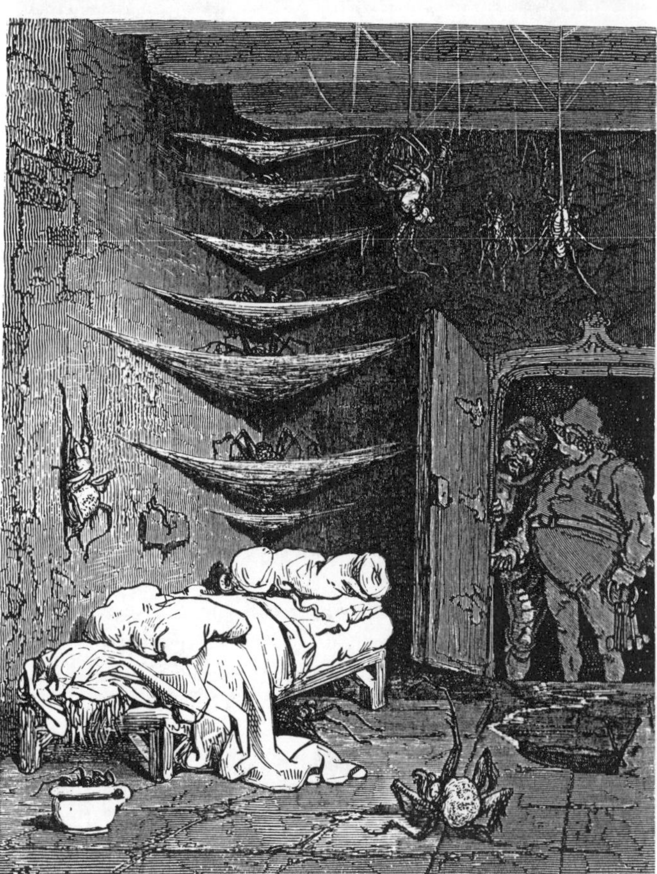

publisher as Furne/Jouvet. It may be the only Doré title that was enlarged by the English publisher, the undated December 1865 Cassell being 10x13. Later Cassell editions are likewise undated, but were reduced to 8½x10½. In the next chapter we will examine how to identify the hundreds of undated Cassell editions. This was the only Doré title for which Cassell did not have U.S. pirate competitors. For the Doré ***Munchausen***, the real bibliographic nightmare comes in the 1930s, with the dreaded "3 Sirens" series, 10-15 undated editions of basically the same book. The only other real surge of the Doré ***Munchausen*** was a dozen German editions between the wars.

Ernest L'Epine: Captain Castagnette
Ernest L'Epine: Legend of Croquemitaine

This French author is virtually unknown, except for the Doré illustrations of his works. The author may be listed as L'Epine or one of his pseudonyms "Manuel" or "Quatrelles." ***Castagnette*** is the story of "the man with the wooden head," a French military hero fighting in the Napoleonic Wars. He keeps getting parts of his body blown away in combat. He is so courageous that after getting both legs blown off by a cannonball, he proceeds to use his leg stump as a club in ensuing battles. The loss of both arms barely slows him down. The filling of his head with sawdust does not seem to diminish his military effectiveness. Finally he is completely blown to bits, only his medal remaining. This black comedy is a cross between his ***Rabelais*** and his ***Russia***.

Croquemitaine is the story of a warrior woman, Mitaine, who is Charlemagne's godchild. Roland is also in the story. The title means "he who would croque (kill) Mitaine." It is about the bogey-man, or our imagined perils. Mitaine, who has a pet lion named Oghris, has to single-handedly take on "The Fortress of Fear." One of my favorite Doré engravings is the scene where a brave knight has come to an inn that is full, and demands any available hole in the wall. The innkeeper opens the door to a little room full of montrous spiders. This book is also quite a rollicking parody. There have been about a dozen Doré illustrated editions of each of these titles.

Doré returned to Hachette for these books. ***Castagnette*** is a thin 9x12 edition with eight plates and 34 vignettes. It sold in 1862 for only 6 *fr*, and was serialized in ***Journal pour Tous*** a year later. It is one of the few Doré books published in French in America - in 1964 for the National Textbook Co. of Chicago. The first English edition was 1866. ***Croquemitaine*** is a larger 10x13, with 20 plates and 157 vignettes, selling in 1863 for 15 *fr*. This title was more popular in English than in French. The translator Tom Hood's name was listed much larger than L'Epine on Cassell's title-page. The 1872 reprint edition was reduced to 8½x11, and the title changed to ***Days of Chivalry***. In 1953, Rodale Press published just the third section under the title ***Fortress of Fear***, with 45 illustrations.

Vicomte de Chateaubriand: Atala

Francois Auguste Rene, Vicomte de Chateaubriand, was born into French nobility in 1768, of a lineage that had fought with William the Conqueror at the Battle of Hastings and with Louis IX in the Crusades. But the privileges attached to such a lineage ended just as Francois reached adulthood, and in 1791 he fled to America. In the next decade he learned the meaning of poverty and humiliation. His source of solace wavered between philosophy and religion, until the death of his mother and sister in 1798. As he put it, "I wept and I believed." He is famous for three books, ***Atala***, ***Rene***, and ***The Genius of Christianity***. ***Atala***, published in 1801, is in many ways the origin of "the noble savage," decades before Cooper. For a century it was considered a great romaticist classic, but in this century it is virtually forgotten. It is set in 1720 in Louisiana. It is primarily a love story amidst the background of Indian warfare and early missionary endeavors in America.

Doré did 30 plates and 14 large vignettes for this 1863 Hachette folio. In my opinion, these (and ***Tennyson***) are his best scenic engravings, here featuring lush tropical vegitation in the virgin forest. In fact, at some points in the story nature overwhelms the plot. It contains some of his best white-on-black effects. These truly are b&w paintings. Prior to this no one thought such things could be done with wood engravings. It is a fairly short novel, and it also suffers from bizarre plot twists, especially the death of the Indian maiden Atala.

The 1863 folio sold for 50 *fr*. Amazingly enough, there are no French reprints, not even cheaper editions. How can there be 15 English editions and only one French edition of such a great French classic? In 1864, Frederick Leypoldt of Philadelphia published 12 of the plates in his ***Atala Album*** portfolio. The first official English edition was Cassell's 1867 folio. Leypoldt preceded Cassell on several Doré works. Here are the rare Leypoldt U.S. Doré first editions:

1863	*Sleeping Beauty in the Wood*	(6)
	The Dante Album	(10)
1864	*The Atala Album*	(12)
	The Wandering Jew	(13)
1865	*The Dante Album* (reissue)	(76)

Cassell published four editions of *Atala*, one of their slowest selling Doré titles. In the 1880s, there was a flurry of U.S. pirate editions by Fine Art Pub. Co., Belford & Clarke, and the Catholic publisher P.J.Kenedy. Then it just died out. There were Italian, Swedish, Spanish & Portuguese editions.

Miguel de Cervantes: Don Quixote

Doré again combined business and pleasure on a lengthy trip through Spain in 1862 with his friend, Baron Charles Davillier. But this time Doré doubled his pleasure and his business by beginning two great works, a travel folio of ***Spain***, and ***Don Quixote***. The travel book had text by Davillier, and was serialized in ***Tour du Monde*** from 1862-1873 before it was published in book form in 1874. But more about that later. Here is how Davillier related to Jerrold the origin of their travels, per Jerrold (p.124-125):

> For a long time past my old friend Doré had talked to me of his desire to see Spain. At first it was only a vague project, cast out between two puffs of a cigarette. But it soon became a fixed idea, one of

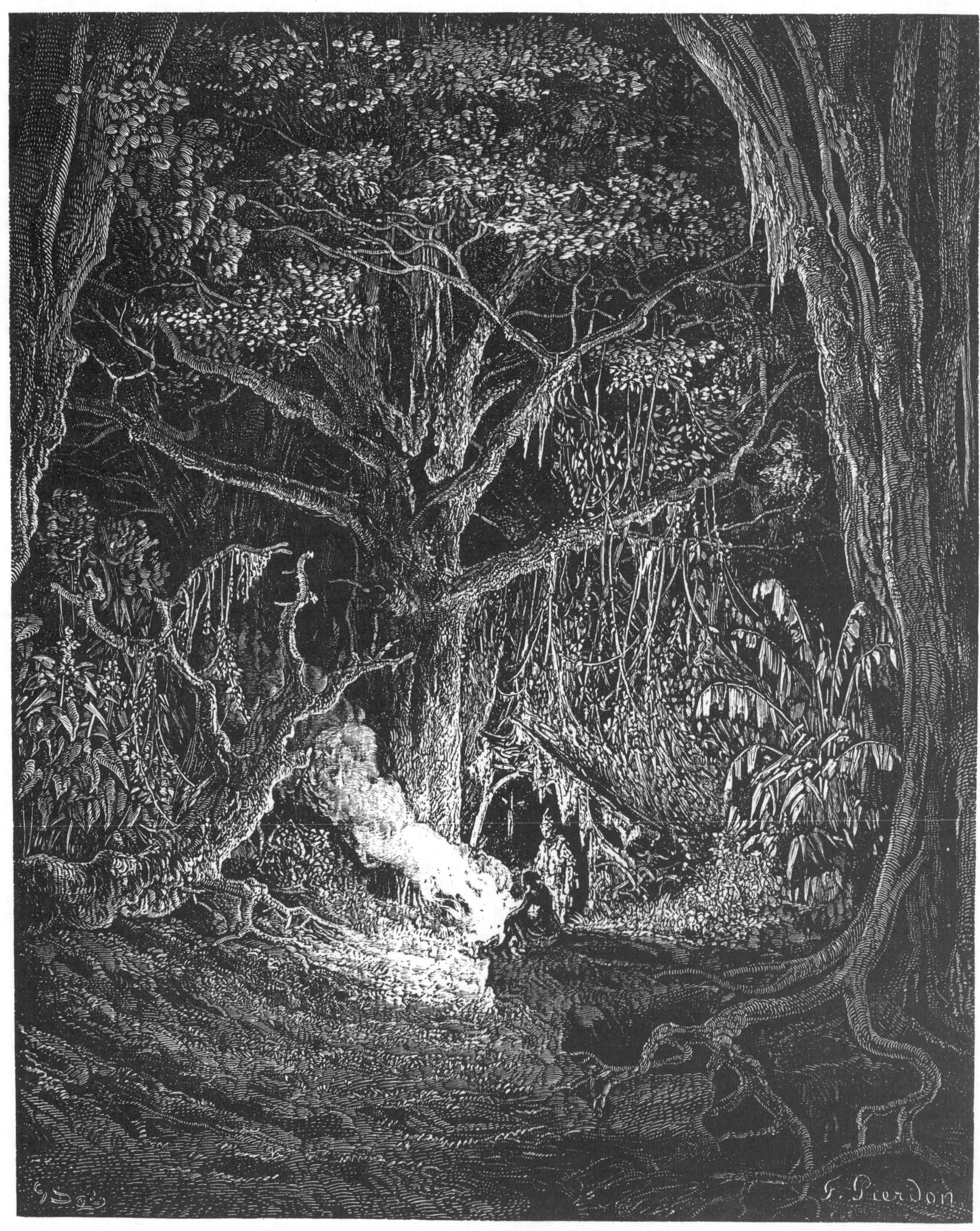
F. Pierdon

> those dreams which will not leave the mind at rest. I never saw him that he did not ask me point blank -
>
> "When do we start for Spain?"
>
> "But, my dear friend," I answered, "you forget that I have wandered over the classic land of the castagnette and the bolero at least twenty times."
>
> "The better reason," he said. "If you have seen Spain so often, there is no reason why you should stop now."
>
> I could find no argument to rebut such reasoning, and a few days later we took our tickets for Perpignan."

Doré had an unparalleled ability to visit a place and soak in the very essence of the personality of the people and the scenery. His photographic mind saw everything - the sights, the sounds, and the people of Spain. Before the trip, Doré's plans for ***Don Quixote*** were modest, but the trip inspired him to ever greater accomplishments, per Jerrold (p.127/129):

> When he returned from Spain, he arranged with his friend and engraver, Pisan, to make, at his ease and at his own cost, some forty drawings to illustrate the exploits of Cervantes' most whimsical hero. But, as the subject fastened itself upon him, he became impatient to realize all his conceptions; and he burst one morning, in the early summer, into M. Pisan's atelier, to announce that he had made arrangements with a publisher to have his *Don Quixote* out before the end of the year, and in two volumes. Then artist and engraver fell to; and, as M. Pisan has remarked to me, they were both worked to death. But is was always so. Yet with all his haste, Doré never became careless. At the last moment he would have a drawing engraved two or three times. It must be, to his eye, as good as he could make it. He respected the public, and he respected himself.
>
> ... His romantic dreaming mingled with that of Cervantes. He apprehended the very heart and soul of the romanticist's conceptions, and, by the help of his store of types, his life-long analytical studies of the human countenance, and the play of human foibles and passions, could embody them. The fantastic, the quaint, the heroic, the romantic, the purely humorous and the picturesque, are assembled, in an extraordinary degree. From the highly fanciful picture of Don Quixote in his study, to a tail-piece describing a corner of a Spanish farmyard, with a few children and chickens in the foreground, Doré's illustrations not only embellish, but interpret, and give fresh meanings to the text.

Don Quixote was in many ways Doré's greatest work. There was no time in his life when he was happier and better suited to the task. Doré and the Don were both dreamers. Doré ended up doing 120 full-page plates and 257 vignettes, in a massive 2V folio for Hachette, priced at 160 *fr*. Just a couple years earlier, that same man was telling Doré people would not pay 100 *fr* for a book. One other factor that increased the quality of this work was that all 377 illustrations were engraved by Pisan, whom many believe to be Doré's best engraver. It was the only major Doré title engraved by one man. It is hard to believe that Doré and Pisan completed all 377 engravings in just a few months. Like most Doré folios, the plates are just under 8x10. The vignettes are also rather large, averaging about 5x7½ (oblong). By comparison, the 766 illustrations by Tony Johannot in 1836 were almost all small vignettes, and even his handful of full-page plates are smaller than Doré's vignettes. Johannot's engravings were appetizers compared to Doré's gourmet feast.

There are over 300 editions of ***Don Quixote*** with Doré illustrations. What makes that so remarkable is that while there are very few illustrated versions of ***Dante*** and ***Milton***, everybody illustrated ***Don Quixote***. Prior to Doré, the most famous sets of illustrations were by Coypel in the 1720s, and by Johannot. There are probably 50-80 editions of each of those. Some people like Daniel Vierge's illustrations from the turn of the last century, but there are ten times as many Doré editions as Vierge. Here are some of the other major ***Don Quixote*** illustrators: Wm. Hogarth, Jean-Honore Fragonard, Thomas Stothard, Robt.Smirke, Richard Westall, C.R.Leslie, Horace Vernet, George Cruikshank, John Gilbert, Henri Pille, J.J.Grandville, Celestin Nanteuil, A.B.Houghton, Ad.Lalauze, Gordon Browne, Walter Crane, Edmund J. Sullivan, W.Heath Robinson, Moreno-Carbenero, and Salvador Dali. That list is about 10% of all the ***Don Quixote*** illustrators.

The 160 *fr*. price may have been a little steep. It was not reprinted until 1868, when Hachette issued a parts edition, culminating in an 1869 2V folio edition for only 40 *fr*. Finally in 1882, Hachette issued a much cheaper 7x11 abridged edition with only 168 illustrations, that sold well. But French is only fifth on the list of language editions of Doré's ***Quixote***, behind English, Spanish, Italian, and German. There were also editions in Portuguese, Russian, Dutch, Greek, Polish, Finnish, Hungarian, Bulgarian, Czech, Estonian, Lithuanian, and Japanese. There are very few Oriental Doré editions.

Don Quixote was the first Doré folio to be published in England. In December of 1864, Cassell began a 30-month parts edition. In that 2½ year period, Doré went from being virtually unknown in England to being the most famous illustrator in the world. All that is in the next chapter. Suffice it to say that Cassell issued a steady stream of ***Don Quixote*** in parts editions (British & American; monthly, bi-weekly, & weekly) and book editions. They even did a children's version by Clara Mateaux entitled ***The Story of the Don***. The English version contained only 364 illustrations. They left out a couple chapters they considered too risque. The Cassell edition was actually fairly cheap. They reduced the size down to 10x13, stuffed all the story into one fat volume, and printed it on thin, cheap paper. The inferior paper is the one major drawback to the first English edition. But the price was only $15 (the ***Inferno*** was $25). The cover of the first English edition (publisher's cloth) was an elaborate gilt design from edge to edge. There is one mystery about that first edition.

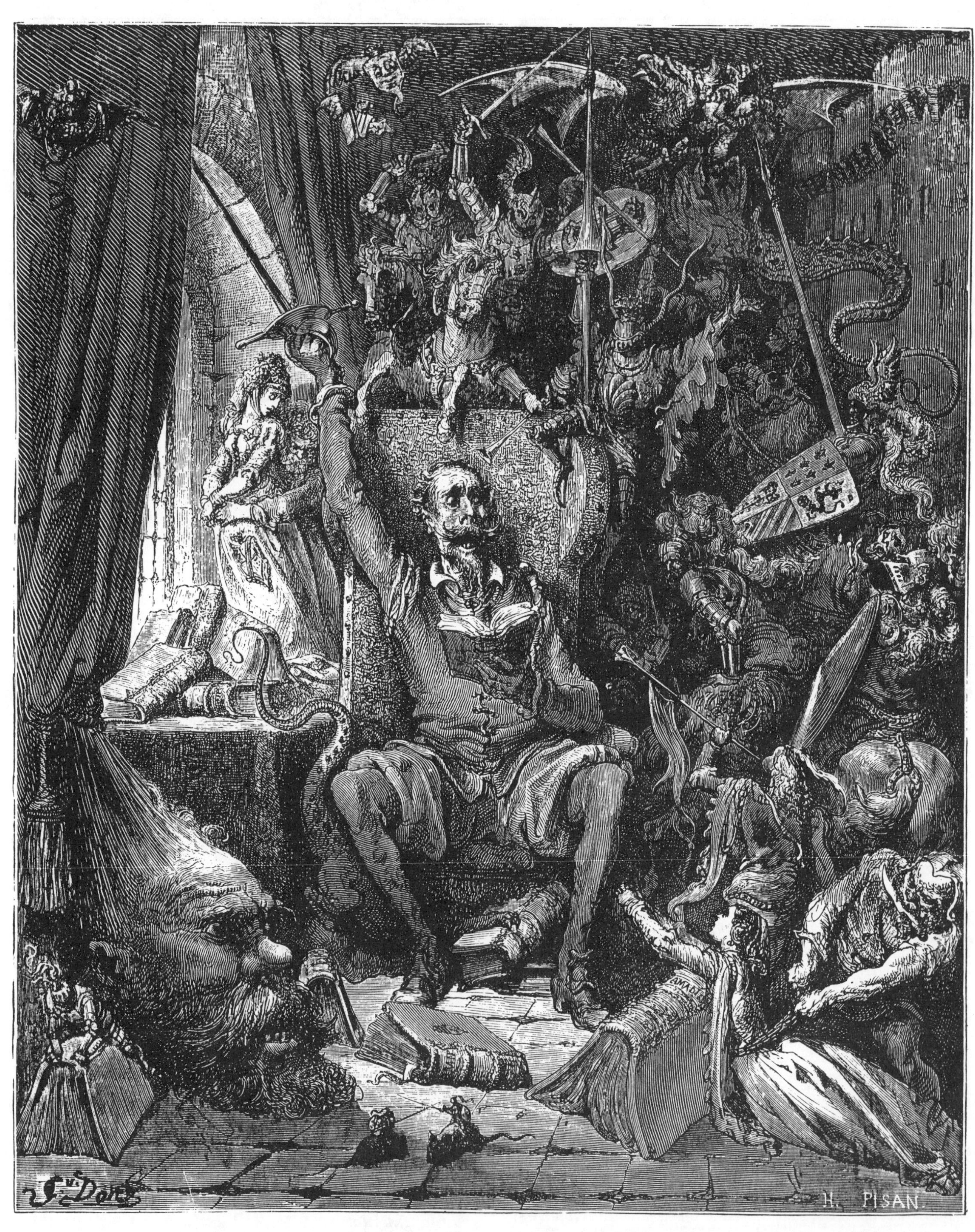

DON QUIXOTE IN HIS STUDY (1863 wood engraving full-size)

There is an extremely rare version of the first English edition that lists both Cassell (London) and Gebbie & Keppel in Philadelphia. But Cassell had opened a New York office right after the Civil War ended, and began listing that New York office on the title pages of their editions in the fall of 1866 (which is when they published the first ***Quixote*** book edition). So the "standard" first edition lists Cassell in London and New York. Why would they publish another edition which adds a second U.S. publisher? Perhaps the Gebbie version was bound from the first parts edition (which was London only since it began in 1864) and that the title page was printed by Gebbie, in place of the normal title page for the parts edition.

Cassell published about 30 editions of the Doré ***Don Quixote***. But many U.S. pirate publishers quickly picked up on the popularity of the Doré illustrations. Altogether, there were over 70 English editions in 25 years. But many of those editions have nothing more than Doré's name and a handful of poorly re-engraved, reduced illustrations. One even got the famous windmill scene backwards, making Don Quixote left-handed. Almost all of the small editions (about 6x8) have only a few Doré illustrations. The larger editions (at least 9x12) are usually major Doré editions. This century has seen few English Doré *Don Quixote* editions.

In the 25 early years that saw 70 English editions, there were only five Spanish editions. But in this century there have been nearly 100 Spanish editions with Doré's illustrations to ***Don Quixote***. The land of Cervantes has taken Doré to heart. The first Spanish edition is more bizarre than that first U.S. edition. The Barcelona publisher Maravilla published volume one only in 1865. In 1875, another Spanish publisher, Riera, reissued volume one, and then published volume two in 1876. So reference books list the first Spanish edition of Doré's ***Don Quixote*** as 1865-1876. So Riera's first volume is considered the second edition, and his second volume is considered the first edition, even though the first volume was published before the second volume. Anyway, it was a major 2V folio edition containing all 377 engravings. Shortly after the turn of the century, a Spanish artist named Salvado Tusell made watercolor renditions of 350 of the Doré illustrations. There were several editions with those color illustrations. since then there has been an unending stream of Spanish Doré editions (including some in Catalan), from the U.S., Spain, England, Mexico, Argentina, and Puerto Rico.

Several Spanish editions deserve special attention. The 1879 ***Iconografia de Don Quijote*** is a fabulous reference work, containing a sampling of 101 engravings from all major sets of ***Don Quixote*** illustrations over the previous 257 years, including three by Doré. There are many ***Don Quixote*** bibliographies, but the 1946 ***Interpretacion Pictorica del Quijote por Doré***, by Miguel de Romera-Navarro focuses on illustrated editions and why the Doré illustrations are the premiere visual expression of Cervantes' masterpiece. Among the treasures at the Biblioteca Cervantina in Barcelona are three 22x30 silver relief plates of Doré scenes. Those are shown in their 1935 ***Catalogo Bibliografico de la Biblioteca Cervantina***. The title-page of a 1940s edition from Argentina boasts 406 Doré illustrations. They simply reused parts of 29 vignettes. There are many U.S. Spanish editions with Doré illustrations, including a brand new 1994 educational edition by the National Textbook Co.

Among the more interesting Portuguese editions is the one by the great Brazilian children's writer Monteiro Lobato, called ***Don Quixote das Crianca*** (retold for young people), published in the 1930s in Sao Paulo, with several reprint editions. It was also very popular in Italy and Germany, and there was a 2V folio published in German in 1868-69 in New York by J.W.Schmidt. The first country to reprint the 1863 French edition was Greece in 1864. There was also a U.S. Greek edition in the 1920s, published by the National Herald of New York. The 1948 Lithuanian edition was actually published in Germany. The 1915 Japanese edition was so popular that there were three editions within 18 days. There is even a U.S. children's ***Don Quixote*** LP from the 1960s (?) by United Artists in a series called *Tale Spinners*, the cover of which is a painting copied from Doré's windmill engraving. A 1977 program for ***Man of la Mancha*** contains this quote, "In particular, Gustave Doré, some of whose drawings are reproduced on other of these pages, may be considered the Don's definitive illustrator."

Sinbad - from Arabian Nights

It is a shame that Doré did not do more ***Arabian Nights*** illustrations. He did do 20 engravings for ***Sinbad the Sailor*** in 1857, but they have the look of his 1860s folio engravings. We list them here because the book edition came out in 1865. They were originally a ***Sindbad le Marin*** serial in Hachette's ***Semaine des Enfants*** in 1857. There are 10 (nearly) full-page plates and 10 vignettes. One of the plates is an oblong double-page spread. In 1862, Hachette reused the engravings in their other magazine, ***Journal pour Tous***. Finally in 1865 they issued a book edition of ***Les Mille et un Nuits*** (1001 Nights), with 171 illustrations by many artists, including Doré's 20 ***Sinbad*** illustrations. It was a 2V large 8vo, priced at 16 *fr*. In 1868, it was serialized a third time in ***Magasin Illustre***. There were a handful of French reprint book editions.

In 1874, Cassell published a new English edition of ***Arabian Nights Entertainment***, edited by James Mason, with about 350 French illustrations, most of which are not that significant. But it does contain almost all the Doré engravings for ***Sinbad***. Some of his largest illustrations were too big for the 8x10½ edition. It was also issued in parts. The U.S. book edition sold for a modest $4. What is surprising about that book is that Cassell did not mention Doré, either in the book or in their catalogues, even though the book features a Doré frontispiece. In fact, they even removed his name from most of his engravings. All this was at the time when the first page of Cassell catalogues listed nothing but Doré. Two of Doré's engravings which were not in that book edition were inserted into an 1889 edition of ***The Doré Gallery***, where they do list ***Arabian Nights*** as one of Cassell's Doré titles featured amongst the 250 full-page plates. Doré's engravings were also used in Mary Braddon's ***Tales from Arabian Nights***.

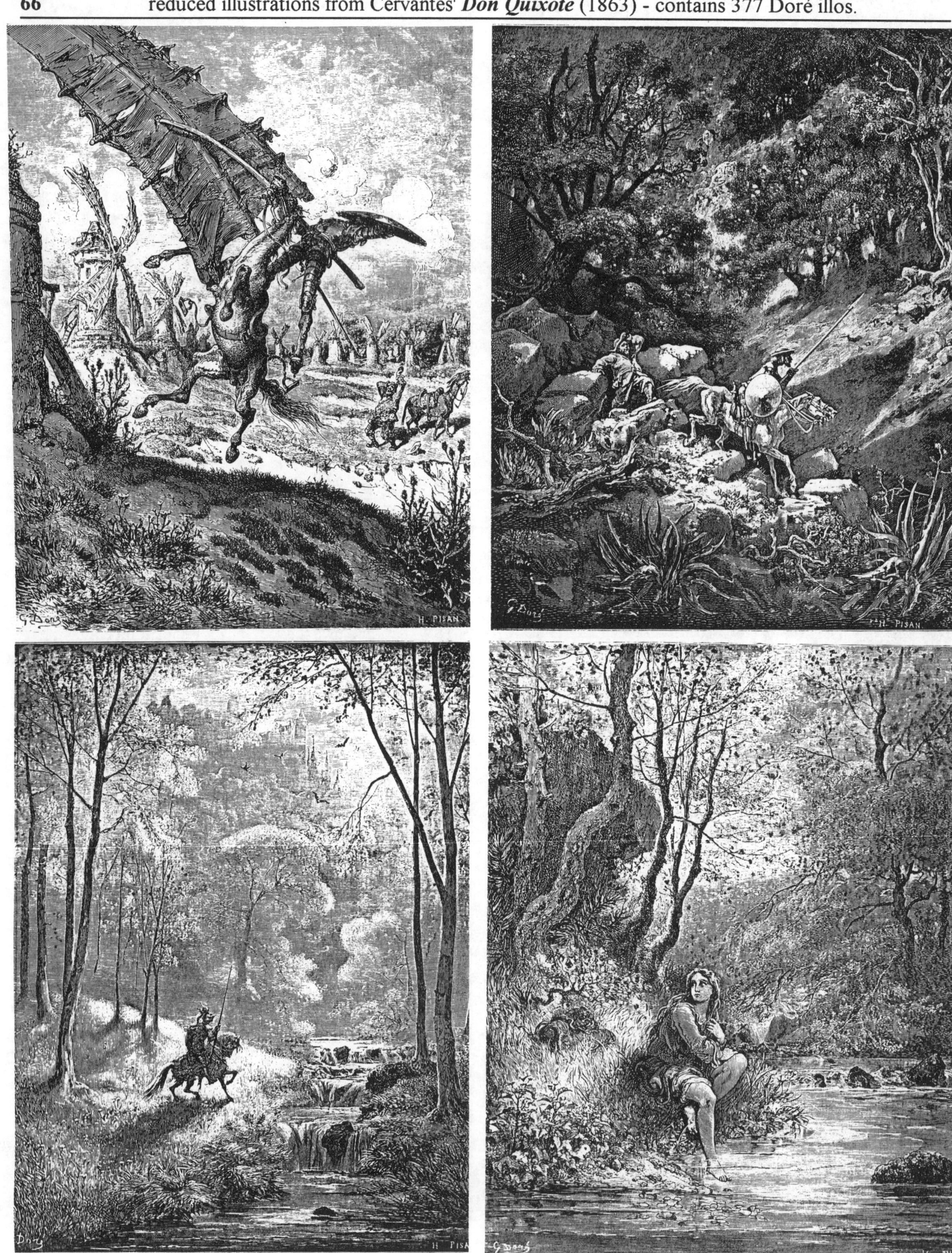

After 1863, there was a lull in Doré titles as he geared up for his next big production. Just as in the late 1850s, Doré was privately working on ***Dante***, so now he was working on ***The Bible***. The big difference was that by 1863 he no longer needed to do large quantities of vignettes for smaller works, just because publishers offered them. He was now steering his own ship. The period 1864-1865 saw only 25 new Doré book engravings, as compared to 604 in 1863. But this was a very happy time for Doré, perhaps the happiest period of his life. For many years he gave up his obsession with painting. He appeared content with being France's greatest illustrator, and concentrated on each upcoming project with new vigor.

This was also a good period for him socially. He had regularly scheduled soirees almost every evening of the week, at his own home (Sunday), or at the homes of composers like Rossini (Saturday) or Richard Wagner (Wednesday), or at the homes of famous writers like Theophile Gautier (Thursday) or Alexandre Dumas (almost anytime) or others. Rossini had a very good effect on Doré. He was like a father to him. In many ways Rossini was the king of Paris in those days. Most of his composing (and wild living) had been finished decades earlier, and he was determined to enjoy the twilight of his life. The festive musical evenings at his home were legendary. Anyone might be called on at a moment's notice to sing or play music. One night a wild-looking man in priestly garb appeared out of nowhere, and proceeded to play Rossini's music on the piano with a fervor that shook the house. When he finished he asked Rossini, "Is that how you meant it to sound?" Rossini replied, "My God, the man has a demon!" It was Franz Liszt. Doré was perhaps the only person who was part of the inner circles of both Rossini and Richard Wagner. Doré often sang or played the violin at Rossini's, and Rossini often spoke in glowing terms of Doré's musical talents. One of Doré's most prized possessions was a photo of Rossini, dated August 29, 1863, and inscribed,

> Souvenir of tender friendship offered to Gustave Doré, who joins to his genius as a painter and draughtsman the talents of a distinguished violinist and a charming *tenorino*, if you please.
> G.Rossini.

When Rossini died on November 13, 1868, Doré made two death-bed sketches that were then made into paintings and engravings. Those works of art received high praise from all around, especially from the Italian delegation to Rossini's funeral, per North-Peat (p.312):

> Several members of the deputation from Pesaro called on M. Doré to view this interesting souvenir of their great compatriot. So affected were they by this splendid sketch, and the marvel-lous fidelity with which the *maestro's* features had been delineated, that they were melted to tears.

Today, one of those paintings hangs in a place of honor in Pesaro's Rossini Conservatorio. Doré's painting is featured on a postcard sold there. We will have much more on Rossini in the chapter on Doré's romances, since many of Doré's amours were famous singers who were also close to Rossini.

The parties at the Doré home were quite an event in their own right, presided over by Madame Doré, whom it was said dressed like an accomplished gypsy. The interaction between Doré and his mother was a sight to be seen. At times, Doré would get out of hand in his wild expressiveness, and his mother would rein him in or scold him like a schoolboy, which seemed to actually make him behave. They had an ongoing squabble about his insistance upon drinking only expensive champagne. She was always trying to get cheaper wine introduced as the standard, but a few minutes into the evening, he would begin talking in the tone of a sad little boy, and he would say to her in the midst of everyone, "And the champagne, mother dear; is it not time that we had it? Pray let it come on at once. We are all dying to drink to your health." She would just shrug her shoulders and give in. As his mother got older, his brother Ernest's daughter Madeline would assist in the hostessing chores. At these parties Doré would often enter walking on his hands or doing handsprings. He was indeed an amazing acrobat and gymnast. One time he was walking with some friends near a cathedral. On an impulse, Doré climbed over the fence, climbed up the wall and the steeple, and did a handstand on top of the spire. A crowd had gathered, and they became terrified. When he descended, the police had arrived, and they gave him a stern warning not to do that again. To Doré almost everything was a game, or at least that was the case until the Franco-Prussian War crushed his homeland, and then so many of his older friends died. There was no comparison between the Doré of the 1860s and the Doré of the 1870s. He went from a boy to an old man in one decade.

But at the parties of the 1860s, the entertaining became more and more elaborate - impromptu plays, concerts, and games. Doré loved to plan surprises for the guests, and then howl with delight at their discovery. One evening the carafes were actually Swiss music boxes, and as soon as they would lift their flask to drink, the music would begin to play. One time Doré served a giant *pate de foie gras*, going on and on about what a rare delicacy it was. He then asked a guest to do the honors, and when it was cut open a bird flew out, followed by a guineau-pig. One evening the guest was the postmaster-general, and every detail of the food and dining room was some part of the interior of a post office. He often poked fun at his guests, but always in a pleasant, light-hearted way. Such festivities became the stuff of faded memories, as the years went by. Roosevelt compared it to the scene after Doré's death, when the old nurse Francoise was the only one there, and she had this to say to Roosevelt (p.272):

> I do my best to keep things clean, but it is too much for my aged eyes. Then, too, there is no reason why I should, for they are all gone; only I am left; and some day some one else will be here in my place. C'est clair; c'est bien clair.

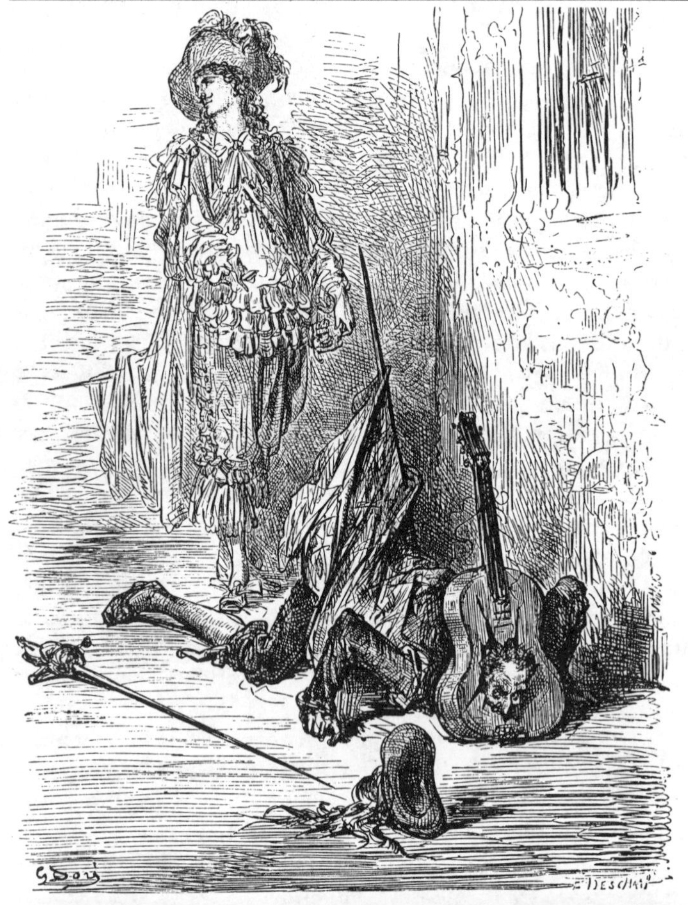

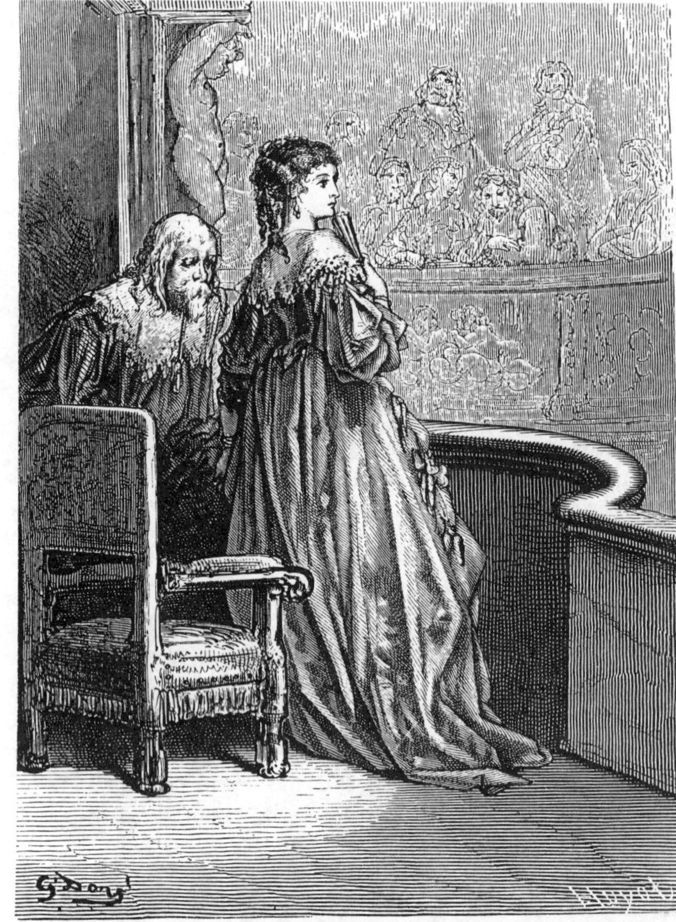

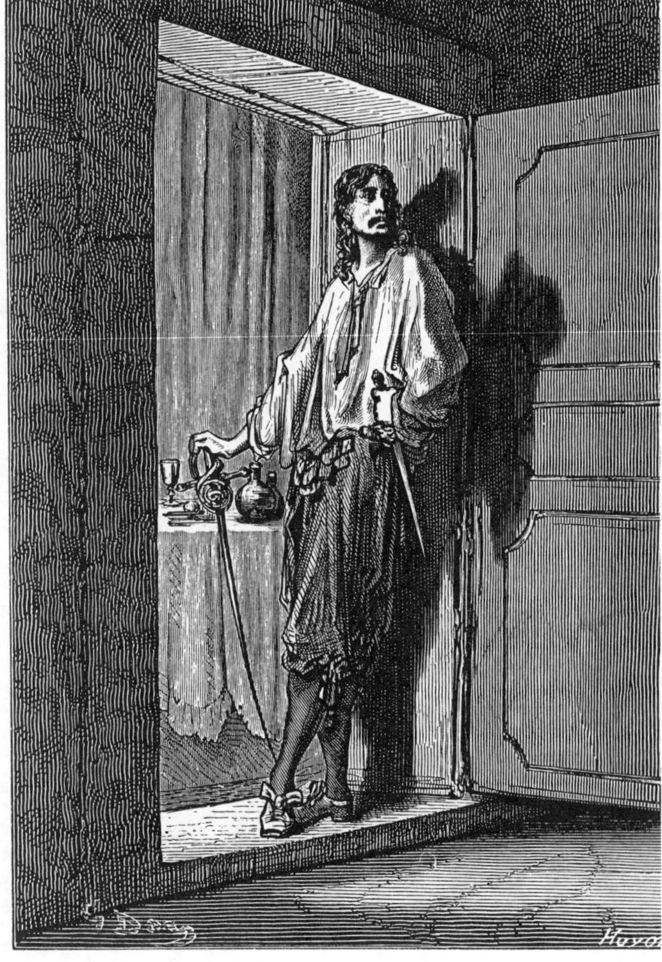

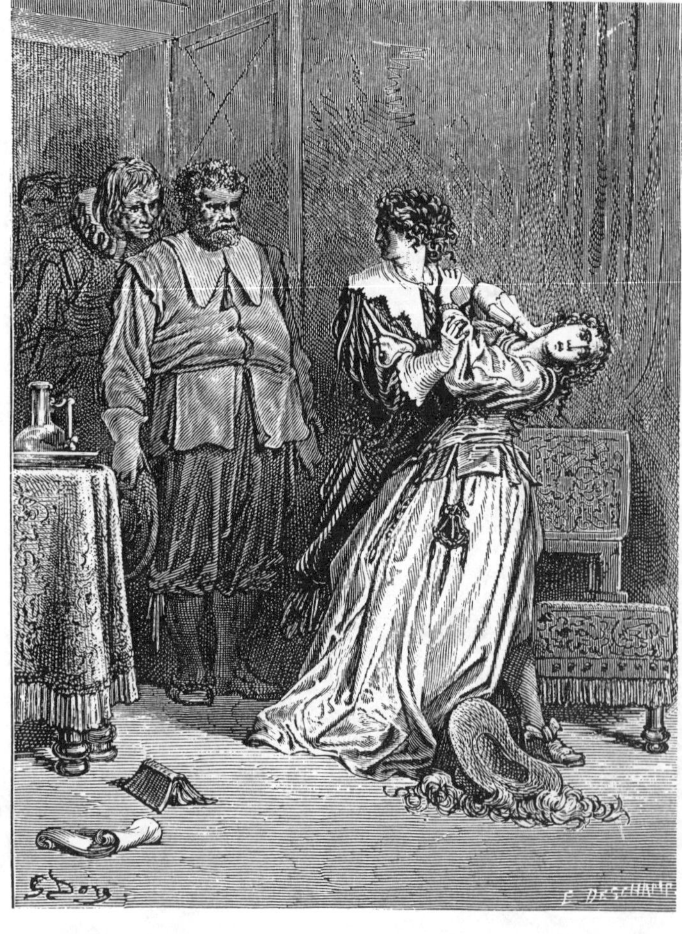

6. LO, I TURN TO THE BRITISH (1866-68:CASSELL)

The mid-1860s were probably the happiest time for Doré. He seemed content with his illustration success and mellowed in his obsession with painting. An example of that was related by Paul Dalloz about an Italian vacation. In Venice, Doré put up a cold front about going with the others in the group to visit the Fine Arts Academy, per Roosevelt (p.235):

> Ah, bah! paintings; Italian masters; some of them are not bad, but I can live without them ... I can see paintings anywhere ... I shall stop at home, I don't feel equal to visiting galleries ... Go without me; I shall stop at home and write letters. I have a headache, too. Pray go without me.

So they did. But as they gazed at all the Italian masters, Dalloz caught sight of a man in a little side room, totally absorbed by a beautiful Bordone - *Marriage of the Doge with the Adriatic*. The man analyzed it from every angle in rapt concentration. Dalloz soon realized that it was Doré. Instead of going up to him, they hid and watched him. Eventually Doré got up and snuck out the side door. That evening they had great sport with Doré as they spoke of visiting the academy. Dalloz began to describe in great detail the very painting Doré had examined. Finally, Doré could not take it any more, exclaiming:

> Wretch! You saw me. Never mind; *c'est rudement bien fait!* Heavens! what would I have not given to have been the author of such a picture? If I had only painted it! *c'est rudement bien fait.*

It was very rare for Doré to ever admit any inadequacy as a painter. By the way, his mother was not on that trip. Doré settled into a state of contentment, maximizing his b&w talent. Roosevelt claims (p.237), and others have backed her up, that from 1850-1870, Doré earned 7,000,000 *fr*. He may have been "only" an illustrator, but was there a painter in the world who during that time earned a similar sum? Another close friend, Mr. Bordelin, told Roosevelt the following story (p.238-239):

> I have seen Gustave earn 10,000 *fr* in a single morning. He would have 15-20 blocks before him, and would pass from one to another with a rapidity and sureness of touch that were amazing. He rarely finished any drawing at a single sitting, but kept up a continual hither and thither, backwards and forwards, between them. One morning he made no fewer than 21 splendid designs, finishing the last on the stroke of twelve. He then thrust his pencils from him with a laugh, threw back his head with that peculiar gesture which always sent his hair waving with it, and said to me gaily, "Not a bad morning's work, my friend. Here are enough bank-notes to keep a whole family for a year. Do you think I have earned the right to a good breakfast?"

But his life was about to change dramatically, for better or for worse. From 1856-60, there were only four English Doré editions with about 40 engravings. From 1861-64, there were <u>none</u>. But from 1865-68, England saw 20 major Doré folios and quartos with over 2000 new Doré engravings. By 1868, Doré was literally the most famous artist in the world. From 1865 on, half of Doré's new titles were published in England. A famous quote was, "In every English-speaking home where they can spell the word 'art,' you will find Doré editions." Here is a quick list of English Doré titles from 1865-68:

year	illos	author: *title*	publisher
1865	24	(Tom Hood): ***Fairy Realm***	Ward/Lock
	24	J.G.Edgar: ***Cressy & Poictiers***	Beeton
	42	L'Epine: ***Cptn.Castagnette***	Beeton
	76	Dante's ***Inferno***	Cassell
	158	***Baron Munchausen***	Cassell
1866	50	Milton: ***Paradise Lost***	Cassell
	12	***The Wandering Jew***	Cassell
	177	L'Epine: ***Croquemitaine***	Cassell
	377	Cervantes: ***Don Quixote***	Cassell
	12	***A Dozen Specimens of Doré***	Beeton
	303	Doré: ***200 Sketches***	F.Warne
	9	Tennyson: ***Elaine***	Moxon
1867	2	Hugo: ***Toilers of the Sea***	S.Low
	115	H.Blackburn: ***The Pyrenees***	S.Low
	44	Chateaubriand: ***Atala***	Cassell
	238	***The Bible***	Cassell
	9	Tennyson: ***Vivien***	Moxon
	9	Tennyson: ***Guinevere***	Moxon
1868	20	Doré: ***Historical Cartoons***	J.C.Hotten
	60	Dante: ***Purgatory & Paradise***	Cassell
	329	LaFontaine: ***Fables***	Cassell
	9	Tennyson: ***Enid***	Moxon
	37	Tennyson: ***Idylls of the King***	Moxon

Theophile Gautier: Captain Fracasse

In 1866, Doré finally a set of engravings for his close friend and supporter Gautier. This title that was popular in France but little known elsewhere. First published in 1863, it is a swashbuckling tale of a young nobleman fallen on hard times who takes up with a travelling theatre group, with plenty of intrigue, romance, and sword-fighting. In the 1950s, there was a famous comic-strip version of it done by the great French illustrator Rene Giffey. Doré did 60 full-page plates, the engraving image size being about 4½x6½. There are eight predominant sizes of Doré's full-page plates:

3½x5½	***Balzac, Hugo, Saintine, Taine***
4½x6½	***About, Gautier***
5½x7½	***Lafon, Munchausen, Rabelais*** (1854)
6x9	***L'Epine, Sinbad, Spain***
7½x9½	(the standard size for his literary folios)
8x10½*	*oblong (most lithographic albums)
9½x12½	***Coleridge, Poe***
12x16	***Wandering Jew***

Fracasse was issued in 60 weekly parts in 1865-66, and in an 1866 book edition for 24 *fr*. It was rather expensive for the size. In 1874 F.Polo published a 5 *fr* edition. There were several French editions, a couple Italian editions, and even one published in Mexico. The only English edition was a tiny 16mo by H.Holt in 1880. It contained only six reduced Doré illustrations. Even though these 60 plates were high quality illustrations, expectations were so high for Doré editions by 1866 that they seem rather tame in size and dramatic impact.

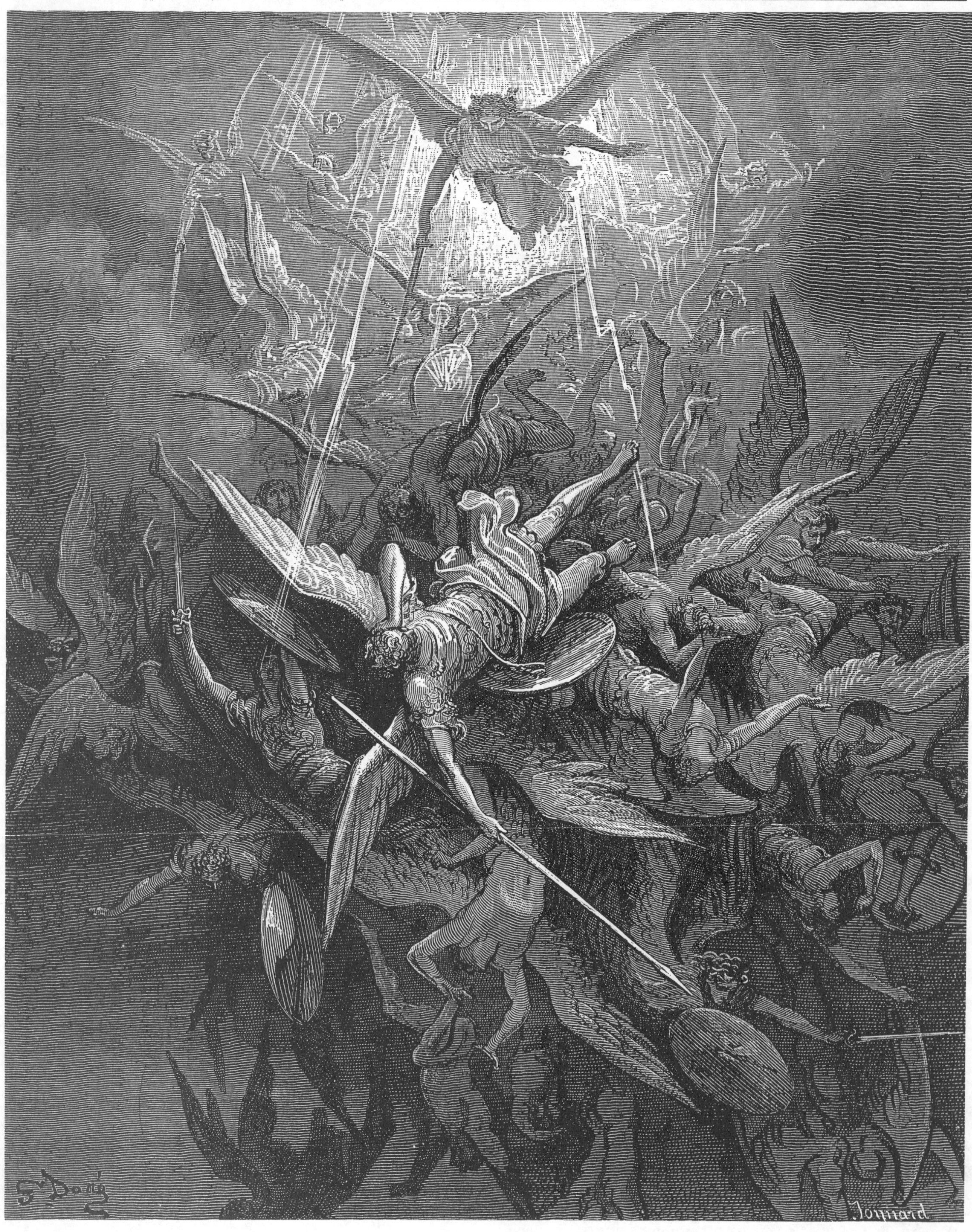

The House of Cassell

In 1865 no one could have predicted that in the next 30 years a British publisher would issue over 200 Doré editions. Cassell was certainly not his only British publisher, but they marketed the heck out of their Doré editions, featuring them on the front page of their catalogues for 20 years. In 1866, the firm was actually called Cassell, Petter & Galpin. John Cassell started his publishing company in the 1840s. He was heavily involved in the temperence movement, and was essentially a religious publisher. He was highly respected, but he went bankrupt in the 1850s. Petter and Galpin were the two major creditors who then owned the company, but they left Cassell on as a courtesy, and because his name was well known. They treated Cassell very kindly, and after he died in 1865, they supported his widow far beyond any legal obligation. The company first made contact with Doré in 1861, while they were producing their heavily illustrated ***Family Bible***. Their art editor was in Paris, and he sent the following note back to John Cassell, according to the excellent 1958 reference work, ***The House of Cassell***, by Simon Nowell-Smith (p.83):

> Can you make it convenient while in Paris to see M. Gustave Doré? Although his style of compositions is not in general suited to the illustrations of the Bible, there are subjects, now and then, which it would be an advantage to have from his pencil. Such is the vision of the Resurrection of Dry Bones in the Book of Ezekiel. No one could do it so well as Doré, if he would undertake to avoid anything grotesque, and give sufficient solemnity to its weird figures. There may be a few more subjects before we get to the end of Revelation.

You have to chuckle at the idea of Doré's style not being suited to the Bible. I wonder if that editor lived long enough to see Doré's ***Bible*** engravings become the most popular illustrations ever done? Initially John Cassell did not think much of Doré - "He is the last man in the world to whom a time block should be given." But after Cassell died, Doré would make Cassell's partners wealthy. Doré did do three engravings for ***Cassell's Family Bible*** (two from Ezekiel plus the Vision of the Four Chariots in Zechariah). The scenes were completely different from the ***Doré Bible*** engravings with the same titles.

Cassell thought no more of Doré until they were looking around for illustrations to ***Don Quixote*** in 1864, and stumbled upon a gold mine. The firm had decided to expand into the literary market, particularly illustrated editions. By this time the electrotype (or electro or cliche) had been invented, which made it possible to reproduce wood-engravings so that they could be used indefinitely. To save on expenses, Cassell was buying electros from French publishers who were swimming in engravings, rather than commission their own. They signed a contract with Hachette for Doré's ***Quixote*** electros, and began a 30-month parts edition in December of 1864, at a cheap 7d per part. We have already remarked about the unfortunate low quality of that edition. Meanwhile, English art magazines had begun to discover Doré's French folios. In February of 1864, the ***Art Journal*** finally reviewed Doré's 1861 ***Dante's Inferno***, in an illustrated article. They knew so little about Doré that they listed his first name as "Gustavus." It was a very favorable review, and they recalled their review of his ***Wandering Jew*** seven years earlier. In August of 1864, they had another complimentary illustrated review, this time of ***Atala***. Then in February of 1865, they reviewed CP&G's first installment of ***Don Quixote***. Then they did not mention Doré for a year. But by then everyone in London knew about Doré.

John Cassell died in May of 1865, just as the firm was announcing their first Doré book edition - ***Dante's Inferno***. The 12x15 edition was priced at a hefty 50s, and came out that December. The ***Quixote*** parts edition also announced that the French edition of the ***Doré Bible*** was published in December of 1865, and that Cassell would shortly begin an English parts edition, at 2s.6d, their highest priced parts edition ever. Why would Cassell publish another major illustrated Bible, after their 1862 *Illustrated Family Bible*? The simple answer is that they quickly realized what a major event the ***Doré Bible*** was going to be, and as the major London religious publisher, they could not let it go elsewhere. It was a fortunate decision, since both illustrated Bibles sold very well over the next 40 years.

Many British publications described 1866 as "the Doré year," a golden year for his British publishers. In March, the ***Doré Bible*** parts edition began, amidst much fanfare. In September, Cassell announced four new Doré book editions, ***Milton***, ***Don Quixote***, ***Wandering Jew*** (Cassell's first edition), and L'Epine's ***Croquemitaine***. In December of 1866, they even managed to squeeze in the first U.S. edition of Tennyson's ***Elaine***. In 1867 they published the massive 2V book edition of the ***Doré Bible***, plus ***Atala*** and ***Fairy Realm*** (after acquiring the rights from Ward/Lock). In 1868 they finished their major series of Doré folios with ***LaFontaine's Fables*** and ***Purgatory & Paradise***. Of the 2,000+ new Doré illustrations published in England from 1865-68, Cassell published 3/4 of them. Most of the other publishers "borrowed" Doré illustrations. Both ***Edgar*** and ***Blackburn*** contained ***Taine*** engravings. ***200 Sketches*** reprinted 1849-52 vignettes from ***Journal pour Rire***. Beeton's ***Dozen Specimens*** contained 12 Doré folio engravings from ***Dante***, ***Perrault***, and ***Castagnette***. ***Historical Cartoons*** was an English version of his lithographic album *Folies Gauloises*. The two small ***Hugo*** and the folio ***Tennyson*** engravings were commissioned in London, but were few in number. Moxon's ***Tennyson & Hood*** editions were Doré's only steel engravings. Other publishers dabbled in Doré, but CP&G was considered Doré's English publisher. The 1873 ***History of Booksellers***, by Henry Curwen, published by Chatto & Windus (who had not then published any Doré editions), said this about the House of Cassell, after the death of John Cassell in 1865 (p.274):

> ... Messrs. Petter & Galpin have launched out into a vastly superior style of book-publishing, and in placing the works of Gustave Doré before the English public have taken very high rank as Fine Art Publishers.

By 1867, ***The Art Journal*** was full of articles about Doré, in January, February, April (2), July (2), August, October, and November. By then the articles had a similar theme - "this new work by Doré is incredible; how can one man produce so many

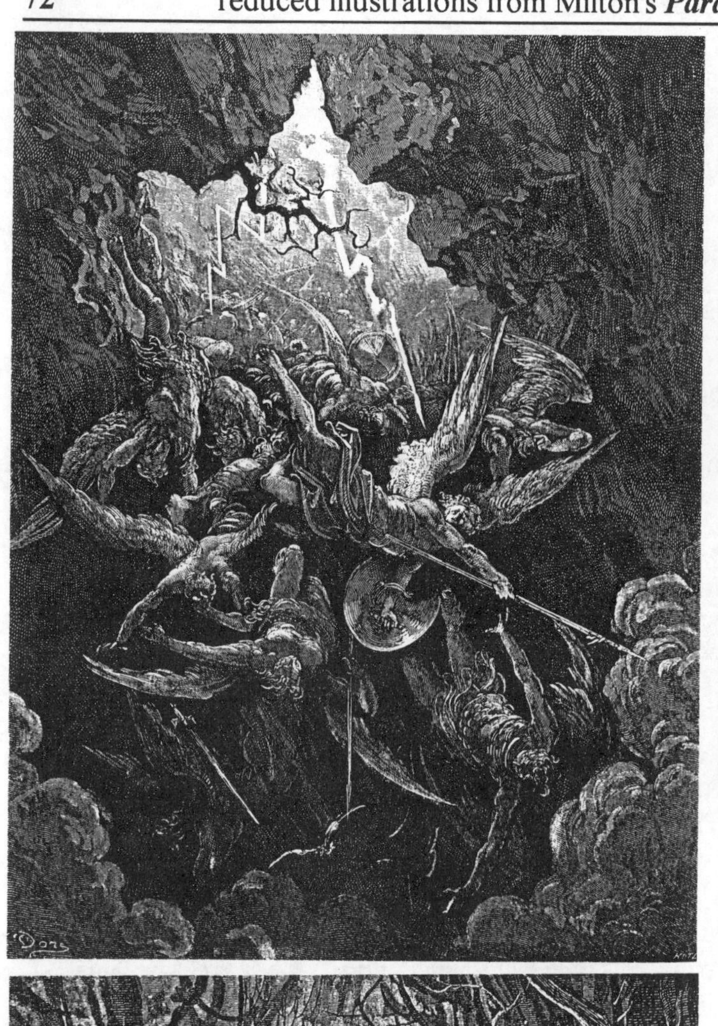

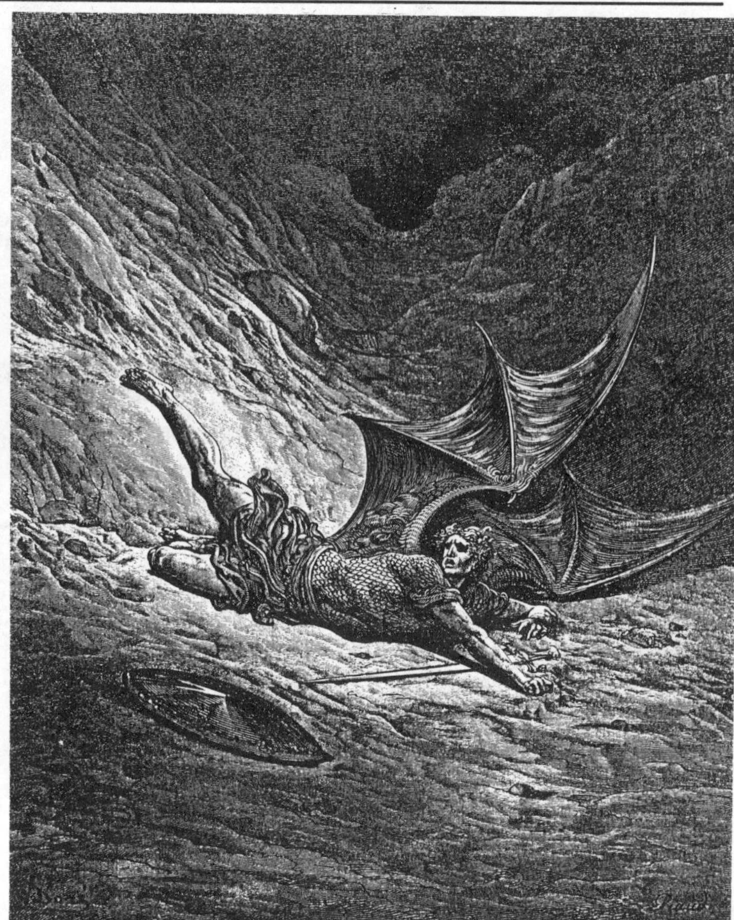

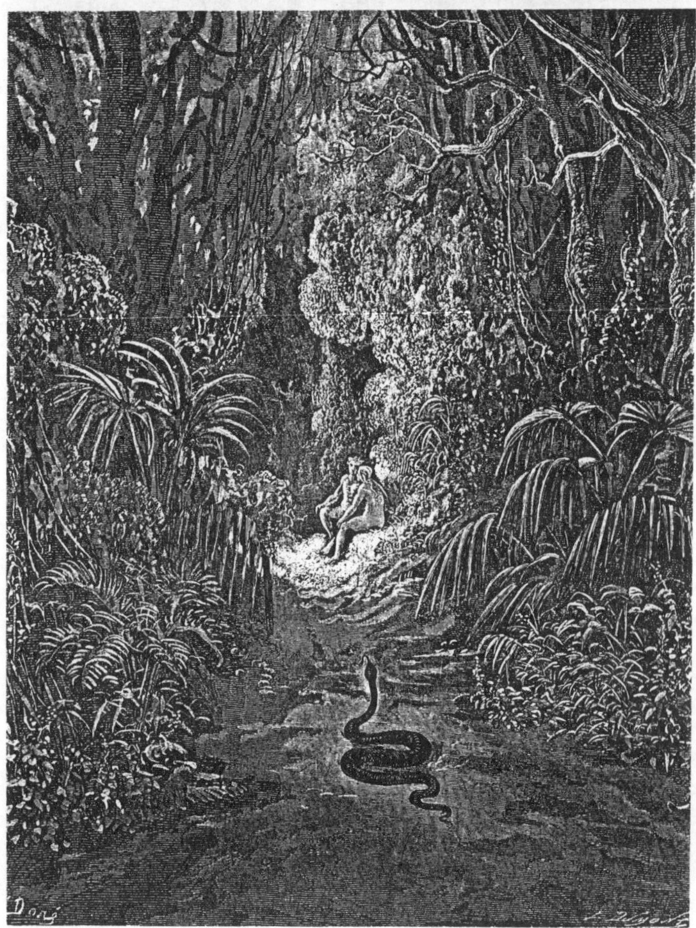

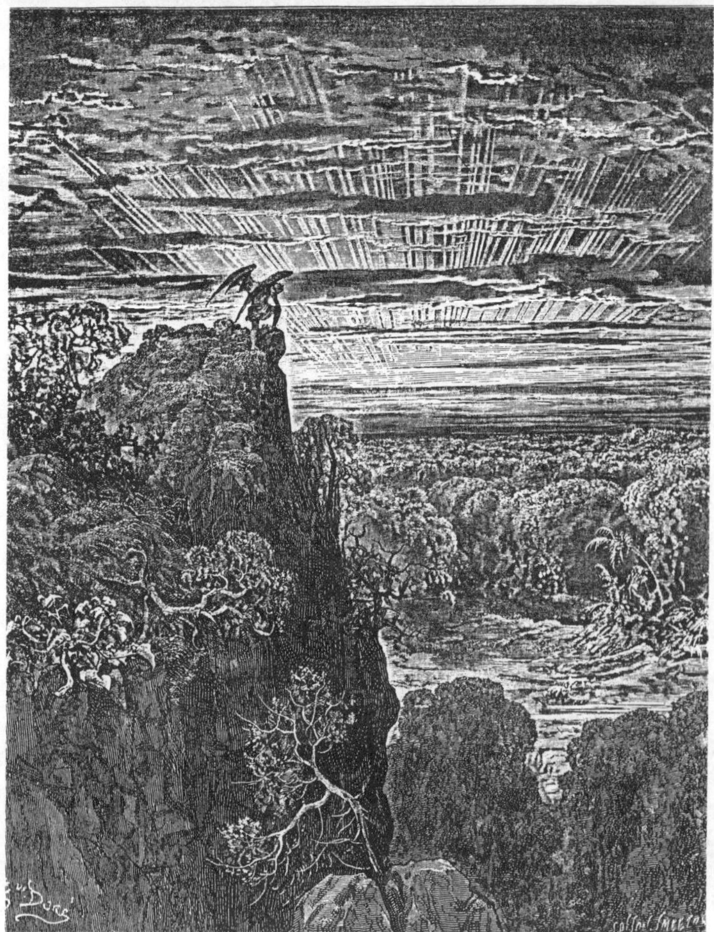

artistic masterpieces in such diverse fields? Doré has elevated illustration to a level never before dreamed possible; but how can he keep up this pace of production? He has got to slow down for the sake of his own health." One of the July articles was not about illustrations at all, it was about Doré the painter. Doré had again started submitting large paintings to the Salon, and while they were still rejected there, British correspondents began writing that Doré was not just a great illustrator, but also a great painter. French and British art critics looked at Doré's paintings in the Salon and wrote opposite things about them. In the next decade that dichotomy became increasingly radicalized; the more British art critics asserted Doré as France's greatest living painter, the more French art critics put Doré down and ridiculed the British art critics for praising him. French art critics seemed to have the attitude of how dare Doré turn to the British, just because we rejected him. It become ugly and personal and tore Doré apart.

But none of that could be foreseen in 1867, when Doré was just delighted to read any positive review of his paintings. It led to Doré's first trip to London in 1868, and the setting up of the Doré Gallery (the exhibition, not the book), an amazing phenomenon in Victorian England. But we will cover that in future chapters. Here we are looking at Doré the illustrator, up through the end of the 1860s. Cassell, Moxon, and others were marketing Doré in every way imaginable. Before the dust of the U.S. Civil War had settled, Cassell was the first British publisher to open an office in America. That New York office was first listed in catalogues from December of 1866. The true Cassell first U.S. Doré editions were 1867-70 parts editions.

In 1870, Cassell published the ultimate Doré collector's edition, ***The Doré Gallery***, with 250 full-page folio engravings from 10 different previous Doré titles. They even repackaged that repackaging in 1887, with 80 of the 250 ***Doré Gallery*** engravings offered as ***Masterpieces from Doré***. In 1889 they repackaged all 250 ***Doré Gallery*** engravings as two new titles: ***The Life & Works of Gustave Doré*** and ***The Later Works of Gustave Doré***. Of course they were repackaging engravings from individual titles. His ***Bible*** engravings were re-used in dozens of religious titles. They had children's books written to his engravings from ***Don Quixote*** and ***Purgatory & Paradise***. In 1903 they offered a set of ten ***Dante Pictorial Postcards***.

The biggest problem with Cassell editions is that over 95% of them are not dated, a major headache for libraries and antiquarian bookdealers. Often they will boast a luxurious first edition, only to be irritated by someone such as myself pointing that their copy is about the 10th edition. Many bookdealers base their selling price of undated Doré folios on the quality of the binding and paper. If you need that type of bibliographic information, consult my ***Gustave Doré - Adrift on Dreams of Splendor***. It catalogues 3000 Doré book editions, and has a special section on how to date all those undated Doré editions.

The prices of most Cassell Doré editions stayed high through the 1870s, but dipped in the 1880s due to competition from cheap U.S. pirate publishers. British prices were usually listed in Shillings (12d=s; 20s=£), but they sometimes used the old currency of Guineau (=21s) or Crown (=5s). Major titles went from 50s folio editions in the 1860s-70s to 21s quarto editions in the 1880s to 10s octavo editions in the 1890s. The U.S. drop was even sharper. The $25 folios editions dropped to $4-$6 quartos in the 1880s. That is why he was actually more popular after his death. A $25 book was very expensive, but almost any family could afford a $4 book, especially titles that they had dreamed of owning for decades.

John Milton: Paradise Lost

We are covering ***Milton*** before ***The Bible***, even though ***Milton*** actually came out a year later, to keep it in the context of Cassell, who commissioned it. When Cassell saw the Doré ***Bible*** illustrations in the fall of 1865, they were so impressed they not only made arrangements with the French Catholic publisher Mame for Cassell to be the English publisher, but they personally approached Doré to do ***Milton***. The price must have been very high. When ***Milton*** came out the next year, it sold for a whopping 100s, double the price of ***Inferno***, even though ***Milton*** had 26 less engravings. The initial U.S. price was $50. That must have staggered war-ravished America, because the next year (1867) the price dropped to $40.

Again there is confusion about the first edition. There was no initial parts edition. The first edition can be found in 12x17 or 12x15. The 12x17 may be a deluxe version, or the 12x15 may have been bound from a parts edition a couple years later. But an 1871 catalogue lists a second parts edition as a 4to, yet there are no known copies before the 1880s smaller than 12x15. There are several 12x15 Cassell Doré titles, and all are listed as folios, not 4tos. So how can the 1871-72 ***Milton*** parts edition be called a 4to? The simple way to tell the 1866 first edition is by the cities listed on the title page. The first edition lists only London and New York. They added Paris in 1871. Cassell advertised several Deluxe ***Milton*** editions, including a dated 1882 edition, with gauffered edges. It is 3/4 calf, with an engraved design carved into the gilt edges which matches the gilt design on the spine.

Doré's *Milton* was very popular, with about 100 editions worldwide. Cassell issued about 30 editions, and U.S. pirate publishers issued about 25 editions in the 1880s-90s. What is really amazing is that there have never been any French Doré *Milton* editions? That book came to symbolize Doré turning to the British. But other than France, Doré's ***Milton*** continues to be popular. Some Franklin Library editions have illustrations by Doré, some have Blake. There was a literary journal begun in the 1960s called ***The Milton Quarterly***. When they did a review of ***Milton*** illustrations, they had nothing good to say about Doré. But guess what illustration is regularly featured on the front cover? You guessed it, a Doré engraving, and without giving him credit. There are also editions in German, Dutch, Spanish, Portuguese, Italian, Russian, and Greek. Amazingly enough, the 1887 Greek edition is the first Greek edition of ***Paradise Lost***. Doré's ***Milton*** illustrations also feature heavily in recent books about angels.

The Holy Bible

In chapter four of ***Tom Sawyer***, Tom pulls some of his characteristic shenanigans in Sunday School. On page 46, Mark Twain interrupts his narrative of this midwestern boy to

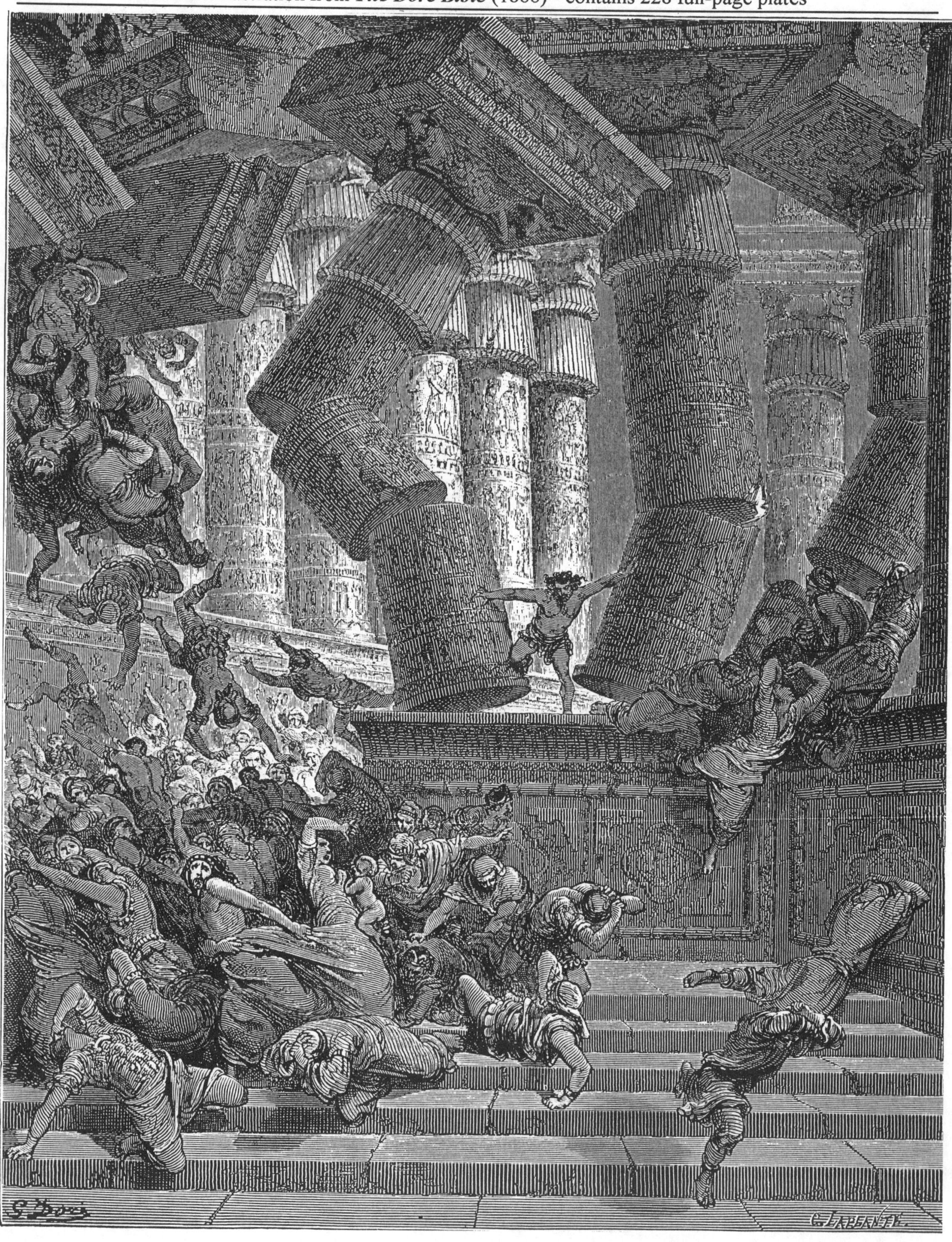

make the comment, "How many of my readers would have the industry and application to memorize two thousand verses, even for a Doré Bible?" ***Tom Sawyer*** was not a religious book, nor was Twain a religious writer, and what did a French religious illustrator have to do with rural America? In the 1870s, ***The Doré Bible*** was perhaps the most treasured (and expensive) book in the world. It may be the only Bible edition ever named after an artist. Bible editions are usually named for ethnic groups, denominations, languages, translators, editors, publishers, etc. Not since the Renaissance have religion and art so intermingled as in ***The Doré Bible***. Nearly 700 editions of Bibles and religious books have used the Doré engravings..

In the 1850s, Doré had complained about Meissonier being paid 200,000 *fr* for a painting. But that was not nearly as extraordinary as a decade later when Doré was paid that exact amount for a set of engravings! Yes, Doré was paid 200,000 *fr* by the Roman Catholic publisher Mame in the city of Tours, for 228 full-page folio engravings, which measured just under 8x10. That comes out to 877 *fr* per engraving. Even that was topped by the U.S. publisher Harper who paid Doré $6,000 for 26 ***Raven*** engravings, which comes to 1154 *fr* per engraving. Remember how outlandish people thought it was for Philipon to pay Doré 50 *fr* per page back in 1848? The ***Doré Bible*** also contained beautiful ornamentation on every page by Doré's friend Hector Giacomelli. Giacomelli did about 20 different patterns which are repeated. The giant 2V folio was 200 *fr*, or 300 *fr* for the Deluxe version. When the English edition was offered in 1867 (2V, 7" thick, 40 lbs.), it sold for $64-$150. That Deluxe full morocco ***Doré Bible*** was probably the most expensive book sold in America in the 19th century (of course, not counting sets, like ***Audubon's Birds of America***).

These were not Doré's first ***Bible*** illustrations. As early as 1857, Doré did a couple ***Bible*** engravings for ***Journal pour Tous***, which found their way into earlier ***Bible*** editions. We already mentioned the three illustrations Doré did in 1861 for ***Cassell's Family Bible***, but Doré's engravings are lost in the 900 total. Their only real significance is in comparison with the 1866 set, which were actually done between 1863-1865. Some of them are dated 1863. The Mame first French edition was dated 1866, but was actually published in December of 1865. It contained 228 full-page engravings. Its reception was even greater than ***Dante's Inferno*** or ***Don Quixote***. Within a year, Mame published a second edition. Unfortunately, it was also dated 1866. Did they not realize what a problem they would create for libraries a century later? But there are two simple ways to tell the editions apart, even though they are both 2V, 12½x17, 1866 editions. The second edition contains 230 engravings instead of 228, and the second edition adds to the title page the names of the translators (from the Latin) Bourasse & Janvier, and H.Giacomelli. But there are actually many more changes in the second edition. They did not just add two engravings. It was a major overhaul of the engravings, and it is hard to understand why they did it. They deleted 13 of the original illustrations, added in 15 new ones, had 22 of the illustrations re-engraved (the same basic scene, but a different drawing), and had 11 of the engravings touched-up. Some of the touch-ups are almost microscopic.

Mame's obsession with revised engravings went beyond the second edition. In 1868, they put together a 4V folio set containing 312 photogravures of Doré's original drawings or engravings. That set was not for publication. It was Mame's reference set, and many of those illustrations were never published. That set was in the collection of Samuel Clapp of London, and was recently sold to the Musee d'Art Moderne in Strasbourg, where it went on display in 1993. Here is the breakdown of the 312 illustrations:

- 228 - engravings published in 1st edition
- 28 - **new** illustration drawings
  - 15 engraved and published in 2nd edition
  - 7 engraved but never published
  - 6 drawings never engraved
- 45 - **redrawn** & re-engraved 1st edition illustrations
  - 22 published in 2nd edition
  - 23 engraved but never published
- 11 - **touched-up** 1st ed. engravings published in 2nd ed.

But those are by no means all the variations of the Doré ***Bible*** engravings. Doré ran into a major hurdle with English religious taste. Doré made six engravings which showed God the Father (looking amazingly like Moses). That was a major British no-no, which left Doré bewildered. But Cassell was adamant, and you can actually see some engravings where they scraped God off, or cut out that section of the block. Doré once joked that the real reason the engravings were altered was because his likeness of God did not resemble his publisher. But there were many other variations later on. All it took was a publisher who did not like any particular detail. Some U.S. publishers even had a few Doré wood engravings redone as steel engravings. Almost all Doré engravings list the engraver, so re-engraved plates can be identified by a different engraver.

The 3000 copies of the first French edition (containing 228 engravings) sold out in the first few months of 1866, even at the lofty price of 200 *fr*. With sales of 600,000 *fr* in a few months, the 200,000 *fr* paid to Doré did not seem so bad. The second edition (containing 230 engravings, of which 15 were new) came out at the end of 1866. Foreign editions soon followed. Most foreign editions contained the 230 engravings from the second French edition. But the first English edition had 238 engravings, using most of the illustrations from both French editions. There is an excellent (and currently available) Dover edition with 241 different illustrations. No one has ever published all 243, or all 265, or all 312. Perhaps the museum in Strasbourg might some day print all 312. There are few French editions of the ***Doré Bible***. Besides the 1866 editions, Mame published an 1874 and an 1882 edition. In recent decades there have been a few more French editions. But Mame did borrow ***Bible*** engravings for a dozen other religious titles, much like Cassell did. The other French religious titles were by Bourasse, Cruchet, Boissonnot, Lamennais, and Pinault. The 1903-05 Boissonnot titles are significant because they contain four of the previously unpublished engravings. The ***Doré Bible*** has been published in dozens of languages. It is hard to understand why there is no listed Portuguese edition, with strong Roman Catholic influence in Portugal and Brazil. Perhaps there are editions with Doré's engravings that just do not mention his name. Here are the known languages:

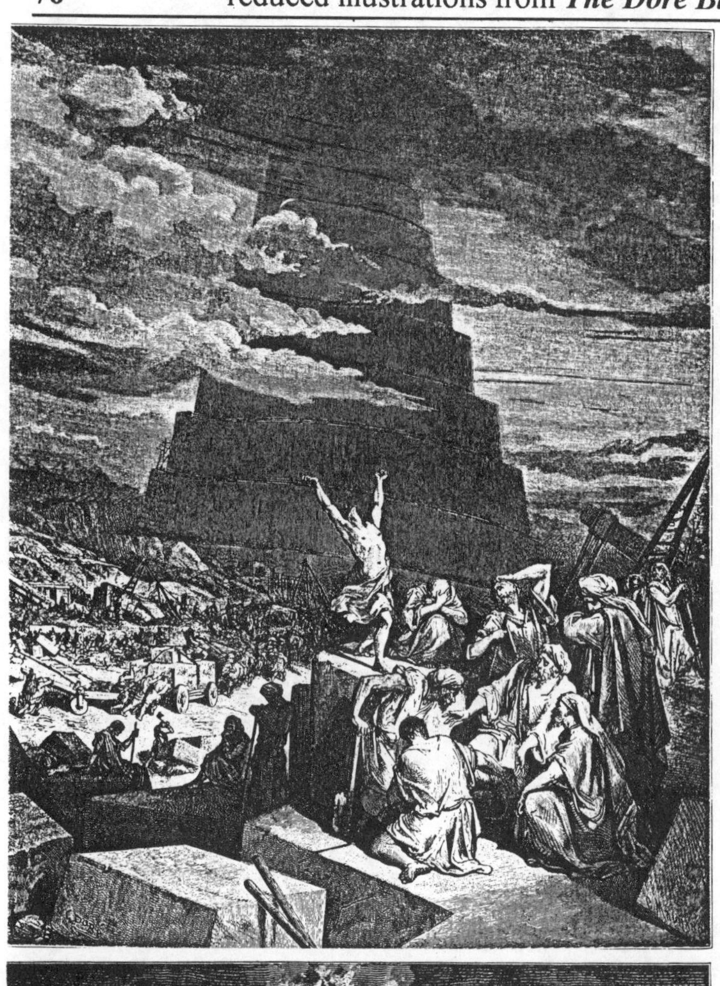

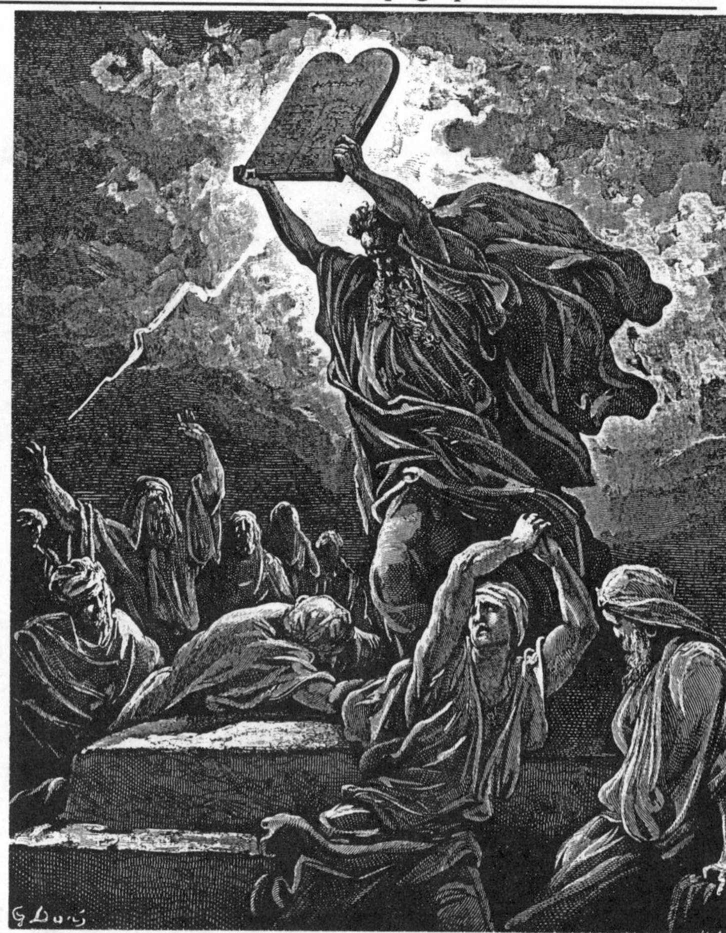

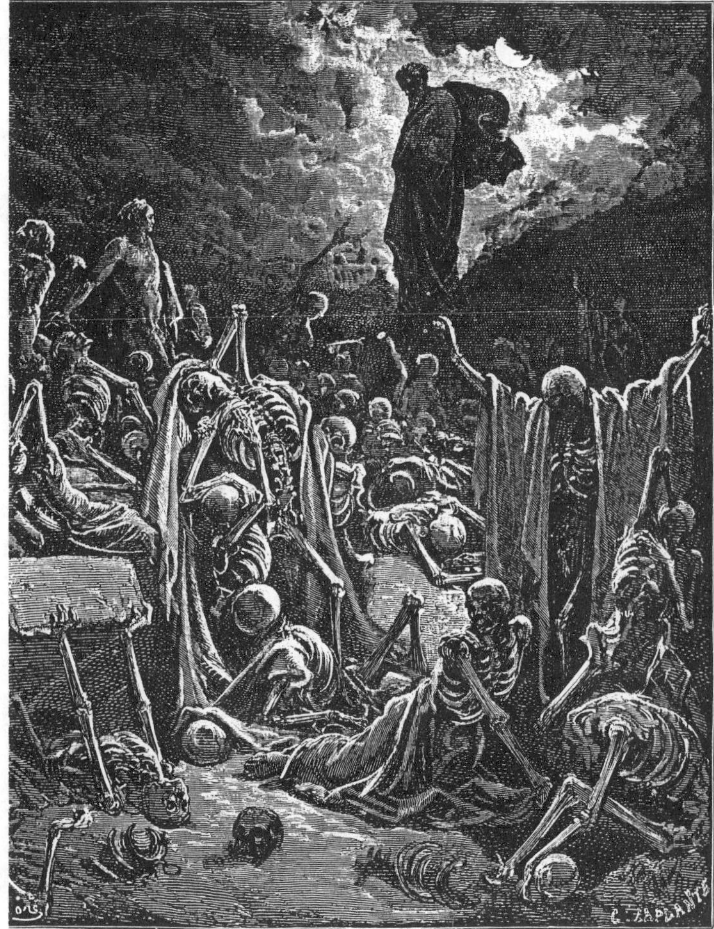

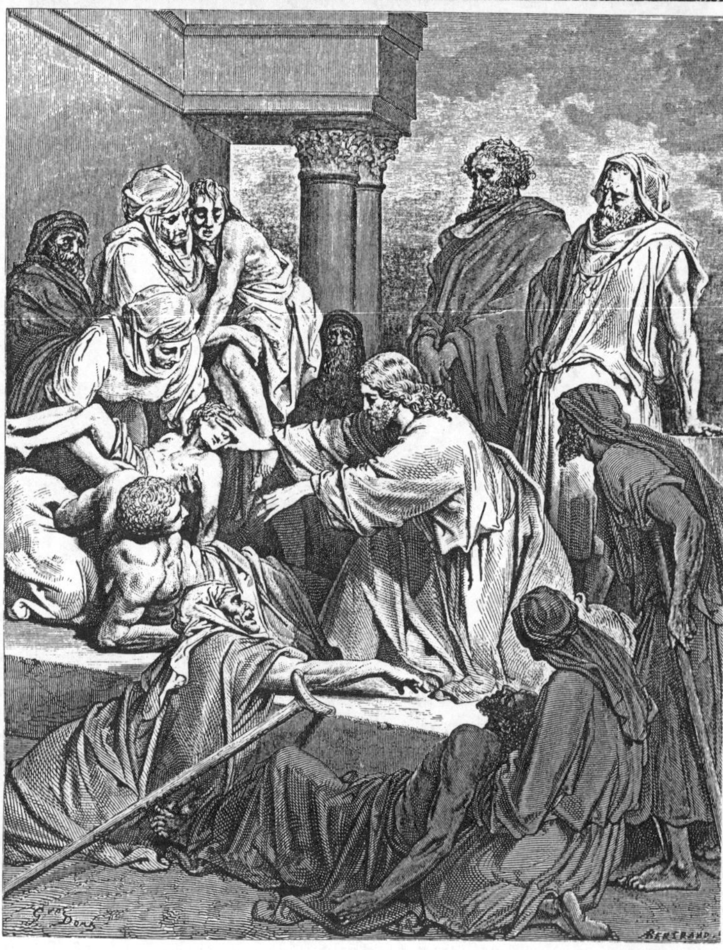

French	Russian	Hungarian
English	Polish	Norwegian
German	Czech	Esperanto
Dutch	Slovak	Yiddish
Spanish	Finnish	Hebrew
Italian	Greek	Ukrainian
Danish	Serbian	Armenian
Swedish	Croatian	Portuguese?

Cassell announced the ***Doré Bible*** in November of 1865. They offered Londoners the French edition for £10 (200s), listing Cassell as the "sole English publisher" of the French edition. Perhaps they meant distributor. They never published a French edition. Two years later the English version was £8 (160s). They announced that the English parts edition would begin January 1, 1866, for "half-a-crown" (2.5s). But it did not begin until late March, 1866. There were rave reviews in ***The Art Journal*** (including two engravings) and the other English publications that had not already reviewed the French edition. The parts edition ran through 1870, but the book version came out in December of 1867. The U.S. parts edition began in 1868, with different content quantity, in an effort to catch up to the British parts edition. In 1872 they began a cheaper parts edition in London and New York - 56 months for 50¢ or 7d, a major price drop. But that edition had 33 less engravings. The parts editions could be bound into 2V, 3V or 4V. There are very few early parts editions still unbound. Subscribers put a small fortune into that parts edition, and they had little desire to then let it set around in flimsy paper parts. The first English edition of the ***Doré Bible*** was considered a great treasure in the homes of Victorian England and America. Plus, it is the only version of the ***Doré Bible*** with 238 engravings. Cassell issued the ***Doré Bible*** in parts in 1866-70, 1872-76, 1880-84, 1888-92, and 1898-1902. The 1892 cheap edition had only 194 engravings and sold for a very low 15s. In 1903 they offered a Deluxe version on the installment plan. You got the ***Bible*** by sending in 5s down, and you then had to make 10 monthly payments of 10s each. If at any time you missed a payment, they took the Bible back. They did not say what effect a repossessed Bible would have on your eternal soul.

Most European countries published luxurious editions of the ***Doré Bible***. Most were 12x17 in 2V. German editions by Hallberger were particularly beautiful. They are undated, but the editions are numbered, alternating between the Allioli Catholic translation and the Luther Protestant translation. In 1874, they also came out with a Jewish ***Doré Bible*** edition. It is in German with additional Hebrew headings. It deletes the New Testament, but includes the Roman Catholic Apocryphal books, which primarily deal with Jewish history between the Testaments. Cassell was a Protestant publisher, but their ***Bible*** editions also include those Apocryphal books, to show the 21 Doré engravings therein. Not until the 1930s did a Protestant version of the ***Doré Bible*** delete the Apocryphal illustrations. When Israel again became a nation, there were a number of editions of ***Doré Bible*** illustrations published by Sinai Publishing Co. in Tel Aviv. Those also include the Apocryphal engravings, referred to as "Supplement." The only actual Roman Catholic theology expressed in ***Doré Bible*** illustrations is one at the end of the New Testament, entitled ***Crowned Virgin*** (in heaven). Cassell simply deleted that engraving.

An indication of the true significance of the ***Doré Bible*** illustrations is how much they have been used by so many different groups. The Roman Catholic Church has always had high praise for Doré's illustrations. Recent Bible editions by the Daughters of St. Paul still feature them. There were also over 100 Protestant Bible editions containing Doré engravings published in the U.S. before the end of the 19th century. Besides mainline Protestant denominations like Lutherans and Southern Baptists, the illustrations have been used extensively by evangelicals from D.L.Moody to Billy Graham, and by the Mormon church as recently as 1994 in missionary publications in the Philippines. They are also widely used by non-religious groups, from astrology to new-age to mystics. The ***Doré Bible*** illustrations have also been used in recent books on angels, computers, old age, the medical profession, libertarianism, and Plato. They are even used in a graphics package with a Johann Sebastian Bach audio CD. The front cover of the December 18, 1995 ***Time Magazine*** features a ***Doré Bible*** engraving.

The real proliferation of ***Doré Bible*** engravings began with the U.S. pirate publishers. There was a virtual explosion of U.S. publishing after the Civil War, especially subscription and cheap publishing (usually combined). Publishers on the East Coast lost sight of the westward moving U.S. population. Rural folk had no bookstores to browse in, but they still had a tremendous thirst for books. Some enterprising (and not a few unscrupulous) new publishers figured out how to take the books to the people. Vast armies of book salesmen spread out over the midwest, with sample "dummy" books, taking orders. The subscription publishers started out with the old standards: religion, history, literature & art. While some U.S. religious books as early as 1868 borrowed, re-engraved, and reduced ***Doré Bible*** illustrations, the first book produced in any mass quantity was an 1870s quarto ***Pictorial Family Bible***, similar to Cassell's version a decade earlier in England. There was a network of dozens of publishers in various midwestern cities. A book would be published by one big company, and then each small publisher could buy into it and insert their title page. Many of these were very small companies, with salesmen out on commission. But nothing made you look like a major publisher than having your imprint on ***The Family Bible***. The first version of the ***Pictorial Family Bible*** was in English, but with waves of immigrants coming to America, they soon added German and Scandanavian editions. Those editions were not technically the ***Doré Bible***. They were Bibles with hundreds or thousands of cheap illustrations, and the fame of Doré made the inclusion of some of his ***Bible*** illustrations a big feature (most had 30-100 Doré engravings). The quality of ***Family Bible*** editions was lower than official ***Doré Bible*** editions.

By 1879 someone finally thought of the idea of printing engravings only from the ***Doré Bible***, editions of which were ponderously bulky. ***The Doré Bible Gallery***, usually with 100 engravings in a 4to format, proved to be the most practical and successful. Overnight the cost of an edition featuring Doré ***Bible*** engravings dropped from $64 to $6. All editions of ***The Doré Bible Gallery*** were published in the U.S. The U.S. pirate publishers actually thought of it first, and the U.S. Cassell

(top row) reduced illustrations from ***The Doré Bible*** (1866) - contains 228 full-page plates
(bottom row) full-size illustrations from Hugo's ***Toilers of the Sea*** (1867) contains two plates

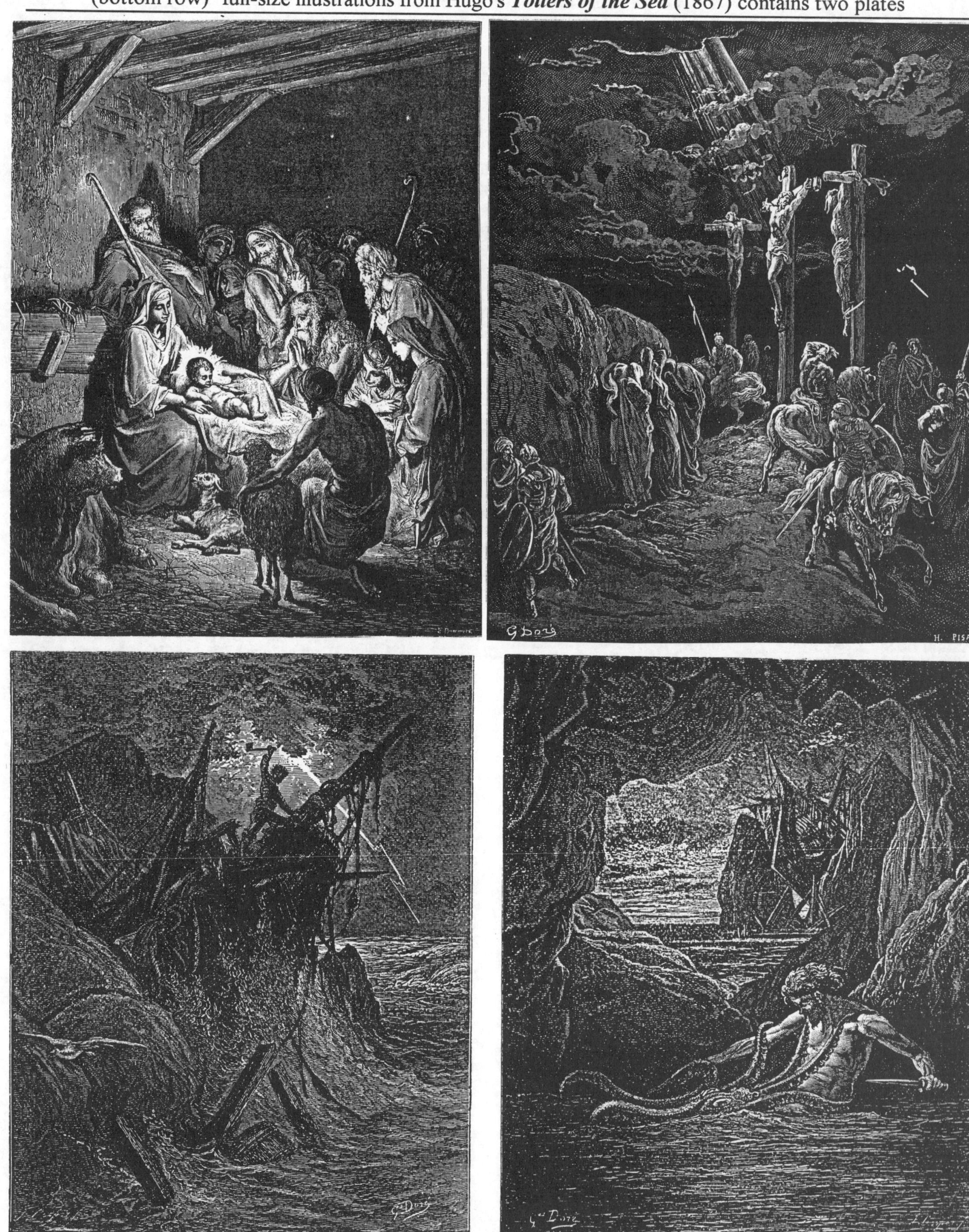

office had no choice but to follow suit. In the next 15 years there were 40 editions of ***The Doré Bible Gallery***, issued by 18 different publishers. Some of the editions were lower quality. Usually each publisher's first edition was fairly high quality, but deteriorated with subsequent editions. Belford/Clarke of Chicago published five editions between 1886-91, the 1891 edition being much smaller and cheaper. But it still turned out to be very historically significant. A 10-year-old boy liked his copy of that edition so much that he later described it as his favorite book. He also said that it was the greatest influence on his adult accomplishments. Here is what would be written about him in his 1973 biography by Charles Higham (p.7):

> He loved the classics, and the works of Gustave Doré: the most fingered book at Pompton Lake was the Doré Bible Gallery, a collection of illustrated sacred texts published by Belford-Clarke in 1891. He loved to pore over pictures like "Ruth and Boaz," "The Judgment of Solomon," "The Sermon on the Mount," and "The Prodigal Son." From these the whole visual inspiration of his great religious films sprang."

That little 10-year-old dreamer was Cecil B.Demille.

Stories about the influence of the Doré *Bible* engravings are legion. They were so popular that Doré expanded on them in enormous paintings which later filled The Doré Gallery (not the book, the exhibition in a building of the same name) in London. It was considered the greatest collection of religious paintings in the world. Some of those paintings were as large as 20 feet high by 30 feet wide. In 1947, Cecil B. Demille purchased some of those paintings. But we will deal with that in a later chapter. In the last third of the 19th century, there were probably a hundred articles written about Doré's Biblical illustrations and paintings.

It did not take long for publishers to start "borrowing" Doré *Bible* illustrations for other religious books, especially in America, where it was like taking candy from a baby. There are nearly 200 religious books which contain some Doré ***Bible*** illustrations. Many early editions prominently featured Doré even though they only contained a couple of his illustrations, whereas many later editions used many of his illustrations without mentioning him. Of course the French publisher Mame quickly began using Doré illustrations in other books, the first being the 1868 ***Les Saints Evangiles*** by Bourasse & Janvier. But American publishers were soon to follow. I believe the earliest American pirated illustrations were in the 1868 ***Illustrated Bible Biography***, by Lee & Shepard of Boston, which featured 20 Doré ***Bible*** engravings. Other publishers quickly followed, and 1869 saw John Kitto's ***Illustrated History of the Holy Bible*** (by Henry Bill) and Lyman Abbott's ***Jesus of Nazareth***, by Harper. Titles from the 1870s on are way too numerous to mention. Even as late as the 1890s there was another surge in the popularity of Doré ***Bible*** engravings. After the Doré Gallery of religious paintings was in Chicago in 1896, and broke all attendance records, Chicago religious publishers went wild adding Doré ***Bible*** engravings to their books. A good example is Rhodes & McClure. Prior to 1896, they had published only one edition with Doré ***Bible*** engravings, an 1891 edition of ***Forbidden Fruit*** by E.U. Cook. From 1896-1910 they published 45 editions containing Doré ***Bible*** illustrations, in works by D.L.Moody (21), Sam Jones (13), and E.U.Cook (11). The editions averaged about 30 Doré ***Bible*** illustrations each, but the printing quality is poor.

Quiz question: what first edition of Charles Dickens contains Doré illustrations, even though neither of them knew anything about it? The reason neither of them knew anything about the first edition in question is that it was not published until a half century after both of them were dead. In the 1840s, Dickens wrote a story for his children, with instructions that it should not be published while any of the children were still alive. After the last of the children died, the grandchildren gave permission for it to be published in 1934. It was entitled ***The Life of our Lord***. It had only 85 small text pages, but it was published with great fanfare and serialized in various newspapers. Some first editions contain Doré illustrations. But many editions just say "illustrated," and some of those contain a selection of religious paintings which does not include Doré. Few editions that contain Doré illustrations mention his name.

Victor Hugo: Toilers of the Sea

In the 1860s, Victor Hugo was in self-imposed exile. He did not return until Napoleon III was deposed after the Franco-Prussian War of 1870-71. Yet his influence on France was immense. From exile he was turning out major novels like ***Les Miserables*** (1862) and ***Toilers of the Sea*** (1866). The British publisher of ***Toilers of the Sea*** arranged to have Doré do two small illustrations ($3\frac{1}{2}$x$4\frac{1}{2}$) for the first edition, yet Doré's name is listed as large as Hugo on the title page and spine. They are very nice illustrations, but barely an appetizer, by Doré's standard. But the publisher could assert "Illustrations by Doré." After Hugo returned from exile, he and Doré would be close friends, but even in 1866 he was a great fan of Doré. When Hugo first saw the two illustrations in October of 1866, he sent the following letter to Doré in Paris:

> Hautville House, October 18, 1866
>
> Young and powerful Master -
>
> This morning in the midst of a tempest worthy of it, your magnificent *translation* of the *Toilers of the Sea* came to my house.
>
> You have put everything in this picture, the wreck, the ship, the rock, the hydra, the man. Your octopus is frightful, and your Gilliat is grand. In this you have added a rare page to your charming and terrifying in-folio volumes.
>
> This splendid specimen of my book exacts the rest. God, yourself, and the publisher willing, it is certain that we may accomplish that result. To you I shall furnish the opportunity to create another monument. I send you my laudations and thanks in the most cordial of effusions.
>
> VICTOR HUGO

Doré was always proud of that letter, particularly Hugo's use of the word "translation" instead of "illustration." But even though they remained close friends, Doré never illustrated any

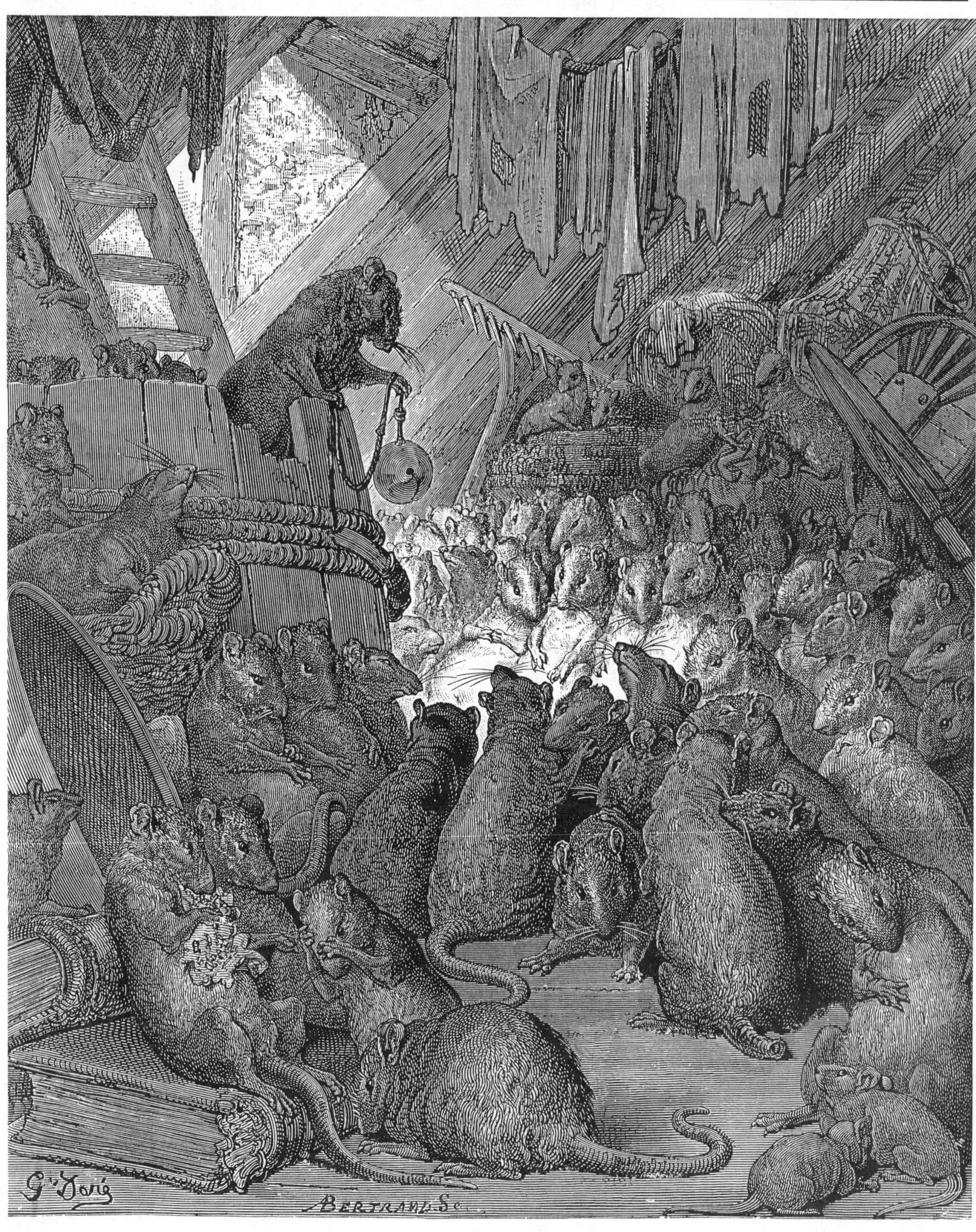
G. Doré
BERTRAND Sc.

more of his books. Doré cut back on illustrating in the 1870s to concentrate on painting and sculpture. ***Toilers of the Sea*** had many later illustratrations by Chifflart, Vierge, and Hugo himself. Editions with the Doré engravings are quite rare. But Doré did do other drawings of Hugo's works. In 1856, Doré did four illustrations for Hugo's ***Les Contemplations*** in the magazine ***Musee Francais-Anglais***. He also did drawings and paintings of ***Hunchback of Notre Dame***, including a beautiful watercolor of "The Court of Miracles" from ***Hunchback***. That is the scene where the thieves and beggars of Paris gather at night, and miraculously the blind see and the lame walk. The king of beggars is going to hang Gringoire for the crime of being a poet, when Esmeralda saves his life by agreeing to marry him. Doré's scene is gorgeous. First he did a large drawing (24x32) which is black-on-white or essentially a daytime view. In 1882 he made it into a 26x36 watercolor, switching it to nighttime. Like so many of Doré's paintings, it is monochromatic (orange). It may be considered an enlarged colored illustration, but it is still very powerful.

200 Sketches, Humorous & Grotesque

We mentioned this in chapter three. It contains 303 wood engravings first published in ***Journal pour Rire*** from 1849-1852, and reprinted ad nauseum in France by Philipon. ***200 Sketches*** was published simultaneously in December of 1866 by Frederick Warne of London and Roberts Brothers of Boston. It also lists the logo of the Dalziel Brothers, Engravers & Printers. I do not know if Dalziel re-engraved them or just printed them, but there was also an edition in French, published by Dalziel. Several of Doré's original captions were changed to make them more contemporary. It was the only glimpse English audiences had of his early comic strip art. It is a vivid example of how in the late 1860s, English publishers were tripping over each other in the mad rush to publish books with Doré's name on it. Here are the British and American publishers who issued Doré editions between 1865-68:

London:	S.O.Beeton	New York:	D.Appleton
	Bell & Daldy		M.Doolady
	Blackwood		Harper
	Cassell		G.Routledge
	Wm.Collins		J.W.Schmidt
	Dalziel	Boston:	DeVries/Ibarra
	J.C.Hotten		Lee & Shepard
	S.Low		Roberts Bros.
	Moxon		J.E.Tilton
	Tinsley	Philadelphia:	Gebbie & Keppel
	Ward/Lock		F.Leypoldt
	F.Warne		Porter & Coates

Jean de LaFontaine: Fables

LaFontaine's Fables was the 1668 French version of ***Aesop's Fables***. Although the content of the two versions is very similar, about the only time you ever see an English edition of ***LaFontaine*** is when it is featuring a set of French illustrations. Though there were crude woodcuts for *Aesop* as early as the 15th century, the first major illustrated version was a set of 112 etchings by Francis Barlow in 1665. The most famous 18th century illustrations were by the Frenchman Jean-Baptiste Oudry. There were two famous 19th century sets of illustrations (prior to Doré), the French set in 1838 by J.J.Grandville, and a British set in 1848 by Sir John Tenniel, whose illustrations were a major factor in his getting the commission in 1865 to illustrate ***Alice in Wonderland***.

On November 13th, 1866, Hachette published the first of 58 weekly parts of Doré's ***LaFontaine***, finishing just before Christmas of 1867. The parts set was 11x15, and contained a total of 84 full-page plates and 248 vignettes. Of course, most people who got the parts then had them bound into a book. In December of 1867, Hachette offered the book edition for 30 *fr* (with Deluxe versions from 35-50 *fr*), dated 1868. But the book edition is different from the parts edition. Hachette had eight replacement engravings inserted into the book version. But to complicate matters, Hachette also offered in December, 1867 a Deluxe 2V (13x17) vellum paper edition, and dated it 1867, even though it was published at exactly the same time as the one volume 11x15 plain version. So since the smaller version is in the same format as the parts edition, it has been asserted that the 1868 edition is the official first edition, and the Deluxe 1867 edition is the second edition. Why are people so obsessed with asserting an "official" first edition among two different versions published at the same time? Why not just say that they are both first editions - a regular edition and a large paper Deluxe edition? The 1867 Deluxe 2V edition sold for 200-240 *fr*, in comparison to 30-50 *fr* for the 1868 edition. How did Hachette convince people that that the 2V edition was worth six times as much as the 1V edition? To complicate matters further, the 2V 1867 version deleted 13 of the 1868 engravings, and added in 15 new ones, making a total of 334 in the 1867 Deluxe version. So all three versions - the parts edition and the two book editions - each have some engravings not in the other two. Altogether that comes to 355 engravings: 332 (from the parts edition) + 8 (new in the 1868 version) + 15 (new in the 1867 version). In the 1870s, Hachette switched to a cheap 8vo version with only 92 vignettes, of which there were several 19th century editions. Then there were no French editions for 70 years. Recent decades have seen various French editions, including a 4to published in Quebec in 1993.

But there is one more French mystery edition. It is listed in the American Catalogue, but no library catalogue lists a copy. There is no listed date, but it would be about 1868. It was listed as being published by D.Appleton of New York. It lists both a French and an English version, both in a 2V folio. But the really staggering part is the price - $100-$150. That is as much as the ***Doré Bible***! At the same time the Cassell 4to edition was only $15. My theory is that the English-language mystery edition never existed, and the French-language edition would have been Hachette's deluxe edition with an Appleton title-page. I believe Appleton put out an announcement to test the waters about the U.S. market for a Deluxe U.S. edition, but dropped it due to reaction to the price. It may have been like Cassell's announcement of "their" French ***Doré Bible*** edition.

The English version of ***LaFontaine*** was another eagerly awaited Doré work. ***The Art Journal*** could not wait for either an English edition or a French book edition. In April of 1867, they reviewed the French parts edition! By this time English publishers were closely monitoring Doré's every move. When

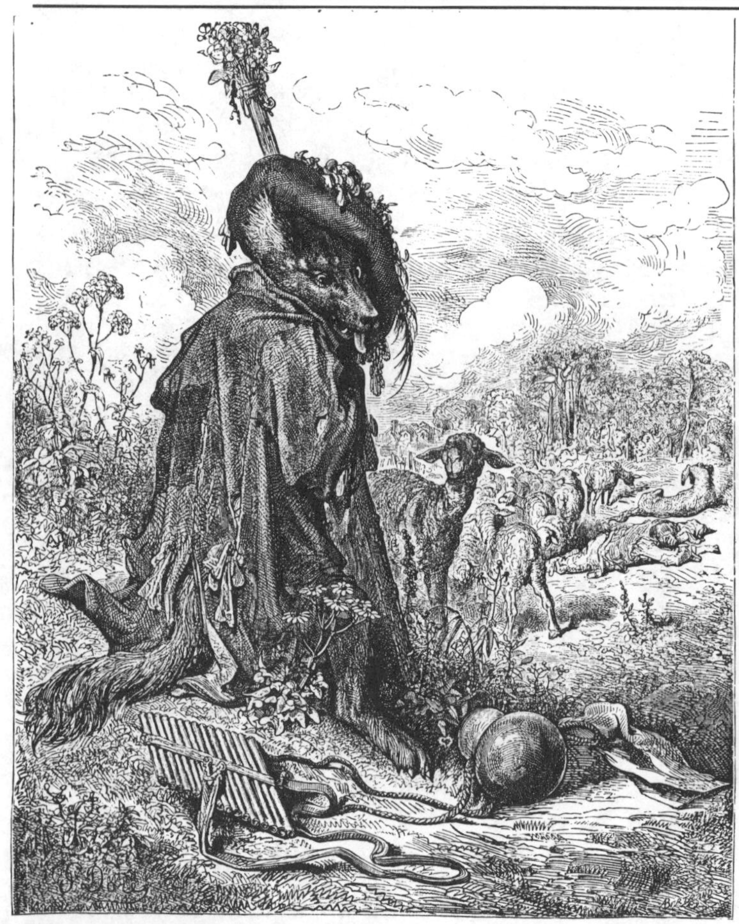

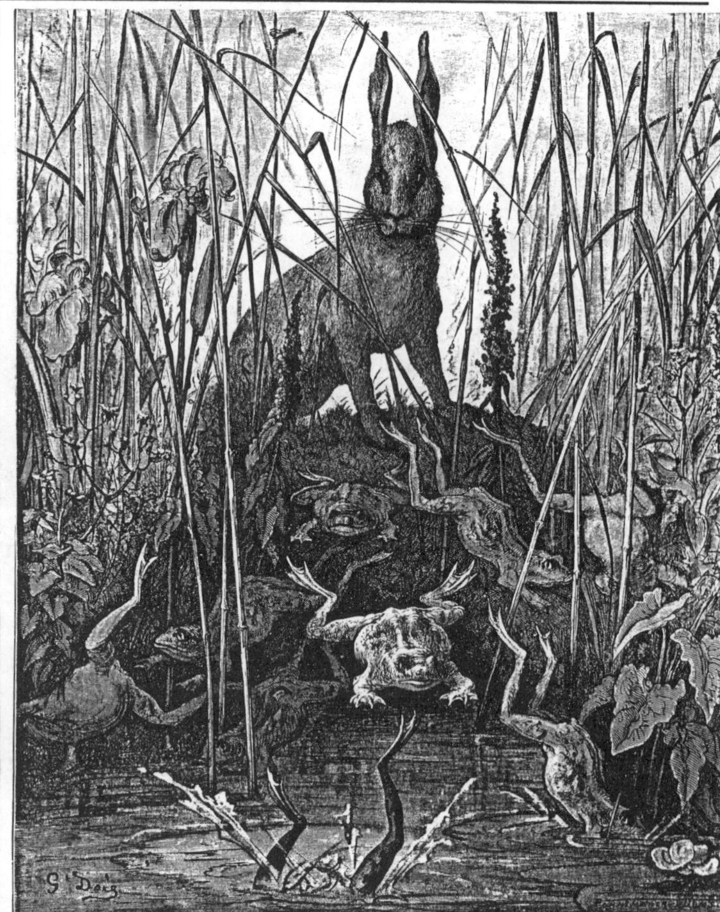

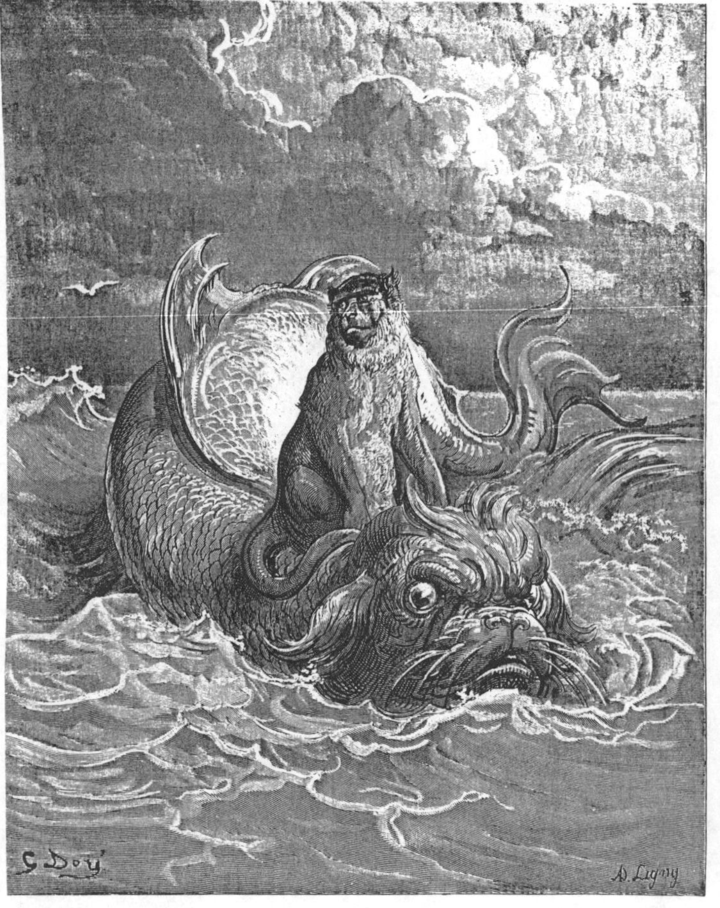

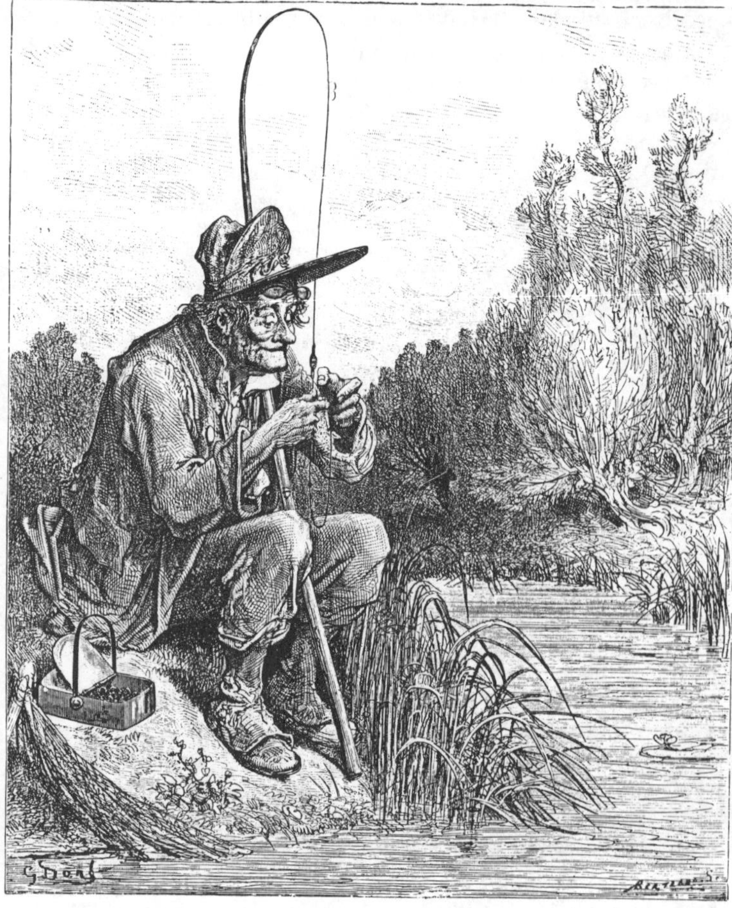

Cassell published the last part of ***Don Quixote*** in May of 1867, they announced a 30-month ***LaFontaine*** parts edition. At first they could not decide what title to use, so they called it ***Cassell's Illustrated Book of Fables***. The U.S. parts version was only 22 issues, and it may have started in June of 1867 or a few months later, in which case the 22-month schedule may have been to finish at the same time as the British version.

It is a challenge reconciling the engravings in Cassell's English version with the three French versions. It would have been way too simple to just follow one of the French editions. Here is what Cassell included: 4 of the 8 engravings that are only in the French parts edition; 5 of the 8 engravings that are only in the 1868 French book edition; and 10 of the 15 engravings that are only in the 1867 French book edition; then for good measure they deleted 14 engravings that are in all three French versions. That is how they ended up with 329 engravings in the Cassell editions. There were at least three Cassell parts editions, and several book editions up through the 1870s, but it fell out of popularity in the 1880s. Later on, Cassell tried two format variations of ***LaFontaine***, both of which bombed. In 1888 they announced a 2V Deluxe edition for $25, which would include, besides the Doré engravings, 100 etchings by the 18th century master Oudry. The problem was that the only Deluxe feature was the set of Oudry etchings; the high quality printing of which only contrasted with the low quality of the paper and the printing of the Doré engravings. Then in the early 1890s, Cassell Pub. of New York came out with a cheap Doré edition, with only 87 of the 329 engravings and 43 of the original 240 fables. ***LaFontaine*** is about tenth on the list of Doré's most popular titles, with about 70 editions. Some of the U.S. pirate publishers issued it in the 1880s, some following the French set of engravings. Recent editions delete many engravings. A few ***LaFontaine*** engravings were used in ***Twelve Old Friends*** (1885) by Dinah Mulock Craik. There were a few foreign-language ***LaFontaine*** editions, in German, Dutch, Portuguese, Spanish, Italian, Polish, and a 1992 Hebrew edition, with text by Ivan A.Krylov.

Dante's Purgatory & Paradise

Doré finished ***The Divine Comedy*** in 1868, adding 42 engravings for ***Purgatory*** and 18 engravings for ***Paradise*** to the 76 he did in 1861 for the ***Inferno***. It marked the end of his prodigious output of folio engravings. From 1866-68 he did about 800 engravings. From 1869-71 he did about 40. These 60 new engravings have always played second fiddle to the ones for the ***Inferno***, but they are spectacular in their own right, with flights of fancy that are still inspirational to the religious and non-religious. Two of the most oft-reprinted engravings are "The Eagle lifting Dante out of Purgatory" and "Epyrean," with its dazzling circles of angelic light.

In 1861, Hachette had told Doré that nobody would pay 100 *fr* for a book. Seven years later, that same price looked like a bargain. Doré's ***Purgatory & Paradise*** was published in the same format as the 1861 ***Inferno***. But in 1861 they had been afraid to even think about a Deluxe edition. After all, the regular edition itself was a Deluxe edition. By 1868, Deluxe editions were the name of the game. So they issued individual Deluxe volumes of ***Purgatory*** and ***Paradise*** in 100-copy numbered Limited editions on vellum paper, priced at 100 *fr* each. Both the Limited edition and the regular edition had text in French and Italian, just like the ***Inferno***, and Hachette again published a version of ***Purgatory & Paradise*** in Italian only. But there were only a couple of French reprint editions. Once again, there was a mysterious listing of a U.S. French edition by D.Appleton that nobody seems to have, at a very high price compared to the Cassell edition.

The Cassell editions of ***Purgatory & Paradise*** follow the same pattern as ***Inferno*** editions - 12x15, then 10x13, then 8x10, then 4x6½, ending in 1913. Cassell also published two children's book versions of ***P&P***, written by Rose Emily Selfe, entitled ***How Dante Climbed the Mountain*** (1887) and ***With Dante in Paradise*** (1900), each with just a few reduced Doré engravings. The U.S. cheap publishers also issued several ***P&P*** editions in the 1880s. While English publishers tended to keep the two volumes separate, most foreign language editions quickly combined the two volumes into ***The Divine Comedy***. There were numerous such editions in Italian, German, and Spanish. The Italians have now pretty well "taken over" Doré's illustrations to ***The Divine Comedy***, much like the Spanish have now done with ***Don Quixote***. But in the 1910s-1920s, the Germans exploded with some 15 editions of Doré's ***Dante***. There are ***Dante*** editions in Dutch, Portuguese, Swedish, Finnish, Russian, Bulgarian, Yugoslavian, Latvian, and even Chinese. There have been about 180 editions of ***P&P***, and about 200 editions of ***Inferno***, but most are combined editions.

Lord Tennyson: The Idylls of the King
Thomas Hood: Poems

(note: even though *Hood* was an 1870 title, we include it here because these two works were Doré's only steel engravings, all published by Moxon, essentially a series)

The publisher Moxon could hardly have produced more expensive books. They got the Poet Laureate of England, the world's greatest illustrator, and the most expensive type of engraving (steel), published in a large folio format. Alfred, Lord Tennyson was perhaps the second most popular writer in England, after Charles Dickens. Moxon was the only publisher ever to commission steel engravings from Doré. Moxon's total cost for these editions must have been staggering. And if you think that Philipon, Hachette, and Cassell had no shame in their over-marketing of Doré illustrations, Moxon could have written a book on it. They published 42 Doré folio editions of ***Tennyson*** and ***Hood*** in 12 years, and Moxon did not even have a U.S. office. All of those were London editions.

Moxon's strategy was to publish a series of individual stories from ***Idylls of the King*** and then combine them. They would offer each story in three formats: a regular folio book edition with steel engravings, a portfolio of photogravures of the original art, and a set of India Proofs, each proof signed by Doré, Tennyson, and the engraver. The folios also came in a range of bindings, from morocco-grain cloth to some of the most beautiful full morocco bindings you have ever seen. They also offered individual engravings, in b&w and hand-colored. At least they did not publish it as wallpaper.

full-size illustration from Dante's ***Purgatory & Paradise*** (1868) - contains 60 full-page plates.

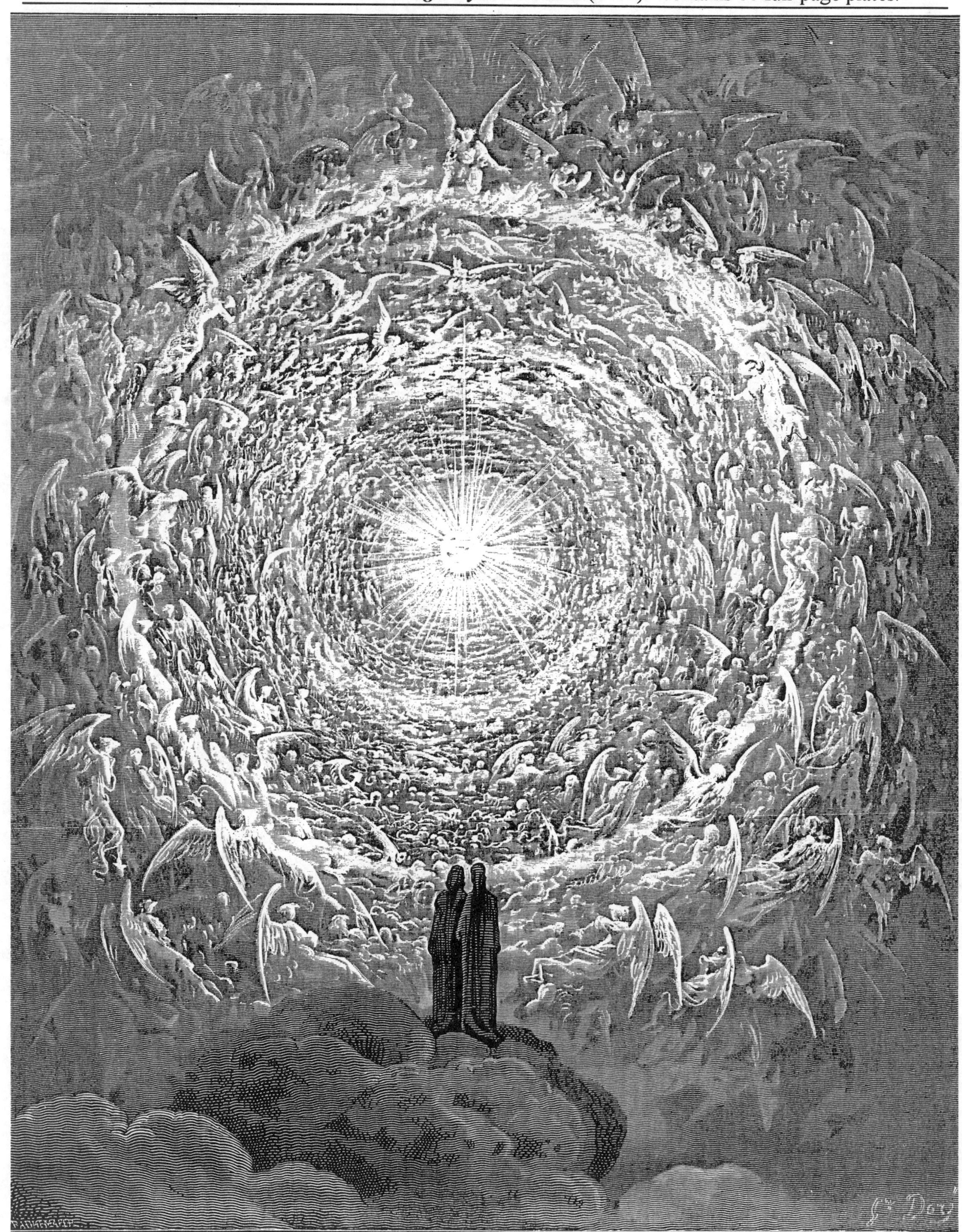

This had to be one of the earliest instances (1867) of offering both photogravures and engravings. It allows you to compage the original art to the engraving. We see thousands of old engravings, but how often do we know how engravings compare to original art? Also, since the engravings are dated, we can compare the printing dates to the publishing dates. Here are the engraving printing dates compared to the title page dates for the four ***Tennyson*** stories and ***Hood***:

Elaine	December 1, 1866	1867
Vivien	December 2, 1867	1867
Guinevere	December 2, 1867	1867
Enid	November 1, 1868	1868
Hood	November 20, 1869	1870

Each title had nine steel engravings. Steel engravings give more of a speckled look to the scenes, different from the grainy look of wood engravings. It makes for a serene, dreamy, mystical look that is a little different for Doré. Some of them make you feel like you are floating through time and space, peering down on characters and scenes below. ***Elaine*** came out in December of 1866 to rave reviews. The book version was priced at only 21s, less than most Cassell Doré folios, but these Moxon folios had so few engravings. The portfolio with the photogravures was 63s, and the proofs were 105s. The books and portfolios were 12½x17, and the proofs were 21x28. The portfolios looked just like the book editions, but when you opened the cover, all the pages inside were loose. Since Moxon did not have an American office, they contracted with Cassell to publish and distribute an American edition, but only the regular book edition. But major problems quickly developed between Moxon and Cassell, due in part to the facsimile of a handwritten letter from Tennyson which appeared only in the Cassell edition:

> *Oct. 28th / 66*
>
> *Gentlemen,*
>
> *My publishers inform me that they have arranged with you for the exclusive publication in America of Elaine with the steel plate engravings of M. Gustave Doré.*
>
> *As the publishers of M. Dorés other works in America you seem to have the prescriptive right to the publishing of this.*
>
> *I trust it to you with confidence & a hope (if I may judge from the past success of my works in America) that this arrangement will fulfill your expectations.*
>
> *I have the honour to be, Gentlemen,*
> *Your loyal servant*
>
> ***A. Tennyson***
>
> *Messrs. Cassell, Petter & Galpin*

Moxon must have felt that Cassell was trying to upstage him with the letter. Moxon did not have any congratulatory letter from Tennyson in their edition. Notice that Tennyson does not even mention the name Moxon, and he seems almost too complimentary to the publishing firm that was Moxon's major rival. Behind the scenes, Tennyson was having a major falling out with Moxon, and a few years later he would leave them altogether. Also, in Cassell's December 1866 British parts edition of ***Don Quixote,*** they mentioned that they were publishing the Doré edition of ***Elaine***, and they listed a British price! That certainly made it appear that British customers could purchase Cassell's U.S. edition. Twelve months later, when it came time for the U.S. edition of the next two Doré ***Tennyson*** folios, Cassell was completely out of the picture. G.Routledge became Moxon's U.S. publisher. You can just see Moxon saying, "so much for Cassell's prescriptive right."

Some critics have claimed that Tennyson did not like the Doré engravings. This is based on early articles in publications like ***The Athenaeum***, who just despised the Doré ***Tennyson*** illustrations. Their attacks on Doré were quite personal, as in December 21, 1867 (p.844-45): "We suspect, indeed, that M. Doré has never read Tennyson, and never thought of Tennyson while engaged upon his work." In 1876, eight years after Doré had finished ***Tennyson***, ***The Athenaeum*** was still ranting and raving, on February 19 (p.271-272): "It was a misfortune for artist and poet that they were thus brought together." But the quote usually referred to by Doré critics is in the Tennyson biography by his son Hallam in 1897, describing the visit by Tennyson to Doré in Paris, as a friend recalled (V2 p.77): "We were much pleased with the good Doré, although Tennyson had not been entirely satisfied with the publication of the folio edition of the *Idylls*, which Doré illustrated." But a recent book by Peter Levi: ***Tennyson*** (1993) sheds more light on the issue. It turns out that for all the laudatory remarks made about the 1857 ***Tennyson*** illustrations by the Pre-Raphaelites, published by Moxon, that they were not popular with the public or Tennyson himself. Levi points out that it was one of the many events that led up to Tennyson eventually breaking off with Moxon completely (p.256):

> The ghastly "Illustrated Edition" by various Pre-Raphaelite hands was already a cause of anxiety, because it was intended as a Christmas book but failed to appear until the following May, and then sold badly. There were 10,000 copies, and halfway through July Moxon had sold 1300 and was still smiling, but six years later, when half the edition was sold off to Routledge, total sales had amounted only to 2210.

Tennyson's relations with Moxon were deteriorating all through the 1860s. Their relations were so bad it is amazing that they were ever able to pull off the Doré editions. Notice in the above Hallam quote that it did not say that Tennyson was unhappy with Doré's engravings; it says he was unhappy with the publication of the Moxon editions. Tennyson was so unhappy with Moxon that about two months after Doré's edition was finished, he left Moxon and went to the publisher Strahan. Moxon was then going bankrupt, and had lost the rights to Tennyson's works, but Moxon continued to market

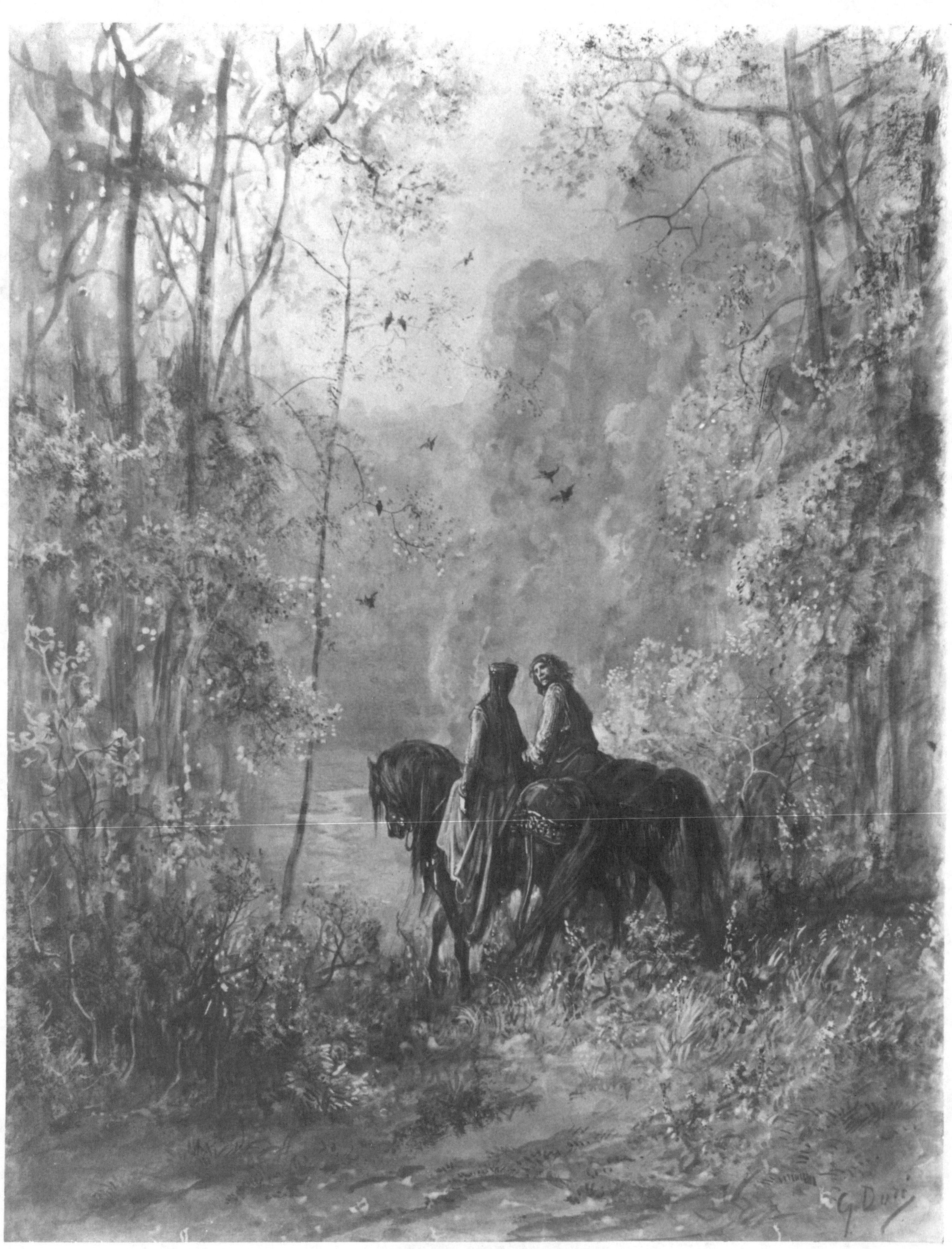
G. Doré

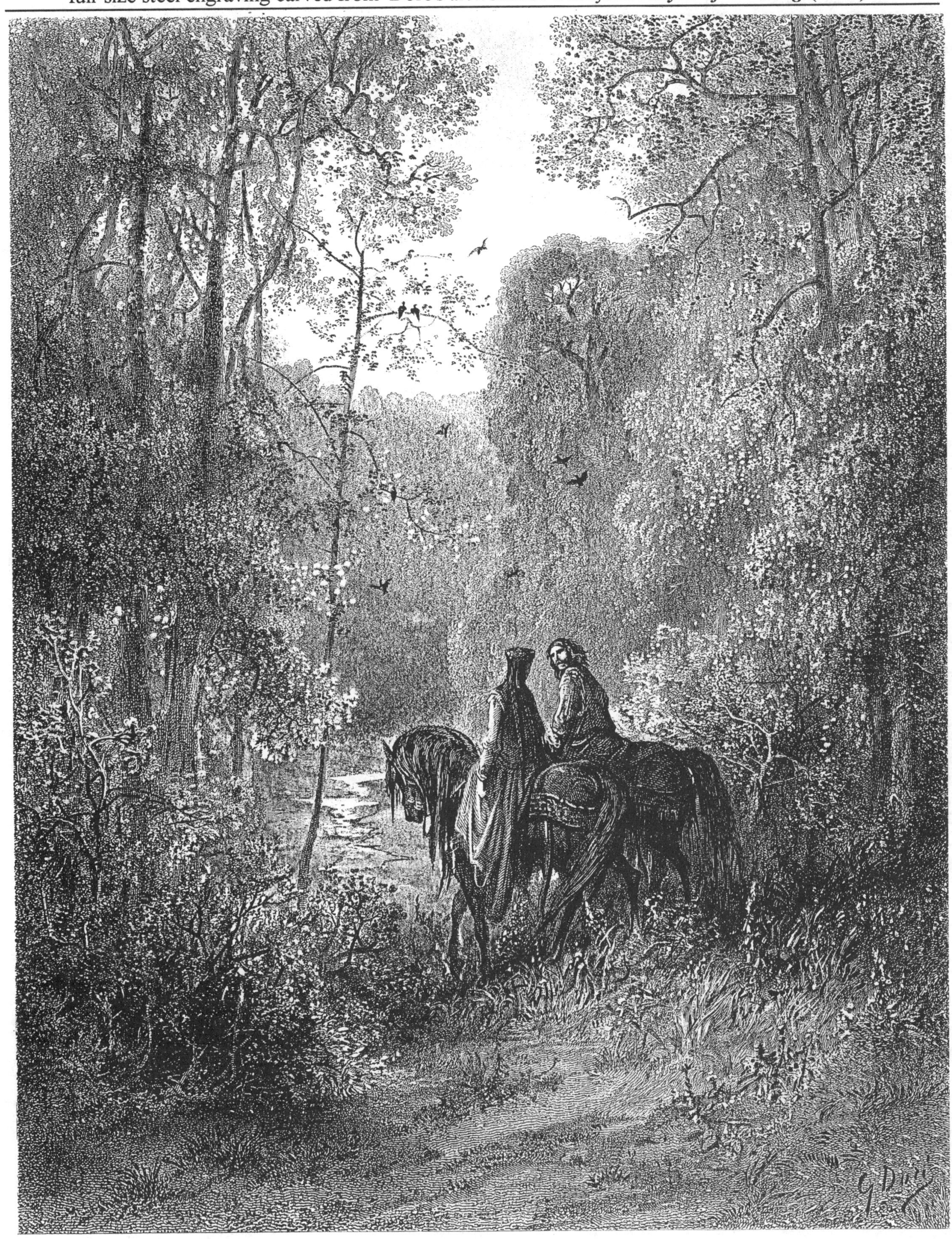

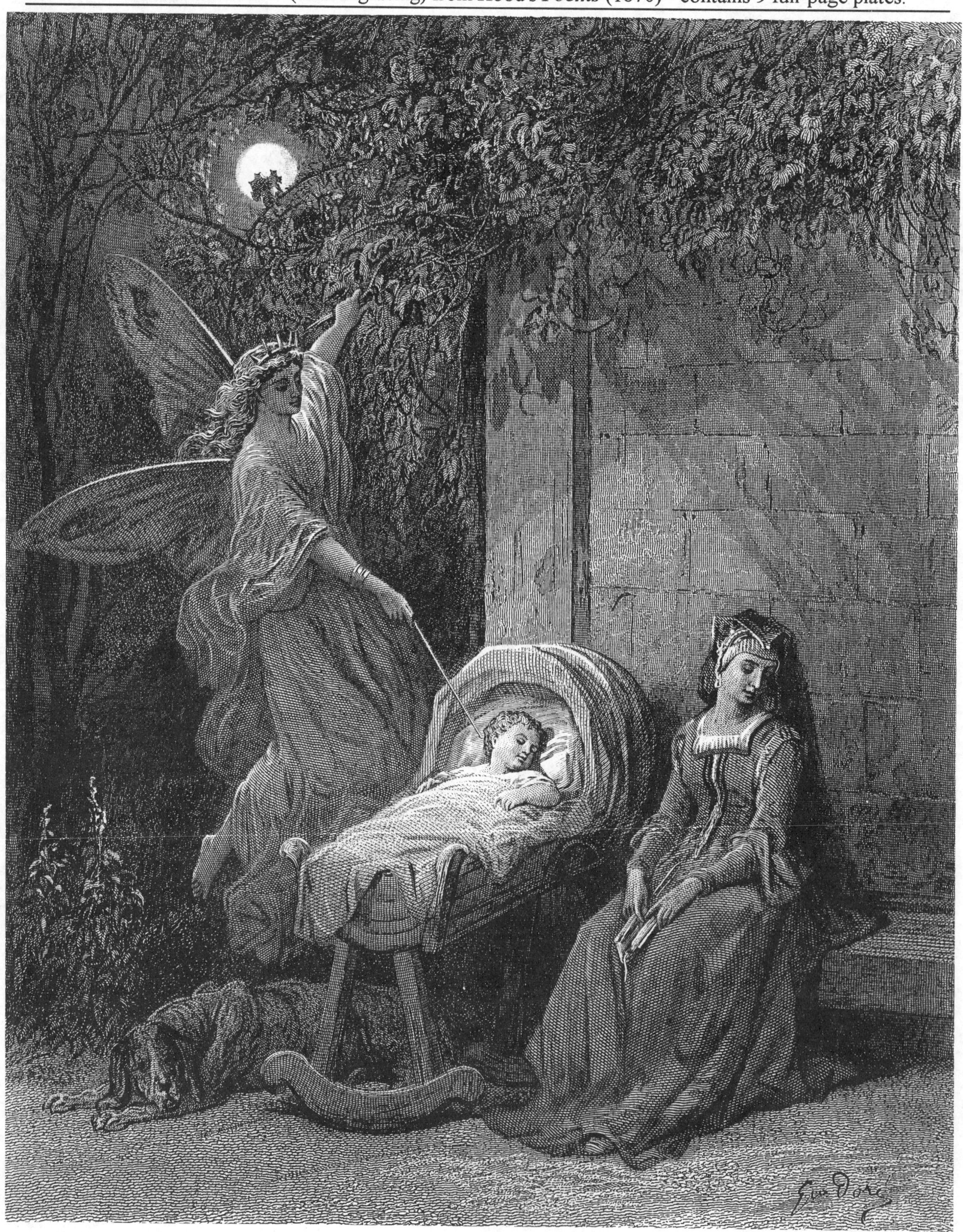

the Doré illustrations by entitling editions things like ***Doré's Illustrations to Tennyson***. Finally in 1880, Moxon gave up completely and sold the rights to Ward, Lock. So what did Tennyson actually think of Doré? Levi points out (p.6 & 249):

> ...The laureate hated most of his illustrators, though he was polite to Doré and did no worse than grunt about Tom Hughes... His anger over the illustrated poems (ed.note: the 1857 edition) should be set off against his warm admiration (with a few exceptions) for what Doré did for him: he was surely right to admire those four tall, stately volumes.

So the real point in Tennyson's letter to Cassell was that there was no way he would write such a letter to Moxon. But for those who criticize Doré and praise the 1857 edition by the Pre-Raphaelites, they do not mention that Tennyson's attitude was exactly the opposite of theirs. So it does not mean much to take a Tennyson statement open to several interpretations and claim it to be a blanket rejection of Doré, when all the documentary evidence points in other directions. It is true that Doré did make a couple technical errors in the ***Tennyson*** illustrations, such as an incorrect coat of arms and a detail about a boat riding too high on the water, but what percent of the public either knew or cared about such details? These were very popular illustrations. What other set of illustrations to Tennyson has been reprinted 100 times?

But getting back to 1867, Moxon published two more ***Tennyson*** titles that year - ***Vivien*** and ***Guinevere***. Those were both rather thin volumes, so Moxon offered not only individual editions but a joint ***Vivien & Guinevere***. Then in 1868 they came out with ***Enid***, and at that same time they published a combined volume of all four stories as ***Idylls of the King***. In addition to the 36 engravings from the four stories, Doré provided a new frontispiece for the ***Idylls***, showing Tennyson with Arthurian characters around him. That edition not only had a main 1868 title page for ***Idylls***, but individual title pages for each of the four stories. That presents us with yet another mystery. There are two versions of that 1868 ***Idylls***, and the only difference is in the dates on those individual title pages. The "correct" version has all five 1868 title pages. But the other version has dates as follows: ***Idylls***-1868, ***Elaine***-1867, ***Vivien***-1867, ***Guinevere***-1868 & ***Enid***-1869. The inclusion of one 1869 title page means it must be a later printing. Since all combination editions have individual title pages, you can make any combination title you want by just binding those titles together. There is one edition that has an 1867 ***Elaine*** bound with an 1869 ***Enid*** into one volume.

After Moxon lost the rights to print Tennyson's texts, they began coming out with all kinds of strange editions, with text made up or arranged to facilitate Doré's engravings. They had editions with text by Sir Thomas Malory, editions with background on the Arthurian Legends by G.R.E. (Emerson), and one edition with the lengthy title: ***The Doré Gift Book of Illustrations to Tennyson's Idylls of the King***. Most of those editions are undated, but were advertised around 1878. The long title edition is often mis-dated as being 1868. Any edition listing G.R.E. is from the 1878-1880 period. Ward, Lock then took over with cheaper editions, which they advertised in publisher's catalogues up through 1884. In 1889 there was a U.S. pirate edition by Henry Altemus. About 1900, Putnam began publishing little 5½x7½ editions, but of high quality. They are cute little editions. Meanwhile, as early as 1871, U.S. publishers began adding a few Doré engravings to general editions of Tennyson's poetry. There were not many foreign-language editions. Hachette published French folios in 1867-69, but they were not reprinted. There were also German and Dutch editions. Spanish editions used different text by Don Jose Zorrilla y Moral, entitled ***Ecos de Las Montanas***.

The poetry of Thomas Hood (elder, the father of the Tom Hood who wrote the English text for Doré's ***Perrault*** and ***L'Epine***) was written between 1825-1845. Evidently Moxon switched to Hood in 1869 because they had lost the rights to Tennyson's works. Doré's engravings are okay, but the poems he was supposed to illustrate were so disjointed that they have little meaning as a set of engravings. Moxon offered them in the same variations, but within a couple years they reduced the engravings for inclusion in little pocket-size books of poetry (it was Moxon's Poets#7) with six of the nine original Doré illustrations, but almost all of Doré's detail is lost. While there are about 25 editions of ***Hood***, it is the only Doré folio for which there are no foreign editions, and most of the English editions are the little 5x7½ poetry books. But they kept using Doré's name. They issued a second small volume of ***Hood*** (Moxon's Poets #21), and listed Doré's name on the title page, even though it only contained one Doré illustration. That was called "Hood. Second Series." Sometime it is hard to tell from a listing whether it is the folio version or the little pocket-sized reduced version. Here is a simple way to tell the difference - the folio with nine full-size Doré engravings has 63 pages, the 5x7½ "first series" with six Doré reduced illustrations has 400 pages, and the 5x7½ "second series" with only one Doré reduced illustration has 475 pages.

We close this chapter with a quote from the first great U.S. illustrator, Felix O. C. Darley, who was famous for his western and literary illustrations. In 1867-68, Darley visited Europe and from his diary produced an illustrated 1868 book, ***Sketches Abroad with Pen and Pencil***, published by Hurd & Houghton. Darley met Doré in Paris on December 17, 1867:

> On Thursday evening, we went to a reception at the American Minister's, where we found the house filled with Americans. Doré the artist, was also there; a remarkably mild looking young man of thirty, or thereabout, his face exhibiting no indication of the vigorous genius for which his works are so remarkable.

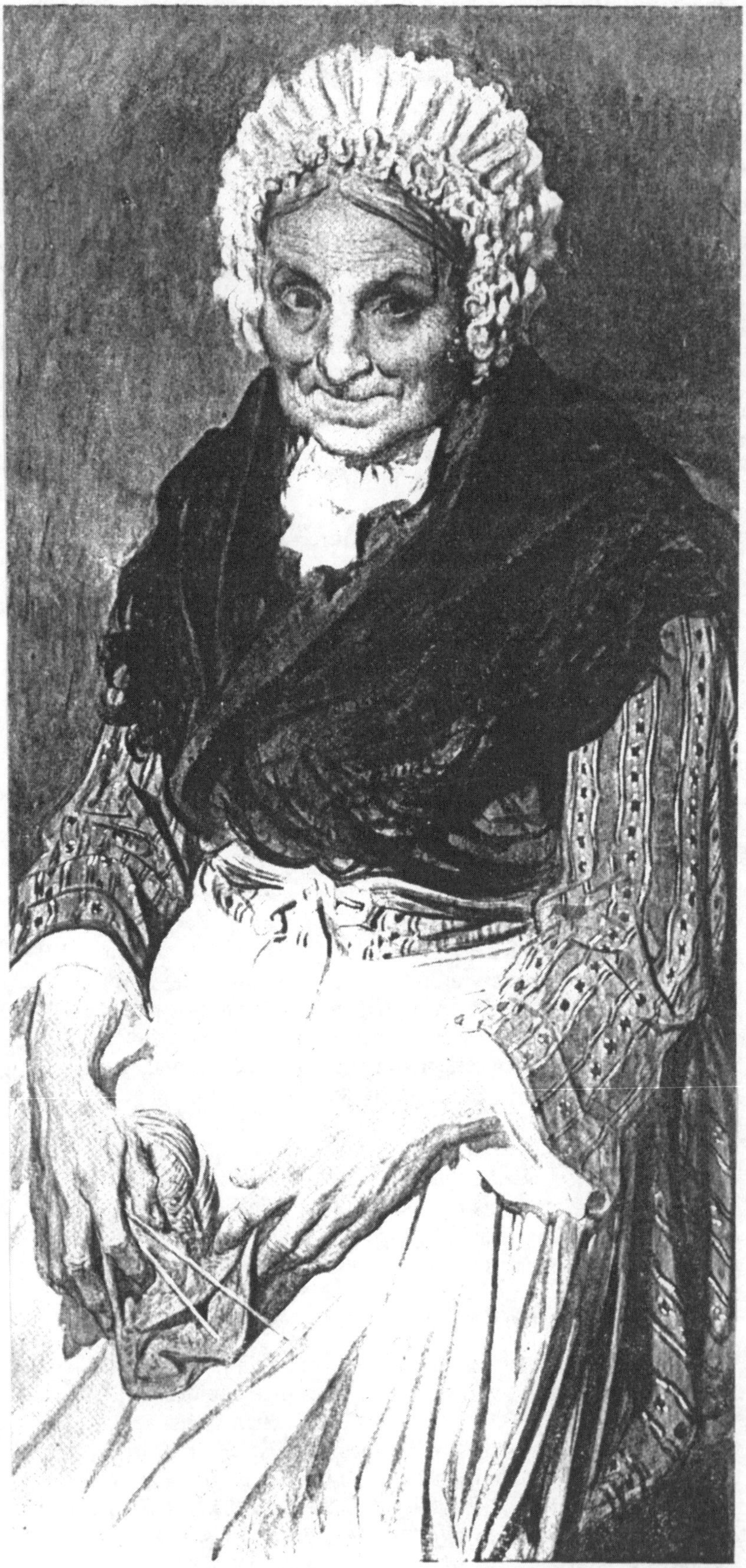

Doré watercolor paintings of his mother (1879) and his nurse Francois (1881)

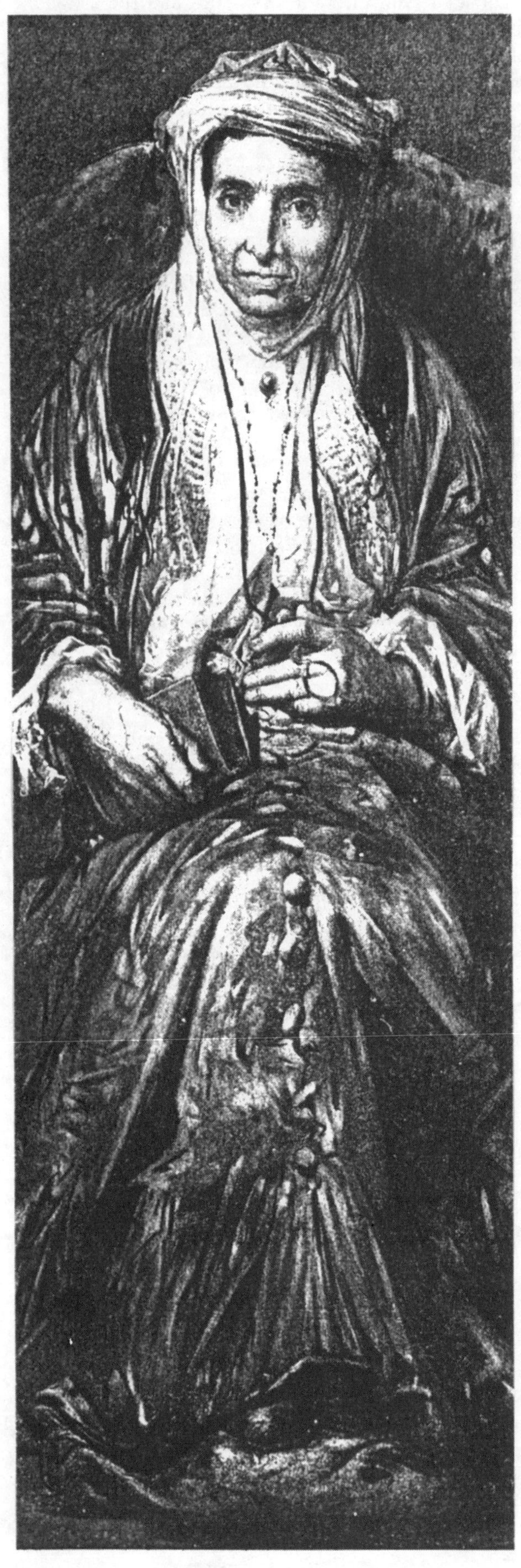

7. TO ALL THE GIRLS DORÉ LOVED BEFORE

In this chapter we will look at Doré romances with six famous women. This chapter has a specialized bibliography:

Bernhardt	=	Sarah Bernhardt: *Memories of my Life* (1968)
Cone	=	John F.Cone: *A.Patti, Queen-Hearts* (1993)
Courtesans	=	Joanna Richardson: *The Courtesans* (1967)
Dalmazzo	=	G.M.Dalmazzo: *Adelina Patti's Life* (1877)
Dolph	=	Chas.Dolph: *The Real Lady-Camellias* (1966)
Engel	=	Louis Engel: *From Mozart to Mario* (1886)
Ferris	=	George Ferris: *Great Singers* (1907)
Gautier	=	Judith Gautier: *Le Collier des Jours* (1909)
Gold	=	A.Gold/R.Fizdale: *The Divine Sarah* (1991)
Goncourt	=	Edmond/Jules de Goncourt: *Journal* (1956)
Holden	=	W.H.Holden: *The Pearl of Plymouth* (1950)
Horne	=	C.F.Horne:*Great Men/Famous Women* (1894)
Houssaye	=	Arnese Houssaye: *Confessions* (1970)
Jerrold	=	Blanchard Jerrold: *Gustave Doré* (1891)
Klein	=	Herman Klein: *The Reign of Patti* (1920)
Lauw	=	Louisa Lauw:*14 Years w/Adelina Patti* (1884)
Marie	=	Marie L.: *Reminiscences of G.Doré* (1893) (LC call # ND553.D7 H6-Print Div.)
North	=	A.North-Peat: *Gossip-Paris 1864-69* (1903)
Pearl	=	Cora Pearl: *Grand Horizontal* (1983)
Richardson	=	Joanna Richardson: *Gustave Doré* (1979)
Roosevelt	=	Blanche Roosevelt: *Gustave Doré* (1885)
Siedl	=	Anton Siedl: *Music of-Modern World* (1895)
Skinner	=	Cornelia Otis Skinner: *Madame Sarah* (1967)
Strasbourg	=	(Doré exhibition book-Strasbourg) (1983)
Vaudoyer	=	J.L.Vaudoyer: *Alice Ozy* (1930)
Woon	=	Basil Woon:*The Real Sarah Bernhardt* (1924)
Weinstock	=	Herbert Weinstock: *Rossini-Biography* (1968)

Besides romantic interests, there were other important women in Doré's life. Much more important than any romance was his relationship with his mother (Alexandrine Doré). For almost all of the 51 years of his life, Doré slept but a few feet away from his mother. He literally could not live without her. Roosevelt and Jerrold both contain extensive references to the amazing bond between mother and son, and out of respect for Doré speak in glowing terms about his mother. But the level of emotional domination was almost incestual. Primarily because of it, he never grew up. How long can you go on in life being a playful child, just because mother nods approvingly? In the last decade of their lives, when the harsh realities of life were too much for him, all she did was reinforce his paranoia. At some point, someone needed to smack Doré in the face and say, "Get a life! Stop acting like a baby just because French art critics will not accept you as a painter. Thousands of painters would give anything to trade places with you. How can you be so unsatisfied with so much? If the French are so mean to you, why not move to England, marry some sweet young Victorian virgin, start a family, and forget about the French art critics." After she died in 1881, he no longer had the will to live.

A far more sympathetic figure was his nurse Francoise. Toward the end of Doré's life he painted large watercolor portraits of his mother and Francoise. Francoise was the epitome of unselfish devotion. She told Roosevelt that Doré was practically born in her arms and died in her arms. Oh how quickly those 51 years must have gone by for her. I cannot get out of my mind the scene of Blanche Roosevelt visiting the aged Francoise who is all alone after Doré's death, and she is dusting but has no idea why, as though Doré might come back.

Doré never married and never had any children. He could not marry while his mother was alive. It was said that shortly before his death, he was talking about getting married, but we are never told to whom. Another mystery. One thing that was not a mystery was his attitude toward children. He loved them, nay, adored them. One such reference is in Roosevelt (p.285):

> For many years he spent his New Year's Day at the foundling hospital, whither he carried presents of toys, money, and clothing to the poor little waifs whom fate had cast adrift on the fair but barren shore of Parisian life. He used to get up before the break of day and take carriage load after carriage load of presents to all the children's asylums in his neighborhood. He would distribute the toys himself, sit by the infants' tiny cots, and amuse them until from those accustomed haunts of suffering shouts of baby laughter arose. He told them Bible stories, and fairy legends, tales of angels and nymphs, of giants and pigmies; he helped them to eat their bonbons, set their skip-jacks in motion, wound up their locomotives and spun their tops for them. He entered into their joys and sorrows; in short he was one of them, and there was not a thought or feeling within the range of babyhood's fancy which did not awaken a responsive echo in his own breast.

Doré was not without a host of female admirers. He was wealthy, famous, handsome, charming, and kindhearted. Not one of his amours ever wrote one negative word about him. Two of his famous lovers left him to marry other men, but both of those marriages were very unhappy. The other thing that is not mentioned in their writings about Doré is one word about his mother. In 1860s Paris, everyone knew that if you invited Doré, he would be the life of the party. Theophile Gautier's daughter Judith was very fond of Doré, and she mentioned him often in her memoires, such as the following amusing incident (Gautier, p.185-86):

> His childish face with its pink and white complexion, fine moustache and long blond hair combed well back, hid, beneath an impassive countenance, a mischievousness which was always ready to seize upon any occasion as the opportunity for some prank... Generally he made his entrance on his hands with his feet in the air.... (on one occasion) Doré carried his Machiavellian habits so far as to send (close friend Arthur) Kratz ... and only arrived himself after dinner ... when he organized experiments a la Robert Houdin, unearthed the most carefully hidden things, read sealed letters, guessed thoughts that were whispered far away from him ... he confounded and stupefied us. We did not suspect that Kratz, who seemed so detached, or so interested in a private conversation, was telling him aloud all he ought to know ... with the aid of words agreed in advance.

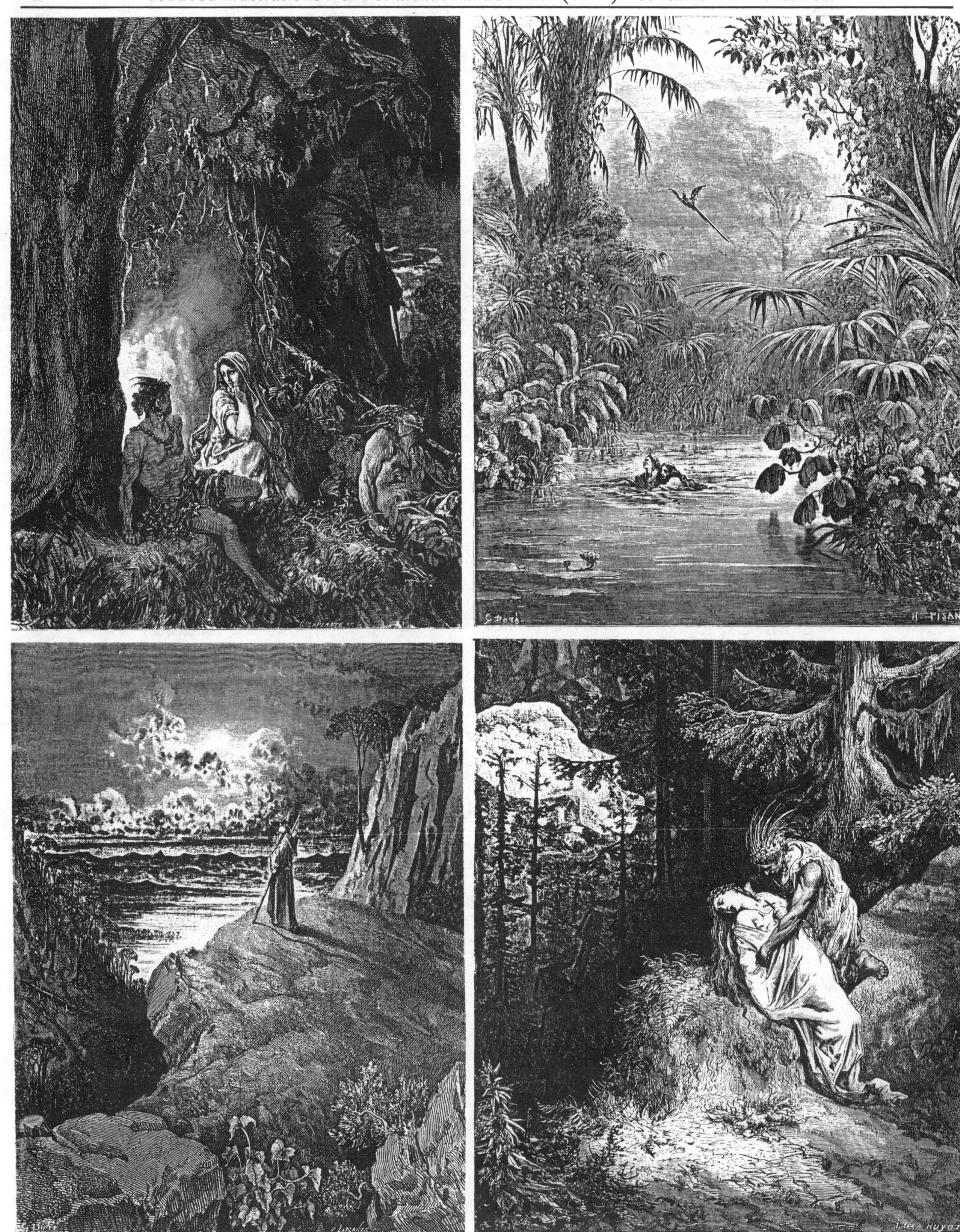

Many British women admired Doré but none could really be called romances. After Doré died, Amelia Edwards wrote a major article of personal reminiscences of Doré in ***The Art Journal***. Doré biographer Blanche Roosevelt was such a big fan of Doré that her work is usually described as "gushing." Lady Warwick drew a very nice portrait of Doré, and he was warmly received by Queen Victoria and the ladies of her court. But Doré could not seem to get romantically interested in English women. He thought of them as just friends. But there was one other girl, a French girl, with whom Doré was in love, not included amongst these six romances because we are never told her name. Doré fell in love with a Parisian girl in 1851, as related by Paul Lacroix to Roosevelt (p.288):

> When Gustave was about nineteen he fell desperately in love with the daughter of a gentleman in the Government service, and raved about her beauty from morning till night. I never knew any man so profoundly infatuated with a woman as he was with Mademoiselle X______. Nothing would do but he must marry her. He proposed for her to her father, and was immediately rejected. Monsieur's reply was not unamiable, but extremely matter-of-fact. He told Gustave that he wished his daughter to marry a rich man. His words were these, as nearly as I can remember:--
>
> "You are a young man of whom everyone speaks well, one who *possibly* has some prospects before him as a draughtsman. I do not doubt your talent, but your future is uncertain. That of my daughter, must be secure; and I wish to give her to one who has a settled position."
>
> He little dreamt then of the name and fortune "the draughtsman" would so soon make for himself! Gustave was utterly stunned by the refusal, and vowed that he could never love another woman, that he would kill himself, and I don't know what besides. For my part I think he was lucky to have met with such a father and daughter; for the girl of eighteen who preferred a secure position to a charming young lover with a fine future before him, could have been no fit wife for a man like Doré. I therefore congratulated him on his escape.

Alice Ozy (*Julie-Justine Pilloy*) (1820-1893)

This was Doré's only romance with an "older woman." It was in the early 1860s, and was his first serious romance and her last. Alice Ozy was an actress/courtesan who had retired from the stage in 1855, and so at the time of their affair, she was just a courtesan. A courtesan is rather difficult to explain today, but for that French generation it was an elitest way of life. We would call a courtesan a prostitute, but it was more than that. Prostitution was legal in France at that time, and in 1864 it was claimed that in Paris alone there were 4000 registered artists, 30,000 registered prostitutes, and 100,000 unregistered prostitutes, in a city of under two million people. There was a great deal of government corruption and moral decay under Napoleon III. But there were also many legitimate people like Doré who became wealthy through honest industry. It came about that the mark of the male Parisian elite was to engage the services of a courtesan. With so many prostitutes available, the elite began to divide them into levels, to avoid low-class prostitutes. The elite prostitutes who rose to the top of the social ladder formed the courtesan class - part whore, part mistress, part socialite. Courtesans were condemned by legitimate upper class women, who were the wives of the men who frequented the courtesans. Early on, courtesans were still excluded from all dignified gatherings. But on one (in)famous day, a courtesan went to such a gathering and began mingling with men she knew. The other women sent an attendant to demand that she leave, but she refused: "I may not belong with these women, but I do belong with these men." With that the dam burst and soon you could not tell a princess from a whore, literally. The elitest men who allowed it all to happen thought they were having quite a party in life, with the wife and kids at home, plus an limitless stream of high-class whores at their beckon. But the party was short-lived. France's leaders were drained of moral resolve, and in the Franco-Prussian War of 1870-71, the leaders cared more about their whores than they did about their soldiers. France (including Paris) was crushed and the courtesan way of life died with it. Then some of those same men put on the airs of moralists, and by the 1880s, it was fashionable to denounce former courtesans in very personal terms. The 1883 book, ***The Pretty Women of Paris***, contained this description of a former courtesan, Caroline Letessier:

> She was one of the queens of prostitution some 15 years ago, and when she passes in her carriage, a fearful wreck, we are forced to ask how it is that she could have accumulated the riches she possesses, for she is very ugly and has always been so. A pair of watery, moth-eaten, red-rimmed eyes; a big nose, with gaping nostrils ...; a bumpy forehead; her skin rough and pimply, cracked by the use of doubtful paint; her face shining with glycerine when at home, and covered an inch thick with red and white at night - such are the ruins of the whore of the Empire...

Out of 130,000 prostitutes there were probably less than 100 true courtesans, who migrated from one wealthy patron to another, or had several at a time. But for the dozens who were the cream of the crop, it was very lucrative. A greedy, ruthless courtesan could reduce a millionaire to a pauper in a matter of months. But most courtesans spent it as quickly as they took it in. The courtesan lifestyle came to compete with royalty in terms of clothing, jewelry, horses, and carriages.

Most courtesans were barely out of childhood when they entered their "profession." Alice Ozy, born Julie-Justine Pilloy was abandoned by both parents when their marriage fell apart. At the age of 13 her beauty changed her life, when she was seduced by the shop owner where she was employed. Then a young actor saw her and wisked her away to become part of his lifestyle. She was fascinated with the stage, and soon learned that almost all actresses were courtesans, and the purpose of being an actress was so that wealthy men would see you. She first appeared in the theatre in 1840, and shortly thereafter her theatre company was summoned by King Louis-Philippe for a command performance, where the King's 19-year-old son, the Duc d'Aumale fell madly in love with her. Overnight she joined the top rank of courtesans. The next two decades saw a parade of Parisian luminaries through her boudoir. The young

94 (top row) photo of Alice Ozy, Chasseriau sketch of Ozy, Doré marble ***Madonna*** at Ozy's grave.
(bottom row) photo of Christine Nilsson; engraving from photo of Hortense Schneider.

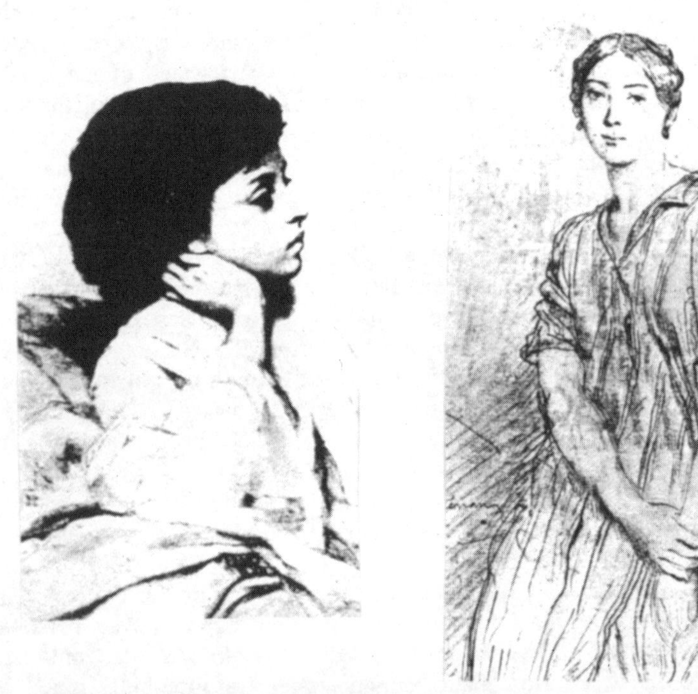

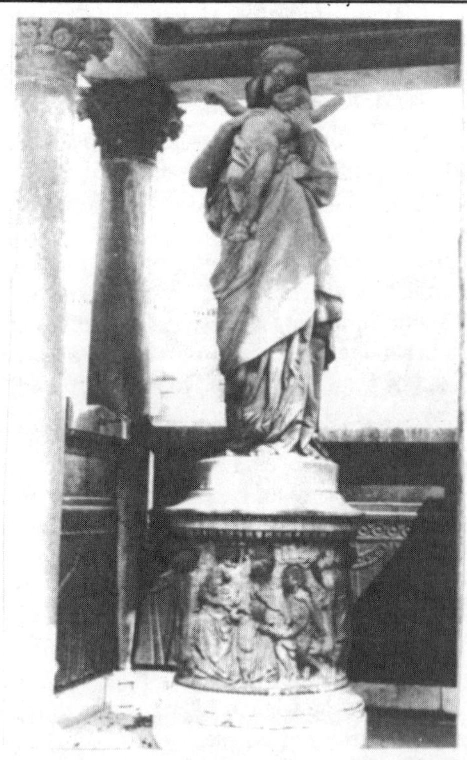

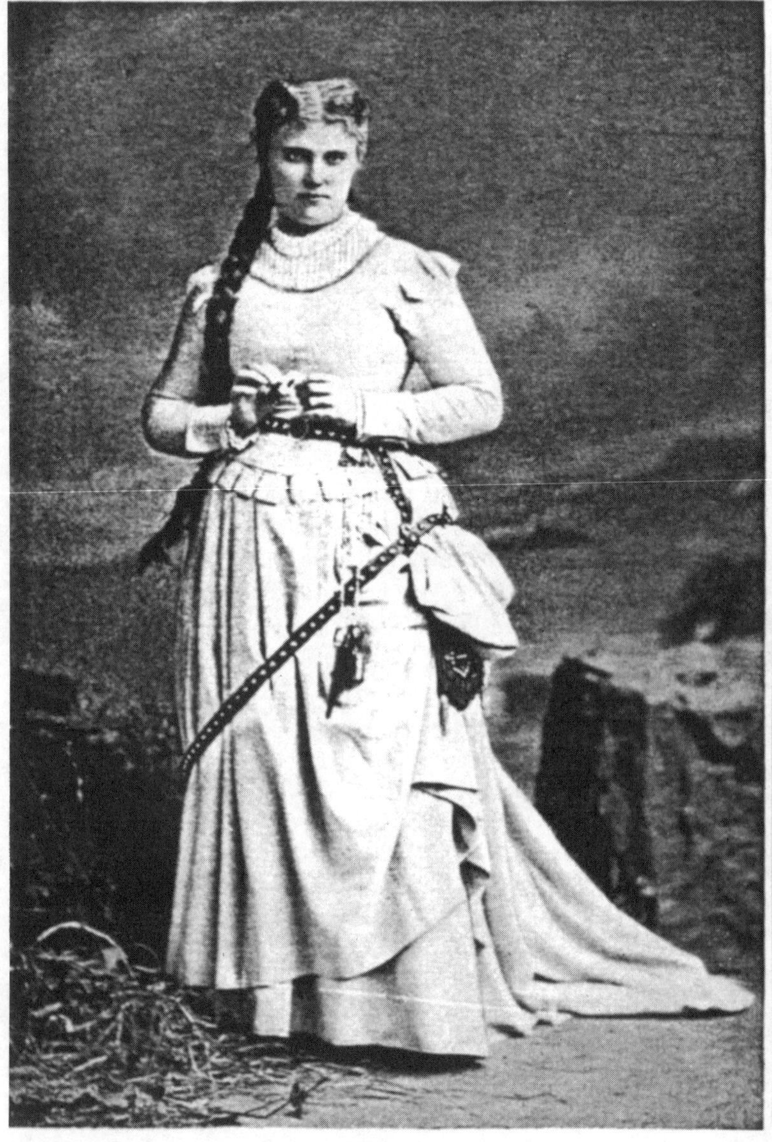

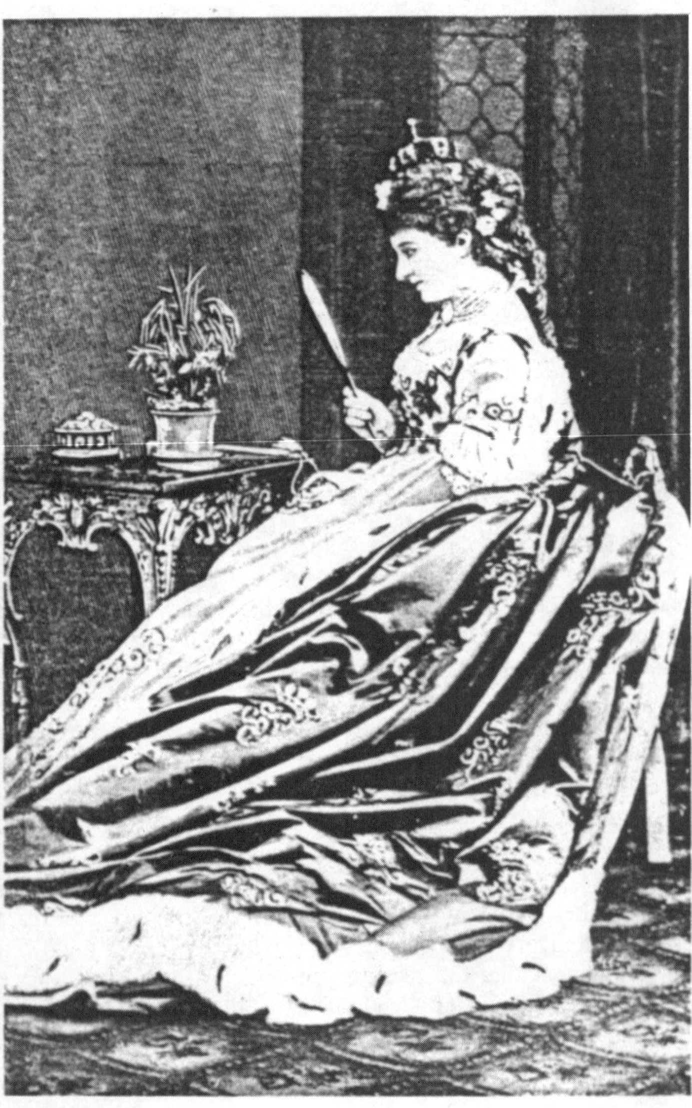

artist Theodore Chasseriau immortalized her in his 1850 nude painting, ***Baigneuse Endormie***. She attracted the literary elite from Theophile Gautier to Edmond About. But she was most famous for having turned down Victor Hugo. She was having an affair with his son at the time, and somehow felt that taking on Victor would be incest. By the time she took on Doré, she was over 40, and knew her days were numbered. She was one of the more practical courtesans; she asked for stocks rather than jewels. She was by then very wealthy, and their romance was mellow, closer to friendship than passion. After a couple years they parted, but remained friends. Alice then lived 30 more lonely years, with great wealth but few friends. She "outlived her happiness." In her will she gave 3,000,000 *fr* to charity. One other stipulation in her will was to have a Doré work of sculpture on her tomb in the Pere-Lachaise cemetary in Paris. They selected his white marble ***Madonna & Child***.

Hortense Schneider (1833-1920)
Christine Nilsson (1843-1921)

There are few details about these two romances. It is hard to pinpoint when they took place. They could have been in the mid-1860s or early 1870s. Reference books refer to rumors about Doré pursuing these two ladies, mainly from newspaper accounts, and Roosevelt included them in her book (p.289):

> By public report he had been successively betrothed and married to a great many female celebrities ever since his *Rabelais* set Paris talking about its young illustrator. At one time it was alleged that he was madly in love with Adelina Patti, and had threatened to kill himself in her boudoir; at another that his assiduities at the feet of Christine Nilsson had compelled the fair Swede to forbid him her house; again, that he adored Hortense Schneider, and I don't know whom besides.

All three of the women listed were opera singers. In fact, all six of the women in this chapter were on the stage. Little is known about the childhood of Hortense Schneider. The first anyone heard of her was in 1855 when she was a flower girl at Bordeaux. She later made her stage debut at the Athenee Threatre there. That exposure led her to become the mistress of the actor Berthelier, who took her to Paris. There he made the contact that would make her future - an engagement at the Bouffes-Parisiens, directed by the king of comic opera, the composer Jacques Offenbach. He was quite pleased with her talent for comic opera, and as Offenbach's popularity grew, she followed him from theatre to theatre. By the mid-1860s, she was considered the supreme interpreter of Offenbach. She had men flocking after her in droves. She was known as "the pathway of kings" because of her international following, which included the kings of Bavaria, Portugal, and Sweden, the Grand Duke Constantine of Russia, Bismarck, Moltke, etc. She was famous as a singer and a courtesan, but both of her specialty fields went out of fashion after the Franco-Prussian War. She then married a Mr. deBionne, and dropped out of the public picture for the last 45 years of her life. Any romance with Doré would have been either 1864-66 or 1871-72.

Christine Nilsson was the youngest of seven children, born in a little peasant hut in the forest of the estate of Count Hamilton of Sweden. Three years later at a town fair, a judge named Tornerhjelm noticed a crowd gathered in the street. He pushed his way to the center of the commotion and could not believe his eyes - a tiny barefoot girl singing like an enchanted bird, and playing a borrowed violin. Yes, 3-year-old Christine Nilsson earned 3½ pence that day for her family. The judge was a music enthusiast and took Christine under his wing. She got the best musical training to be found in Sweden, and then was sent to Paris for further training. She could not decide between voice and violin, but at her first concert the audience's responce to her singing was so overwhelming that she set aside the violin. She made her London debut in 1866, and was considered the second best opera singer in the world (to Adelina Patti, whom we will cover shortly). Europe's royalty lavished expensive gifts on her, but she never forgot her roots. She paid back her benefactors for all they had done. On one occasion she was asked by nuns to sing at a school for poor girls. Shortly after she had agreed to that engagement, she was visited by a royal emissary from Queen Victoria, with an order for her to give a Court Concert at Buckingham Palace on that very same evening. Every singer dreamed of receiving such an order. What did she do? - per Engel (V2, p.320):

> She told Her Majesty's bandmaster that she was very sorry not to be able to accept the Queen's invitation for that evening, as she had an engagement which she could not evade; and that at any future opportunity she would be happy to receive Her Majesty's command, but that she could not sing at Court that evening.

When Queen Victoria learned the circumstances of the refusal, she immediately rescheduled, and was from then on one of Christine's biggest supporters. In 1870, Christine took an extensive tour of America, which brought her $200,000. In 1872, she married a French merchant, Auguste Rouzeaud. Unfortunately, he died a paralytic in 1882. She retired from opera in 1880 to care for him. In 1887, she married a Spanish nobleman, Count A. de Miranda, and took up residence in Paris. Her life was relatively free of scandal, despite all the men who pursued her. If there was a romance with Doré, it probably occurred in Paris prior to her 1866 London debut.

Adelina Patti (1843-1919)

These last three are the serious relationships, and all three of them wrote about Doré. Adelina Patti was the most popular singer of the 19th century. She gave concerts for over 60 years. It is unfortunate that by the time Patti made sound recordings, she was already in her sixties. Many people wrote about the quality of Patti's voice and the effect it had on audiences. Patti's life story is fascinating. There is an amazing number of similarities between Doré and Patti:

- both were astounding child prodigies, from the age of 5
- both began professional adult careers by the age of 16
- both had amazing natural talents which could not be taught
- both were spoiled because of their talent and early success
- both had great singleness of purpose from a very early age
- both were instinctively theatrical from a very early age

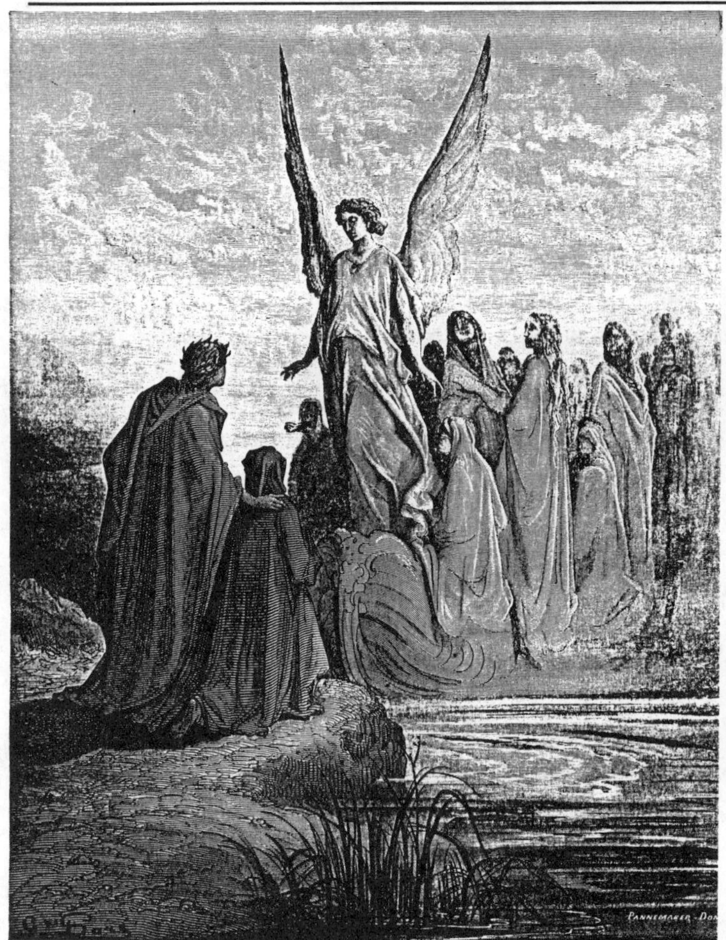

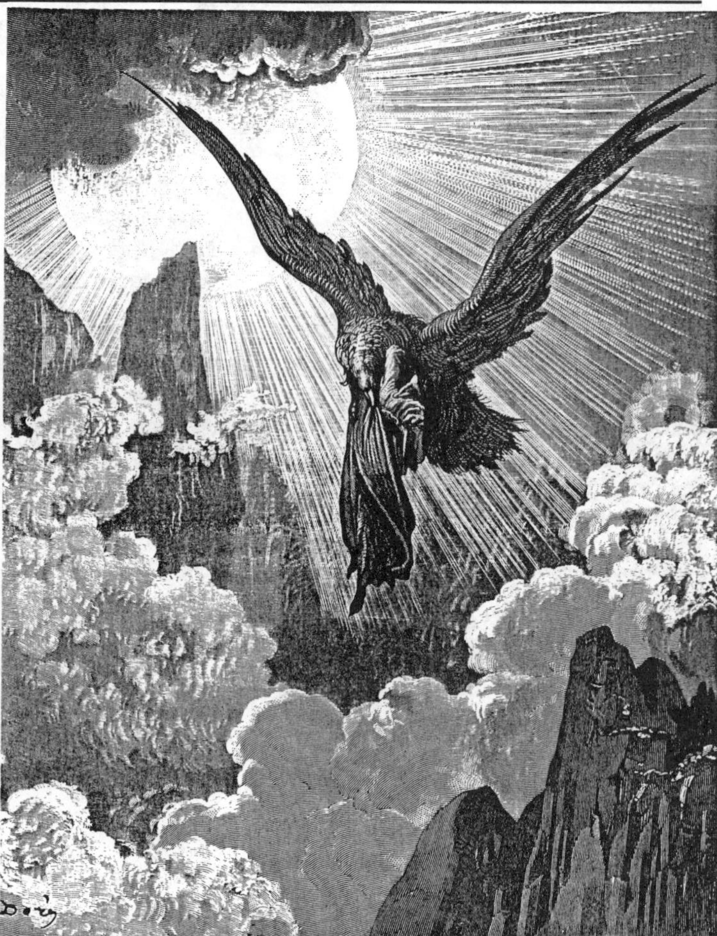

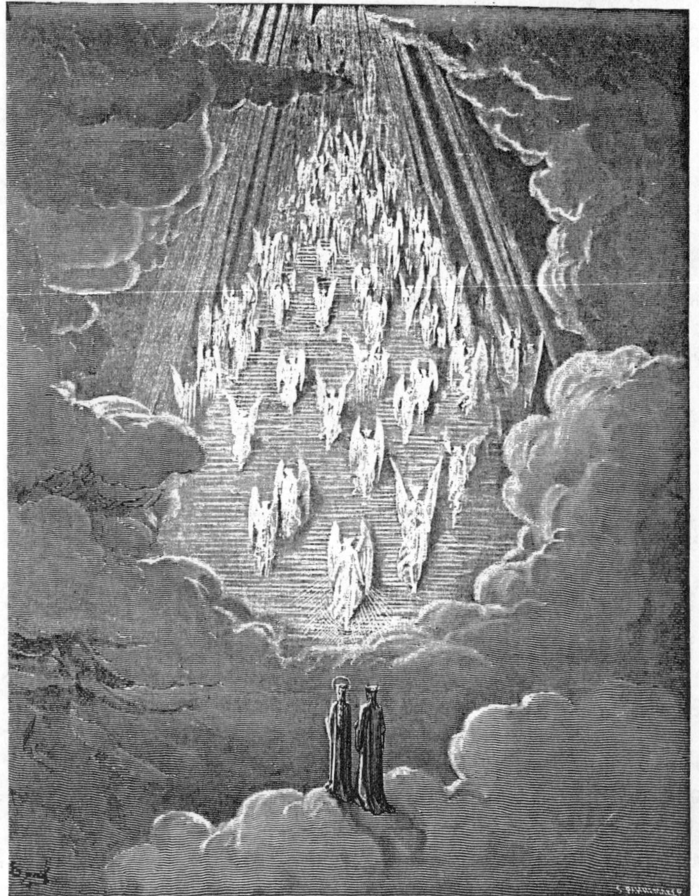

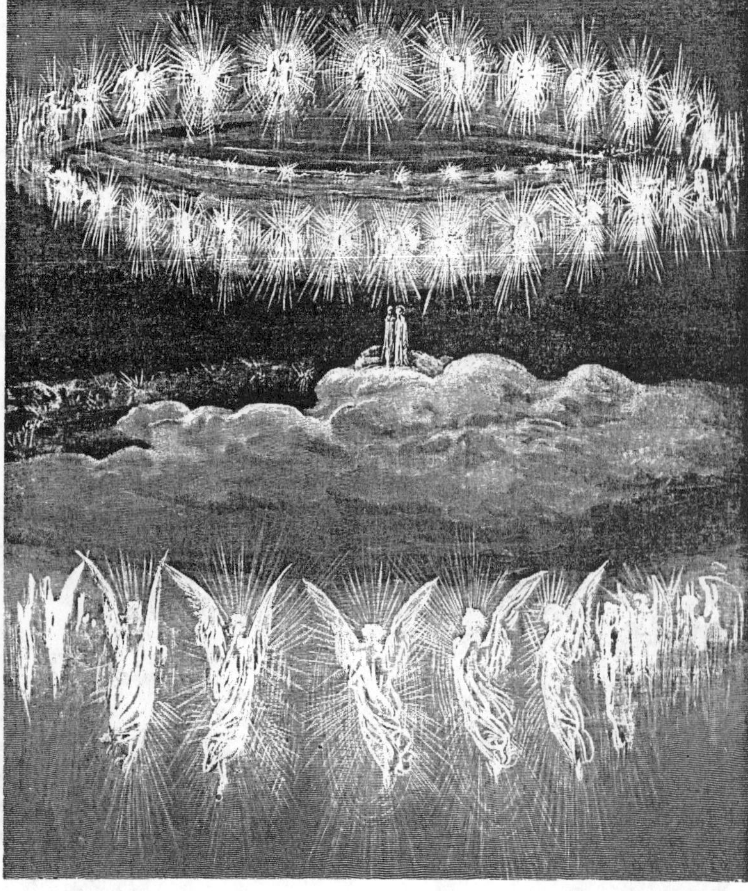

- both were involved in the artistic expression of literature
- both supported family (due to misfortune) at a young age
- for both, 1861 was the key year to their worldwide fame
- both were foreigners who took London by storm in the 1860s
- both were the highest paid in their profession in the world
- both had the most prolific professional output in the world
- both very close to Rossini and first met at his home in 1862
- both socially/culturally sophisticated but never had children
- both were distant from their same-sex parent, but close to & had their business managed by their opposite-sex parent
- both were largely forgotten by the 1920s

But there were also major differences in a few key areas:

- Patti's early success was due to her family's backing
- Patti's talent could only be experienced personally
- Patti was satisfied with being successful in one field
- Patti got married and became an independent adult
- Patti outlived Doré by 36 years

Patti's life reads like an operatic fairy tale. Her parents were Italian opera singers. They were touring Spain when she was born. Her mother went into labor with her while singing an opera. Their large family moved to America when she was three to "make their fortune," but both parents soon "lost their voices" and quickly faced poverty, having to sell household items to make ends meet. While her older siblings were taking voice and instrumental lessons, little Adelina played with her dolls and always went to hear her mother sing. Unbeknownst to them, late at night Adelina would line up her dollies as an audience and pretend to be an opera singer. One day when she was about five or six, a sister was having difficulty practicing trills. Adelina piped up with "Why don't you do it like this?" and then to their utter astonishment proceeded to execute a faultless trill. No one had paid attention to her as she went around the house singing. Soon after that, her parents finally decided to hear what she sounded like, per Klein (p.15-16):

> One day they thought they would make her go through a whole piece, and, in order to see her the better, they made her stand upon a table. She began without hesitation, not knowing the meaning of the word nervousness. They had no idea what she was going to sing. Imagine their wonder, not unmingled with amusement, when she started the long sustained note and "turn" that form the initial phrase of *Casta Diva!* It was to be nothing less, if you please, than that most exacting of arias - the noblest of Bellini's inspired melodies...

They immeditately began instrumental and voice training (primarily to extend her repertoire). No one taught her to sing, though years later many tried to take credit for it. Patti always said that her voice was "a gift from God." Besides lessons, they were eager for other musical professionals hear her sing, such as Luigi Arditi and Giovanni Bottesini, per Cone (p.23-24):

> Arditi and Bottesini noted the air of importance with which the tiny songstress first selected a comfortable seat for her doll in such proximity that she was able to see her while singing, and then, having said, *La, mon bonne petite, attends que ta Maman te chante quelque chose de jolie*, she demurely placed her music on the piano.
>
> Adelina's selection was not a child's simple song but the difficult aria *Ah! Non Giunge* from *La Sonnambula.* Upon its completion Arditi and Bottesini wept geniune tears of emotion, tears which were the outcome of the original and never-to-be-forgotten impression her voice made. After having heard her sing several other arias,... (they were) amazed, nay, electrified, at the well-nigh perfect manner in which she delivered some of the most difficult and varied arias without the slightest effort or self-consciousness.

The major topic of discussion in the family was when she should make her concert debut. The two people who directed her career were her father and her sister's husband, Maurice Strakosch. Finally, in November of 1851, at the ripe old age of eight, she climbed up on a table at Tripler's Hall in New York and knocked them dead. The next day the ***Tribune*** wrote:

> The peculiar feature of the evening was the debut of Adelina Patti, a mere child... yet a Jenny Lind in miniature, a petite nightingale, whose performance was indeed surprising. She sang the difficult and eccentric *Echo Song* with remarkable effect, and entirely astonished her audience not only by her powers of voice, but by the self-possession and ease which could not have been looked for in one so young.

When Adelina gave a concert, she was like a tiny adult. But the next day she was a little girl again, inviting playmates in to see all the flowers she had received. She gave a few more concerts that year, and then at the age of nine, began a concert tour. Here is how the tour began, per Klein (p.27):

> At the opening concert at Baltimore only 100 persons paid for their seats. But the 100 went away amazed - and talked. At the second concert the total rose to 300; and so the tale grew until, at the sixth, every seat had been sold before the doors opened. The room was capable of holding 2000 people, so the receipts mounted quickly and the prospects of the tour became very rosy indeed ... Strakosch came across an old friend, Ole Bull, the Norwegian violinist, who was also paying Baltimore a visit. For once the latter had noted a falling-off in business. "What is the cause?" he asked. "Little Miss Patti," they told him, the phenomenal child soprano. Ole Bull went to hear her, and instantly perceived that there would be wisdom in converting so powerful a competitor into a partner ... and the joint tour began without delay.

The tour lasted three years, covering the East Coast (even President Pierce attended) to Canada to St.Louis to Mexico to Cuba. By the time she was 11, she had earned $20,000 and eased all their financial problems. They even bought a house. But what a burden to put on a little girl's shoulders. She was often lonely and depressed. There are sad stories about how in the middle of a concert she would call out to little girls in the audience to come and play with her after the show.

 reduced illustrations from Tennyson's ***Idylls of the King*** (1868) - contains 37 full-page plates.

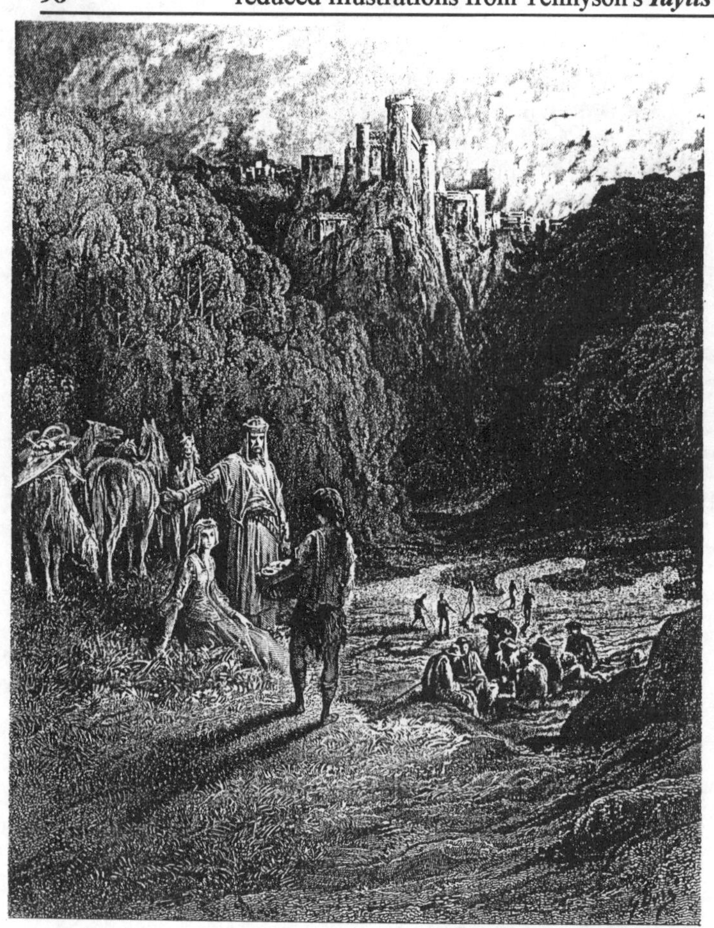

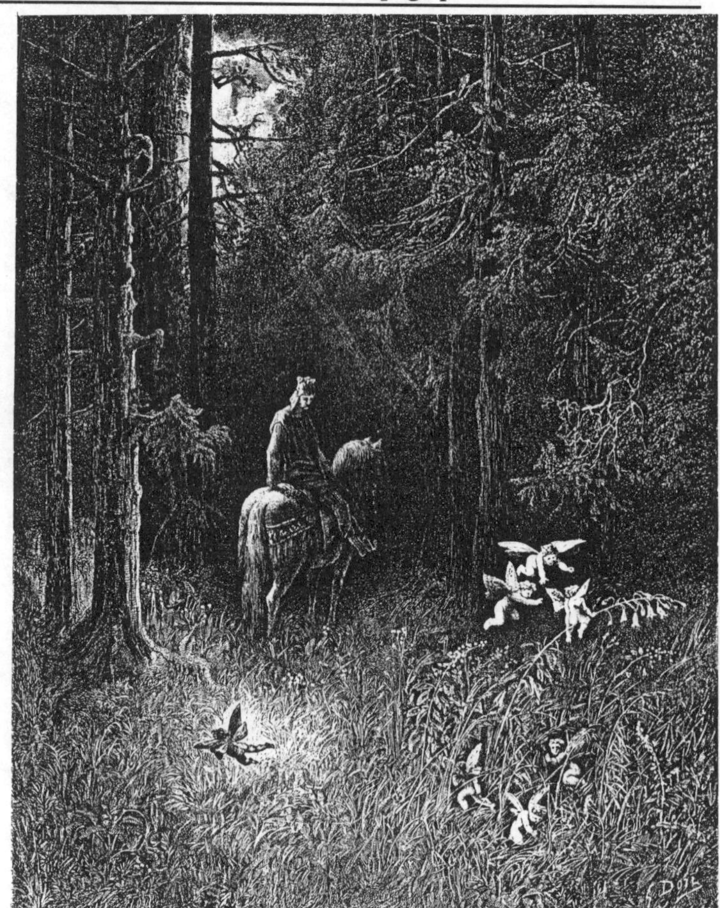

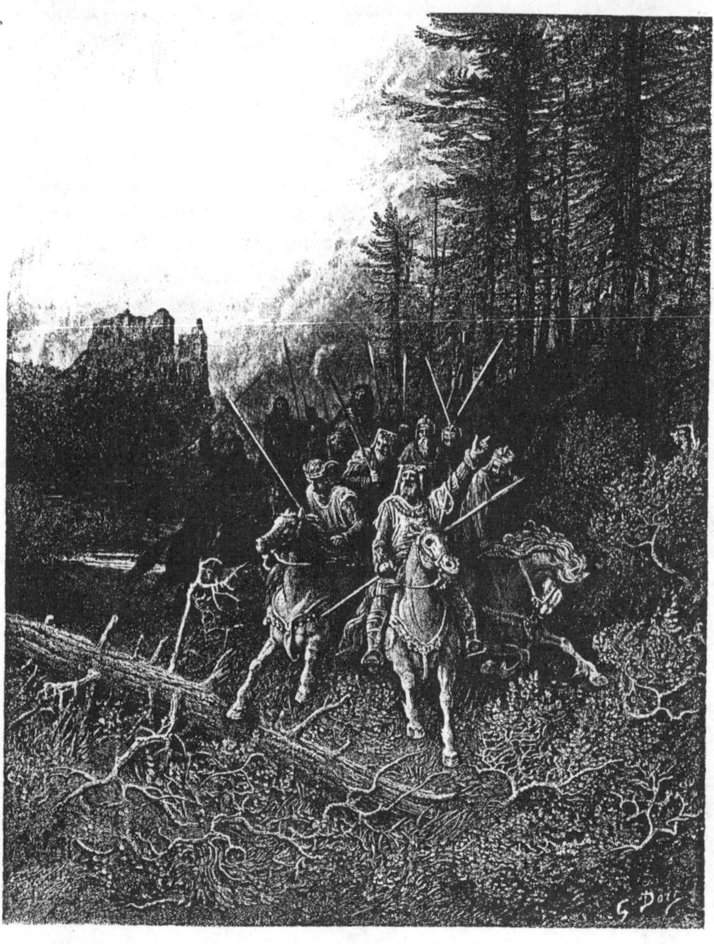

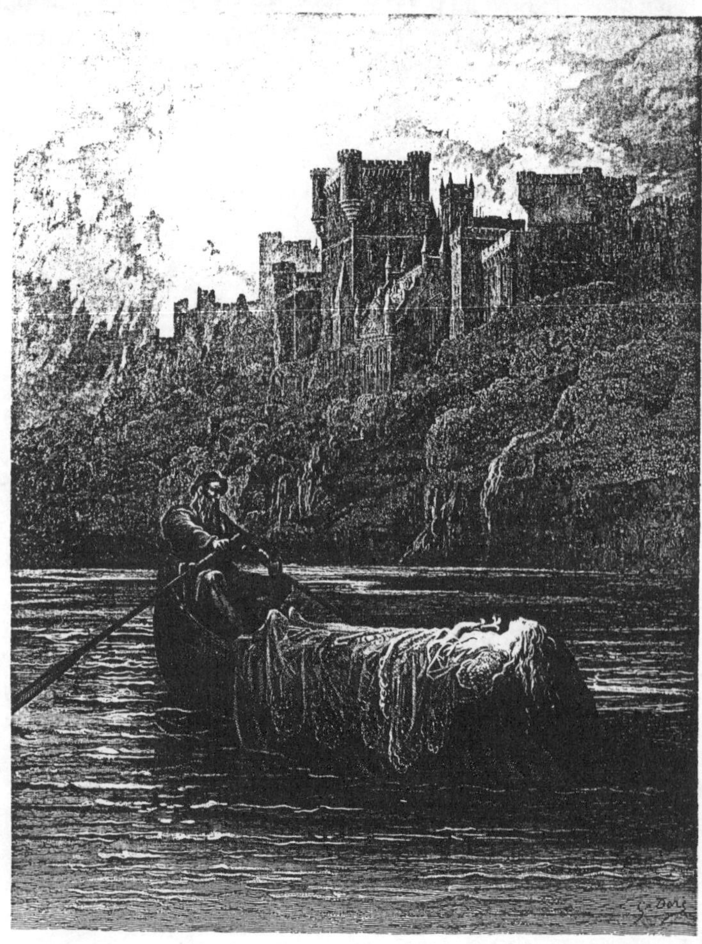

In 1854, after her tour had ended, Mario and Grisi, the king and queen of opera, came to New York to give a concert. Adelina went backstage after the show and gave them some flowers. Mario picked her up, kissed her cheek, and said, "I shall keep these always, little one, in memory of you." Seven years later Adelina would be starring opposite that same Mario in ***Romeo & Juliet***. But first the big issue when she would make her adult operatic debut. On November 24, 1859, she took her tiny little 16-year-old frame to the center stage of New York City's Academy of Music for the lead in ***Lucia di Lammermoor***. We will not bore you with endless stories of audiences going wild, for that became commonplace over the next 50 years. In reviews her name changed from Adelina Patti to Miss Patti to Mlle. Patti to Diva Patti to La Patti. She began another U.S. tour, getting $100 a performance. She was in Cuba when the Civil War started, so they left for England.

In 1861, most Brits still looked down their noses at U.S. culture, and Miss Patti's being praised in America meant very little to them. She finally got an audition with Frederick Gye of Covent Garden Theatre, but on such short notice that she had to agree to a rather one-sided contract. Patti would sing three performances for nothing, and if well-received, she would get $100 per performance the first year, up to $250 by the fifth year. One consolation was that her leading man would be none other than Mario. The date of her London debut was set for May 14, 1861. For the next 50 years, British music enthusiasts would brag about having been there that night. There was no advertising and little mention in the papers. Most attendees were there because it was an extra subscription night. When she walked out onto the stage she was greeted with frigidity. Why, this American stranger looked like a little girl (she had just turned 18). They were too shocked to applaud. The silence lasted only through her first song. It is a shame there were no recordings back then, because we can never really know why so many people described that night as the greatest musical event of the century. The audience, including the likes of Charles Dickens, went absolutely wild with joy. By the end of the evening, the reign of Patti had begun. The reception was so overwhelming that she barely made it back to her hotel room before she burst into tears. By the next afternoon every ticket for her next performance was sold out. The manager soon begged her to do extra performances for $500 per night. A month later, that little dark-eyed American nightingale was asked to sing at a State Concert at Buckingham Palace.

Almost overnight, Patti conquered Europe. Countries and their royalty fell before her, from France to Belgium to Holland to Germany to Austria to Spain to Italy to Russia. Kings and Emperors tripped over one another as to who could give her the most expensive diamonds, rubies, emeralds and pearls. One journalist, when asked what Patti's musical style could be compared to, wrote: "It is impossible to compare it to anything ever heard before; she resembles no one." Her Paris debut on November 16, 1862 followed the same pattern as her London debut. The sophisticated French were not impressed by what the unsophisticated British had to say about her. But their aloofness quickly evaporated, and again the audience went crazy. No audience could stand before her melodious charm. A few days later she was invited to a soiree at the home of the true musical king of Paris, Gioachino Rossini. At Rossini's party Patti so embellished her version of *Una voce poco fa* that Rossini asked her who had composed the song. She reluctantly informed him that the composer was himself. That celebrated squabble was short-lived, and they were close friends until he died. She also became close friends that night with a man who was the life of the party. His name was Gustave Doré.

The musical stir caused by Patti in Paris was similar to that a few years earlier when Rossini moved there. Paris saw ten years of Rossini's Saturday evening parties from December 18, 1858 to September 26, 1868. The Rossini biographers pointed out that Doré was in Rossini's inner circle and was one of the main souces of entertainment at his parties. Weinstock tells how Rossini introduced Doré to Giulio Ricordi (p.344): "M. Doré, whom the world believes to be a great draftsman, but who is in fact a great singer! ... and therefore my colleague too." In the same recollection by Ricordi, Weinstock points out that Doré often took part in the festive music at Rossini's (p.345): "Next, Gustave Doré sang a song; Rossini was right: Doré had a very beautiful baritone voice and sang with great taste and expression." Weinstock also wrote about Rossini's last birthday party (1868), when ten close friends had supper with him, and Doré gave a gift to Rossini's wife (p.352-353):

> As a souvenir of the occasion, Doré gave Olympe a fan that he had painted. On it, a bust of Rossini rose from a bed of greenery, with vines twined around five parallel lines of ribbon forming a musical staff. Numerous *amorini* were depicted as playing instruments among the foliage, their heads being placed in relation to the five ribbons so as to become the opening notes of Arnold's aria in *Guillaume Tell: O Mathilde, idole de mon ame.*

Rossini was very close to Doré and Patti, musically and emotionally. They were both there when he died, and Doré made two death-bed paintings of Rossini, and Patti sang at his funeral service. The year 1868 marked a major change in the "mood" of Doré's life. But let us remember the pleasant earlier days. Much of the information about Doré and Patti was from Lauw, Patti's travelling companion for 14 years (p.29):

> After Adelina had completed the season in London we returned to Paris, where we remained during the winter, and Adelina was again the "star" of the Italian opera. She had set apart her Sundays for her recreation and for reception evenings, in her house, and which became some of the most interesting in Paris. Christine Nilsson was seldom missing. The celebrated illustrator, Gustave Doré, counted among the most assiduous visitors of these Patti-evenings, in which with his masterly "jodlern" he delighted the entire company, and even made Adelina so unfaithful to her firmly declared resolution not to sing in private circles that, to the terror of Strakosch, she began bravely joining with him.

It is difficult to tell when Doré really fell in love with Patti. They were very close from 1862-1868. In 1862 Doré was probably still involved with Alice Ozy, and later on with either

Painted Fan given by Doré to Madame Rossini on Gioachino's 76th (& last) birthday - February 29th, 1868; the cupids form the opening notes to Arnold's aria in *William Tell* in celebration of its 500th performance.
oil painting of ***Rossini on his Death-Bed*** (1868) - now in the Conservatorio Rossini in Pesaro, Itay.
oval lithograph of Doré's side-view sketch of ***Rossini's Death Bed*** (1868) - sketch at Musee Carnavalet, Paris.

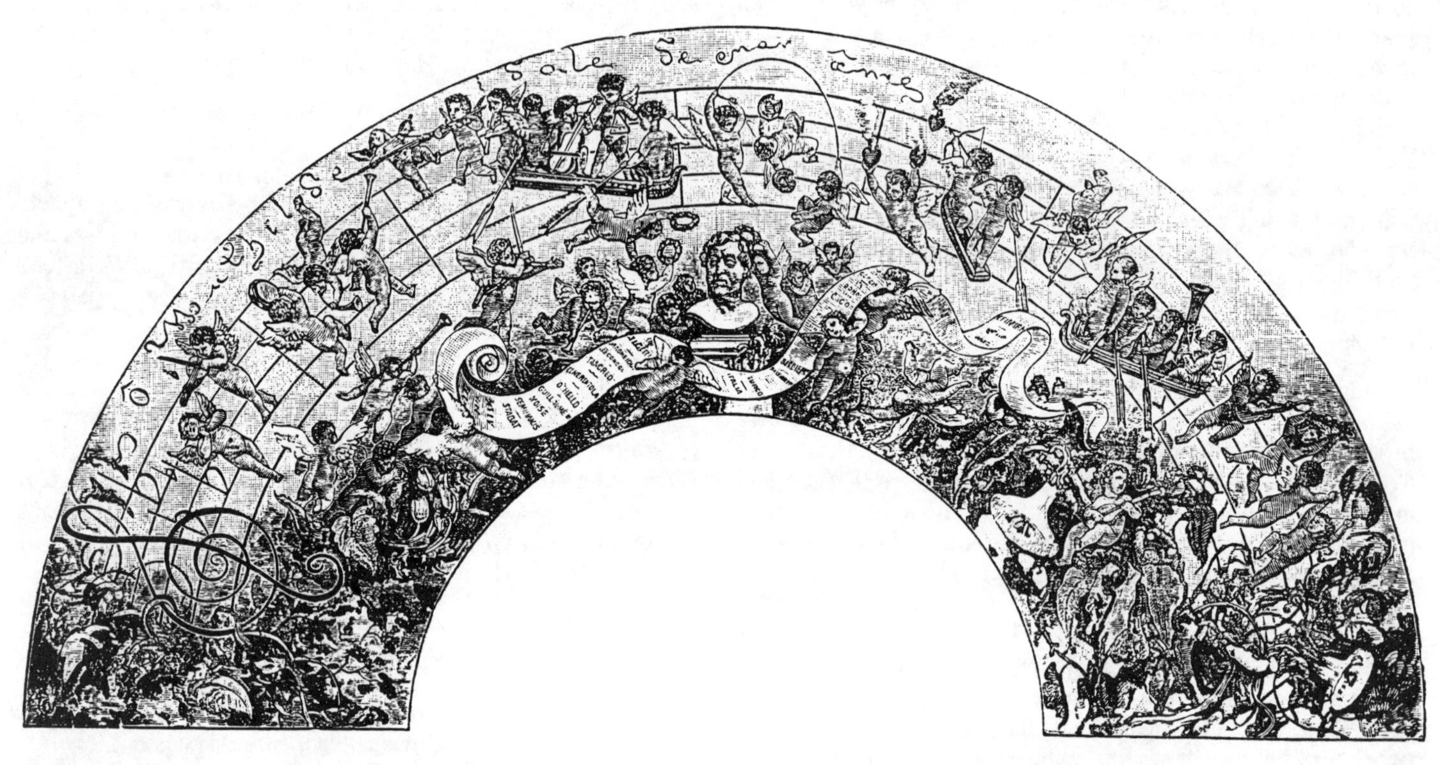

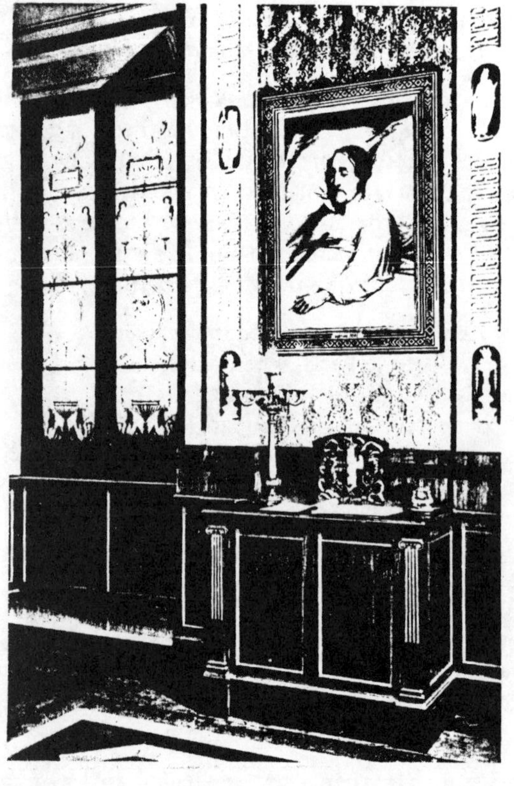

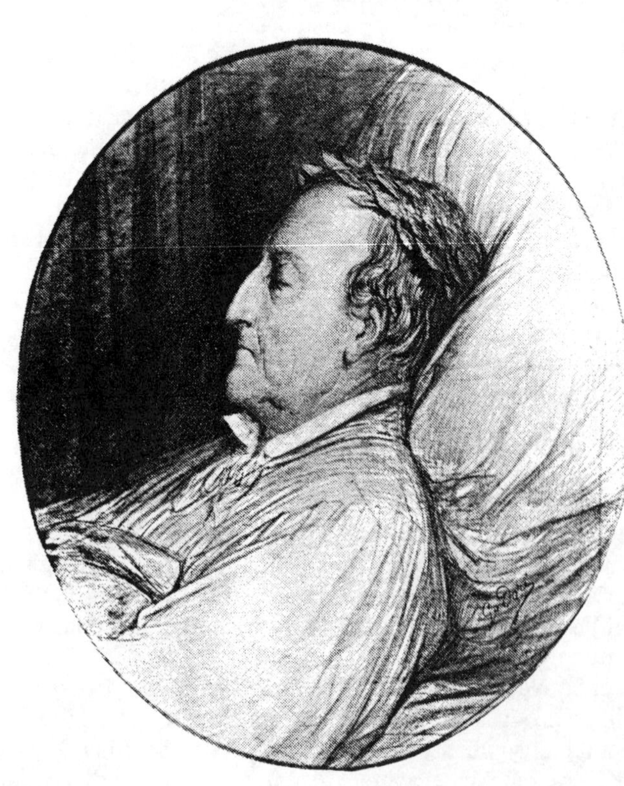

Christine Nilsson or Hortense Schneider. By 1867 the circle of serious Patti suitors had been narrowed to two, the Marquis de Caux and Doré. It was probably 1867 when Lauw wrote (p.32):

> Doré besieged Adelina to allow herself to be painted by him, and soon two beautiful half-length portraits of Patti were displayed in his studio. In color and drawing they were, indeed, masterpieces, but the likeness to Adelina was scarcely recognizable.

Those paintings were described in Roosevelt and Jerrold, and even written up in ***La Vie Parisienne*** (March 28, 1868, p.222) "... the laughing Mlle. Patti herself, a circlet of gold in her black hair, a red rose behind the ear, her shoulders emerging from the glossy satin of her bodice." Without ever stating her name, both Roosevelt and Jerrold describe Patti as Doré's one true *grande passion.* But by the time that March 28, 1868 article was written, it was already too late. Patti had decided to marry the Marquis. Patti biographies point out that despite her family's strong objections to the Marquis, she was bullheaded and determined to become the Marquise. Here is how Jerrold expressed it (p.307 & 308):

> There was the most delicate and highly-finished portrait of a prima donna, apart upon an easel, for some time. But it suddenly disappeared - the lady had married. A tender chord had been broken.... The *grande passion* about which he talked and wrote, and which really troubled his repose and made him unhappy for a time, was a dream that never, as I have already remarked, took the shape even of a declaration. The beautiful face that disappeared from the easel faded also out of his life.

Roosevelt points out that many rumors were flying around about Doré marrying Patti. One of Doré's British friends, Col. Sampson, had the misfortune of inquiring about it, evidently during the time period when Doré knew she was going to wed another, but the public did not know. Here is how Sampson related that conversation, per Roosevelt (p.354-355):

> I once asked Doré if there was any truth in a rumour very current at the time, that he was engaged to be married to a certain celebrated prima donna. We were alone in the Rue Bayard studio at the time, and he said nothing for the moment; then, suddenly waving his hand in the direction of a dozen or so easels, each having upon it some unfinished work, he exclaimed, half sadly, half mockingly, "No; my wives are there! Better that they should be canvas ones, mon cher!"

In May of 1868, both Doré and Patti were in London. Doré was on his first London visit, where an exhibition of his paintings was displayed. No one understood his gloom on what should have been a grand tour. Some sources claim that Doré threatened to kill himself. But Patti went to London, and when the opera season ended in July, she married and became the Marquise de Caux. Then a couple months later, Patti and Doré were together again at Rossini's death - a doubly sad moment.

But Patti's marriage was one of the most famous unhappy relationships of the century. The Marquis was from a recently impoverished, but very old line of nobility. His family thought it was a major step down for him to marry a "woman of the stage." Her family thought him to be a gold-digger from the start, fond of gambling, carousing, and putting on aristocratic airs. He was at the time an emissary of Napoleon III and the Empress Eugenie, and they asserted a strong influence in the affair. The Empress advised Patti to work a few more years and then they would arrange for her to get a position as a lady of the court. The marriage lasted about as long as the Second Empire, which two years later was blown to bits by Prussian cannons. After the Franco-Prussian war, his aristocracy was as empty as his pockets had been before the marriage. Then his aristocratic ego could not handle the fact that he was now nothing and she was still the most popular (and the wealthiest) singer in the world. He shortly began having affairs while she remained faithful to him, per Houssaye (p.284-285). He made her life unbearable and turned Lauw against her. Patti eventually had an affair with one of her co-stars, the tenor Ernest Nicolini. All of a sudden she was evil, and Lauw left her and wrote her scandalous book. Patti and the Marquis were separated in 1877 but not divorced until 1885. Patti had to pay him over a million francs to get rid of him. Then she married Nicolini, who died in 1898, and in 1899 Patti married a man half her age. Her third husband was 45 years younger than her first husband. But Patti's operatic dominance continued until after the turn of the century. She last sang publicly at a charity concert in 1914, 63 years after they set her up on that table in Tripler Hall in New York. There is an excellent new Patti biography, John Cone's 1993 ***Adelina Patti, Queen of Hearts,*** by Amadeus Press. After Patti died in 1919, her husband married a young woman, so even though Patti was born in 1843, her husband's daughter is still alive over 150 years later.

After Patti separated from the Marquis in 1877 she again saw Doré from time to time, until she left on her U.S. tour late in 1881. But by then she was already in love with Nicolini, so Doré was once again playing second fiddle. Doré biographers assumed that Doré destroyed the two paintings of Patti after she married, but John Cone found them in Wales. Patti bought a castle in Wales, which is now a museum. But there was another major source of information about Doré and Patti. She wrote a book (under a pseduonym) about her relationship with Doré, which no one knew about for over a century:

Marie L.: Reminiscences of Gustave Doré

Allow me to speculate about how this, the only book ever written by Patti, came to be written, and was then lost. In 1892, Patti probably read that the Doré Gallery exhibition in London was going on a tour of the U.S. (her homeland). She had many letters from Doré and wanted to do something in his memory, but not in public way, having been tainted over her Nicolini affair, whom she was then married to. So she came up with the idea of sharing fond personal memories of Doré under a pseudonym. She arranged with Henry Heyman, the manager of the Doré Gallery in New York, to publish such a little booklet about Doré, using the pseudonym, "Marie L." "Marie" was both her middle name and a character she played in the

photo of Adelina Patti at age 10 (1853) while she was on her three-year American concent tour.
photo of Adelina Patti (early 1860s) after her operatic career sky-rocketed her to worldwide fame.
photo of Adelina Patti (1863) debuting in Brussels as Marie in *The Daughter of the Regiment*.
photo of Adelina Patti (late 1860s) *prima donna assoluta*, when Doré was madly in love with her.

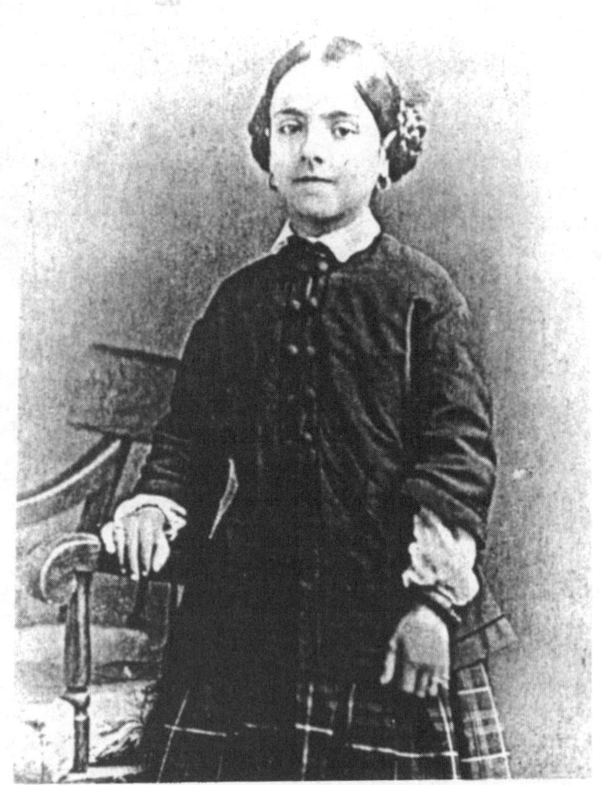

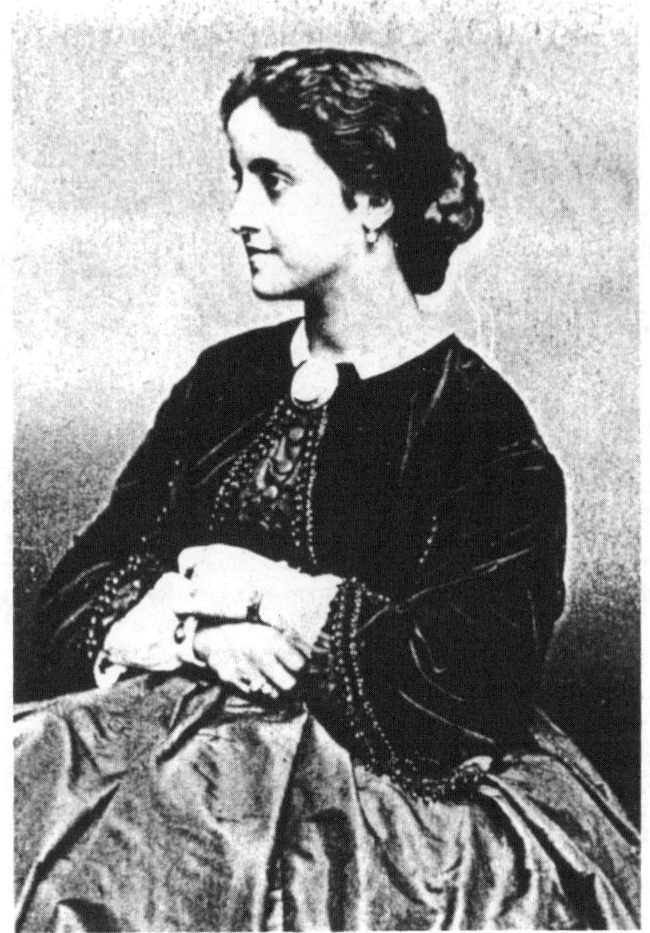

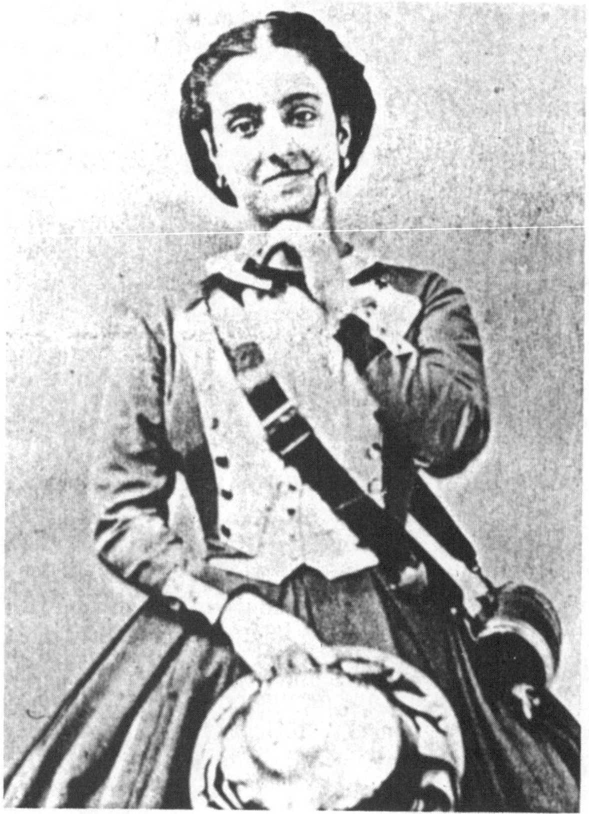

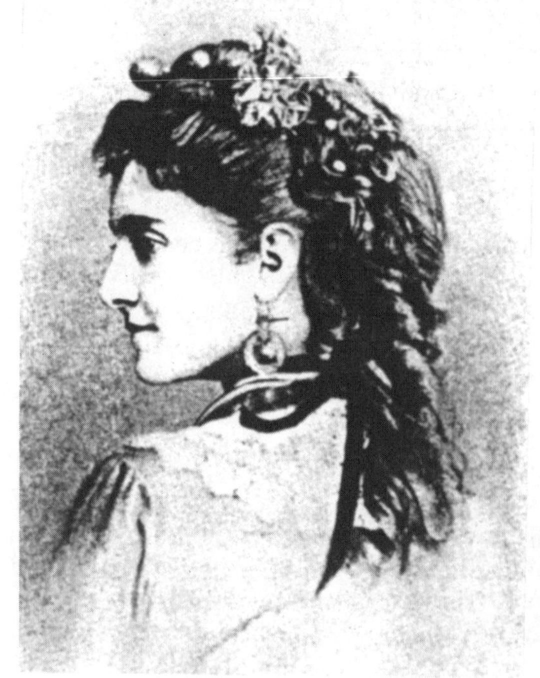

opera ***The Daughter of the Regiment***. So this 5x8 green 40-page paperback booklet was "published by The Doré Gallery, Carnegie Music Hall, New York" in January of 1893. The only copy known to exist was sent to the Library of Congress, where it was stamped "Jan 25 1893." On the inside front cover, Henry Heyman wrote the following introduction:

> The following reminiscences, written as they are from actual personal recollection, by one who was the great master's only *grande passion* and who knew him all the varying phases of his ardent and artistic temperament, need no long explanatory or apologetic preface at my hands.
>
> The writer being an American lady (whom doubtless many will recognize under her *nom de plume*) - is the fact which induces me to place the first issues before the American public, though the perusal of these pages will interest all those on both sides of the Atlantic who sympathize with the struggles of a *grande ame* in the pursuit of a great artistic mission.
>
> HENRY HEYMAN
> Manager Doré Gallery
>
> New York, January, 1893.

That introduction reveals the author's identity too easily. Only one famous American opera singer had a romance with Doré. Patti was probably furious and demanded that all the copies be destroyed. The idea was to hide her identity. She went to great lengths in the text to hide her identity So all the copies were destroyed, but one had already been sent to the Library of Congress. But what happened to Patti's copy and all her letters from Doré? Shortly after her death, a household servant, claiming to act on Patti's dying request, built a bonfire on the front lawn and burned all her personal effects. But the copy in the Library of Congress somehow got mislabeled, and for a century listed Henry Heyman as the author. I was able to get the book on inter-library loan and I photocopied all of it.

The book's content is rambling and personal, jumping back and forth. It takes in-depth knowledge of Doré and Patti for it to make sense. But it is a fascinating look into the lives of two of the most famous artistic personalities of the 19th century. For example, many people wrote about when Patti first sang at Rossini's. But the stories were second-hand. This book gives a first-hand account, by none other than Doré himself, in his own colorful style. The authoress tries to hide her identity by referring to "Patti" in the third person. But it is Doré telling the story about Patti to other people at Patti's party. The days also give it away. The authoress says Doré told this story at her party, the day after Rossini's party. We saw that Rossini's parties were on Saturday and Patti's were on Sunday. Besides, what other famous American opera singer was giving parties in Paris in 1862, and having a romance with Doré? This passage is at the end of the book, even though it describes Patti and Doré's first meeting (p.39-40):

> It was my custom to give a *petit diner d'artistes* every week. Where poets, painters, musicians, and composers, men of literature and famous women met, with that lovely *sans gene* only known in Parisian life, where friends come and go without the pasteboard of invitation.
>
> In that artistic mode, Doré was often in his happiest mood.
>
> He lost sight of everything but mirth; and sometimes his wit became so absolutely sparkling that it cast its scintillations over our coterie, leaving a memory never to be effaced. When inspired with such moods, his badinage was a picture, terse in form, in color rare, and as graphic as his wonderful brush could have painted it.
>
> As an illustration of this he once told as he had heard Patti sing, the evening previous in Rossini's salon. I quote his words.
>
> "Imagine Patti bristling across the room like a thistle in a gale. Imagine Rossini (*ce cher pacquet d'harmonie*), ensconced in his easy chair, both hands in his vareuse pockets, his shoulders drawn up, his brown wig no larger than a big chestnut, his eyelids snapping as if an invisible shower-bath were dripping over him. While the Diva *cascadait ses roulades inconnues au Maitre*! The invisible shower-bath became colder and colder as she trilled."
>
> "When the Diva ceased Rossini was below zero."
>
> "Maestro, how did that please you?" asked the bristling young thistle.
>
> "What was it?" asked the frozen composer - like a ghost from Lapland.
>
> "Why, your own *Una voce poco fa*, from the *Barbiere di Seviglia.*"
>
> "Ah!" wheezed the Laplander, "*Je ne le reconnaissais pas*!"
>
> "And then," added Doré, quaffing his champagne and brimming over with laughter, "we all entered the frigid zone."

The book is very personal. Doré keeps referring to her as "goldenrod" and she calls him "stork" (but in French). She tells how she would go to his studio and enter quietly without ringing or knocking. He would be working high up on some painting, and she would play the piano while he painted. There are no dates in the book, but sequences can be dated by what paintings he was working on at the time. Most of the paintings are in the 1867-68 period, just before she left him to marry the Marquis. Both of them were incurable romantics, but Doré was much more in love with her while she expresses great fondness for him. She speaks of love dreamily, such as in reference to the beauty of her native America (p.9): "There is something in my native land that would tell you love can never go." Doré replies, "Paris teaches a religion of love quite different from yours." The conversation continues from his studio to a flower garden to a symphony to an intimate dinner to her boudoir. So much of the conversation deals with Doré expressing his love for her and his fear that he is losing her. She does not want to hurt him, and replies expressing fondness and friendship. She clearly enjoys him, but often interrupts her own narrative to give her thought, "I resolved to live only for my art," the exact phrase Patti biographers often use concerning her. Patti really had two levels of motivation. She did not want to lose the affectionate relationship with Doré, but she was more and

104 Doré oil painting of ***Adelina Patti*** (1867) - now in Chrstine Scott Plummer collection.
Doré mixed media sketch of ***Adelina Patti*** (nd, late 1870s?) - now in Glynn Vivian Art Gallery in Wales.
photo of infamous Adelina Patti (1868) to the Marquis de Caux; Patti's father Salvatore is to her right, brother-in-law (and manager) Maurice Strakosch is behind Patti & DeCaux; they were the only family members willing to attend the wedding; they made DeCaux sign a prenuptial agreement.
photo of Adelina Patti (1876) at her debut as *Aida*; shortly thereafter she left DeCaux and again saw Doré.

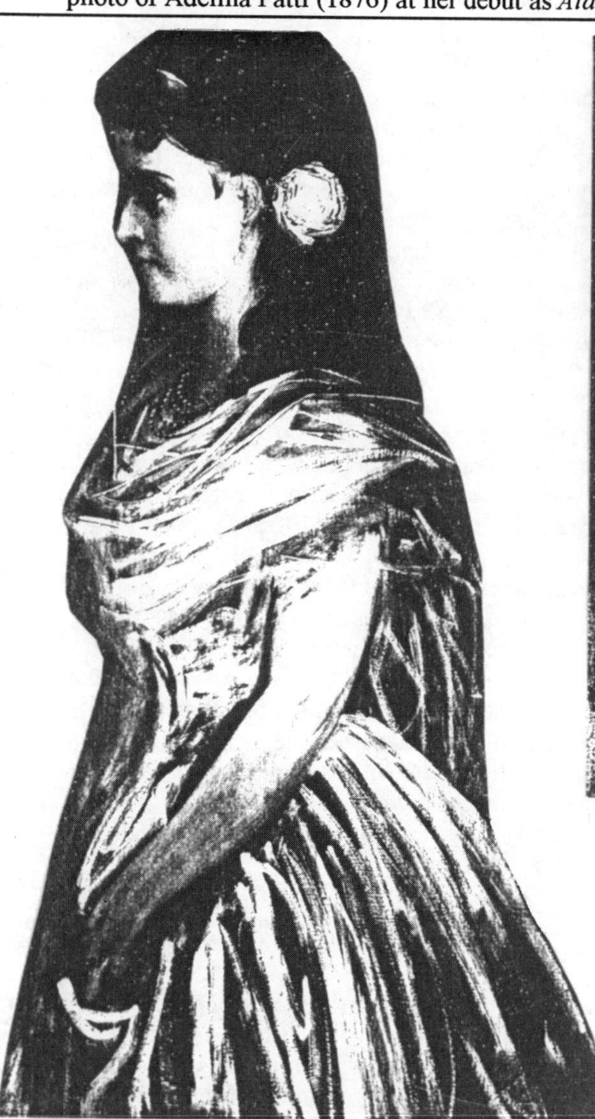

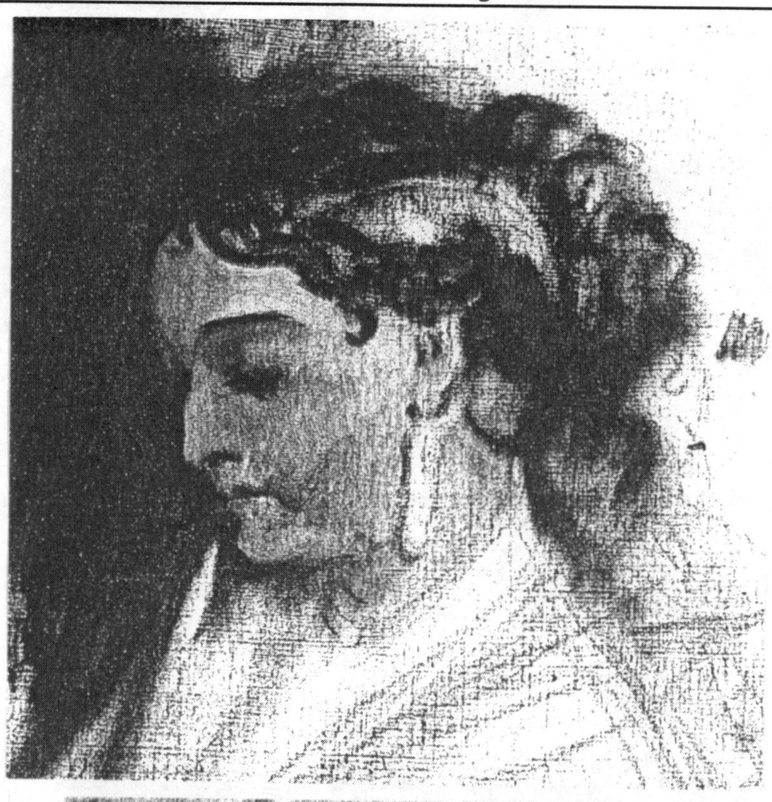

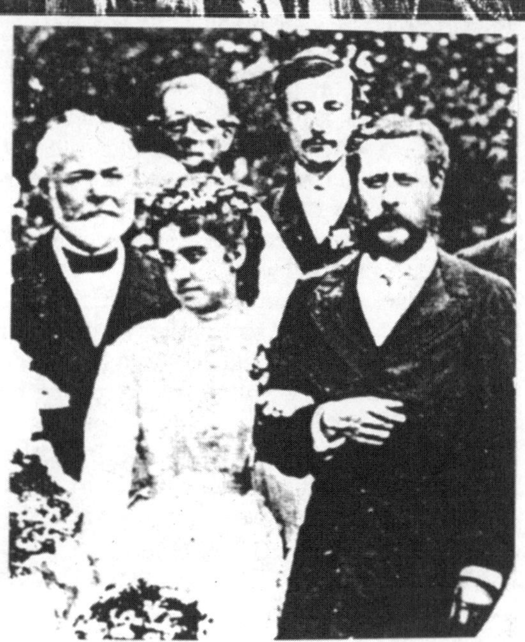

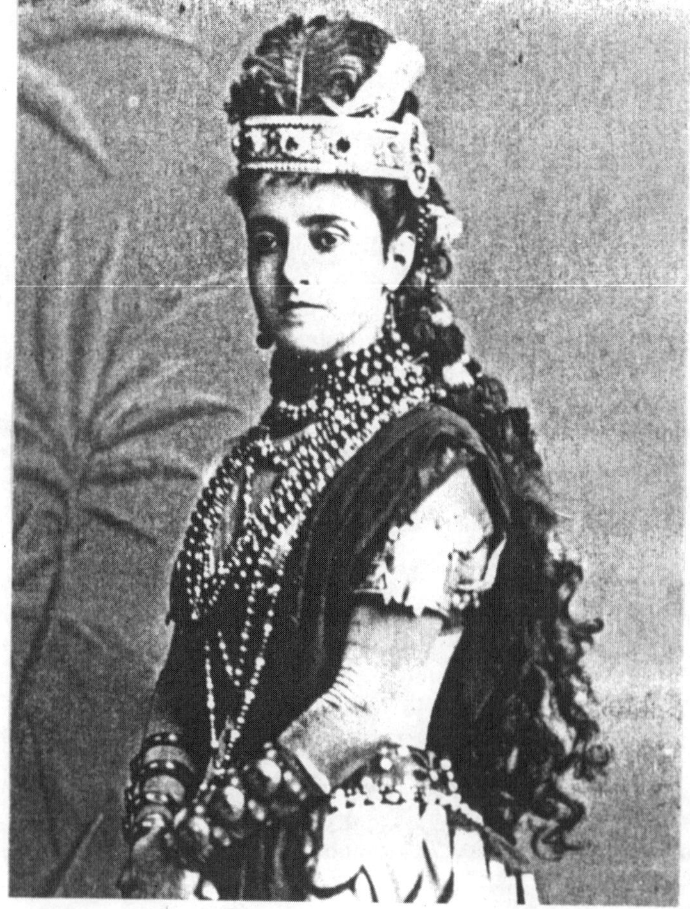

more determined to marry the Marquis. But on the deepest level, her career was more important to her than any man. Her marriage did cause her to lose contact with Doré for a decade. There are also lighter moments in the book, as when they play a game of words about a nude painting Doré is working on, ***Andromeda*** (which recently sold for $600,000). The heroine is chained to the rocks with a dragon about to devour her (p.13):

> "I am going to paint on *Andromeda*. I want you to help me."
> "Cynic!" I exclaimed. The warm blood flooding my face angrily.
> "Not for worlds would I wound thee, Rameau d'or, not by a single tear obscure that 'melancholy gaze' of thine eyes I love so well." ...
> "Could it be," I ventured in a spirit of *diablerie*, "could it be that such a length of arm, such length, from hip to toe, of poor *Andromeda*, could be natural?"
> "You do not like tall women? How tall is *Andomeda* supposed to be?
> I amused him, I am sure. His mood changed to high revelry. He answered me:
> "If you were chained to that rock, with such a dragon about to devour you, would you not stretch every nerve and sinew to more than their natural length, to recoil from it?" ...
> "I want to give the color of your hair to *Andromeda*; may I?" ... "I will only take the color and the ripple, not its glorious length."

Pages 24-26 appear to be the time when she tells him she is going to marry the Marquis. She speaks of his eyes being full of tears, of his asking her what he can do, and her trying to console him by telling him to dedicate himself to his art, as she has done. They then sit and say nothing for a long time. Finally, he grabs some flowers and departs, saying, "At least these can be mine!" A decade passes before the next chapter, which she begins "Thirty days and more had sped, or rather been lost in what is known as social duties." But perhaps the most significant part of the book is from 1880-81, based on paintings mentioned. That is where she determines to go see Doré again. By then they had both known great sadness and suffering. She goes to his studio, and he is overjoyed (p.29):

> "Thou wert not lost then, only missing - Cher ange! Rameau d'or! Thou fragrant blossom! Come, scatter thy golden sweetness over my solitary hours as thou wert wont ... When day after day passed and you came not, I thought you were lost to me. Out of the trouble of such a fear there arose the most elevated and agonized inspirations."

They share their sorrows: "I buried my face in my arms, on the keyboard of the piano, and sobbed aloud;" and Doré replies, "Pauvre amie! I have been painting thy sorrows too!" He tells how he inserts her into paintings in ways no one can tell, such as the painting ***The Day Dream*** where a young monk is playing an organ, with a wispy dream of young woman behind him. Patti was the dream girl. Then she says (p.35): "A great change came. Was the end of so sweet a life at hand? Was it possible? America - the broad Atlantic between us!" She refers to her departure on her U.S. tour in the fall of 1881. She never saw Doré again. He died in January, 1883. She says she could not leave without one more visit to his studio. By then Doré's mother had died, and he was even more sad and lonely. She described the weather that dark, windy and rainy night when she could not find Doré and searched for him, until (p.36):

> The spell of heavenly peace stole over me. He stood beside me.
> "Found at last," he said joyfully.
> "I have sought thee through thorns and brambles and wild despair and death," I sighed.
> "We are safe now, we are in love," he said.
> "We are safe now, we are in heaven," I replied.

Notice that she does not say, "we are in love." If there is any theme to the book, it is romance vs. friendship. The book concludes with letters Doré wrote to her in the U.S., the last of which did not reach her until after his death. But the most amazing thing in the book was in one of his last letters (p.37):

> I see thee ever as I saw thee last. Ah! How well do I remember! The filmy white frill about thy throat. The gray Tartan, for the ocean, wrapped about thee. The melancholy glance of thine eyes. Thy sweet face telling me of unshed tears. Some day, in some strange land or country, perchance, thou mayest see *The Flower Girl* and recognize thyself as thou wert at our sad parting. Should it offend, forgive me. I see thee ever as I saw thee last."

Why would that painting offend her? In fact, in 1893 when the Doré Gallery published the book, they had that very painting on display. Patti probably saw it there. But there is something very strange about the painting. Patti, being Italian, had black hair. But the girl in the painting has frizzy red hair. The hair on the girl in the painting is Sarah Bernhardt's hair!! The dark eyes are definitely Patti's. I am now convinced that Doré combined the features of his two lovers! The combination of features so disguised the character that for a century no one realized what it was? We will get to Sarah shortly, but she left on her American tour in 1880. Then Patti came to visit Doré, rekindling the old flame, and then Patti left for America in 1881, and Doré never saw either of them again. His mother had also died recently. I believe that the ***Marie L.*** book deletes the part of the letter where Doré told her that ***The Flower Girl*** had Sarah's hair, Patti's eyes, Sarah's nose, and Patti's mouth. It explains why Doré would said, "If the painting offends you, please forgive me." That painting ***The Flower Girl*** was last sold by Sotheby's of London in 1979.

Doré and Patti were kindred spirits, but their egos were too big. One difference was that Patti was able to recover and learn from and unhappiness, while Doré seemed overwhelmed by negative emotional intensity. In this booklet, Patti expressed her personal affection and high respect for Doré (p.40):

> One of the most extraordinary peculiarities of this great and gifted child of God was his electrical transposition from the lofty summits of his magnificent and glorifying creations, to an almost childish candor and caprice, of which history furnishes no parallel.

 Doré oil painting ***The Flower Girl*** (1881) which combined the features of Adelina Patti & Sarah Bernhardt.

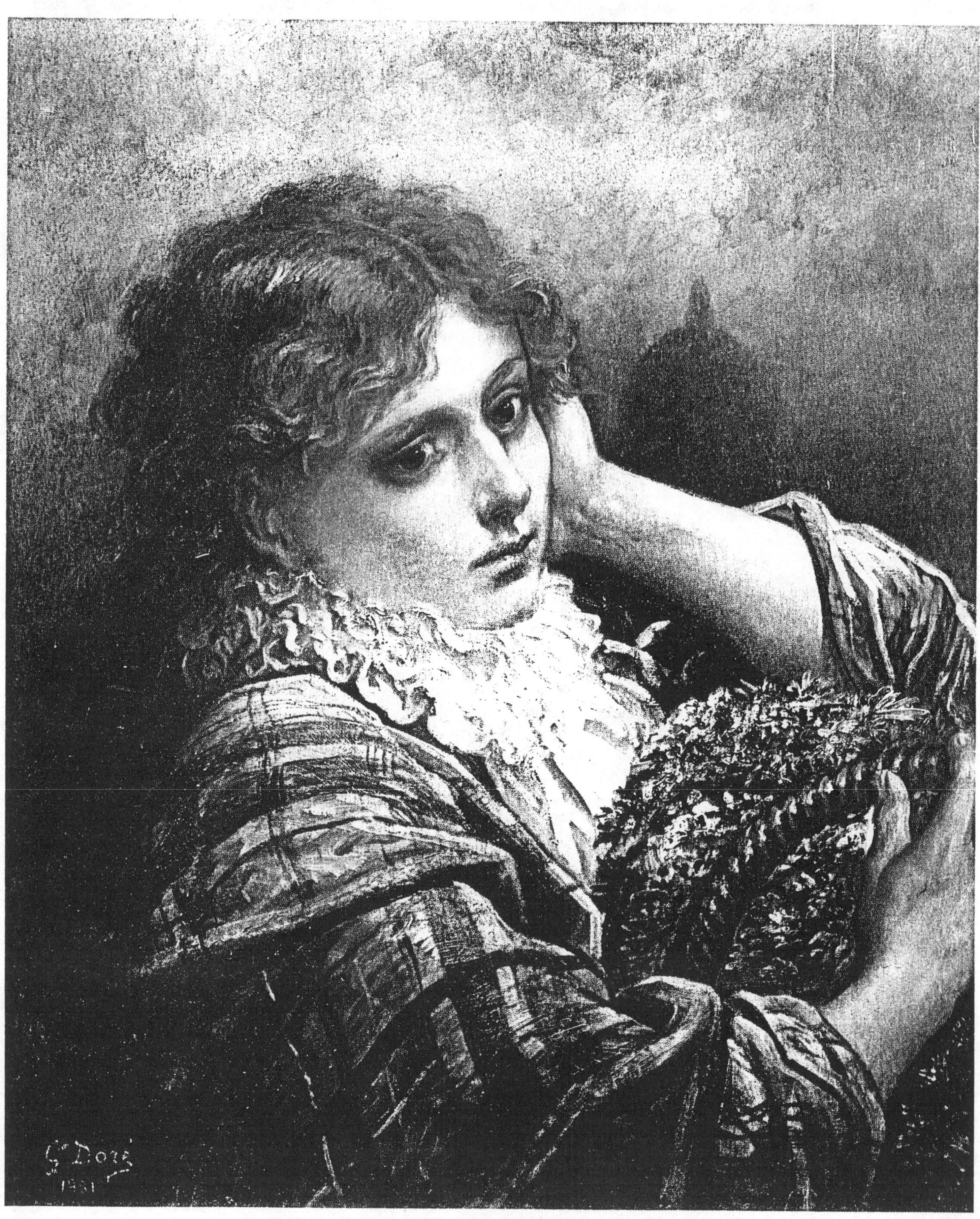

Cora Pearl (Eliza Emma Crouch; 1837-1886)

Doré's next romance was a major change of pace. He went from the most famous singer in the world to perhaps the most famous prostitute in the world. His relationship with Cora Pearl was an immediate reaction to his being jilted by Patti. It probably began within weeks after that tearful evening when he left Adelina's boudoir with only a handful of flowers. What is amazing is not that Doré turned to a prostitute to drown his sorrows over Patti, but that he actually considered marrying her. It was one of the few times when the emotional dominance of his mother proved beneficial. Otherwise, Doré might have married Cora Pearl just out of spite.

Cora Pearl was born Eliza Emma Crouch in Plymouth, England, into a family whose boast of three generations of musicians and composers did little to support a large family. One day when she was a teenager a man passing her on the road made her an offer she could not refuse and she simply walked away from her home and became a prostitute. Later on another man took her to Paris. She enjoyed Paris and refused to go back to England. She found a steady stream of men looking her way and set up shop as Cora Pearl. She was much more on the prostitute side of courtesan than Alice Ozy, who was more of a mistress/lover. In fact, Cora came to be regarded as a symbol of ruthlessness. She had no interest in romance or marriage. She was, by all accounts, very good in bed, and expected to be well reimbursed for services rendered. And so she was. She garnered and squandered great fortunes.

There are three major sources of information about her. The standard text is W.H.Holden's 1950 book, ***The Pearl of Plymouth***. But the real sources are two books, both claiming to be her memoirs. After her death, there appeared in Paris in 1886 the ***Memoires de Cora Pearl***, which we would now label R-rated. There was talk that she blackmailed various men by sending them pre-publication chapters, which they dutifully paid her to suppress. But in 1890 there appeared an English book entitled ***The Memoirs of Cora Pearl***, published under a fictional imprint because it was X-rated. It may be the nastiest book written in the 19th century by a woman. Alas, I was forced to skim through it for Doré research, there being no index. You will not find that 1890 version in any library. It appears that there was only one known copy known, owned by a Swiss collector. In 1983, that collector allowed an editor, William Blatchford to transcribe the original, and re-published as ***Grand Horizontal***, with a historical introduction. There was much speculation as to whether the 1890 title was a forgery. The section on Doré is amazingly accurate. The 1890 version was written about 1873, just after she was banned from France.

In the 1860s, Cora was probably the most (in)famous courtesan in Paris, having serviced just about every prominent man in France - the Emperor Napoleon III, Prince Napoleon, the Duc de Morny, Prince William of Orange, Prince Achille Murat, etc. She boasted that she went to prominent functions where every man there had had sex with her. She threw the wildest parties in Paris. She once held a party for about 15 famous men, and there boasted that she would serve up a meat dish that no man would slice. She went to the kitchen and soon the servants carried in a huge platter, and when they raised the lid, it was her - stark naked. She claimed that right then and there all 15 of those men had sex with her. But like most of the courtesans, the Franco-Prussian War put her out of business. They were the accursed reminder of all the evils of the Second Empire. In 1872, Cora was actually still in business, and she latched onto a young man named Duval who had inherited ten million francs, which she spent in a few months. When he was out of money, she kicked him out. He came back with a gun. It is uncertain whom he meant to shoot, but he shot himself. As he lay dying on the floor, she uttered the most famous words ever to come from the lips of a courtesan - "Pig, you are getting blood on my carpet!" Shortly thereafter, the chief of police informed Cora that she should consider herself lucky that she had only been banned from France. She managed to get by for a few years by selling her valuables, but by 1880 was impoverished. Her final years were spent in the gutter, when she could no longer attract anyone. One day a young couple passed her, and the man froze at the sight of her. It was Duval! Cora never knew he had survived and become a responsible adult. He had started a business and was raising a family.

So how did Doré get involved with such a person? It was all Adelina's Patti's fault. When Patti left Doré in the spring of 1868, he was so distraught that he sought solace in a readily available refuge - the arms of Cora Pearl. We will quote here the entire section from her 1890 memoirs about Doré. It is remarkable that she had nothing bad to say about Doré, unlike most of the other men in the book. Two details may seem questionable. First, it says that Doré asked Cora to model for him (Doré did not use models). But it is clear that it was just a pretext to get her alone. Secondly, it says that Doré asked Cora to marry him. It does not say it there, but this is when Doré's mother put her foot down. Many Doré biographers thought Alice Ozy was the courtesan Doré wanted to marry. But his affair with Alice ended in the early 1860s. It was Doré's rejection by Patti that made him want to marry Cora. Here is the section from ***Grande Horizontal*** (p.124-126):

> It was in the spring of 1868 that I met an artist whose name has now become familiar and who was even then beginning to be known - Louis Auguste Gustave Doré. He was introduced to me by a friend who advised me on buying pictures, and was at that time working on illustrations for the English poet Tennyson's verses about King Arthur. He was a serious, intense fellow in his thirties, who had already drawn the pictures for works by Dante and Milton, but that this had not made him too solemn was demonstrated by the fact that when we first met he remarked: "Ah, the lady whose breasts are reputed to be the shapeliest in Paris. May I be permitted to draw them?"
>
> Whereupon I made an appointment, and the following day went to his studio, where I posed for him (and I may say, have recognized my breasts as those of many a Biblical heroine since!). He became very silent as he drew me, and at last laid down his pencil, came over to me, and without more ado began

two different undated Doré oil paintings, both entitled ***In Fairyland***.

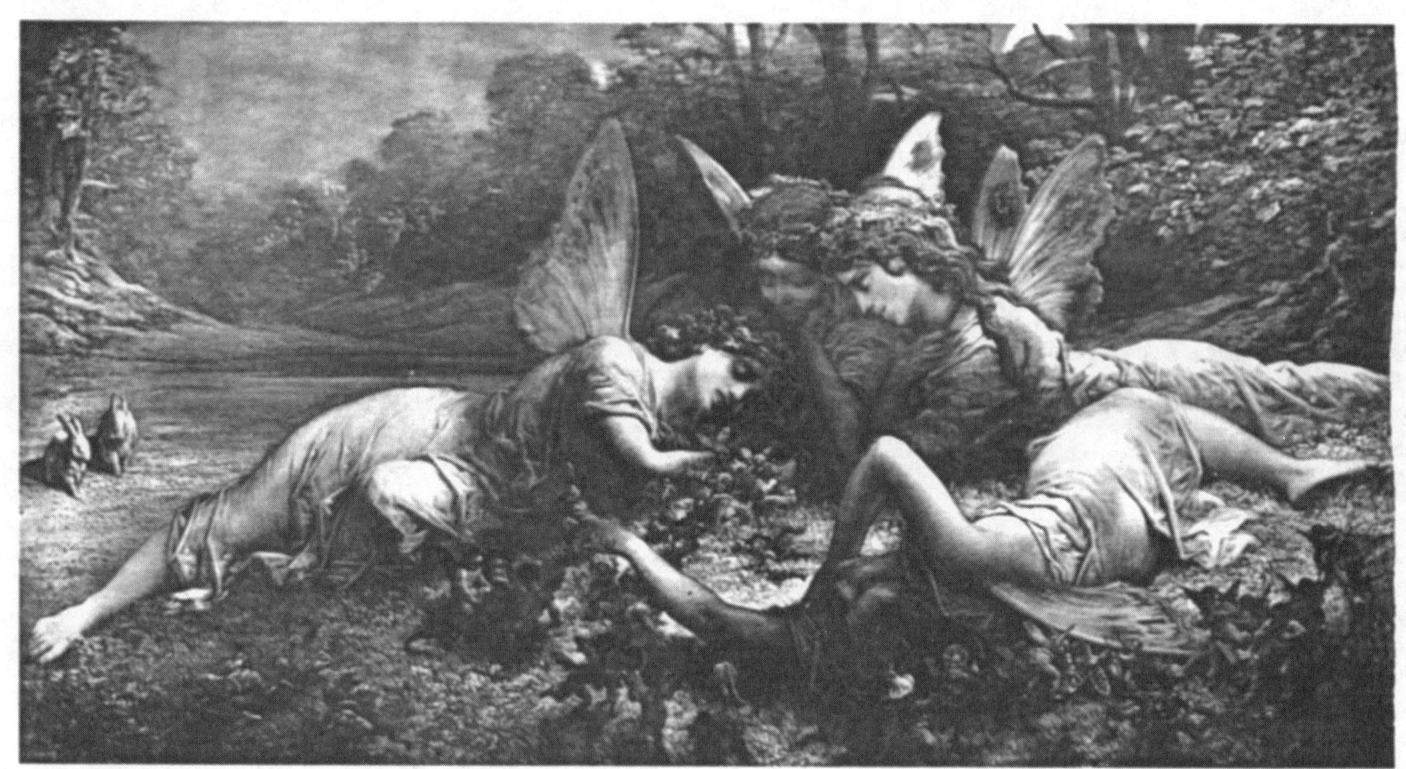

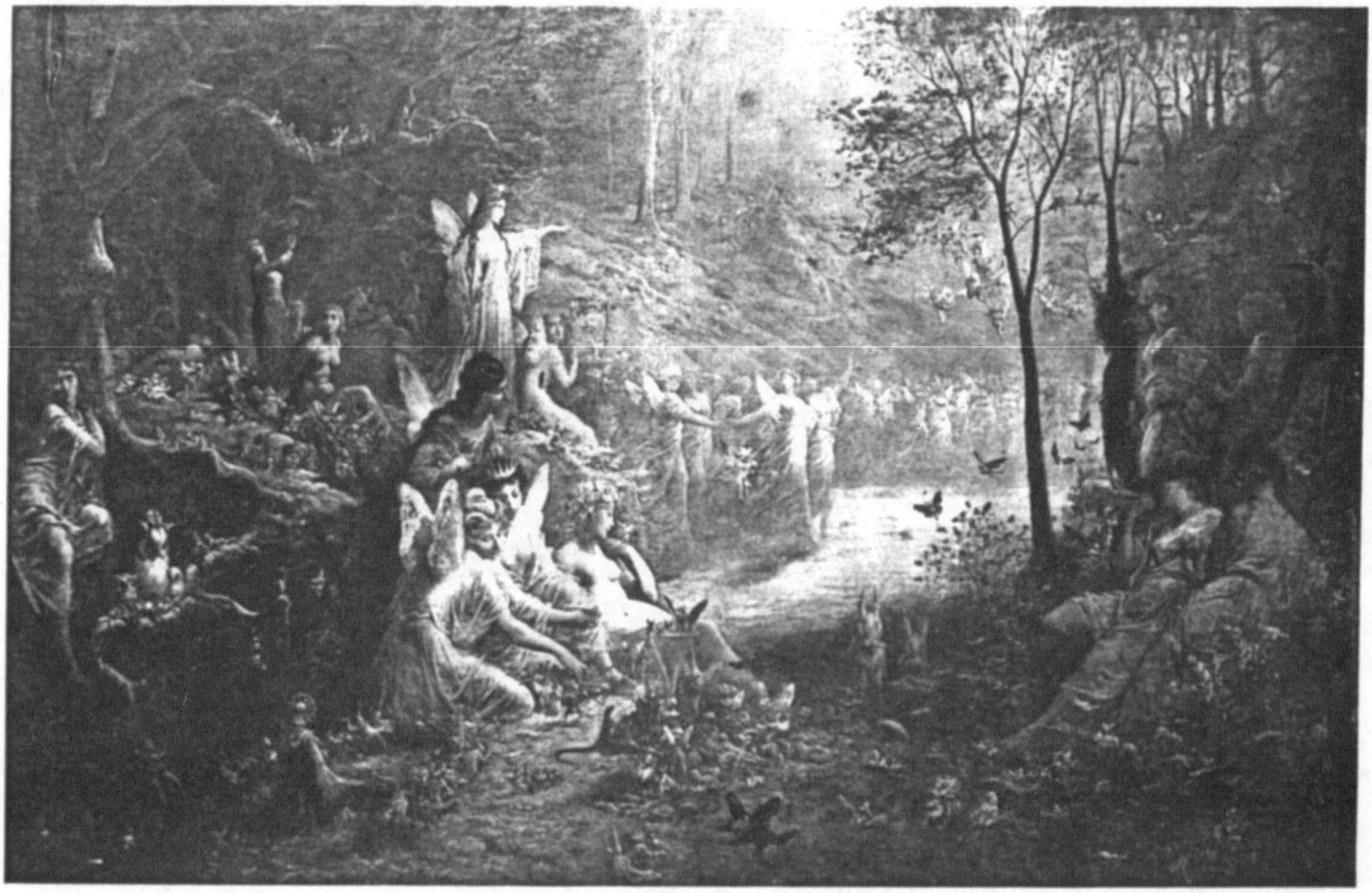

> to press kisses upon me, whereupon I returned them with interest, for he was a fine and intelligent man, who soon turned out to be as well-shaped and well-equipped as some of the heroes of his less public drawings, commissioned by, among others, the Prince.
>
> We continued to meet for two years, and at one time he continually pressed me to marry him; but the idea of marriage has never commended itself to me, and we continued as lovers. He was always particularly passionate when we first met; but after one or perhaps two bouts would go for his paper and pencils and sketch me; he made several sketches of my most intimate parts which were in detail the finest I have seen; but he would never leave them with me, and I have often wondered what occurred to them.
>
> Doré was, in the variety of his conversation, the lightness of his spirits, the invention of his amorous attentions, the loving appreciation of my company, one of the most charming men I have known, and had I been of a more settling disposition - or less convinced that marriage is a recipe for boredom and eventual neglect - who knows but that I might have become Madame Doré? But it was not to be, and eventually, becoming weary of the clandestine nature of our relationship (which he concealed from his growing company of patrons), we parted, not without regret. I gave him a photograph of myself, in remembrance, which I am told he still treasures. I had no wish to send Doré away.

That photograph was shown in a 1948 Paris exhibition. Even though Cora and Adelina were very different women, they both expressed admiration for the same personal and artistic Doré qualities. Unfortunately for Doré, he had qualities which made many women have very strong affection for him, but none of them wanted to marry him. When they banned Cora from France in 1873, they held a sale of her possessions. Among her valuables there were only four books - all Doré folios. She even had the Doré Bible. But she was fortunate not to be alive to read her obituary notices, per Holden (p.128):

> (Cora Pearl) was once one of the darlings of Paris. She is dead, and she died in destitution, though she was the mistress of a prince and the paramour of a millionaire. Yet Cora Pearl, as she called herself, possessed neither beauty, wit, nor culture. What was the secret of the fatal influence she exercised over men? There is no clue to the mystery in the dreary pages which record the history of her miserable life. She was not only vile and vulgar, but vain and vapid.

It is intriguing how moralizers of the 1880s felt it necessary to assert that the courtesans were ugly. They were not satisfied with saying that they were immoral. There is no mystery about their popularity - they were attractive, charming, glamorous, and willing to do anything for money. You may assert that those qualities are bad, or produced negative consequences, but it is quite a stretch to say that because such qualities are undesirable we must also pretend that they do not exist.

Sarah Bernhardt (1844-1923)

Sarah Bernhardt was the most famous actress of the 19th century. Sarah and Adelina both loved, admired, and respected Doré, but left him for what proved to be unhappy marriages. All three of them could be summed up in the word "dramatic." They were like Poe characters, with supercharged sensibilities, coupled with artistic genius. But while Doré and Patti were both recognized for their talent at a very young age, Sarah was just the opposite. The phrase Sarah heard most often as a child was "that girl is an idiot." Sarah's mother was a courtesan. Sarah never knew her father, but he was not poor, because he left her an inheritance. Sarah was raised in a Catholic school. She was not really religious, but was mystical about all the dreamy aspects of nunnery. When told that she had to marry to receive her inheritance, she replied, "I will marry God!" Sarah was a wild, uncontrollable child. Her mother had very little use for her. Sarah also had very poor health, and it was thought that she would die of consumption at a young age. She was obsessed with death, and loved to pretend to be dead. She gravitated toward anything that was inherently dramatic. But her mother saw her dramatic tendencies as temper tantrums. The one thing fortunate for Sarah was her mother's patrons who had strong ties to the theatre, like the Duc de Morny and Alexandre Dumas. They were not hostile toward Sarah and thought her to be amusing. One day when Sarah was about 15, they had a meeting to try to decide what to do with the recalcitrant Sarah. After several outbursts, the Duc de Morny finally said, "she should be on the stage." Sarah had no idea what the stage was, but agreed to go see a play. That event changed her life, although she did manage to embarrass her mother by crying during the performance. After that, Sarah forgot about being a nun and wanted to be an actress. Sarah's biggest hurdle to becoming a successful actress was that she was too dramatic, and she often came very close to abandoning acting and falling back upon her mother's occupation.

Her mother's friends were able to get her in the academy and then into theatre groups. But she still had to prove herself there, and she kept shooting herself in the foot. One time she slugged an older actress who had knocked over Sarah's little sister. Another time they performed for the Emperor Napoleon III and Sarah chose to recite poetry by Victor Hugo, only to watch bewilderedly as the Emperor walked out (Hugo was a political exile). She learned all too quickly the secret of being a part-time actress and a full-time courtesan. Finally she began to learn to control her dramatic expression. Her first real break came in 1868 at the Odeon Theatre when politically rebellious students created a ruckus because they wanted a play by the exiled Victor Hugo, instead of one by Alexandre Dumas, who was in the audience. Sarah stopped in the middle of her performance and pleaded with the students, "Please, it is not the fault of M. Dumas that M. Hugo is in exile." Her dramatic spontaneity struck a chord with the students and she quickly became their favorite, while also making a strong supportor of Alexandre Dumas. But just as she was becoming popular in Paris, a fire destroyed all her possessions, and she was sued by the landlord. She was destitute. The Odeon Theatre put on a benefit to try to raise a portion of the 40,000 *fr* she needed. Then an angel of mercy appeared, in the form of none other

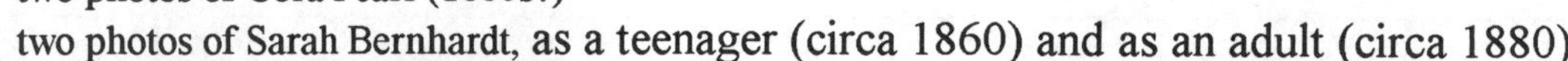

(top row) two photos of Cora Pearl (1860s?)

(bottom row) two photos of Sarah Bernhardt, as a teenager (circa 1860) and as an adult (circa 1880)

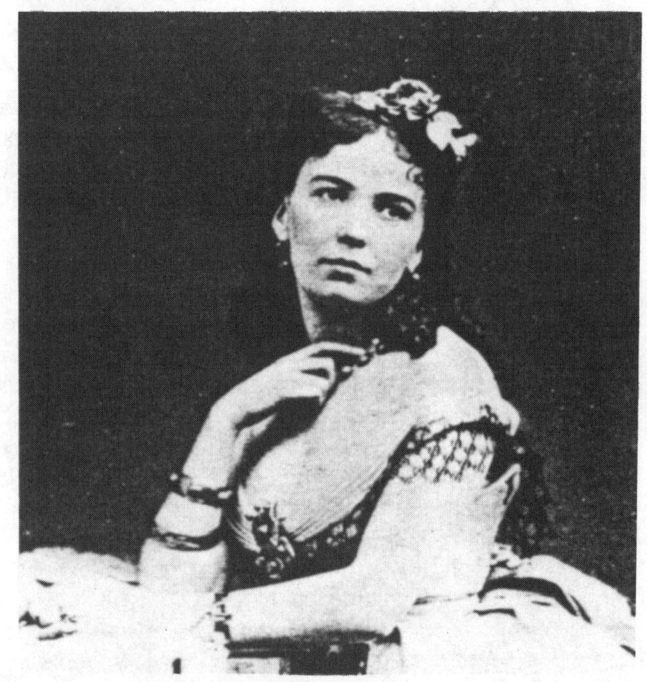

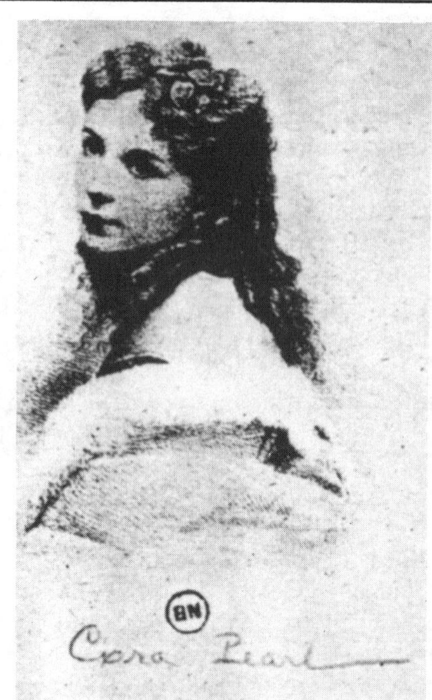

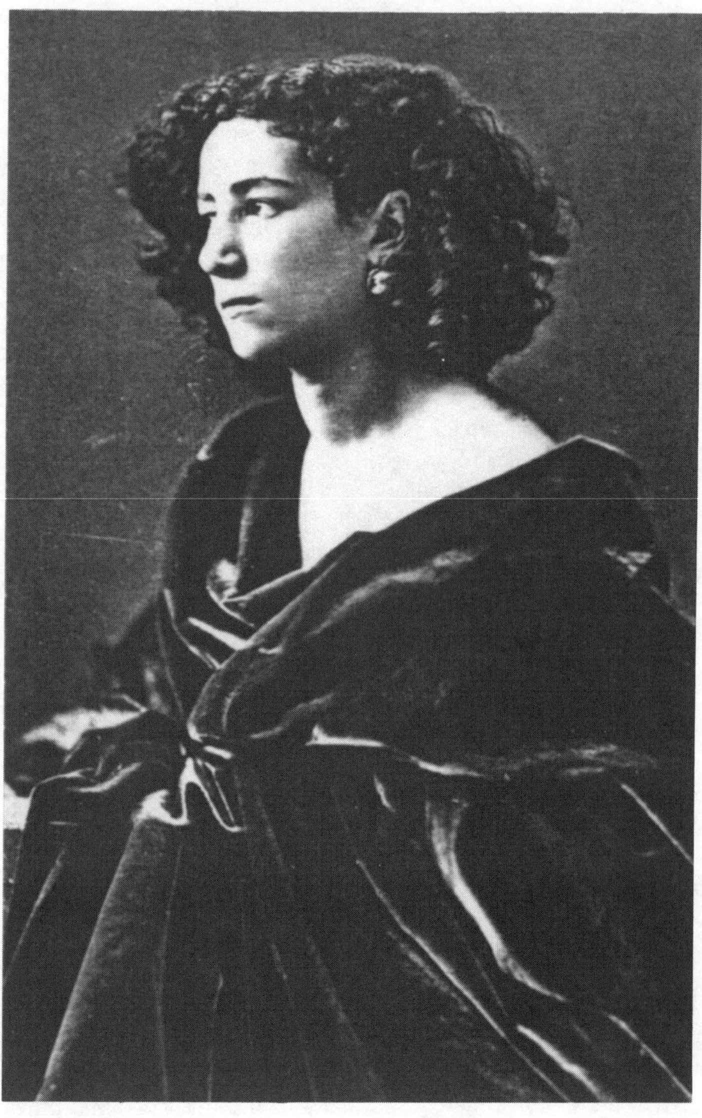

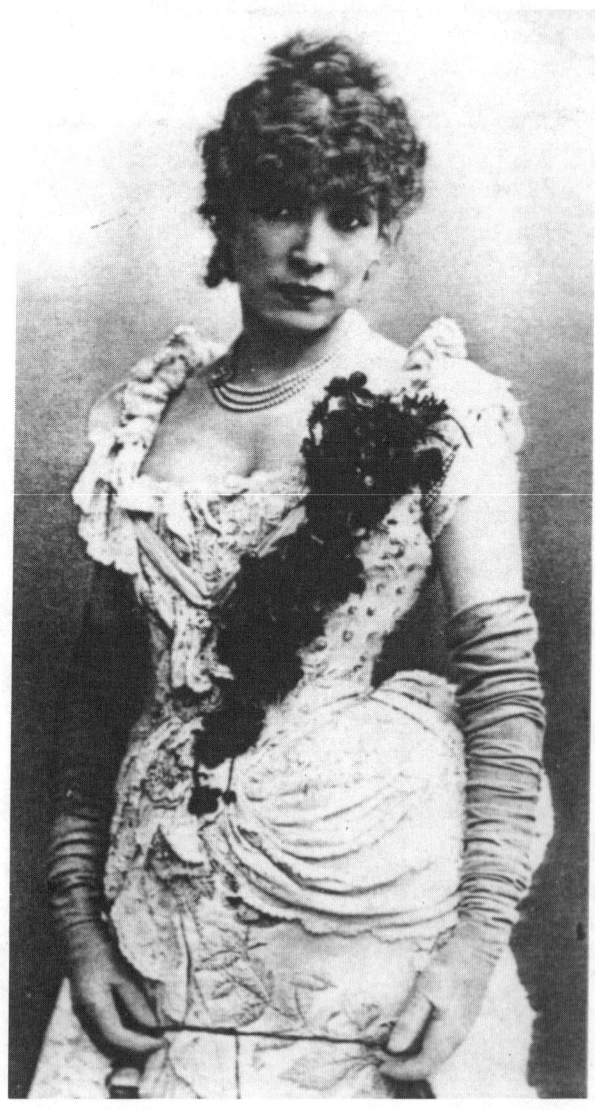

than Adelina Patti, who agreed to sing at the benefit. In 1869, Patti was the most famous and highly-paid singer in the world, while Sarah was barely gaining a reputation in Paris. This was the first time Patti had ever sung at a benefit. Some have suggested that Sarah had known (biblically) the Marquis prior to his marriage, and thereby had some influence in the matter. Sarah was later quoted as saying privately, "I made them both sing." Patti's name was enough to make the proceeds more than cover the losses. Sarah was speechless, per Lauw (p.51):

> After the concert (Sarah) in a modest black woolen dress, timidly approached the great songstress, handed her a little bouquet, and, unable from embarrassment to say a word of thanks, kissed her hand. Who could then have dreamed that this, at that time, insignificant actress would become the celebrated Sarah Bernhardt of today, and would make the world hold its breath by her art and her eccentricities.

During the Franco-Prussian War Sarah endeared herself to her countrymen by turning the theatre into a hospital. One young soldier she cared for told her that getting wounded was a blessing, because he was her biggest fan. Nearly 50 years later that same man would make special arrangements for Sarah (who by then had a leg amputated) to be carried to the front lines during World War I to inspire the troops. By then he was not a young recruit. He was then Commander-in-Chief of Allied Forces General Ferdinand Foch. Sarah's patriotism was legendary. After their crushing victory in 1871, Prussia took Alsace-Lorraine and five billion francs as indemnity. Sarah refused to ever perform in Prussia again. Years later, Sarah was at a banquet in her honor in Belgium, at which the Prussian ambassador to Belgium was present. He appealed to Sarah to give a German performance, and made the mistake of saying to her, "Just name your price." At that she literally screamed at him across the table, "Five Billion Francs!"

After the war, Sarah helped to reinvigorating Paris. Her popularity in Paris continued to grow, and in 1872 she was asked to return to the Comedie Francaise, from which she had been fired earlier. It was during the 1870s she become the most famous actress in France, then England, then America, and then the world. The 1880s would see her no longer an employee, but an employer with her own theatre group touring the world. She retained that position for nearly half a century, much like Adelina Patti. You might say that Sarah was a late bloomer, but she was still going strong long after Patti had retired. Another similarity between them was that they both barely made it onto recordings, long after their prime. Patti made a few audio recording about 1905 (in her sixties), and Sarah made a couple of films a decade later (in her seventies). That is one major difference between them and Doré. When you look at a Doré folio, you see his artistic creations at the prime of his career. But if you hear Adelina or see Sarah, you can only guess how they enthralled audiences in their prime.

There is an new excellent Sarah Bernhardt biography - ***The Divine Sarah***, by Arthur Gold and Robert Fizdale (1991, Knopf). Most biographers begin the Doré/Bernhardt romance about 1876, Gold pushes the date back to 1872 (p.129):

> (Doré) saw her at the Comedie Francaise and, struck by the beauty of her performance, sent her one of his Biblical drawings. The gift led to an invitation to Sarah's dressing room and, as she found love-making the quickest road to friendship, to her bed. It took very little time for Paris to learn about their liaison and the romantic trip they made to the wild shores of Brittany.

In her own memoirs, in which the description of her affairs is much more subdued, Sarah first mentions Doré platonically in 1876, when she was having lunch at Victor Hûgo's. She was pleased to be there, but things did not go so well, and she passed out. But she was famous for passing out at will (p.291):

> ... But what a terrible lunch we had! It was really bad and badly served. My feet were frozen by the draughts from the three doors, which fitted badly, and one could positively hear the wind blowing under the table. Near me was Mr. X______, the German architect, who ... had such dirty hands and ate so badly that he made me feel sick.... and the boredom I was afflicted with - all reduced me to a state of positive suffering and I lost consciousness. When I recovered I found myself on a couch, my hand in that of Mme. Drouet and in front of me, sketching me, Gustave Doré.
>
> "Oh, don't move," he cried, "you are so pretty like that!" These words, though they were so inappropriate, pleased me, nevertheless, and I complied with the wish of the great artist. From that day we were the best of friends.

Of course, they were much more than friends. Sarah was just getting over an affair with a handsome but jealous French actor, Jean Mounet-Sully (who had also had an affair with Adelina Patti a decade earlier). Gold points out how much Sarah appreciated Doré, compared to Mounet (p.129-130):

> Doré must have come as a welcome change from the long-suffering Mounet. The actor had expected to reform her; the artist, who had affairs with such eminently unreformed divas as Adelina Patti, the Swedish soprano Christine Nilsson, and Hortense Schneider, the queen of operetta, expected nothing but pleasure. Mounet had offered the domestic security of his small roof-top apartment and the cloistered life of the theatre; Doré offered the stimulation of high bohemia and the limitless horizons of artistic freedom. Even his studio was to her taste, with its vast murals of forests, ruins, and deserted lakes, and its *trompe l'oeil* views of the Rhine.
>
> Doré, at forty, was rich and handsome; a celebrated artist who wore the *Legion d'honneur*, was welcome at the English court, held a lively musical salon, and hobnobbed with the literary and artistic lions of the day. In a word, a man after Sarah's heart...
>
> Sarah, of course, felt that no man could have too much blood in his veins to suit her. Nor could she resist Doré's macabre fantasies, the torture and death in the desolate landscapes that filled his books and canvasses.

112 Doré oil painting of ***Sarah Bernhardt*** (nd, late 1870s?) - present location unknown
Doré sketch of ***Sarah Bernhardt*** (nd, 1870s) - Clapp collection, now in Strasbourg Art Museum.
photo of controversial Sarah Bernhardt (1870s), sculpting and wearing men's clothing.
engraving made from Bastien-Lepage's painting of ***Sarah Bernhardt*** (1879).

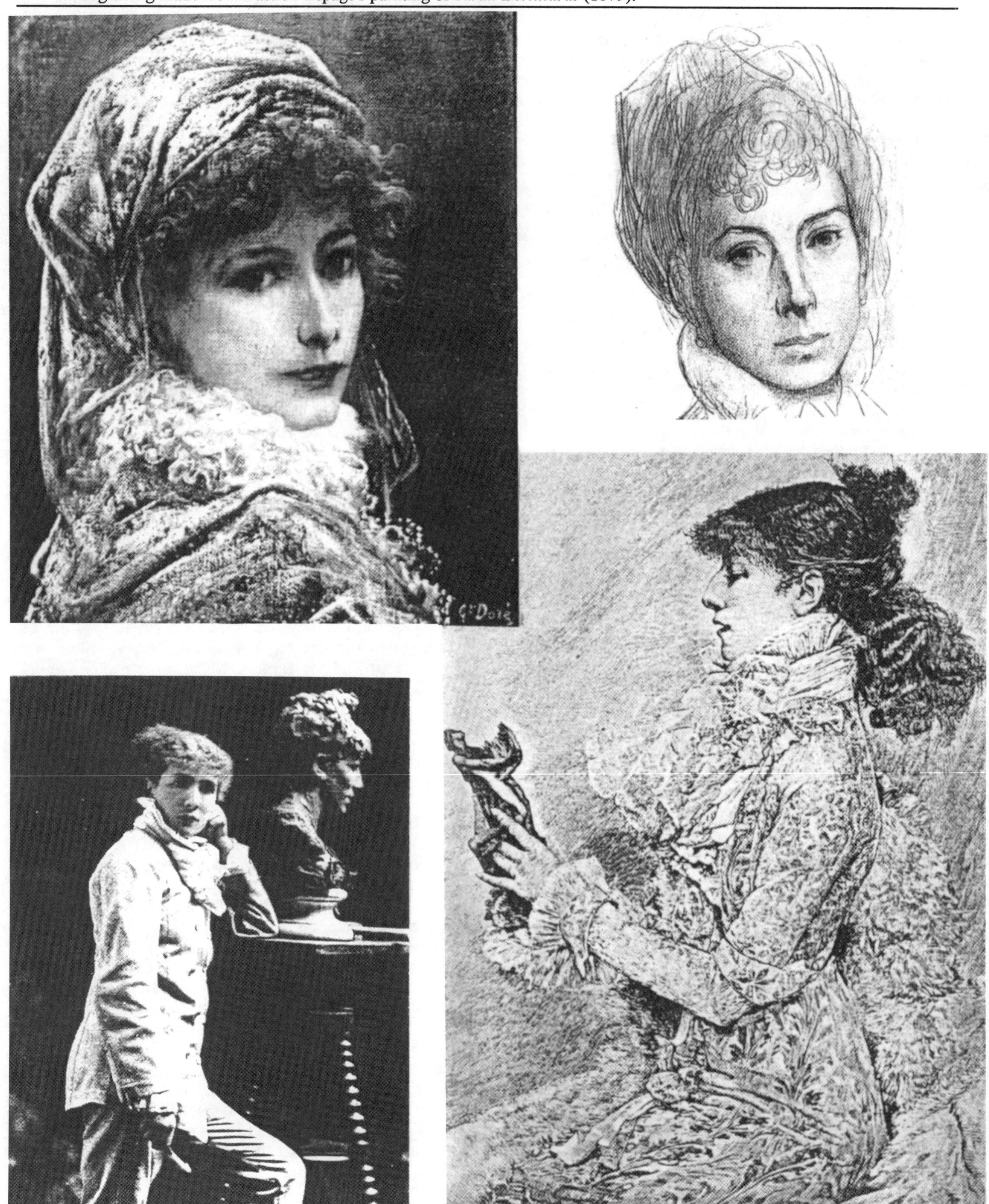

Doré and Sarah had many common interests, especially after Sarah took up painting and sculpture. They went on trips together, often to work on landscape paintings. Woon relates one interesting excursion (p.331):

> Sarah and he spent one August sketching together in Brittany. They both wore corduroy trousers and carried easels, and people who did not know them took them for an old painter and his apprentice, never dreaming that the apprentice was the most famous actress in France.
>
> Sarah told me of an amusing incident that occurred during this painting odyssey. They had been walking all day, and dusk found them near a farmhouse. Entering, they asked for shelter for the night.
>
> After dinner Doré was shown to a bedroom, and the painter supposed that Sarah had been given another. But the next morning, on looking out his window, he was amazed to see her washing herself at the yard pump, her clothes full of straw and filth. She was in a merry mood.
>
> "They took me for your boy pupil, and gave me a bed with the cow in the barn!" she told him.

Sometime in the late 1870s, Doré did a painting of Sarah. But the one project that really bound them together for posterity was the new theatre in Monte Carlo in 1879, where Doré did a sculpture called ***La Danse*** and Sarah did a sculpture called ***Le Chant***, per Gold (p.131-132):

> Their friend Charles Garnier, the architect responsible for Paris's sumptuous new opera house, was now drawing up plans for a casino in Monte Carlo: a theatre with gambling rooms attached. If she could persuade Doré to make a sculpture for the facade, Garnier told her, he would commission her to make a companion piece. Sarah hastened to her desk and wrote to Doré, distorting the facts somewhat to suit her purpose:
>
> "My friend, I've been charged with a mission. I'll be blunt and go right to the point. Here it is: Garnier is building a large theatre in Monaco. There are to be a pair of sculptural groups on the facade. He has asked me to do one, and told me he has great hopes that you will do the other, but he is afraid you might turn him down. Could it be true, dear friend, that you would not want me as a partner? It would make me proud! Send an answer quickly to your friend who loves you with all her heart! Say at once whether Garnier dare approach you without the risk of being refused by Your Highness!"
>
> Doré was understandably reluctant to agree to these conditions. He was ambitious for his sculpture, having taken it up fairly recently, and tempted by Garnier's offer, but he had no desire to associate his work with that of an amateur. Bernhardt, though a novice at sculpture, was a past master at intrigue. Without consulting Doré, she forced his hand by hinting to the press that they had both agreed to decorate the casino. When her "adored one" read what was news to him, he accused her of double-dealing. Once again Sarah rushed to her desk, this time in the hope of covering her tracks.
>
> "My beloved Master,
> You know perfectly well that the newspapers invent stories, and always get everything wrong. It's all lies ... I would never do anything without letting you know beforehand. I love you very much."
>
> When Doré finally accepted, Sarah, elated by her adroit manipulation of art, love, and business, decorated one of her engraved calling cards with the following message and sent it to him:

> You have made two people happy, Garnier and
> **SARAH BERNHARDT**
> who sends you a kiss.
> S.B.
> Garnier will come to see you, I think,
> tomorrow or the day after.

They were very close until Sarah left on her U.S. tour in 1880, and then Adelina followed the next year. Neither one of them would ever see Doré again. He died a very lonely man. For all his famous lovers who thought him charming, he was to the end an incurable romantic, destined not for a flesh-and-blood lover, but for a dream lover. At the time of his death, he was doing the illustrations for Poe's ***The Raven***, expressing "sorrow for the lost Lenore." Just as the narrator of Poe's poem followed Lenore in death, so did Doré.

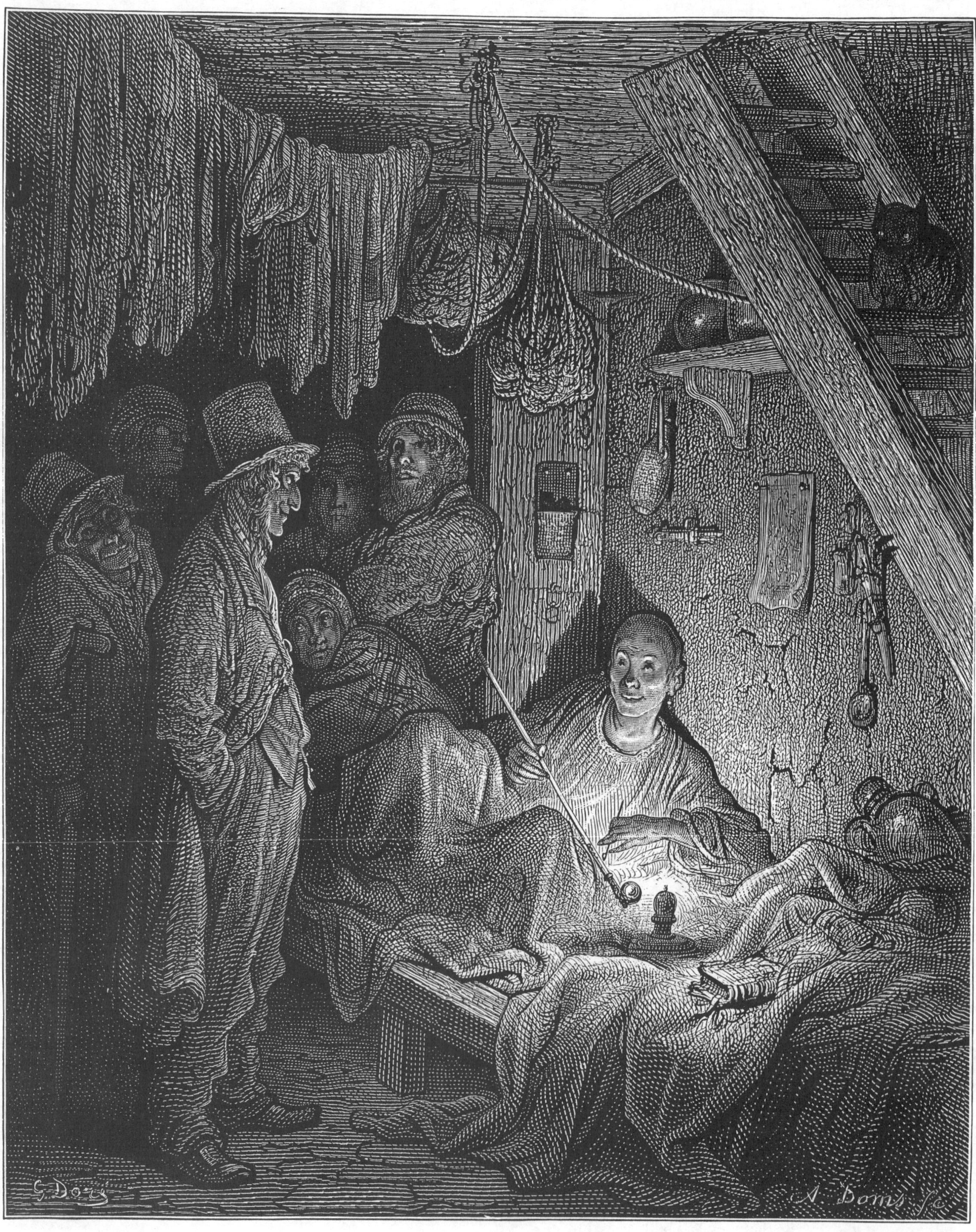
G. Doré
A. Doms Sc

8. DORÉ'S LATER FOLIOS (1872-83)

We will go through the last decade of Doré's life three times; to cover Doré the illustrator, Doré the painter, and Doré the sculptor. When we left Doré the illustrator in the fall of 1869, he had just finished his fifth set of steel engravings for Moxon's ***Hood***. Doré did 20 major sets of book illustrations during the 1860s, but only seven in the last decade of his life. Doré was no longer messing around with filler work. He now considered himself a painter, and took on illustration projects with reluctance. All the later ones were major folios, and the engraving size was increasing. Many vignettes were as big as 6x8. For works with fewer plates (***Coleridge*** and ***Poe***), the plates were 9½x12½, rather than his normal 7½x9½. Here are his last folios, with full-page plates (B) and vignettes (b):

1872	B.Jerrold: ***London, a Pilgrimage***	54-B,126-b
1873	F.Rabelais: ***Works*** (614 new illos)	61-B,658-b
1874	C.Davillier: ***Spain*** (mag.illo repros)	132-B,174-b
1876	S.T.Coleridge: ***The Ancient Mariner***	38-B, 4-b
1877	J.Michaud: ***The Crusades***	100-B
1879	L.Ariosto: ***Orlando Furioso***	82-B,536-b
1883	E.A.Poe: ***The Raven***	24-B, 2-b

Blanchard Jerrold: London, a Pilgrimage

Technically, Doré was also listed as an author of this work; in fact, he was listed first. Of course he did not write the text; he could barely speak English. ***London*** was much more visual than textual. It was not the first time text was written to his illustrations. ***London*** was eagerly awaited by the English public, having been postponed by the Franco-Prussian War.

The idea for ***London*** began with his first trip to England in 1868, which we will look at in the next chapter. Jerrold, in his Doré biography, devotes a whole chapter to how this book came into being. Jerrold humbly admits that ***London*** was his idea from the start - to match Doré's artistic genius with an in-depth view of all segments of London society - rich and poor, common people working and playing, famous sites and slums, nobility and criminals. Many nights Doré went incognito, with undercover police for protection, to see the parts of London not listed in any tour guide. One day Doré would be the guest of honor at some gala ball, and the next day he would wander through the slums where ragged children played in the mud. One famous engraving was the opium den in Charles Dickens' recently unfinished ***Mystery of Edwin Drood***. Doré did many engravings of the homeless, particularly those who slept on the London Bridge, clinging together for warmth.

The result was a book often hailed as the greatest visual expression of the social class struggle ever published. Many people who do not even like Doré admit the genius of this work. Many people have asserted it to be Doré's greatest work, but it certainly has to share the top billing with the likes of ***Dante's Inferno, Don Quixote,*** and ***The Bible***. There is no greater tribute to Doré's genius that the diversity of these four works, from horror to comic adventure to religion to social commentary. In each field, they are the greatest set of engravings ever created. But let us settle one issue here. There seems to be some debate about whether Doré was a socialist or a religious fundamentalist. He was neither. He was a mystical hedonist. Whether he was illustrating the suffering of the poor or the suffering of Christ, he was actually taking his own personal suffering, which plagued the last dozen years of his life, and expressing it through whatever character his hand was called upon to create. In his earlier years, the dominant theme of his work was playfulness. From 1870 on, immense sadness permeated his creations.

When it first came out, ***London*** was not nearly as popular as Doré's works from the 1860s. It was published in London by Grant in twelve monthly parts during 1872, and then in a massive 13x17 book edition. But they never reprinted it. There is also an extremely rare U.S. parts edition, published as a supplement to ***Harper's Weekly*** from 4/13/72-5/31/73. Harper did not then publish it as a book edition, but anyone with the parts could have had them bound. Harper finally came out with a book edition in 1890, in a smaller 11x13½ format. Though the title-page title is the same, the cover is entitled ***Doré's London***. In 1876, Hachette published a French edition with different text by Louis Enault. For some time that caused a major rift between Jerrold and Doré. There was an 1882 Russian edition, with different text by A. Vatsin, in a small format with just a few Doré illustrations. A few of the ***London*** illustrations were also inserted into an 1880 edition of Dicken's ***Pickwick Papers*** by the New York publisher G.W.Carleton. ***London*** was not reprinted for nearly a century.

But it was not forgotten. A poor, wild-eyed redhead, who fancied himself a painter, greatly admired the ***London*** folio, but could not afford the steep price. He mentioned his admiration of those engravings (and how he had tried to copy them, but it was very difficult) in letters to his brother Theo. In 1890, shortly before he died, he took one of Doré's simplest ***London*** engravings, "The Newgate Prison Yard," and made it into an oil painting, entitled ***Prisoners Exercising (after Gustave Doré)***. Today that painting is in the Pushkin Museum in Moscow. He was, of course, Vincent van Gogh. Here is one of his comments, from his letters (V3, p.332):

> What is happening to the wood engravings? The beautiful ones are getting scarcer and scarcer, and more and more difficult to get hold of ... The other day I saw a complete set of Doré's pictures of London. I tell you it is superb, and noble in sentiment - for instance that room in the "Night Shelter for Beggars" - I think you have it, or else you will be able to get it.

Jack & Charmian London were big admirers of Doré, and mentioned him several times in their writings, the most significant of which was in his 1903 book, ***The People of the Abyss***, the text of which is similar in content to ***London***. Near the end of chapter six, Jack London wrote:

> We went up the narrow gravelled walk. On the benches on either side was arrayed a mass of miserable and distorted humanity, the sight of which would have impelled Doré to more diabolical flights of fancy than he ever succeeded in achieving.

Doré's illustrations were so applicable to Jack London's text that in 1980, the publisher Joseph Simon issued an edition of ***The People of the Abyss*** with 20 Doré illustrations. Even the cover is a Doré illustration.

 reduced illustrations from Jerrold's ***London, a Pilgrimage*** (1872) - contains 180 Doré illos.

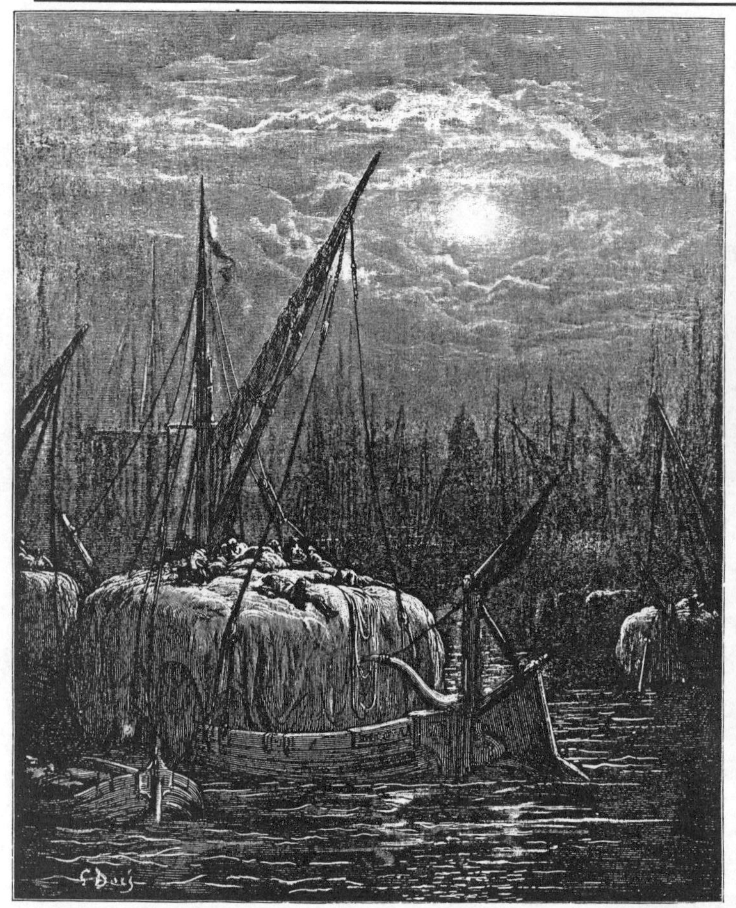

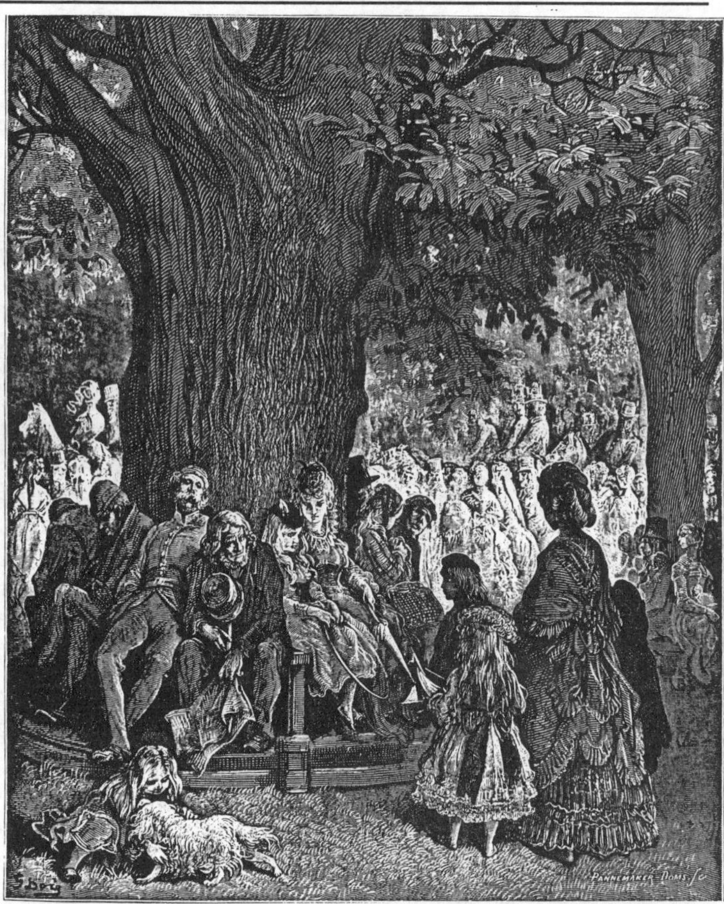

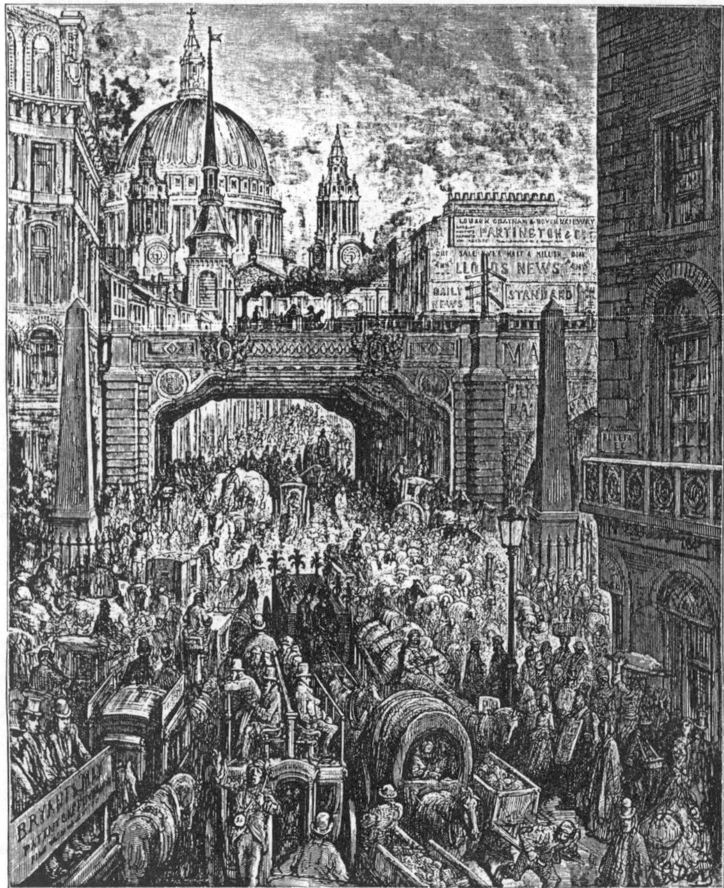

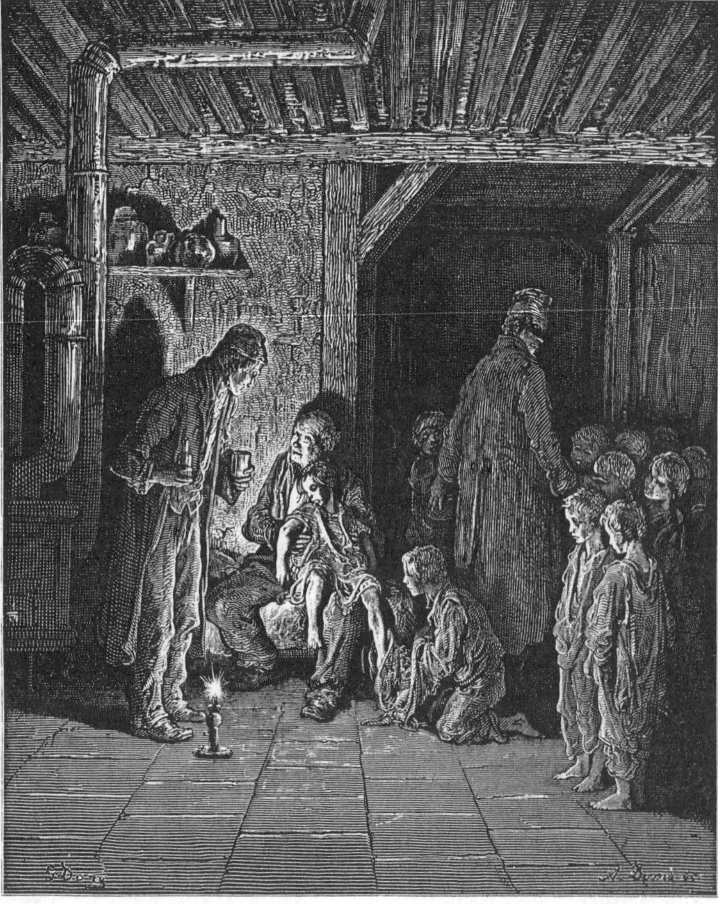

The American revival of interest in Doré began in the 1960s. But long before that, the film industry had been relying on Doré's *London* engravings for background scenes in films based on Dickens' works; for example the David Lean films ***Great Expectations*** (1946) and ***Oliver Twist*** (1948). In 1968, Benjamin Blom reprinted a facsimile edition of ***London***. Other publishers followed suit. Twice as many editions of ***London*** have been published in this generation as were published in the 19th century. Many articles have been written about its social significance. In his 1969 book, ***Civilization***, Kenneth Clark relates ***London*** illustrations to Dickens' works (p.328):

> Dickens' early illustrators were too comical and pictorially incompetent to convey his feelings about society. The images that fit Dickens are by the French illustrator Gustave Doré. He was originally a humorist; but the sight of London sobered him. His drawings were done in the 1870s, after Dickens's death. But one can see that things hadn't changed much. Perhaps it took an outsider to see London as it really was, and it needed someone of Doré's marvellous graphic skill to make this great slice of human misery credible.

Clark's work has been made into an 11-hour video, and that video may also contain Doré illustrations. Besides 180 wood engravings for ***London***, Doré also made a large number of drawings, etchings, and paintings of London scenes. In 1978, 24 ***London*** illustrations were made into slides, entitled ***Social Contrast in the Second Half of the 19th Century***, by A/V Productions of England, distributed by Gould Media of New York. ***London*** engravings have been used in other books, on topics ranging from sociology to history to literature to geography. But how is it possible that there were zero editions of ***London*** for about 80 years, and then all of a sudden it is Doré's greatest work?

F.Rabelais: Gargantua & Pantagruel

We already covered ***Rabelais*** back in 1854. The 1854 J.Bry edition was a thin 7½x11 with "only" 105 engravings. The 1873 Garner edition was a 2V 13x18 folio with 719 engravings (inluding the earlier ones). Early English editions contained only 50 of the early engravings. Finally in 1978, Dover reprinted 252 of Doré's ***Rabelais*** illustrations. Then in 1979, Franklin Library put 158 of Doré's ***Rabelais*** illustrations into their 2V 6x9½ edition. There were a few French reprints of the 1873 edition, but with fewer illustrations, some with 674 and then in 1928 down to 286. Some recent French editions do have the full 719 illustrations in a small 4to. There is also a 1979 German edition with 682 illustrations, but it is only a small 8vo. If you see a Doré edition of ***Rabelais***, check how many illustrations it has. But 1870s French ***Rabelais*** editions are some of the most beautiful books ever published.

Baron Charles Davillier: Spain

This book came out in 1874, but it had been serialized for 12 years! When he went to Spain in 1862 to do ***Don Quixote***, Doré was fascinated with the Spanish people and culture. So in 1862, ***Tour du Monde*** began a serial on ***Spain*** with Doré's engravings and text by Baron Charles Davillier. Altogether, Doré did 164 full-page plates and 160 vignettes for ***Spain***. The 1874 Hachette edition was 10½x14, with 306 of the 324 magazine engravings. Publishers keep using ***Spain*** engravings in any book about Spain, with texts ranging from Alexandre Dumas to Theophile Gautier to William Prescott to Ernest Hemingway to Edmondo de Amicis.

So many people wrote text to Doré's illustrations that a phrase became common, "the author has illustrated Doré's engravings very well." Every publisher wanted to offer a set of illustrated travel books. In 1869, Cassell began a 6-year serial, ***Illustrated Travels***, using many French illustrations, including Doré's ***Spain*** engravings. Captain Mayne Reid wrote to Cassell about those French illustrations, per Nowell (p.105-106):

> Don't you think it would be judicious to take the French artists' and gravers' names from the pictures in *Illustrated Travels*? They take away from the idea of originality as your readers may easily know them to be French, and there is no reason why they should know it. I adopted the plan myself with some of your cuts which I purchased from Mr. Turner in New York for my magazine there. The least touch of the chisel will do it without damaging the picture in any way.
>
> A reader who suspects an article to have been *written to an illustration*, and not vice versa, will doubt its geniuneness; and many readers know the names of these French fellows familiarly enough.

The first English book edition of ***Spain*** finally came out in 1876, with only 235 engravings. There were just three English book editions; 1876 S.Low, 1876 Scribner, and 1881 Bickers. But English readers had been seeing those ***Spain*** engravings in a dozen other books which borrowed them. In 1870 ***Harper's Magazine*** began to use them. Also in 1870, ***Spanish Pictures drawn with Pen & Pencil*** used about 30 of them. There were also early editions in Spanish (no!), Italian, German, Dutch, Danish, and Russian. ***Spain*** is much more of a travel book than ***London***, but it is still much more than a travel book. It captures the heart and soul of Spain and the Spanish people. It should be noted that the pictures of pretty young senoritas tend to look like Adelina Patti. Doré also did many paintings and unpublished drawings of Spain. At times Doré biographers disagree about whether certain paintings are of characters from Spain or London, especially the poor and homeless. But both ***Spain*** and ***London*** are invaluable visual expressions of what life was really like in 19th century Europe.

Samuel T.Coleridge:Rime-Ancient Mariner

In 1798, 500 copies of a little anonymous book of poetry were published, entitled ***Lyrical Ballads***. It contained 19 poems by William Wordsworth and four by Samuel Taylor Coleridge, one of which was ***The Ancient Mariner***. Critics thought it was awful - "A rhapsody of unintelligible wildness and incoherence." When they went to issue a reprint in 1800, they were going to leave that poem out, but Coleridge tried modernizing some of the archaic wording, so they left it in. Not until 1817 was Coleridge listed as author of the poem.

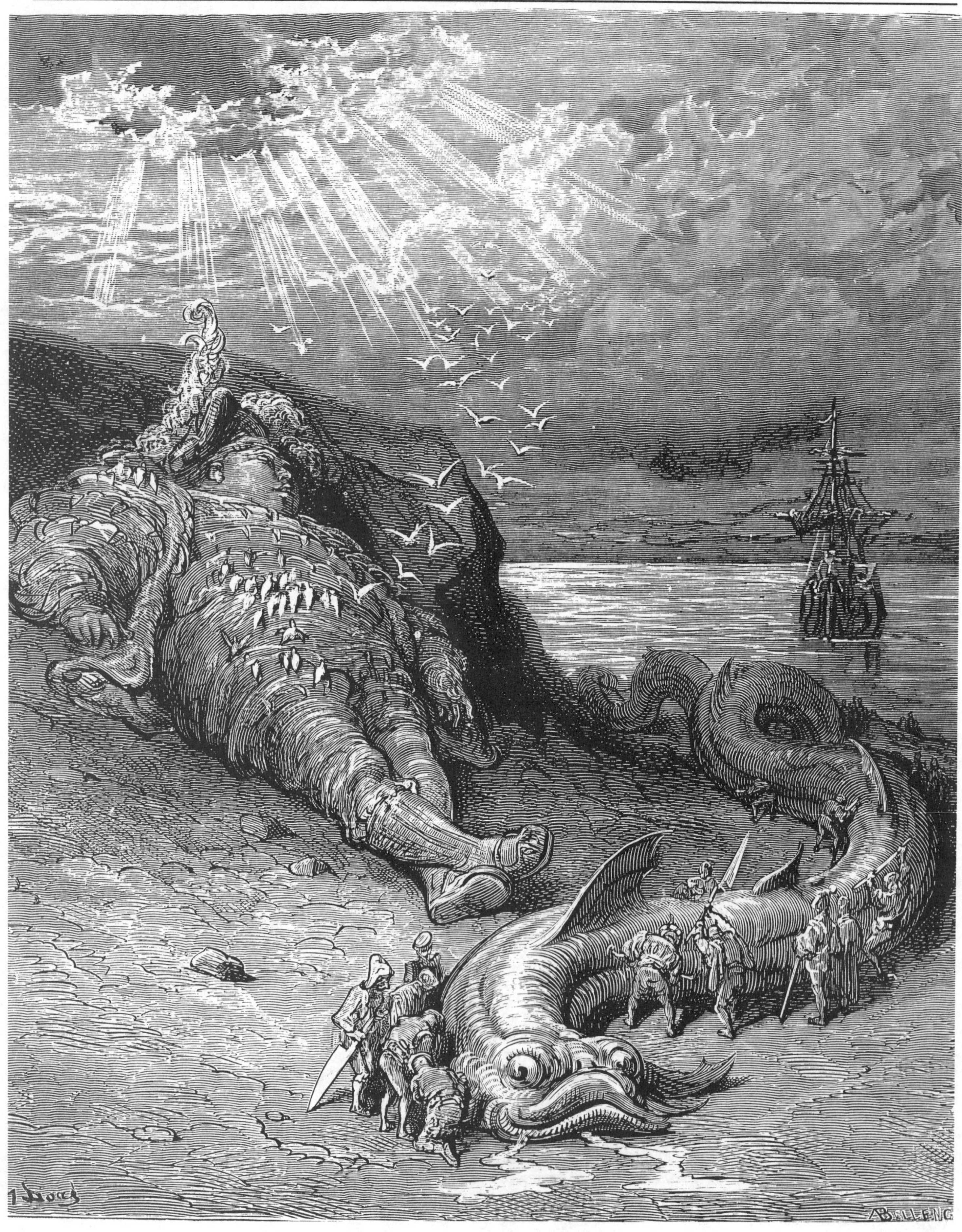

When Coleridge died in 1834, the poem was not considered to be particularly significant. But in 1837, a Scottish publisher issued a large folio of it, with 25 etchings by David Scott, who seemed obsessed with close-up anatomical drawings of hands and feet. Both he and that edition died in obscurity. In 1857, another publisher tried a more practical set of vignettes of ***The Ancient Mariner***, which featured Birket Foster. Those had a life because they could be reprinted cheaply. Finally, in 1863, another Scottish artist, J. Noel Paton, won a contest by the Art Union of London with 20 beautiful oblong outline illustrations of the poem. But that was a subscription edition and few people saw it. Finally in December of 1875, Doré did a set of engravings that would make the poem famous. Few people today realize how much the popularity of that poem was due to the many Doré editions which finally made it come to life.

There is a great deal of confusion about the first edition of this major Doré folio. There are listings with differing dates, differing publishers, and differing formats. But there is just one British folio edition, but at the same time they also offered a very expensive set of India Proofs. The edition came out in December of 1875, but it was dated 1876. There is no edition dated 1875. LeBlanc got his information from the English Catalogue, which lists editions according to the year in which they were published, not according to the date listed on the title page. This has proved to be one of the great follies of literary research, and has produced many a phantom edition. Not only do dozens of rare book libraries have the 1876 edition (none have an 1875 edition), but the January 15, 1876 edition of the ***Illustrated London News*** has a review of the book, stating that it just came out. The real absurdity of the two edition theory is that the same people who assert it claim that the book was a commercial failure. Their twisted logic goes like this: the book was very expensive--it was a financial disaster--they reprinted it the next year. Here is the wording from the bottom of the title page:

LONDON

DORÉ GALLERY

BEEFORTH & FAIRLEFS, 35, NEW BOND STREET

HAMILTON, ADAMS & C°

32, PATERNOSTER ROW

ALL RIGHTS RESERVED

MDCCCLXXVI

The main thing that has confused people is the listing of two London publishers. It has been stated that Doré published this book himself, but Doré did not own The Doré Gallery, Fairless & Beeforth did. Hamilton may have functioned more like their distributor. That first British edition was 16x20 and sold for 84s (= $21), while the set of India Proofs was 210s. Those are high prices for such a thin book, and the binding is very plain - the decorative border is stamped in blind, not in gilt, and there is no cover illustration. All the pages of the book are individually sewn into pieces of material. The paper and printing are high quality, but the binding is impractical, and it is easy for the pages to tear where they are sewn to the material. It is quite likely that the British edition did not sell well because of the price and the binding.

Such was not the case with the U.S. version. Harper published a handsome, well-bound volume, just over 14x18, at a fairly low cost of $10. Their first edition came out in December of 1876. In their review of their own book in ***Harper's Weekly***, they came to the amazing conclusion that their Doré title "is far better in an art point of view, and far better as an illustration of Doré's peculiar power, than his famous Bible." There are two versions of the December 1876 version, one dated 1876 and one dated 1877. Harper normally dated major books the year following the December in which they were issued. Also, a survey of rare book libraries shows that the 1876 version is very rare, the great majority of copies having the 1877 date. It would make no sense for almost all U.S. libraries to pass on the highly publicized first edition, but to then purchase an unadvertised reprint. The high quality and low cost of the Harper edition made it very popular. There are Harper editions dated 1876, 1877, 1878, 1881, 1882, 1883, 1884, 1886 & 1888. Those were not pirate editions. They were printed from electrotypes made from the original blocks. Their gilt cover design was also major improvement on the English edition. So why did the U.S. version sell so well, while the English version sold so poorly? Perhaps the Doré Gallery folks really did not know how be be a book publisher. Their edition looks like they tried to insert paintings into a book binding. The Harper version was a better product at a much lower price. After Doré's death they discovered 450 unbound copies of the Doré Gallery edition in his atelier. Perhaps he was planning to do a specially bound version but never got around to it.

Finally in 1883, the U.S. pirate publishers got cranked up. Eight U.S. publishers issued editions in all shapes and sizes in the next decade. They also began combining the Doré illustrations with other earlier sets. In 1883 there was a set that featured Doré with the 1857 Birket Foster vignettes. In 1886 there was a version that combined the full sets of Doré and the 1863 J.Noel Paton illustrations. In 1887, Doré's illustrations even appeared in J.W.Buel's non-fiction book, ***Sea & Land***. In the 1892 book ***Discovery & Conquest of the New World*** they doctored Doré's ***Mariner*** engravings and listed them as being illustrations of Columbus! There were also foreign-language folio editions in French, German, Italian, and Russian.

This is another Doré title rediscovered in the 1960s, after almost no editions from 1900-60. Since 1963 there have been nearly 30 editions, not to mention illustrations borrowed for ***Moby Dick, Frankenstein,*** and Time-Life's ***Enchanted World*** series. In a later chapter we will analyze those who during the 1960s and 1970s re-asserted Doré's true significance, such as Anthony Burgess, author of ***Clockwork Orange***. The revival of interest in Doré's ***Mariner*** illustrations began with the Martin Gardner ***Annotated Ancient Mariner*** in 1965, in which he insisted on using Doré's illustrations. He even used the complete set of engravings twice. In his introduction, Gardner asserted that some non-Doré ***Mariner*** illustrations which were then in fashion were just plain awful (particularly those by Alexander Calder), and that even though Doré was then "out of style," his illustrations were still by far the best ever done for ***Rime of the Ancient Mariner*** (p.2-3):

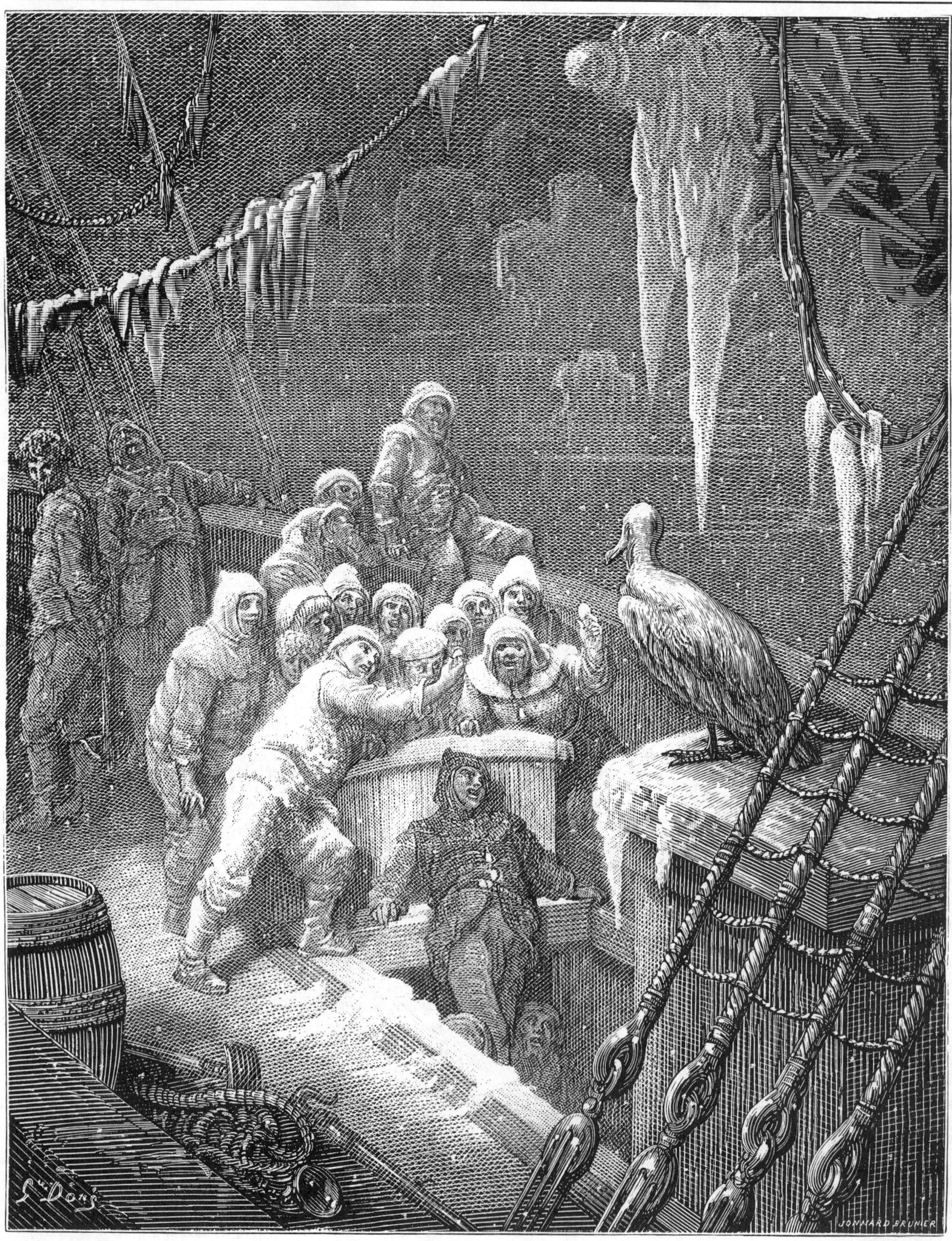

> I make no apologies for reproducing the Doré illustrations. They are something of a gamble, for Doré has been out of fashion for many decades.... To me, at any rate, Doré's crowded, romantic illustrations for *The Ancient Mariner*... are a refreshing visual holiday.

The ***Annotated Ancient Mariner*** was a smaller 8½x11, with the 9½x12½ illustrations reduced to 7x9, plus another set reduced down to 2½x3½ to fit in with the text. But the quality is surprisingly good for the size. It was published by several different U.S. and British publishers. It re-established Doré as the premiere ***Mariner*** illustrator. The next year, the Italian publisher, Edizione d'Art "FELIX" of Milano published an English-language edition worthy of Doré and Coleridge. It came in a slipcase stamped Time-Life Books and International Book Society. It was a silk-bound 12½x17 folio, printed on high-quality paper with full-size illustrations, most of which are very high quality. It also has an excellent introduction to Doré and the poem by Anthony Burgess, who is impressive in the depth of his understanding of Doré, at a time when most of the intellectual community was dismissing Doré outright with the terse "too melodramatic." Here are excerpts from the beginning and end of his introduction:

> The build-in resistance to the spirit of poetry which, regrettably, seems to be part of our modern society, happily is not matched by a resistance to visual art. Generations of readers in the past came to associate Gustave Doré's illustrations with classic works (by Balzac, Cervantes, Rabelais and Dante, among others) and today Doré is justly growing fashionable again. His illustrations to Coleridge's poem need no advocacy, no explanation. Though it would be dangerous to regard them as a substitute for the poem, they immediately and marvellously invoke the eerie, magical, superstitious world which Coleridge created. Even if we start with Doré we end with Coleridge. The draughtsman's art is great, but it is put to the service of another art. Waterspouts, foundering ships, dark looming figures seem to leap from Coleridge's poetic imagination to Doré's wood blocks. It is a wonderful wedding of poet's and craftsman's line - all the more remarkable in view of the differences in time and style and, above all, genius which separated the two men.
>
> -----------------------
>
> Coleridge died in 1834, before the Victorian Age started. Louis Christophe Gustave Paul Doré was born a couple years earlier and died in 1883, having lived through - and even helped to mould - an era of taste very different from that of the first Romantics. Doré, unlike Coleridge, was an artist of great facility whose quality shows few variations. His capacity for hard work, moreover, contrasts sharply with the poet's Hamlet-like indolence ... In all he illustrated nearly a hundred books, including the Bible, *The Divine Comedy*, *Don Quixote*, the Fables of LaFontaine - anything classical, larger than life, or grandly comic. His influence on the European imagination has been considerable: when most of us think of Cervantes' Spain we are really thinking of Doré's; the Doré Inferno is more terrifying than Dante's.

The one-two punch of Gardner and Burgess put Doré's ***Ancient Mariner*** back on the artistic/literary map. In 1970, Dover published their low-cost edition (with introduction by Millicent Rose, author of a 1946 Doré biography). The Dover edition has been in print continuously ever since. In recent decades, many people have claimed that ***The Ancient Mariner*** was one of Doré's greatest works, which may be true, but that category is beginning to get a little crowded. There have been several recent editions, including a "comic-book" version.

In 1952, an educational film company made the Doré illustrations into a b&w filmstrip, and then into a 29-minute b&w film. In 1975, Lumiere Cine made that Doré film into a 52-minute colorized film, entitled ***The Strangest Voyage***, with an extensive Coleridge biography. In 1988, that color film was made into a 60-minute stereo color video, and the Coleridge biography even uses other Doré illustrations from ***Milton, The Bible,*** and ***London***. The 1988 video is available from Kultur Intl. Films (1-800-4-KULTUR). At the end of the video there is a commercial by John Huston in support of Kultur.

Joseph Michaud: The Crusades

This set of 100 full-page folio engravings was Doré only straight historical work, and he showed his versatility once again. Many books dealing with the Crusades have borrowed his engravings, and many people consider the Doré set the best illustrations ever done for the Crusades. Doré had quite a fascination with knighthood, and his works cover almost every imaginable facet of it - ***Rabelais, Jaufry the Knight, Don Quixote, Croquemitaine, Tennyson, The Crusades***, and still to come - ***Ariosto***. That is over 2000 knighthood engravings.

Joseph Michaud put most of his life into this 7-volume reference set, published between 1812-22. Although they are comprehensive, they do have a strong French bias, particularly in relation to people like Richard the Lion-Hearted. It is quite a lengthy work, and in many ways the engravings are superior to the text. ***Michaud*** was published in 1877 by Furne/Jouvet, first in 25 parts and then as yet another massive 2V folio, priced at 150 *fr*, or on special paper at 170 *fr*. This was the last non-Hachette folio. Like so many other Doré titles, ***Michaud*** originated in France but saw few French editions. An 1883 edition was advertised, but LeBlanc was unable to find a copy. There have not been any French editions since.

Now we come the most perplexing Doré edition of them all, more so than the first French editions of ***Balzac*** or ***The Bible***, or the first British editions of ***Tennyson*** or ***The Ancient Mariner***. The first (undated) American edition of ***Michaud*** seems simple enough (no British edition has ever been found). It is a 2V folio (11x14½), 5" thick and weighing about 30 lbs. The binding, the paper, and engravings are all high quality, but the books are so heavy they often fall apart. The publisher was George Barrie of Philadelphia. But the listed dates for this undated edition range from 1878-1896!

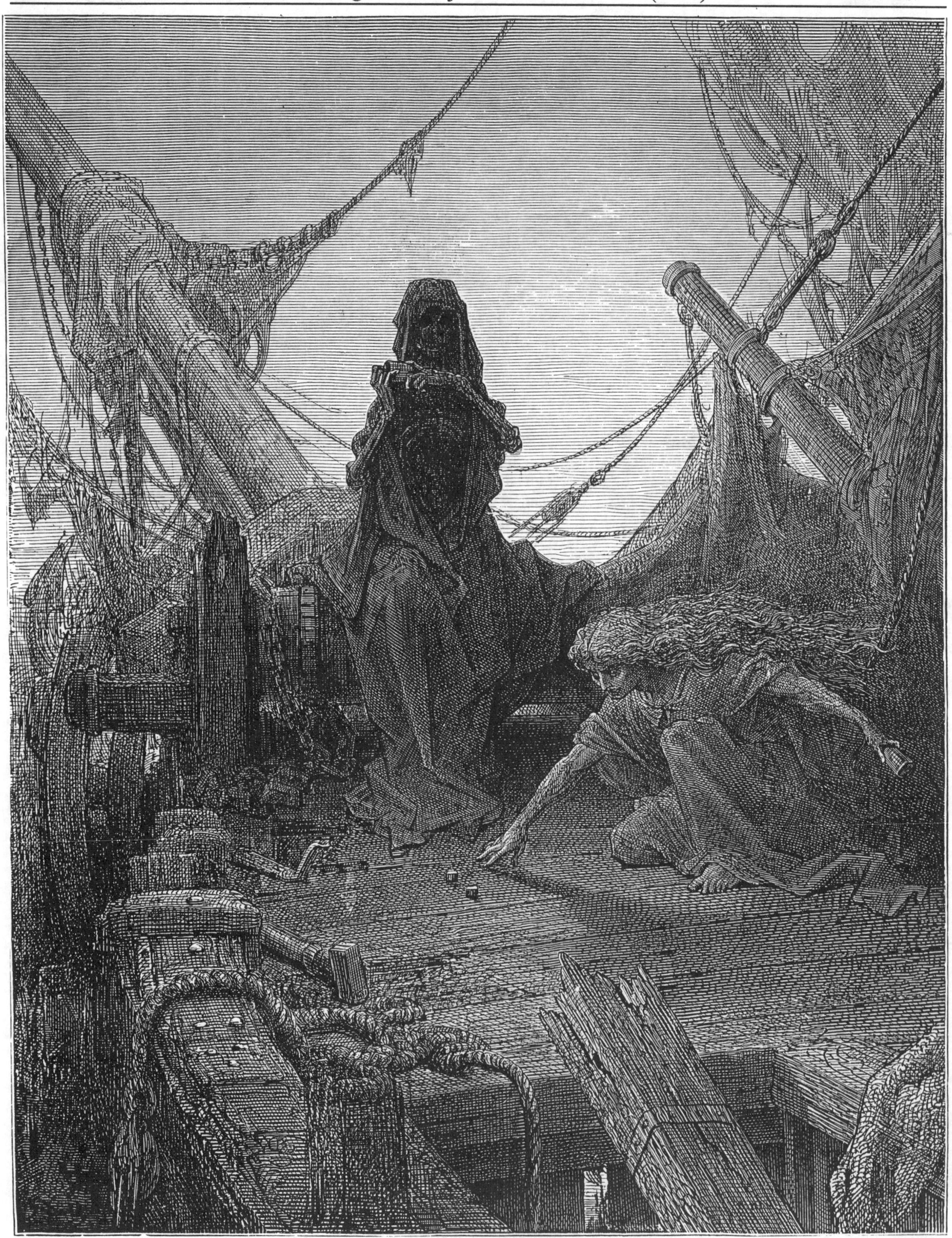

If a publisher issued an undated book which did not sell well, could they simply re-offer it as is 15 years later? That appears to be the only theory that explains this crazy edition. Copies of this edition in rare-book libraries range in height from 14" to 15½" (a range of ½" is common). But first we need a little background on this publisher. You may recall that bizarre 1866 edition of ***Don Quixote*** which listed both Cassell (London) and Gebbie & Keppel (Philadelphia). Gebbie shortly thereafter dropped Keppel and in 1873 published the first U.S. edition of Doré's ***Wandering Jew***, with the publisher listed as George Gebbie. Then Gebbie took on George Barrie, and in 1878, Gebbie & Barrie published the U.S. edition of the Paris International Exposition folio, contained some engravings of Doré works of sculpture. In 1880, Gebbie sort of retired, and the company was then called George Barrie. But Gebbie did not stay retired long, and started Gebbie & Co. anew, as a competitor to his former partner. In 1885, Barrie was at 615 Sansom St., and Gebbie at 619 Sansom St. in Philadelphia. In 1890, Barrie moved to 1313 Walnut St. in Philadelphia. By the turn of the century, both companies were out of business.

This edition of ***Michaud*** was issued in subscription parts, either 25 monthly parts for $1 each, or in five parts at $5.50 each. There is a amazing lack of any advertisements or official listings of the book edition. Some libraries list an 1893 date for the 2V folio, while others list an 1896 date. The parts edition would have run for over two years. So it would be very simple to ascribe a date somewhere between 1893-96 for the parts editions and the book version. But there are problems with that. First of all, nobody was publishing Doré editions in that size and at that price in the 1890s. By then there was a flood of cheap Doré editions in the $4-$6 range. The format of the Barrie edition of ***Michaud*** is consistent with the 1870s, but not with the 1890s. A second factor is the fact that by 1893, the Doré ***Michaud*** illustrations had already been borrowed and inserted into two other text versions of the Crusades. In 1886, Pollard & Moss had published an Alfred Trumble title, ***Sword & Scimetar, a Romance of the Crusades,*** with 80 of the 100 Doré illustrations, in a thin 11x14 edition for $10. Then in 1892, P.W.Ziegler published a title by James Boyd, ***The Story of the Crusades,*** with all 100 Doré illustrations, in a smaller 8x11 format. It would be very unlikely for two revised versions to come out before the official version. But those revised version would be quite logical if the official (and expensive) version had come out a few years earlier. The ad for the Trumble edition certainly sounds like there was a previous ***Michaud*** edition: "The story of the Crusades is in this volume told for the first time in a form to be of popular interest. All previous chronicles have been of the ponderous and circumstantial character that has value to the historian alone."

There is another major problem with the late date theory. After Doré's death, a major Paris exhibition was held in 1885. The exhibition booklet is usually called ***Duplessis*** (he wrote the introduction). In ***Duplessis*** (page 160), it lists editions of ***Michaud***, including: "Philadelphia, Gebbie & Barrie, 1878, 2V folio." In 1878, the company was still Gebbie & Barrie. But every known copy of the ***Michaud*** folio lists George Barrie as publisher, which means the edition could not have been before 1880. But if the U.S. edition was actually published in the 1890s, how could Duplessis be listing it at all in 1885?

Suppose Gebbie & Barrie had begun the 25-month parts edition in 1878, and by the time the book version came out in 1880, George Barrie would have been the only name on the title page. Duplessis could have somehow combined parts and book edition information. That would also make sense about the size and price of the book, and how revised versions could have begun in 1886. But why do rare-book libraries list dates in the 1890s? The parts edition lists a 1313 Walnut St. address (the book edition lists no address). Various reference works list 615 Sansom St. as Barrie's 1880s address, and 1313 Walnut St. as Barrie's 1890s address. So that parts edition had to have come out in the 1890s. Libraries could have used that address as evidence for an 1890s date.

I subscribe to the double-issue theory, that Barrie offered it in 1880 but it was too expensive and did not sell well. In the 1890s they discovered a quantity of copies and reoffered it in parts and book editions. Parts covers were then printed, with the tell-tale 1890s address. The 15½" pages had to be trimmed to fit the new parts covers, accounting for the smaller copies. The parts editions would then have been rebound into 14½" book editions. So you could tell which version you had simply by the height of the book. But this does not answer whether there was an 1878-80 parts edition, why ***Duplessis*** had the publisher's name wrong, and why there were no reviews, ads, or catalogue listings. After all, it was certainly a major edition.

Doré ***Crusades*** illustrations appeared in many historical works, such as the 10V ***Story of the Greatest Nations*** by Ellis & Horne, with 24 Doré illustrations, 15 from ***Michaud***. But this century has seen very few editions. In 1969, Centron Educational Films of Lawrence, KS produced a 16-minute, 16mm color/sound film ***The Crusades***, using the Doré illustrations. There have also been editions of Doré's ***Crusades*** in German, Dutch, Spanish, Italian, Norwegian, and Russian. In the Netherlands in the 1970s, background booklets for a comic-book series called ***Toppers in Strip*** used Doré's ***Crusades*** illustrations for ***Richard the Lion-Hearted*** and Sir Walter Scott's ***The Talisman***.

Ludovico Ariosto: Orlando Furioso

By the late 1870s, printing technology was about to do away with the wood engraving. It is hard to imagine what Doré could have accomplished had he not been so tied down to the need to make an engraving out of each drawing. We get just a glimpse of that in his last major French folio. His 618 illustrations for ***Ariosto*** were not wood engravings, or even steel. They were *gillotage*, a new type of zinc engraving, for which Doré only had to make drawings. Some have said that it caused Doré to go wild in ***Ariosto***, like a raging river that had burst a dam. ***Ariosto*** is pure fantasy. It is amazing to see all the effects Doré was able to create in ***Ariosto*** without the aid of color. It is the most underappreciated of all Doré's works, principally because it is also the rarest. There were no English editions. Most people had never seen any of these illustrations before Dover's 1980 edition came out.

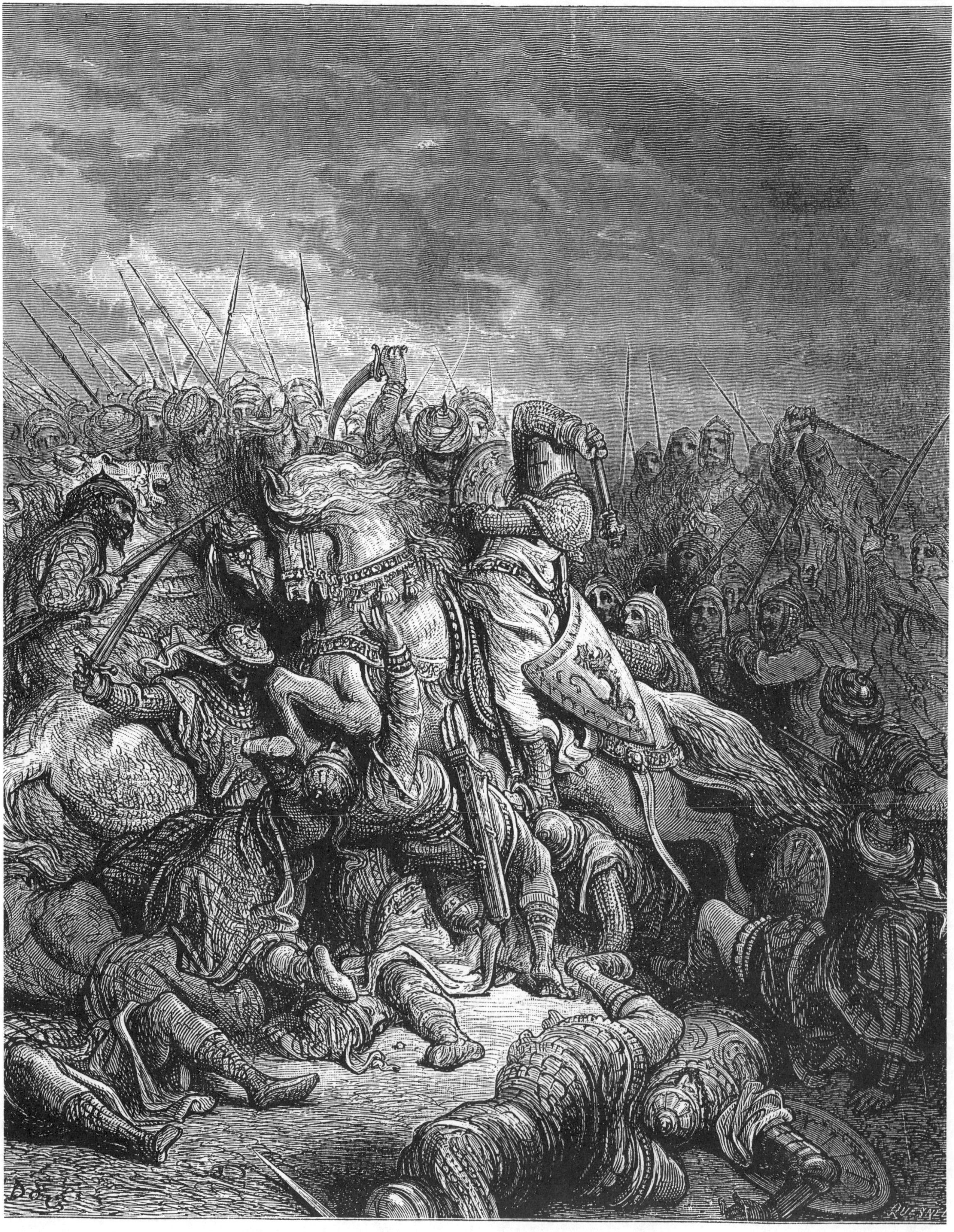

Very few people are familiar with ***Ariosto***. It is basically the Italian Renaissance version of the Song of Roland. First published in 1516, it is a vast panorama of knightly adventure that just floats off into fantasy. It combines many basic themes from Charlemagne and King Arthur. Much of the conflict involves Christians and Moors in Europe, but it spreads out to involve the whole world, not to mention the moon, etc. Here you find a knight riding a hippogriff (part horse, part eagle), monsters of every sort (scenes strikingly similar to ***Star Wars***), superhuman madmen uprooting trees and dragging around dead horses, many romantic scenes (probably more than any other Doré book), naked women chained to rocks about to be devoured by dragons, wild battle scenes shifting quickly to palatial ornamentation to the serenity of nature. Every deed is noble and magnificent. Of course, we are really describing the 618 Doré folio illustrations more than the text itself.

Doré returned to Hachette for this work, but it would be his last French folio, and his most expensive 1V folio. The regular edition was 12x17½, with 13x19½ Limited Editions - 50 on Whatman paper (250 *fr*), 40 on China paper (300 *fr*), and 15 on Japan paper (350 *fr*). The special editions came in 15 parts in slipcases. There are 82 full-page plates, including the 9½x12 frontispiece. With 618 engravings on 658 pages, ***Ariosto*** is "fully" illustrated. Most foreign editions were 2V folios. It is unfortunate that there were no English edition. The 1980 Dover edition was illustrations only - 208 of the original 618. There were folio editions in German, Italian, Spanish, and Portuguese, and an edition published in Mexico in 1955.

Edgar Allan Poe: The Raven

This edition was published virtually to the day that the copyright expired. It was the only American author Doré ever illustrated, and the only set of Doré engravings that was ever commissioned by a U.S. publisher. Harper had been getting on famously with their elephant folio edition of ***The Ancient Mariner***, and they wanted to make it and ***Poe*** a matching set. Doré was doing the ***Poe*** illustrations late in 1882, and finished them shortly before he died in January of 1883. It contained 24 full-page plates (9½x12½) and two ovals. In many ways, they are different from any other Doré work. As we mentioned previously, Adelina Patti and Sarah Bernhardt had both left for American tours, and Doré's mother had died in 1881. Doré was in a state of deep depression from then until his death. It is amazing that he took on the commission to do ***The Raven***. Perhaps it was because of the poem's theme of death; Doré was dying inside while doing the illustrations. They have a heavy sadness about them, as though the central figure can barely lift himself out of his chair. Some of them have a fuzzy look about them and may have been unfinished. Did Doré actual finish them and send them to Harper before he died, or did they just take what was there after his death, assuming it was finished? Doré would probably have been incapable of doing this work 30 years earlier, but in 1882 it was much more than Poe's story, it was Doré's story. After Doré died, Harper set to work during 1883 having American engravers carve the images, without any input from Doré. What a shame that Doré was not there to direct them in person or inspect them on completion. It is too bad Doré never could be coaxed to visit America.

The Doré ***Raven*** folio was published in December of 1883, simultaneously in the U.S. and England. Since Harper had commissioned the work, they would be considered the "true" first edition. But once again, this edition is the source of confusion. Harper's title page lists 1884, while the copyright page lists 1883. The British edition (by Sampson Low) lists 1883 on the title page. So the British edition gets listed as 1883 and the American edition gets listed as 1884, prompting many people to believe that the British edition came out first. Both versions are 14½x18½, but they look quite different. The British edition has a simple, small raven illustration on the cover, taken from an engraving detail. The American edition has a striking non-Doré illustration filling the front cover from edge to edge. Harper had commissioned U.S. artist Elihu Vedder to do a charcoal title-page illustration showing Poe and Doré, and an unnamed female American artist to do that cover illustration. Her initials "D.W." are in the lower right corner. Harper added an Edmund C. Stedman introduction, and after covering Poe and Doré, he mentions those illustrations (p.14):

> ... Vedder's symbolic crayon aptly sets them face to
> face, but enfolds them with the mantle of immortal
> wisdom and power. An American woman has wrought
> the image of a star-eyed Genius with the final torch,
> the exquisite semblance of one whose vision beholds,
> but whose lips may not utter, the mysteries of a land
> beyond "the door of a legended tomb."

The British edition included the full Stedman introduction, but did not include Harper's title-page or cover illustrations. That must have left British readers scratching their heads. There is no doubt that the U.S. cover is far more aesthically desirable than the British. Like Harper's ***Ancient Mariner*** folio, ***The Raven*** also sold for $10. But while they had several ***Mariner*** reprint editions, there were no ***Raven*** reprint editions. In fact, there were no ***Raven*** editions by any country for 80 years. How could Harper's "twin" Doré folios sell so differently? Perhaps they did a large first printing. Perhaps it was too late for such a deluxe edition. The Harper edition certainly came out with ample advertising and rave reviews. Lafcadio Hearn (he of Japanese fairy tale fame) thought it was practically the best book he had ever seen. This is the only Doré folio of which there are no early or folio reprint editions. The U.S. pirate publishers could not touch it since it was a U.S. commission.

No reference work ever listed the identity of D.W., that American woman who did the ***Raven*** cover. In 1883 there were no female American book illustrators. In England there were a few, like Kate Greenaway, but the first female American illustrators came out of Howard Pyle's Brandywine school in the 1890s. I searched for D.W. for years and finally gave up, only to find her by accident. Her name was Dora Wheeler, and the ***Raven*** cover appears to be the only book illustration she ever did. She was in the arts & crafts movement, where her mother, Candace Wheeler, was one of the leaders. One of Candace Wheeler's claims to fame was that she authored her last book in 1921 - at the age of 93! Dora's first claim to fame was winning postcard design contests by Louis Prang in the early 1880s. One of her 1882 postcard designs is very similar to the ***Raven*** cover, albeit much simplified. It appears that Harper must have seen her postcard

full-size illustration from Ariosto's ***Orlando Furioso*** (1879) - contains 618 Doré illos.

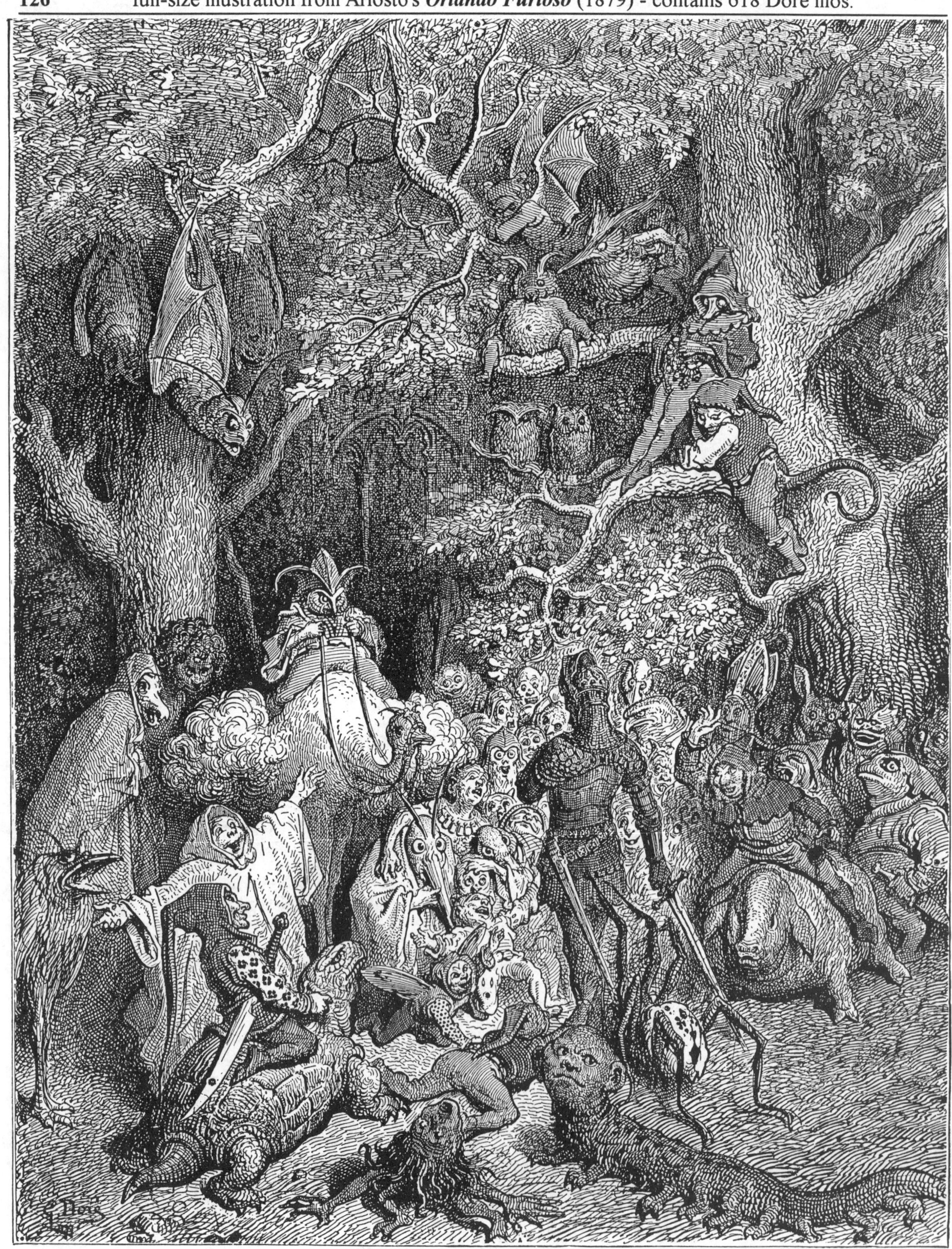

and commissioned her to do a similar but expanded version for the ***Raven***. Dora was also later known for tapestries and portrait paintings. There are several reference sources for information about the Harper ***Raven*** edition and others about Dora Wheeler, but none of them ever mentions her having done the ***Raven*** cover. For a century the artist of the ***Raven*** cover was just one more Doré-related mystery.

As we mentioned, this was the only Doré folio that was a critical success and a commercial failure. How it went 80 years without a reprint edition defies explanation. But after it was resurrected in the 1960s, this generation has seen editions in English, French, German, Spanish, Italian, and Greek, not to mention a video. MCE Publishing recently issued a facsimile reprint of Doré's ***Raven***. The Edgar Allan Poe Museum in Richmond, VA has a room dedicated to displaying the Doré engravings. They have several copies of the 1884 ***Raven*** folio. They took a copy that was falling apart and had the individual engravings framed and hung around the room with another intact copy on display under glass. They even sell Doré ***Raven*** T-shirts. They also have another related display there. A poor British sidewalk artist named James Carling (1857-87) went to New York in 1882 and tried to compete with Doré for the Harper ***Raven*** commission. It is doubtful that it was an official competition. I can find no record of Doré ever competing for commissions, especially in 1882 in far-off America. Carling probably heard that Harper was planning an illustrated ***Raven*** edition and submitted 43 drawings of variable artistic quality to Harper. They have some similarity to Doré's set, but at times Carling went off on wild artistic tangents. It is fascinating to compare the sets. Carling's set was rejected and he returned to England, where he died at the age of 29 and was buried in a paupers' grave. Carling had a brother Henry in Chicago who then took possession of the never-published illustrations until his own death in 1936. By a strange twist of fate, Henry's daughter Stella shortly thereafter made contact with and sold the drawings to the Poe Museum in Richmond, where they were put on display. In 1982, Roscoe Brown Fisher edited and published a book which finally showed Carling's illustrations. To this day, the two sets of illustrations by Doré and Carling can be viewed in adjoining rooms at the Poe Museum in Richmond. Doré was very successful and Carling was very unsuccessful, yet both had very unhappy lives and untimely deaths. The curse of ***The Raven***? Hardly. They fell prey to a much bigger curse called *life*.

There is also a ***Raven*** video. In 1954 a b&w experimental film was made from the Doré ***Raven*** engravings. In 1973 Lewis Jacobs colorized it and in 1978 it was made into a video. It is only 11 minutes long, with sound and color, narration by Gregg Morton, and background music by Ravel. It was made by Texture Films of Chicago. It contains, not only the 26 Doré ***Raven*** illustrations, but another 30 Doré illustrations from ***Dante***, ***Milton***, and the ***Bible***, but primarily from the ***Inferno***. There is a famous Doré engraving where the eagle is lifting Dante out of Purgatory. By focusing in on just the central part of that illustration, the ***Raven*** video used it for the scene "take thy beak from out my heart" because the angle at which the eagle is grasping Dante is pointing at the center of his chest.

(Versailles & Paris in 1871)

There were a few other minor Doré works in his latter years. Some were magazine reproductions, like the 1867 ***Mayflower Page*** by Ponson du Terrail, the 1869 ***Golden Knives*** by Paul Feval, or the 1879 ***Golden Rangers*** by Gabriel Ferry. There was an 1886 English version of ***Ferry***. In 1869, Doré contributed an etching to the art book ***Sonnets et Eaux-Fortes***, which contains work by many famous writers and artists. The 1883 ***Society of French Aquarellists*** will be covered in the next chapter under fine arts, along with the illustrated catalogue for The Doré Gallery exhibition in the 1890s. But there is one other Doré book which was not published until 1907. It is not an official Doré book, just some unpublished sketches compiled 24 years after his death. Since Doré also did hundreds of paintings and drawings, any group of those could be put together to make "new" Doré books. But would they then count as Doré original art sketches or as Doré book illustrations? In 1907 they took 95 crude unpublished Doré sketches pertaining to characters related to the Franco-Prussian War, and made a new Doré book - ***Versailles et Paris en 1871***. There was also a German version a dozen years later.

We have yet to cover Doré the painter and sculptor. But if he had never been a painter or sculptor, his place in history would be no less secure. In fact, his place in history is actually less secure because he was a painter and sculptor, because that is where almost all the controversy was. He did not seek controversy. It haunted him. His talent was a gift. But it was a gift with a curse attached. His inability to grow up meant that he could only cope with life's problems up to a certain level. Up to that level he could entertain both himself and the public. After he reached that level, he still had the ability to make the public happy, but not himself. His adoring public could never understand how he could not be happy with his success. Who can understand the heart of the restless genius? It is driven by a dynamo that both gives life and takes it away, all in the same motion. That dynamo makes a great servant, but a terrifying master. For two decades that dynamo was Doré's servant. For the last decade it was his master.

 reduced illustration from Poe's ***The Raven*** (1883) - contains 26 full-page plates (9½ x 12½).

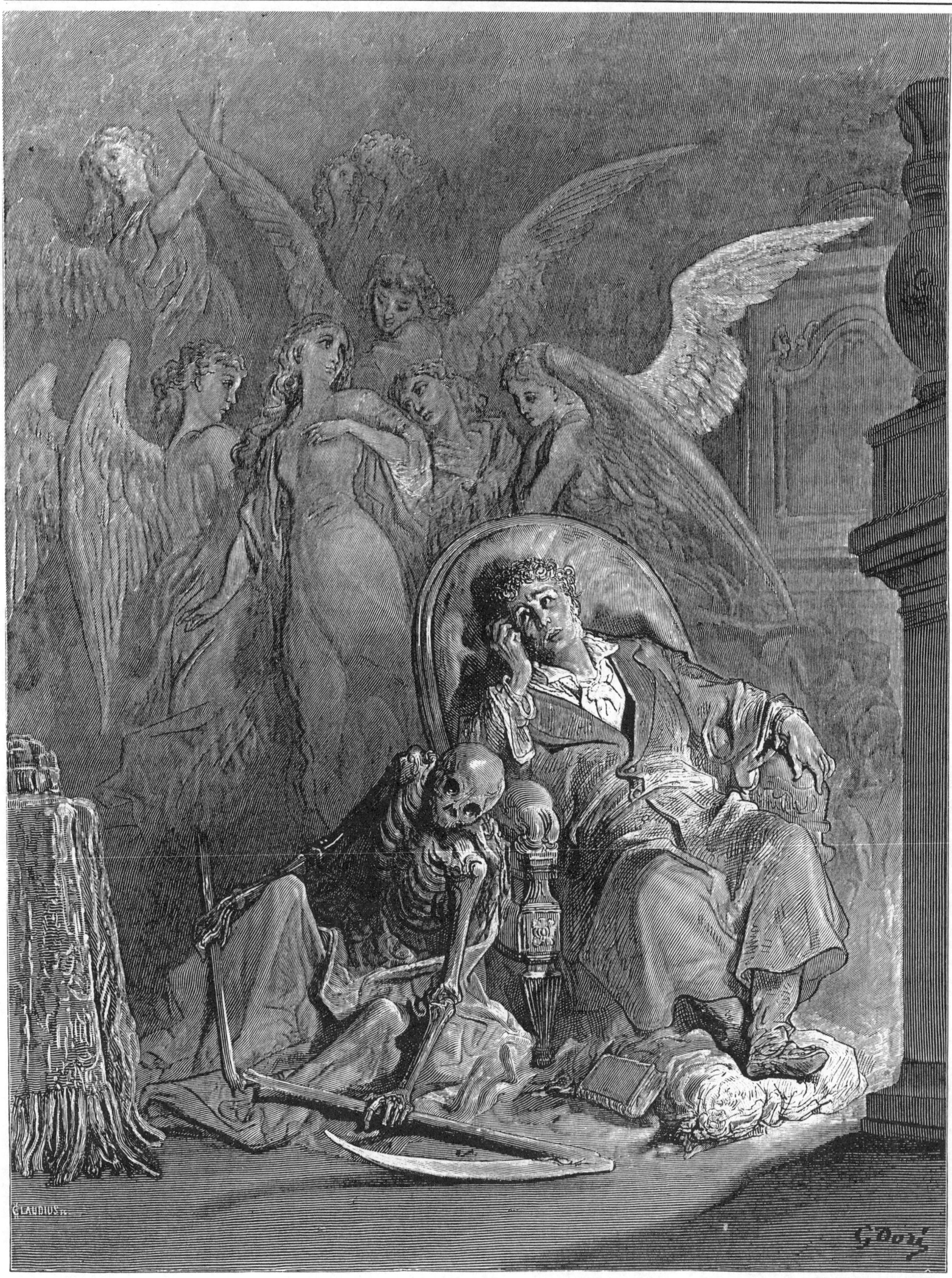

9. DORÉ THE PAINTER - THE DORÉ GALLERY (1868-83)

During the last 15 years of Doré's life, England hailed him as France's greatest living painter, while France did not hail him as a painter at all. Both countries agreed on his status as an illustrator, although those who attacked him as a painter also began attacking his illustrations. But his fans were legion. They felt that the dramatic impact of his paintings overrode any defective coloring. They seemed satisfied with enlarged illustrations. It is no wonder there was a brisk market in steel engravings of his paintings.

Doré began doing oil paintings in his teens, but his ego could not handle the criticism from friend and foe alike. By the late 1850s he seemed resolved to being "just" a successful illustrator. He submitted ten paintings to the 1857 Salon (and received an Honorable Mention) but in the years 1858-64 he submitted only five paintings total. That was the period when he concentrated on his folio engravings. In 1861 he received the Legion of Honour, but as an illustrator. The only really significant painting Doré did during this period was his 1863 ***Paola & Francesca*** (6'4"w x 8'10"h), which sold in 1989 for $600,000. It is a powerful nude painting of the souls of the murdered lovers from ***Dante's Inferno***. There is also a 12x17 steel engraving of that painting.

During the period 1865-68 he became world-famous as an illustrator. After a dozen ***Art Journal*** articles reviewing his folios, there appeared a very different article in July of 1867. It was about Doré the painter, with a very different tone from French magazines. The British art establishment had not built up prejudices against Doré paintings. They saw him merely as an exciting illustrator who had burst on the scene. The French art establishment knew Doré as a cocky young kid who became famous as a comic-strip artist without paying his dues, and who then had pretensions of artistic greatness. So by 1867, when Doré was again exhibiting in the Salon, the British art journalists were actually examining the Doré paintings while French art journalists dismissed them as soon as they saw the name of the artist. The two major paintings were ***Jephthah's Daughter*** (a Biblical scene) and ***Tapis Vert***, an enormous painting of the roulette table at the Baden-Baden resort, with dozens of famous people in the scene. The British review was mixed (they thought ***Tapis Vert*** promoted gambling), but they accepted him as a painter, independent of his illustrations.

The year 1867 was really the beginning of Doré's career in the fine arts, and from that point on he was really more of a British artist than a French artist. In 1866 he accepted literary folio commissions from two major British publishers (Cassell & Moxon), and London was awash in Doré engravings, with the public clamoring for more. So while both French and British art journals may have described Doré's paintings as enlarged illustrations, to the French that meant they were awful, while to the British that meant they were great. In 1867, two independent groups approached Doré about setting up an exhibition of his paintings in London. The first was headed by a Parisian friend, Mr. Arymer. It was set up in the Egyptian Hall in Piccadilly, London at the end of 1867. It did not work out too well or last too long, for reasons that had very little to do with Doré. The catalogue for the display in the Egyptian Hall read ***Catalogue: Gustave Doré, Exhibition of Paintings.*** Arymer's Egyptian Hall exhibition featured, besides a few smaller items, three large horizontal Doré oil paintings:

- Dante in the 9th Circle of Hell	10'2" h x 14'0" w
- Jephthah's Daughter	10'9" h x 16'1" w
- Le Tapis Vert	17'0" h x 34'0" w

There are at least five different listings of the dimensions for ***Tapis Vert***. From 1868 on, there were more articles in the ***Art Journal*** about Doré the painter than Doré the illustrator. But the Feb. 1, 1868 article started off very negative (p.27):

> It is scarcely necessary that we should here recapitulate the well-known characteristics of Doré's works - their bold originality, versatility, creative power, and productivity. His designs have grown familiar - perhaps too familiar - to every eye; in England, however, the public had yet to become acquainted with Gustave Doré as a painter in oils. The present exhibition, therefore, has excited not a little curiosity, though it will scarcely have satisfied the expectations grounded on the artist's reputation as a draughtsman. The first impression on entering the room is that Doré, however great he may be in design, has never taken the trouble to become a painter, in the true Art sense of the word, that he has never cared to obtain mastery over the material, that the technical manipulation of oil remains to him an unresolved mystery, that the distinction in the use of transparent, glazing, and opaque pigments is by him either unknown or unrecognised. And certainly, if these large and remarkable pictures are thus something short of satisfactory to artists, they will be still less acceptable to general visitors.

With such a review, it is hard to believe that paintings by that artist would be on continual display in London in a gallery devotedly exclusively to his works for the next 25 years! It appears that the "general visitors" did not get their marching orders from magazine articles. But there was a big difference between this British article and ones in France at the time. A French article would have stopped there and dismissed all the paintings; this article went on to give several complimentary details about the major Doré's paintings (p.27):

> ... Yet it must be admitted that Doré, in this awe-inspiring picture, falls not very short of Dantesque sublimity; there is grandeur in the terror here wrought out unrelentingly; there is fearful reality in that fissure of riven ice, where flows molten fire wherein the worm dieth not. Few painters save Doré could have come off victor in encounter with the difficulties here involved. Delacroix's well-known picture of *Dante & Virgil* will no doubt always take higher rank; it is every way better as a picture. The imagination of Doré, however, is unapproachable; not even our own Martin could have come near to it; it is not only exhaustless, but ghastly and appalling, and it calls to its aid even the grotesque.
>
> *Jephthah's Daughter*: here the painter is in another mood; we paid tribute to the poetic ardour

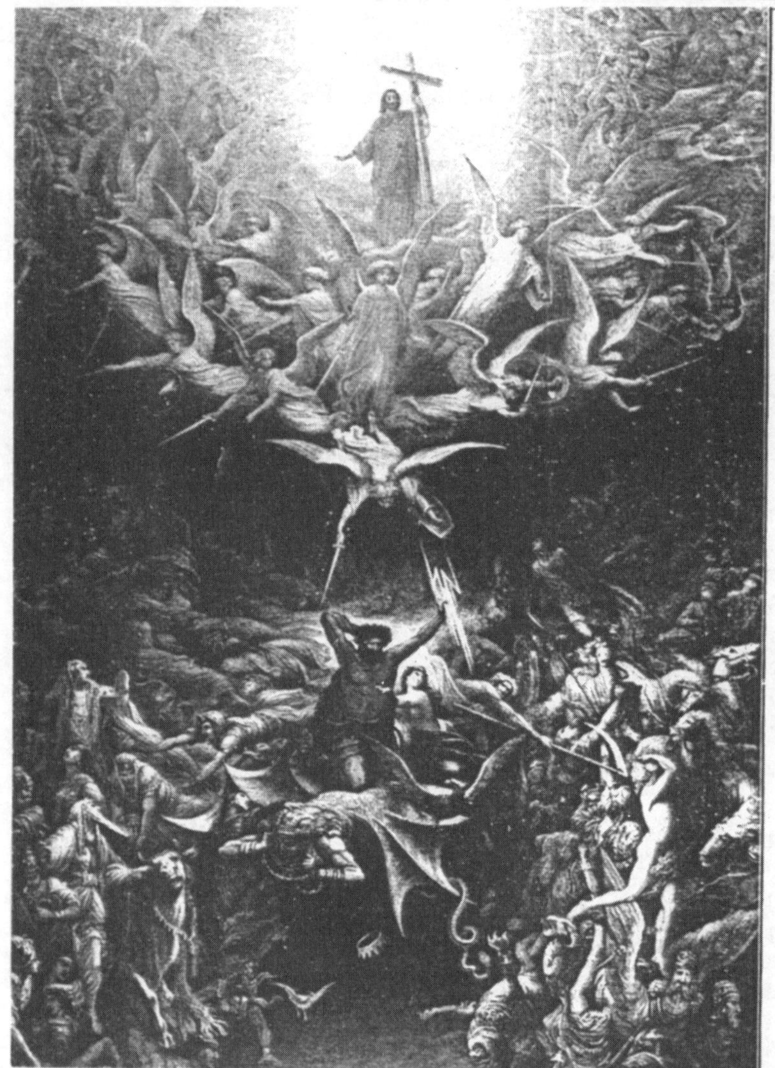

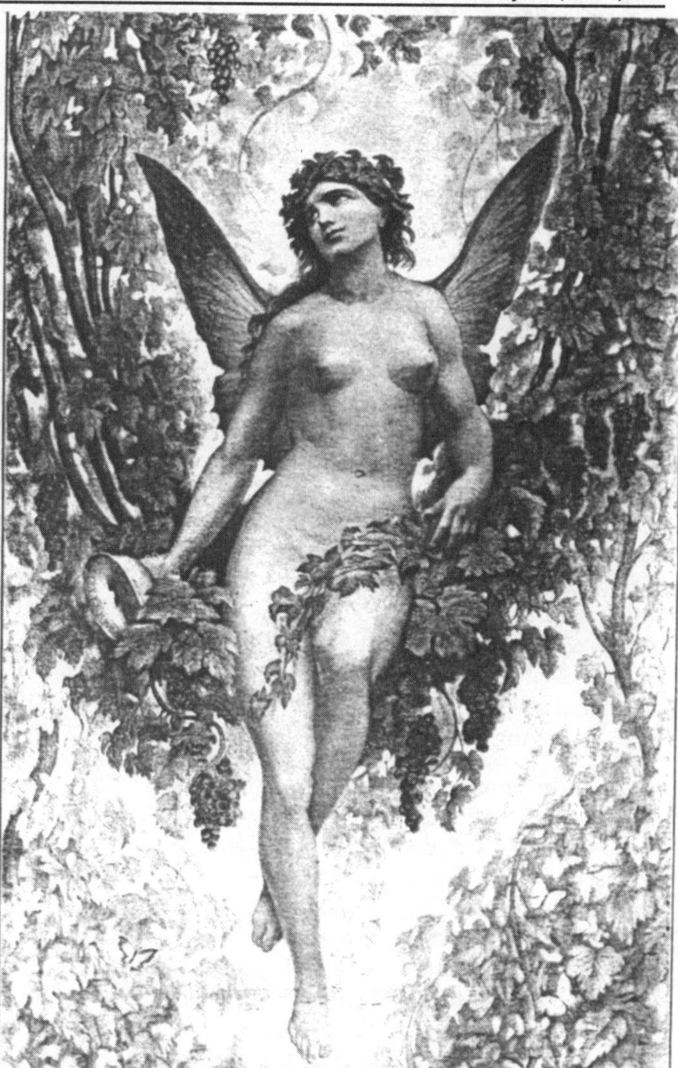

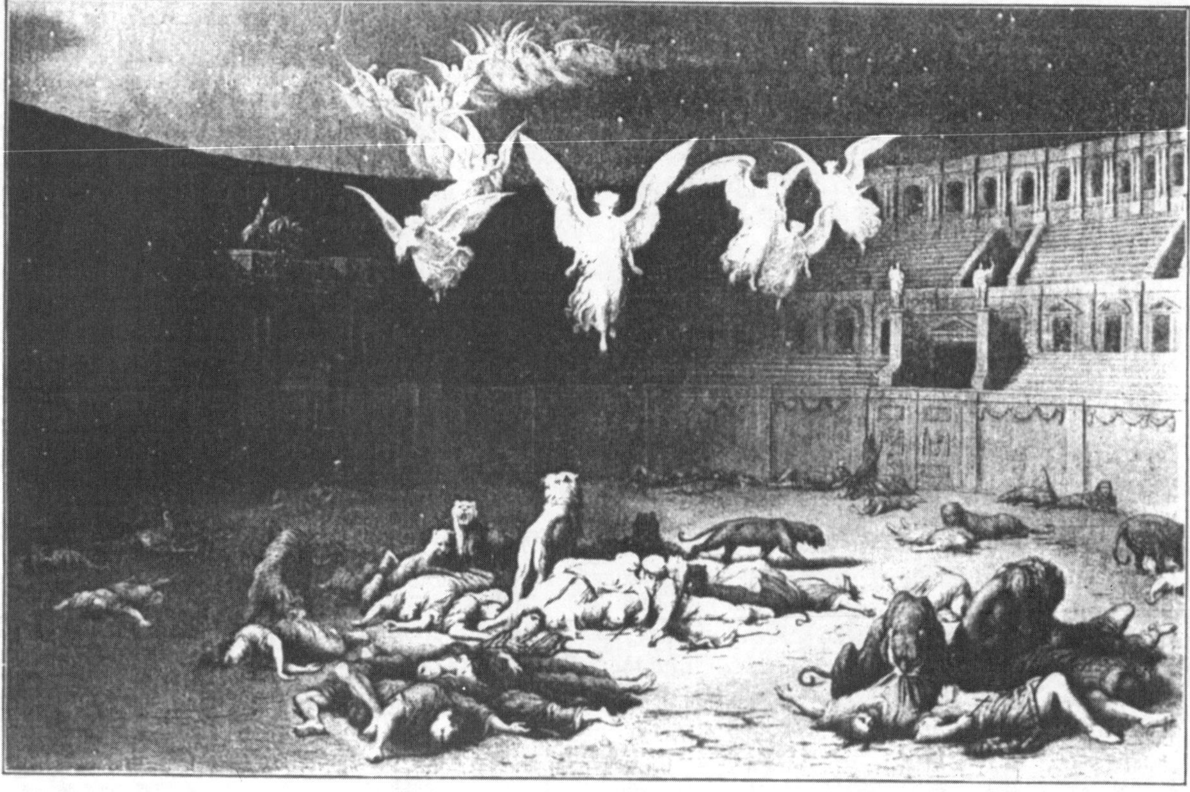

of this work, when exhibited last season in the Paris *Salon*. It is in London better seen, and nearer view enhances its beauties. Certain technical defects, which we have already dwelt upon, are less painfully apparent than usual. The picture, almost as a matter of course, has power and breadth; it is good as an idea, beautiful as a poem.... The treatment, in fact, is throughout artistic.

Le Tapis Vert (*Baden-Baden*): we can but reiterate the reprobation with which we greeted this shameless performance in the French *Salon*. This chronicle of vice, which some critics have excused under the plea of fidelity to contemporary history, is nothing else than the prostitution of talent. Folly is not reproved by reason, vice is not lashed by the whip of satire; the picture panders to the basest types and practices of humanity ... The picture contains indications that Doré might succeed as costume painter ... The cry was raised, which we re-echo, "What will Doré do next?"

So it turns out that all they really objected to was the subject matter (gambling) of one of the paintings. Yet of those three major paintings, ***Tapis* Vert** was the only one that would stay on display for the next 30 years, and even be made into a steel engraving. The Egyptian Hall exhibition lasted only a few months. It was overshadowed by the much larger exhibition of Doré paintings at the German Gallery, which would later be moved to a new location known simply as The Doré Gallery. There has been a great deal of confusion about the name "The Doré Gallery," It was actually used to refer to several different things, so let us set the record straight to begin with:

The Doré Gallery - an **exhibition** of Doré paintings, primarily large religious paintings, which were on continuous display in London from 1868-92, then toured America from 1892-98, then returned to London, where it was terminated sometime after 1900.

The Doré Gallery - a London **location**, 35 New Bond Street, which contained the Doré exhibition, but after 1900 added works by other artists and groups.

The **Agency** of the Doré Gallery - a British **bookseller**, J. Ichenhauser at 68 New Bond St., who arranged the sale of items for The Doré Gallery in Europe while the exhibition was touring America.

The Doré Gallery - a **paperback catalogue,** issued almost every year, describing that Doré exhibition.

The Doré Gallery - the **publisher** of those catalogues, of 25 steel engravings/etchings of exhibition paintings, of the 1876 Doré folio *The Rime of the Ancient Mariner*, and the 1893 *Reminiscences of Gustave Doré* by Marie L. (published in New York)

The Doré Gallery - an 1870 **folio book** published by Cassell, with 250 full-page engravings from a dozen Doré titles, also called *Cassell's Doré Gallery*. It was not connected with the above exhibition. Cassell usurped the name because of its popularity.

The Doré **Bible** Gallery
The Doré **Scripture** Gallery
The Doré Gallery **of Bible Stories**
The Doré Gallery **of Bible Illustrations** - four book titles, each of which reprinted Doré *Bible* engravings.

The Doré Gallery was conceived of in December of 1867 by two entrepreneurial Londoners, James Liddle Fairless and George Lord Beeforth. This was after Mr. Arymer arranged for the Egyptian Hall exhibition, and after Doré had agreed to his first visit to London in the Spring of 1868. Fairless & Beeforth decided to set up a Doré exhibition in the German Gallery to coincide with his five-month London visit. What was to be a five-month exhibition lasted over 23 years! They lined up Doré landscape paintings, two of his nudes (***Paolo & Francesca*** and ***Andromeda***, and in what would prove to be the key to the success of the exhibition, they commissioned a large religious painting - ***The Triumph of Christianity over Paganism***.

The Neophyte (& The Day-Dream)

Another major feature of the German Gallery exhibition was the display of two different versions of ***The Neophyte***. It is a fascinating personality study of a young monk who has just entered a monastery and is having second thoughts. The faces of the elderly monks clustered around the neophyte are quite amusing. The idea originated in 1855 with a lithograph Doré did in the magazine ***Souvenirs d'Artistes*** entitled *Frere Angel*, a scene from Georges Sand's ***Spiridion***. That illustration shows only four monks. Doré redid this scene many times, and each time he added more monks. In the two oil paintings in the German Gallery, one had one row of monks, the other had two rows. Doré did many sketches of the scene and even a sheet music cover. He then etched it nine times, each one larger than the. The first etching was 9½x11½, and by the time he was satisfied with it and published it in 1876, it was 23½x29! He then switched to another version that showed the neophyte playing the organ, and daydreaming about a lost love. That title was called ***The Day Dream*** (***Reverie du Moin***). It was also an oil painting. ***The Neophyte*** was one of Doré's most popular works, with versions in museums and collections such as the actor Charles Boyer and industrialist Armand Hammer.

Triumph of Christianity over Paganism

Fairless & Beeforth commissioned this large religious painting as something special for their exhibition. It was very significant in two ways. First, it was Doré's first commissioned oil painting. What a proud moment for Doré. They paid him £800 (=$4000 =20,000*fr*) for a painting ten feet high, based on one of his apocalyptic ***Bible*** engravings. Secondly, it was the first of a series of large Doré religious paintings, which would become the dominant theme of the Doré Gallery. Though Doré was actually a mystic, he came to represent Protestant religious fervor in England and America. There is one major difference between the popularity of Doré's ***Bible*** engravings and his religious paintings. The engravings have been reprinted in nearly 700 book editions, but his religious paintings, though praised *ad infinitum* at the time, were virtually unknown within a couple generations. Here are the major religious paintings commissioned by Fairless & Beeforth:

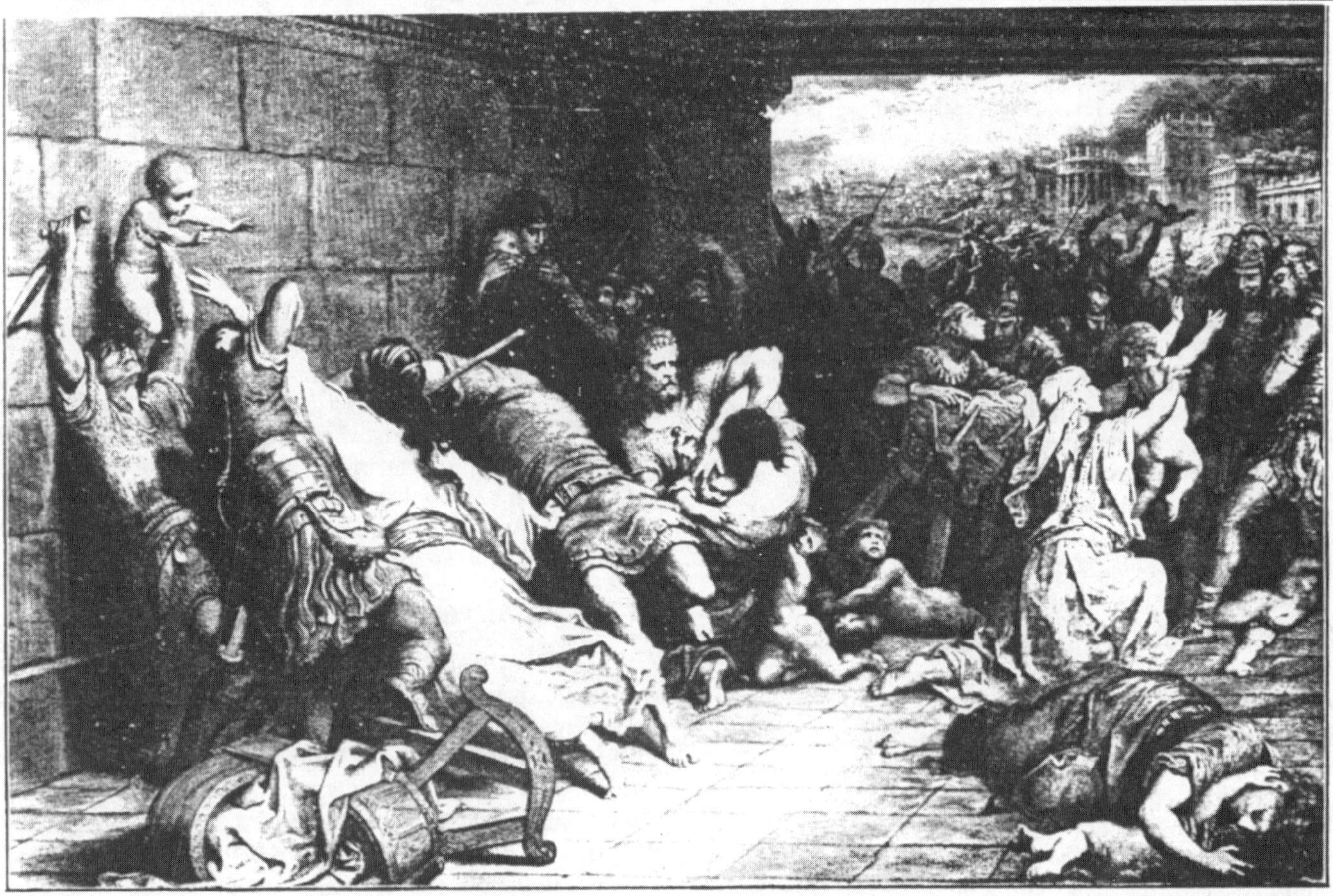

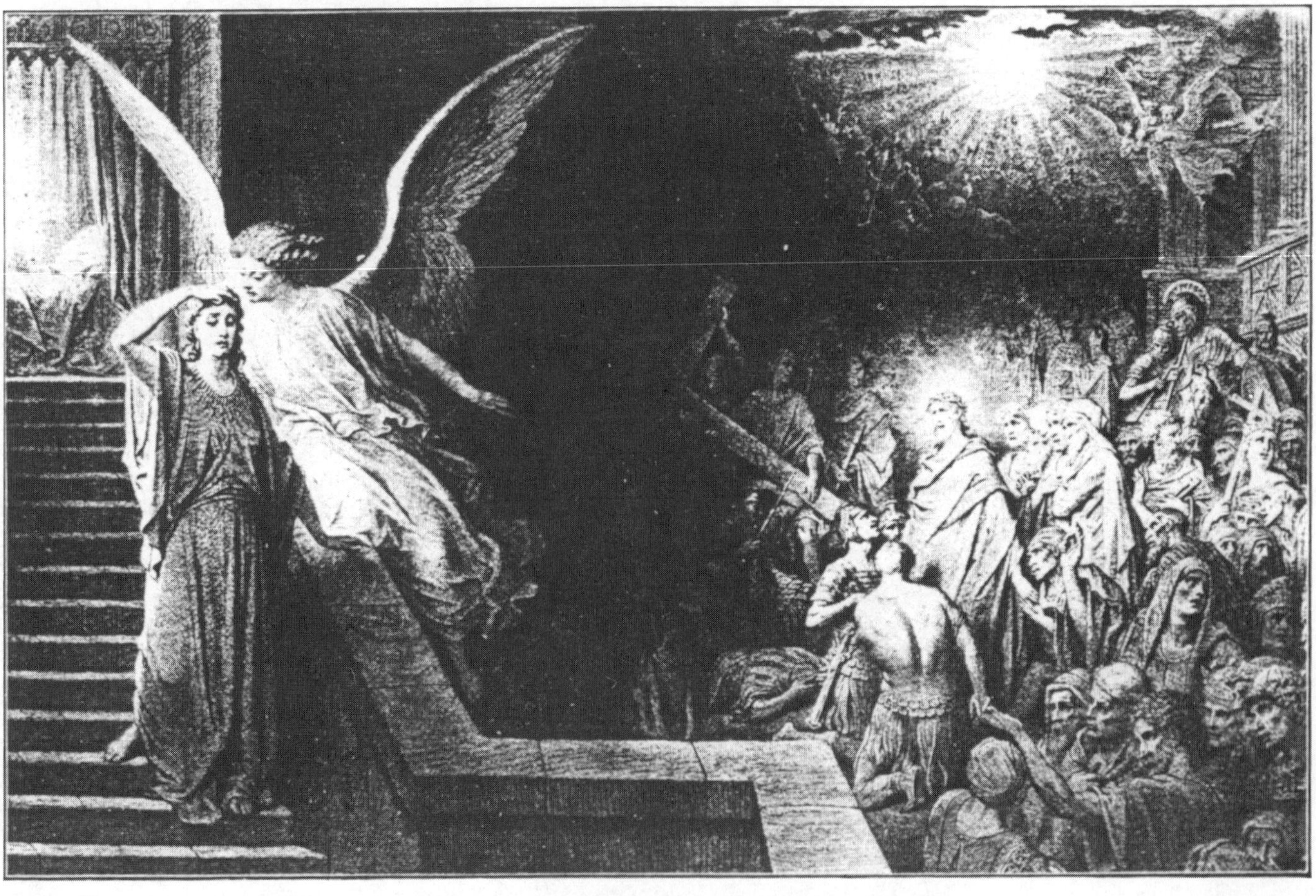

1868 ***The Triumph of Christianity over Paganism***
1870 ***Christian Martyrs in the Coliseum***
1872 ***Christ Leaving the Praetorium***
1872 ***The Massacre of the Innocent***
1873 ***The Night of the Crucifixion (Les Tenebres)***
1874 ***The Dream of Pilate's Wife***
1874 ***Soldiers of the Cross*** (the Crusades)
1875 ***The Battle of Ascalon*** (the Crusades)
1875 ***The House of Caiaphas***
1876 ***Christ's Entry into Jerusalem***
1877 ***The Brazen Serpent***
1877 ***Ecce Homo! (Behold the Man)***
1878 ***Moses before Pharaoh***
1879 ***The Ascension***
1881 ***The Head of Christ***
1883 ***The Vale of Tears***
1883 ***Calvary*** (unfinished)

Some massive canvasses were as big as 20 feet high by 30 feet wide. All of them (except for the unfinished ***Calvary***) were made into 22x32 steel engravings. There were four different ***Head of Christ*** etchings. A trip to the Doré Gallery was like a religious pilgrimage. Ministers preached impromptu sermons in front of the paintings. British Evangelist Charles Spurgeon urged his congregation to visit what became known as "the greatest collection of religious paintings in the world." Roosevelt reprinted Doré's original contract with Fairless & Beeforth for the *Triumph of Christianity*, dated December 7, 1867. Here are some excerpts from that contract (p.331-332):

> The said Gustave Doré undertakes to paint, in a highly finished and his best manner, for the said James Liddle Fairless and George Lord Beeforth, an oil painting representing the *Fall of Paganism*, for the sum of £800 of lawful money of Great Britain, to be received from them jointly on the completion of the said picture. The sum of £800 is to include payment for the copyright of the said picture in France, Great Britain, America, and every other country where such right is recognized, ...
>
> Also for the same sum to make a water-colour drawing of the said picture, fit for the engraver to engrave from, and all the original sketches which he may make in connection with the said picture, which he engages shall be ready, with the original picture, not later than March the first, 1868.
>
> Gustave Doré also undertakes to lend to the said James Liddle Fairless and George Lord Beeforth his bust, to exhibit along with the above-named picture, during the continuance of its exhibition, on the understanding that it is to be returned uninjured at its close.
>
> Gustave Doré also undertakes to sign, in the usual manner, with his autograph, the remark proof and the artist's proof of the engraving of the *Fall of Paganism*.

The exhibition at the German Gallery, 168 New Bond St., ran from April 17 to September 26 of 1868. Doré arrived for his first British tour on May the 18th to find London abuzz over his achievements. London welcomed him with open arms, from the nobility to the common people. Doré was treated like a visiting dignitary, as an illustrator and a painter. Once again, the review by the ***Art Journal*** was not 100% positive, but it was a major improvement over the negative articles appearing in France about similar works. Here are some excerpts (p.141):

> The name of this artist has appeared so often in our pages, that each repetition may almost provoke the exclamation *toujours perdrix*! It is, however, impossible to overlook the tacit challenge which the spirited and prolific French artist now offers to his English brothers in Art, and the appeal he makes to the taste of the English public. When London is full, and when the works of the Royal Academy and the other Exhibitions are covered with the efforts of our own painters, M.Doré opens the German Gallery in Bond Street, and covers the walls with the work of his own brush. Of the principal painting it must be said that it is extremely unfinished. The allegorical style is not in favour at present in England; but the grouping is clear and well wrought out in design....
>
> The landscapes, as usual, are superior to most of the figure pictures.... but the most noticeable part of the Exhibition is the original style in which M. Doré has attempted four or five life-sized subjects. If we call it fresco-painting we shall give a wrong impression, but it is a sort of fresco painting on canvas. Doré has thrown the plaster of his walls rough-cast on his work. The faces alone have something of the finish of true fresco; but the effect, from the proper point of view, is wonderfully vivid and life-like ... the *Gitana*, though the baby is commonplace, has a face worthy of Murillo. It is impossible for the artist to persevere in such a style of work without so educating his powers as to give assurance of nobler results than any which have yet been admired or criticised from the pencil of M. Doré.

Catalogues for the early Doré exhibitions are extremely rare. But in the summer of 1868, Doré and his exhibitions were a major hit. Roosevelt and Jerrold detail social aspects of Doré's British tours. Even Cassell put on a Doré exhibition of their own, displaying original Doré ***Bible*** engravings. When Doré returned to France, the German Gallery exhibition did close, but only to make plans for a larger permanent display.

THE DORÉ GALLERY

From September 1868 to April 1869, Fairless & Beeforth were busy securing larger quarters: 35, New Bond Street (now Sotheby's) and arranging for more Doré paintings. They were so encouraged by the 1868 display that they took out a 10-year lease on the new quarters. The new exhibition would no longer be named after the building; it would be dedicated to the artist. Back in December of 1867, they asked for a loan of the Doré bust for a few months. The "few months" became 30 years, long after all the original parties had died. But just as Doré was gaining respect as a painter, a stream of personal sorrows began to unravel. It began with Patti's marriage in the summer of 1868. While Doré was being wined and dined by the likes of the Prince of Wales, his broken heart was being walked on at a wedding procession just down the street. Then Doré arrived

sketch of interior & photo of front entrance of The Doré Gallery in London in the 1870s
photo of the current front entrance of the same location - now Sotheby's of London.

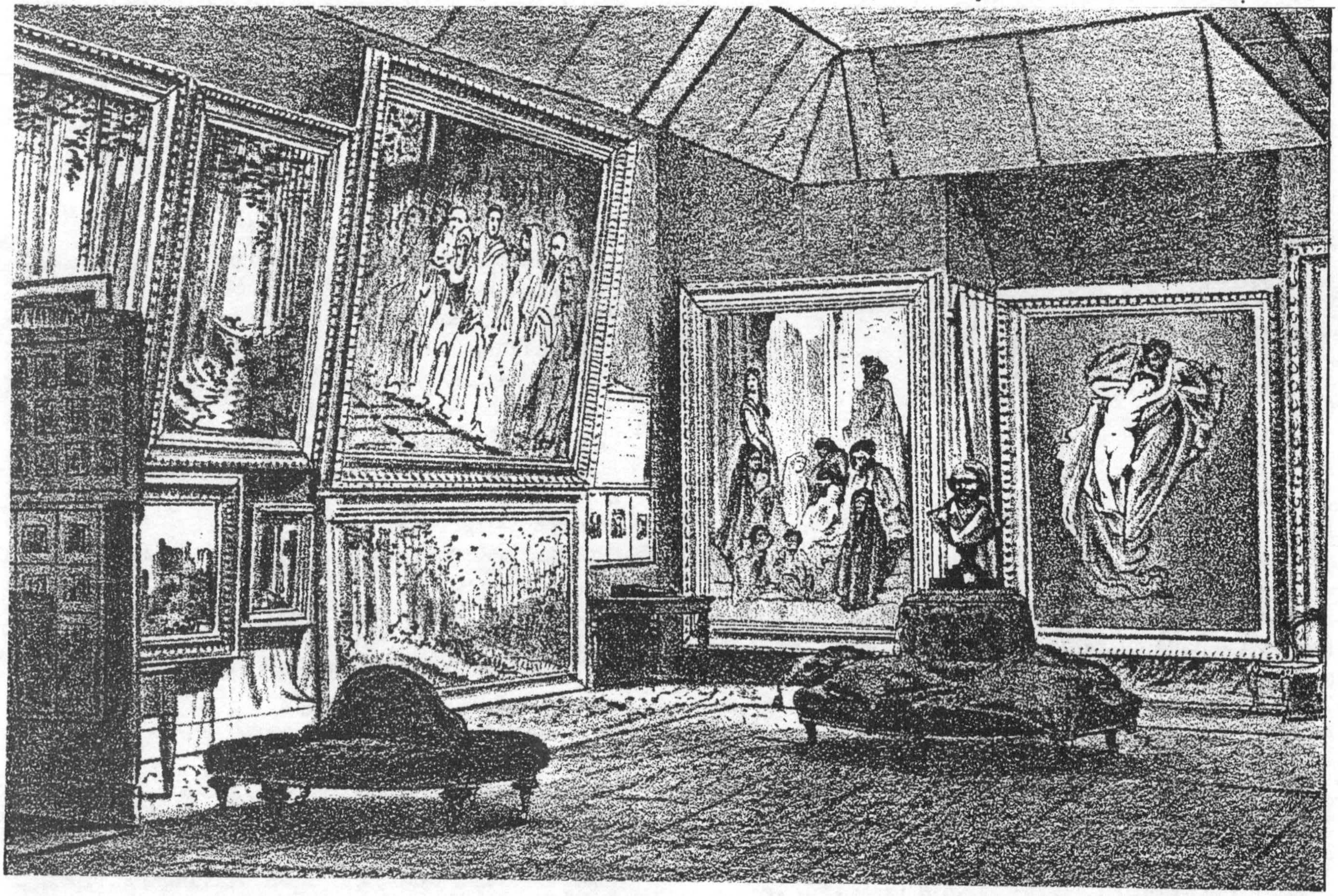

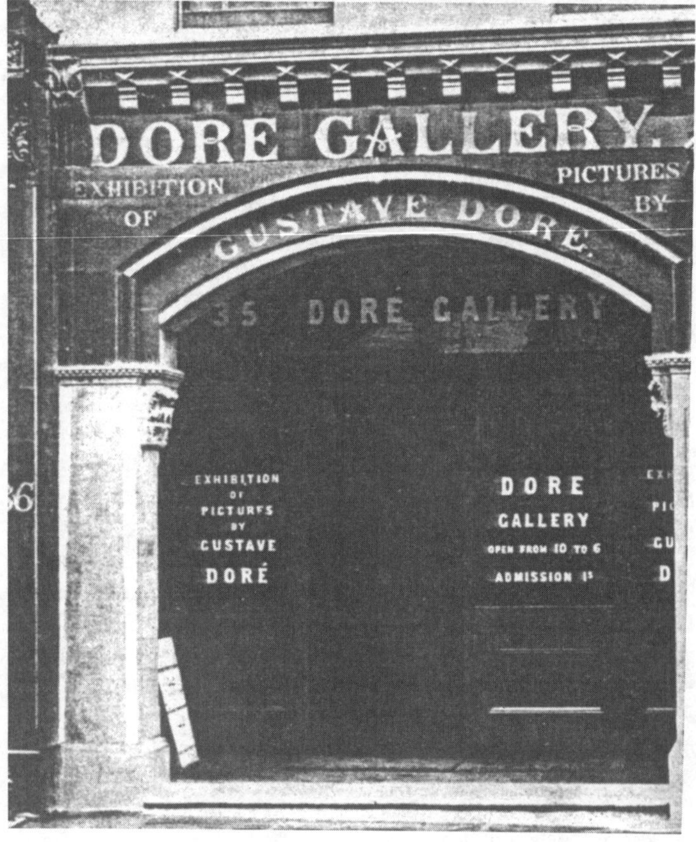

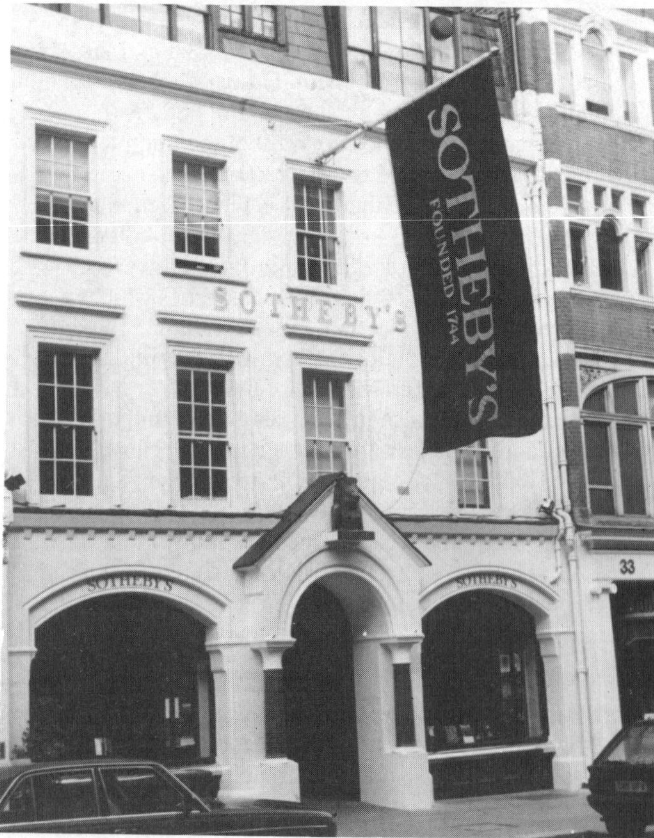

back in Paris to find Rossini dying. Doré the boy genius had been privileged to share the twilight of some of the great geniuses of an earlier generation. But the last rays of Rossini's genius flickered out on November 13th, 1868, and Doré was called on to make the death-bed sketches. The final salt in the wound came from a cold-hearted journalist who asserted that Doré (who was like a son to Rossini) was "profiting from the dead" by making an etching of the death-bed sketch.

But the winter of mourning passed, and the springtime of Doré the painter blossomed in London. On April 23th, 1869, The Doré Gallery opened. It was open continuously at 35, New Bond St. until September of 1892, when it toured America. The 1869 exhibit featured 24 paintings, with many more on the way. Besides items from the 1868 show, and some from Arymer's ill-fated display, there were several new items. The title of the catalogue now read ***Descriptive Catalogue by Tom M. A. Taylor of Pictures & Drawings by Gustave Doré on exhibition at The Doré Gallery***. Fairless & Beeforth kept the major items on display and sold minor paintings and smaller replicas of the major paintings. Some items were loaned to the gallery and returned to Doré. The commercial enterprise had income from entrance fees, catalogues, and engravings. Doré got 15% of the fees plus payment for the paintings themselves. Altogether Doré received about $300,000 for some 40 major paintings, the highest price being $30,000 for ***Christ Leaving the Praetorium***. Not bad for a "shockingly bad painter." The Doré Gallery opening generated a great deal of excitement. Again, the *Art Journal* was one of the most balanced, making a concerted effort not to be either fawning or condemning, as many others were. Here are some of their excerpts (p.184):

> For the third time M. Doré makes his appearance as an English exhibitor. In the first instance he brought before us that vivid representation of a German gaming table, the *Tapis Vert*, the peculiar lighting of which in a room at the Egyptian Hall, Piccadilly, attracted so much attention, and raised so much debate. Last year he invited us to see the *Triumph of Christianity* (of which we gave a description), at the German Gallery, in Bond Street, together with a collection of paintings, many of them of Spanish subjects, the greater number of which, it appears, have been sold, although the prices named were high. In the present year the French artist has made a more determined effort, if not to naturalise himself on our soil, at least to show that his Art is cosmopolitan. A gallery has been taken, and very tastefully fitted up, at No. 35, New Bond Street, for the exclusive exhibition of oil-paintings by M. Doré, and we learn with extreme satisfaction that the welcome already given to his productions has assumed so substantial and tangible a form as to have led to an arrangement being entered into for the use of the gallery for this purpose, for the term of ten years.
>
> The greatest triumph which, so far at least as the present collection extends, has been reaped by M. Doré's pencil, is the representation of the deathbed of Rossini ... The real grandeur of the portrait cannot be expressed by description. But it is proper to call attention to the rare and peculiar harmony of the tone, and the perfect distinctness, both in apparent texture and in shade, of so many white surfaces...
>
> The picture which, next to the Rossini, will be viewed with most curiosity, is the scene from *Midsummer Night's Dream*, called *Titania*. We wish that we could speak of its merits and great beauty as undeniable. That it exhibits great defects is no less certain. The thing which strikes us most forcibly is the regret that, in a picture which evinces so brilliant an inspiration, M. Doré should have allowed himself so far to experiment, instead of following that beaten and time-honoured road in which he has showed that he can so surely proceed with the stride of a giant.
>
> The great superiority of the present appearance of *The Neophyte*, as compared with last year, is due to the circumstance that we now see the original picture, of which last year only showed us a *replica*...
>
> The wonderful power evinced by Doré of giving the effect of height, of distance, of length, or of number, by the arrangement or repetition of the lines of a picture, is evinced in the landscape *Die Engelshorne...*
>
> But the painting by which M. Doré will take the highest rank, not as regards this exhibition alone, but as far as any untravelled English critic has had an opportunity of forming an opinion, is that of *Paolo & Francesca di Rimini*... Let M. Doré paint thus and his fame will take care of itself.

Roosevelt contains a list of 28 paintings which were sold from the gallery from 1869-85. Their new-found praise for ***Paolo & Francesca*** is hard to understand, since it was already on display in the German Gallery. None of the new items in 1869 were really major items, and ***Paolo*** quickly came to be considered the feature attraction. This is also borne out by a September 1869 article announcing that ***Paolo*** would be the first Doré Gallery painting made into a steel engraving. That 12x17 steel engraving by Francis Holl was completed in May of 1871. It turned out to be the smallest and simplest of two dozen engravings made from Doré Gallery paintings, most of which were 22x32 and took 4-5 years to engrave. The steel engraving of ***Triumph of Christianity*** was finished in 1872, with most of the others completed in the late 1870s. Those engravings proved to be a major source of income.

There is often confusion about dating Doré paintings. As many as four different dates can be found for a painting. First, they could have some historical data telling what year(s) Doré worked on or completed a painting. Then, someone might be going by the date actually written on the painting itself, which might be different from when he actually completed it. Then other sources might be listing what year it was exhibited in the Paris Salon, which might be thought of as when the painting was "unveiled" or released. But other reference works related to the Doré Gallery might list what year that painting was first displayed in the gallery. And all of that does not include the replica paintings, which are often confused with the original. At least all known Doré replica paintings are different sizes.

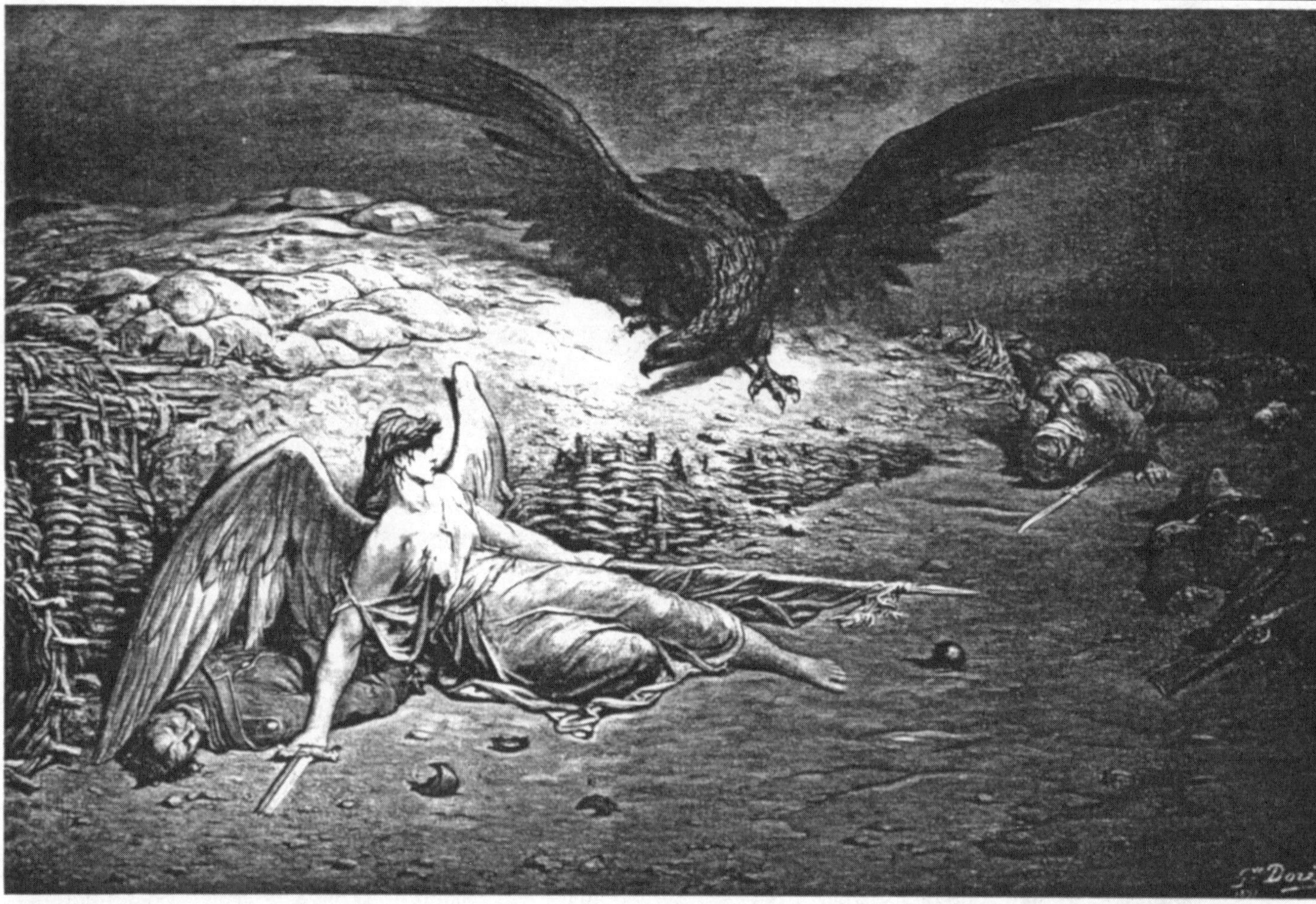

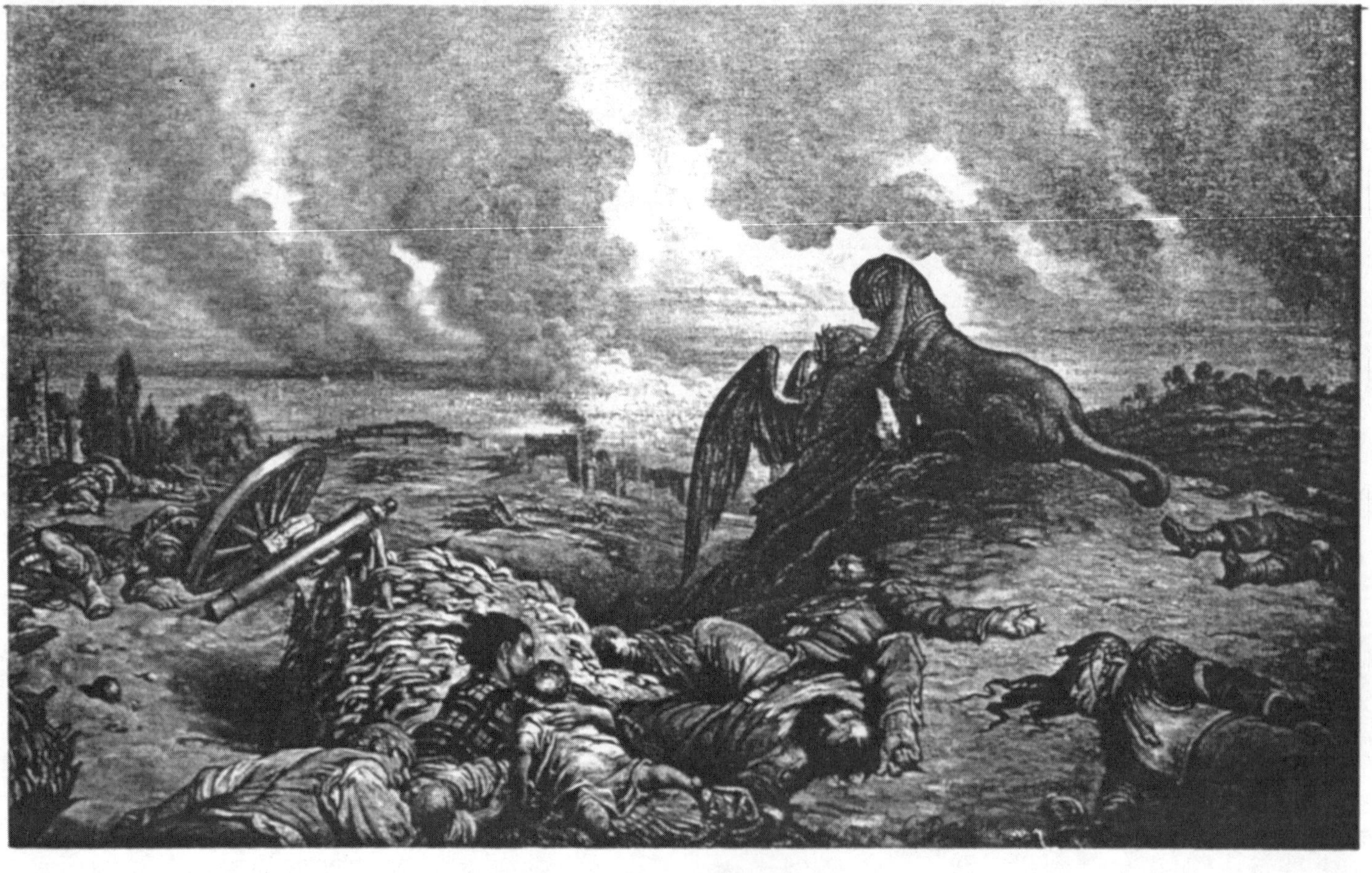

Christian Martyrs in the Coliseum

British reviews list this painting as coming to the Doré Gallery in 1870, yet the Paris Salon registry lists it as # 625, in 1874. Then in 1875, it is listed again in the Doré Gallery catalogue. Did they actually take down a four-year-old painting out of the Doré Gallery, ship it to back to Paris, put it up in the Salon, and then ship it right back to the gallery and hang it right back up? Why would they do that when Doré was doing so many paintings at that time? ***Christian Martyrs*** is now in an art museum in Peurto Rico. There also confusion about the titles of two Doré paintings - ***Christian Martyrs*** and ***Massacre of the Innocents***. The first is about adult Christians being mauled to death by lions in the coliseum. The second is about Jewish children being stabbed to death by Roman soldiers. When Roosevelt (p.334) stated that in February 1870, Doré painted ***Massacre of the Innocents*** in two days, she probably meant to say ***Christian Martyrs in the Coliseum***. ***Massacre of the Innocents*** was exhibited in the 1872 Paris Salon, and was then put on display in the Doré Gallery in 1874.

(The Franco-Prussian War)

This section is about the event, not a painting with such a title. Doré had witnessed & illustrated three previous wars (the 1848 revolution in France, the 1854 Crimean War, and the 1859 Italian War of Independence), but nothing could possibly have prepared him or his Parisian friends for the onslaught of the Prussians. France had fared very well in its previous wars under Napoleon III, but by 1870 France was low on leadership. Meanwhile the Germans were lean, hungry, and mechanized. On July 15, 1870, Bismarck managed to provoke Napoleon III into declaring war over the ascension to the Spanish throne. The French deluded themselves into thinking they could win a war with Germany. The French had paid no attention to the formidable new military equipment Germany displayed at the 1867 Paris Exposition. Doré the patriot was also caught up in the nationalism of the summer of 1870. He quickly produced paintings like ***To the Rhine***, ***The Call to Depart***, and his most famous military painting, ***La Marseillaise***, the lithograph of which has been reprinted in many history books.

The first month of the war was sort of a party, with lots of farewell celebrations. Early reports seemed encouraging. But then in rapid order came Gravelotte, Metz, and Sedan. By September 1st, the war was over. Napoleon III surrendered his 130,000 men at Sedan and left Paris defenseless. In the winter of 1870-71, Hell came to Paris. The people froze, the people starved. Sarah Bernhardt sent a little boy on an errand, and then saw him blown to bits right in front of her. The seige began September 20th, the bombardment began December 27th, Paris capitulated on January 28th, and the Prussians marched in. The French gave up Alsace-Lorraine (including Doré's home town of Strasbourg) and agreed to pay five billion francs in reparations. We have already related how that stuck in the craw of French patriots like Doré and Sarah Bernhardt.

But surrender only led to the commune, which took over Paris in March of 1871. Finally in May, 130,000 French Army troops attacked the barricaded Parisians. Nearly 30,000 people were killed as they cleared Paris block by block, in one of France's darkest hours. Doré was in Paris all during the ten months of hell, with his major paintings buried in long metal tubes. In ten months, Doré went from a playful youth to an old man at heart. And with the deaths of Rossini, Alexandre Dumas and Theophile Gautier, Doré seemed to lose his capacity to enjoy life. Doré was a great patriot, but was not particularly a supporter of Napoleon III. Though Doré was much admired by the royal court, they also played a major role in luring Adelina Patti into the arms of the Marquis de Caux. Doré did not forget things like that. In 1869, Doré was invited by the Empress Eugenie to accompany the royal court at the opening of the Suez Canal. Doré shocked them by declining. Both the Emperor and the Empress personally invited Doré a second time. The stunned Emperor saw Doré say "no" to his face. As Roosevelt records (p.358), Napoleon III bit his lip and said, "Pray let us say no more about it." During the war, Doré wrote several letters to British friends, per Roosevelt (p.361):

> September 13, 1870
>
> Dear Harford, - How shall I ever thank you enough for your kind and affectionate thoughts, and all the good they do to my soul? With the day of distress came the souvenir of a sincere and dear friend, and such precious wishes!
>
> In writing to you thus, I profit by the last day upon which letters will be able to go by train to England; the enemy is at the very gates of Paris, and from one moment to another we may be in the throes of the first bombardment. Our misfortune is immense, and our anguish terrible. How shall we ever emerge from this gulf of blood and abandonment into which poor France is plunged? No hope and no solution gleams on the horizon; and yet it seems hard to think that our beloved France, so innocent of this war, should be the object of universal execration.
>
> I shall carry my flask with me, dear friend, when I go to the ramparts - this well-chosen object which your affection has prompted you to send to me. I think it will be to-morrow, for, as I have told you, the peril is most imminent. My dear and well-loved friend Harford, I beg you to address your prayers to Heaven that this drama now in progress may have as prompt an ending as possible, and that the grief that already overwhelms us may not put all France into mourning.
>
> No news of my poor brother, the captain; we are in mortal disquietude. I have tried everything, even the help of several members of the Geneva Society, who they say ought to know certain things; but have signally failed. Adieu, my dear Harford, my heart is very heavy, but it is with the best of my affection that I embrace you.
>
> Your devoted friend,
> G.Doré.

Doré did many paintings about the horrors of war, or shall we say, the horrors of losing a war. Doré did at least 50 oil paintings, watercolors, mixed media sketches, lithographs, etchings, and sculpture, plus an album of 26 drawings. He did

Christ Leaving the Praetorium (1872) - top: Doré working on painting; bottom: steel engraving of painting.

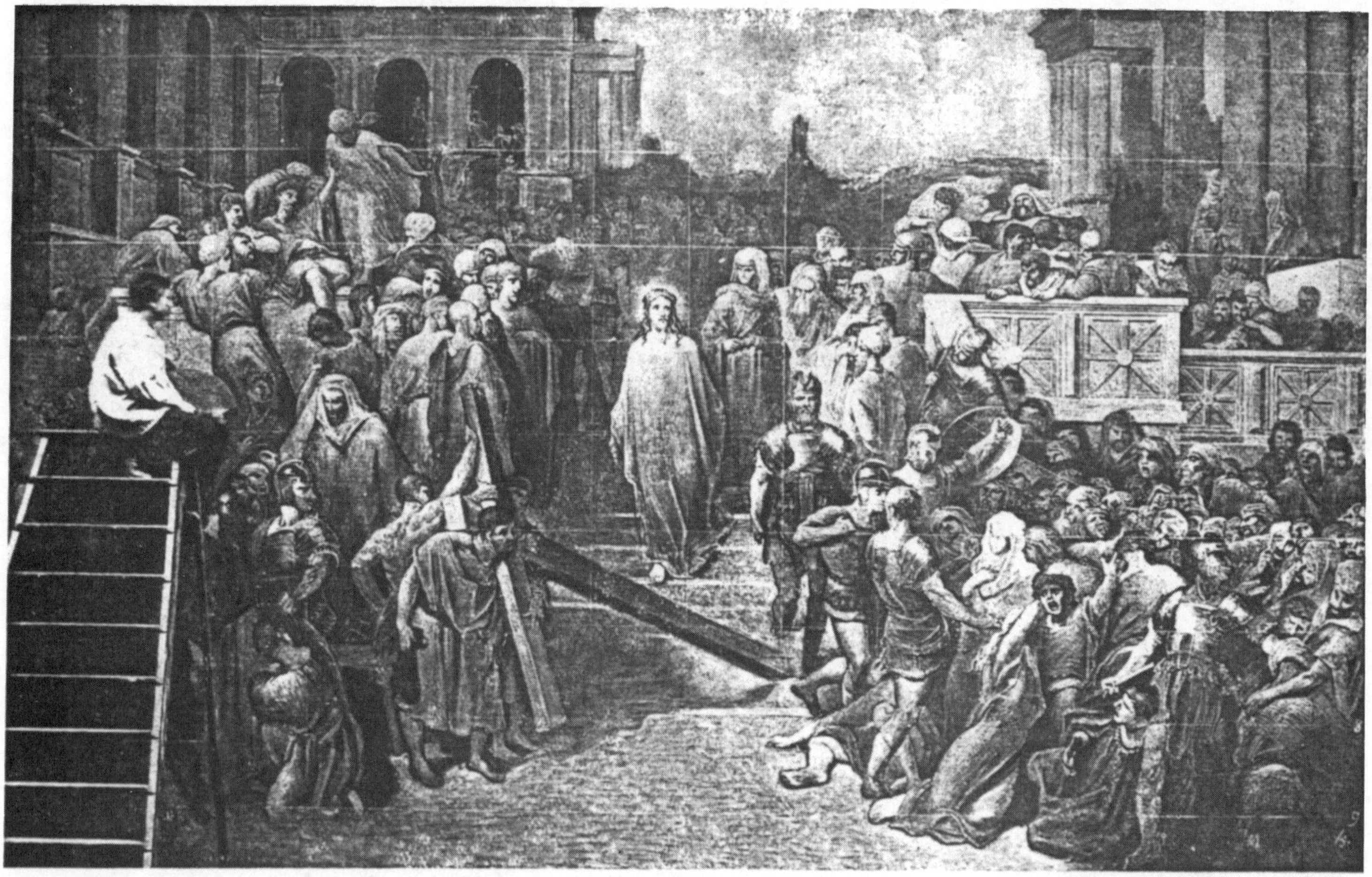

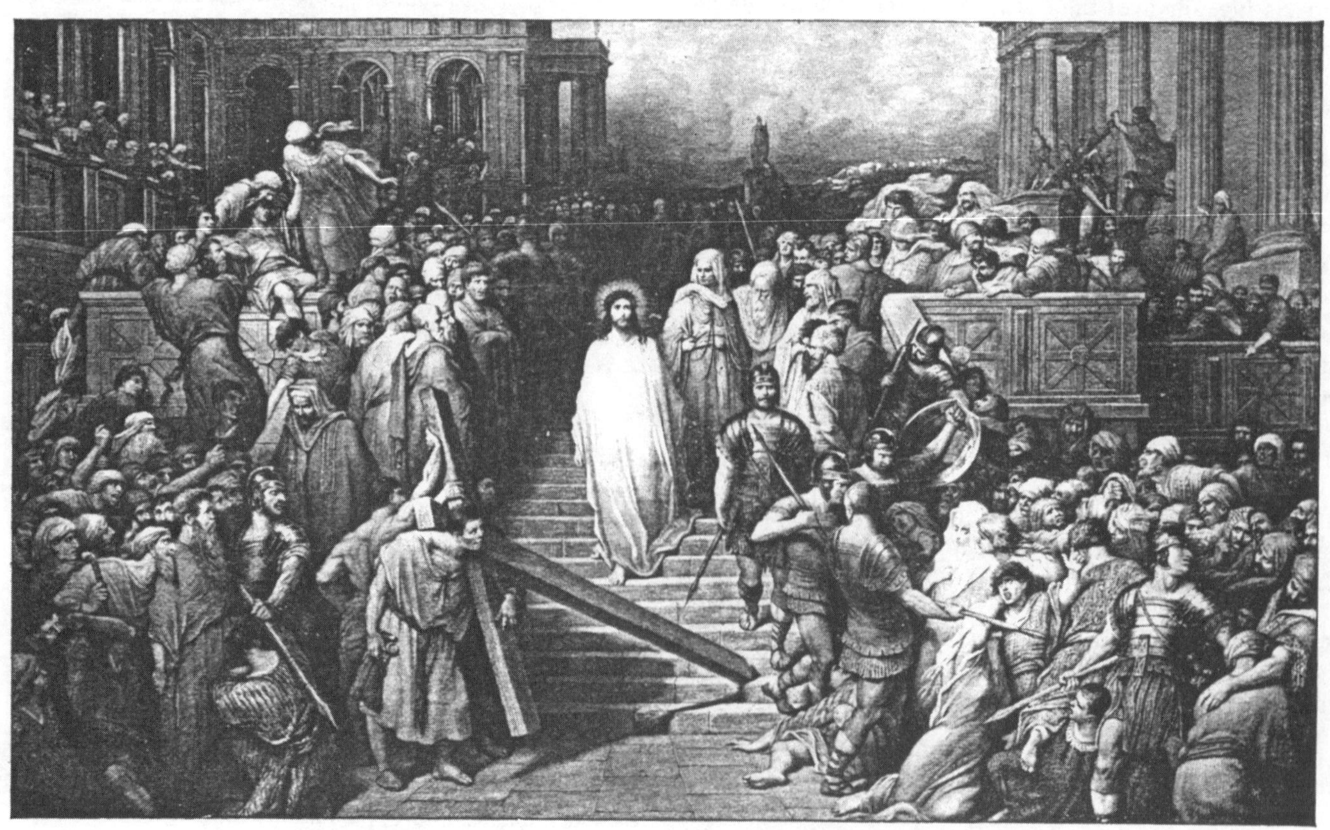

not want to publicize these items during his lifetime. He said, "why would I want people to see the suffering of my country?" They are now in museums in Paris (Musee du Louvre, Musee d'Orsay, Musee Carnavalet), LeHavre, Strasbourg, Mulhouse, Colmar, and at Vassar College; and in private collections in Europe and North America. A partial list includes:

- ***Gathered herds in the Bois de Boulogne*** (Louvre)
- ***Sister of Charity bearing wounded boy*** (LeHavre)
- ***Scene of the Bombardment of Paris*** (Mulhouse)
- ***The National Defense*** (sculpture) (Canada)
- ***Alsace Weeping*** (or Murdered) (Colmar)
- ***The Black Eagle of Prussia*** (Switzerland)
- ***The Enigma*** (The Sphinx) (d'Orsay)
- ***France and her Children*** (England)
- ***The Defense of Paris*** (Vassar)

Several Doré reference works, such as Valmy, Farner, Forberg, Kaenel, and Strasbourg-1983 show those paintings. It would be interesting to see an edition of Emile Zola's ***The Downfall*** (***La Debacle***) illustrated with Doré paintings. Even though he did nearly a hundred works of art about the Franco-Prussian War, they have never been used to illustrate the text of any book, except for ***La Marseillaise*** in a few historical books.

Christ Leaving the Praetorium

No matter how devastating the war was, it did end and life almost returned to normal. For Doré in late 1871, that meant London. It meant his folio ***London, a Pilgrimage*** and it meant the Doré Gallery in London. The war caused Doré to put on hold what was then considered his greatest painting. It was his largest commission and his largest painting. It would be hailed as the greatest religious painting in the world. The 1875 Doré Gallery catalogue (which had 25 pages describing 25 items) devoted 11 pages just to quotes about ***Christ Leaving the Praetorium***. It became so popular that Doré painted two smaller replicas of the painting, and two large mixed-media sketches. Those five works of art are now in museums in the U.S., Puerto Rico, England, France, and Austria. It was also made into a chromolithograph and a large steel engraving. Yet the painting has major coloring defects, and many people think it looks better in b&w.

The idea for ***Praetorium*** came from Rev. Frederick Harford, a minor canon of Westminster, who would become one of Doré's closest British friends. During Doré's 1868 British tour, a group discussion came up about famous religious paintings. The question arose about major biblical scenes that had never been painted. Harford asserted that the only major scene he could think of that did not exist as a painting was the scene where Christ sets out from Herod's palace (the Praetorium) for Calvary, through the assembled mob. This immediately struck Doré's fancy, since it would be very original and very theatrical, and he determined to do it on a life-size scale. He stretched out a monstrous canvas in his studio 20 feet high by 30 feet wide, and went to work. Jerrold contains several of Doré's preliminary sketches for details of the painting. At the center of the agitated crowd, the figure of Jesus seems to almost float down the steps, as though a movie camera focused in on him and switched to slow motion. The contrast between Jesus and the crowd is very powerful. The Doré Gallery catalogue identifies characters in the crowd - the haughty high priests, the glassy-eyed centurion, the shadows of Pilate and Herod in the background, Judas hiding his face from Jesus, the mother of Jesus fainting away, supported by the other Marys. Doré even forced himself to slow down his normal pace to concentrate on accuracy. Early in 1870 it was nearly done, and Doré made plans to exhibit it in the Salon that year and then take it to the Doré Gallery. His plans went awry by two years. Part of the reason was the war, but even before that, in February of 1870, Canon Harford visited Doré, and Doré was anxious to show him the nearly completed canvas. Roosevelt picks up the narrative from there (p.334):

> ... The picture was not what it is at present. Instead of the heavy sky and sombre pall of cloud looming up in the background, which at present intensify the fatal and lugubrious aspect of that sad morning, Doré had painted a sunshiny sky, and all the roseate luminousness of a fair spring day. Canon Harford said little about the picture, and, remembering their conversation and Doré's decision as to how he was to depict the scene in its every detail, felt that Doré had either forgotten his original intention, or had slightly changed his conception of the work; for the fair morning he had painted almost nullified the idea of sadness and fatality that should have been indicated by Nature's aspect on the day of that dread tragedy. Doré noticed his friend's reticence, and remarked, "You say nothing about my picture; *our* picture of *Christ leaving the Praetorium.*"
>
> The reverend gentleman hesitated to pronounce an absolute opinion, but with a few apt words recalled their conversation respecting the artistic conception of the subject, and contrived to convey to the artist his impression that the picture did not absolutely represent Doré's original preconceived idea of what it should be.
>
> Madame Doré, who was present in the studio, was horrified that any one should dare to speak so plainly to such an artist as her son. Doré seemed overwhelmed, but listened with profound seriousness to the sentiments expressed with regard to his picture. As a matter of fact he was too creative, original, and unpractised in mere mechanical art to stick absolutely to any settled scheme. He could develop his ideas in a thousand different ways, each bearing to him a strict relation to the radical one; but perhaps the very redundance of this faculty of development might lead him astray.
>
> After the brief conversation above referred to, a painful silence fell upon the studio. Doré looked at his erring picture again and again, and seemed buried in profound reflection. Then, at last, a sad, determined look overspread his countenance; he sprang up his ladder like a cat, and, before a word could be spoken by any one present, seized a brush and commenced vigorously painting out the picture. Madame Doré nearly had a fit, and screamed out with irrepressible anguish, "Oh, Gustave! how can you?

 Christ Leaving the Praetorium (1872) - full-size detail of steel engraving (full image dimensions 22x33)

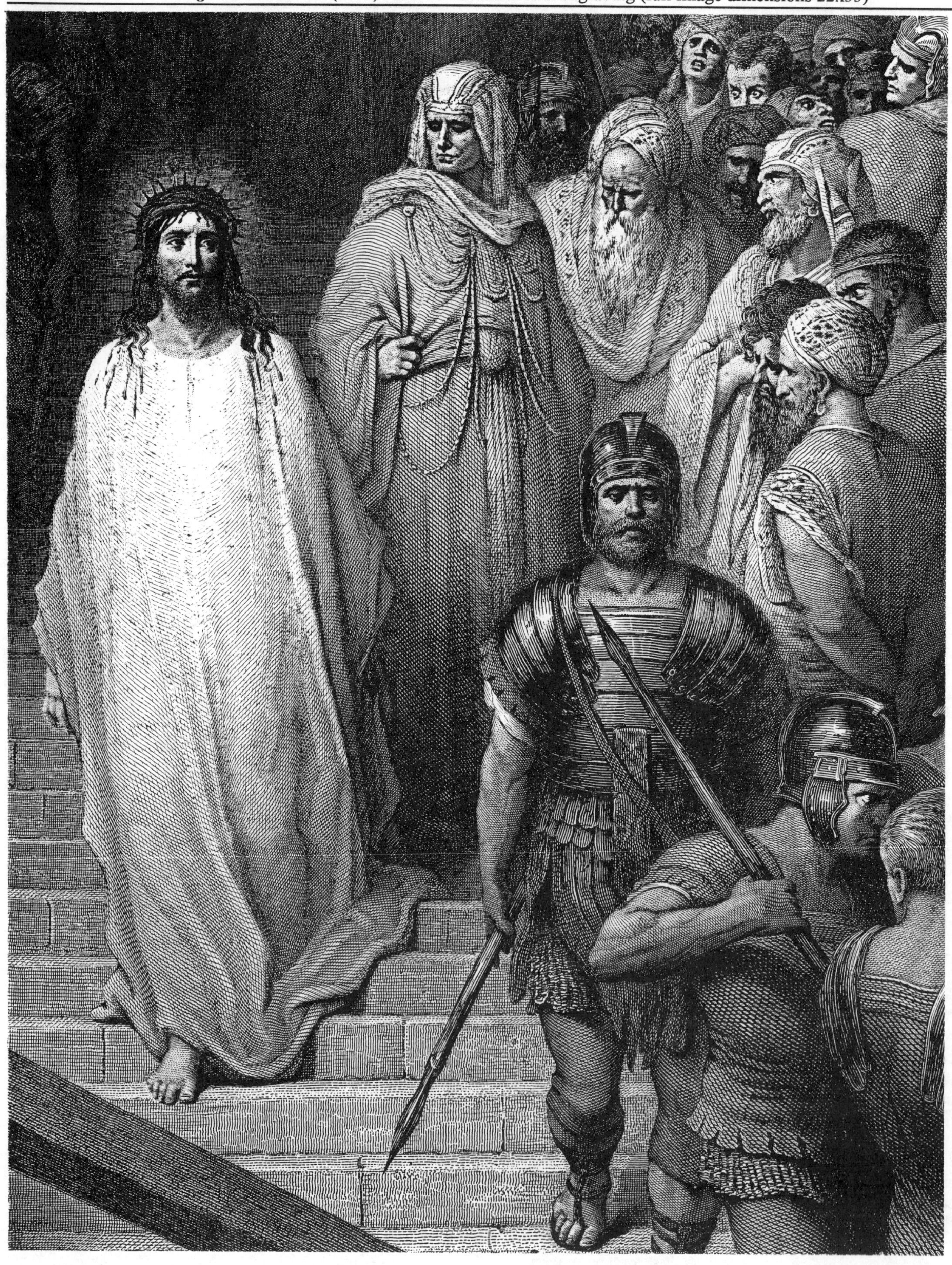

Stop, stop, do stop, it hurts me to see you ruin your glorious picture. Don't do it. You are both wrong!"

"It is quite right, mother, and my friend is quite right!" exclaimed Doré, emphasizing each word by a frantic lunge at the picture, "quite right! and I am glad he has told me the truth. There, now!" He gave one final flourish of the brush, totally obliterating the unfortunate sky, and then descended his ladder. He grew very pale as he added, in a helpless sort of way, "That is done with, and my work for the Salon? Nothing remains of this; what am I to do?" He then painted the *Massacre des Innocents* in two days.

The giant ***Praetorium*** canvas went into a metal tube during the war. After the war, Doré repainted about a third of it, finishing it April 21, 1872. Doré dated it "1867-72," even though the discussion that initiated the painting took place in May of 1868 during his first trip to England. Perhaps he was too shell-shocked to remember when he began the painting. He never did get to display it in the Salon, but it was on display in his atelier for a couple weeks (where it was very well received) before being shipped over to the Doré Gallery, where it filled one wall of the gallery. The gallery immediately commissioned Herbert Bourne to begin work on a 22x32 steel engraving, which took five years to complete. Roosevelt and Jerrold wrote extensively about reaction to the painting. Roosevelt (p.337):

> It would be useless for me to attempt the description of a picture so generally known as this one. Its reception in England was of the most enthusiastic nature. The Doré Gallery was crowded from morning to night; preachers, painters, connoisseurs, art-critics, press-men, and the public in general kept up a constant talk and excitement about the work. The unanimity with which it was praised was astonishing, and for a wonder the art-critics outvied one another in descanting on its general merits. One review said, "The most marvellous picture of the present age is to be seen in New Bond Street;" another, that "for grandeur and boldness of mass and outline, and for energy and passion of expression *Christ Leaving the Praetorium* suggests a comparison with the masterpieces of Michel Angelo."

Jerrold added these comments (p.304-305):

> ... The effect of the genius of the artist is direct and commanding. Crowds upon crowds have taken their seats before the picture, and remained long before it, speaking together in whispers. To them Doré has been, in truth, "the preacher painter;" and his weak points have been lost in the marvelous force and majesty - the thought and emotion - of the scene as a whole... that which is immortal in the work, and will put it on a level with the masterpieces of the Italian masters of the 16th century.

Roosevelt and Jerrold were actually rather restrained in their praise, compared to some articles in British periodicals at the time. Doré Gallery catalogues were full of bewildering quotes. Here is a catalogue quote (p.7) from the ***Examiner***:

> ... Whatever faults or defects may be alleged against M. Doré, it cannot be said that he has employed his extraordinary artistic genius on trifling or commonplace subjects. In gravity and magnitude of purpose, no less than in the scope and power of his imagination, he towers like a Colossus among his contemporaries. Compared with such as work as *Christ Leaving the Praetorium*, which has just been added to the collection of M. Doré's paintings in the Doré Gallery, New Bond Street, the pictures in Burlington House look like the productions of a race of dwarfs whose mental faculties are as diminutive as their stature. And it is not alone the efforts of the English School of painting that appear puny in the presence of so great and gigantic an undertaking; the work of all the existing schools of Europe sinks into equal insignificance, and we must go back to the Italian painters of the 16th century to find a picture worthy of being classed with this latest and most stupendous achievement of the young master.

Here is a catalogue quote (p.10) from the ***Morning Post***:

> The grandeur and versatility of M. Gustave Doré's genius have never been displayed to such a striking effect as in his new picture, entitled *Christ Leaving the Praetorium*. This magnificent painting ... is doubtless the finest pictorial illustration of the ineffable tragedy of the Redemption that art has produced in modern times.

In another catalogue quote (p.11-13), the ***Daily News*** of May 24, 1872 claimed to be able to look into Doré's heart and see the complete purity of his motivation in doing the painting:

> ... This very remarkable work of the young master of the French school is now to be seen... It should be understood, however, that this grand undertaking in no way takes its original from a commercial source, but is wholly and freely a work of genuine artist feeling, inspired by the painter's own native vigour and ardent ambition to pourtray (sic) a subject of the most elevated character of sacred history. No doubt it was designed and would have been painted without one farthing of the large amount now paid as its price; it needed no such temptation to impel a painter of such metal as Gustave Doré, who must be as enthusiastic in his art as Tintoretto; and like that great painter of the one great representation of the *Crucifixion*, as entirely above all thought of recompense but that of fame, and the gratification of his own high-souled ambition...
> ... The picture could not be fully appreciated by any description, even were it possible to convey in words the peculiar emphasis with which Doré throws into the countenance of his figures every expression of emotion. No painter of the time approaches him in this quality, and few surpass him in giving strong action and varied motion in the attitude of his figures.
>
> We are not disposed, however, to dwell upon any weak point in a work of such unquestionable power and such noble aspirations as this; neither

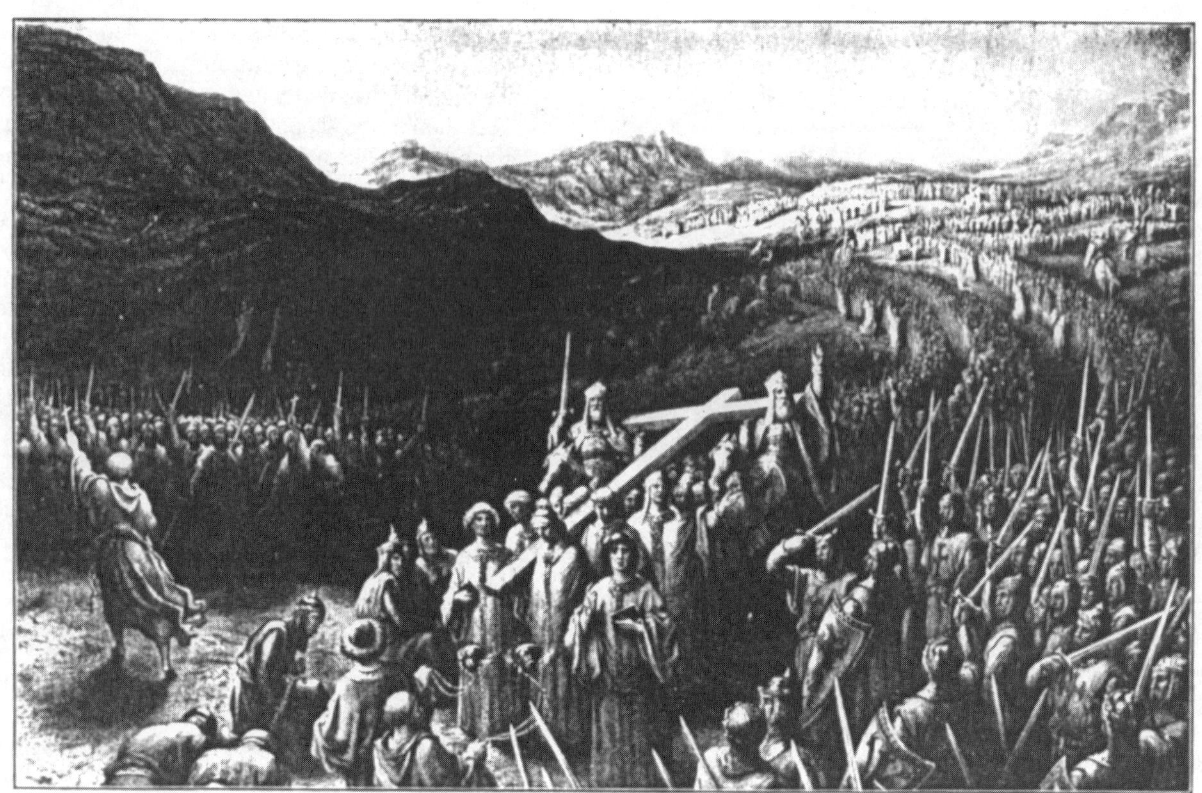

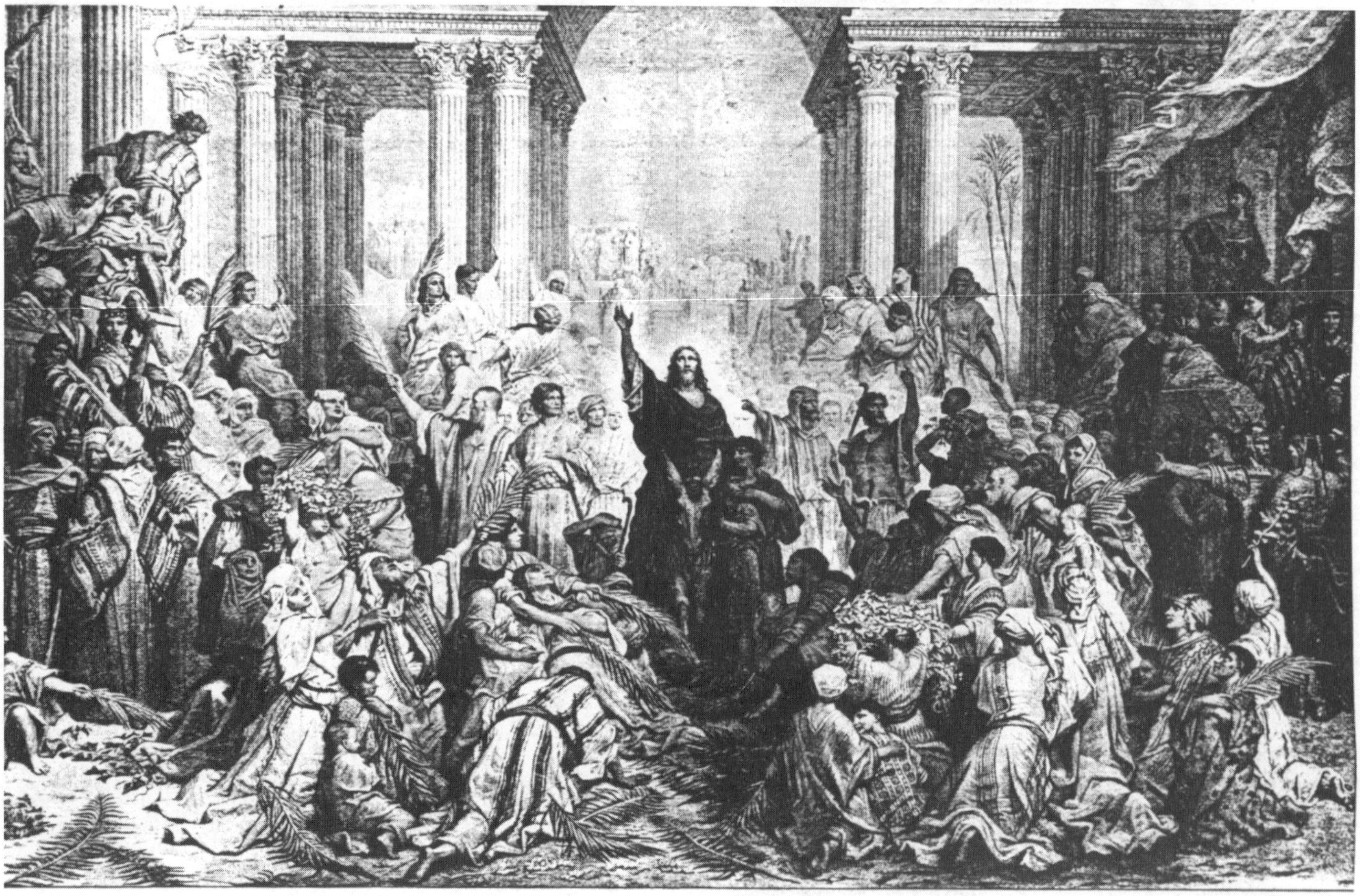

can we complain of the preponderance of the complex forms and colouring of the picture over the higher requisites of simplicity and grandeur, as necessary to these great themes of art. A painter, like an orator, must be allowed his manner; if he can impress us with his art, he deserves our praise and our gratitude. It must be owned, whatever one may think of the style of M. Doré, he is always impressive ... Apart from any consideration as to the technical merits or demerits of the picture, it possesses the greatest interest, and deserves the warmest recognition, as the work of the most serious and earnest purpose by a painter in the very prime of his artistic career, at a time when all the world of painters are occupied with the trivialities of technical nicety and the pleasing prettinesses of genre painting.

Notice how many reviewers refused to even discuss any technical defects in the painting. How could Doré the rejected French painter so quickly become Doré the British painter who was above criticism? Simple! He touched a nerve. He did not plan it, he just happened to be the right man at the right time. He came to symbolize Protestant religious fervor in Victorian England. He made their beliefs & feelings come alive through dramatic content (not to mention size). To say that Doré was theatrical and melodramatic is really a compliment. This was the third major stage of Doré's output - from comic-strip satire to literary folios to large dramatic religious paintings. For each stage there was a defining moment, from ***Hercules*** to ***Inferno*** to ***Praetorium***. And success at each stage was dependent upon the popularity achieved by the previous stage - his popularity as a comic-strip artist made the French willing to consider his literary folios, and the popularity of his literary folios made the British willing to consider his paintings. The British saw no difference between Doré's folio ***Bible*** engravings and religious paintings. They were all beautiful, dramatic illustrations.

Doré eventually did one other work that was as large as his ***Praetorium***. It was his 1876 ***Christ's Entry into Jerusalem*** (which we will look at shortly). Those two became the twin pillars of all Doré Gallery exhibitions from then on. But there are much large religious paintings that those. The apparant record (on canvas) is ***The Crucifixion*** (completed in 1897) by Polish artist Jan Styka. It is 45 feet high and 195 feet long. For many years nobody knew what to do with it, and finally the Forest Lawn Memorial Park in Glendale (just outside of Los Angeles) bought it and built a theatre just to house/display it, where it is now a major tourist attraction. The original 1872 ***Praetorium*** was in a private collection for most of this century, but in 1982 it was displayed in Heinrich von Ferstel's Gothic revival in the Votivkirche Cathedral in Vienna, Austria. Other versions are in the Musee des Beaux-Arts in Nantes, France and in Bob Jones University. Recent ***Praetorium*** interest has been highlighted by two major articles, in ***Apollo Magazine*** (May 1985) and in the ***Revue du Louvre*** (April 1987). In ***Revue***, Nadine Lehni, curator of the Musee d'Art Moderne in Strasbourg (which has the largest Doré collection in the world) discusses recent Doré acquisitions by French museums. She explains the different versions of ***Praetorium***.

Massacre of the Innocents
Night of the Crucifixion (Les Tenebres)
The Dream of Pilate's Wife
The House of Caiaphas

After the success of ***Praetorium*** in 1872, Doré began to concentrate on large religious paintings, turning out about one per year. It was also during this period that he began doing etchings and watercolor landscapes. It was about this time that Doré remarked that he only needed about three hours sleep a day. Back in 1867 the ***Art Journal*** had expressed fear that Doré's artistic pace would literally kill him. If anything that pace accelerated in the 1870s. It finally caught up with him.

Massacre of the Innocents was also finished in 1872. It was 12 feet high x 17 feet wide. Doré exhibited it in the 1872 Salon, and it arrived at the Doré Gallery late in 1874. ***The Night of the Crucifixion*** was originally entitled ***Les Tenebres*** ("the darkness"). It was only 4'3" high by 6'2" wide. Doré exhibited it in the 1873 Salon. It is now in an art museum in Puerto Rico. ***The Dream of Pilate's Wife*** was also highly praised. It shows an angel coming to Pilate's wife in her sleep to show her the suffering of Jesus. There is also a replica of it. One is 10 feet high by 13 feet wide, and the other is 6'4" high by 9'7" wide. Both versions have recently sold in the $50,000-$70,000 range. One is in the Joseph Tanenbaum collection in Toronto. ***The House of Caiaphas*** was a diminutive 3'6" x 5'9" and it was displayed in the 1875 Salon before going to the Doré Gallery. ***Caiaphas*** is now in the Houston Art Museum. It is the scene where Judas goes to the high priests and offers to betray Jesus. Besides religious paintings, quite a few Doré landscapes (both oil and watercolor) were also added to the gallery. The 1875 catalogue lists eleven landscapes, one of which, ***Loch Lomond***, is now in the St.Louis Art Museum.

Christ's Entry into Jerusalem
Ecce Homo! (Behold the Man!)
The Brazen Serpent
Moses before Pharoah
The Ascension

These were all added to the Doré Gallery between 1877-79. Doré began to do major paintings in pairs. ***Entry*** was the sister painting to ***Praetorium***, and was displayed in the Paris Salon in 1877. Again there was a great outpouring of British enthusiasm over ***Entry***, making a striking contrast to the lack of enthusiasm by French art critics, who by 1877 were really fed up with Doré's British popularity. Doré might well have paraphrased three famous Biblical quotes, "He came unto his own, and his own received him not," "An artist is not without honor save in his own country," and "Because ye deem yourselves unworthy of my artistry, lo I turn to the British."

Doré was often referred to as the "painter-preacher" during the 1870s. Doré was officially Roman Catholic, but was actually more of a mystic. He certainly followed a circuitous pathway to becoming such a "painter-preacher." The dominant theme of his early comic-strip art was social satire. His early

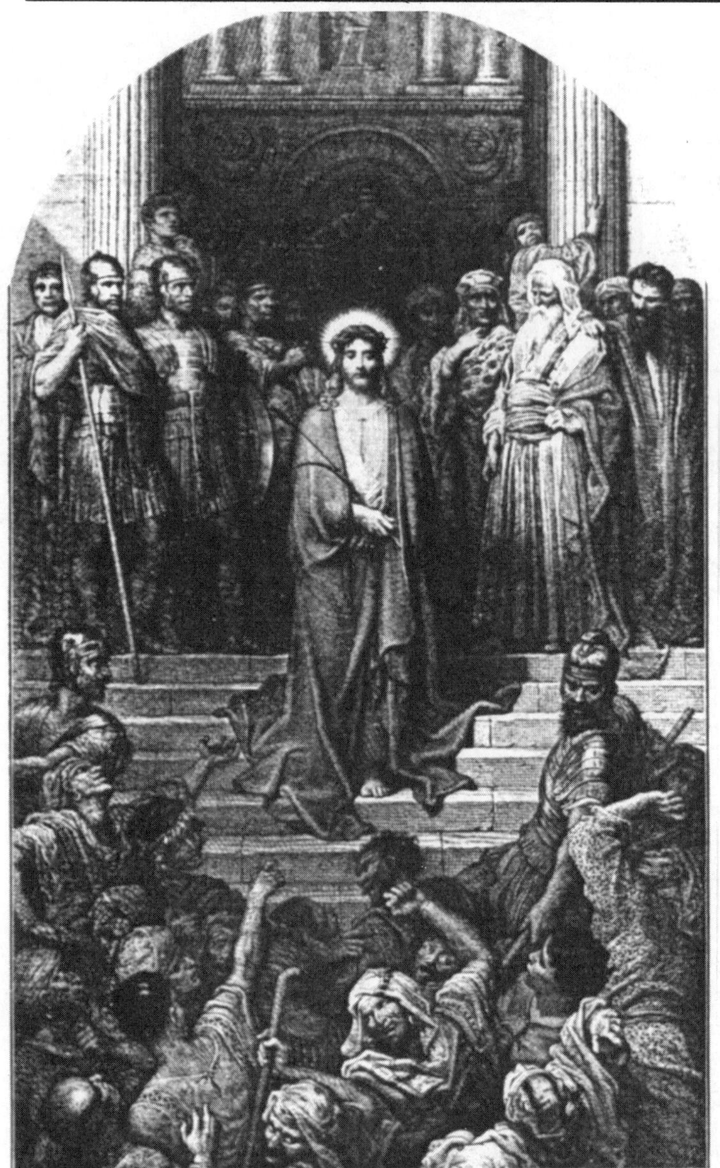

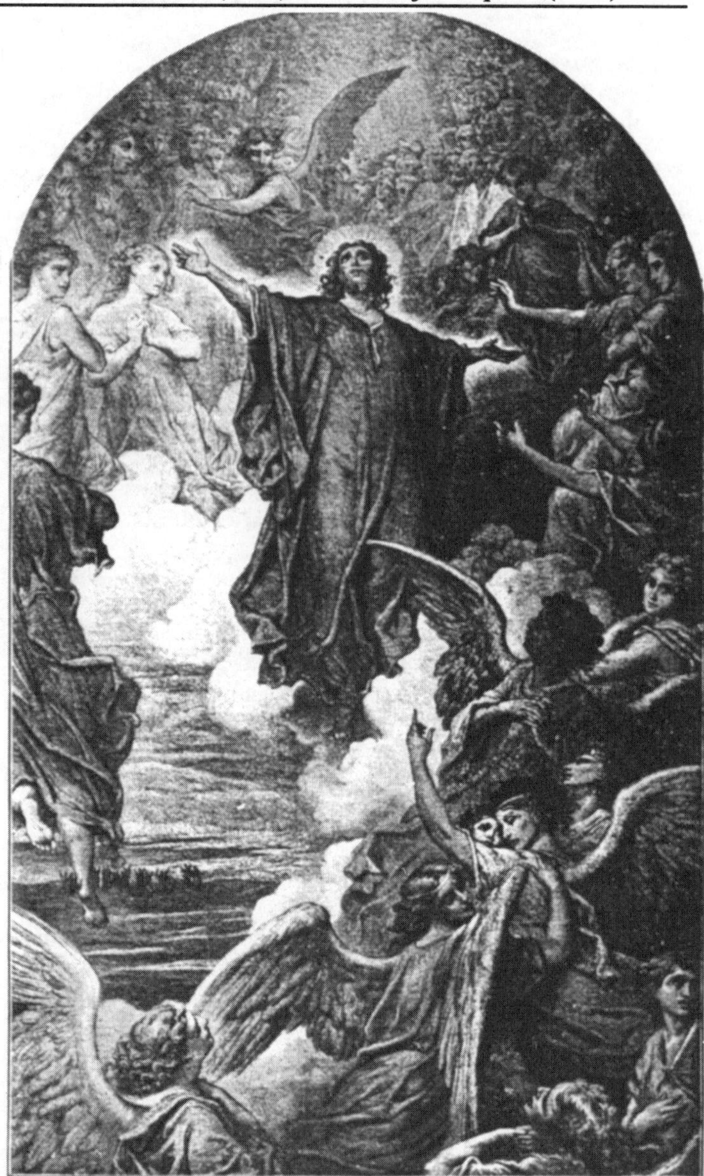

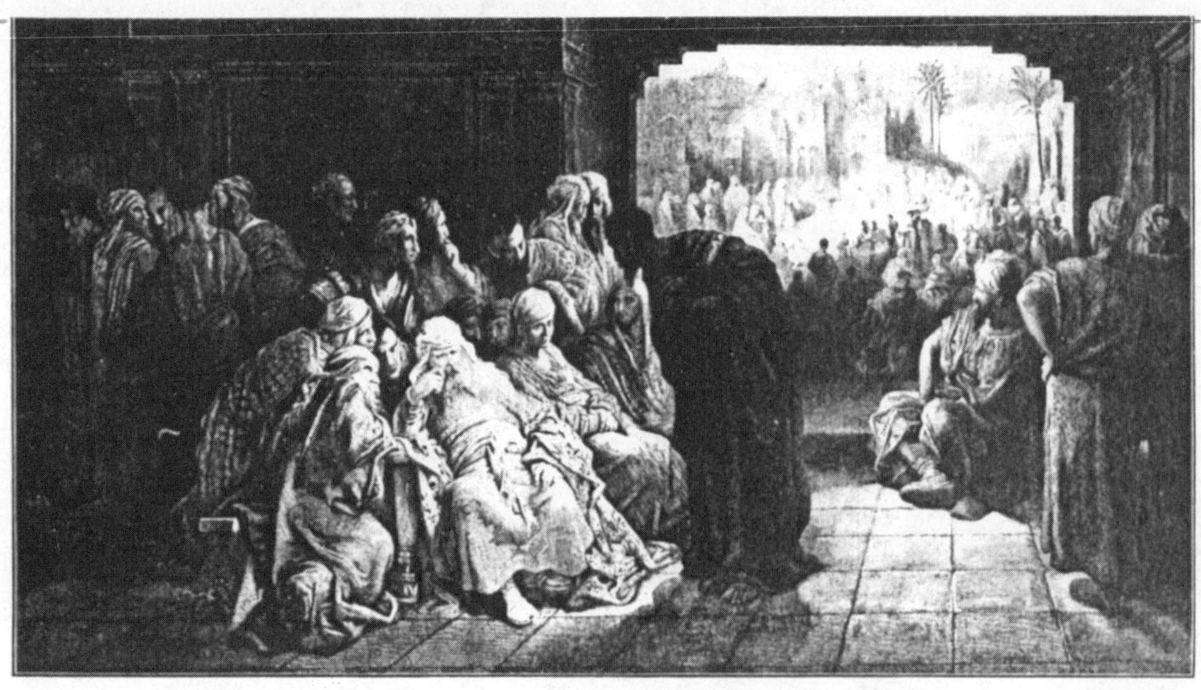

literary art was decidedly racy (***Rabelais, Balzac***, etc.). Some of his early literary folios did have religious content (***Dante, The Wandering Jew, & Chateaubriand***), but he was actually selecting titles for dramatic literary content. The coincidental timing of his ***Bible*** engravings with his British fame led the British to push him to make religious paintings. Doré was not a religious man seeking to evangelize, but a painter in search of an audience. But once the door was open, the enthusiastic reception to the dramatic content of Doré's religious paintings overshadowed both his technical painting defects and his personal religious beliefs. He certainly was not anti-religious either. On his first visit to England, Doré was asked about his religious beliefs. His reply came from the famous Bible chapter on love, according to Roosevelt (p.306):

> My friend, I am a Roman Catholic, a professed Roman Catholic. I was baptized in that Church, and I stick to it. That is all very well and good; but if you wish to know my real religion, I will tell it to you. It is contained in the 13th chapter of St. Paul to the Corinthians.
>
> Then he began quoting, and, to the reverend gentleman's amazement, recited it through from the beginning to the end, without hesitation or missing one word....

Some ministers did more than just encourage audiences to visit the Doré Gallery. Some preached sermons from the pulpit about Doré paintings. The Rev. E. Paxton Hood sent Doré the printed text of such a sermon in 1873. Doré wrote him back the following letter (quoted in William Tirebuck's ***Great Minds in Art***, p.76):

> Friday, September 5, 1873
>
> Dear Sir - I have just received some printed copies of the sermon that you have done me the honour to deliver on the subject of my picture, *Christ Leaving the Praetorium*. I hasten to tell you, sir, how grateful and flattered I am by such an act, and I regret not being in London at this moment the better to express to you, personally, my thanks for your kind and obliging words. Be good enough to believe, dear sir, that in looking back to the hours of success which have been given me in the course of my career, I have never felt so honoured and proud as in learning that my name has been pronounced in a religious place and before a Christian assembly, and I have never found a satisfaction more tender and true, or an encouragement more high and powerful.
>
> GU. DORÉ.

There is no reason to doubt his sincerity in such a letter. Both Doré and Sarah Bernhardt loved all the mystical aspects of religion. One of the proprietors of the Doré Gallery once told Doré that he should be proud of his genius and varied talents. Doré replied, according to Roosevelt (p.304):

> Not proud, Monsieur Beeforth, I am simply glad of them. I am not vain; but only grateful. God has been very good to me, and I thank Him every day of my life for my gifts. I would not change places with any man in the world. Understand me, not from vanity, but because, when I look around me and see how full the world is of hapless people and hopeless talents, I go down on my knees to thank Him for having given me so much to work with, and so much to be grateful for.

What was frustrating to Doré's fans was his proclivity for leaving a field just about the time he had a large following in it. When the French loved his comic-strip art, he wanted to do literature. When the French loved his vignettes, he wanted to do folios. When the French loved his French folios, he was already planning British folios. When the British loved his folios, he wanted to do paintings. When the British loved his religious paintings, he wanted to do landscape watercolors. When his landscape watercolors began to be popular, he wanted to be a sculptor. For all the radical polarity of opinion about Doré, friend and foe alike agreed on the public's true motto for Doré, "What will he do next?" This group of five religious paintings represented the end of that era for him. By then his emotional energy was in sculpting. But the religious faithful continued to think of Doré as their artist.

Once again, there were many versions of ***Entry***. There were two smaller oil paintings, and a watercolor version. The two Moses paintings were also very large. ***The Brazen Serpent*** (1877) was 18'4" high by 29'6" wide, while ***Moses before Pharaoh*** (1878?) was 17'6" high by 26'6" wide. The Moses paintings were similar to ***Bible*** engraving scenes. But these paintings were a major influence on Cecil B. DeMille's film ***The 10 Commandments***, where Yul Brenner looks strikingly similar to the Pharaoh in ***Moses before Pharaoh***.

Ecce Homo! and ***The Ascension*** were finished two years apart but came to the Doré Gallery at the same time. They are the same size and shape - a curved top 13'6" wide by 20' high, like a stained-glass window, many of which are based on Doré ***Bible*** engravings. ***Ecce Homo!*** is dated 1877. It was displayed in the Paris Salon in 1878. Then it came to the Doré Gallery in 1879 with ***The Ascension***. Once again, they were very popular, and Doré had just about completed replica oil paintings of them 6'9" wide by 11' high at the time of his death. LeBlanc (p.534) lists a third oil painting version of ***Ecce***. The steel engravings for these two are only 12½" wide by 22" high. Versions of ***Ecce Homo!*** are now in the Petit Palais in Paris and in Swansea, England. The replica version of ***Ascension*** is at Bob Jones University. They were able to acquire that painting in 1964 for $36. They were fortunate enough to catch Doré when he was "out of style."

The Head of Christ

This originated as one oil painting, but there were four different drawings made into etchings. This was another theme Doré returned to again and again. Doré finished one etching and left 14 unfinished etchings at his death, so the gallery had three more etched and offered for sale. The four sub-titles were ***Bearing his Cross, Hail-King of the Jews, Salvator Mundi,*** and ***Road to Calvary***. Since all are facial close-ups, some titles do not make any sense. The title ***Road to Calvary*** is especially

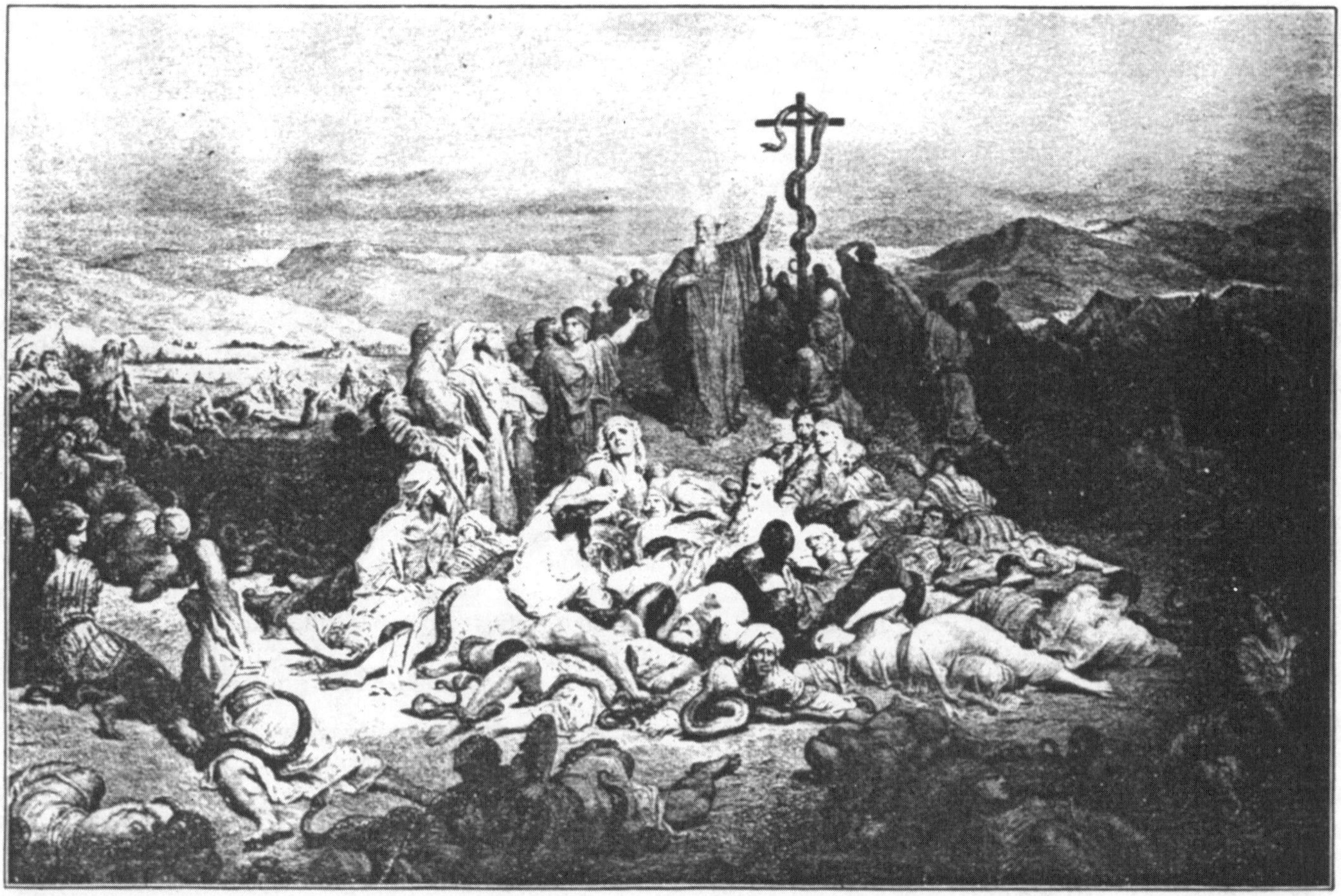

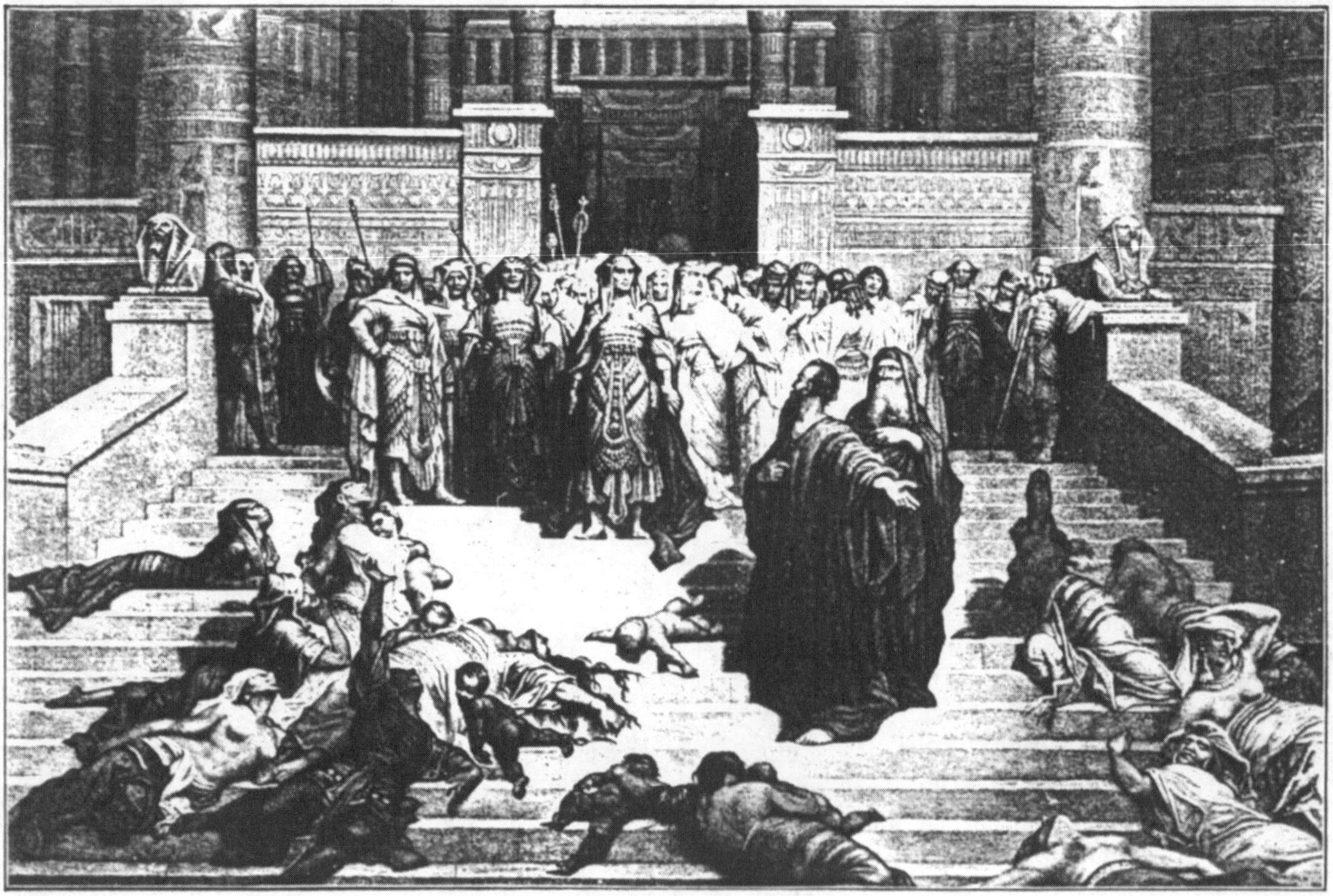

confusing, since that was also a large oil painting by that title. But they were very powerful and popular etchings.

The Vale of Tears
Calvary

Doré had nearly completed these oil paintings at his death. They were then purchased and displayed in the gallery. The oil painting version of ***Vale of Tears*** is 14 feet high by 21 feet wide. There was also a drawing, a sketch, a watercolor, and a steel engraving. All were featured in the Doré Gallery catalogue. The watercolor was also used on the front cover of the 1983 Doré exhibition in Strasbourg. The oil painting was acquired by the Petit Palais in Paris in 1985. The unfortunate thing about ***Calvary*** is that it was never made into a steel engraving, and so was never illustrated in any Doré Gallery catalogue, or in any Doré reference book. The 51"h x 76"w oil painting version is now at Wellesley College. The other Doré paintings with similar titles can be differentiated by size.

Steel Engravings & Etchings

Before any of Doré's paintings were engraved, he had already done drawings for 46 steel engravings for Moxon from 1866-69 for ***Tennyson*** and ***Hood,*** but they were book size (7½x9½). From 1871-86, the Doré Gallery had 20 large steel engravings made from Doré's paintings, plus five etchings. All 25 of those items were illustrated in some U.S. Doré Gallery catalogues in the 1890s. But there were a few other Doré paintings made into steel engravings, while some other Doré paintings were engraved as lithographs. So his paintings could be engravings as etchings, lithographs, or steel engravings. In 1866, Doré did two paintings entitled ***War*** and ***Peace***, which were made into steel engravings in 1867. They were then published simultaneously in Paris, London, Berlin, and New York. While those two were also very large, two smaller steel engravings were made of ***The Homeless*** and ***Alms-Giving***, which were published in New York in art books.

The first gallery painting made into a steel engraving was ***Paolo & Francesca*** in 1871. At 12x17, it was barely larger than the ***Wandering Jew*** wood engravings (12x16). When ***Praetorium*** came to the Doré Gallery in May of 1872, their was tremendous interest in the planned engraving of same, per an article in the ***Art Journal*** (1872, p.289-290):

> ENGRAVING OF *CHRIST LEAVING THE PRETORIUM* (sic) - Unusual pains are being taken to make this great engraving a worthy translation of the picture. It is entrusted to Mr. Bourne, of whose admirable skill in reproducing the expression of an original the visitors to the Doré Gallery can judge by specimen - some of them engraved for the *Art Journal*. The picture has been reduced, in sections, by photography, and a photograph on canvas is now being finished in black and white chalk. No precaution seems to be omitted, and we hope to have to congratulate Messrs. Fairless & Beeforth on an engraving worthy to hang by the *Francesca da Rimini*.

The ***Praetorium*** engraving was not finished until June 1, 1877, and cost about $8,000. That may sound very expensive, but Roosevelt (p.425) mentions that in about a 3-year period, the steel engraving of ***Christ's Entry into Jerusalem*** alone had sales of about $20,000. These engravings sold for almost as much as many Doré book editions. In Clapp (p.62), he lists the selling prices of these steel engravings as being £6.6s for the small ones (like ***Paolo***) and £13 for the large ones. That is about $30-$70 each. You could have had the ***Doré Bible*** for less than the ***Praetorium*** steel engraving. To reconcile all that with Roosevelt's figures, if the ***Entry*** engraving sold for about $70, then they sold about 300 of them in three years, or about one every four days. Needless to say, these engravings were for the well-to-do. They are now quite scarce. The first list of Doré Gallery engravings was in the 1885 ***Duplessis*** catalogue for the Paris Doré exhibition. They list 20 of the 25 eventual Doré Gallery engravings. The 1890s illustrated U.S. Doré Gallery catalogues list all engravings with the name of the engraver.

Misc. Oil Paintings & Watercolors

It is impossible here to really cover Doré's hundreds of landscape paintings - mainly of Alsace, the Alps, the Pyrenees, and Scotland. Most have general titles and are difficult to tell apart. It might be difficult to imagine Doré the super-dramatic artist doing peaceful landscapes. Perhaps they were some sort of therapy for him. The Doré Gallery included dozens of Doré landscapes, basically as fillers for the major featured paintings. They sold many landscapes from the gallery. Some were there only a couple months. His landscapes were about the only thing that escaped the lash of the French art critics. It has even been asserted (Gosling, p.80) that Doré (the "unschooled") did "landscapes in the Barbizon-school manner." What a major concession. Can it be possible that Doré was actually accepted as a fairly good landscape artist? Is it possible that here was a field in which he was not simultaneously the best and the worst, depending on who was doing the judging? In a recent book about the Pyrenees, published by the Musee des Pyrenees, the front cover features a Doré landscape.

A few other paintings in the Doré Gallery deserve note. There were two versions of ***Titania***, from ***A Midsummer Night's Dream*** in 1869 and 1874. One of those paintings was purchased by James Duncan, the Laird of Benmore, who had his own London art gallery, in an interesting story by Roosevelt (p.339-340). Doré had been burned 20 years earlier by his mother demanding high prices for paintings, so except for the major feature paintings commissioned by the Doré Gallery, Doré sold most of his paintings at low prices. When Mr. Duncan came to Doré's studio in the early 1870s, both Doré and Mr. Duncan were surprised. Doré was surprised to see one man wanting to buy so many of his paintings, and Mr. Duncan was surprised that major works of art could be had at such bargain prices. At a certain point Doré decided to take a major leap of faith. Instead of letting ***A Midsummer Night's Dream*** go for, say, a thousand dollars, Doré asserted that he really did not want to sell that item, and could not part with it for less than $11,000 (2000 guineas). To Doré's amazement, Mr. Duncan did not hesitate to snatch it at that price.

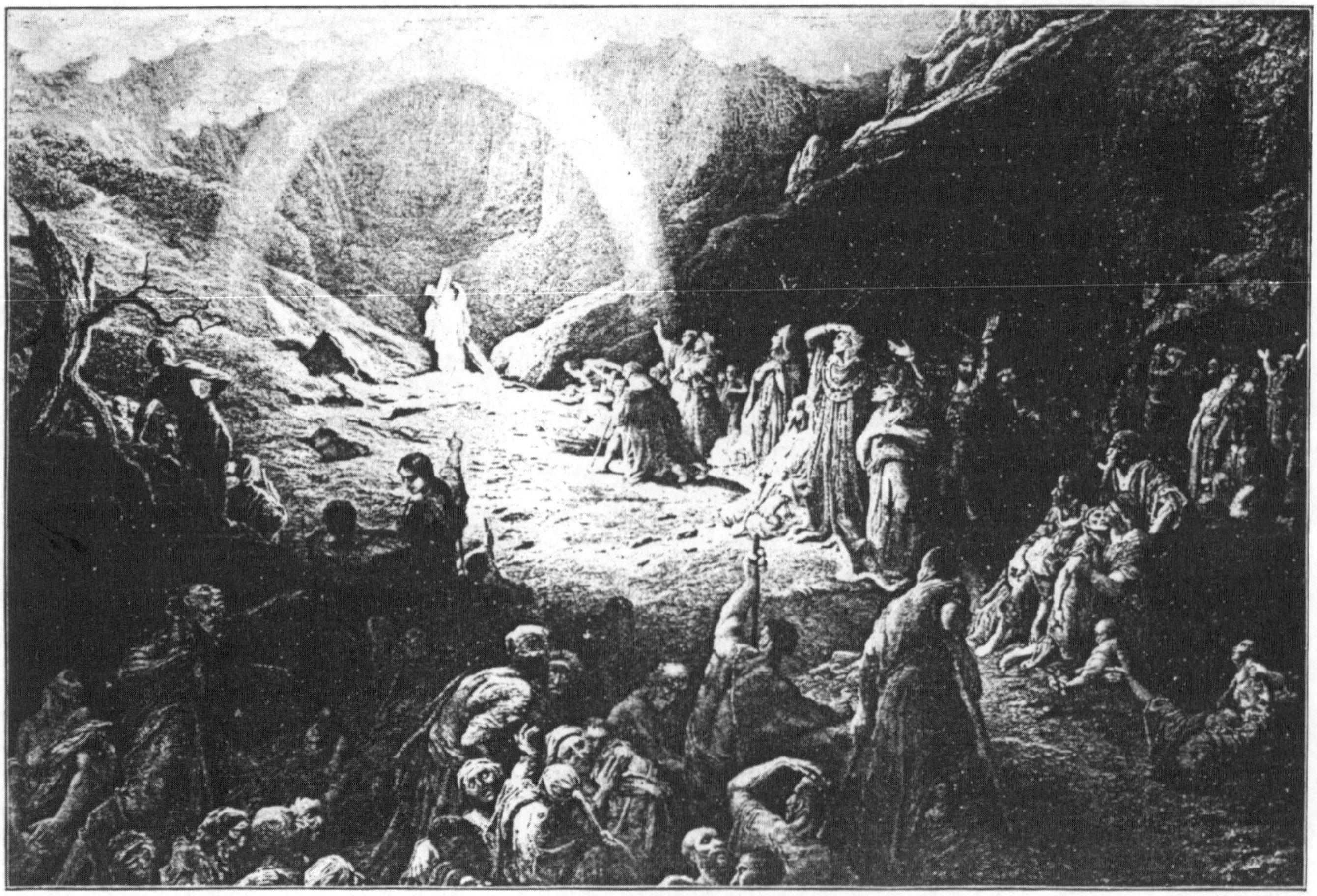

steel engravings of Doré oil paintings ***The Battle of Ascalon*** (1875) & ***The Vale of Tears*** (1883)

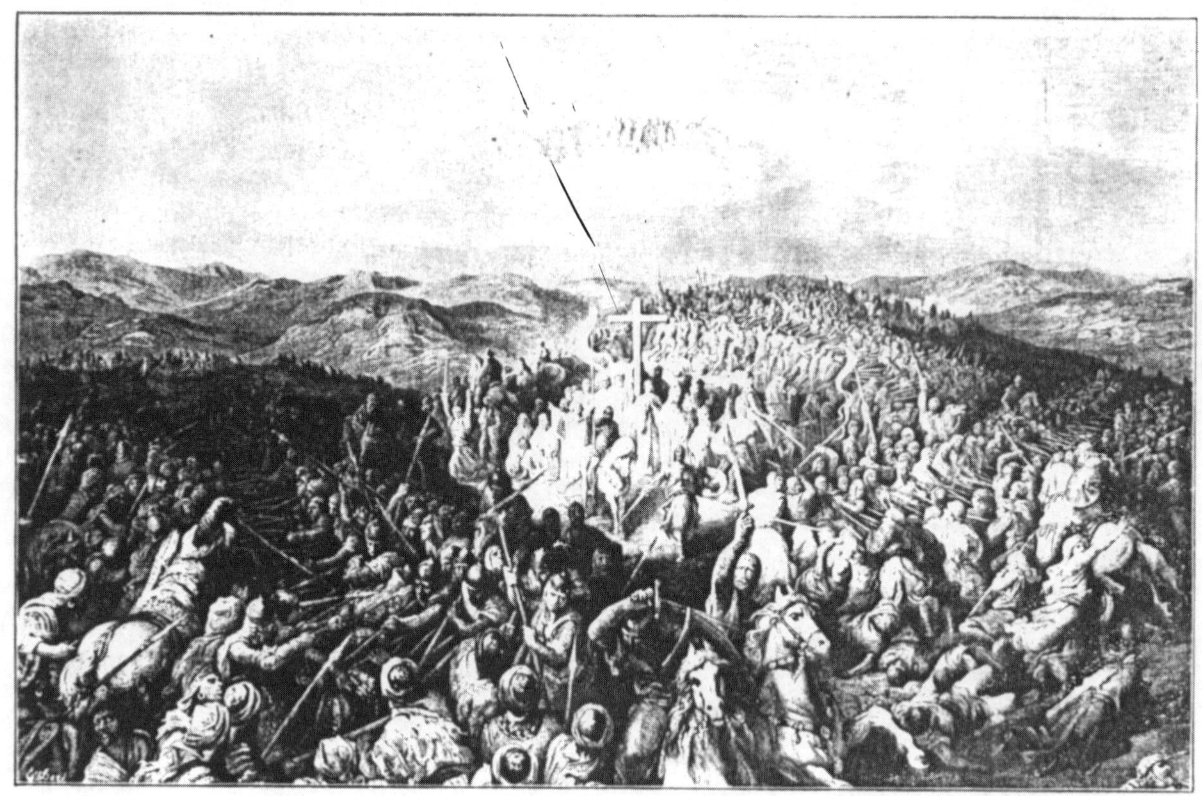

In the section on the Franco-Prussian War, we mentioned a poignant 1872 painting called ***Alsace***. It has also been called ***Alsace Weeping*** or ***The Death of Alsace***. Doré was greatly moved by the loss of his home to the Germans. In the Fall of 1872, the following ***Art Journal*** article appeared, about the French government ordering a Doré painting removed (p.289):

> M. DORÉ'S *ALSACE* - We can readily believe the statement (which has been positively made, although we do not assume the responsibility of verification) that the government of M. Thiers requested M. Doré to remove from the *Salon*, at Paris, the noble picture of *Alsace*, which is now exhibiting at the Doré Gallery in New Bond Street. The heart of the man who does not feel as he looks at the picture that he *has* a heart, must be callous. To a Frenchman, the pathos is only too deep and real. Remarkably chaste and severe in its treatment, this fine work forms a chapter apart in the long roll of M. Doré's imaginations. A tall, nobly formed woman, with the flaxen hair of the Alsace peasantry, clad in their picturesque national dress, but scarfed and hooded with crape, stands before a blank wall, holding - and holding erect - the flag of France... The desolate, abandoned, but still noble and defiant, figure; the grand contour of the physiognomy; the magic lines in which the drapery of the flag is thrown, while the truncheon is firmly grasped, and the point towers towards heaven as if it were the *oriflamme* itself, must be seen to be appreciated. Once seen, it will not readily be forgotten.

Many Doré Gallery paintings sold quickly. ***Alsace*** was sold in 1874 to the Baroness Burdett-Coutts. In 1870 another painting briefly appeared, entitled ***Le Psalterion***, a picture of a young man playing a lute. It was quickly purchased for $2000 by Queen Victoria. It was one of the few bright spots for Doré during the war. The gallery also rediscovered early lost Doré oil paintings and put them on display, like the 1855 ***Death of David Rizzio*** and the 1867 ***La Prairie***. Replica paintings were never listed in the catalogues, but in the 1880s, they began to list the sketches connected with the major paintings. They had probably been exhibiting these all along, but just did not count them as separate items until the 1880s. An 1872 ***Art Journal*** article states that the preliminary sketches for ***Christ Leaving the Praetorium*** were exhibited along with the painting. At least three sets of book illustrations were also listed as items in the gallery. The 1868 catalogue lists the ***Dante's Inferno*** illustrations, in 1882 the ***Ancient Mariner*** illustrations were listed, and in the 1890s the ***Tennyson*** illustrations were listed. Unconnected with the Doré Gallery, Cassell exhibited the original ***Bible*** illustrations upon Doré's first London visit in 1868. When Doré visited London, he was very fond of "his" gallery, per Roosevelt (p.190):

> ... Then we would issue forth on the day's travels, generally calling at the Gallery in Bond Street to begin with. Doré was never tired of glancing into his Gallery; it was his sole consolation, as a painter.

From the moment Doré first came to Paris, he loved the Salon. In 1848, at the age of 16, he exhibited two drawings there, and then in 1850 exhibited his first oil painting. His early interest climaxed with ten paintings exhibited in 1857. Then his interest in the Salon subsided, as he concentrated on his literary folios. But his folios led him to the British, and the British led him back into painting. From 1868-76, Doré exhibited only oil paintings at the Salon, mainly landscapes and religious works. But from 1877-82, his Salon emphasis switched to sculpture. His last religious paintings at the Salon were in 1878. He did win a Third Class Medal for Sculpture in 1880, but by then it meant very little to him. In 1879 he was made an Officer of the Legion of Honour. In the last years of his life, he actually made inroads into French art establishment respectability in both sculpture and watercolor, but by then his basic attitude had become entrenched negativism, and nothing was able to shake the bitterness. What a shame.

In 1879, when Doré joined the Societe des Aquarellistes Francais, he was welcomed as an honored watercolorist. He took part in their exhibitions for five years, in which time he exhibited 58 watercolors, his major topics being landscapes and literary scenes. Each year they put out a little catalogue, and seven of Doré's watercolors were reproduced in them. In 1883 they put out a major elephant folio, featuring Detaille, Doré, Leloir, Beaumont, de Neuville, Isabey, Jacquet, Lemaire, Tissot, Vibert, and many others. Doré was given 16 pages, showing 14 sketches and five watercolor photogravures by Goupil. The main feature there was his large watercolor of his mother. He also selected a scene from ***A Midsummer Night's Dream***, an Alpine landscape, and two views of the London poor. They treated Doré very respectfully.

Had Doré just been a landscape painter, he would never have been controversial. But his "heavy" paintings could never break free from his premier reputation as an illustrator. In 1882, Edward Strahan put it very well in ***Etudes in Modern French Art*** when he wrote (p.73): "Doré is injured in his reputation as a painter by his supremacy as a designer."

150 plaster model (11'6" high) of ***Glory*** or ***Genius killed by Fame*** (1878) - now in Mauberg Museum.
wood engraving of ***Fate & Love*** (1877) - six known versions, three presently in French museums.

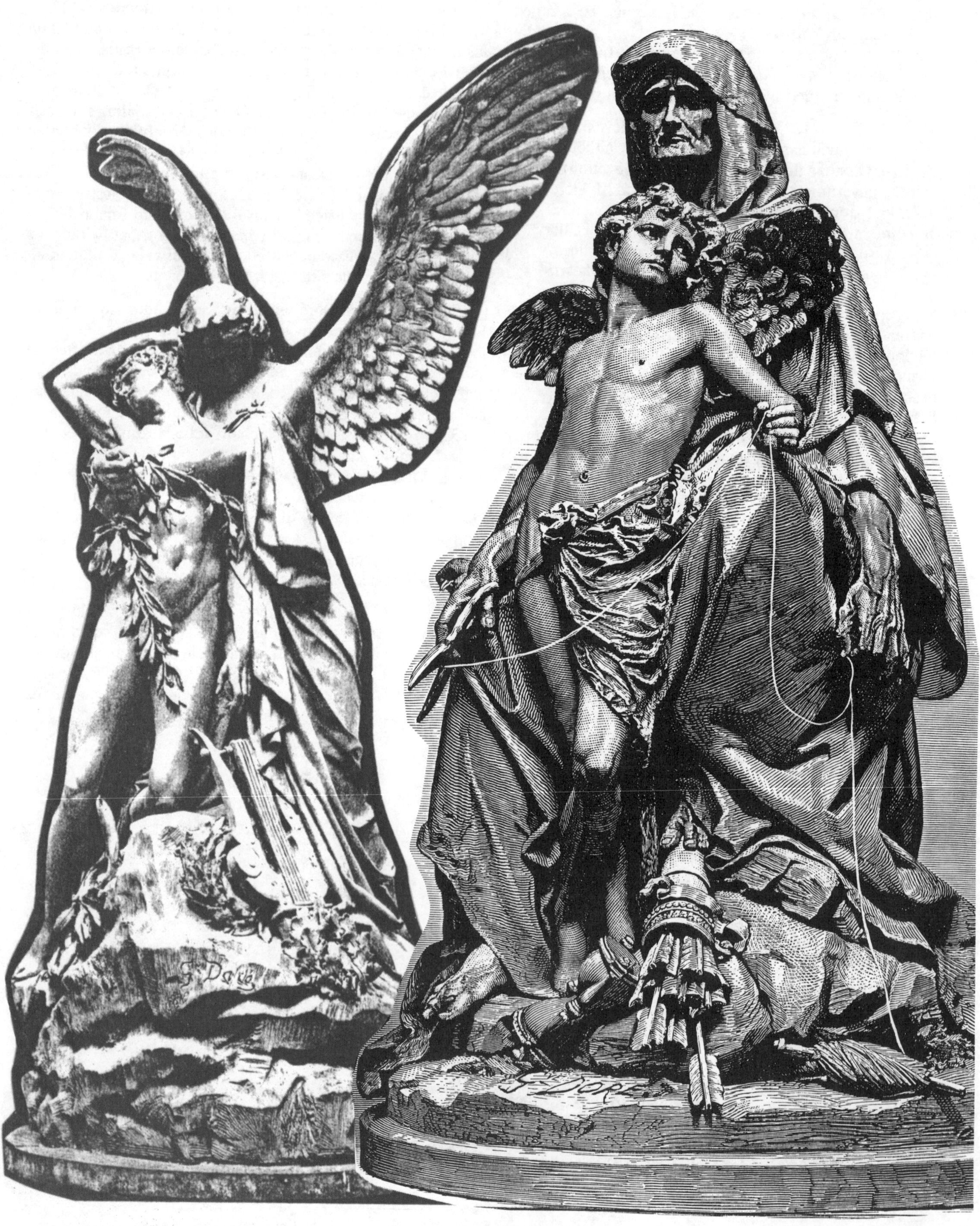

10. DORÉ THE SCULPTOR (1877-83)

Sculpture had a feature that was very appealing to Doré - no color! But to him subconsciously everything was illustration - paintings were enlarged color illustrations and sculpture was 3-dimensional illustration. But there was no immediate market for his sculpture as there had been for his paintings in London. There the religious audience really drove him into painting. So while the Doré Gallery did display a few works of sculpture, it was as a courtesy to him. They never featured or promoted any of them. Most of his sculpture themese were French, and while the French response to his sculpture was not as negative as to his paintings, it was hardly enthusiastic. The other drawback of sculpture was the expense. So when Doré finally turned to sculpture, the French wanted Doré to stick to what he was doing in the 1860s (illustration), and the British wanted him to stick to what he was doing in the 1870s (religious paintings).

Doré did about 30 works of sculpture, with variations. The definitive research on his sculpture has been published (in French) by Samuel Clapp (a major London Doré collector) and Nadine Lehni (Conservateur of the Museee d'Art Moderne in Strasbourg). They were the two key players in the various 1983 Doré centennial exhibitions. In 1993 the Strasbourg museum bought out Clapp's Doré collection and exhibited it there. In 1991, the two of them published their Doré sculpture research in the ***Bulletin de la Societe de l'Histoire d'Art Francais*** (p.219-253), entitled *Une Introduction a la Sculpture de Gustave Doré*. That is the major source for this chapter.

Although the French art world had seen Doré's 30-year career move from comic-strip satire to lithographic albums to literary vignettes to literary folios to oil painting to watercolor to etching, they still had one more shock in store for them in 1877. Doré was compared to Alexander the Great in ***The Chefs-d'Oeuvre d'Art of the International Exhibition, 1878***, per the English editor, Edward Strahan (p.64):

> The year 1877 found Doré, after a little weeping for new worlds to conquer, bethinking him that the domain of sculpture was still left to his prowess, and surprising the public with a group of statuary called *Fate & Love*. The work was exhibited in the Salon, and was on the whole favorably received. For the Universal Exposition he chose to continue the new-found line. He prepared the monumental composition of figures and foliage, modeled around the circumference of a vase, which he called *La Vigne*.

Here is a summary of Doré's major works of sculpture, with date completed, French title, number of known versions, and English title or description, all from Clapp/Lehni:

Year	French title	Versions	English title or description
1877	Parque et l'Amour	(6)	Fate & Love
1878	La Gloire (Glory)	(3)	Genius killed by Fame
	Ganymede	(2)	(from Greek mythology)
	La Nuit	(3)	The Night (with star circle)
	La Vigne	(3)	(ornamental vase)
1879	L'Effroi	(7)	Maternal Love (the Terror)
	La Danse	(5)	Dance (Monte Carlo theatre)
	Defense Nationale	(5)	(from Franco-Prussian War)
	Le Temps	(3)	Time mowing down the hours
	Persee/Andromede	(2)	Perseus & Andromeda
	La Mort d'Orphee	(3)	Death of Orpheus (high-relief)
	La Belle et la Bete	(2)	Beauty & the Beast
1880	Madone	(15)	Madonna & Child
	Pyramide Humaine	(4)	The Human Pyramid
	Le Petit Puck	(2)	Little Puck (with owl)
1881	Saute-Mouton	(4)	(game of leap-frog)
	Le Christianisme	(1)	Sister of Charity
1882	Miroir	(2)	(ornamental mirror)
1883	Alexandre Dumas	(2)	(monument in Paris)
	+ D'Artagnan	(3)	(part of Dumas monument)
	+ La Lecture	(2)	Group reading (monument)
	Amour/Tetes de Mort	(4)	Cupid reclining on skulls
	Venus Couchee	(3)	Mother with sleeping child

Fate & Love
Genius killed by Fame (Glory)
Ganymede

Doré's first two works of sculpture were allegorical, but everybody missed the point, or did not want to say openly, that they were both about Doré's own life. By 1877 Doré was not a happy camper, and his first two works of sculpture expressed that fate and fame were killing him. Was not the hooded figure in ***Fate & Love*** Doré's mother? Was he not crying out that his mother's all-encompassing love was smothering him? Then in ***Glory***, was not Doré the genius whose fame was destroying him? In each of his first three works, Doré sculpted the figure of a youthful boy, and who was more of an eternal child than himself? Was he not saying that he never grew up because of his mother and his too-early fame? In ***Ganymede*** it was Doré's own creative imagination that transported the eternal child to new worlds. Doré began expressing very different ideas in his sculpture than he had with illustration or painting. For the first time his art was introspective, and critics found them too hard to understand. They asserted that the purpose of sculpture was not to pose riddles. After nearly a century of abstract art, such comments are now nothing short of hilarious.

Fate & Love (also known as ***Time cutting the Thread of Life***) made quite a sensation at the 1877 Salon. It revived the overworked saying, "What will Doré do next?" The group shows the youthful Love leaning back against the mysterious hooded figure of Fate, while Fate is cutting the thread of life. He also exhibited it at the 1878 Paris Universal Exhibition, where it received a 3rd Class Honorable Mention Medal. Strahan's ***1878 Expo*** folio has an 8x10 wood engraving of it. Clapp & Lehni list 16 references to it between 1877-79. It was then put on display in the Doré Gallery from 1879-91. The original plaster design was about 7½ feet high, but like most Doré works of sculpture, there are versions of it in plaster, terracotta, and bronze, and in varying sizes down to about two feet high. Today, versions of it are in private collections and museums in Paris, Bourg-en-Bresse, Strasbourg, and London.

In 1878, Doré was everywhere in the world of art, with four works of sculpture (in three different exhibitions), new large religious paintings in the Doré Gallery, plus watercolor landscapes, a new-found delight in etching, while in his spare time he turned out 600 zinc engravings for his ***Ariosto*** folio. He exhibited ***Glory*** in the 1878 Salon, per Roosevelt (p.436):

152 plaster model of ***Ganymede*** (1878) - present location of both versions unknown
plaster model (7'5" high) of ***The Night*** (1878) - present location of all three versions unknown

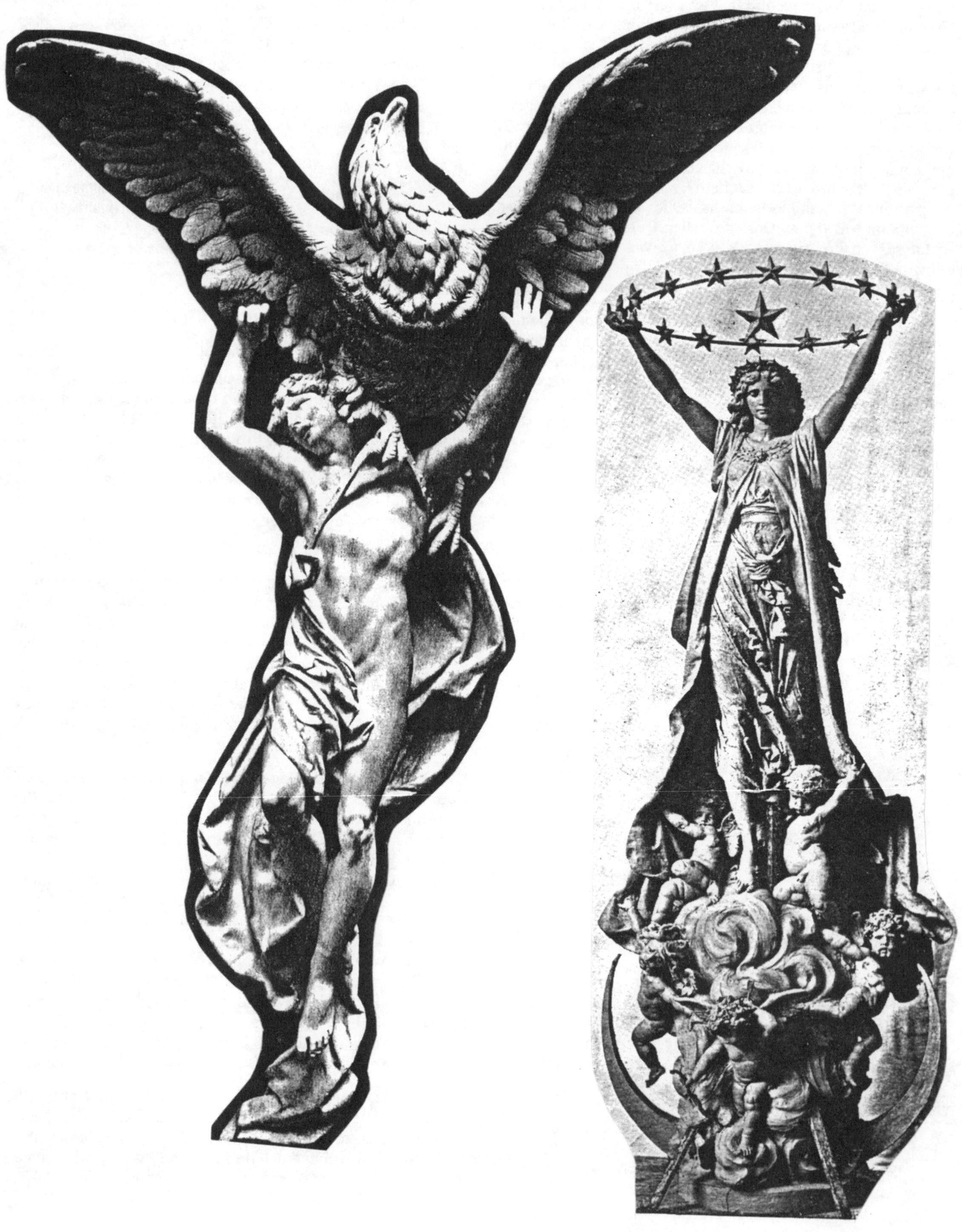

> ... this group occupied the place of honour in the garden, where all the sculpture sent to the Salon is exhibited. Crowds surrounded the work, and people who read the name of G.Doré on its picturesque pedestal thought how strange was the coincidence that there should be two G.Dorés. Few connected the sculptor of *La Gloire* with the creator of the *Neophyte, Rabelais,* and the *Wandering Jew*. Critics praised the work enthusiastically; and yet the jury of the Salon, after giving the place of honour to a young man who exhibited sculpture for the second time only, probably thought that this distinction was reward enough. One of the most beautiful works of the day was, so to speak, practically ignored by the Parisian tribunal of taste.

The English titles for ***La Gloire*** ranged from ***Genius killed by Fame*** to ***Glory killing Ambition***. The winged Glory embraces the youthful Fame and wraps him in laurel leaves, but at the same time is plunging a dagger into his heart. The same message that ***Fate & Love*** communicated subtly, ***Glory*** states aggressively. The message is made powerfully, because at first glance you usually do not see the dagger. The youthful Fame never saw it coming. It is no wonder the French art critics did not want to talk about its meaning. Doré's message could very easily have been directed at them - "you are killing me!" The original plaster was eleven feet high, a reduction of which was displayed in the Doré Gallery from 1879-91. The original is now in the Musee des Beaux-Arts de Maubeuge. ***Glory*** has become rather popular of late, having been shown in many exhibitions, and illustrated in several books.

Doré exhibited ***Ganymede*** (the mythological cupbearer of the gods) in the 1878 Exposition du Cercle de l'Union Artistique, place Vendome. Not much is known about this work. It is almost a cross between ***Glory*** and Doré's engraving in ***Dante*** showing an eagle lifting Dante out of Purgatory. ***Ganymede*** was exhibited in the Doré Gallery from 1879-91. Per Clapp & Lehni, its present location is unknown.

La Nuit (The Night)

Like ***Ganymede***, the present location of ***La Nuit*** is unknown. ***La Nuit*** was Doré's first romantic theme. It was exhibited in 1878 in both the Exposition du Cercle de l'Union Artistique and the Exposition Universelle. Were two different versions displayed simultaneously? It was about seven feet high, and Doré's flair for the theatrical was especially evident in this work, as explained by Roosevelt (p.440):

> ... *La Nuit*, another of Doré's superb creations, occupied a place in one of the interior galleries of the Champ de Mars buildings. This *Torchere*, as it is called reminds us of one of Marlow's poems, describing Helen arrayed in starry robes and bearing a circlet of light above her head. As we have been assured, it was in fact that very poem which inspired M. Doré; and certainly his inspiration was a most happy one.
>
> By an ingenious contrivance, flames of bluish light, emanating from concealed gas-jets, shed a glow of mystery and weird beauty over this statue. *La Nuit* stands on a crescent issuing seemingly from a group of cupids. Her attitude is a peculiar one, the outstretched arms firmly sustain the circlet, whilst the drooping countenance is studded with tear-drops. Again, the vision of sadness makes itself manifest! M. Doré embodies past hopes and future fears in all his creations; but the former idea usually predominates the latter.

La Nuit was briefly displayed in the Doré Gallery in 1879 (although apparently it was never listed in the catalogue). It was included in the 1885 Paris Doré sale. There was a major (illustrated) write-up about it in an 1887 French book, ***Album des Fontes d'Art de L. Thiriot***, and then it just disappeared, with no reference to an actual copy for over a century.

La Vigne (ornamental vase)

This work is now in the garden near the front entrance to the M.H.DeYoung Memorial Museum in San Francisco. It is, to say the least, unconventional. The idea for this ornamental vase, in the shape of an Italian wine bottle, came from a Doré ***Rabelais*** engraving. The last two full-page plates for the 1873 ***Rabelais*** folio dealt with the oracle of the divine bottle. That idea grew into an oil painting, entitled strangely enough, ***La Gloire*** (now in a Munich Art Museum, per Renonciat, p.271), and then into this behemoth work of sculpture. The original plaster model was 14½ feet high. It was quite a sensation at the 1878 Exposition Universelle. No one had seen anything like it. The bottle was covered with hundreds of little nymphs, satyrs, fauns, cupids, and other creatures, playing on the vines. Here is how Strahan's ***1878 Expo*** folio summarized it (p.65):

> Such is the purpose of the composition: but a description can hardly give an idea of the gracious forms accumulated around the flanks of the vase, the intensity of life animating the crowds of gallantries and follies everywhere distributed, the contrasts of indolence and passion, of beauty and uncouthness. In arranging so many details into clear and harmonious groups, and composing in sculpture a world of figures such as animate his most crowded drawings, Doré has made a plastic study of an absolutely novel kind, and opened to decorative art a broader horizon.

Blance Roosevelt personally attended that 1878 exposition, and she experienced the delight of coming upon the Doré vase by accident. Here is how she reported it (p.438-440):

> ... After looking at many of the marvels the world's fair afforded, I remember coming by accident upon this vase, which struck me spell-bound. Although tired beyond expression, I sate (sic) me down at a little distance to gaze upon it at my ease, and was soon rapt in contemplation of so curious and extraordinary a composition...
>
> To look at M. Doré's vase is to revel in fancy and recollection. It would be difficult to describe this unique creation, or to say exactly what it means. It tells a different story to every one; the story, mayhap, that each spectator locks up within his own breast. The vase is called *The Poem of the Vine*,

photo of 1894 San Francisco display of ***The Doré Vase*** (bronze, 1878, 14'2" high) now at front entrance of M.H.deYoung Memorial Museum (shown here on front cover of their magazine)

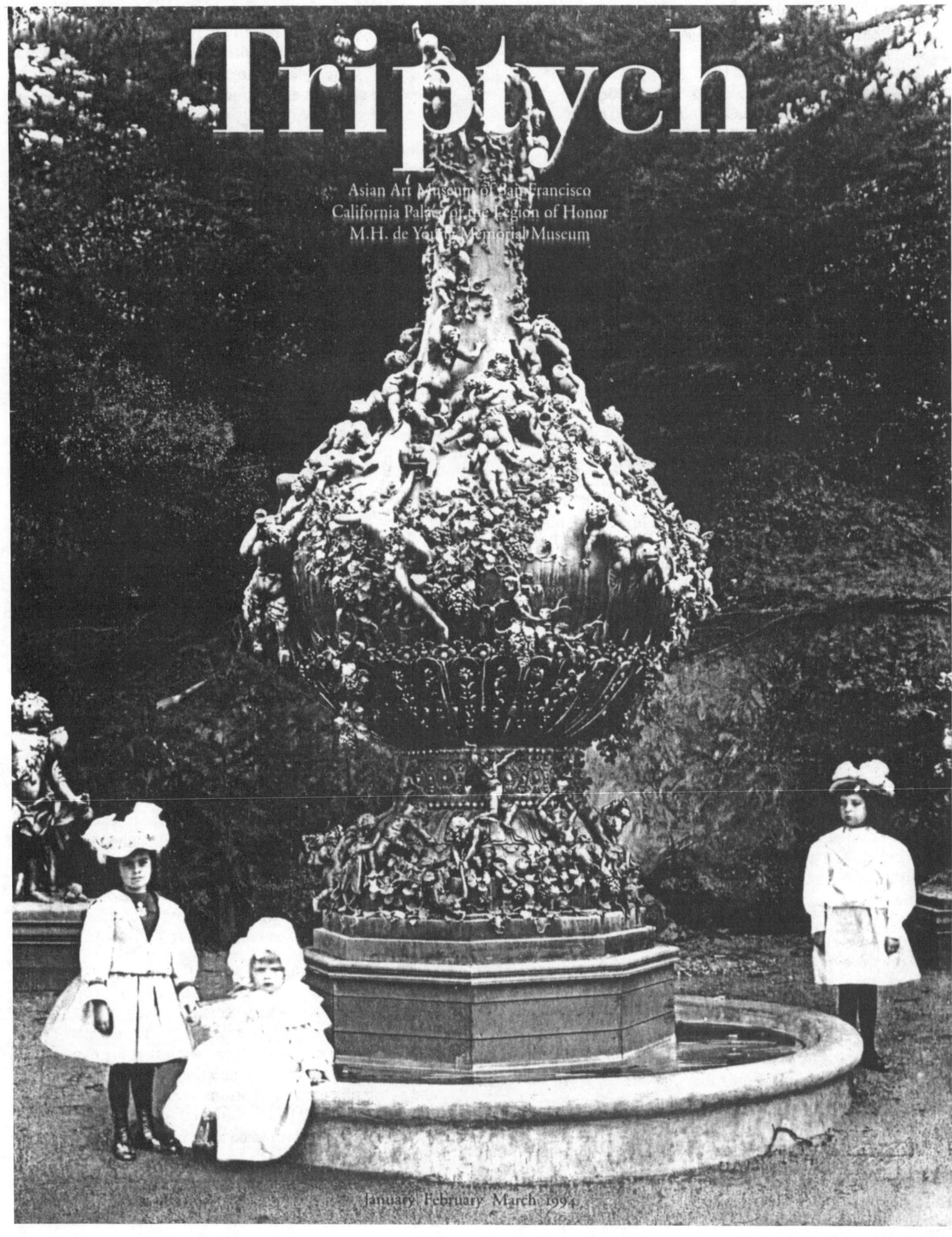

> and is necessarily allegorical...
>
> When the exhibition closed, not only did Doré neither receive any medal or recompense from the government, but amongst the many foreigners upon whom medals were bestowed for sculptures there was not one name, unless we except the Italian sculptor Monti, whose works were not vastly inferior to Doré's. Although decorative art is not necessarily expressed in sculpture, this vase must be ranked in both categories. There was a great deal of comment on this lack of appreciation evinced by the French for their fellow-countryman.

Roosevelt was not alone in expressing outrage at Doré's omission from medal-winners. The *Art Journal* felt compelled to bitterly attack the French art establishment (1879, p.186):

> Doré has also suffered in many respects from the jealousy and injustice of his own countrymen and contemporaries. His genius has found fuller and warmer recognition abroad than it has at home. The Institute (the French Academy of Fine Arts), though finding it impossible to ignore his vigorous and fruitful talent, has ever accorded to it a grudging and partial recognition only. The spirit of the rulers of artistic France is nothing if not *routiniere*. Those who refuse to bow to its decrees, or to abide by its laws, are outcasts unworthy of the gifts and glories of the sanctuary. Theodore Rousseau, Jean Baptiste Millet, Jules Dupre, and even Corot, in his earlier days, sought in vain at the hands of the reigning clique for rewards, or even justice. It was, therefore, no matter of surprise to those who knew the inside workings of these matters, when Doré was passed over unnoticed by the Art jury of the Universal Exhibition, and that, too, in the teeth of the fact that his vase had been hailed as the most original and creative work of sculpture of which the Exhibition could boast. The grade of Officer of the Legion of Honour, which was accorded to him a little later, formed but an inadequate substitute for the Medal of Honour, to which he was undoubtedly entitled. Had the suffrages of the spectators been collected, we have no doubt of the result. There is a wealth of fantastic grace and imaginative detail lavished on that single work that might furnish forth the whole sculpture department of a single *Salon*.

Doré hoped for a commission to have the work done in bronze but none resulted from the 1878 exhibition. The plaster version disappeared. There was a claim that it was destroyed in the bombing of Reims in 1917 in WWI. But Doré was able in 1882 to talk the Thiebaut Freres Foundry in Paris into casting it in bronze. The bronze version was 13 feet high and weighed 6000 pounds, and was exhibited at the Salon the same year. Though it got a lot of attention (30 references to it in books & periodicals from 1878-85), no buyer came forward. Thiebaut kept it for himself. There was also a small terracotta version, exhibited at the Exposition du Cercle de l'Union Artistique in 1883, but nobody knows what ever became of it.

In 1893, Thiebaut decided to exhibit the bronze version at the Columbian International Exposition in Chicago. There it attracted the attention of a wealthy Californian, M. H. de Young (editor/publisher of the San Francisco Chronicle), who paid $10,000 for it. Mr. de Young was so impressed with the Columbian Exhibition that he planned a similar exhibition for San Francisco - immediately! In one of the greatest feats of exhibition organization in history, San Francisco pulled off the California Midwinter Exposition of 1894 from scratch in less than eight months! There the Doré vase was prominently featured. Isaiah West Tabor took a beautiful photo of the Doré ***Vase*** there with little children in front of it. It had been illustrated many times - an 1878 wood engraving, four photos in Delorme (1879), and a Champollion etching, but all of them showed the vase by itself. The Tabor photo is the only one that lets you to see how massive and impressive the vase really is. Even in 1894 it was remarked how much the children loved it.

In 1931, the ***Vase*** was officially donated to the M. H. de Young Memorial Museum in San Francisco. In the 1970s it was transferred to the Palace of the Legion of Honor. In 1990, there was a 24-page booklet entitled **The Doré Vase** by Arthur Chandler, published by San Francisco State University. At the beginning of 1994, ***Triptych***, the official publication of the San Francisco Museum Society, did a major article on the 1894 Midwinter Exposition, and the cover featured the Tabor photo of the Doré ***Vase***. In April 1994, San Francisco held its annual Landscape Garden Show, with an article about the show in the April 20, 1994 *San Francisco Chronicle* (p.E4):

> This year's show-sponsored garden, the Court of Honor, features a huge bronze urn called *The Poem of the Vine*, created by sculptor **Gustave Doré** and brought to San Francisco for the 1894 Midwinter Fair in Golden Gate Park by M. H. de Young, who paid $10,000 for the urn and later gave it to the Fine Arts Museum. A museum official said, "That was a really good buy." After the landscape show, the urn, which was last housed in the rotunda of the Legion of Honor, will be moved to the gardens in front of the de Young Museum.

In July of 1994, the Doré vase was placed at the front entrance to that museum in Golden Gate Park.

The Terror (Maternal Love)

In 1879, Doré produced seven major works of sculpture. That was also the year he joined the Societe d'Aquarellistes Francais, and the year of his ***Ariosto*** folio. ***The Terror*** is the dramatic scene of a Negro (Nubian) woman who is attacked by a snake, with its fangs caught in her skirt. Instead of defending herself, she instinctively raises her baby above her head. It is also called ***Maternal Love***. Doré exhibited the original plaster model in the 1879 Salon, but the French art establishment did not think much of it. L.Pate in ***L'Illustration*** dismissed it as "sort of illustration in plaster," and dismissed its maker with "Doré has two great enemies; first painting, then sculpture."

The size of theoriginal plaster version of ***The Terror*** was never listed, but it was very large, and its present location is

156 patinated plaster model (8'2" high) of ***La Danse*** (1879) - now at front entrance of Monte Carlo Opera Theatre
bronze ***La Defense Nationale*** (1879) - copies in collections of Tanenbaum (Toronto) & Gabus (Switzerland)
bronze ***The Terror*** (1879) - copies in Strasbourg Museum, University of Chicago, and Tanenbaum collection.

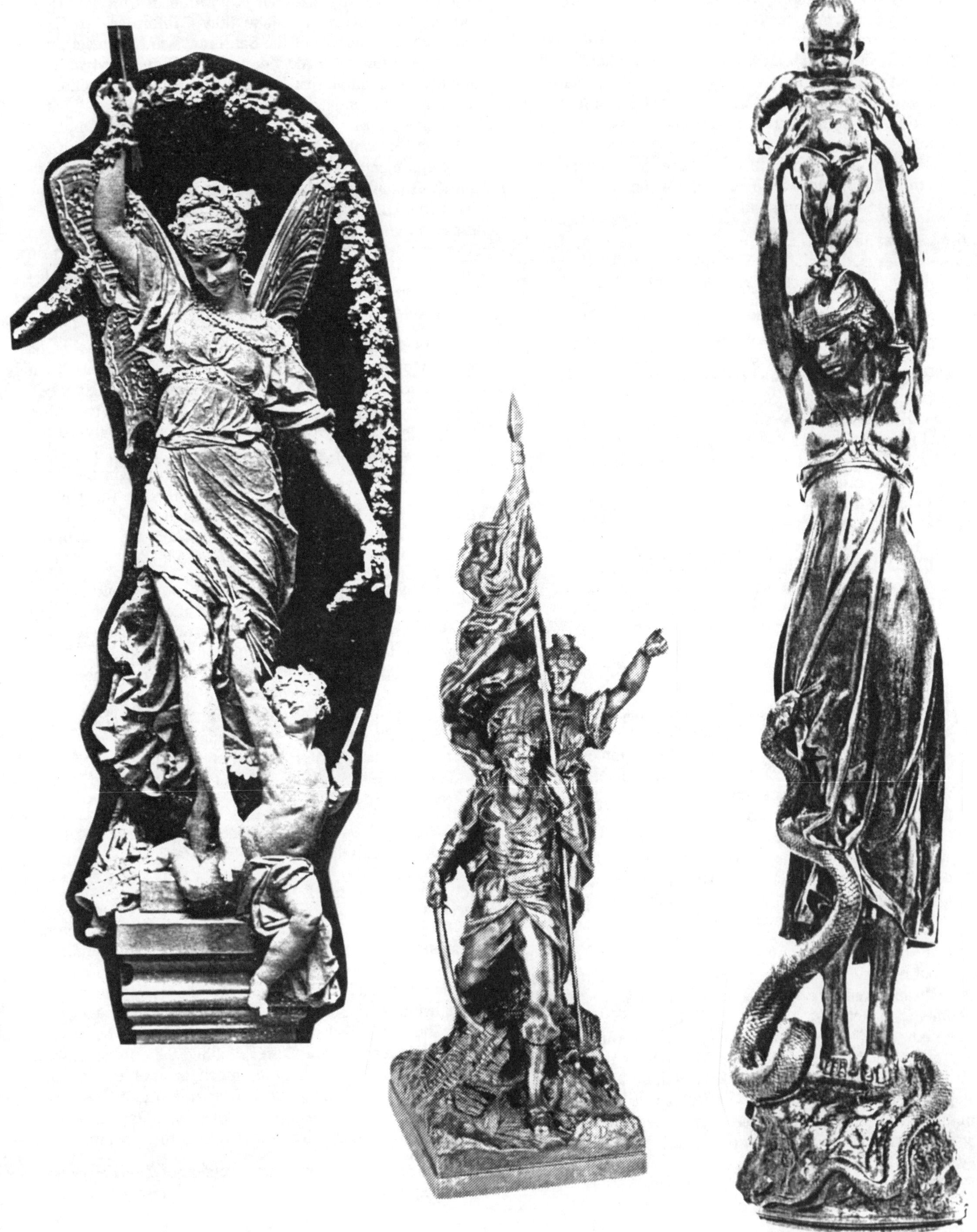

unknown. The known versions are reductions varying from two to four feet high. One reduction was in the Doré Gallery from 1879-91, Presently known versions are in Strasbourg, Paris, London, Chicago, and Toronto. It was one of five Doré works of sculpture shown in the 1980 Los Angeles exhibition book, ***The Romantics to Rodin; French Nineteenth-Century Sculpture from North American Collections***. There Doré is treated as just another great 19th century French sculptor. It is refreshing to see him treated objectively.

La Defense Nationale (...de Paris)

The background of this work of sculpture is described in the 1980 L.A. exhibition book, concerning a related work of sculpture, ***The Call to Arms***, by Rodin (p.331):

> The Prefecture de la Seine announced a competition in the spring of 1879 for an allegorical group of two figures that would commemorate the recent defense of Paris. The group would be placed at the *rond-point* of Courbevoie, to the west of the city, where a monument had been destroyed during the Franco-Prussian War.

Neither Doré nor Rodin were among the finalists. That was before ***The Thinker***. Perhaps the best work of sculpture related to the Franco-Prussian War was Mercie's 1874 ***Gloria Victis!*** The undated bronze version of Doré's ***Defense*** was about 4½ feet high, and somehow it was displayed after Doré's death at the 1889 Exposition Universelle. It is now in the collection of Joey & Toby Tanenbaum of Toronto. A smaller bronze is in the collection of Pierre-Yves Gabus of Switzerland, which was shown in the 1985 Doré exhibition there.

Perseus & Andromeda

This was a theme Doré returned to over and over. He first illustrated the scene in ***Malte-Brun's Geography*** in 1857. Then Doré did an 8x10 lithograph for it in the 1862 ***Album Gustave Doré***. Then in 1868 he did the oil painting which was 8½ feet high. Many a devoutly religious Victorian man felt an urgent need to save that beautiful naked girl chained to the rocks. A 12x17 steel engraving was made of that painting in 1881. The theme also popped up in Doré's ***Ariosto*** engravings, except that it was Orlando saving Olimpia, or Ruggiero saving Angelica. How is it possible for so many beautiful naked women to get chained to rocks, with sea-monsters about to devour them, and knights in shining armor arrive just in time to save them? That does not happen every day in St. Louis.

Doré's 3-foot high plaster model of ***Andromeda*** was a "miracle of equilibrium." The entire weight of the knight and his winged creature are borne by the enormous lance piercing right through the mouth of the sea-monster. But, as Clapp & Lehni point out (p.227-28), the title is wrong. The character in the sculpture cannot be Perseus because he is riding on a hippogriffe. That is the winged creature in ***Ariosto*** that is half-horse, half-eagle. The actual scene in the sculpture is Ruggiero saving Angelica. But it is amazing that it survived so many years without breaking at the lance. The knight appears to be suspended in mid-air. ***Andromeda*** was never exhibited, and was barely even mentioned for 50 years. But in 1931, it was sold to Jean Cocteau, the famous French writer & painter. In 1954, Cocteau used that plaster model, the only version in existence, to convert it into a bronze piece. The plaster model was destroyed in making the casting for the bronze version.

La Danse (Monte Carlo)
Time mowing down the Hours
The Death of Orpheus
Beauty & the Beast

These are the other four major works from 1879. We already covered ***La Danse*** in the chapter on Doré romances. It was the work Sarah Bernhardt talked him into doing for the theatre in Monte Carlo, so that she could do the companion piece ***Music***. ***La Danse*** is about eight feet high. It was recently restored by M.Sartucci and featured in the 1990 Musee d'Orsay (Paris) exhibition book, ***L'Opera de Monte-Carlo au temps du Prince Albert 1er de Monaco*** (pages 61-65). Known reduction versions (three to four feet high) are in Paris and New Jersey.

There are many title versions for ***Time mowing down the Hours***. It is also called ***Time destroying Love*** or ***The Fall*** or ***Time mowing down his children*** or ***Alice Ozy's Clock***. It was a tribute to his former lover Alice Ozy, who was turning 60. It shows Father Time standing over a large clock, mowing down rows of cupids, representing the hours. There is another version without the clock. The original plaster was exhibited at the Exposition du Cercle de l'Union Artistique in 1879. Then a 4-foot bronze version was exhibited there in 1882. Upon Alice Ozy's death in 1893, the bronze was donated to the Musee des Arts Decoratifs in Paris, where it still remains. The plaster was exhibited in 1985 at the Shepherd Gallery in New York.

The Death of Orpheus was similar to the ***Andromeda*** theme, except that there are dozens of aggressive, war-like naked women. He also did oil painting & watercolor versions. Doré exhibited the oil painting in the 1879 Salon. It was 17 feet high by 23 feet wide. It shows a group of Maenads around the dead body of Orpheus. One version of the sculpture shows a woman holding up the head of Orpheus. The sculpture was in high-relief, which is like bas-relief, but the image protrudes further from the background. There are also engravings of similar scenes in ***Ariosto***.

Doré's ***Beauty & the Beast*** sculpture has nothing to do with the famous fairy tale. It shows a nymph and a satyr. It was one of Doré's smallest works of sculpture, just over a foot high. Doré got all of his sculptural nudes out of his system in 1879. Besides the major titles we have listed, he also did three other lesser-known works that same year, all having to do with nymphs: ***Nymph pursued by Cupid***, ***Nymph taking the Fauns from the Nest***, and an individual ***Nymph*** from the Orpheus group. It is hard to believe that in 1879, Doré did nine works of sculpture, at least five major oil paintings, a few watercolor landscapes, plus over 600 engravings for ***Ariosto***. Most of the themes in the paintings and sculpture were rather racy, right out of ***Ariosto***. You might say that 1879 was the year that the folks at the Doré Gallery finally figured out that there was a side to Doré very different from being a painter-preacher.

158 plaster model of ***Time Mowing down the Hours*** (1879) - copies in Paris Museum & Shepherd Gallery-NY
bronze ***Madonna with Child*** (1880) - 15 versions, many in private collections in Paris + Notre Dame Univ., University of New Mexico, Tanenbaum collection (Toronto), and The Shepherd Gallery (New York).

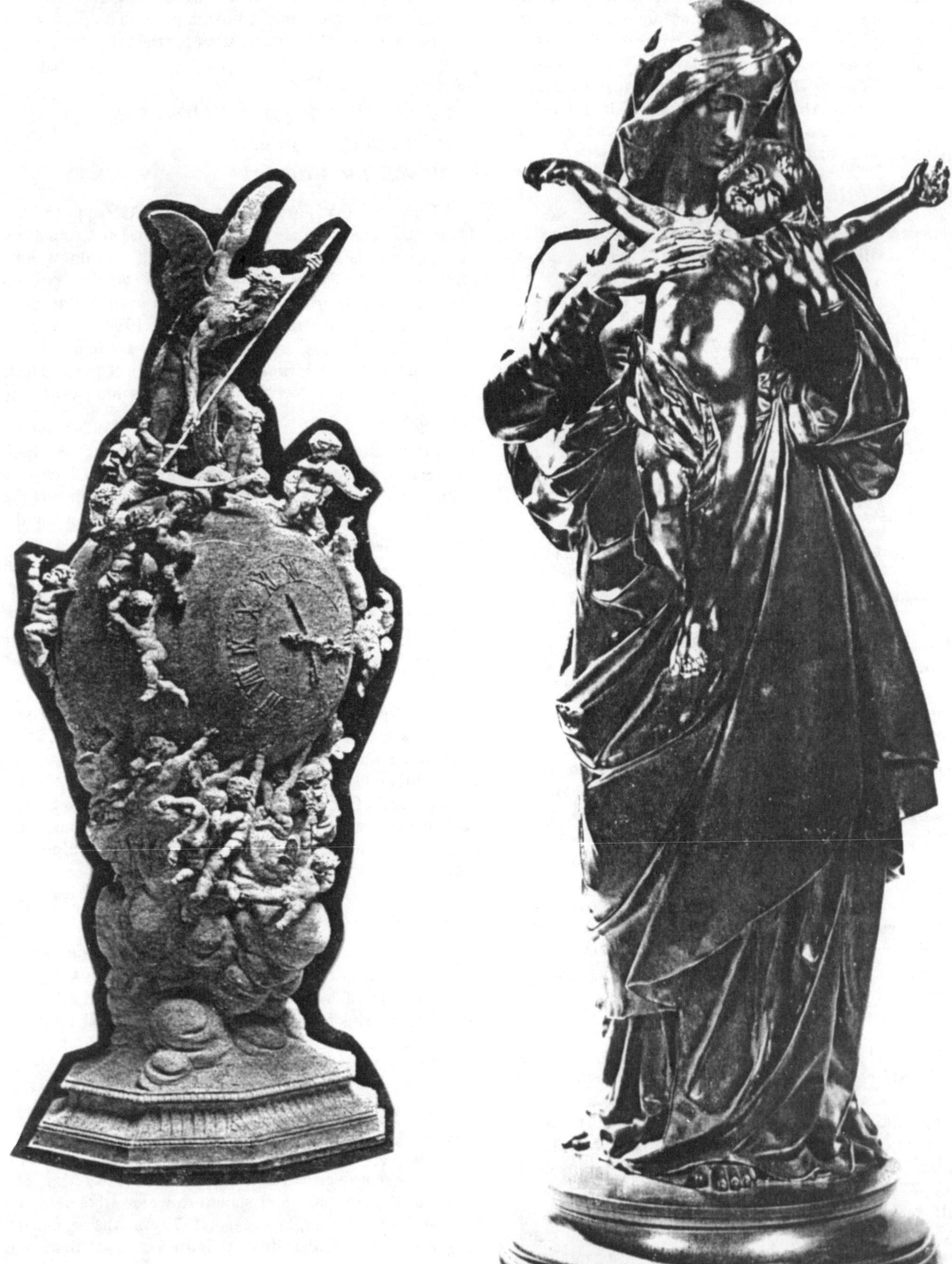

Madonna & Child

Perhaps this 1880 work of sculpture was penance for all of his wild sculpture from 1879. But instead of returning to the Protestant British religious audience, he turned instead to his French Roman Catholic background. Two of his 1880 works of sculpture had Roman Catholic themes, and the Doré Gallery expressed no interest in them. His 1880 ***Madonna*** was his only truly traditional work of sculpture. It must have been popular, because there are at least 15 versions of it, more than twice as many as any other Doré sculpture. In Doré's ***Madonna***, Mary just happens to be holding the baby Jesus out in front of her with his arms outstretched in the positioin of the crufixion. The original plaster version was about eight feet high. It was exhibited in the 1880 Salon, and to his shock it was awarded a Third Class Medal. Many people felt that the jury gave him that medal to make up for not having given Doré a medal for either ***Glory*** or ***La Vigne***, both of which deserved a medal. Not only did he win a medal, but he almost passed out from shock as he read one complimentary review after another, such as this one in ***L'Art***, quoted in the L.A. exhibition book (p.239):

> A third-place medal - and that is really quite little - rewarded the effort of M. Gustave Doré. M. Doré modeled a life-size Madonna, standing and holding the infant Jesus in her arms; the latter, in stretching out his little arms like an unruly child, evokes the spectacle of the last scene of the passion drama. M. Doré had until now shown himself more intemperate than reasoned. This time he must be accepted in earnest as a creator of statues. What energy of will in this nature which nothing astonishes and nothing fatigues, in this imagination which conceives of the most diverse scenes and which moves with such abundant verve from the pencil to the modeling clay.

It was as close to praise as Doré ever got from the French art establishment. ***Madonna*** was then cast in several sizes in plaster, bronze, terracotta and marble. When Alice Ozy died in 1893, she specifically requested in her will that a work of sculpture by Doré be placed on her tomb in the Pere Lachaise Cemetary (where Doré was also buried), so they had a 6-foot marble version cast by Fagel & Mathet. Doré's ***Madonna*** is still popular. It has been exhibited in recent years at Notre Dame University and in New York, Los Angeles, Strasbourg, Paris, Bourg-en-Bresse, Germany and Switzerland. There are also versions at the University of New Mexico and in Toronto.

The Human Pyramid

Doré's second major sculpture of 1880 was exactly the opposite of his ***Madonna***, which was very traditional and was immediately popular. By contrast, ***The Human Pyramid*** (also called ***The Acrobats***) was unconventional and received little initial notice. The original plaster was never exhibited or sold, and its present location is unknown. But in recent decades bronze versions have been illustrated several times and have received critical praise. ***The Human Pyramid*** and ***La Vigne*** are probably Doré's two most original works of sculpture. ***The Human Pyramid*** has been described as being unique among 19th century works of sculpture, according to the 1980 L.A. exhibition book (p.241):

> Throughout his life, one of Doré's passions was gymnastics. His studio on the Rue Bayard was a former gymnasium; there, for a time, the artist retained a trapeze hanging from the ceiling. As an extension of this interest he created what is one of the more curious works in the history of sculpture. A gigantic, three-dimensional illustration, *The Acrobats* depicts a series of ten figures climbing on top of each other to form a human pyramid. Although individual forms are rendered in the traditional, academically realistic fashion, the composition of the work is totally unconventional and, in a sense, non-sculptural. It ignores the time-honored principles of contrapposto and compositional balance, since the subject dictates instead a precarious balance of figures disposed in an additive, vertical arrangement.

Just as he had done with ***La Vigne***, Doré brought another new dimension to sculpture. He came up with a radical new concept - the subject dictated the scene. It was based on a real-life group of ten acrobats in a circus that climbed up and stood on each other's shoulders ten-high. The only minor complaint is that none of the bronzes is larger than four feet high (the size of the original plaster model is unknown). It is too bad it was never cast life-size. A 23" bronze version was exhibited at the 1881 Exposition du Cercle de l'Union Artistique. It was eventually acquired by Fairless & Beeforth, but they did not exhibit in the Doré Gallery. The 36" bronze was purchased by Alexandre Dumas, fils, but its present location is unknown. After the turn of the century, the work was virtually unknown.

The largest bronze version (50" high) was acquired by circus owner John Ringling in the late 1920s, but missing one head and two arms. In 1946 (after his death), his estate was made into three museums in Sarasota, Florida. In the early 1970s, they contacted the London owner of another bronze version, and using it as a guide had Mrs. Joseph McKennon restore the missing parts. Since then, it has been illustrated several times, and was exhibited in the 1980 L.A. exhibition.

Little Puck (with owl)
Sister of Charity bearing wounded boy
Leap-frog
The Mirror
Cupid reclining on Sculls
Mother with sleeping Child

These were all done between 1880-83. ***Little Puck*** was finished in 1880 and was exhibited the following year in the Exposition du Cercle de l'Union Artistique. There was a 24" plaster and an 11" bronze. The winged Puck in the sculpture is the mischievous elf from ***A Midsummer Night's Dream***. He is leaning against his friend the owl. Doré was very fond of owls. He kept some in his studio, and also did oil paintings of them. The location of the plaster version is unknown, and the bronze is in a private collection.

37" bronze ***Perseus & Andromeda*** (1879) - Jean Cocteau destroyed plaster model to make bronze in 1954.
13" bronze ***Beauty & the Beast*** (1879) - now in private collection.
plaster & 51" bronze ***The Human Pyramid*** (1880) - bronze version in Ringling Museum in Sarasota, Florida.

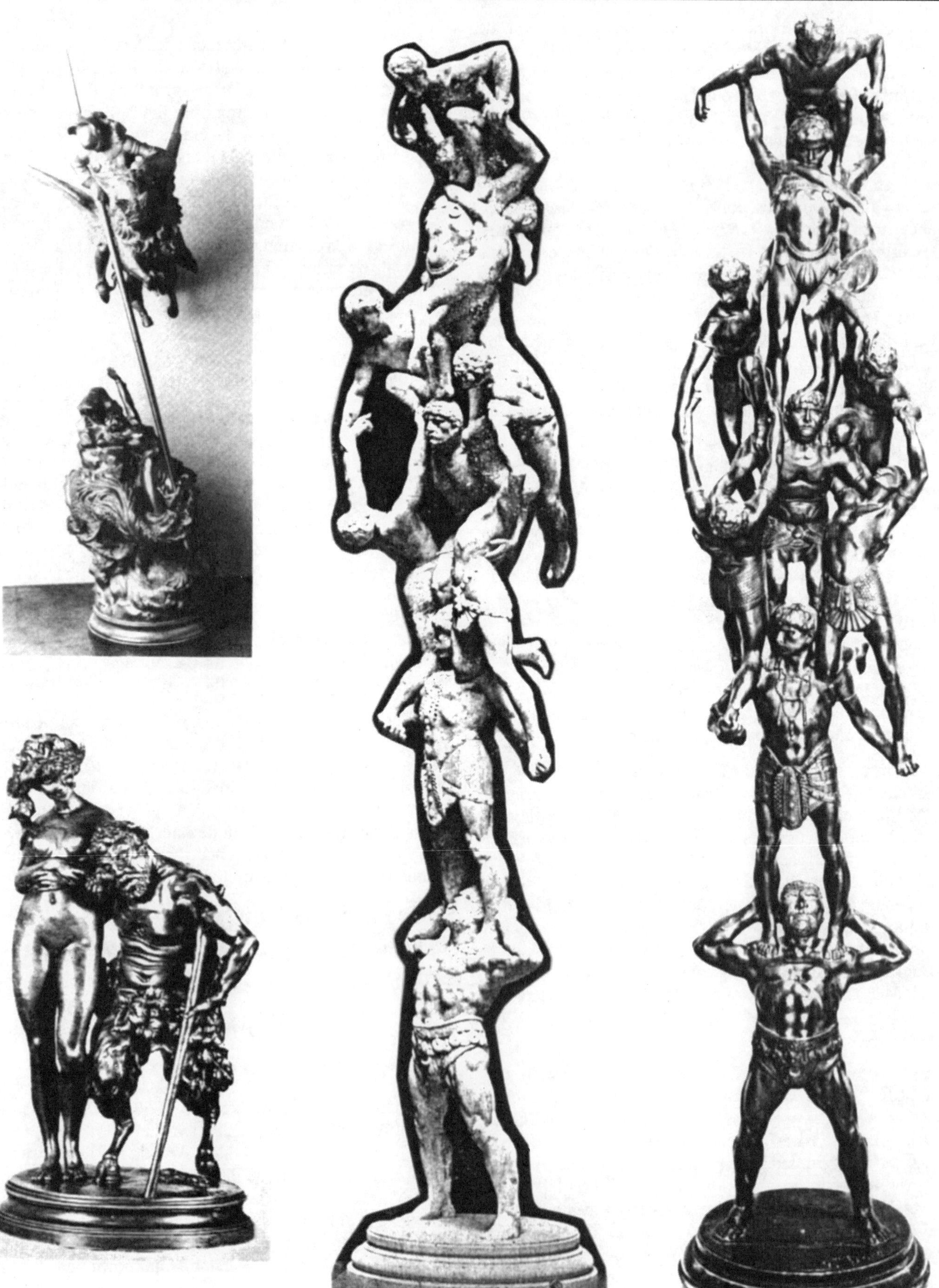

The Sister of Charity is similar to the Doré oil painting from the Franco-Prussian War. The painting is now in the art museum at Le Havre. The French title for the sculpture was ***Christianity***. There is only one version. It was a plaster model about seven feet high. It was exhibited in the 1881 Salon, sold in the 1885 Doré sale, and has not been seen since. The full scene of the original painting is a nun carrying a wounded boy through the streets of Paris during the Prussian bombardment.

Leap-frog is a cute little bronze piece (about 14½" high) showing a knight and a monk playing leap-frog. The French title is ***Saute-Mouton*** or ***Joyeusete*** ("the joke"). Doré finished it in 1881 and exhibited it in 1882 at the Cercle de l'Union Artistique. There are four known bronze versions. Three are in private collections in Paris, and the fourth was acquired by the Boston Museum of Fine Arts in 1992.

Doré's bronze ornamental ***Mirror*** (1882) was a gift for Maria Feodorovna, Empress of Russia. It was about 40" high. It's festive design shows cupids playing amidst drapery around the mirror. Doré was and still is very popular in Russia, as witnessed by the flurry of new Doré editions there after the fall of the Soviet Union. The ***Mirror*** eventually found its way into Jean Cocteau's collection. A second version was exhibited in the Cercle de l'Union Artistique in 1883, after Doré's death. That version was acquired by the Musee de Brou in Bourg-en-Bresse in 1972, and exhibited in the 1983 Doré centennial.

Cupid reclining on Sculls is a perplexing allegorical work, with a very sad-looking cupid. Was Doré expressing his loneliness, after his mother's death and the departure of Sarah Bernhardt and Adelina Patti for America? The L.A. exhibition book thought it was intriguing (p.240): "The juxtaposition of a naked infant and a pile of skulls has a hallucinatory, dreamlike quality which is evocative and rich in allusions and invites various interpretations." It was one of Doré's smallest works of sculpture, with versions only 6"-7" high. It was also one of his more private works; no version of it was exhibited during his lifetime. One copy (with the wings broken off), is now at the Museum of Art at the Rhode Island School of Design. Others are in private collections in London and Paris.

Doré's tiny ***Mother with sleeping Child*** was originally entitled ***Venus couchee avec l'Amour***. It is about 3" high and 8" wide. The first version (terracotta) was a gift to a British friend, Mr. D. Murray. It is now owned by the Musee d'Art Moderne in Strasbourg. The two bronze versions are in private collections. There are several other "minor" works of sculpture by Doré. Many were never illustrated before Clapp/Lehni.

The Monument to Alexandre Dumas
- Alexandre Dumas statue
- D'Artagnan
- La Lecture (group reading)

Doré's last work of sculpture is widely considered to be his greatest. It is a traditional monument, of very high quality (especially ***D'Artagnan***). The planning committee was having trouble raising enough money for the monument. When they accepted Doré's proposed design, he refused any payment for labor or materials, per Roosevelt (p.445):

> Let me do it for love ... Do not speak of money; my payment is in the work itself. This is my contribution to the memory of Alexandre Dumas, my dead friend.

There are three parts to the monument. Dumas is seated on top, pen in hand. Below in front sits a group of three of the "common-people" reading Dumas' works, to symbolize the broad appeal of his writings. Below in back sits D'Artagnan, in full musketeer regalia, with his sword across his lap, basically guarding the tomb. Doré's involvement in this project is also described in the 1957 three-generation Dumas biography by Andre Maurois, entitled ***The Titans*** (p.434):

> In 1880, a Committee had been formed, under the presidency of Adolphe de Leuven, now an old man, for the purpose of arranging for a statue to Dumas *pere* to be erected in the Place Malesherbes. But the public showed ingratitude to the memory of a writer who had provided it with so many thrills over so long a period. The subscription produced only a mediocre sum. Gustave Doré very generously offered to give his work free, and designed the monument which, alas, he never saw in its completed state, because he died shortly before the inaugural ceremony which took place on November 3rd, 1883.
>
> Doré had drawn his inspiration from the dream once described by Dumas *pere* to Dumas *fils*: "I was on the top of a mountain, each stone of which was one of my books." On the summit of a gigantic stone pedestal, the very one of which he had dreamed, was set a bronze statue of Dumas with a smile on his lips. at his feet was a group of three figures - a student, a workman and a young girl - his eternal readers. On the other side, a seated d'Artagnan kept watch.

Roosevelt also relates the circumstances that led up to Doré being chosen to do the Dumas monument (p.444-445):

> ... A committee of gentlemen came to Doré and spoke of their intention to erect a statue to the celebrated writer. Knowing how busy Doré was, they scarcely ventured to suggest to him the desirability of his sending in a design for the proposed statue. To their surprise, however, the sketch they secretly desired reached them the next day, and was unanimously adopted. The original intention of the Committee had been to give the work to Dubois, but he was engaged at Chantilly; and Doré, after listening to many *pros* and *cons*, said, "Gentlemen, you have honoured me by consulting me and by adopting my idea for the Dumas statue; but one thing remains. Let me also be the sculptor, and present to you gratuitously this memorial of a dear friend who lightened some of the sadder hours of my youth by his rare and treasured works. It is little enough towards repaying some of the enjoyment I owe to him.

162 three parts of Doré's ***Monument to Alexandre Dumas*** (1883) in the Place Malesherbes in Paris. statue of Dumas, d'Artagnan on guard, and group of three reading Dumas' works.

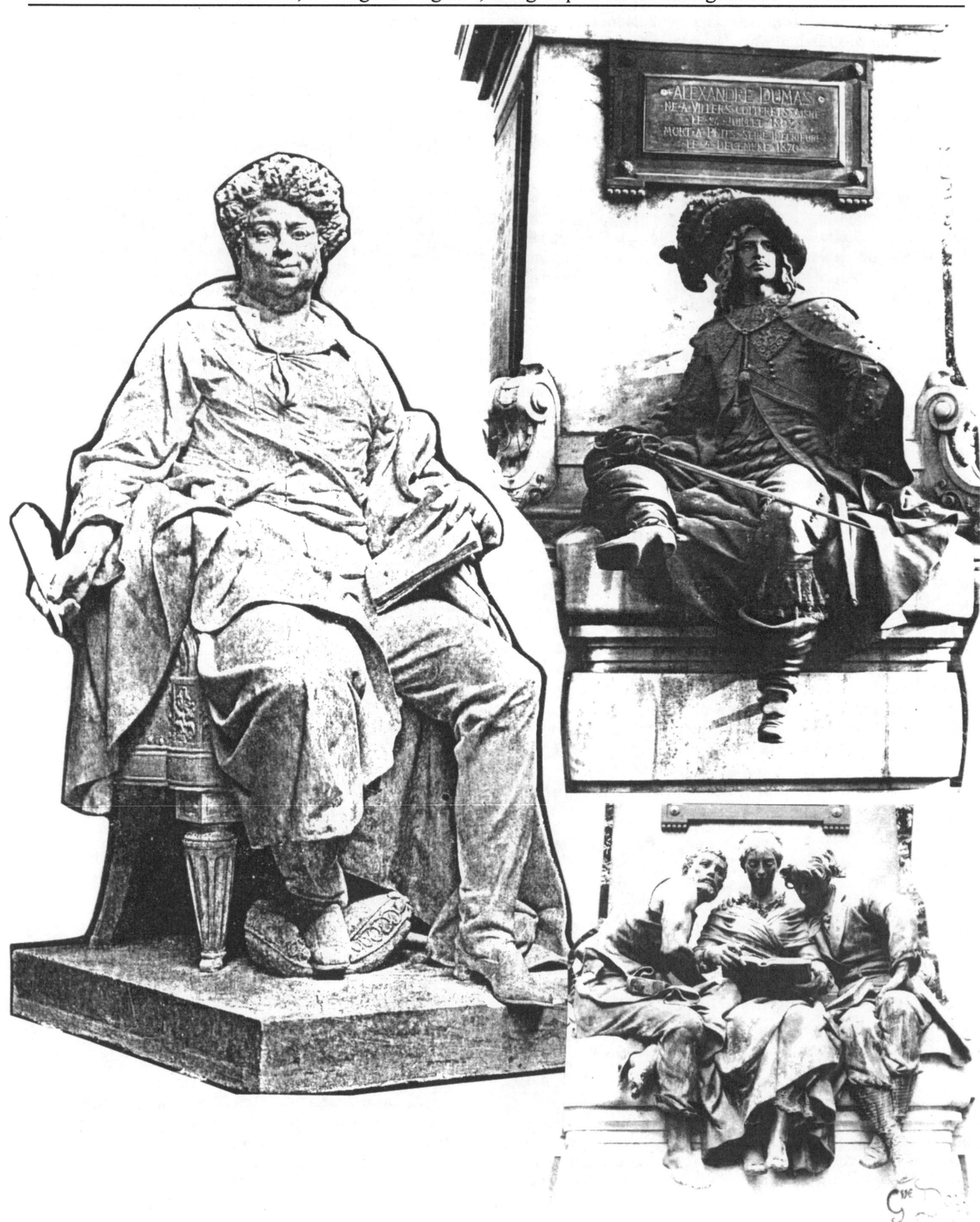

Doré's first letter to mention his involvement in the ***Dumas Monument*** was dated December 30, 1881. During 1882, the last year of Doré's life, marked by despondency and despair, his letters mention three projects which were keeping him going - his ***Dumas Monument***, his painting ***The Vale of Tears***, and his ***Shakespeare*** illustrations. He would not live to see any of them presented to the public. On Friday, January 19, 1883, Doré made what would be his last two sketches - of an unidentified impish little boy. He was regressing back to his childhood. On Saturday night, he was supposed to dine with friends, but he never made it. He had a massive apoplectic seizure. His two brothers and other close friends rushed to his bedside. On Sunday he was a little better, and began to talk about resuming his projects. But early in the morning of Monday the 23th, he uttered a groan and sank back into his pillow, his eyes covered with a glaze. They all immediately knew he was gone. He had just turned 51. The funeral was on the 25th, and Alexandre Dumas, fils delivered the eulogy. Some of the same art critics who personally attacked Doré during his lifetime praised him at his funeral. We will cover the articles about Doré's death in the next chapter.

The ***Dumas Monument*** was erected in November 1883, ten months after Doré's death. Once again, those art critics hailed Doré the sculptor, both in their periodicals and at the unveiling. You could hardly find a breath of a criticism. The quality of the monument was unassailable, Doré's motivation was as pure as the driven snow, and the art critics could not remember why it had been so important to them to personally attack and belittle Doré's artistic abilities. The bronze Dumas monument was erected in the Place Malesherbes in Paris. It is still there. In 1993 it was closed off for a few months, to give it a much-needed cleaning and restoration.

Besides the bronze versions in the monument itself, there was also the original plaster model of ***Dumas***. It was owned by Alexandre Dumas, fils, who died in 1895. In 1897, Mme. Henriette Alexandre Dumas donated the plaster model to the Musee des Beaux-Arts in Rouen. Unfortunately, in 1944 it was destroyed in the bombing. There are also plaster and terracotta ***D'Artagnan*** models, about 25" high. In 1979, that plaster version was donated by Rene Claude to the Societe des Amis d'Alexandre Dumas. It is on display in the Maison Alexandre Dumas, Chateau de Monte-Cristo, in Port-Marly. The other (terracotta) version is still in the Doré family.

The Clapp & Lehni research is invaluable for reference information and illustrations. Why has it not been published in English? We can only hope that some day Clapp & Lehni will be able to do that same level of research on Doré oil paintings, watercolors, and mixed-media sketches. Doré's output of 38 works of sculpture (with over 80 versions) was tremendous for a sculptor whose entire career lasted from 1877-83, and who was also a full-time painter and illustrator.

164 Doré engraving: *Newgate Prison Exercise Yard*, from ***London, a Pilgrimage*** (1872) + (inset): van Gogh painting ***Prisoners Exercising (after Gustave Doré)*** (1890) Pushkin Museum, Moscow.

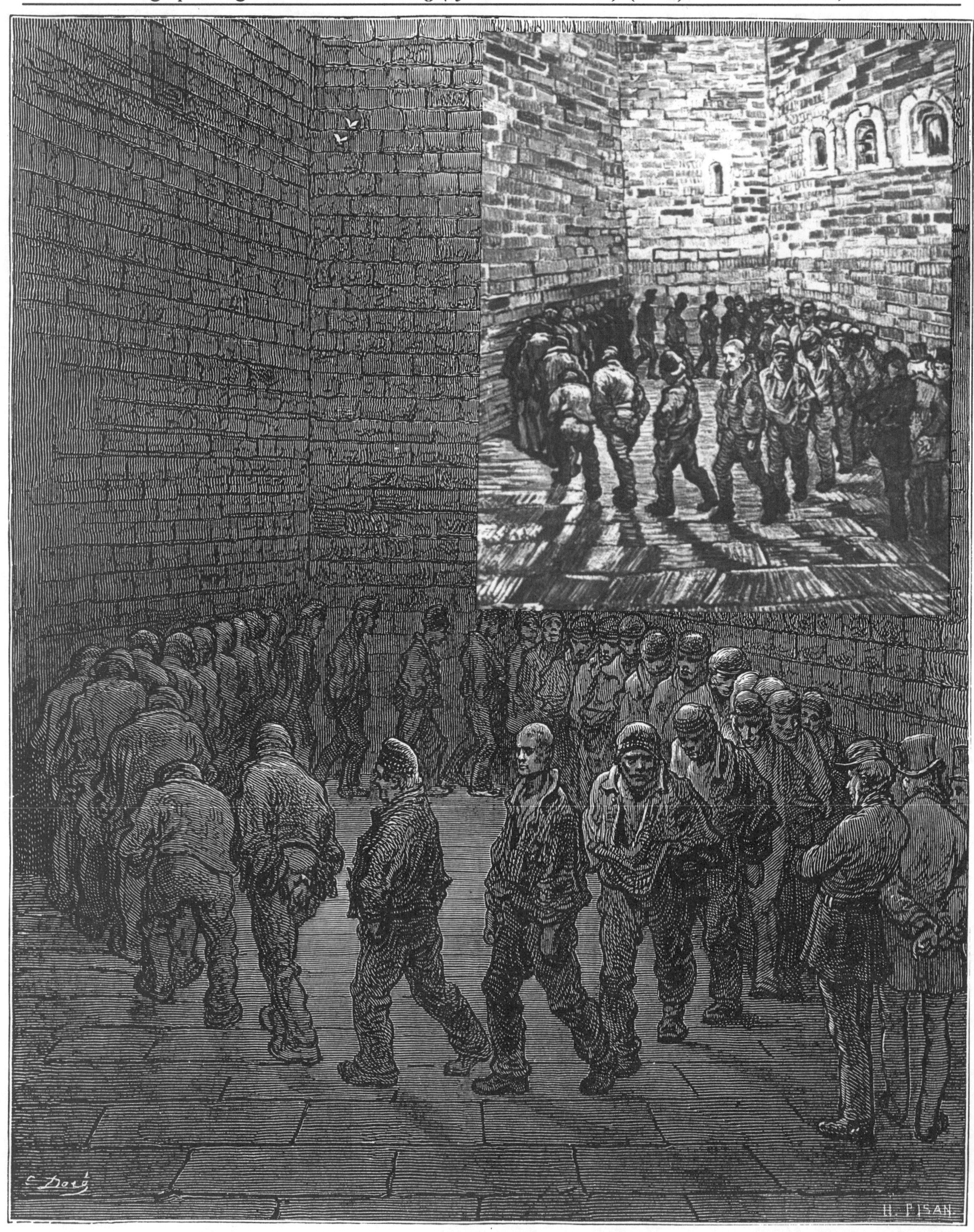

11. FLEETING FAME; ENDURING INFLUENCE

Doré left a large surplus of works of art at his death on January 23, 1883, and the public was still enjoying new Doré items for the next 2-3 years. His fame did not diminish with his death - it actually increased in England and America. By the turn of the century his fame finally began dying out. By 1920, he had become a story that the elderly talked out.

1883 Posthumous Works & Eulogies

Three major Doré works came out in 1883 in three fields of art - his ***Raven*** folio, his oil painting ***The Vale of Tears***, and the ***Dumas Monument***. Reviews of those were in a sense also eulogies, but his death shocked the world, and there was no shortage of tributes pouring in. The funeral was January 25, and Doré was buried with full military honors, due to his rank as Officer of the Legion of Honor. Alexandre Dumas, fils spoke at length to the thousands of friends and dignitaries at the funeral. Here are excerpts, per Roosevelt (p.478-481):

> ... If ever in this world a man had a right to count upon the present and believe in the future, that man was the prodigious artist whom we have just lost. Never have volition, energy, grace, and talent, never has life itself - that life which seems to come direct from God in human guise - been crowned with more radiant and convincing symbols....
>
> What rapidity! What originality of conception! What an inexhaustible, far-seeing imagination! What a miraculous knowledge of cause and effect! What a grandiose, dramatic, troubled appeal from earth to heaven of lights and shadows, of chaos, of the fantastic, the invisible, the visionary! What a world of gods, goddesses, saints, martyrs, apostles, virgins, archangels, heroes, giants, fairies, spectres of celestial and monstrous types, divine or droll, taking all at once birth, form, colour, movement, and life in this luminous brain for ever blotted out and obscured! ...
>
> In France, in France alone, people often passed ironically, or, what is worse still, indifferently before those grand canvases of which the composition and the idea were always majestic. Doré suffered horribly through not having been understood. Who was wrong? He who suffered of he who did not understand? The painter who aspired to the applause of the world, or the passer-by who refused it to him?
>
> ... how many of the misunderstood, how many who have been scorned and ridiculed, long since dead of despair, we must come to seek here, in order to entice them to achieve the glory which their own epoch refused to them! ... let us be respectful towards those who, like Doré, having lived but fifty years, have been able during forty to give the greatest example that can be given to mankind of incessant work, the passion of the ideal and the eagerness of its eternal spirit....

Another early tribute to Doré was a poem in the February 1883 ***Household Magazine***, by G. Weatherly:

> Doré is dead. Still is the wondrous hand
> That seemed to run with Time, and win the race;
> And now no more will his keen fancy trace
> The glorious visions of each age and land.
> And lo! the mourners meet in concourse grand:
> Dante and Milton, one in lasting fame;
> Cervantes, too, and many a one whose name
> Upon a later muster-roll will stand.
>
> Doré is dead! alas, that it is so!
> But though the giant powers rest with night
> The giant works remain with us to show
> That Genius dies not with Life's fading light,
> But lingers ever, while the world shall last,
> Linking the Present to the mighty Past.

There were major Doré articles in leading publications. The February 1883 ***Magazine of Art*** contained an illustrated article (p.221-27), with this closing paragraph:

> It must be remembered that Doré, by the very nature of his talent and accomplishment, was an artist essentially popular. He worked not for the few who can imagine for themselves, but for the many who crave their pictures ready-made. He may be said to have read in pictures; and his facility in reproducing his reading in a graphic form has enabled millions of people to realise a great number of things that, but for him, must always have remained obscure and unintelligible. For these he has identified himself for long with some of the greatest books in all literature.

Perhaps the most bizarre Doré item was a little biography published right after his death. A cheap U.S. publisher, John B. Alden of New York, was issuing a "semi-weekly magazine" called ***The Elzevir Library***, which was actually a series of very cheap books, mostly literary works. Their #16, dated February 23, 1883, was an illustrated biography, ***Paul Gustave Doré***, by Frank H. Norton. The cover price was THREE CENTS! It was a 4x6 paperback booklet with 21 text pages, a nice engraved portrait, and four very cheap illustrations from the ***Doré Bible***, referred to as "greatly reduced outline drawings." There seems to be only one known copy of this priceless gem. You could have bought 5,000 of them for the price of one deluxe edition of the ***Doré Bible***. Norton asserted that Doré was the foremost figure in French art, and that in 1874, besides the London one, there were also Doré Galleries in Paris and New York. He had apparently looked at the Cassell folio ***The Doré Gallery*** and saw that the title page listed, sure enough - London, Paris & New York. But there is an ever greater *faux pas* in Cassell's ***Doré Gallery*** folio itself. Did you know that Doré was still in the prime of life after he died? The first edition of Cassell's ***Doré Gallery*** folio was in 1870 and included a Doré memoir by Edmund Ollier. When Cassell did a memorial edition of that work after Doré's death, they added a notice of his death to the memoir. But they did not check the memoir text itself, because in it Ollier discusses what other works Doré might do in the future, "since he is still in the prime of life."

But the best biographical Doré tribute was by his close friend Amelia Edwards, in a 2-part article in the ***Art Journal*** (1883; p.361-65 & 389-94). Edwards was a British writer who gained fame as an Egyptian expert. She tells many personal stories of her friendship with Doré, including (p.365):

oil painting: ***London Bridge*** (1871); etching: ***The Neophyte*** (1876).

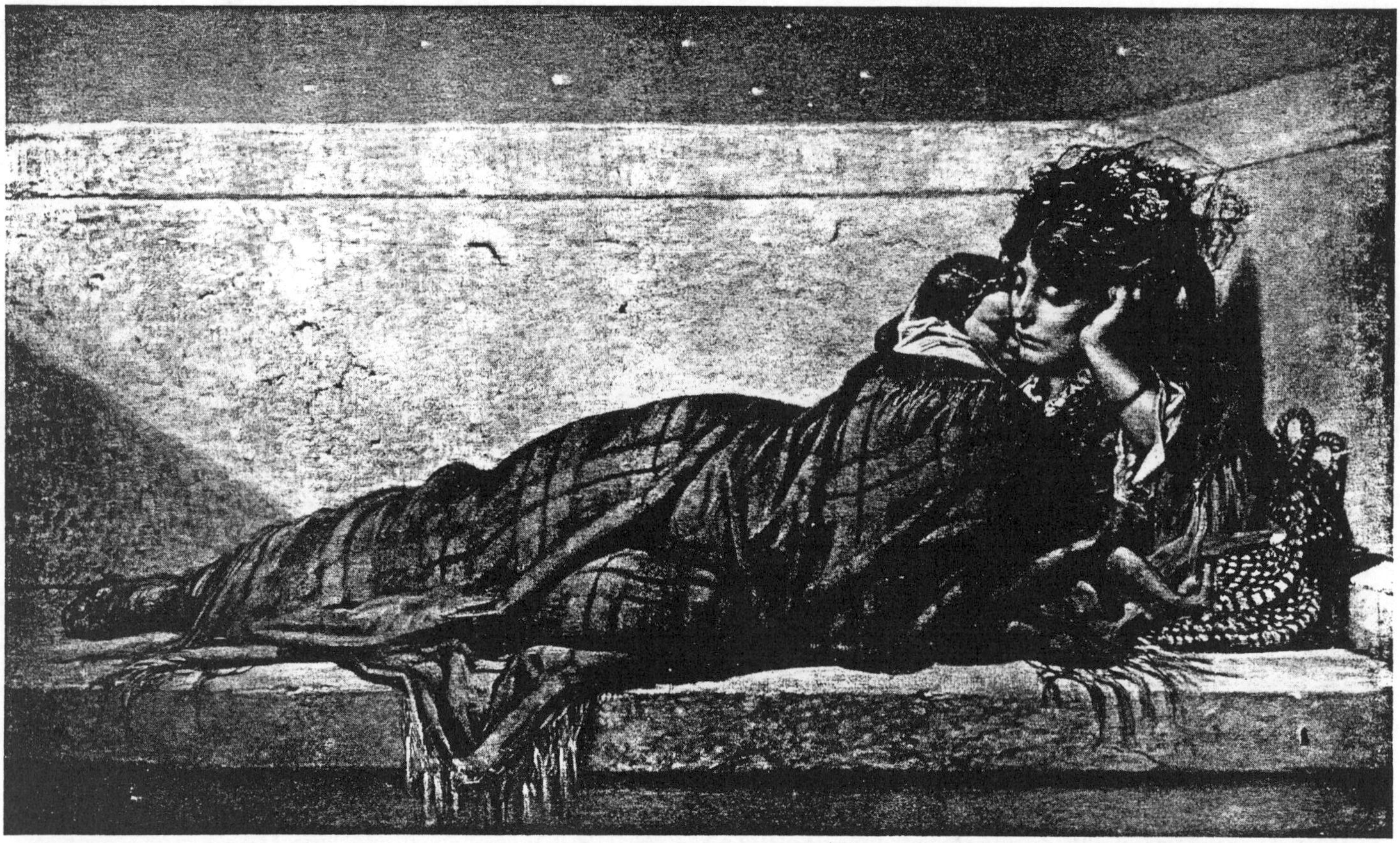

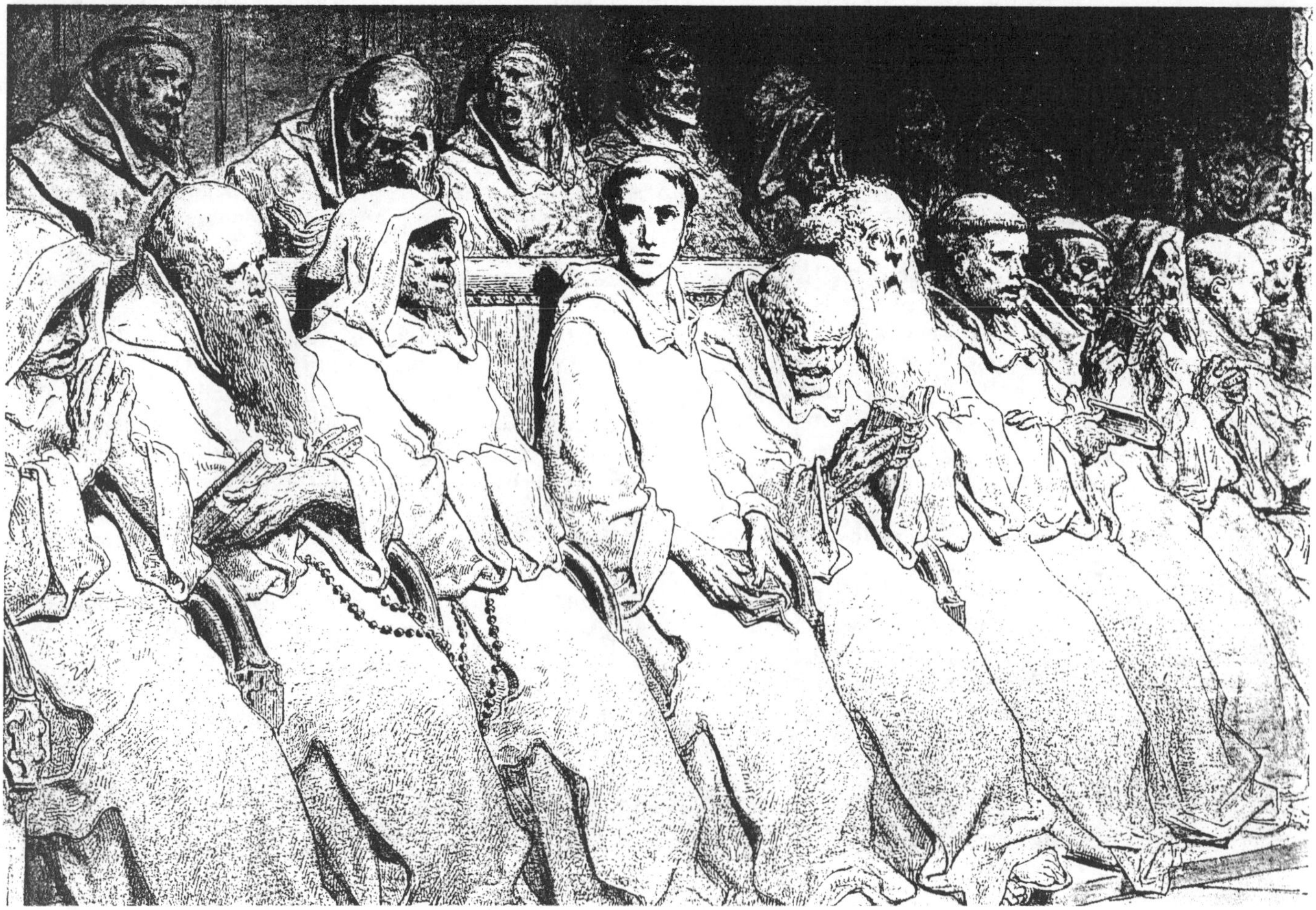

> ... Being much tormented by requests for Doré's autograph, I asked him one day to oblige me by writing his name on half-a-dozen slips of paper. "Bah! les autographes!" he said, smiling. "I will send you something to-morrow, which you can cut up and give away."
>
> The "something" came, a little oblong sketch-book full of admirable pencillings, and every leaf signed. Three of those pencillings - most faithfully rendered, even to the crumbling of the blacklead pencil, are here reproduced. They show in every touch the immense rapidity of the artist's hand, and the curious way in which, by a few final strokes, he evoked the figures from a cloud of apparently wild flourishes.

Doré had sent her dozens of signed original sketches, and she was gracious enough to show some of them in her article. Her article is more of a complete biography than Norton's "book." She goes into great detail about Doré's illustrations for ***London, a Pilgrimage*** (p.365):

> Doré, in truth, delighted in London street-scenes and London riverside haunts; and he assured me that he thought the London poor the most picturesque figures in Europe. All his work for the illustrated *London* was executed *con amore*; many of the smaller drawings being miracles of sharp and delicate finish. I saw a number of the small blocks in progress when he was at the Golden Cross Hotel in 1871 (working hard for the publishers all through the time of his stay in town); and I was amazed at the amount of labour lavished, not upon drawings to be copied by a draughtsman, but upon the very wood destined for the engraver. The drawings thus made were necessarily, in a sense, sacrificed; and they of course lost much of their original character and touch in the process of cutting. By far the greater number of Doré's book-illustrations were produced in this manner; and that is why his drawings are scarce and valuable. When he took the trouble to make finished designs (as for the *Inferno* Series, still on view in Bond Street) the immense superiority of the drawing over the engraving is seen at a glance. He was a most generous giver. He used to say that he could not keep his drawings - that they were "for his friends."

Most of Amelia Edwards' article is taken from letters she received from Doré. It was heavily illustrated with drawings, etchings, and works of sculpture. She also relates many of her conversations with Doré from the gallery, concerning Doré's ***Neophyte*** and ***Triumph of Christianity*** paintings (p.392):

> "He finds that he has made an emormous mistake," said Doré, coming into the Bond Street Gallery one morning, and finding me before the picture. Convent life is not what he expected it to be."
>
> "And he despairs," I replied, "because his mistake is irreparable."
>
> Doré shook his head. "He will be over the wall to-night," he said, smiling....
>
> "See this, now!" he said, stopping before *The Triumph of Christianity*. "They say this picture wants finish. I say that it wants nothing but distance. Any picture looks coarse if you go nearer than the artist intends. From my point of view, it is finished."

Edwards also mentions that besides the Legion of Honor, Doré had also received the Knight Companion of the orders of SS. Maurice and Lazare, St. Sylvestre, and the Crown of Italy. She also relates that each year Doré came to London, he would promise her that he really would learn English "the next year." As late as 1879, he promised (p.394) to "really study English, which, at the present rate, I shall begin to speak fluently in about 25 years; that is to say, when I am about to die!"

There were numerous lauditory remarks by the British in July of 1883 about Doré's ***Vale of Tears*** painting, and by the French in November of 1883 about his ***Dumas Monument***. When the Doré ***Raven*** folio came out in December of 1883, there was an excellent review by Lafcadio Hearn in the New Orleans Times-Democrat. During Poe's lifetime, the publisher Harper had rejected his work, but in 1882-83 they paid Doré $6,000 for his 26 folio engravings. Hearn praises the edition and the engravings, and expresses regret that the illustrations turned out to be posthumous. Hearn asserts that the poem is "weird" but that "Doré has materialised the weirdness into palpable ghastliness - the ghastliness of Death made visible - gazing with eyeless sockets, grinning with fleshless face." But probably the most significant part of the review has to do with the production of the engravings, and whether or not Doré had actually completed all the illustrations:

> It has been well said of Doré's work that its unfinished character in no sense impaired its power: his pictures did not need perfecting in order to satisfy the imagination - for they invariably surpassed it....
>
> On the whole, it may be said that Doré has interpreted Poe in an unexpected manner - yet with such force that however reluctantly we may first receive his version of *The Raven*, we shall never be able to dissociate the pictures of the great artist from the stanzas of the great poet, after having once fairly examined the former....
>
> The question remains: Has Doré been well-represented by the American wood-engravers? Certainly the work before us is a veritable triumph of American art-execution; and some of the plates, at least, will rival the best Parisian work, perhaps surpass it! A few are not altogether above the possibility of criticism - there are effects which Doré might have modified had he lived to correct all his proofs. The best *set* of engravings of Doré's works are still, we think, to be found in the French plates to his Chateaubriand; but it is only fair to remind the reader that these were executed under his personal supervision. American engravers have in this case shown a capacity which even surpasses their well-deserved reputation, for the task of engraving *The Raven* plates involved work of a unique and excessively difficult kind, and uniformity of execution could not be expected on the part of so many different artists.

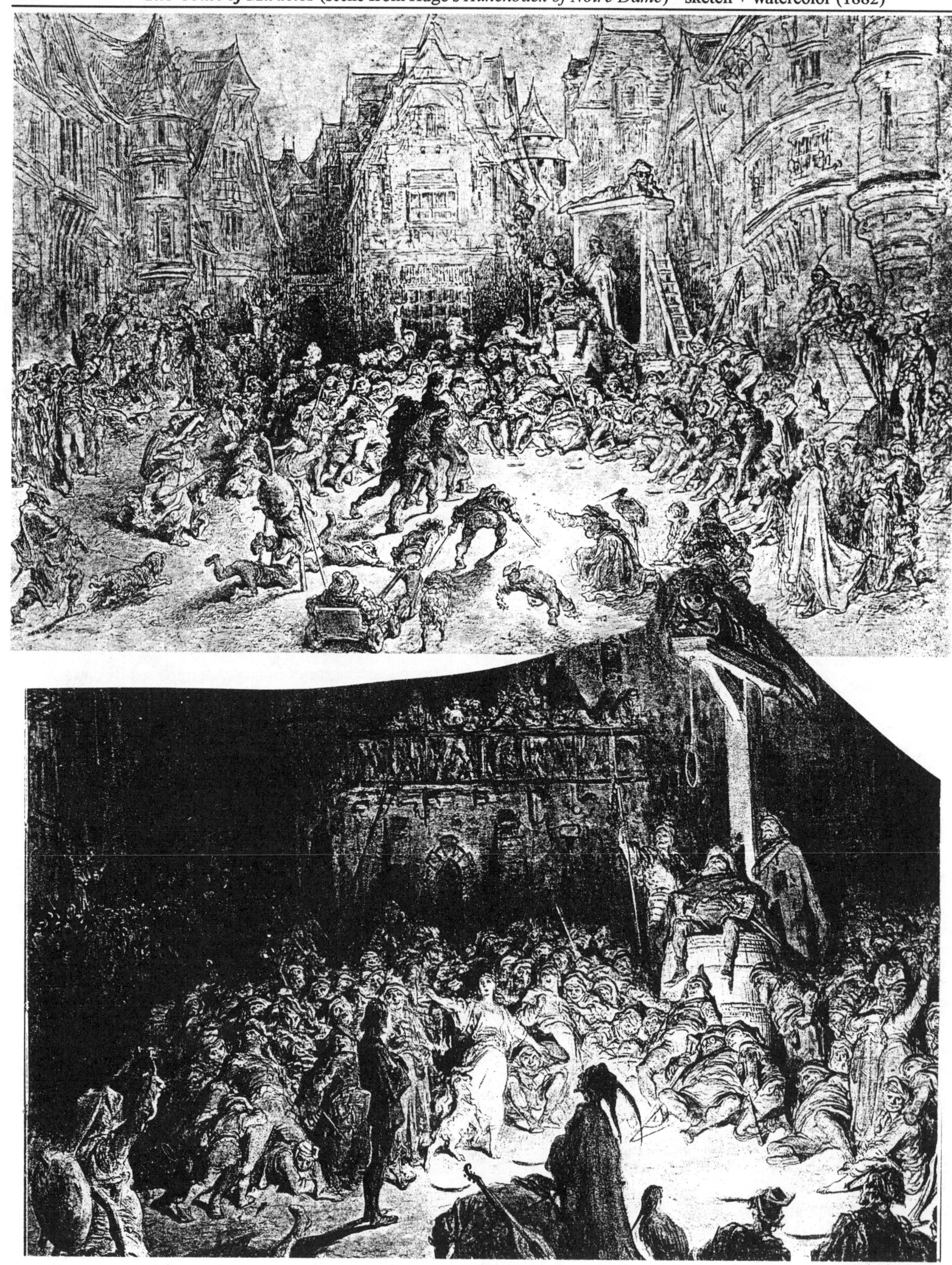

Doré's French influence

Although Doré remained popular in Britain and America for a couple decades after his death, in France he was quickly forgotten as a painter and sculptor. His illustrations continued to be reprinted in France for many years, but without any particular fanfare. It was not until the centennial exhibitions of 1983 that Doré gained major respect in France as a painter and sculptor. Praise for his ***Dumas Monument*** by the French art establishment was an oasis in the desert of French artistic rejection. His French swan song consisted of two events in the spring of 1885. One was an exhibition and the other was a sale (in French "vente"). The titles of the two booklets are similar. Here are the titles pages; the first is the **exhibition**, usually referred to as "Duplessis" (for the editor), and the second is the **sale**, usually referred to as "Vente Doré 1885."

- Catalogue des Dessins, Aquarelles et Estampes de Gustave Doré, exposes dan les Salons du Cercle de la Librarie (Mars 1885), avec une notice bibliographique par M. G. Duplessis. Paris, Cercle de la Librarie.

- Catalogue des Tableaux, Etudes et Esquisses, Aquarelles, Dessins et Sculptures laisses dans son atier par feu Gustave Doré, dont la vente aura lieu Hotel Drouot, les 10, 11, 14 et 15 Avril, 1885. Paris, Imprimerie de l'Art.

Duplessis is a 218-page, 5x7½ paperback booklet with a 60-page biography and a list of 355 items on display. Though it has a few errors, it is a crucial early Doré reference work. We have referred to ***Duplessis*** display items, such as the U.S. ***Crusades*** folio and the engravings loaned by the Doré Gallery in London. It was held in March of 1885. The next month they had the big Doré sale at the Hotel Drouot. That catalogue was larger in page size, but only 60 pages long. Besides works of art, it included the sale of those 450 unbound copies of the first British edition of the ***Ancient Mariner*** folio. Most of the items sold for pitifully low prices. They should have held that sale in London. In fact, the Doré Gallery bought some of those items for their display. What is more amazing is why Doré's British fans did not go to Paris to get bargains. Doré's 19th century French connection died, not with a bang, but a whimper.

Vincent van Gogh

Doré never heard of van Gogh. In 1883, who had? Who could have dreamed that a century later it would be considered a major asset for the then-unknown van Gogh to praise and copy the then-famous Doré? The 3-volume ***Complete Letters of Vincent van Gogh*** list 15 references to Doré. The earliest reference is in an 1877 letter, expressing his great admiration for Doré's ***London*** engravings. There are also references to ***Bible*** engravings, etchings & paintings, and his admiration of Doré's character. He refers to Doré (V3, p.329) as one of the "great black-and-white artists of the people." He also writes (V3, p.332), "The other day I saw a complete set of Doré's pictures of London. I tell you it is superb, and noble in sentiment..." Then he takes up the defense of Doré in earnest, in a letter that will forever make van Gogh one of the premier crusaders for Doré's respectability (V3, p.333):

> Of course you have heard, like myself, a lot of cheap talk - with regard to "the illustrative" - aimed at Doré - and of course at Morin too. But I believe that, notwithstanding this, you still like the work of these artists - and yet, unless one is on guard, such things may influence one. Therefore, now that I am sending you these sheets, I don't think it superfluous to tell you that I find in these soiled wood engravings a certain flavor of the days of Gavarni, and of Balzac and Victor Hugo - something of the now almost forgotten *Boheme* - for which I feel a deep respect, and which, every time I see them again, stimulates me to do my best and to attack things energetically.
>
> Of course I too see the difference between a drawing by Doré and one by Millet, but the one does not exclude the other.
>
> There is a difference, but there is also a resemblance. Doré can model a torso and put together the joints better, infinitely better, than many who revile him with pedantic self-conceit - witness that one sheet which to him was no more than a rough sketch of sea bathers.
>
> I say that, if somebody like Millet had criticized Doré's drawings - I doubt if he would ever have done it, but suppose he had - well, then he would have had a *right* to do so; but when those who with their ten fingers cannot do a tenth of what Doré can do with a single finger revile his work, then it if nothing but humbug, and it would be more appropriate if they held their tongues and learned to draw better themselves.
>
> It is so ridiculous that nowadays this nonappreciation of drawing should be such a general phenomenon.

Although van Gogh wrote about the difficulties of trying to copy Doré's "Convict Prison" about 1880, it was not until early 1890 when van Gogh was at the asylum at Saint-Remy-de-Provence that he completed his oil painting ***Prisoners Exercising***, and unlike others who "borrowed" from Doré without giving him credit, van Gogh listed his work as "after Gustave Doré." The oil on canvas was 80x64 cm, and is presently in the Pushkin Museum in Moscow. Besides van Gogh's coloring, he also painted his own face on the convict in the front center. That painting later became a film scene by Ewald Andre Dupont in the 1925 film ***Variete***. Doré's original illustration seemed simple compared to many other scenes in ***London***, but it has a powerful symbolic quality.

Doré's British influence (The Doré Gallery)

Cassell had begun publishing lower-cost Doré editions even before his death, due to low-cost American competition. Nor were they a major reduction in quality, like so many cheap pirate editions. The major change was to reduce the height of the editions from about 15" to about 13," but the gilt covers were still very attractive. In the 1890s, Cassell tried out some cheaper 8vo editions, but after the turn of the century, offered larger editions one last time. By 1906, the few titles remaining were offered pocket-size, and those editions ended by 1913.

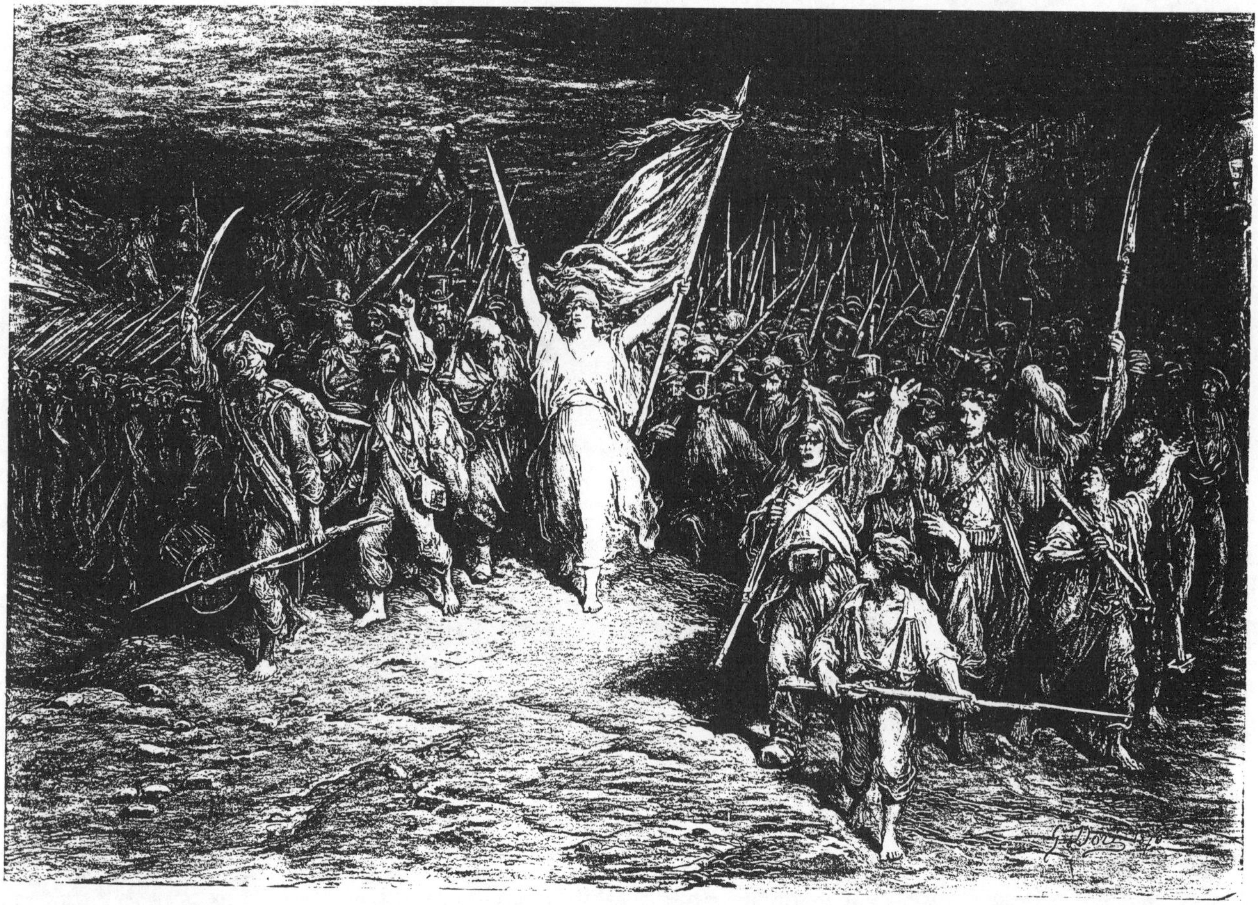

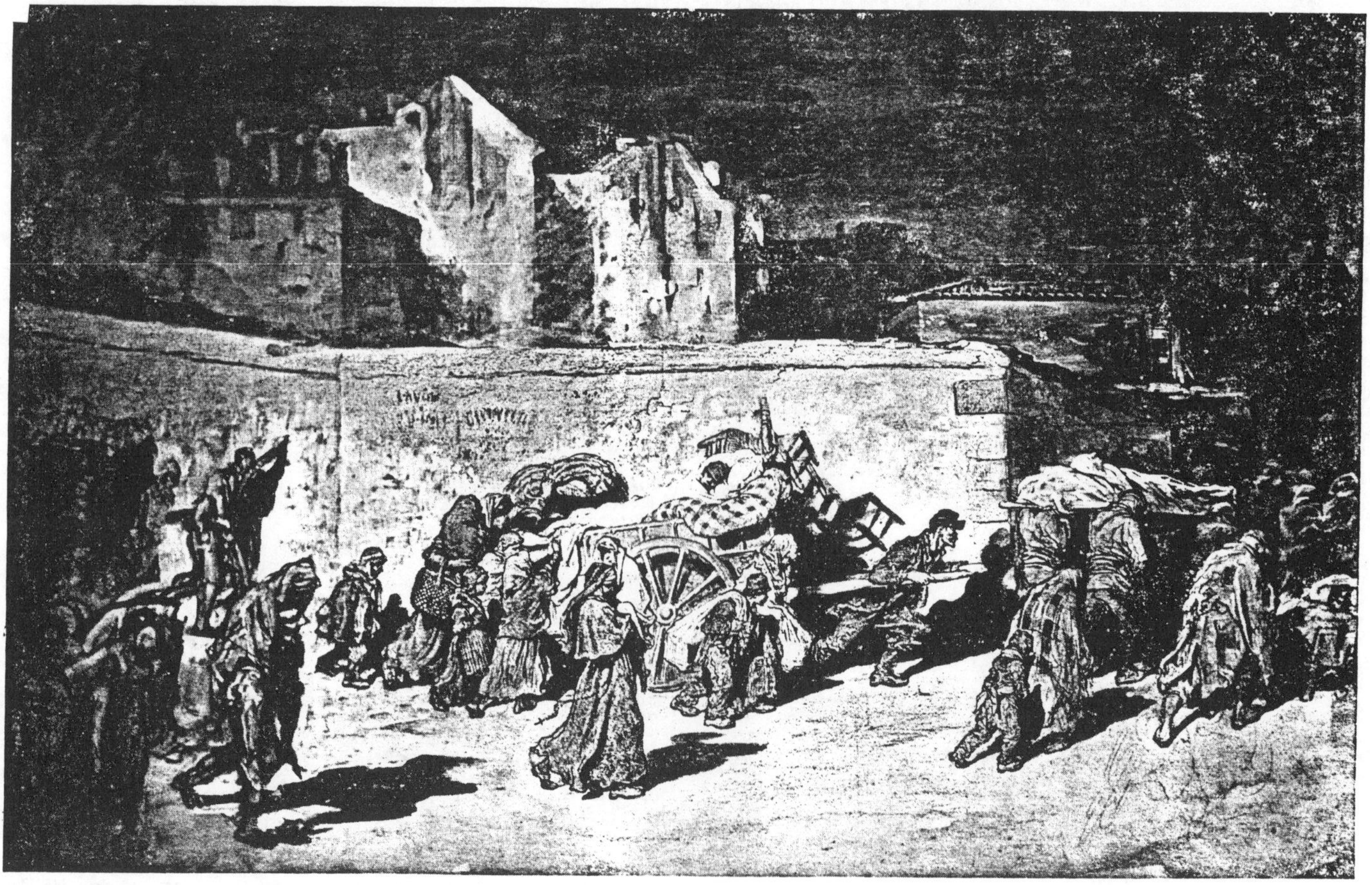

scenes from Franco-Prussian War: ***La Marseillaise*** - lithograph (1871); ***The Bombardment*** - mixed-media sketch.

Altogether, Cassell published over 200 Doré editions between 1864-1913. That is an edition every three months for 50 years. No one ever dreamed that an illustrator could be so popular. But a generation later, Doré had faded into obscurity.

At Doré's death, the Doré Gallery was going still strong, and if anything, his death only increased interest in the Doré Gallery, and they were able to continue adding new items for several years. In their catalogues they also starting listing the drawings of the paintings as separate items, so it looked like the number of Doré items had greatly increased. But finally they ran out of new Doré items. The first sign of the end was a new painting in 1891 by another artist. It was a large religious painting by Edwin Long: ***The Market Place in Nazareth***. Apparently Fairless & Beeforth sold the Doré Gallery about the same time, because their names are deleted from the 1891 catalogue, and the Doré Gallery was then listed as "Ltd." The next year, the exhibition was loaned for an American tour.

Doré's American influence

The cheap U.S. pirate publishers kept Doré very popular in America after his death. The drop in quality was not nearly as important as the major drop in price from \$25-\$50 down to \$2-\$6! Lower middle-class Americans could now afford his editions. Do not forget, it was one of those cheap editions that was such an inspiration to 10-year-old Cecil B. DeMille. But the decrease in quality escalated, and many turn of the century editions look awful. So the cheap Doré editions had died out, and the U.S. Cassell operation was virtually nonexistent.

Then in 1892 the Doré Gallery came to America. The few Americans who had seen it in London made it legendary. At some point (probably in the late 1880s), an unknown group of people actually set up a fake Doré Gallery in Chicago. It was very different from the official Doré Gallery which visited Chicago in 1896. Apparently, someone Chicagoan had visited the real Doré Gallery in London and purchased four of the popular 22x32 steel engravings of Doré's paintings - ***Christ Leaving the Praetorium, Christ's Entry into Jerusalem, The Dream of Pilate's Wife & Christian Martyrs in the Coliseum***. They returned to Chicago, set up a room displaying the four engravings, and announced it as being "The Doré Gallery." They even published a little catalogue very similar to the one issued by the real Doré Gallery in London. But the catalogue for the fake gallery was entitled "Descriptive Catalogue of the Reproductions." As is so often the case with this type of Doré item, there is only one copy of that catalogue known to exist, owned by the Henry Francis DuPont Winterthur Museum in Delaware. The catalogue does not even tell what city that "Doré Gallery" is in. But it gives the address - 233 Wabash Ave., at the corner of Jackson St, which is easily identifiable as downtown Chicago (Jackson St. is now 300 S.), only a couple blocks from the Art Institute of Chicago. They managed to put together an 18-page catalogue for nothing more than four engravings. Their catalogue refers to information obviously gleaned from Roosevelt (1885). They managed to give a brief Doré biography and a description of the engravings without ever mentioning that there was a Doré Gallery in London!

By 1892, most Americans assumed that Doré's paintings must be as good as his engravings; why else would there be the Doré Gallery in London? U.S. magazines and art reference books probably spoke more favorably of Doré than did their British counterparts. A good example was the June 1891 Doré article in ***Cosmopolitan*** by Mary D. Wellcome (p.171-183), written eight years after Doré's death. Besides being very positive, it also shows ten Doré book illustrations and five of his oil paintings, but the captions do not differentiate between engravings and paintings. Most Americans didn't either.

The Doré Gallery in America

But the real story of how Doré briefly came to be considered the world's greatest painter by the American public began with an article in the August 10, 1892 ***New York Times***, quoted here in its entirety (p9-c4):

> THE DORÉ COLLECTION COMING HERE
>
> Mr. Henry Heyman, acting on behalf of the syndicate owning the famous Doré collection of paintings, completed arrangements on Monday with the managers of Carnegie Music Hall for the transfer of the collection in its entirety to Recital Hall, from the Gustave Doré Gallery, at 51 (sic) New Bond St., London, where it has been on exhibition for twenty-one (sic) years, having in that time been seen by over three million people.
>
> Mr. Heyman, who sailed for Europe today to fetch the pictures, has secured a six months' lease of Recital Hall, with an optional lease of another six months. The exhibition will probably open in October.
>
> The collection consists of thirty-eight canvases, the masterpiece being *Christ Leaving the Praetorium*, a painting 20 feet in height by 30 feet in width.

The New York exhibition, entitled ***The Doré Collection***, first ran from October 1892 through March 1893. It was hailed as "the greatest collection of religious paintings in the world." Reviews ranged from the sublime to the ridiculous. One that was probably both was in ***The Recorder*** of October 2, 1892: "*Christ leaving the Praetorium* is without doubt the most marvelous ever conceived by human brain." But the best review, and one of the most balanced article ever written about Doré as a painter, was the article in the ***New York Times*** of October 3, 1892. Here are a few excerpts (p4-c7):

> Doré was above all things a caricaturist and a designer in black & white for the press. He won his great triumphs in France on this score. Later in life he began to paint, and he painted with an energy and recklessness of space that took people's breath away. In his own Paris, he was distinctly not the success as a painter that he thought was due to his genius, for Doré was most certainly a genius in his way. But he found that the English appreciated fully the somewhat literary side of his pictures, and were not repelled, as the French were, by a something heavy and Germanic in his technique and often in his compositions. The people who admired Frith and Edwin Long and still consider Leighton and Millais

 four different etchings of ***The Head of Christ*** (1881-86) - some completed by others.

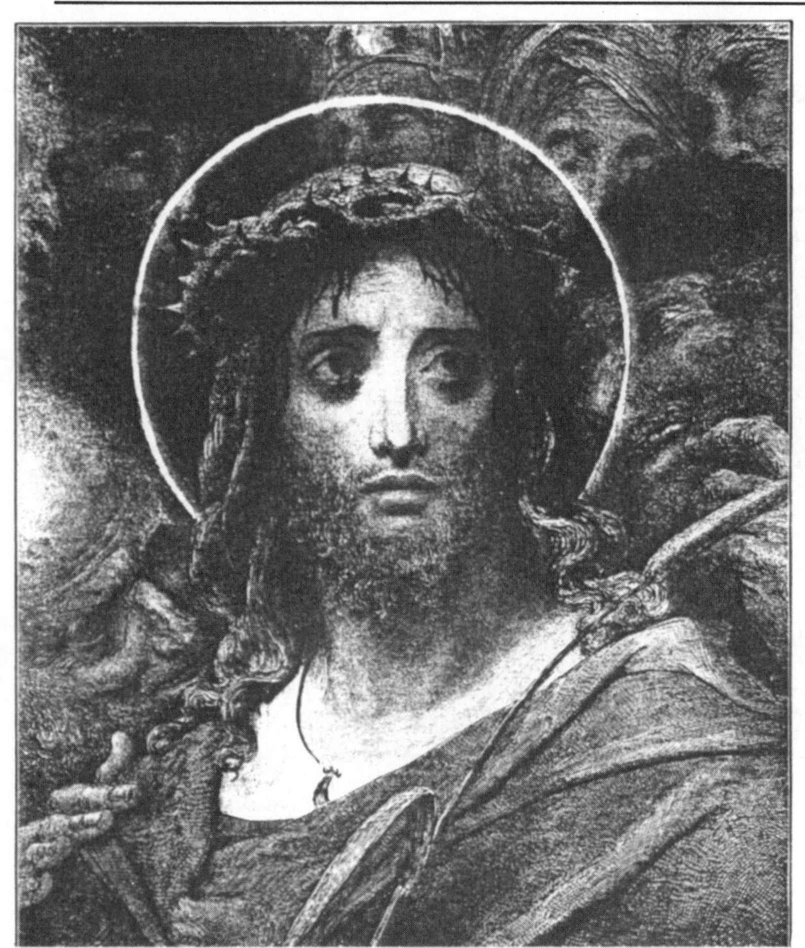

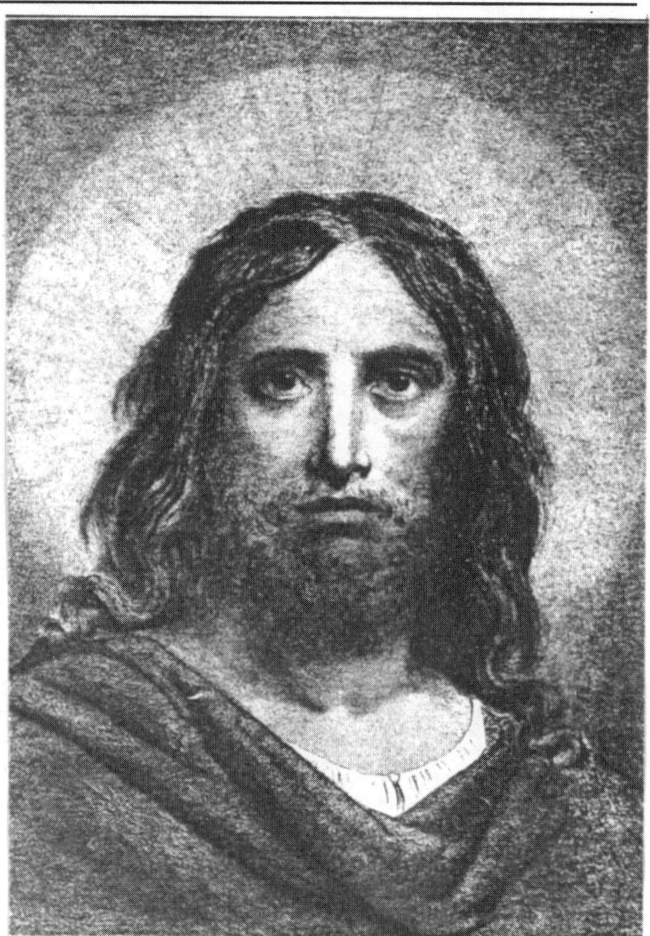

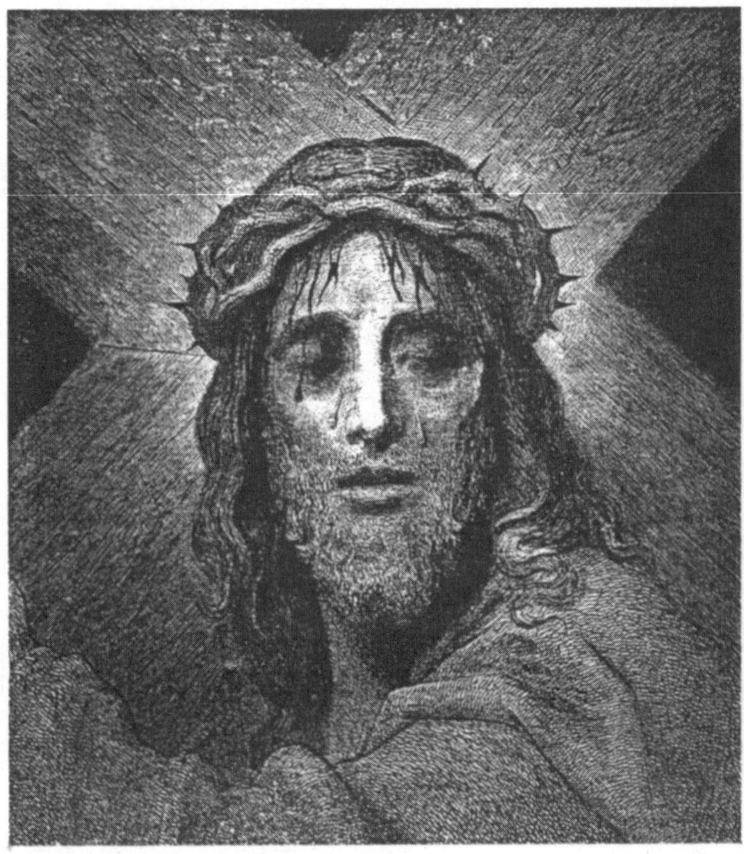

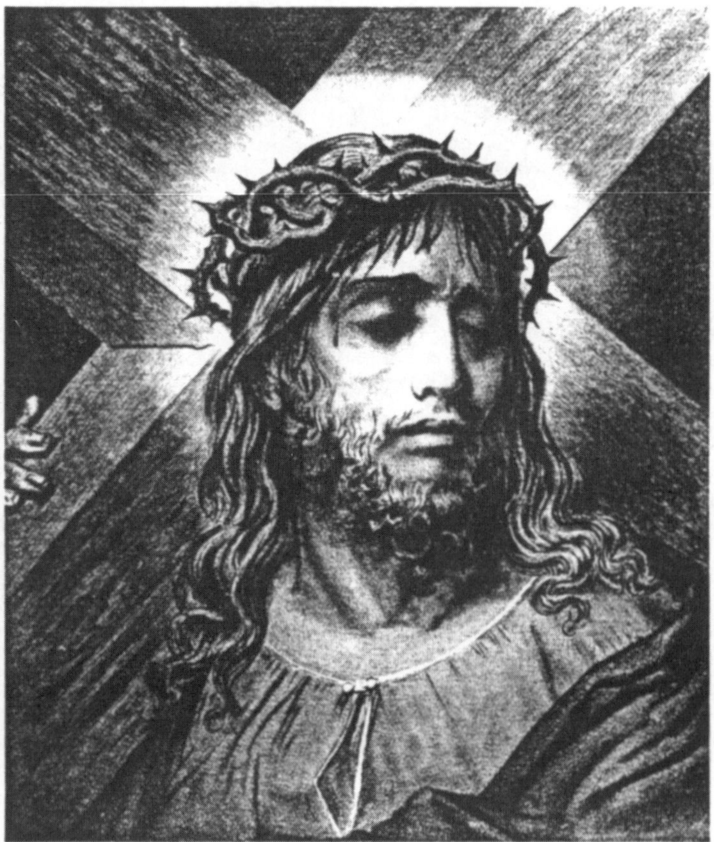

great as painters in the narrow, technical sense of the term, were not likely to trouble poor Doré with hypercriticism. His work was so successful that promoters took possession and made a museum of him. Curious to relate, a large number of the huge canvases in the London Doré Gallery were made for that museum and have never been seen by the common run of Parisian art connoisseurs.

It would be too much to say that any number of those connoisseurs regret the fact. But it is nevertheless true that Doré in time learned to paint far better than Paris was disposed to believe. Naturally very limited in his sense for color, Doré learned a great deal. He was a man of great inventiveness and prodigious industry....

On the whole, the ability of Doré to paint is a matter for surprise. He is never a great painter, but he is a great artist in so many other ways that the result is highly interesting. Decidedly, the fashion of this day does not lie in his direction any more than it does toward such steel engravings as have been wrought with infinite care and at great expenditure after his works. But there will always be among our people, as among Britons, thousands of persons who will be touched by the story of *The Christian Martyrs in the Arena* to the one who will turn way because the handling is not up to the latest ideas.

Another perplexing comment in the article was in regard to ***Christ leaving the Praetorium*** - that "the picture is known everywhere by engravings." That would be the case in London, but in New York? At first the exhibition gave out a 4-page brochure and then a 48-page catalogue. Keep in mind that in January of 1893 they published the "Marie L." book. When the exhibition's 6-month lease expired in March of 1893, they did not renew it. Instead they moved into larger quarters that June, with better lighting. The second New York exhibition ran from June 1893 at least until the end of 1893, probably into 1894, and possibly even into 1895. The later N.Y.. catalogues are undated, and I have never find any article telling when the New York exhibition closed. But there was a very significant feature to the undated New York catalogue - it was illustrated, showing the 25 engravings offered for sale at the exhibition. That illustrated undated New York catalogue also changed the name of the exhibition to the more correct Doré Gallery. Although any copy of a Doré Gallery catalogue is quite rare, the illustrated ones are much more significant and desirable.

In 1896, the Doré Gallery came to Chicago, for what would prove to be Doré's finest hour as a painter, even if it did come 13 years after his death. It is a shame Doré did not live to see his exhibition of paintings break every attendance record at the Art Institute of Chicago, and all those records still stand. If only Doré had followed Sarah Bernhardt and Adelina Patti to America. The 1896 Chicago exhibition was the only time the Doré Gallery was ever seen in midwestern America, where in 1896 Doré was still revered as the most popular artist in the world. In New York the Doré Gallery daily attendance topped 3000, which was thought to be very impressive. The exhibition in Chicago was supposed to run from January 21 to March 22 of 1896. On the first day in Chicago, over 7000 attended. But the real omen of things to come was on the 12th of February, when the capacity of the Institute was severely tested with an all-time record of 12,729 people visiting the Doré Gallery exhibition in eight hours. Overall, the first month's attendance averaged just over 3000 per day. Then came the final weekend before the planned departure of the exhibition. On Saturday, March 15, 1896, a truly astonishing 15,916 people marched through the gates during the eight-hour display. On Sunday afternoons, the gallery was only open for four hours, but on March 16, over 7000 attended. So in a 12-hour period, over 23,000 people had jammed the Doré Gallery exhibition. During the second month of the exhibition the average daily attendance had jumped to almost 5000.

This produced a major dilemma for the directors of the Art Institute. Bringing the Doré Gallery in the first place had been controversial, with some art critics asserting that Doré's paintings were not "real art." But it had proved to be by far the most popular exhibit ever to come to the Institute. For an art museum having financial woes, it had proved to be a lifesaver, because it was making a level of profit they had hardly dared to dream of. On March 24, the directors of the Institute issued a press release - the Doré exhibition had been extended "indefinitely." Art critics howled that attendance would now drop way off; that the attendance records were only due to the anticipated closing of the exhibition. Boy were they wrong! On April 12th the attendance exceeded 16,200! That is still the all-time daily attendance record for any exhibition in the history of the Art Institute of Chicago. The exhibition stayed until October 4th of 1896. From the day they extended the exhibition until its close, the <u>average</u> daily attendance exceeded 7000! In 8½ months, over 1.5 million people had visited the exhibition. And to think that the British had been bragging that nearly three million people had visited the London Doré Gallery in 23 years! When the last day of the Chicago exhibition arrived, there had inadvertantly been no advertising or article announcing the closing. October 4 was a Sunday, but the attendance was still nearly 10,000 in four hours. And as a final coup-de-grace (which would make any self-respecting art museum employee shudder), on that final day, over 4000 people came through the "gates" in <u>one hour!</u> That is a rate faster than one per second.

How could all this happen? Fortunately, the Art Institute has a massive file of old articles pertaining to their activities. It includes hundreds of articles about the Doré Gallery, not just in Chicago, but in every town big enough to have a newspaper. You could describe the Chicago reviews as mixed, but the common people could not have cared less what the experts said. It is the oldest debate in the field of art - is the average person unsophisticated, or are art experts elitists? Perhaps a little of both. It was noted several times that a great number of the people who visited the Doré Gallery in Chicago had never been to an art museum in their life. They came from every little town and farming community in the upper midwest. These were simple people who had been enthralled with Doré the illustrator for decades; folks who had book salesmen knock at their door out in the countryside and sell them cheap Doré quartos. Vincent van Gogh was quite correct when he referred

 three different Doré oil paintings of ***Children in Poverty*** (one dated 1874, two undated).

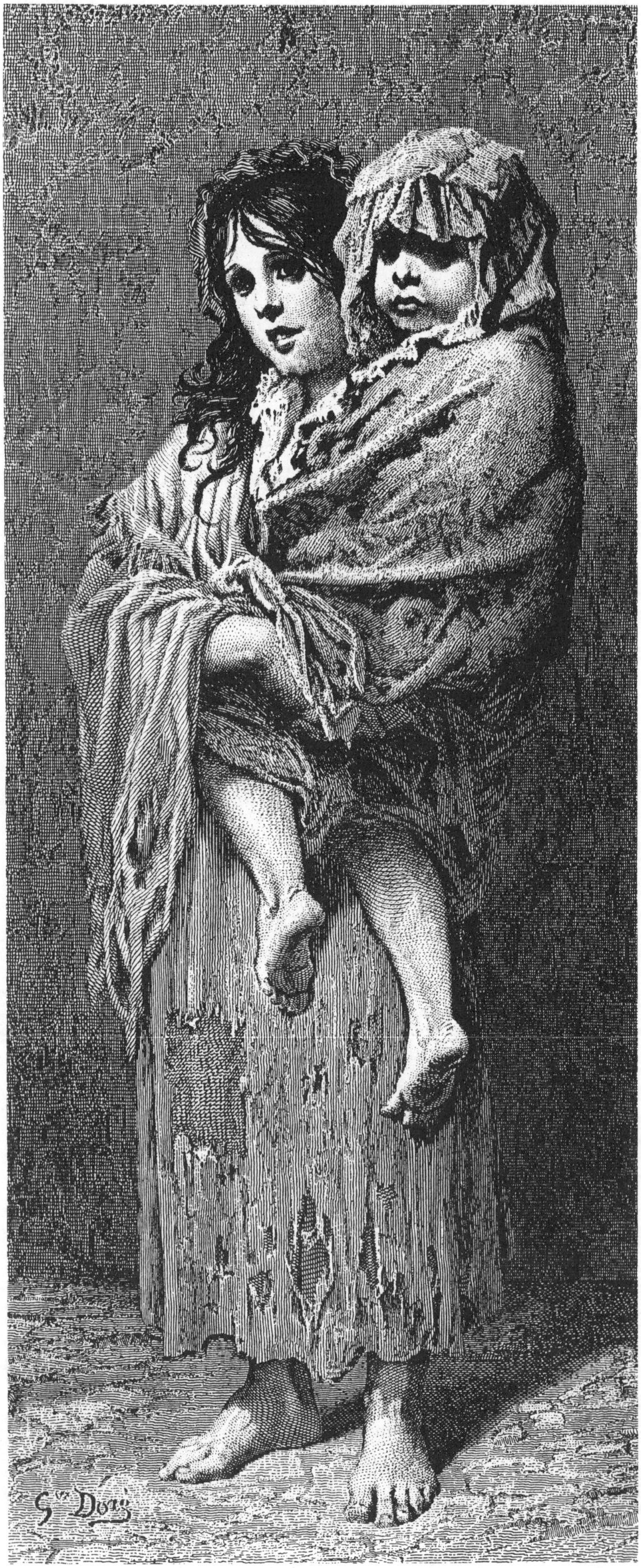

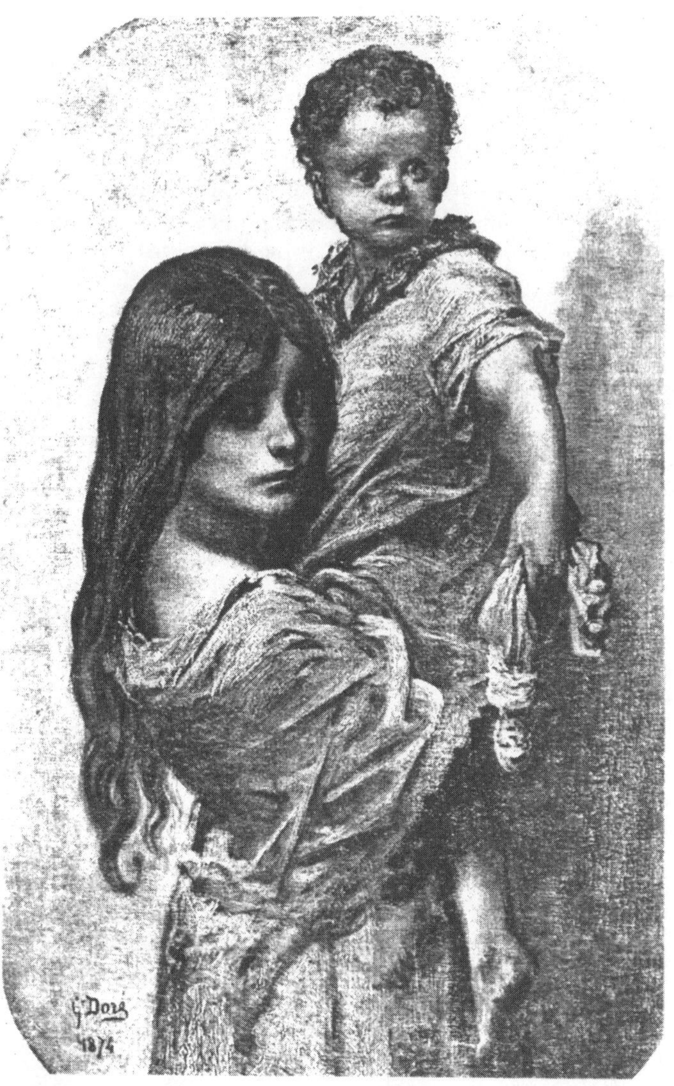

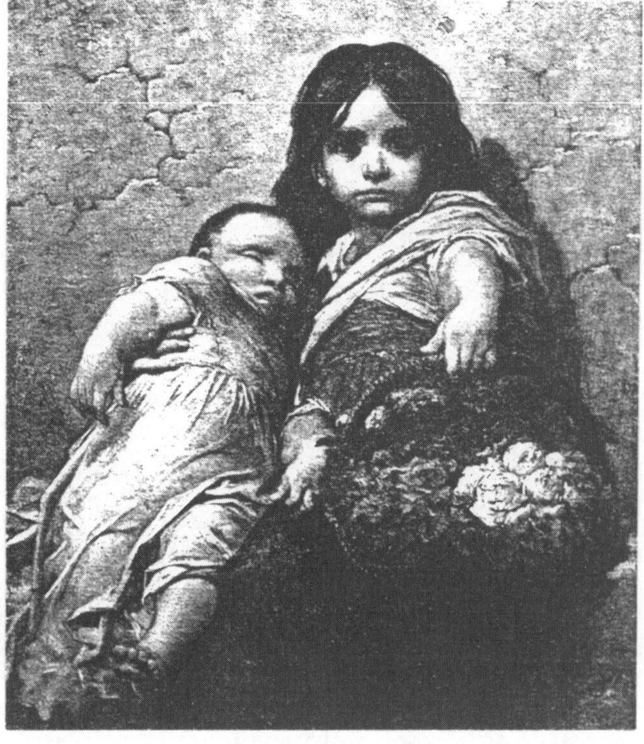

to Doré as "an artist of the people." Most of these people were very religious. They were basically the rural cousins of the Londoners who made pilgrimages to their Doré Gallery. Here is a typical example of the opening lines from a small town newspaper article, from the March 23, 1896 ***Kewanee Star*** (Kewanee, Illinois is about 130 miles west of Chicago):

> Every Kewanee person who goes to Chicago should if possible arrange to visit the Art Institute and see especially the famous Doré collection of religious paintings. These are the most magnificent paintings of the kind in the country.... From the artist's standpoint they are criticised for a lack of perfectness in coloring, but for the wonderful conception of the author they have no superior.

One of the articles that best expresses Doré's true appeal was in the October 5, 1896 ***Chicago Evening Journal*** (just after the exhibition closed), quoted here in its entirety:

> For answer to the Doré critics we have a record of the attendance at the Art Institute that is unprecedented. The great paintings by the Frenchman were exhibited for the last time in this city yesterday, and though there had been no advertisement of their proposed removal, from 8,000 to 10,000 people visited the galleries. Their drawing power has continued unabated, from Jan. 1 to the present time and their popularity has shown no signs of waning.
>
> The critics will probably reply with their stock argument that the triumph, such as it is, is a triumph of degrading sensationalism. They will also murmur something that is unintelligible concerning true art. But a sensationalism that is as steady and as certain as the earth in its course, a sensationalism that leads to nothing unseemly, but arouses a profound spiritual interest and appeals to all classes of society save perhaps true artists, is a curious kind of sensationalism. Upon analysis it is more than likely that it would be found to be helpful rather than harmful, and it is not so certain that in some respects it is not far more decent and far less dangerous than various phases of true art itself.
>
> For example, in another room of the same building there is a picture of a couple of naked women painted by Bouguereau. They are impossible women, seated in defiance of all laws of probability upon the seashore. They are painted for their nakedness, and nothing else. Now it is permissible to submit for the earnest consideration of the advocates of true art this proposition: That representations of the supreme moments in the life of the Savior of mankind, strikingly, impressively, grandly, if not artistically, done, are worth far more to the visitors to the institute than Bouguereau's naked and artistic, but wholly impossible, women.

Doré seemed to touch every nerve possible in the world of art - the illustrator vs. the painter, elitism vs. the common people, religious vs. secular, Catholic vs. Protestant, French vs. English, the populist vs. the art establishment, violence vs. the idyllic, conventional vs. unconventional, instant fame vs. artistic obscurity, commercialization vs. government-funded art. He was as controversial as he was famous. It is fortunate that various groups did not come to blows over him. It is also interesting that the above article would refer to nudes, because Doré not only did nudes, but some of the most prominent paintings in the Doré Gallery were nudes. You could just as easily say that Doré's ***Andromeda*** was but a literary excuse for showing a naked woman chained to a rock with a sea-monster about to devour her. No sexual symbolism there.

There are at least three variations of the catalogue for the Doré Gallery in Chicago. Newspaper articles mention that they kept running out of catalogues. With 1.5 million attendees, they must have reprinted the catalogue several times. Here are the three main versions, in probable order of appearance:

1) ***Descriptive Catalogue of Gustave Doré's Great Paintings***
   The Art Institute of Chicago, Chicago, 1896
2) ***Illustrated Descriptive Catalogue of the Doré Gallery***
   Art Institute of Chicago, January 21 - March 22, 1896
   Published by Illinois Engraving Co., Chicago
3) ***Illustrated Descriptive Catalogue of the Doré Gallery***
   Published by Illinois Engraving Co., Chicago

The first catalogue has no illustrations (except for a portrait), and is largely based on the New York catalogue. It was probably printed up before the Chicago exhibition began. The 1892 New York catalogue listed only 38 items. Chicago catalogues list 64 items. Once again, this is due to listing the preliminary sketches and drawings related to the major oil paintings. They probably had those items on display in New York but did not list them as separate items. They also added the proofs of Doré's ***Tennyson*** engravings that had been displayed in London, but were not listed in the New York catalogue. But there was one other major difference. In Chicago they did not at first display the enormous oil painting ***Le Tapis Vert***, probably due to space problems, and fear that the gambling theme would be unpopular in the midwest. They did include the smaller drawing of that picture. The second version of the catalogue was probably printed in February, the major purpose of which was to add illustrations of engravings on sale.. The third catalogue was probably printed in April or May, since it deleted all dates. But they also deleted mention of the Art Institute. There is one other amusing feature to that third catalogue. It adds a new item, number 35½! Since the exhibition was so popular, they added the full oil painting for ***Tapis Vert*** that had been omitted. The first article mentioning it was in March. But to avoid revising the catalogue, they just found an empty part of a page (below #35), and inserted ***Tapis Vert*** there as #35½. So while all three catalogues go up to #64, the third catalogue actually lists 65 items.

Those files from the Art Institute of Chicago also reveal what happened to the Doré Gallery in London while all the Doré items were on tour in America. The April 23th, 1896, ***Chicago Times-Herald*** reprinted ***Barron's London Letter***, which pointed out that with the Doré items gone, the London Doré Gallery had been renamed the Lemercier Gallery, and they exhibited there 365 religious watercolors by James Tissot. Tissot was, like Doré, a French artist who became more popular in England than France. In the 1880s, he spent several

oil painting - ***Scottish Lake after the Storm*** (nd, 1870s) - now in Grenoble Museum.
watercolor - ***The Lake at Ischl in the Tyrol*** (1876) - Clapp collection, now in Strasbourg Museum.
watercolor - ***Le Trou d'Enfer a Luchon*** (1882) - now in Museum of the Pyrenees in Lourdes.

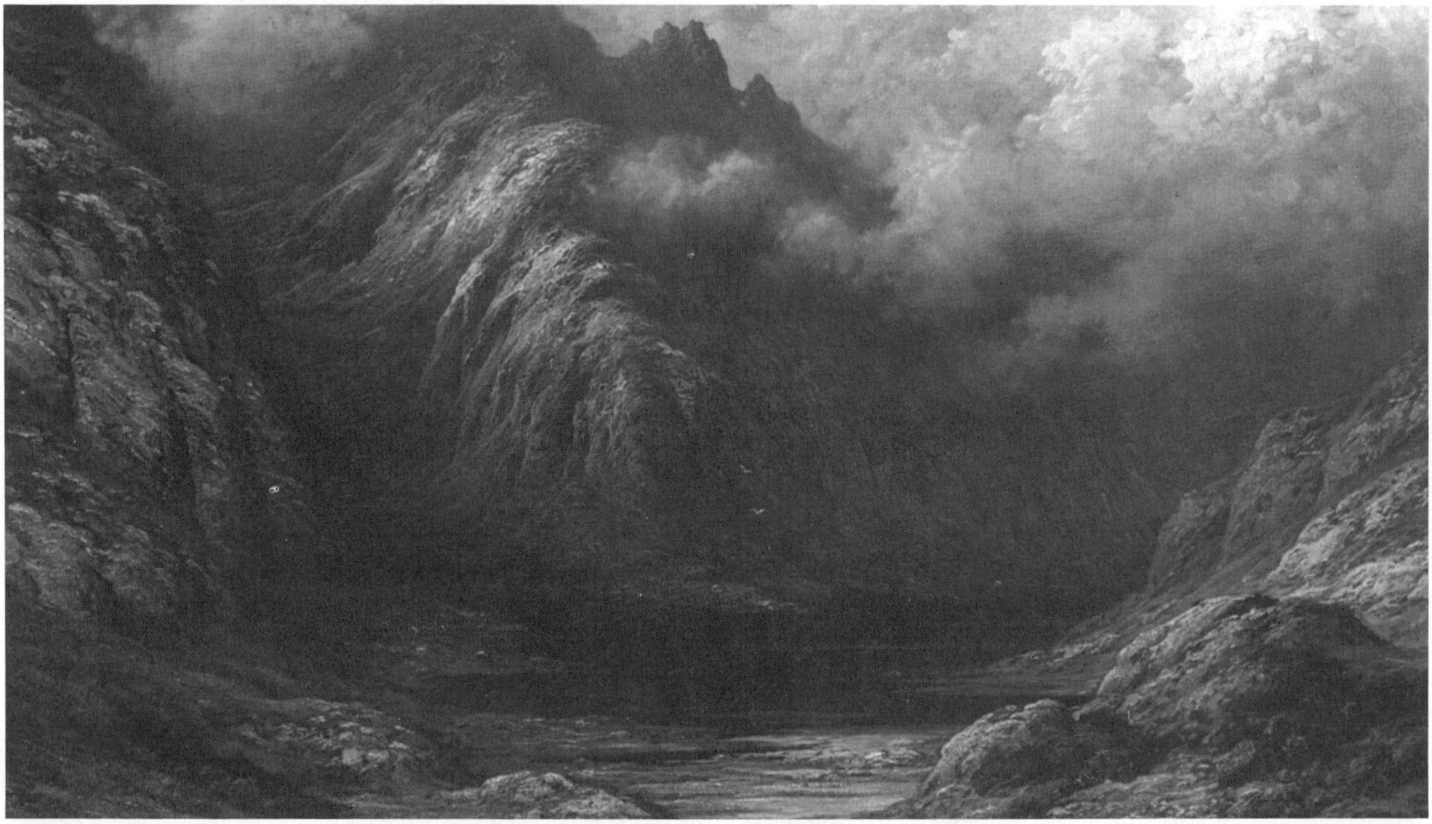

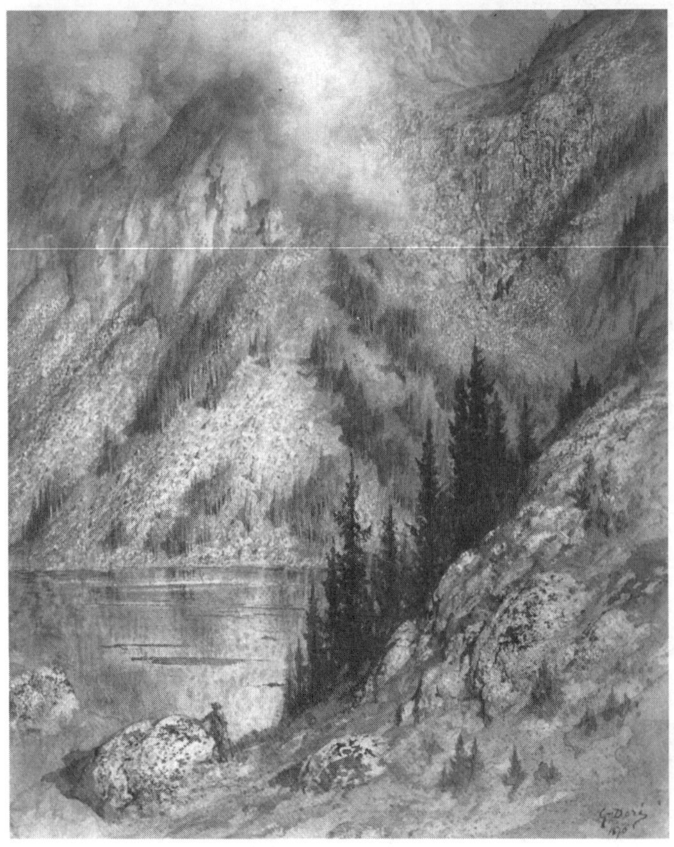

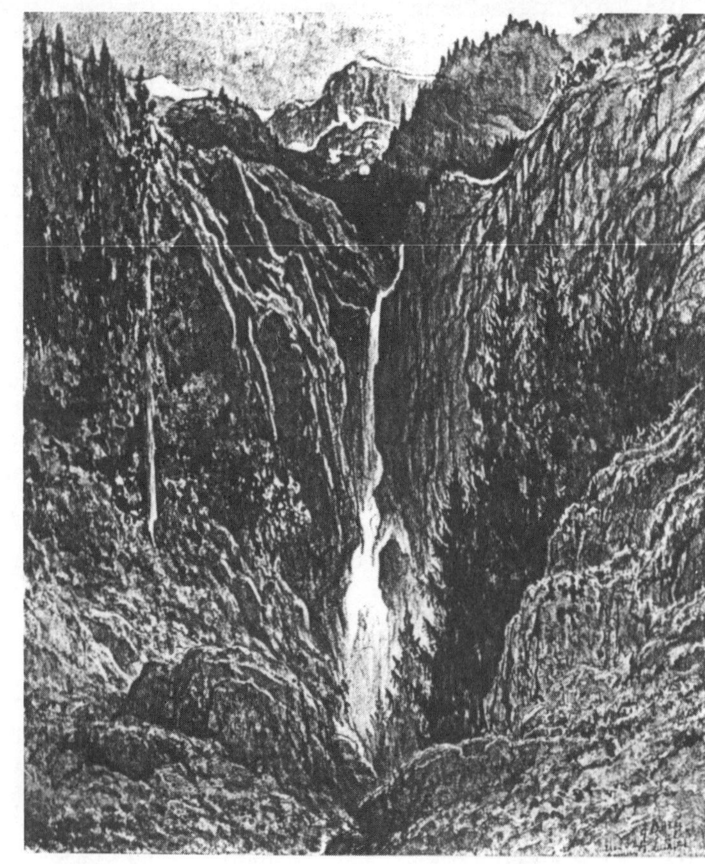

years in the Holy Land, and produced what was probably the most thorough visual treatment of a Bible theme ever. If you thought that Doré's 238 ***Bible*** engravings were comprehensive, Tissot did 365 watercolors just of the life of Christ. But they are quite different from either Doré's ***Bible*** engravings or his religious paintings. First of all, Tissot's watercolors were small for paintings. They were about the same size as Doré's folio engravings. Then Tissot's content was much more cultural and geographical, resembling in many ways a tour guide of the Holy Land. They are also much less dramatic than Doré's religious art. Some people thought that Tissot was competing with Doré. Tissot's watercolors were exhibited in England and America for many years and made into an expensive 2-volume (color) folio, ***The Life of our Lord Jesus Christ***.

The articles at the close of the Chicago Doré Gallery claim that the exhibition was headed for Boston. They state that a Mr. W. D. Normand was in charge of the collection, and would be supervising its Boston opening about November 1st, 1896 at the Copley Hall in downtown Boston. But after extensive research, I have been unable to find any record that such an exhibition ever took place. If someone reading this in Boston knows anything about this, I would certainly love to hear from them about it. We do know is that by 1898, the Doré Gallery was in Philadelphia, where an illustrated catalogue was published by Gimbel Brothers. There is little information about the Philadelphia exhibition also. There is a great deal of information about New York and Chicago, and almost nothing about Boston and Philadelphia. But we do know that the Doré Gallery was in the U.S. six years, and in that time was seen by more people than saw it in London in 23 years.

There has been another mystery about what happened to the collection at the end of 1898. Two conflicting theories are asserted in Doré reference books. One theory asserts that the collection went back to England and then disappeared, finally turning up in a 1964 London Christie's auction. The other theory asserts that the collection stayed in America; that the British owners died and the U.S. manager put them into storage; where they were discovered in 1947 and auctioned by a New York warehouse company. Gosling (1973) refers back to a September 22, 1947 article in Time Magazine:

> In 1899 the art importing company which brought them to the U.S. stored them in a Manhattan warehouse. The company kept up storage payments until 1927, then went out of business. Not until last spring did the storage company get around to unpacking the crates to see what was in them.

Contrast that with Richardson (1980), who does not even mention the Doré Gallery going to America. Here is how she summarizes its demise in London (p.153):

> By 1902, thirty-five years after its inception, the Doré Gallery was losing its popularity. The proprietors began to let off rooms for other purposes. Doré's big pictures were still in view, but visitors could also see Russian peasant art, Picasso or Sickert. In April 1914 the gallery was hired by the Italian futurists. During World War I, the Doré canvases were shipped to America. Some say they were lost at sea; whether or not that is so, they have disappeared.

Richardson's source for that last sentence was Rose (1946), but the paintings were discovered in New York in 1947. So what really did happen? The first piece to the puzzle can be found in the Sept.-Oct. 1898 British magazine, ***The Artist*** (p.247):

> THE DORE GALLERY - Time and travel have dealt kindly with the famous Doré pictures, which, after an interval of eight years, have now returned to their well-known Bond Street home.... from what we hear, the present generation is as eager to see and discuss them as were its predecessors of more than twenty years ago, when these pictures were first exhibited.

The second piece to the puzzle can be found in an undated London Doré Gallery catalogue which lists pictures by Doré "and other well-known artists." Besides Doré items, it also includes two large religious oil paintings by F. Wilfrid Lawson and one by Rudolf Blind. It can be easily dated by two details - one of the new paintings is dated 1899, and that painting was viewed by Queen Victoria (and she died in 1901). So it is fairly simple to come up with an approximate date of 1900. But the real key is in perusing the list of Doré items in that undated 1900 catalogue - there are only 16. It appears that they split up the Doré Gallery. Since many major paintings had replica paintings and/or large sketch versions, there were enough items for two Doré Galleries. If you compare the full 1896 Chicago catalogue list (64 items) with the 1900 London catalogue (16 items), and then compare each of those with the 1947 New York auction and the 1964 London auction, you will find that almost all of the 1900 London items sold in the 1964 London auction, and almost all of the items that stayed in New York sold in the 1947 New York auction. There are only three exceptions, which are still puzzling

But the 1900 London Doré Gallery did not fare so well. Another generation arose that knew not Doré. Indeed, it was now 32 years since Fairless & Beeforth took a chance on an exhibition of paintings by the famous illustrator. It was now 14 years since the last new Doré items had been added to the London exhibition. It could not go on forever. So while it was still called the Doré Gallery, catalogues between 1907-1914 featured Italian futurists, post-impressionists, and vorticists. After World War I, the gallery was purchased by Sotheby's, and it remains their London showroom to this day. Like dew, Doré's fame evaporated with the dawning of a new century.

Doré and his 19th century critics

Doré's early critics can be divided into two groups - a large group of French art critics (and a few English art critics who sided with them) who continually attacked Doré for his "utter inability to paint like a painter;" and a smaller group of English art critics (led by John Ruskin and Philip Hamerton) who criticized him for his excessive horror, violence and hedonism. That second group was very small in comparison to the praise lavished on him by the English-speaking world. Critics in both groups often resorted to personal attacks, and even attempted to discredit Doré as an illustrator. Also, critics

 oil painting ***Les Saltimbanques*** (1874) now in Clermont-Ferrand Museum (influence on Picasso)

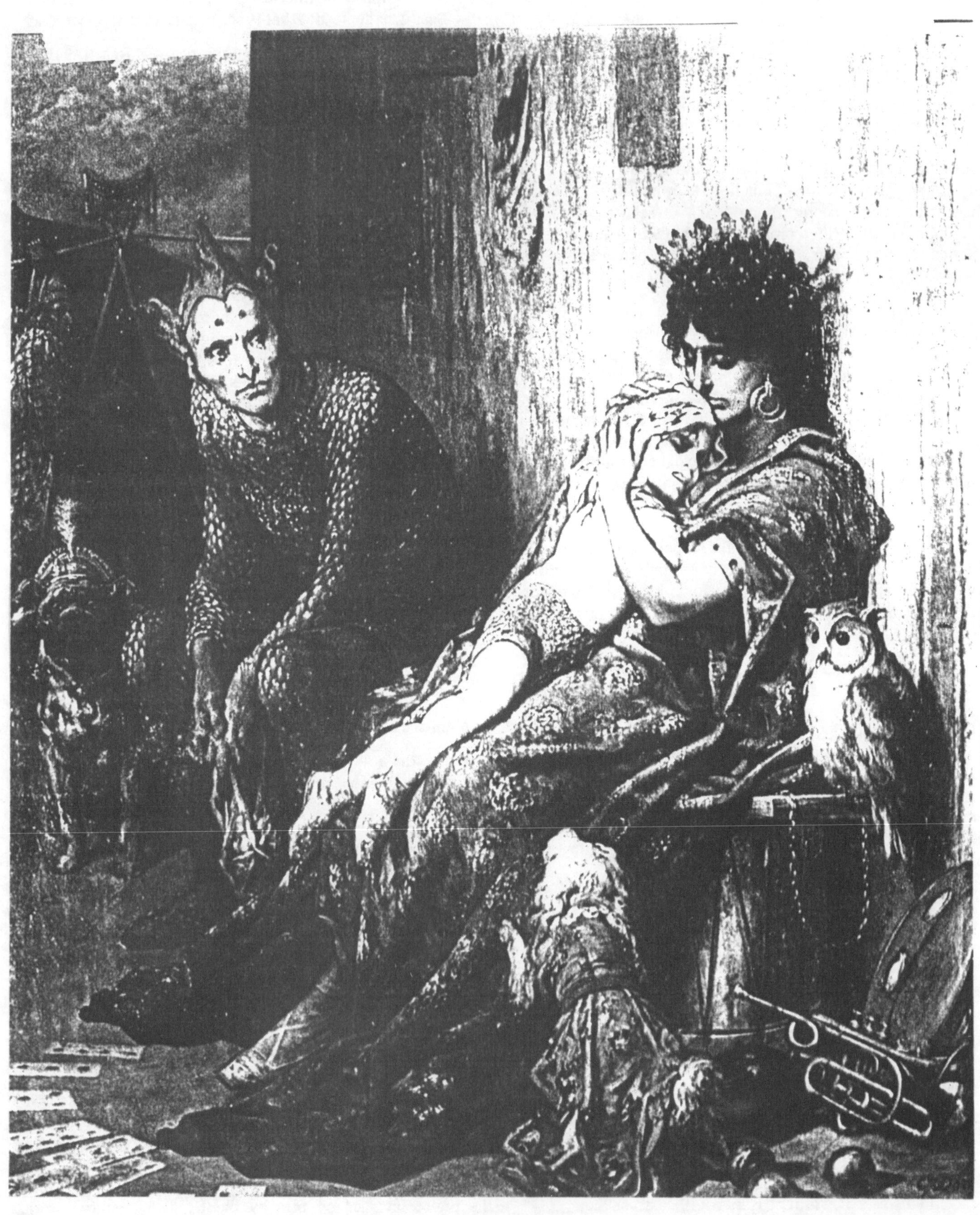

from the second group found it very convenient to borrow from the first group, even though they did not particularly care about the coloring or theatricality of Doré's paintings. All too often, those in the first group did not really review Doré paintings, they simply mocked them. A good example was the prominent French art critic Jules Claretie, author of, among many other books, ***Peintres et Sculpteurs Contemporains*** (1883). Gosling contains several quotes from him. Concerning Doré's ***Battle of Inkermann*** painting (an 1857 Salon entry), Claretie described the soldiers therein as "half-cooked lobsters and a thicket of shrimp." It became fashionable in French art establishment circles to simply mock Doré rather than actually reviewing his artwork. On New Year's Eve of 1882, Claretie wrote in a newspaper article (per Gosling, p.30): "Next year M. Gustave Doré will continue to make crazy paintings and boring sculpture." What he really meant was, "Whatever Doré does, I will describe it as crazy and boring." But Doré finally figured out how to prove him wrong - by dying! Then in the height of hypocrisy, Claretie got up at Doré's funeral service and eulogized him. When the ***Dumas Monument*** was unveiled later that year, Claretie not only did not say it was boring, he could not think of anything bad to say about it. Apparently, Doré's death took all the fun out of their personal attacks. They knew that they could get to Doré; they knew they could drive him crazy with an incessant stream of personal put-downs.

Of course they were making some legitimate points about coloring and theatrics. But Doré's French critics were not satisfied with legitimate analysis of defects, they always had to twist the knife. Compare that to many British and American balanced articles we have quoted, where they criticized some details while praising others. The personalness of the attacks was not limited to the French group. In the 1894 ***Great Men & Famous Women***, Kenyon Cox attacks Doré in ways that are so bizarre there is no way to even debate them (p.301):

> ... Doré never learned, in a true sense, to draw. He had made for himself a sort of artistic shorthand, which enabled him to convey his superabundant ideas quickly and certainly to his public, but his drawing is what is called mannered in the extreme. In is not representation of nature at all, but pure formula and chic. He is said to be a master of drapery, but he never drew a single fold correctly. He is said to show great knowledge of Gothic architecture, but he never drew well a single column or finial ... he never drew a leg with a bone in it.

That is exactly what van Gogh was referring to. What are the artistic achievements of Kenyon Cox and Jules Claretie? Let them lay their greatest works next to the greatest sets of engravings ever done for ***Dante, Milton, Rabelais, Cervantes, Tennyson, Coleridge, Ariosto, The Bible,*** etc. The unknown van Gogh wrote Doré's best defense, when he said about smug elitists who reviled Doré, "... it would be more appropriate if they held their tongues and learned to draw better themselves." Another work van Gogh might have referred to was Clement & Hutton's 1879 ***Artists of the Nineteenth Century***. Their bias is quickly evidenced by the fact that there is not one mention of the Doré Gallery. They refer to Doré's worldwide fame as an illustrator as being "praised *ad nauseam*," but the only art sale they mention is one of his drawings selling for $370. I suppose it would have been beneath them to mention that he was paid $30,000 for ***Christ Leaving the Praetorium***. But what is really negative about the Doré section is the tone of the quotes. Some do contain a little praise, but usually with an accompanying put-down, as this one by the French critic Ch. Timbal (p.213):

> ... Doré must be ranked with those children, well endowed but spoiled by their gifts, who almost succeed in all that they undertake. Already crowned with so many laurels, why rests he not satisfied, and why should those of other men keep him from sleep?

But the extremes of the anti-horror group are nowhere better expressed than in their lengthy quote from Jarves's ***Art Thoughts***. It is so long as to be tedious, so we quote for you here only the most vicious portions (p.214):

> ... If the predominant trait of Delacroix was physical force, that of Doré is fiendish horror. That which devils most enjoy he most heartily depicts... Doré, in translating his *Inferno* into pictorial French, discards all humanity... The advanced theories of peace and good-will to men of our century make no impression on him... He transforms all nature into demoniacal forces... The powers of darkness are let loose. Heaven itself catches the vindictive spirit of Hell. This is art undergoing the delirium tremens, with ravings as blasphemous as they are foul and hideous. This may seem harsh judgment, but an art that distorts and misrepresents the divine attributes, engendering hate or fear in place of love and charity, is not to be dealt with gingerly... Doré's intellect is too deep for light sins... The 425 cuts of *Contes Drolatiques* form a unique monument to his debauchery of design... contaminated by its smut... an object of disgust to the one-sided pious mind. Doré seems to have faith of no kind... There is no religious sentiment in it (Doré *Bible* illustrations) ... Doré cannot draw a saint... Doré makes love, pity, charity, and faith absurd... (true art) must be natural, truthful, and humane. It should have also the instinct of the beautiful. Doré's art has almost none of these qualities. Much of it is heartless, sensual, and perverse. It refuses to elevate, or instruct, or even amuse, except the mind, like the art, be prone to obscene, cruel, or mocking levity; ... If the Devil has ever created such an office as Designer-in-chief to Hell, it is now filled by Doré.

That was written about the most popular religious artist of all time! Was anyone in the Victorian era actually neutral about Doré? How could Doré have been the greatest religious artist with entirely godly motivation, and at the same time a pathetically bad artist with despictable demonic motivation? The one thing that his French and English critics really hated was that Doré was outside of their control or influence. Doré achieved world-wide fame without their help, and in spite of their unceasing condemnation. Doré was a rebel who made the establishment insecure by appealing directly to the people.

180 (top) "early scene sketch" for film ***The Ten Commandments*** (1956) per 1970 book, ***DeMille: The Man & His Pictures*** by Essoe (p.217, no mention of Doré)

(bottom) Doré engraving for the Old Testament from ***The Doré Bible*** (1866).

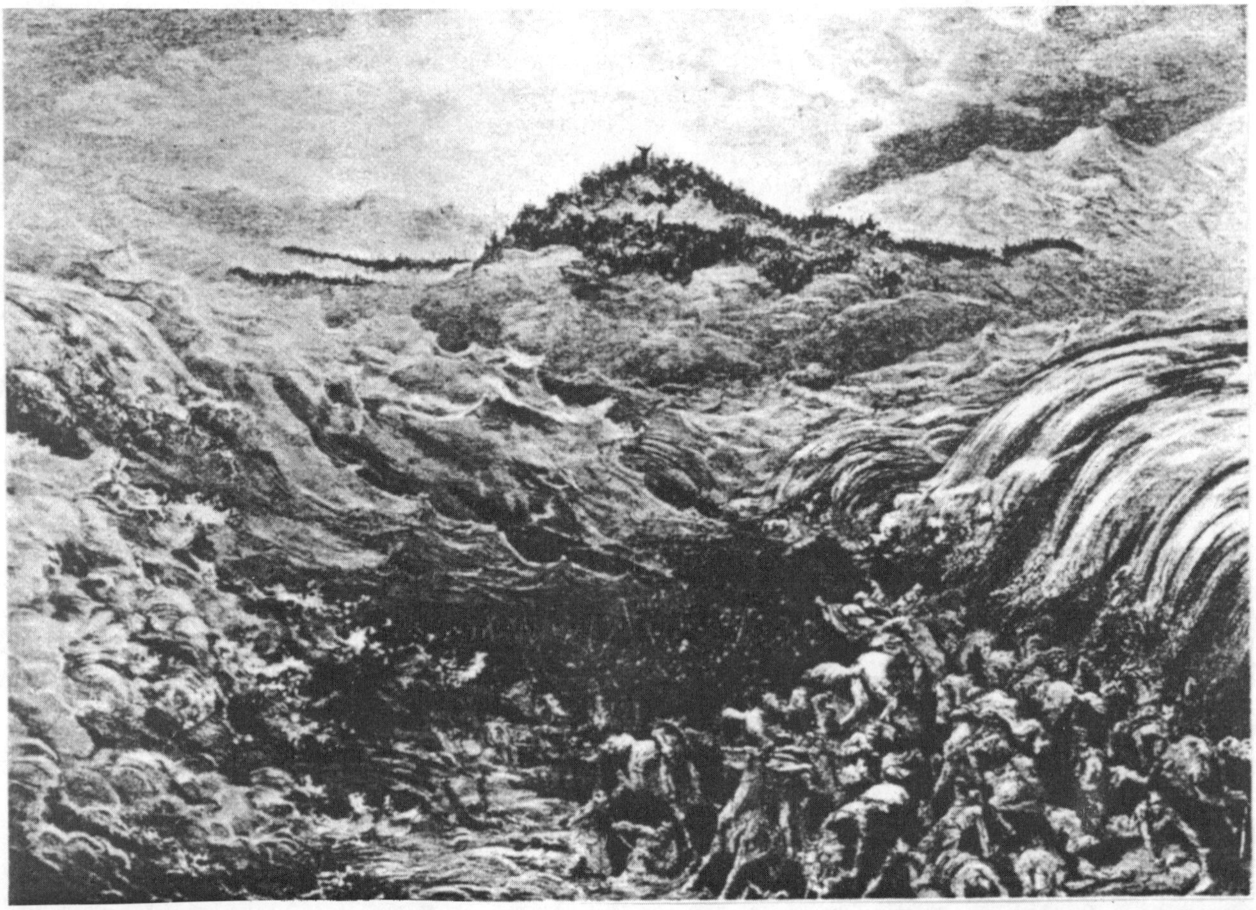

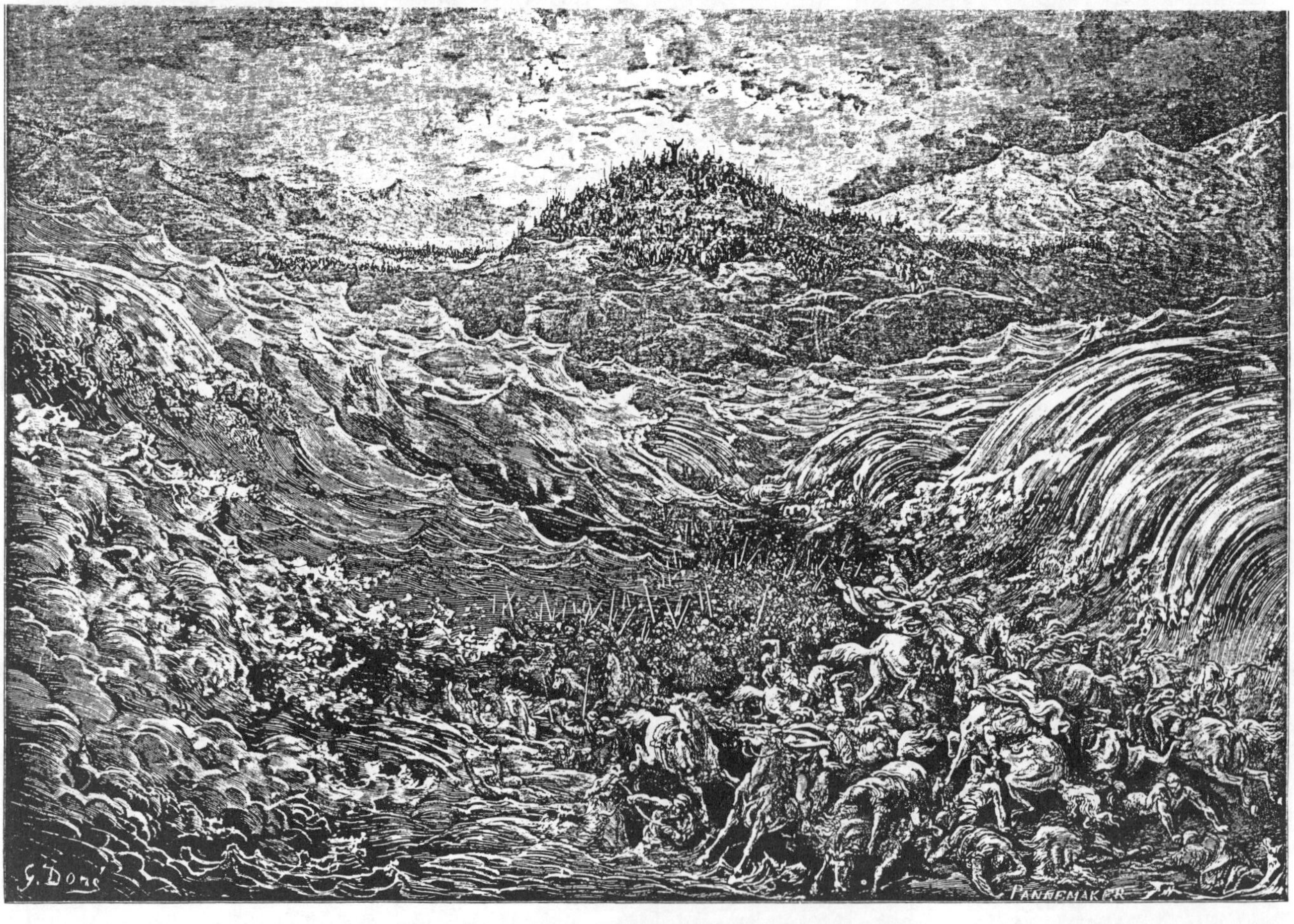

Doré's influence on Theatre & Film

Doré was also one of the earliest influences on the film industry. We mentioned the Parisian businessman who wanted to start a theatre where they would project images of Doré's ***Inferno*** engravings on a screen. Doré loved the theatre. If he had not been an artist, he would almost certainly have been in the theatre. All of his romances were with women of the stage. He also wanted to do scene backdrops. Had he lived another 20-30 years he would almost certainly have ended up in the film industry. Many actors were drawn to the theatrics of his art. Roosevelt mentions (p.427) that the great American actor Joseph Jefferson was a big fan of Doré. Doré also influenced the famous British actor/director/producer Henry Irving (1838-1905). In 1904, Cassell issued a special Henry Irving Edition of Doré's ***Dante***, signed by Irving. In the 1930 Gordon Craig biography of Irving, he has a section (p.121-124) on Doré's influence, from which we quote the following excerpts:

> DORÉ - As a producer, Irving absorbed much from the work of this Frenchman of prolific fancy - a very theatrical fancy - not only a scenical, but a dramatic fancy: Doré was illustrator, and the producer-actor is an illustrator, too...
>
> *Don Quixote* (he lists Doré engraving captions) - this is all Irving. I don't mean that Irving took these designs and did them out again in his acting version of *Don Quixote* - I mean he entered into the very essence of these designs - absorbed every scrap that was in them - added his own power to them and there, as he walks across the stage, say, in *Faust*, or comes on in *Louis XI*, there comes friend Doré, helping him.
>
> He would take a design of Doré's and put it on the stage... since the scene-painter could invent nothing better, he had it carried out, with a few changes.
>
> The Irving sense returns to you over and over again as you turn each page of Doré's *Quixote*, and feel the curious romanticism - the *curious* romanticism - of every touch. In Doré's *Dante*, it is just as evident. All Doré contains seeds of Irving, and all Irving shows the influence of this excellent inventor.
>
> ... I, who owe a debt to Doré, know quite well what it was H. I. found so excellent. Decors? ... oh dear, no. Drama expressed visually? - yes...
>
> It was not Daumier, I think, who gave Irving a clue as to how to *look* the last scene of *Louis XI*. I believe it was Doré's influence again. Had Doré seen him - had he come to supper in the Beef Steak Room, had he and Irving been together even once in their lives, I doubt whether either would have been able to help the other more than it happened without meeting. For there is no mention of Doré in Irving records, neither in Brereton's *Life* nor in Bram Stoker's *Personal Reminiscences.*

Although Doré was consumed with the French theatre, there is no evidence that he ever became enthused about the British theatre. Perhaps it was because he never really learned English. There is not one word about the British theatre in Roosevelt or Jerrold. Of course, his two main lovers, Adelina Patti and Sarah Bernhardt, were very popular in England, and we know that he fraternized with Sarah in England. There is a phrase in the above quote which is a perfect expression of Doré's theatricality. Doré was "drama expressed visually."

As the theatre gradually gave way to the film industry at the beginning of this century, Doré was also going through a transition - from fame to influence. His fame was dying out, but his 10,000 engravings provided an invaluable source of visual expression for both scenery and dramatic action, for an industry that now had to contend with background scenery that extended to the horizon, and dramatic action as big as life itself. Most early film directors and set designers had grown up on Doré engravings, and when it came time to visualize a scene that had never been done before, Doré came to mind. In the 1970 book ***DeMille: The Man and His Pictures***, by Gabe Essoe and Raymond Lee, there is an illustration on page 217 captioned "An early scene sketch for the parting of the Red Sea in *The Ten Commandments*." Though it does not mention Doré, that painting is copied from a Doré ***Bible*** engraving. We know of a van Gogh painting copied from Doré. There is also a Picasso circus painting copied from Doré. So when DeMille wanted scenery background and dramatic action for ***The Ten Commandments***, he knew where to turn. In 1956, it was the most expensive film ever made ($13.5 million), and it outsold all previous films except ***Gone with the Wind***. Many scenes in ***The Ten Commandments*** are based on Doré engravings, but he is not listed in the credits. Higham's biography of DeMille refers to Doré as DeMille's favorite artist and mentions his influence on all of DeMille's religious films.

Many early fims were influenced by Doré engravings. He was a trade secret, and they did not list scene sources. Many film history books from America, England, France, Germany, and even Russia confirm Doré's influence. Leon Barsacq's 1978 book ***Caligari's Cabinet & other Grand Illusions*** (***A History of Film Design***) contains several Doré references:

> In *Variety*, filmed in 1925 by Ewald Andre Dupont, the director made clever use of the last vestiges of expressionism, such as the view from above into the courtyard of a prison, where the circle formed by the prisoners seems to be rotating as though at the bottom of a well. Dupont and the designer, Oscar Werndorff, drew their inspiration for this scene from van Gogh's painting *The Prisoners*, which van Gogh himself had modeled on a drawing by Gustave Doré.
>
> ---
>
> ... *Dante's Inferno* (Fox, 1924), Directed by Henry Otto. The film bears no art director's credit, but the *Inferno* sequence is based on the Doré illustrations.
>
> ---
>
> ... Andrejew, of Russian origin, worked in Germany until 1932. There he designed very personal, atmospheric sets for such films as ... and above all, Pabst's *Threepenny Opera* (1931). For this film he turned for inspiration to Gustave Doré's London illustrations, and succeeded in creating an ambiance both fantastic and realistic.
>
> ---
>
> In designing the sets for David Lean's *Great*

 reduced illustrations from Michaud's ***History of the Crusades*** (1877) - contains 100 full-page plates.

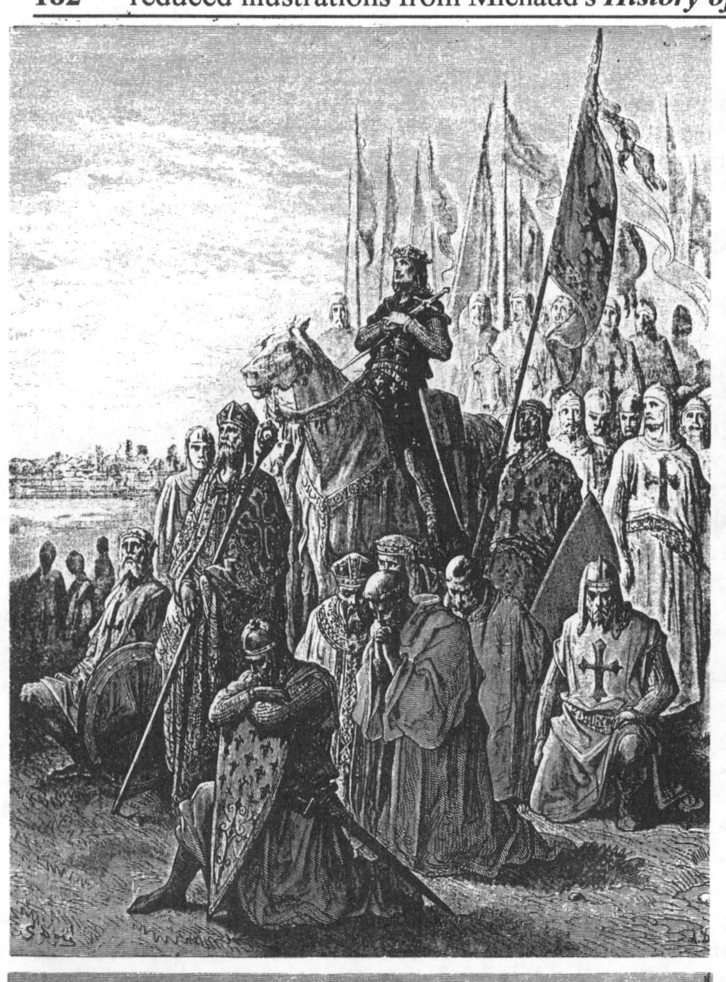

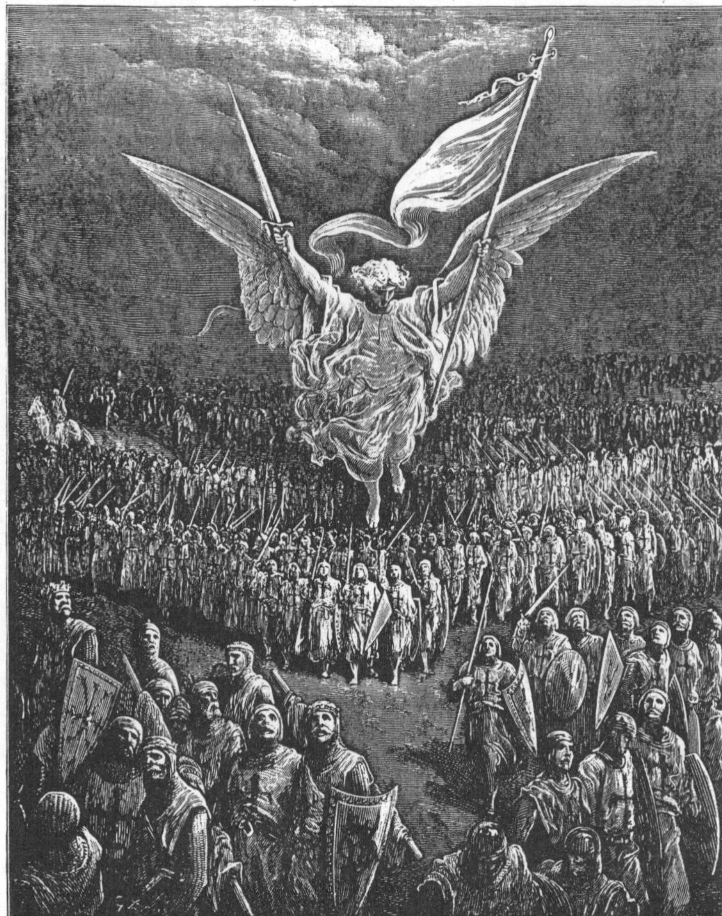

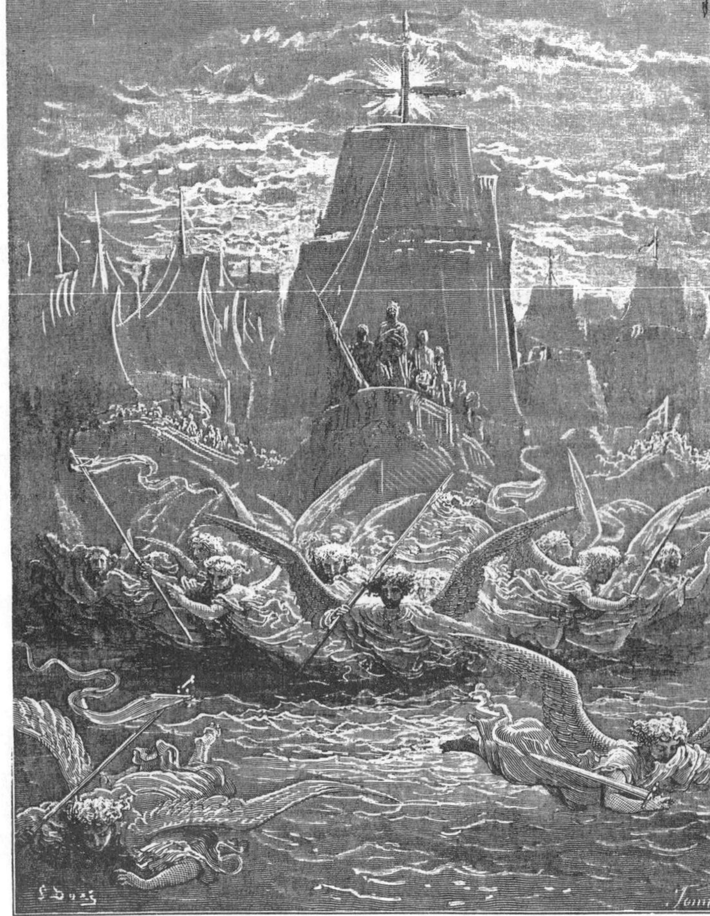

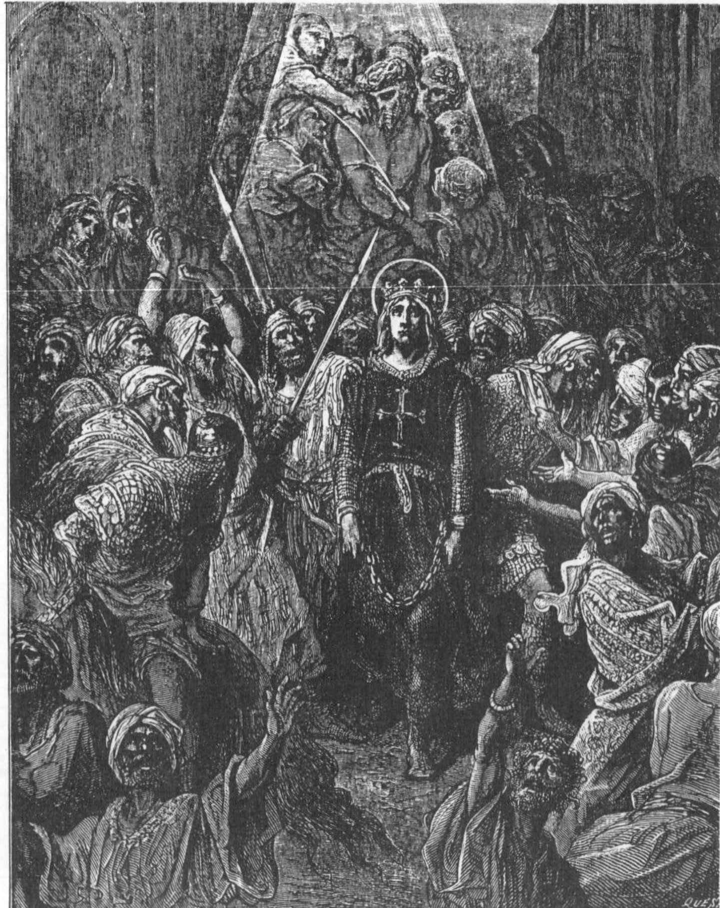

Expectations (1946) and *Oliver Twist* (1948), Bryan was inspired less by English illustrators of Dickens than by Gustave Doré's London.

Unlike the ballet film, the musical gained a new lease on life. One remarkable example is Carol Reed's *Oliver* (1968). Many of the vast, striking sets by John Box representing various districts of London, are based on Doré engravings. The necessary interpretation of reality, using simplified forms and carefully chosen colors, makes these sets a framework perfectly adapted to the production numbers.

The exhibition books for the 1983 Doré centennial also contains sections on his film influence. Here are some other films they list as being influenced by Doré:

- Murnau's *Faust* (German)
- Murnau's *Nosferatu* (German)
- Fritz Lang's *Niebelungen* (German)
- Jean Cocteau's *La Belle et la Bete* (French, 1945)
- Galeen's *Etudiant de Prague* (French?, 1926)
- Paul Wegener's *Golem* (German?)
- Harry Lachman's *Dante's Inferno* (1935)
  (chief designer Ben Carre; starring Spencer Tracy)

There are also unconfirmed reports of Doré's influence on the original ***King Kong*** (the jungle scenes from ***Milton*** engravings), and D. W. Griffith's ***Intolerance*** (1916). We have already seen his influence on ***The Man of La Mancha***. The director George Cukor was a big Doré fan (I have Doré books with Cukor's bookplate in them). It would take a major effect to see how many films have scenes based on Doré engravings. It would really be fascinating to discover how many films have actual Doré engravings as props, such as the 1995 ***Seven***.

The Revival of interest in Doré

The darkest days for Doré's reputation were the auctions in 1947 and 1964, where his paintings sold for a couple hundred dollars down to $18 apiece. All the artwork for which Fairless & Beeforth paid Doré a total of $300,000 for in the 1870s sold for less than $20,000 total about 80 years later. Yet if you added up selling prices for all those items in the 1980s, the total "retail" value would now be about $2 million. Today you would have to pay more for a steel engraving of a Doré painting than you would have paid for the painting itself 30 years ago. To analyze Doré's reputation, you must differentiate between the illustrator and the painter, the differing opinions of the English, French, and other Europeans, and you have to consider three time periods: 1865-1900, 1900-1960, and 1965-present. Before 1900, almost everyone agreed that Doré was the world's greatest illustrator. Most of the English-speaking world also considered Doré to be a great painter. The French art establishment thought Doré was a terrible painter. Most of the French people did not even know he was a painter.

Most European countries never lost respect for Doré the illustrator. The Spanish always considered him the ultimate delineator of Cervantes. Italians have always considered him the greatest illustrator of Dante. When the French seemed to forget about Doré, the Germans were all too happy to try to claim him for themselves, even though it flew in the face of Doré's attitude toward Germany. Some of the best reference books on Doré have been in German, such as Farner (1963) and Forberg (1975). The Russians have never lost their love for Doré. When the Soviet Union fell, there was a flurry of Doré editions in several languages in Russia. Jewish people are among Doré's most ardent collectors and fans, whether in the U.S., Russia, or Israel. When Israel became a nation, there was a flurry of Hebrew Doré editions.

Doré's French reputation did not improve much until the Doré centennial in 1983. There was a surge in French Doré reference books on the centennial of his birth: Valmy-Baysse, Deze, and LeBlanc. His hometown of Strasbourg has always been very supportive, with occasional exhibitions. But until recently the French have not been very excited about their native son. In 1982, Dr. Gordon Ray summed up the French attitude in ***The Art of the French Illustrated Book*** (p.326):

> The French have never taken Doré quite seriously. Most of the books about him are in English, including the principal biographies by Blanchard Jerrold and Blanche Roosevelt. When the Bibliotheque Nationale finally gave him a commemorative exhibit in 1974, it was recorded on a folding sheet, rather than in one of that institution's ample catalogues.

The year after Ray penned those words, Doré finally got some respect in France, with 1983 Doré centennial exhibitions in Paris, Strasbourg, Bourg-en-Bresse, and Le Havre, plus the ones in London and Hannover. The Strasbourg exhibition had 671 items, and their book even had photos of all 202 Doré works of art in French museums. There was also a major 1983 French book on Doré, by Annie Renonciat, with hundreds of illustrations. France even issued a postage stamp to Doré, and there was also a television documentary about him. In recent years French museums have made a concerted effort to buy major Doré works of art, even those large religious paintings from the Doré Gallery, which were so despised by the French art establishment a century earlier. An article in the November 1985 ***Burlington Magazine*** (p.828) reviewed an exhibition in the Petit Palais in Paris, entitled ***Gustave Doré et la Peinture Religieuse Monumentale***, which featured Doré oil paintings ***Ecce Homo, The Ascension,*** and ***The Vale of Tears***:

> ... three works originally produced for the Doré Gallery and recently purchased by the museum as part of its policy of promoting nineteenth century academic art. These gigantic canvases ... had slipped into obscurity following the dissolution of the Gallery ... Their return to France, in the wake of the retrospective of Doré's career mounted by Strasbourg in 1983, marks a further step in the rehabilitation of an aspect of the artist's output generally dismissed by his compatriots during his own lifetime.
>
> ... it would be valuable to investigate whether the selection and rendition of the episodes painted for the Doré Gallery were in any way tailored to English theological sensibilities.
>
> Rather than exploring the meaning of Doré's

four 1992 "comic-book" Doré adaptations by Tome Press: ***The Book of Genesis, The Life & Death of Jesus Christ, Dante's Inferno*** & ***Rime of the Ancient Mariner.***

THE BOOK OF
GENESIS

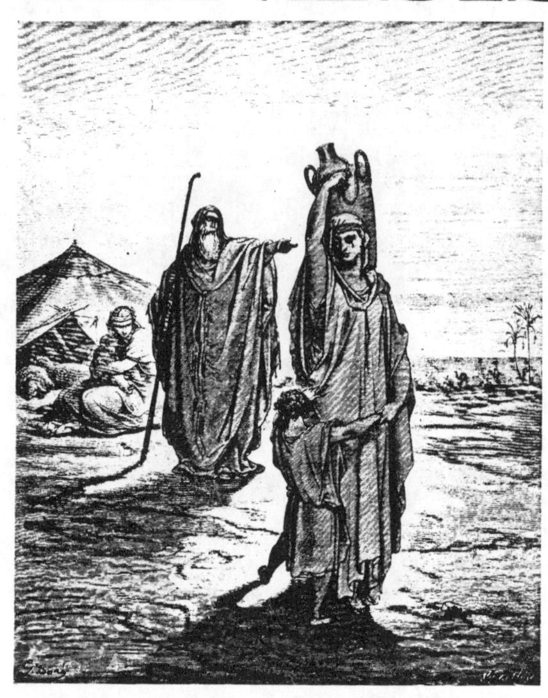

With Illustrations by
Gustave Doré

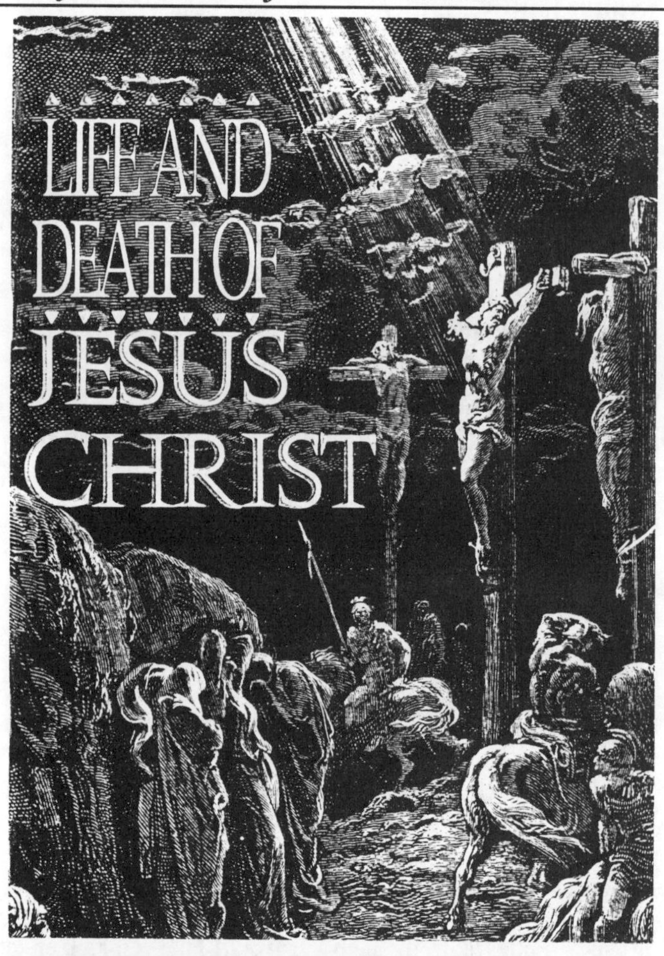

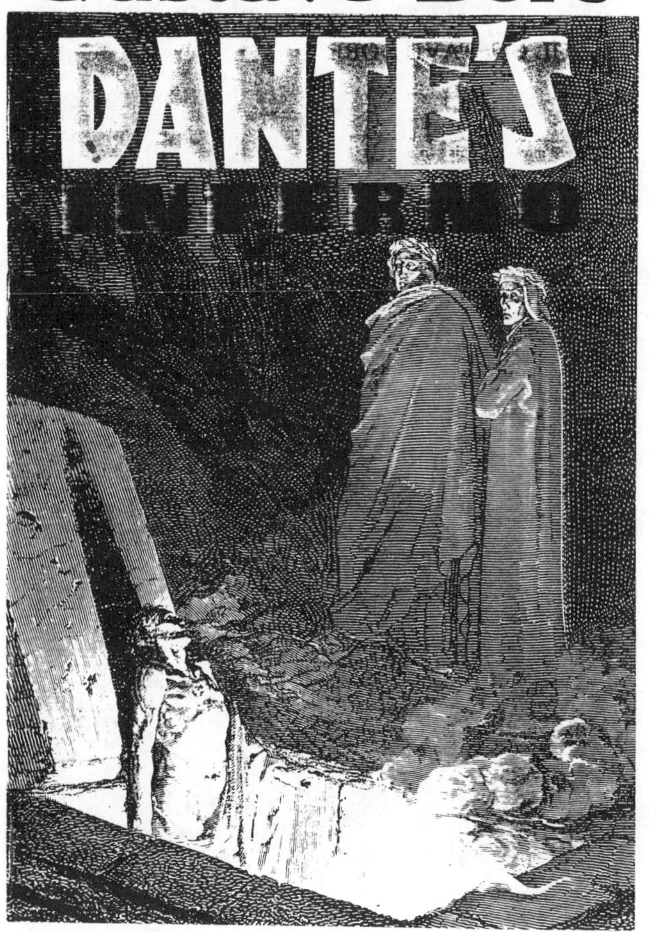

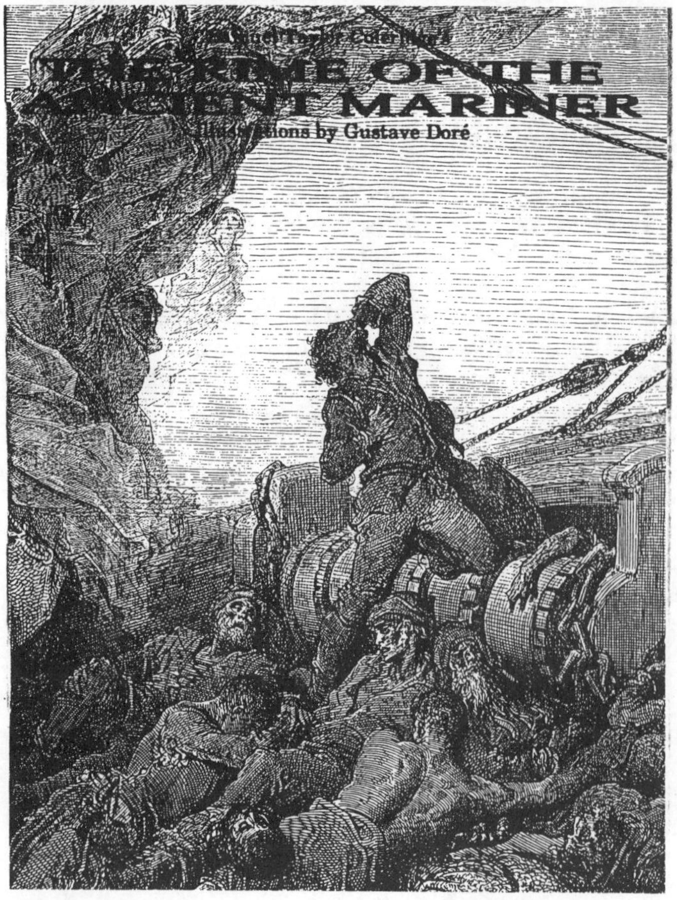

> works, the exhibition organisers chose to present them as part of a small display of French monumental religious painting, which ranged from Scheffer's *Saint Thomas d'Aquin* to Bouguereau's *Vierge aux Enfants*. Dwarfed by Doré's massive canvases, these not inconsiderable pictures ... merely served to provide a decorous chorus-line to Doré's star turn...

Further evidence of Doré's return to French artistic favor was shown in the April, 1987 article in ***Revue du Louvre*** by Nadine Lehni, *Gustave Doré: Recentes acquisitions des musees de Nantes, Bourg-en-Bresse et Strasbourg* (p.284-89), where Lehni states:

> ... As was demonstrated in the exhibition organized by Strasbourg and Paris in 1983, Gustave Doré, that talented artist, the most famous illustrator of the 19th century, was also a painter who suffered all his life because of the rejection of his paintings by the French critics of that era.

She goes on to detail recent purchases of Doré paintings, drawings, and works of sculpture by museums in three French cities. There were other Doré exhibitions in Switzerland in 1985, and another Strasbourg exhibition in 1993, not to mention the 1991 major research article on Doré sculpture. In France and England today, it is quite different from a century ago, when French art critics were personally and obsessively hostile toward Doré, and the English were tripping over one another in praising him. Today very few Brits are obsessed with praising Doré and very few French are obsessed with attacking him. Somehow during that lull he quietly slipped in the side door and took a seat among the hordes of French painters and sculptors. Today the French seem willing to just take Doré at face value, even as a painter and sculptor.

Doré's British fame faded after 1900, and his influence on other artists and the film industry was not in the public eye. When the New York Doré paintings were discovered in 1947 and sold at bargain-basement prices, the art magazines and even ***Time*** and ***Life*** took that as proof positive that Doré was really not much of an artist, and that his amazing popularity in Victorian England showed just how unsophisticated those people really were. But it is still difficult to understand how prices in the 1947 auction stayed so low, with bidders such as the French government, Cecil B. DeMille, Charles Boyer, and several other prominent Americans. Two of the highest priced items in that auction were the nudes ***Andromeda*** and ***Paolo & Francesca***, which together sold for $1,650. Four decades later, those two paintings were auctioned again, and together they sold for $1.2 million! In 1964, the London Christie's auction sold most of the Doré Gallery items that were in England, with even more dismal results, with the average Doré painting selling for about $100. Many sold for as low as $18. Doré's ***Ecce Homo*** (20 feet high by 13½ feet wide), sold in 1964 for $24, and in 1989 it was auctioned again and sold for $77,000. Now that is what I call a good return on investment. By comparison, in 1962 there was a sale (by Alain Brieux of Paris) of 30 of the original wood blocks from ***London, a Pilgrimage***. They also sold for an average of about $100 each. Doré's well-worn wood blocks were actually selling for about the same prices as his large oil paintings.

At this point we need to separate British and American Doré biographies. The two early Doré biographies - Roosevelt (1885) and Jerrold (1891) - were both very supportive of Doré as an illustrator and as a painter. Blanche Roosevelt was an American, and her personal biography is usually referred to as "gushing." Blanchard Jerrold was British, and his biography is more business oriented, although he was very close to Doré. In this century there have been four British Doré biographies, all basically negative. They were by Millicent Rose (1946), Percy Muir (1971, in ***Victorian Illustrated Books***), Nigel Gosling (1973) and Joanna Richardson (1980).

As Herendeen points out (p.306, footnote), "Rose's book might have been the best critical study had she not struggled so hard to avoid what seems to be a prevailing dislike for her subject." Indeed, Rose seems at a loss to find anything about Doré that she likes. First she discredits all of his paintings, as in her closing remark (p.65): "The paintings of Doré still to be found in our provincial galleries are not on the whole of a kind to make us regret the Atlantic disappearance of the bulk of his canvases. But his graphic work remains to us a delight." Or does it? Her final sentence belies the fact that she spent most of her book telling what was wrong with every Doré book. Her pattern was to put down several Doré folios with a sweeping remark, such as in regard to Doré's six major folios between 1866-68 (p.58): "These astoundingly prolific three years were not his best. The dangers of lack of study, already apparent in the ***Inferno***, vitiate the ***Paradise Lost*** which is simply hack work in the grand manner." That was her opinion of the most popular set of illustrations to ***Paradise Lost*** ever made. As van Gogh would have replied, "well Millicent, let us compare your folio engravings of ***Paradise Lost*** with Doré's." Even when she finds a Doré book she seems to actually like, such as ***Rabelais, Perrault, London*** or ***Cervantes***, she then goes into great detail about everything that is wrong with the book. She set the trend of hostile British Doré biographies. Decades later, Dover had her write introductions for their editions of ***London*** (1970), ***Ancient Mariner*** (1970), and ***The Bible*** (1974). In those introductions, Rose rarely mentions how "irritated" she had been with those works back in 1946.

Percy Muir wrote the most hostile review I have ever seen about an artist's works. I actually counted over 100 negative words used to describe everything remotely connected with Doré: "botched - deplorable - failure - irrelevant - vulgar - insufferable - inadequate - disastrous - atrocious - wretched - faulty - bad - very bad - shockingly bad." Muir also made over 50 detail errors about Doré. ***Victorian Illustrated Books*** is otherwise an excellent reference book. Muir added a chapter at the end about foreign influences on British illustration, and he seemed to go berserk when he got to the part about how popular Doré was in England. Muir spends eleven pages telling everything that was wrong with Doré's art. He follows Rose's pattern. He informs readers that Doré was a "shockingly bad painter," and "his reputation as an illustrator has been overrated." And he was not about to say anything good about Doré's ***Bible*** engravings (p.224):

(top row) reduced illustrations from ***Hood's Poems*** (1870) - contains 9 full-page plates.
(bottom row) reduced illustrations from ***The Works of Rabelais*** (1873) - contains 719 Doré illos.

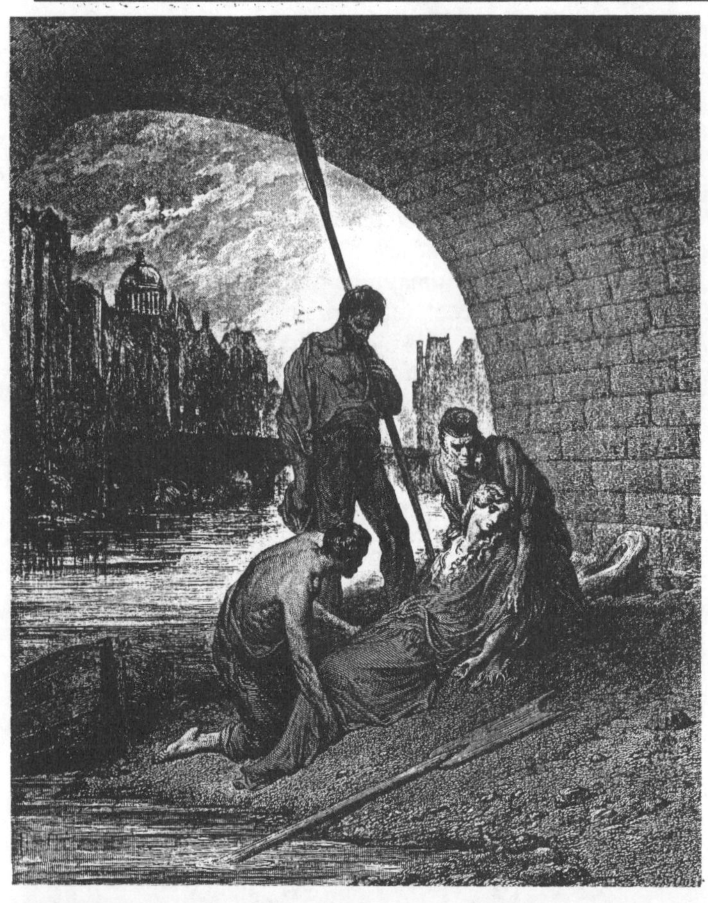

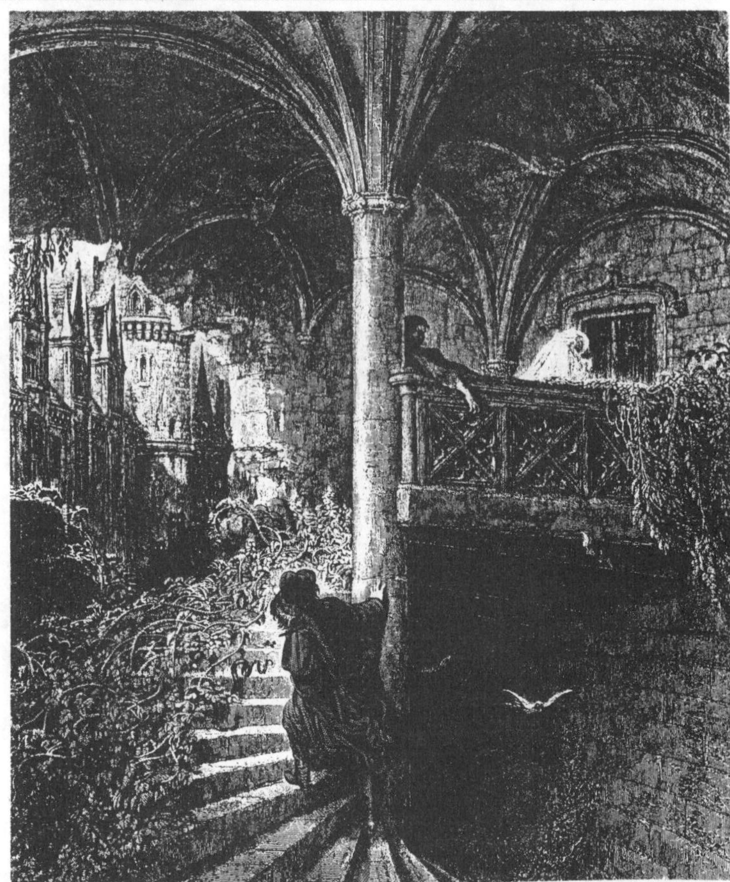

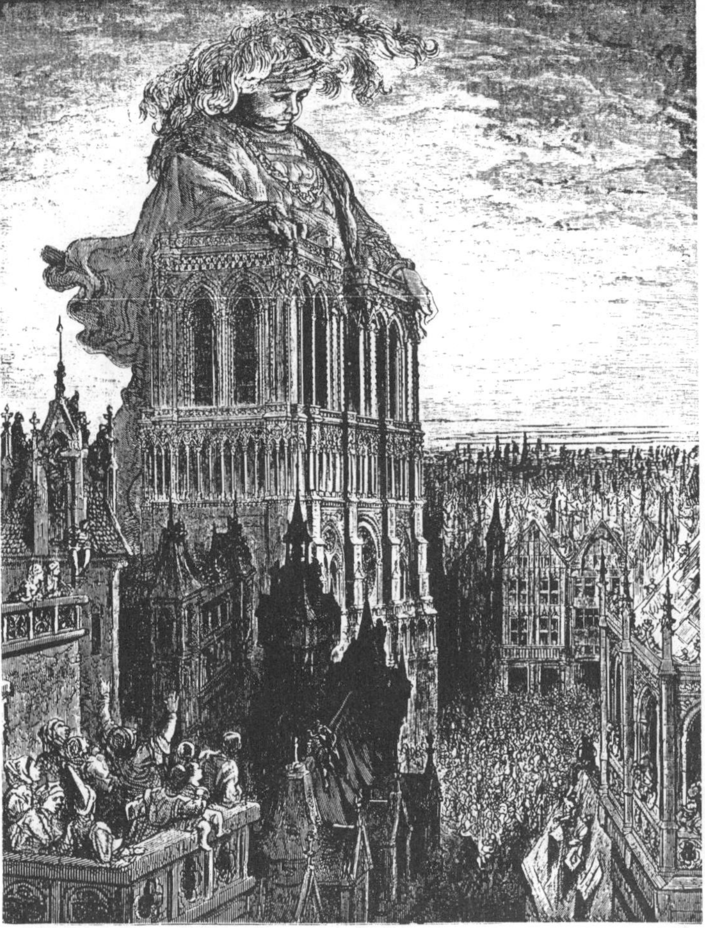

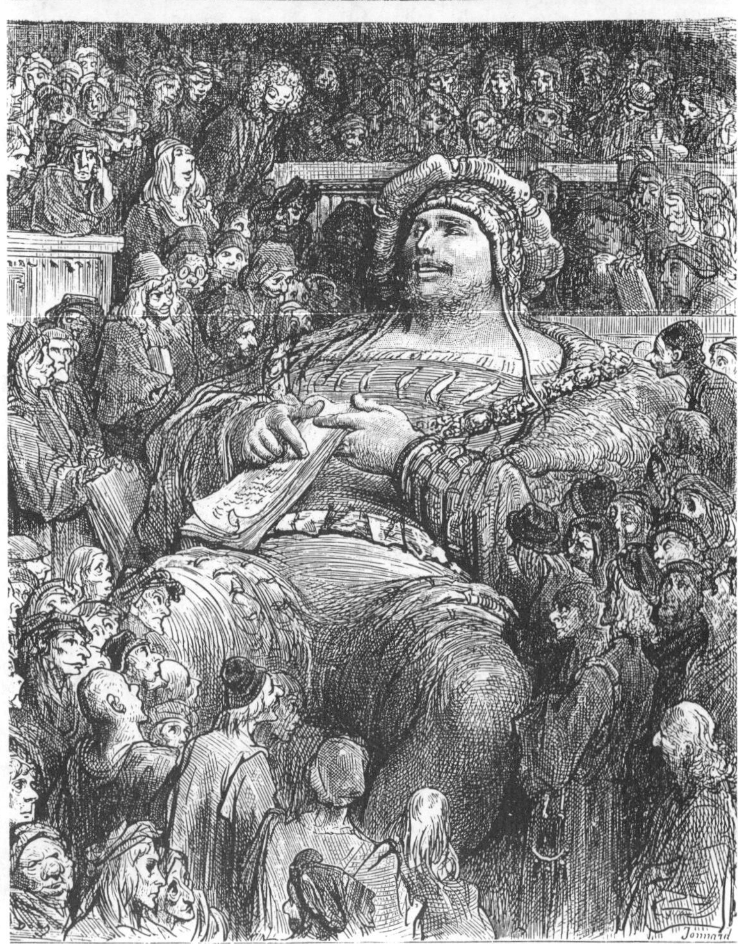

> ... The major impression created by them is that Doré was entirely the wrong man for the job. His weakness for melodrama is especially disturbing in the New Testament where, as Jerrold puts it, one is constantly reminded of "blue-fire and stage carpentry." They are, in short, frequently vulgar in the extreme, and whereas vulgarity can be accepted in connection with the earthiness of Rabelais or Balzac it becomes insufferable in a biblical context. For this reason the Doré Bible has largely failed to retain a high place in the affections of all but the most undiscriminating of Doré enthusiasts.

The "undiscriminating" Doré enthusiasts have made his ***Bible*** engravings the most popular set of illustrations ever done. Muir also uses the common criticism of the Doré ***Bible*** illustrations as being melodramatic. A couple pages later, he informs us that ***London*** was Doré's "one great *tour de force*," but those illustrations are "legitimately melodramatic." In an example of the elitist double-talk common among Doré critics, Muir is saying that melodrama is bad when it is in a book he does not like, and good when it is in a book he likes.

Gosling follows the same tradition. He informs us (p.80) that with a very few exceptions (the ones he likes) Doré's "entire output as an oil-painter must be written off." Part of his evidence for such a conclusion was the then recent auctions of 1947 and 1964. So while Gosling was writing off the Doré paintings, those who were lucky enough to have purchased them saw paintings for which they had paid $24 sell for $77,000 two decades later. Like Muir, Gosling is both negative and erroneous about many of Doré's most popular sets of illustrations. Gosling describes Doré's ***Balzac*** as a "flop," and claims that it was banned in Britain until the 20th century, when there were dozens of 19th century Doré editions. But his favorite word appears to be "failure," and he often describes Doré works as failures when they were the most popular illustrations ever done for that title. He is very hostile toward Doré's religious paintings, and actually tries to evaluate Doré in terms of modern politics, when he compares Doré's ***Bible*** and ***London*** illustrations (p.98):

> Doré's compassion here seems rooted in the solid facts of Freidrich Engel's *State of the Working Classes in England* which had appeared in 1844, and his drawings make - typically, a generation later - the perfect visual counterpart to it. It was doubtless the same admirable sentiment which he tried so hard to produce in his religious paintings. But as soon as his feet left solid documentary ground, his over-active fancy swept him out of his depth. However even here, among portentous disasters like his *Triumph of Christianity* or the operatic *Entry of Christ into the Praetorium* (sic), a few honestly felt images emerge. The doubt-ridden *Neophyte* which so obsessed him that he etched it nine times still makes an effect today.

After Rose, Muir, and Gosling, Richardson seems rather mild. She is basically from the old Ruskin school. Her major complaint with Doré is his excessive horror and violence. She also does not think much of his paintings, but at least she does not make it quite so political. She also delves much deeper into the negative consequences of Doré's relationship with his mother. The 1983 London Doré exhibition book reveals a true British Doré enthusiast - Samuel Clapp. He also contributed to the French exhibition books and the recent comprehensive research on Doré works of sculpture. Clapp's Doré collection was purchased in 1993 and put on exhibition in the Musee d'Art Moderne in Strasbourg.

About the only American biographical work on Doré in the first half of this century was by Hellmut Lehmann-Haupt in 1943, in ***The Terrible Gustave Doré***. The strange title refers to Doré's art as being terrifying to a child. On the whole he is quite supportive of Doré. His main point of reference is his early childhood recollection (growing up in Germany before World War I) of Doré's works, so it is really more from the German perspective than an American perspective, although many of his memories are similar to those of Cecil B. DeMille. Lehmann-Haupt was himself to become quite a distinguished author in the U.S. I managed to acquire a copy of his book which was signed and contained the following inscription:

> THE TERRIBLE GUSTAVE DORE *was written as an escape gesture when the war started in the fall of 1939. It was also a somewhat sentimental tribute to a childhood friend, who had pleased more than he had terrified.*
>
> *The author soon enough discovered that there is no such thing as escape. He now cocks a wary eye at the text of this little book, which in his absence overseas got itself elected into the "50 Books of the Year." The author feels that he has not done full justice to Gustave Doré.*
>
> *August 1, 1949 HL-H*

By the 1960s, Doré had been out of fashion in the U.S. for generations, despite the continued reprinting of his works. But in the 1960s, several people (mostly Americans) stood up and fought the current. One of the earliest was Henry Pitz, who was himself a highly respected American illustrator. In his 1963 ***Illustrating Children's Books***, he made this concise statement about Doré's true significance (p.55-56):

> But the idolized illustrator of the latter half of the century was Paul Gustave Doré. No illustrator up to his time had such widespread influence; his books were sold in great numbers in England, America, and throughout Europe. With a few exceptions his volumes were large-paged, bulky, and generously pictured. His fairy tale subjects were produced for adults as well as children. They were meant for the parlor table and polite family consumption. But we know from countless sources that the children took over Doré, and several generations of them were enchanted by his pictures.
>
> Doré, once the most applauded illustrator of his day, is now treated with indifference. His faults have been exaggerated, his virtues minimized; but he had magnificent gifts that cannot be ignored. No illustrator today could hope to match his incredible fecundity and wide-ranging draughtmanship.

 reduced illustrations from Coleridge's ***Ancient Mariner*** (1876) - contains 42 full-page plates.

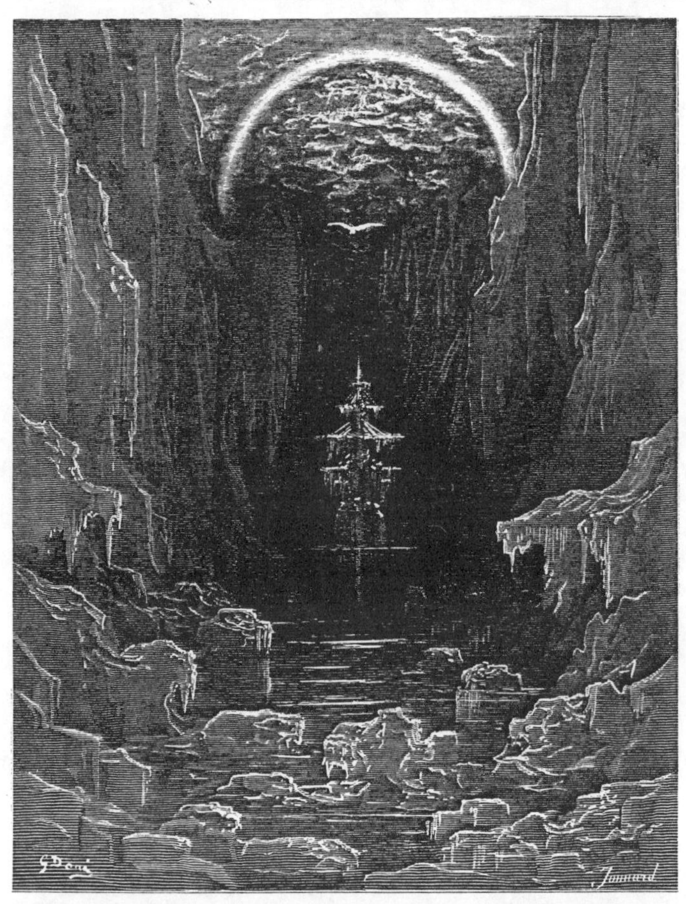

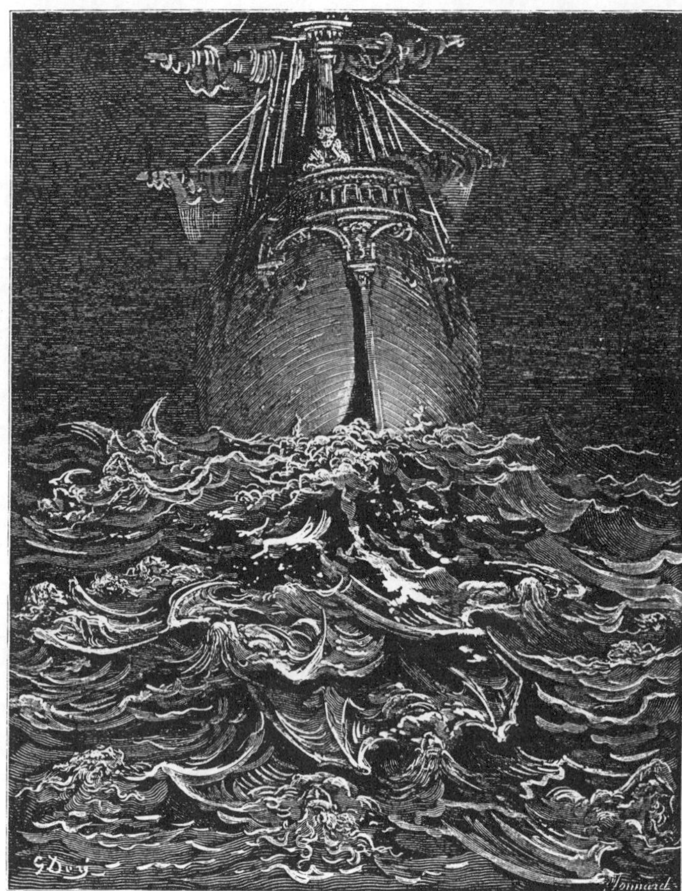

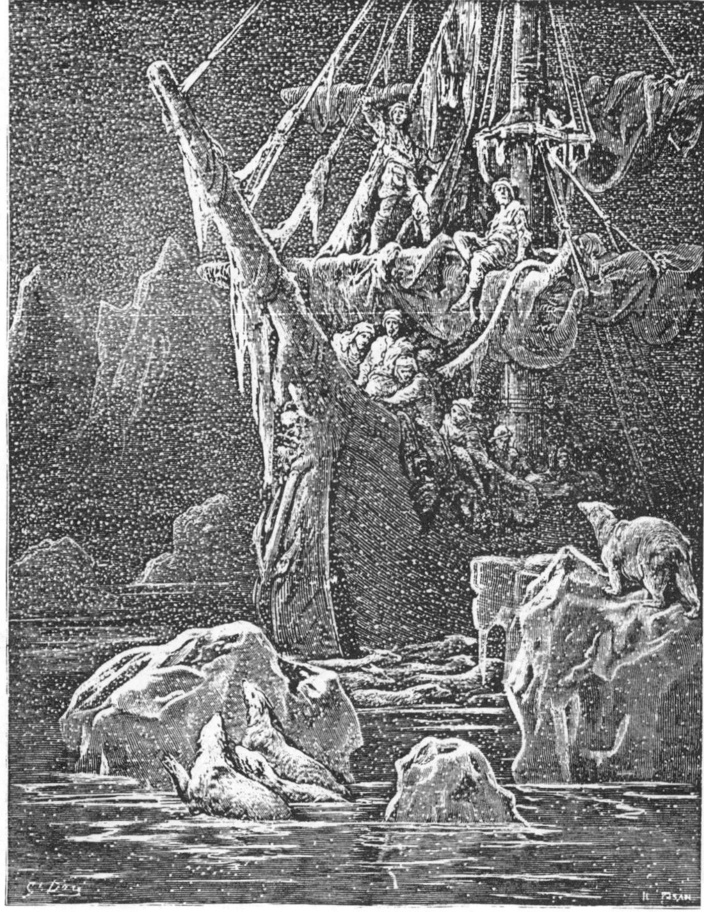

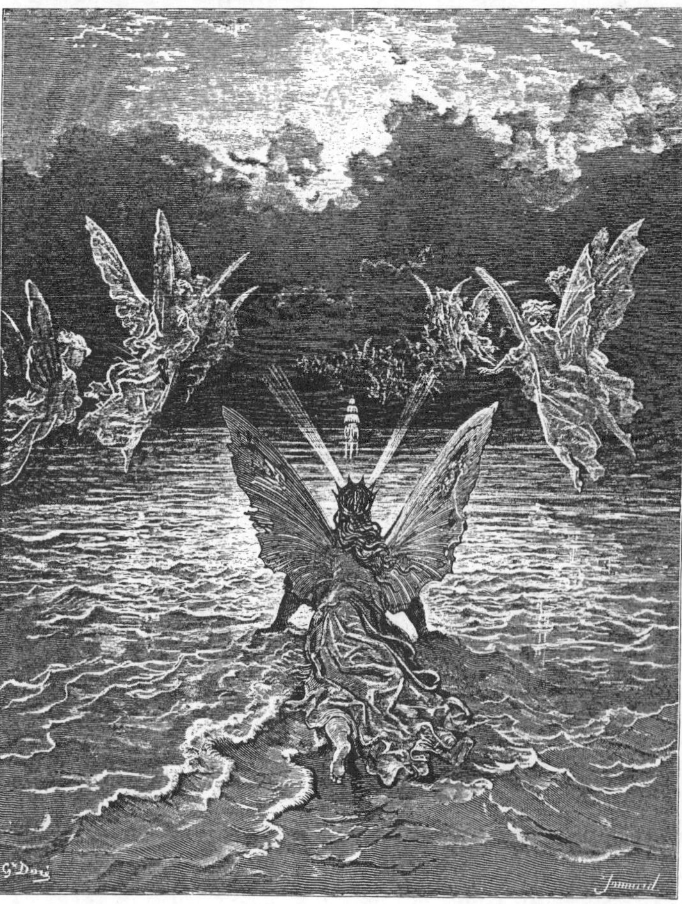

Another 1963 book was Ruari McLean's ***Victorian Book Design***. Its format is similar to Muir, but McLean's attitude about Doré is just the opposite of how Muir treats Doré. McLean only contains a couple of brief references to Doré, the main one being the following (p.160):

> But perhaps the finest and most original book of monochrome wood engravings published in London during this period was the work of a Frenchman, Gustave Doré (1832-83). This was his *London, a Pilgrimage*, with a text by Blanchard Jerrold, published by Grant in 1872. Doré's illustrations, to the Bible, to *Paradise Lost*, to *Don Quixote*, to Dante, Balzac, Rabelais, Perrault, and even the *Ancient Mariner*, make the English illustrations of the 'sixties look puny.

The first two Doré titles to be "revived" during the 1960s were ***The Ancient Mariner*** and ***London***. We already reviewed the powerful support of the Doré ***Mariner*** illustrations by Martin Gardner and Anthony Burgess. But McLean, Kenneth Clark and others also began to assert that Doré's ***London*** engravings were the best visual expression of the social class struggle ever created. By the 1970s, there were numerous Doré anthologies, with important introductions by Eric DeMare, Marina Henderson, and others. Dover began their series of Doré reproductions, with nearly a dozen titles still in print. Doré's ***Russia*** also finally saw print in English, as well as new English editions of many old Doré titles. We also mentioned at length Kunzle's recent research on Doré's early comic-strip art.

In the Spring of 1982, the Pierpont Morgan Library in New York had an exhibition of some 400 French illustrated books, mostly from the collection of Dr. Gordon Ray. They had a similar exhibition of British illustrated books in 1976. The 1982 exhibition resulted in a massive 2-volume 557-page book ***The Art of the French Illustrated Book: 1700 to 1914***, by Gordon Ray. It has a 23-page section on Doré. Ray had some of the rarest early Doré books (such as ***Hercules***), from the famous Michael Sadleir collection. That exhibition was just books and original drawings. While Ray was willing to point out the flaws in Doré's work, he was still an unabashed Doré enthusiast. Here is the end of his Doré introduction (p.329):

> Looking at Doré's total accomplishment, one can hardly deny that he is not merely one of the most popular but also one of the greatest of all illustrators. His output was enormous... He was the last great Romantic illustrator...

Perhaps the best critical analysis of Doré's reputation in Victorian England was in the Spring 1982 issue of ***Victorian Studies***, in a 24-page article by Wyman H. Herendeen of the University of Toronto, entitled *The Doré Controversy: Doré, Ruskin, and Victorian Taste*. Here are a few excerpts:

> ... There is really no solid criticism of Doré and his work; he seems fated to be eternally revived for the popular culture of succeeding generations.
>
> ---
>
> There is no doubt that if Doré's popularity was great, his publicity was even greater. The prolific artist glutted the market with his work - not only with his illustrations of books and journals, but with his paintings, water-colours, and sculptures as well. He attempted to make his name and imaginative vision inextricably associated with the art of the period, much as Picasso did in the twentieth century. Like Picasso, he inundated his public with his name universally known throughout Europe and, nearly to the same extent, North America.
>
> ---
>
> ... Nor should he simply be regarded as another nineteenth-century fashion, for the impact of his art was extremely complex. His popularity aggravated critical opinions: "serious" critics tended to reject him instinctively, while his advocates, however intelligent, were inevitably compromised by the wave of popular enthusiasm. The critic, journalist, and disciple of Ruskin, P. G. Hamerton, identifies this polarity ... "the very popularity of Doré is itself a circumstance to be noted against his chances of recognition by the highest class." Not the mood, but the very substance of the debate is defined by these social and intellectual factions which divided the London art world. They were simply more extreme and complicated where Doré was concerned...
>
> ---
>
> The genial and boyish Doré troubled his critics, whoever they were and whichever faction they represented. As the critics themselves realized, this was to some extent the result of the fame which, hollow or sound, could not be ignored. And so, notwithstanding Doré's sometimes facile effects and his delight in the sensational, he still commanded serious attention; his art provoked harangues from the critics who would have liked to ignore him, and sometimes embarassed those who would praise him. With its vividly imaginative and grossly physical qualities, his art drew critics unwittingly into a steamy realm of moral ambiguity where the voluptuous and cerebral couple, and in this Doré is rather like Keats. But even more than the poet, Doré, in the excesses of his scenes, evokes contradictory responses from his audience, and contradiction is the essential aspect of his technique...
>
> ---
>
> These qualities made Doré defensible and vulnerable from all sides of Victorian taste. On one level, they inspired controversy about technical aspects of his art. He was praised for his realistic detail and precision and criticized for being "dodgy" and inaccurate for the sake of sensational effects. Critics complained that he made minute architectural oversights in his *London*, and that he had woodcutters using saws rather than axes in his fanciful forests. They also objected that he was too accurate in his Spanish scenes, however, and that it would have been better had he never visited Spain, since the realism detracts from the fantasy. When he was meticulous he was "busy," when he worked for general effects he was "careless."
>
> ---
>
> In their confusion, Doré's critics were led to contradictory positions that reveal still profounder

reduced illustration from Poe's ***The Raven*** (1883) - contains 26 full-page plates.

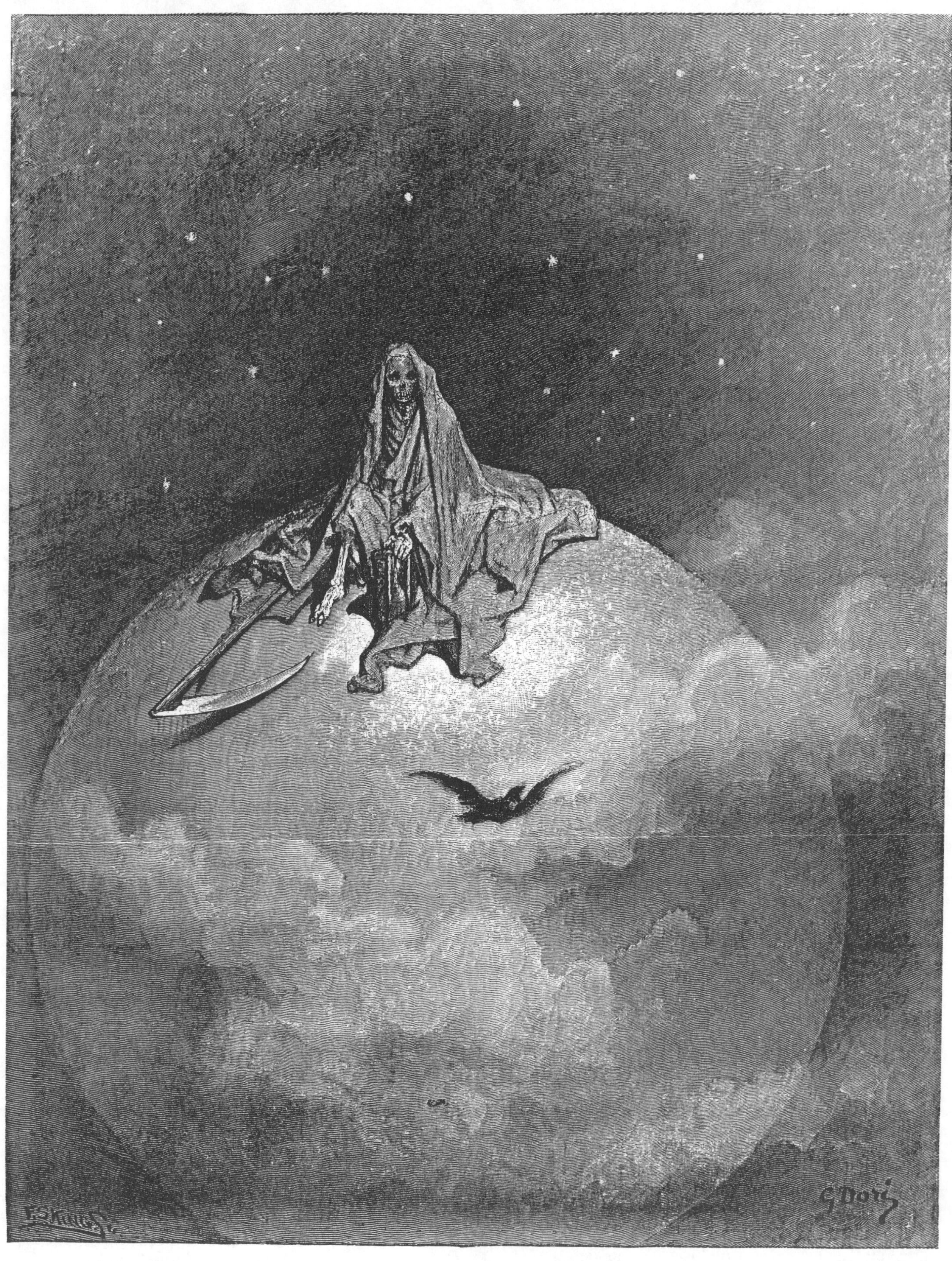

levels of moral and aesthetic disorientation. They lauded his skillful and powerful effects, but at the same time felt compelled, often reluctantly, to disapprove of them. One critic writes with enthusiasm of how Doré's "art revels in all the delirium of a wild and luxurious imagination, or subsides into the fearful dreamings of an unearthly one." ... Ultimately these critics come down on the side of restraint at the expense of artistic expression...

What becomes clear from this critical ambivalence is that Doré's public was not quite certain whether his work was inherently wicked or morally salubrious. Some regarded his paintings, drawings, and illustrations as elevated, refined, pious, and yet powerful, while others found them dangerous, lewd, corruptive - and powerfully so. Thus the Bond Street Gallery was variously regarded as the mecca of the pious London tourist, and the hell-hole of moral and aesthetic degeneracy... While a good many matrons did regard the Gallery as a safe Sunday outing, according to Ruskin, "they had better see the devil" than stop to see Doré's paintings... What becomes clear, though, is that the critics' moral criteria for judging art are useless in the case of Doré, who appears at once moral and immoral, humane and insensitive, ameliorative and disinterested, chaste and lewd.

In Doré the nineteenth century was confronted with an unsettling image of itself and its values. He brings to the surface sensitivities which were commonly suppressed, and in this context, John Ruskin's response to his work is particularly illuminating, for it was generally in terms of his theories that Doré was criticized. Ruskin, more than any other, established and articulated the moral and aesthetic standards of the mid-nineteenth century. As the century advanced and the Impressionists usurped the place of Turner and the Pre-Raphaelites, his theories became outmoded. Ruskin recognized the corruption of his own ideas and read in this the decline of the age and its art. His disillusion and sense of his own failure intensified during the sixties... During the same years, Doré's popularity soared, feeding, it would seem, on Ruskin's own diminishing influence... At this time Ruskin seemed to see in Doré the personification of his nemesis and the symbol of his failure, and his denunciations of the artist became more frequent and vehement... despite his repugnance Ruskin was intrigued by Doré and watched his career closely and with fascination... Doré occupied a special place in Ruskin's imagination, and in his response to the artist we hear the voice of the age anguished in transition.

That Doré should illustrate the Bible and Tennyson was appalling to Ruskin. Doré led the nation towards licentiousness and away from the cultural values Ruskin idealized. Even in these illustrations which others regarded as refined and chaste, Ruskin apprehends an obscenity and sexual corruption that springs from the deepest moral depravity... Doré is a seductive Comus, enchanting rural and urban Britain, defiling her maidens, weakening her sons, leaving the entire realm in debauched confusion. His treatment of sacred and secular subjects - whatever Doré did - was of a kind: "The whole art of Gustave Doré [is] one slimy efflux of the waters of Styx."

For Ruskin all of Doré's work represents the corruption of the times... one of the illustrations of the *Contes Drolatiques* drove him to exclaim that all the illustrations are "in a word, one continuous revelry in the most loathsome and monstrous aspects of death and sin, enlarged into fantastic ghastliness of caricature, as if seen through the distortion and trembling of the hot smoke of the mouth of hell... of all the 425, there is not one, which does not violate every instinct of decency and law of virtue or life, written in the human soul."

It took a century for someone to actually try to understand why Doré produced such radically and dramatically opposite reactions in intelligent Victorian adults. At a certain point (about 1865), Doré entered a domain as an illustrator where no one had gone before. He was not just prolific. He was producing a type of illustration that was unique. And it was not just bigger illustrations with more detail. There was a powerful imaginative quality to them. Many people loved his work, some hated it, but neither group really understood why. It was much more than just being jealous of his popularity. He revealed more about life and human nature than some people wanted revealed. The common people just enjoyed his work. Were they superficial? Most of his critics were intellectuals. Were they elitists? The other element was diversity. Not only were they powerful, but they covered every illustrative topic imaginable. Even today, Doré critics are really people who like certain works and dislike others. That often tells you more about them than it does about Doré. There are few greater challenges than trying to be neutral about Doré's artwork.

Doré is all around you, if you just know what to look for. Now that all his engravings are in the public domain, it seems like everyone keeps borrowing them. Doré was the ultimate literary artist. Most people cannot conceive of ***Dante, Milton, Cervantes, Rabelais, Tennyson, Perrault, Chateaubriand, LaFontaine, Ariosto, The Bible, The Ancient Mariner, The Raven, Baron Munchausen***, etc. without visualizing Doré. Just as Jules Verne's stories take us to other worlds, so Doré's drawings take us to other lands that existed in his creative imagination. Doré was like a comet, lighting up the night sky in a ball of fire and then disappearing into the darkness. But unlike a comet, Doré left gifts behind for us. We can open a Doré folio and see what it was that so enthralled Victorian audiences about Doré's art. I never tire of turning those pages, of dreaming the dreams he dreamed, of visiting the lands that filled his fertile imagination, of seeing the sights that he uniquely saw. Doré never really lived in this world, he lived in the world of imagination.

192 (top row) reduced illustrations from Perrault's ***Fairy Tales*** (1862) - contains 42 full-page plates.
(bottom row) reduced illustrations from L'Epine's ***Croquemitaine*** (1863) - contains 177 Doré illos.

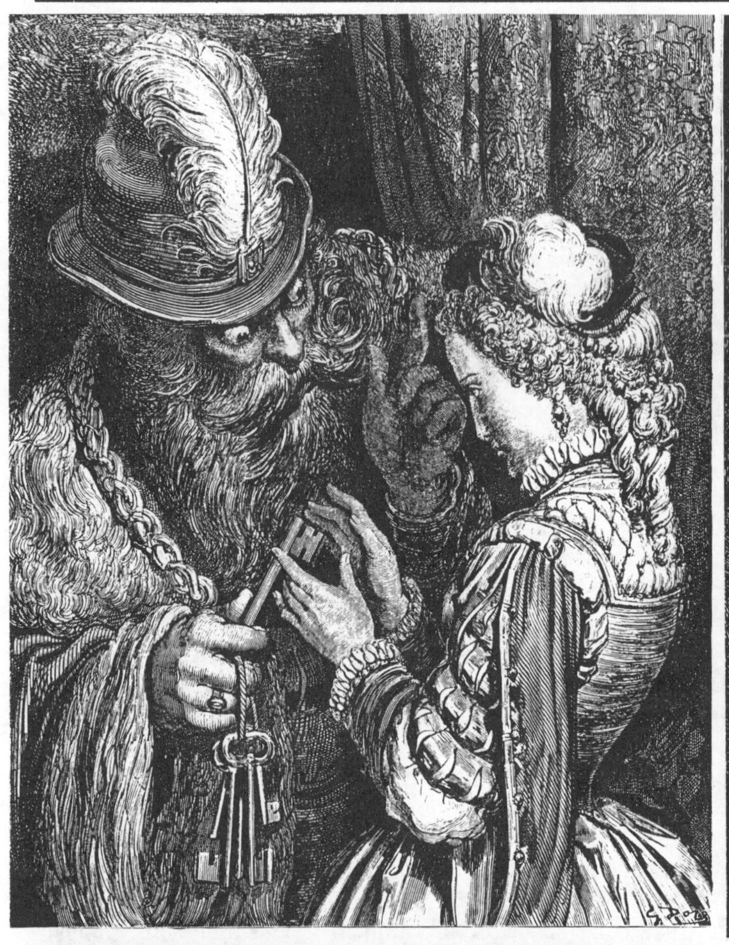

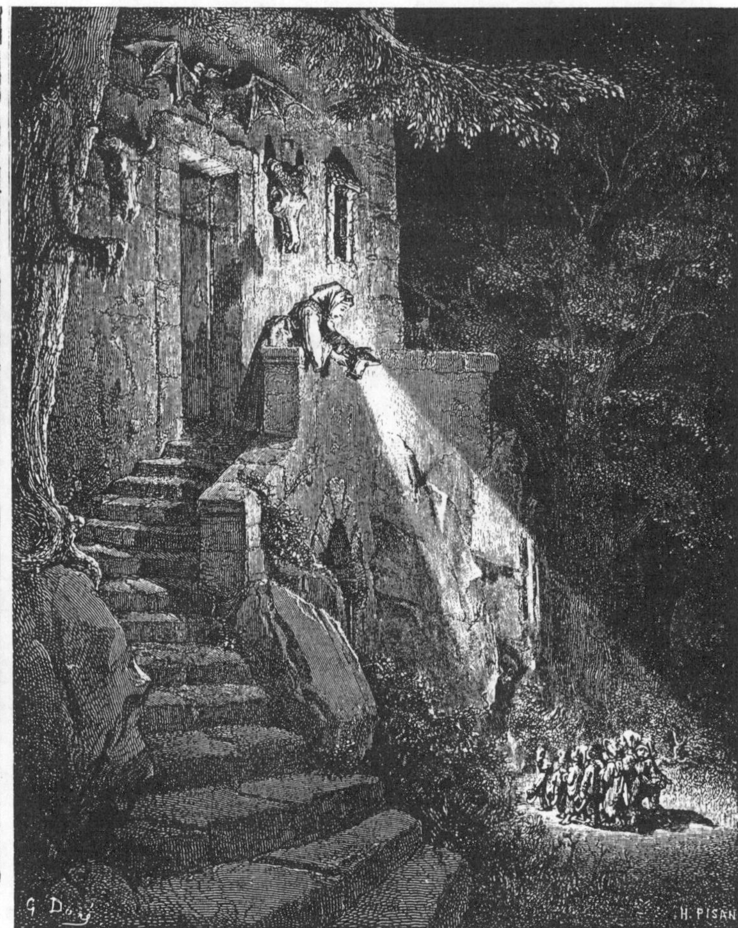

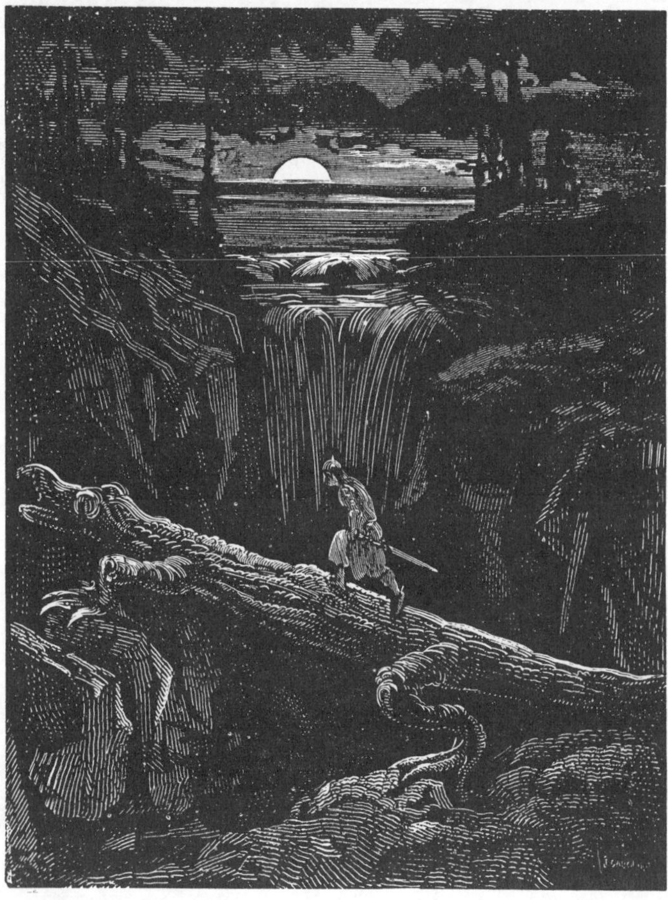

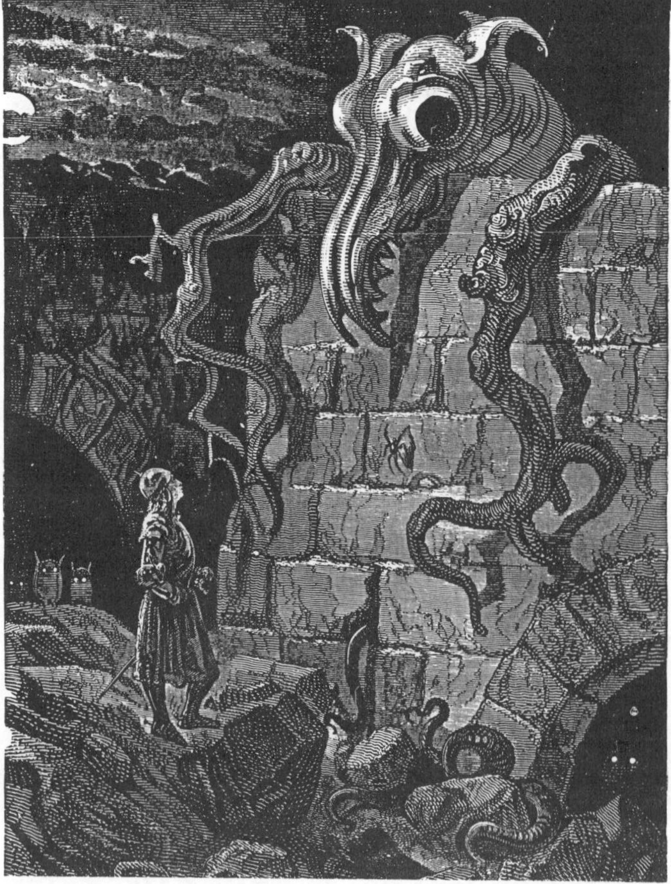

INDEX (Illustration pages listed in **bold**)

196 (top row) reduced illustrations from ***Arabian Nights*** (1865) - contains 20 Doré illos.
(bottom row) reduced illustrations from Shakespeare's ***Macbeth*** (no book edition) - 16 Doré illos.

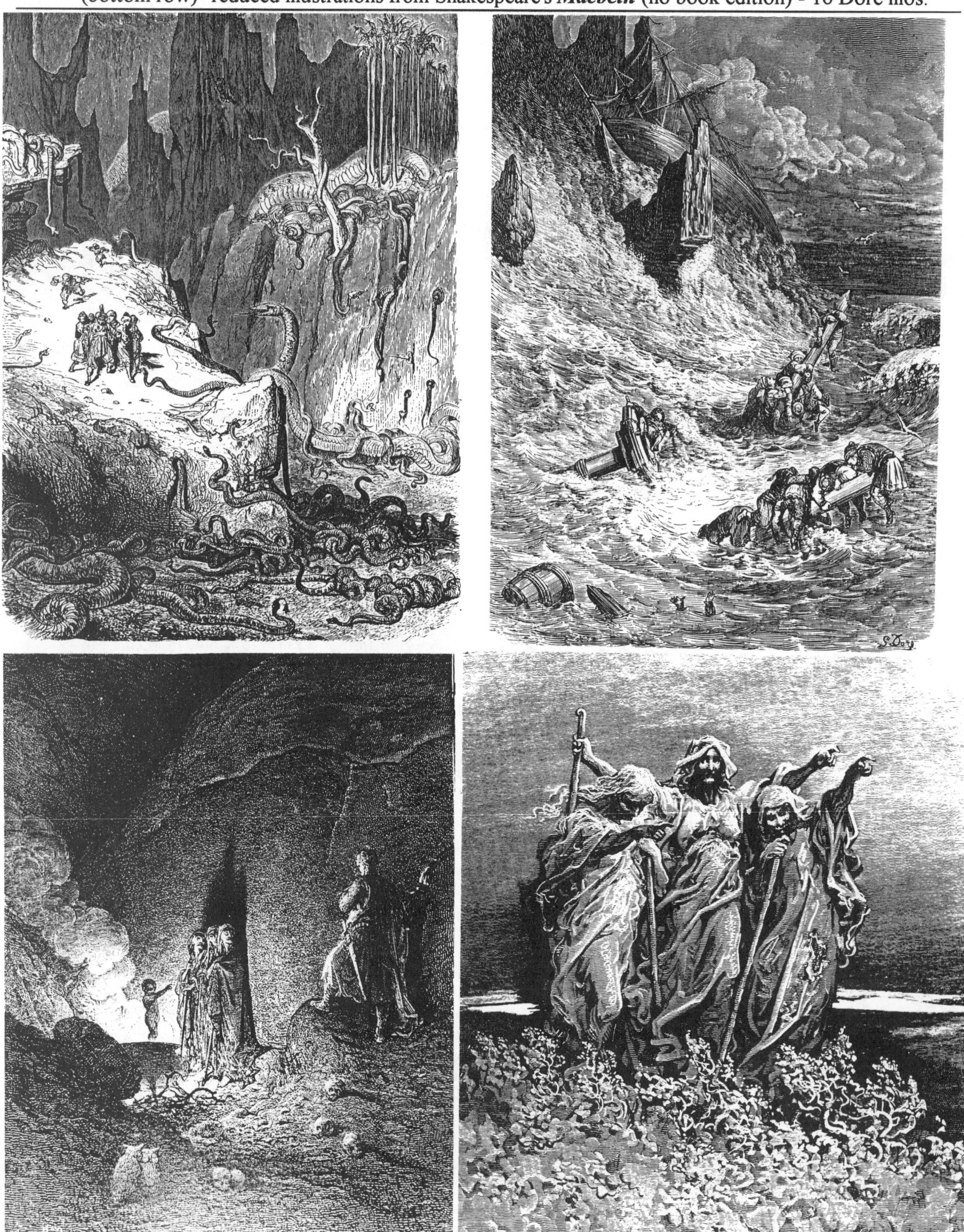

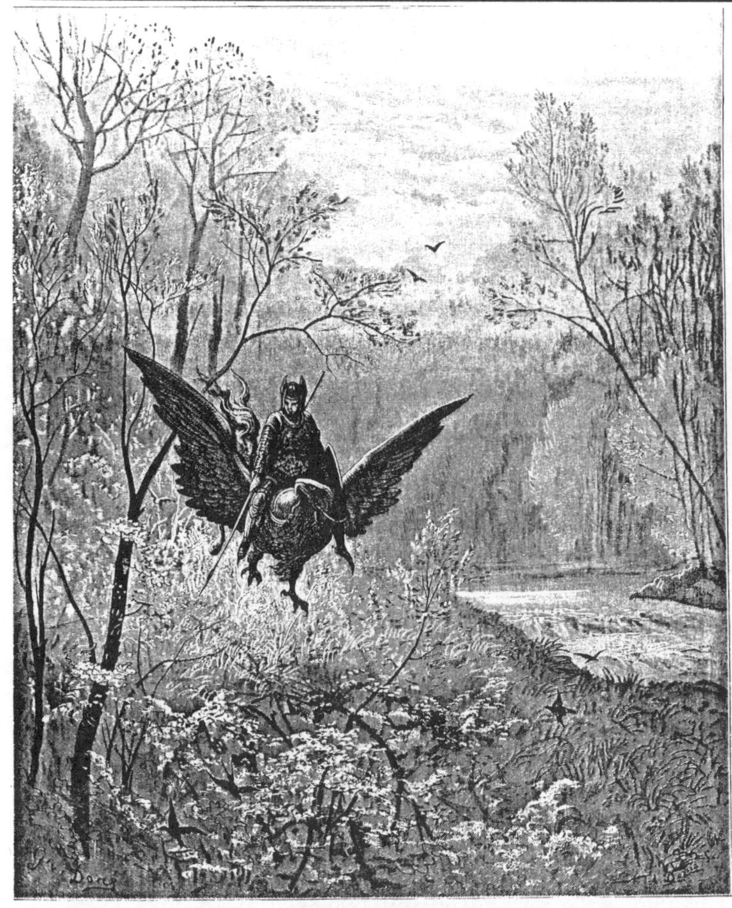

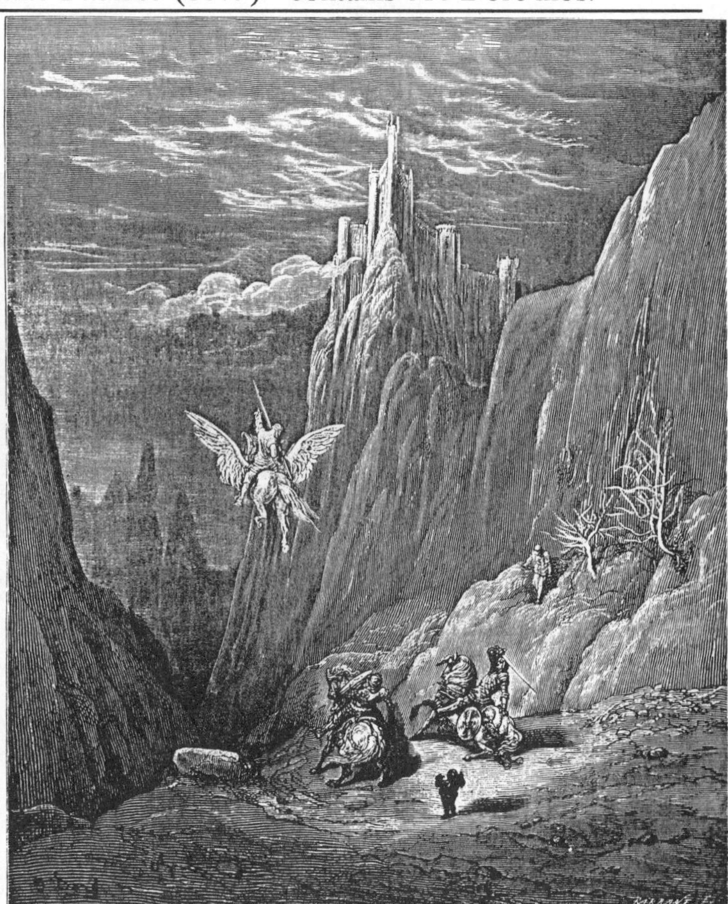

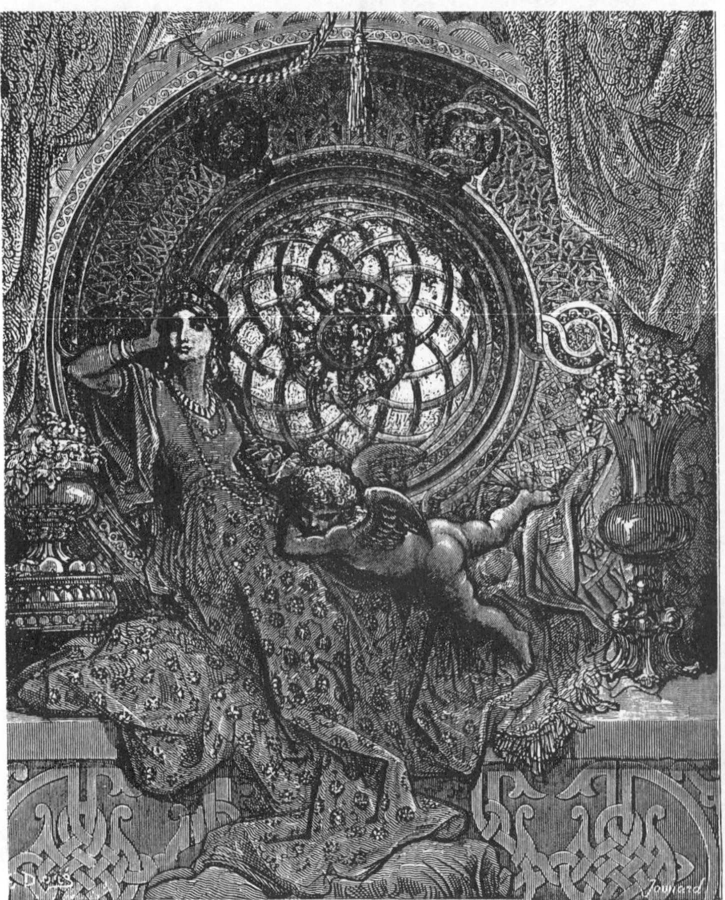

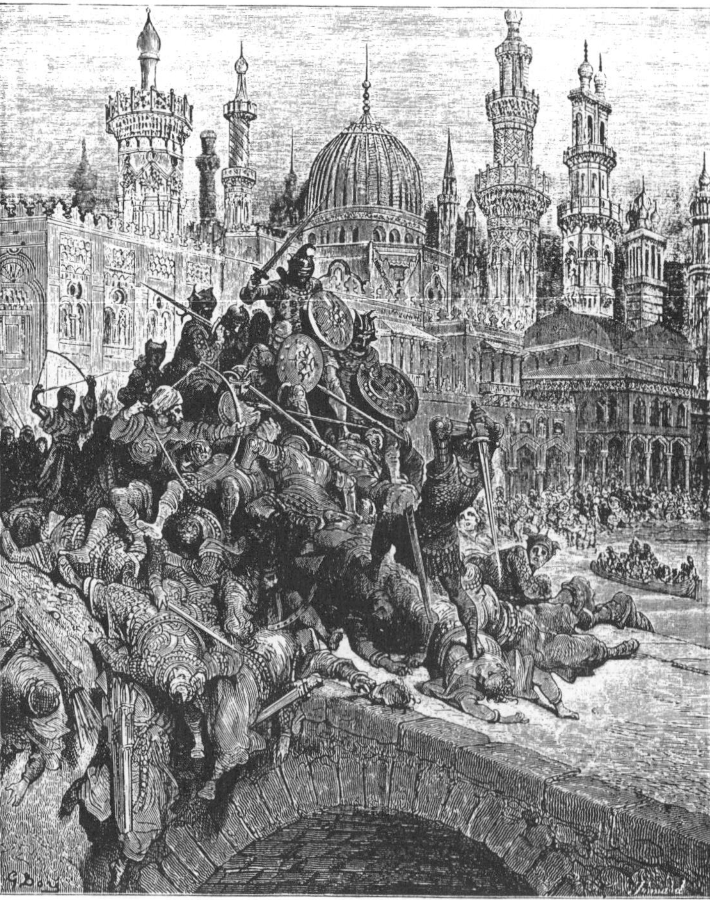

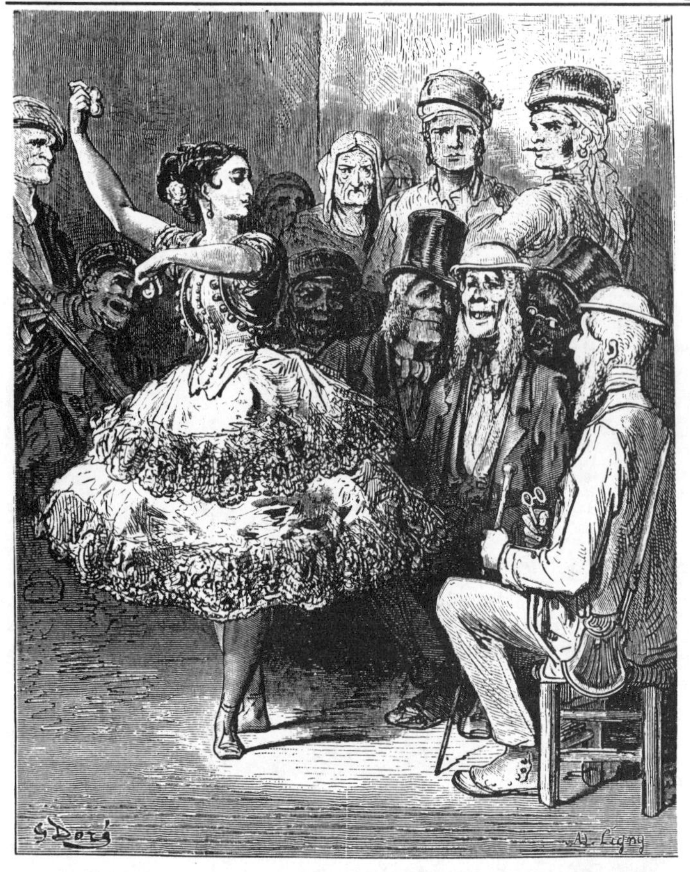
G. Doré

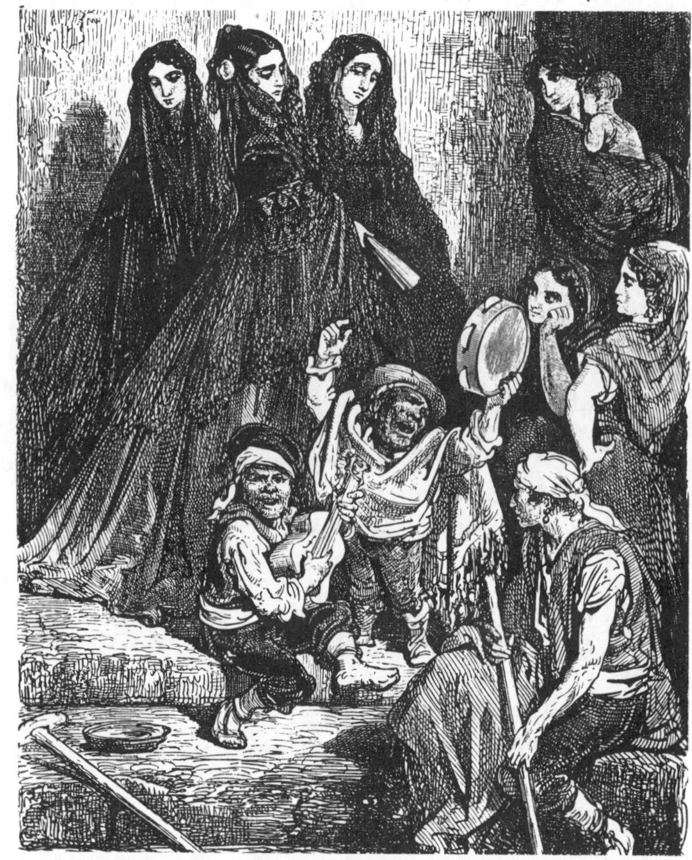

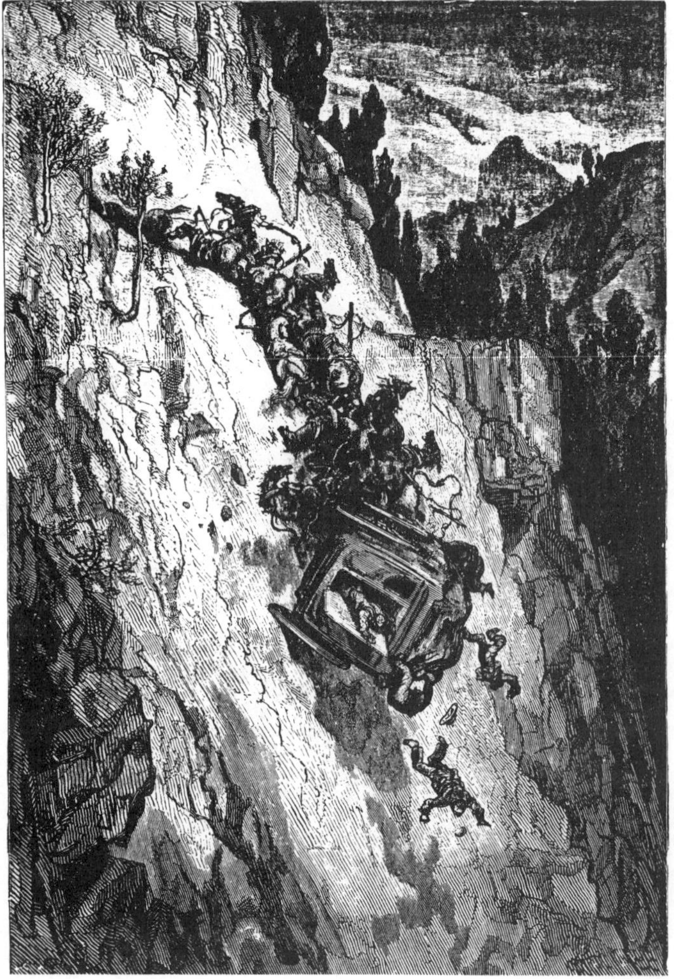

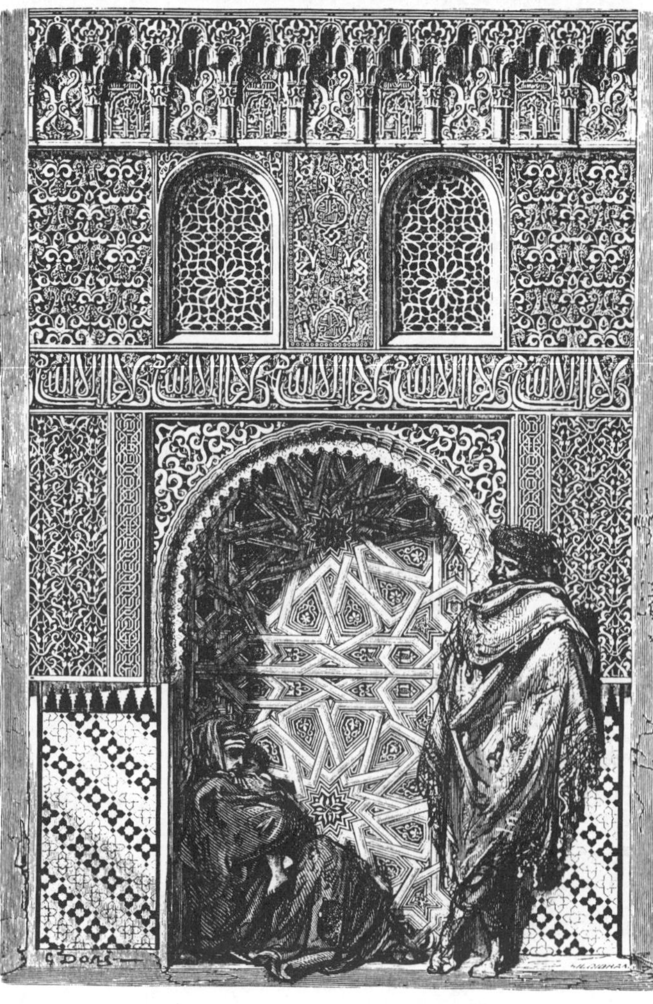
G. Doré

last Doré sketches (child subject unknown), made January 19, 1883 (four days before his death)
Doré's ***Monument to Alexandre Dumas***, as it stands today in the Place Malesherbes in Paris.
sign indicating that the Dumas Monument was closed for cleaning from March-May, 1993.
recent photo of Doré's grave in the Pere-Lachaise Cemetary in Paris, showing fresh flowers.

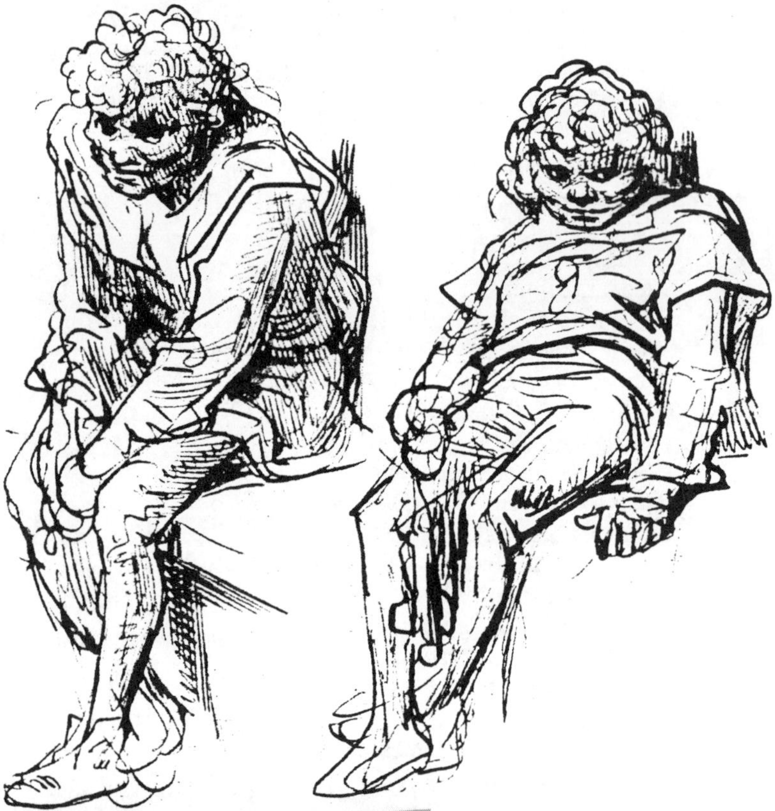

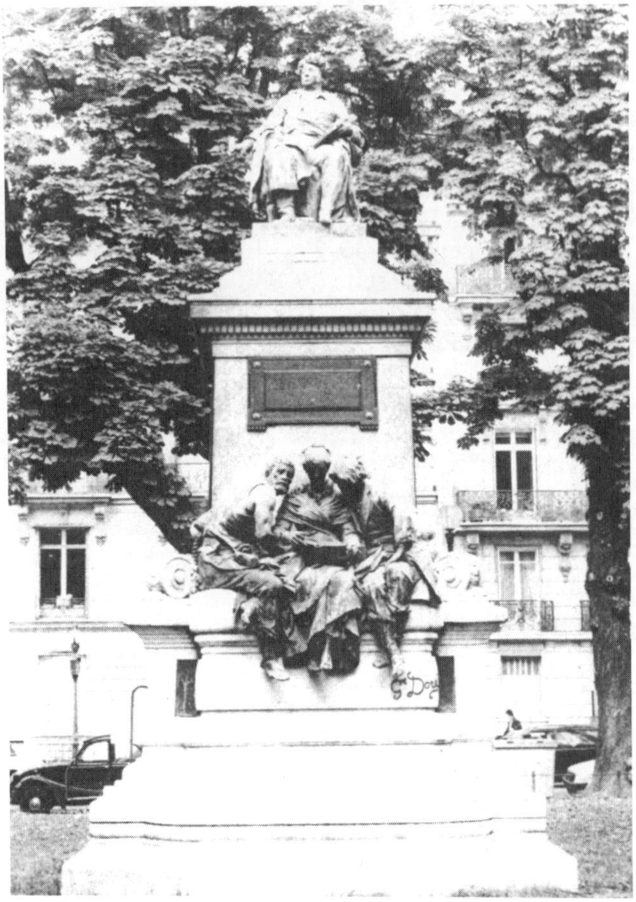

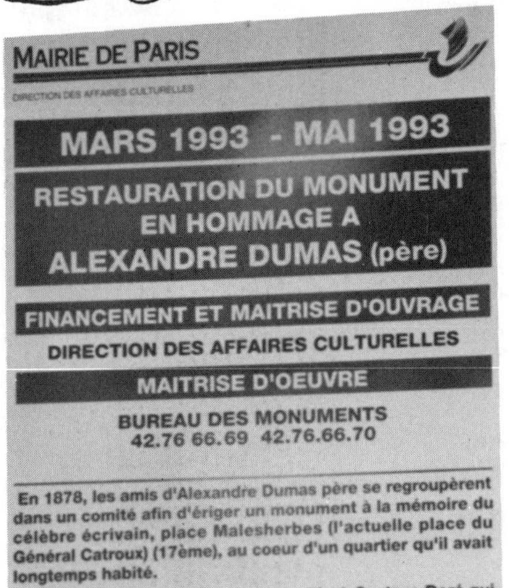

MAIRIE DE PARIS

DIRECTION DES AFFAIRES CULTURELLES

MARS 1993 - MAI 1993

RESTAURATION DU MONUMENT EN HOMMAGE A ALEXANDRE DUMAS (père)

FINANCEMENT ET MAITRISE D'OUVRAGE

DIRECTION DES AFFAIRES CULTURELLES

MAITRISE D'OEUVRE

BUREAU DES MONUMENTS
42.76 66.69 42.76.66.70

En 1878, les amis d'Alexandre Dumas père se regroupèrent dans un comité afin d'ériger un monument à la mémoire du célèbre écrivain, place Malesherbes (l'actuelle place du Général Catroux) (17ème), au coeur d'un quartier qu'il avait longtemps habité.

La réalisation du monument fut confiée à Gustave Doré qui choisit de mettre en avant l'attrait universel de l'oeuvre de Dumas.

Sur un haut piédestal, une représentation en bronze de Dumas, assis dans un fauteuil, dévisage les passants. Sur le devant du socle, trois personnages en bronze symbolisent ses innombrables lecteurs : une femme, un jeune bourgeois et un vieil ouvrier pieds nus. Sur la face arrière, on rencontre l'une des plus célèbres créations de l'écrivain : d'Artagnan.

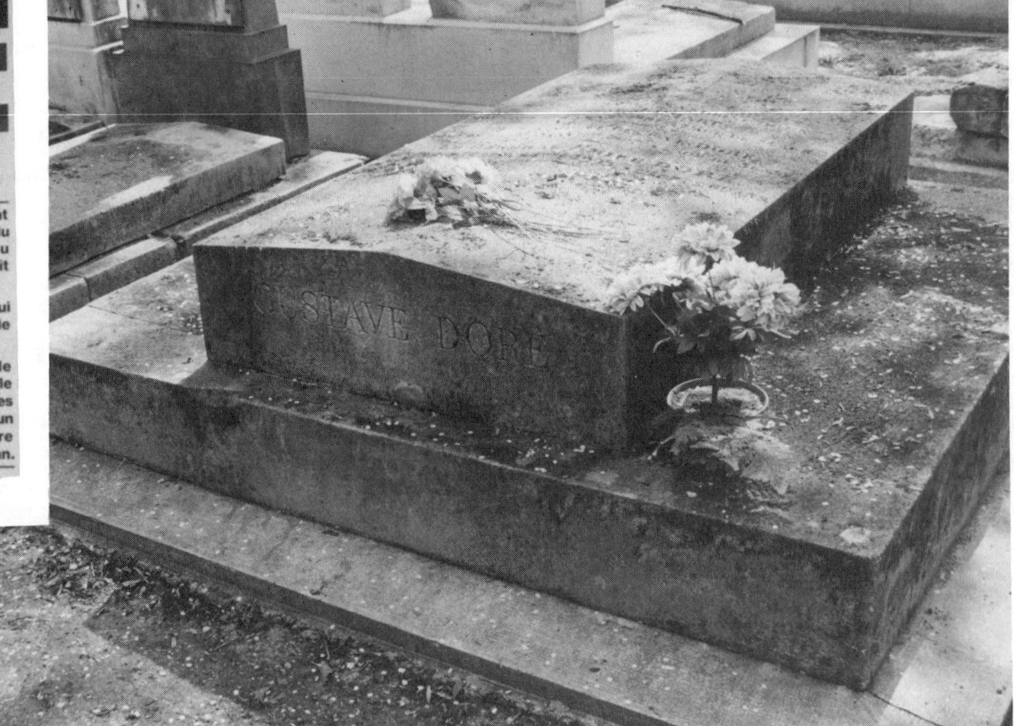